The Borderline Syndromes

THE BORDERLINE SYNDROMES

Constitution, Personality, and Adaptation

MICHAEL H. STONE, M.D.

McGRAW-HILL BOOK COMPANY

New York / St. Louis / San Francisco / Auckland / Bogotá / Hamburg / Johannesburg / London / Madrid / Mexico / Montreal / New Delhi / Panama / Paris / São Paulo / Singapore / Sydney / Tokyo / Toronto

Library of Congress Cataloging in Publication Data

Stone, Michael H
The borderline syndromes.

Includes index.
1. Pseudoneurotic schizophrenia. 2. Manic-depressive psychosis. 3. Mental illness—Genetic aspects. I. Title.
RC514.S819 616.8′9 79-14023
ISBN 0-07-061685-X

Acknowledgment is gratefully made for permission to reprint the following copyright material:

An excerpt from R. C. Rieder, "The origins of our confusion about schizophrenia." *Psychiatry,* 37:197–208. Copyright © 1974 by The William Alanson White Psychiatric Foundation, Inc.

A selection from *Shosha* by Isaac Bashevis Singer. Copyright © 1978 by Isaac Bashevis Singer. Reprinted with the permission of Farrar Straus & Giroux, Inc.

123456789 KPKP 89876543210

The editors for this book were Lawrence B. Apple and Suzette H. Annin. The designer was Christopher Simon, and the production supervisor was Teresa F. Leaden. It was set in Times Roman by University Graphics.

It was printed and bound by Kingsport Press.

For Harold Searles

Contents

Acknowledgments

In any psychiatric text that strives to make a comprehensive statement about borderline conditions, the issue of paternity becomes delicate. This book has as its spiritual father Harold Searles, because, during my residency training, it was his supervision and clinical example that inspired me to devote my professional life to patients in this realm of diagnosis. Whatever skills I have developed for establishing rapport with hospitalized patients, borderline and otherwise, were also derived and licked into shape by my tutelage wth Searles. The book would never have come into being, however, without the stimulus of Otto Kernberg, whose dynamic teaching of structural theory and whose championing of the term *borderline* spurred my interest not only in his diagnostic approach but in all the borderline systems, past and current, and most important, in their interrelationships and differences. Kernberg thus becomes the intellectual father of this endeavor. But there are still others.

My decade of work on the General Clinical Service of the New York State Psychiatric Institute, both as resident and as attending psychiatrist, put me in a unique position—to be able, in a personal way, to learn the diagnostic systems of Hoch and Polatin, of Roy Grinker, Sr. (who lectured there shortly after the publication of his first monograph on borderline patients), and, more recently, of Donald Klein. As a candidate of the Columbia Psychoanalytic Institute, I was to learn of Easser and Lesser's "hysteroid" patient—from Drs. Easser and Lesser themselves. Similarly, my collaboration with Alfred Stanton's McLean-based project on intensive psychotherapy with schizophrenic patients put me in touch with John Gunderson, about whose borderline system I acquired firsthand knowledge, later amplified through his consultative work at the Psychiatric Institute and at the Westchester Division of the Cornell Department of Psychiatry. Through collaboration with Robert Spitzer and his colleagues at the Psychiatric Institute I grew acquainted in a direct way with his approach to borderline conditions. Dr. Spitzer also read portions of the original manuscript dealing with diagnosis; his valuable suggestions were incorporated in the subsequent version.

My involvement with the study of children at high risk for schizophrenia, based at the Psychiatric Institute, gave me ready access to its principal investigator, the psychogeneticist Lucille Erlenmeyer-Kimling. She, in turn, read Part II of this book with her characteristic thoroughness, and provided invaluable suggestions for its improvement. The section dealing with biological markers in the major psychoses was improved in a similar fashion through my association with Drs. David Dunner and Ralph Wharton.

I am indebted to Drs. Eric Marcus, Richard Friedman, and Harvey Greenberg for having read the original manuscript: their criticisms led to a salutary tightening and abbreviation of the first draft. Another reader should be singled out for special mention: Dr. Clarice Kestenbaum, who, as my wife, had no convenient means of escape from the onerous task of correcting this long version. Her participation in the Kimling project, and her directorship of the St. Luke's Hospital Department of Child Psychiatry, have made her unusually familiar with the dilute, incipient, and otherwise borderline versions of the major psychoses.

I owe special thanks to Dr. Edward Sachar, the director of the New York State Psychiatric Institute, for having provided me with an opportunity, free of other duties, to devote myself completely to writing the first draft. To Lawrence B. Apple, Editor in Chief, Behavioral Sciences, McGraw-Hill, I feel no less a burden of gratitude for his ample help and encouragement during the revision phase.

It was easier to put into words this lengthy text than to put into words my deeply felt thanks to Mrs. Angelyn LeGrand, who typed the first draft, and to Miss Roseanne Scaperotta, who typed and proofread the final version. Both approached these forbidding assignments with a cheerfulness and efficiency that took the drudgery out of authorship, converting the latter into the joyful occupation it is supposed to be—but seldom is.

Grateful acknowledgment is made for permission to reprint material from the following sources:

B. M. Astrachan, M. Harrow, D. Adler, L. Bauer, A. Schwartz, C. Schwartz, and G. Tucker, "A check-list for the diagnosis of schizophrenia," *British Journal of Psychiatry,* 121:529–539, 1972. Reprinted by permission of Headley Brothers, Ltd. and B. M. Astrachan.

L. Bellak and L. Loeb, *The Schizophrenic Syndrome,* New York: Grune & Stratton, 1969. Reprinted by permission.

J. Bergeret, *Abrégé de psychologie pathologique,* Paris: Masson, 1974.

W. T. Carpenter, Jr., J. S. Strauss, and J. J. Bartko, "Flexible system for the diagnosis of schizophrenia: Report from the W.H.O. International Pilot Study of Schizophrenia," *Science,* 182(Dec. 21):1275–1277, 1973. Copyright 1973 by the American Association for the Advancement of Science.

H. J. Eysenck, *The Structure of Human Personality,* London: Methuen and Co. Ltd., 1960.

J. Frosch, "The psychotic character," *Psychiatric Quarterly,* 38:81–96, 1964. Copyright 1964. Reprinted by permission of Human Sciences Press, New York.

E. S. Gershon, M. Baron, and F. Leckman, "Genetic models of the transmission of affective disorders." Reprinted with permission from *Journal of Psychiatric Research,* Vol. 12, pp. 301–317. Copyright 1975, Pergamon Press, Ltd.

I. I. Gottesman and J. Shields, *Schizophrenia and Genetics: A Twin Study Vantage Point,* New York: Academic Press, 1972.

"Gunderson's Borderline Personality Disorder," Table 9–3, appears by permission of John Gunderson.

H. Helmchen, "Schizophrenia: Diagnostic concepts in the I.C.D.-8." In M. H. Lader (Ed.), *British Journal of Psychiatry* Special Publication No. 10: "Studies of Schizophrenia," pp. 10–18, 1975. Reprinted by permission of Headley Brothers, Ltd. and M. H. Lader.

R. E. Kendell and J. Gourlay, "The clinical distinctions between the affective psychoses and schizophrenia," *British Journal of Psychiatry,* 117:261–266, 1970. Reprinted by permission of Headley Brothers, Ltd. and R. E. Kendell.

O. Kernberg and E. Goldstein, "A diagnostic study of borderline personality disorder," unpublished grant proposal, 1975.

S. S. Kety, D. Rosenthal, P. H. Wender, and F. Schulsinger, "Mental illness in the biological and adoptive families of adopted schizophrenics." In D. Rosenthal and S. S. Kety (Eds.), *Transmission of Schizophrenia,* Oxford: Pergamon Press, 1968.

D. F. Klein and M. R. Liebowitz, "Diagnostic criteria for hysteroid dysphoria," unpublished.

Figure by A. Miller from Carter, C. O., "Multifactorial genetic disease," *Hospital Practice,* Vol. 5, No. 5, May 1970, and from *Medical Genetics,* McKusick, V. A., Claiborne, R. (Eds.), HP Publishing Co., Inc. New York, N. Y., 1973.

H. Mitsuda, *Clinical Genetics in Psychiatry,* Osaka, Japan: Igaku-Shoin Medical Publications, 1967.

C. Perris, "A study of bipolar (manic-depressive) and unipolar recurrent depressive psychoses," *Acta Psychiatrica Scandinavica,* Supplementum 194, 1966.

Rorschach Plate I is reproduced by permission of Hans Huber Publishers, Bern, Switzerland.

C. Shagass, J. J. Straumanis, R. A. Roemer, and M. Amadeo, "Evoked potentials of schizophrenics in several sensory modalities," *Biological Psychiatry,* 12:221–235, 1977. Reprinted by permission of Charles Shagass.

J. R. Stabenau, "Genetic and other factors in schizophrenic, manic-depressive and schizo-affective psychoses," *Journal of Nervous and Mental Disease,* 164:149–167, 1977. © 1977 The Williams & Wilkins Co., Baltimore.

M. H. Stone, "A psychoanalytic approach to abnormalities of temperament," *American Journal of Psychotherapy,* 33:263–280, 1978.

J. Zubin and B. Spring, "Vulnerability: A new view of schizophrenia," *Journal of Abnormal Psychology,* 86:103–126, 1977. Copyright 1977 by the American Psychological Association. Reprinted by permission.

The Borderline Syndromes

PART I

Borderline Conditions: Early Definitions and Interrelationships

If a man tells me that he is grievously disturbed, for that he *imagines* he sees a ruffian coming against him with a drawn sword, though at the same time he is *conscious* it is a delusion, I pronounce him to have a disordered imagination; but if a man tells me that he *sees* this, and in consternation calls me to look at it, I pronounce him to be *mad*.

Professor Gaubius of Leyden,
Eighteenth century

In the opening pages of some philosophical notes by Ludwig Wittgenstein, later collected as the "Blue Books" (1958), is the phrase, "The meaning of a word is its usage." Thanks to his linguistic analysis, we are able to adopt a more sophisticated view of "meaning"—one that relates no longer to rigid categorical definitions (any of which may miss something important about a particular term, and is therefore only partially "correct") but to overlapping and ever shifting circles of connotation. The contents of these circles are dictated not by heavenly absolutes but by human utility and are therefore "subject to change without notice" from locale to locale and from generation to generation.

The term "borderline" in psychiatric parlance exemplifies these geographical and generational shifts. As we shall see, the term also has acquired different shadings in accordance with the particular psychiatric subspecialty with which the speaker is chiefly identified.

Historically, a phrase like "borderline" has been invoked when clinicians noted that a previously neat two-category universe contained, on closer inspection, some "messy" cases that on the surface were not precisely one thing and not precisely the other. Here "borderline" is used to bridge two formerly noncontiguous areas of meaning, creating a kind of continuum. "Category" is converted into "dimension."

Constitution, in psychiatry, is analyzed as to several possibilities: disturbances of integration, such as the schizophrenias; disturbances of behavioral regulation, such as the manic-depressive disorders, where the emotional thermostat may be set too low or too high; and peculiarities or exaggerations of styles: hysterical, obsessive, paranoid, and so on. The term "borderline" has been incorporated into two universes of discourse: one relating to matters of constitution, the other to the level of adaptation or "coping." A condition that is neither obviously schizophrenic nor obviously manic or epileptic (and so forth) may be spoken of as "borderline." An adaptational level that is in keeping neither with the functional capacities of the ordinary person ("neurotic") nor with the incapacities of the person who has lost touch with reality ("psychotic") is, again, "borderline."

Borderline, in its clinical application, is a term of triage. If one's frame of reference is categorical diagnosis (as opposed to dimensional diagnosis), it often seems natural to speak of three groups. Clear-cut schizophrenics, nonschizophrenics, and an intermediate "borderline" group would constitute an example of a *borderline* notion and its utility.

When psychoanalysts began to recognize the existence of patients who were neither clearly reachable by classical technics nor clearly beyond their powers, another *borderline* group was born—one situated between analyzability and nonanalyzability.

More recently Rosenthal (1975) and others have begun to speak of a borderline or dilute form of illness within the realm of affective disorders. These become the counterparts of "borderline schizophrenia," a concept which Kety, Rosenthal, and their collaborators (1968) have helped to elucidate. Donald Klein's hysteroid dysphorics constitute a borderline group within the unipolar and bipolar-II regions of manic-depressive illness. Some of these patients, while chiefly ill in an affective way, exhibit faint signs in the direction of what is often called "schizoaffective," so they are, in a manner of speaking, borderline twice over. I myself have recently added to this already crowded diagnostic limbo by describing a group of patients who, despite benign outward appearances, are vulnerable in time to a bipolar-I type of manic-depressive decompensation and thus "borderline" with respect to classical manic-depressive psychosis (Stone, 1978).

The chapter that follows is devoted to a comprehensive review of the borderline and related concepts in twentieth-century psychiatry, up to the early 1960s. The systems of Gunderson, Kernberg, Klein, and Spitzer represent the currently most widely accepted borderline concepts. Because of their importance, they will be discussed at greater length in the chapter devoted to the diagnosis of borderline function and borderline syndromes (Chapter 9).

CHAPTER 1

History of Usage of the Term "Borderline"

Early Usages

The scant references to borderline conditions to be found in the nineteenth-century literature, reviewed by Mack (1975) and later by Grinker et al. (1968), are of less interest to us today, because most contemporary usages derive from psychoanalytic papers of the 1930s.

Before the term "borderline" became used more widely, one can see the germ of such a notion in Bleuler's correction of Kraepelinian pessimism about dementia praecox, and in Freud's deemphasis of an organic etiology for what he preferred to call the narcissistic neuroses. E. Bleuler (1950) drew attention to the fact that not all cases labeled dementia praecox deteriorated as Kraepelin initially believed they would. Although clinging to the belief in an organic basis for the group of schizophrenias, as Bleuler renamed these conditions, he did introduce a note of hopefulness about at least a portion of the cases. Freud did not deny organicity in these cases, but his interest in the ideational and psychodynamic aspects of schizophrenic conditions carried them further away from their original organic moorings and from the traditional gloom in which these cases had earlier been enveloped.

Neither Freud nor Adolph Meyer, as Zilboorg (1941) mentions, restricted the diagnosis of schizophrenia to patients displaying delusions, hallucinations, or deterioration. These they considered advanced signs of a condition that was detectable beforehand through a variety of less dramatic indicators. In comparison to Kraepelin, Freud and Meyer accepted the idea of a not yet definitive, and in that sense, "borderline" schizophrenia, though they did not use this phrase.

As Freud's psychoanalytic method and Meyer's optimism began to spread, particularly in the United States, interest shifted away from the abstract categorization of the nineteenth-century German school of psychiatry to the issue of analyzability. The world of mental disorders divided itself into the transference psychoneuroses, susceptible of amelioration by classical psychoanalysis, and the psychoses, which resisted improvement by this means.

Freud's colleagues in the 1910s began to apply the analytic method across the whole spectrum of mental illness. Some, including Brill and Coriat, were outspokenly enthusiastic about the effectiveness of psychoanalysis in schizophrenia, but the majority adopted a more reserved stance. It soon became obvious that there was a large number of patients who were not ill enough to warrant a clear-cut psychotic diagnosis yet who were too ill to benefit from, or even withstand, unmodified psychoanalysis. They were "borderline" between neurosis and psychosis (as those terms were then employed).

Many psychoanalytic articles of the 1920s were devoted to these difficult "in-between" cases, though they were not yet called borderline. An example would be that of the Wolf Man, treated originally by Freud (1918) and later by Ruth Mack Brunswick (1928).

The Wolf Man, a paranoid obsessional patient Freud believed to be just this side of schizophrenia, was much more resistant to psychoanalysis than the classical neurotic. The modern reader will in fact tend to reclassify the Wolf Man as exemplifying a mild form of schizophrenia, but for Freud, as well as for Ruth Mack Brunswick, this patient remained a kind of borderline case.[1]

As I shall try to demonstrate in a subsequent chapter (7), patients called borderline by almost any of the popular definitions appear in many instances to have some degree of hereditary predisposition to mental illness. Often this will allow the clinician to make an educated guess about the patient's vulnerability, the eventual course of the illness, and the type

[1]According to Rangell (1955, p. 287), "neither Freud nor Mack Brunswick raised any specific questions as to the transformation from early neurosis to later paranoid psychosis."

of therapy (including medication) that will prove most effective. The suggestion of a hereditary factor is no new discovery. It was, if anything, taken for granted by the psychiatric and psychoanalytic communities until the second generation of psychoanalysts began to adopt a more linear and purely psychological model of causation.

Thomas V. Moore

It is of interest to note that the first American to write of borderline cases, Thomas V. Moore (1921), thought the hereditary factor was of crucial importance. In 1921 he discussed depression in the following terms:

> Depression is a reaction to incidents profoundly affecting a person's hierarchy of desires, rendering him hopeless. . . . This state can lead to incapacity for work and even to psychosis. That abnormal reactions occur in some men, but not others, depends on inherited constitution. Patients suffering from manic-depressive psychosis have more insane relatives than do normal individuals, and these insane relatives are frequently of the manic-depressive type. In cases of depression there is an hereditary organic factor which makes the patient physically disposed to this type of reaction. (p. 269)

The issue of possible genetic factors in borderline conditions is discussed further in Chapter 7.

Wilhelm Reich

Wilhelm Reich's monograph *The Impulsive Character* was based on his efforts to apply analysis to the patients of a Viennese clinic (1925). There he encountered severe characterological disorders noteworthy for what he called "the grotesque quality of their symptoms." As he put it, "The compulsive thought of killing one's child, as conceived by the simple neurotic, appears trite and innocuous in comparison to the compulsive urge of an impulsive individual to roast his child slowly over a fire" (1925, pp. 16–17).

Elsewhere in the same monograph Reich summarizes his distinctions among three classes of patients, as follows:

> In schizophrenia, with delusions and hallucinations, there is conflict and deterioration in the ego. The conflict is resolved by way of illusory projection of the ego ideal together with the tabooed id impulse.
>
> In the hysteric [psychoneurotic], resolution of . . . conflict is attempted by alternating preference of the ego for one of its two masters, with temporary amnesia.
>
> In the impulsive character, partisanship is simultaneous, and occasionally conflicts are resolved by projection (typical of the schizophrenic) or by splitting (as would be typical of the hysteric). (1925, pp. 113–114)

Reich's idea about the impulsive character's simultaneous involvement with two sharply contradictory feeling states (maintained without conscious discomfort, via *splitting*) has become central to all later theoreticians concerned with borderline cases, including Kohut (1971) and Kernberg (1967).

Oberndorf's Views

In a brief article, tucked away in a journal seldom read by psychiatrists, Oberndorf (1930) summarized the situation with borderline cases as they were then understood. He warned against the dangers of adopting too rigid a view about diagnostic categories, whether they be Kraepelinian or Freudian:

> . . . there is no hard and fast line between neuroses and psychoses. . . . One finds schizophrenic reactions in compulsion neuroses . . . anxiety states . . . fuse with depressions [and] conversion symptoms are found in depressions, in manic excitement as well as in hysterias, etc. (p. 649)

Oberndorf goes on to mention that the "pure types" are so rare as to be negligible and that in office practice, "most of the semi-psychotic and psychotic functional pictures are . . . far removed from textbook descriptions," a point with which one could hardly argue fifty years later.

Oberndorf offered clinical vignettes of a sort that might very well hold up as examples of borderline conditions today. Interestingly, one had a schizophrenic flavor and another, that of a bipolar affective disorder. Regarding the latter, Oberndorf cited the case of a thirty-four-year-old married woman:

> . . . referred for analysis because of fainting attacks occurring at rapidly increasing intervals. Her physician recognized them as hysterical . . . [and] sent her to a hospital [where] two days elapsed before I saw her. At the first interview, for two solid hours long, repressed psychic material gushed forth with a glow of hot lava. A full-fledged manic attack, from which she has not yet recovered, ensued—but . . . the fainting attacks have ceased. (1930, p. 649)

This description is reminiscent of those we encounter years later under the titles "hysteroid" (Easser and Lesser) or "hysteroid dysphoric" (D. Klein) or "borderline structure with hysterical personality, within the context of major affective disorder, bipolar type" (author's impressions).

Elsewhere Oberndorf described a twenty-four-year-old man from a fundamentalist religious background, with severe inhibitions about sex. He swallowed iodine in a suicide attempt after a period of intense anguish over lustful feelings he found totally unacceptable. The few times he attempted intercourse, a nasal tic became activated that he experienced as a reminder of his "sinfulness." In addition he was beset by "bizarre, fantastic, interminable psychosexual religious phantasies, such as would easily have justified the diagnosis of dementia praecox." This man never had productive signs of psychosis and actually made an excellent recovery after gradual resolution of his unconscious conflicts. One will note strong similarities to some of Kasanin's schizoaffective cases or to Bychowski's "latent schizophrenics" (see below).

Though mental illness in relatives was not mentioned, one gets the impression from Oberndorf's vignettes that he was aware of a hereditary/constitutional factor in his borderline cases. Furthermore he seemed to acknowledge that cases could be borderline with respect to either schizophrenic or affective psychoses (see Chapter 7, Table 7–1).

Glover and the Kleinian Viewpoint

In the late 1920s and early 1930s amongst the followers of Melanie Klein in England, there was considerable interest in patients who seemed just beyond the reach of psychoanalysis. Unlike Freud, who never relinquished his regard for biological and constitutional factors in emotional illness, the Kleinians tended to adopt a linear model of causation, in which only the psychological factor was seriously acknowledged. The more severe disorders were seen as having earlier ("pregenital") fixation points along the continuum of psychosexual development. Glover's views (1932) are somewhat ambivalent: he found the term "borderline" in the sense of a new separate entity unsatisfactory, stating that if psychotic mechanisms were present in a patient, they should be accorded a definite label. He would not have called someone with faint signs of schizophrenia "borderline" but rather a "potential psychotic," emphasizing that person's affiliation with the family of schizophrenic disorders. Yet Glover also believed that we were all "larval psychotics, and have been so since age two." The implication was that, diagnostically, we were all on a continuum, and circumstances could push us this way or that.

Kasanin's "Schizoaffective" Cases

In 1933 Kasanin described nine patients of the Boston State Hospital, diagnosed originally as cases of dementia praecox, but whose premorbid personality, emotionality, and course were atypical. He coined the term "schizoaffective" to categorize them. Many were in between Kraepelinian schizophrenia and the manic-depressive disorders; also their course, while not deteriorating, was usually characterized by some residual disability. These patients enjoyed life and had good work adjustments; they were more often sociable than shy; and they were introspective and sexually maladjusted but not eccentric. Their intelligence was average to superior, and in their immediate past was some unusually difficult environmental situation.

Some had brief periods of delusory ideation but showed a kind of double awareness about their psychotic symptoms, such as the man who told Kasanin, "I believe God was telling me to give up my job and move to a different city, but the scientific part of my personality tells me all this is bunk" (1933, p. 108).

Five cases are presented in detail. A close reading of the material reveals that by contemporary diagnostic standards, two were very near to bipolar-II manic-depressive illness; one, pure schizophrenic with thought insertion and no mood disturbance; and two with evenly divided schizophrenic and affective symptoms we would still tend to call "schizoaffective."

Kasanin mentioned that the acute episodes in "schizoaffective" patients were often ushered in by a period of smouldering depression and that improvement often took place before hospitalization became necessary, such that they were more a phenomenon of office practice.

Stern and the Popularization of the Term "Borderline"

The first to give the term "borderline" formal status was Stern, who in 1938 outlined the characteristics of a group of office patients "too ill for classical psychoanalysis."

It is worth mentioning his ten criteria in some detail since they embody in inchoate form most of the features contemporary diagnosticians allude to as distinctive of borderline conditions. These include:

1. *Narcissism*—Stern's patients often betrayed simultaneous idealization and contemptuous devaluation of the analyst, as well as of other important persons earlier in their life.

Often the patients' mothers were cruel or neglectful, and themselves narcissistic.

2. *Psychic bleeding*—This trait refers to the borderline patient's paralysis in the face of crises, his lethargy, and his tendency to give up. These qualities resemble some of the features of Lesse's (1974) "masked depression."

3. *Inordinate hypersensitivity*—Overreaction to mild criticism or rejection may be so gross that it suggests paranoia but falls short of outright delusion.

4. *Psychic and body rigidity*—A state of tension and stiffness of posture readily apparent to a casual observer.

5. *Negative therapeutic reaction*—Certain interpretations by analyst, meant to be helpful, are experienced as discouraging or as manifestations of lack of love and appreciation. Depression or rage outbursts may ensue;

at times suicidal gestures. This reaction overlaps with number 3, inordinate hypersensitivity.

6. *Constitutional feeling of inferiority*—An impression based on Stern's intuition that some hereditary or constitutional factor "deeply embedded in the personality of the patient" is at work fostering the borderline patient's ingrained self-esteem deficit. Some patients exhibited melancholia, others, an infantile personality.

7. *Masochism*—Stern adds that this trait is often accompanied by severe depression.

8. *Organic insecurity*—Here Stern is referring to an apparently constitutional incapacity to tolerate much stress, especially in the interpersonal field.

9. *Projective mechanisms*—A strong tendency to externalize, at times carrying the patient close to delusory ideation.

10. *Difficulties in reality testing*—These are less gross than in the psychoses and express themselves chiefly as a kind of faulty empathic machinery in relation to other people. This difficulty overlaps with the borderline trait Kernberg mentions, involving impaired capacity to fuse partial object representations (of another person) into appropriate and realistic perceptions of the whole person (see Chapter 9).

After Stern's paper a number of years were to elapse before another attempt was made to delineate a so-called borderline syndrome in any methodical fashion. Until the 1954 reformulation of Knight, the term was obviously used by many analysts but not in a way that connoted anything very definite; it was a colloquialism of the analytic fraternity more than a concept to be written of in a scientific article.

Clinicians whose main interest was in hospitalized schizophrenics spoke of borderline cases, which also acquired many other labels of parochial usage in particular regions or centers. Psychoanalysts whose interests were confined largely to office practice had their list of borderline adjectives. One must keep this point in mind, because two trends of usage were developing simultaneously—one concerned with the border between schizophrenia and nonschizophrenia and one with the border between psychoneurosis and the deeper disturbances. These sets of usages approached one another from two widely removed sources, overlapped to a degree, but were by no means coextensive.

Ambulatory Schizophrenia of Zilboorg

In 1941, for example, Zilboorg described a number of cases under the rubric "ambulatory schizophrenia." The term was not meant to denote a separate clinical entity. Actually he believed that all the casual references to borderline cases, incipient schizophrenia, mixed manic-depressive psychosis, or schizoid manics, and so forth, were untenable. At the same time he also regarded the tradition in psychiatry where only "preterminal" or "terminal stages" of dementia praecox were labeled "dementia praecox" as equally untenable. One will notice, incidentally, that writers of this era thought dementia praecox cases went through certain "stages"; the notion that some patients could show its moderate signs only, and never pass to the more deteriorated stages, had not yet firmly taken hold. At all events, Zilboorg regarded schizophrenia as the generic name for a psychopathological *process*. The essential for him was the "trait" not the "state." Therefore if one had the *trait,* and only mild clinical signs, one was just as "schizophrenic" as the patient on the back wards. There was no need for adjectives like "incipient." Ideas of reference, delusions, hallucinations, and flatness of affect all belonged, in Zilboorg's opinion, to well-advanced cases. It was this milder group, with outward normality, dereistic thinking ("thinking *away* from things"), shallow human relationships (acquaintances but no friends), and incapacity to settle upon one job or life pursuit, that Zilboorg called *ambulatory,* where the social facade was fairly well preserved and hospitalization not necessary. His patients were almost all men; some were fetishists or exmurderers whom the governor of New York had sent for diagnostic evaluation. Others were unobtrusive but chronic failures. The women who at all resembled this group, Zilboorg noted, had considerable agitation and depression and therefore did not seem as easily classifiable amongst the schizophrenias. This point is of interest, because at the Psychiatric Institute, even in the heyday of Hoch and Polatin, the term "schizoaffective" was applied much more often to women than to men. In women it is apparently harder to damp out emotionality, whether normal or exaggerated, to the extent that even when they exhibit schizophrenic stigmata, enough affectivity is often preserved to make categorical diagnosis difficult.

The ambulatory schizophrenic of Zilboorg is, in any case, a sicker patient with a poorer prognosis (though some had a "good recovery") than Kasanin's schizoaffective patient, and in a different realm altogether from Stern's patients.

Helene Deutsch: The Beginnings of the Psychostructural Approach

A year after Zilboorg's paper on the ambulatory schizophrenic came that of Helene Deutsch (1942), in which she described and elaborated on an "as if" group of patients, whose most striking features were:

1. A curious kind of depersonalization that was not ego-alien or disturbing to the patient
2. Narcissistic identifications with others which are not assimilated into the self but repeatedly acted out

3. A fully maintained grasp on reality
4. Poverty of object relations, with a tendency to adopt the qualities of the other person as a means of retaining love (hence the "as if," rather than *genuine,* nature of their own personality)
5. A masking of all aggressive tendencies by passivity, lending an "air of mild amiability, which is, however, readily convertible to evil" (1942, p. 305)
6. Inner emptiness, which the patient seeks to remedy by attaching himself to one after the other social or religious group, no matter whether the tenets of this year's group are diametrically opposed to those of last year's

Five patients were discussed in detail: four women and one a homosexual boy of seventeen. Because of the family history of psychosis in four of five, Deutsch was led to conclude that the "as if" personality might represent a phase of the schizophrenic process, "before it built up to the delusional form" (1942, p. 319).

Deutsch was not clear whether the disturbances she was describing really implied a "schizophrenic disposition," but she certainly did feel that the disturbances did not belong to the commonly accepted forms of neurosis, while at the same time, the patients remained "too well adjusted to reality to be called psychotic."

The importance of her contribution lies in its emphasis on the pathology of internalized object relations. Similar conclusions, as Kernberg has mentioned, were reached soon afterwards by Fairbairn (1944) and Melanie Klein (1952).

One aspect of the faulty internalized object relations concerns the formation of value systems and of the ego ideal. There appeared to be an important distinction here between the "as if" person and the true psychotic. Deutsch wrote, for example, "In melancholia, the object of identification has been psychologically internalized, and a tyrannical Super-Ego carries on the conflict with the incorporated object in complete independence of the external world" (1942, p. 318). In contradistinction, "In 'As-If' patients, the objects are kept external and all conflicts are acted out in relation to them" (1942, p. 318).

Elsewhere Deutsch alludes to an integrative defect in the "as if" patient of a magnitude midway between the fragmentation of self- and object representations noted in the full-blown schizophrenic and the much milder impairments in assimilation observed among psychoneurotic patients. "Common to all these ["as if"] cases," she mentioned, "is a deep disturbance of the process of sublimation, which results . . . in a failure to synthesize the various infantile identifications into a single, integrated personality . . ." (1942, p. 316). The diminished capacity for sublimatory channeling, emphasized by Kernberg as an important nonspecific feature of the borderline personality organization, is the counterpart in contemporary metapsychology of Deutsch's original point. The usual expression of this defect is a reduced capacity for work or scholastic achievement, a criterion incorporated in the system of Gunderson (see Chapter 9).

Rapaport, Gill, and Schafer: An Attempt at Classification through Psychological Testing

Psychological testing of a broad diagnostic spectrum of patients, backed up by a control group of healthy young men, formed the backbone of the epoch-making monograph by Rapaport, Gill, and Schafer (1945–1946).

Among the patients to whom they administered their test battery (of which a meticulously recorded Rorschach was an important element) were seventy-five clear-cut schizophrenics. Interestingly, even in the early forties, classical catatonic and hebephrenic patients were apparently quite rare. Rapaport's sample consisted actually of thirty-nine "unclassified" types (our "undifferentiated" type in current usage), twenty-seven paranoid, and nine "simple."

Though the term "borderline" was not used, the authors described (1945, vol. I, p. 21) a group of thirty-three patients whom they chose to call *preschizophrenic*. Characterologically, these patients were schizoid (predominantly), but their adjustment was "so precarious that schizophrenic-like withdrawal . . . or schizophrenic-like ideational productions in the guise of obsessive-phobic thought, had already penetrated into their everyday life."

Rapaport and his collaborators' observations of this group embodied a diathesis-stress model, though such a phrase was not to be used until the early sixties (see Kety et al., 1968). They noted that "any stress or strain could precipitate a schizophrenic psychosis, but under favorable chance conditions, they might continue with such preschizophrenic behavior or ideation without an acute break" (p. 21).

The general characteristics of these patients were:

1. Prolonged premorbid maladjustment, despite some ability to manage in the outside world, and to conceal the grosser abnormalities of personality
2. Marked ("free-floating") anxiety
3. Apart from this anxiety, a constriction of affect in regard to object relations
4. Partial insight with voluntary request for psychiatric help
5. Absence of paranoid projections

Two subgroups were recognized. They were labeled *coarctated* and *overideational*. The coarctated preschizophrenic patients exhibited blocking, withdrawal, inhibition of affect, and some kind of sexual preoccupation. By contrast, the overideational patients showed "an enormous wealth of fantasy, obsessive ideation, obsessions, and preoccupations with themselves and their bodies." The latter variety of preschizophrenic, the researchers admitted, could be very difficult to distinguish at first from (certain) obsessional neurotics. Obsessive ruminations in the neurotics, however, tended to be ego-dystonic and rather unvarying, whereas the preschizophrenics showed a wide range of ever-shifting obsessional ideation. Similarly their inhibited group was distinguishable from psychoneurotics by virtue of anxiety that was "tremendous" in quantity and "incongruous with the situations evoking it."

The preschizophrenics of Rapaport et al. resemble to varying extents the ambulatory schizophrenics of Zilboorg, the latent schizophrenics of Federn and Bychowski, and the borderline schizophrenic of Kety.

Two other groups of patients were described elsewhere in the monograph, to whom the term "borderline," as used by contemporary clinicians, might be applied.

The first of these groups was called the *paranoid conditions* (p. 22), and consisted of patients with rigid, compulsive character structure, good premorbid adjustment, and a varying degree of paranoid ideation (about which they had some degree of intellectual insight). In one subgroup, called *paranoid states,* the paranoid break was short-lived; blunting of affect was not present nor was a formal thought disorder (i.e., no loosening of associations, derailment, and so forth). This subgroup was distinguished from the second group, the *paranoid character,* which consisted of patients also noted to be quarrelsome and suspicious throughout life, in the absence of delusions.[2]

Finally, among the depressive patients studied was a subgroup Rapaport called the *severe neurotic depressions*. These patients had no delusions (and thus were not "psychotic depressives") but did show some irrationality, along with either agitation or psychomotor retardation, not noted in the healthier "neurotic depressive" patients. Many of the patients we are now calling borderline—whether by the stricter criteria of Kernberg or Gunderson or by looser criteria—are nearer to this diagnostic category of Rapaport than to his preschizophrenic types (see cases 15 and 29 in Part IV).

Details of test results in these as well as in less equivocal clinical categories are given in volume II of the monograph. Psychological test findings in patients diagnosed borderline by Kernberg's criteria are currently being investigated by Singer (1977) and Bloomgarden (1978); these findings are further discussed in Chapter 9.

[2]In Part IV in the case illustrations, case 23 most closely fits this subgroup in Rapaport's nosology, although this patient happened not to show insight into his condition.

The "Stably Unstable" Borderline of Schmideberg

One of the analytic writers of the 1940s who did favor the term "borderline" was Melitta Schmideberg (1947). She did considerable work with juvenile offenders but even in her private practice often worked with very sick patients. Borderline, for her, meant in between neurosis and psychosis. Some of her borderline patients she pictured, like her precedessors, as "early cases of schizophrenia." Characteristically these patients:

1. Were unable to tolerate routine and regularity
2. Tended to break many rules of social convention
3. Were often late for appointments and unreliable about payment
4. Were unable to free-associate during their sessions
5. Were poorly motivated for treatment
6. Failed to develop meaningful insight
7. Led chaotic lives where something dreadful was always happening
8. Would engage in petty criminal acts, unless they happened to be well off
9. Could not easily establish emotional contact

They might, for example, appear deeply committed to their analyst one day and precipitously quit the next. Characterologically, many of Schmideberg's borderlines were schizoid or narcissistic. Schmideberg is describing a group with less depressive manifestations and worse functioning than Stern's. How much her group overlaps with Zilboorg's ambulatory schizophrenics is difficult to say. One reason she felt it justifiable to place this group in a separate category was because the patients tended to remain true to their type over long periods of time. As Schmideberg put it, they were "stable in their instability."

Latent Schizophrenia: Federn's Development of Bleuler's Concept

In the same issue of the journal where Schmideberg's article on the borderline personality appeared was another by Paul Federn (1947) on "latent schizophrenia," a Bleulerian term still enshrined in our current American Psychiatric Association diagnostic manual.

Federn relied more on intuition than precision in his description, just as those of us, accustomed during our training to diagnose certain patients as "latent schizophrenics," felt we were engaging more in an act of faith than of accuracy. The qualities Federn drew attention to were the patient's depersonalization and sense of estrangement. He added, " . . . an experienced psychiatrist intuitively recognizes the latent schizophrenic by his behavior, even when neurosis [*sic*] is superimposed. It is often difficult to describe the characteristics of posture, language, and the glare of the eyes. However, a hidden paranoiac or catatonic stigma reveals itself by the patient's behavior and mannerisms, earlier than by his verbal productions" (1947, p. 141). As a kind of afterthought, Federn mentioned that the family pedigrees of his "latent schizophrenics" were often replete with full-blown schizophrenics.

Hoch and Polatin: Pseudoneurotic Schizophrenia

Much more systematic in their attempt to define the borders of the "in-between" patient were Hoch and Polatin (1949). They believed they had isolated a new syndrome within the larger realm of schizophrenia, to which they gave the label *pseudoneurotic schizophrenia.* Hoch was at pains, especially in his 1959 paper with Cattell, to point out that theirs was not a "borderline" group of an ill-defined sort between neurosis and psychosis but a genuine variant of schizophrenia—one that occasionally eventuated in a more classical form of the illness but usually continued on the same course and with the same appearance. Like Kasanin and Zilboorg they inveighed against the Kraepelinian concept of dementia praecox as a deteriorating illness and sided with Bleuler who long ago warned against a taxonomy based only on outcome.

Again emphasizing *trait* over *state,* Hoch and Polatin regarded as essential to their new classification the "basic mechanisms of schizophrenia," by which they meant the classical Bleulerian primary symptoms of autism, pervasive ambivalence, and disturbance in association and affect. Besides these core symptoms, the "pseudoneurotic" patient was typically maladjusted socially and sexually, and cold emotionally—yet exquisitely sensitive to criticism and seething with ill-concealed rage. The most well-known aspects of Hoch and Polatin's description are of course the widespread symptoms mimicking the classical neuroses: compulsions, phobias, depressions, and so on, all occurring in a jumble and in such intensity as to cripple the patient's functioning. This caricature of all the neuroses they named *panneurosis,* and it was apt to be accompanied by pervasive anxiety (*pan-anxiety*) and chaotic sexuality combining promiscuity and perversions: their so-called pansexuality.

Thought disorder in the pseudoneurotic patient was not one of incoherence and irrelevance but one replete with condensations, concreteness, and allusiveness. Instead of clear-cut delusions and hallucinations were what Hoch and Polatin called *overvalued ideas* (a term later incorporated by Kernberg in his description of the borderline). These involved statements such as, "It is as if I were to hear a voice." Psychological tests revealed Rorschach responses characteristic of schizophrenia in general.

The theoretical framework of Hoch and Polatin, it should be noted, rested on the notion of schizophrenia as a *disintegrative* reaction, not one of regression to some early fixation point, as some analytic writers saw it (particularly the Kleinian and Sullivanian groups).

Of the five cases presented *in extenso* in their earlier paper, three have an unmistakable schizophrenic ring (eccentricity, formal thought disorder, and chronicity) and two have a mixture of schizophrenic and affective signs that we might regard as more in keeping with a "schizoaffective" label or even a bipolar, type II, manic-depressive psychosis. One patient even had a dream of being dead, thus defying Freud's dictum that the dreaming ego cannot conceive of its own death (see Chapter 9).

Of these five cases, four were young women (aged twenty-one to thirty-eight) and all were of superior intelligence. Over the years "pseudoneurotic schizophrenia" has remained a kind of trademark for the bright young and rather flamboyant schizophrenic patients selected for intensive psychotherapy at the Psychiatric Institute (and at similar institutions in the East). During the years of my training there, diagnostic standards were not yet as well defined as they are today: some patients who showed predominantly affective signs, and few if any schizophrenic stigmata, still received this appellation. Over the decades, patterns of symptomatology have changed so that nowadays few patients exhibit the multiple "neurotic" symptoms described by Hoch and Polatin, for which reason their label has grown less useful than it once was.

Early Uses of the Term "Borderline Schizophrenia"

In the early 1950s one begins to see the phrase "borderline schizophrenia" in the articles of a number of psychoanalytic writers. Noble (1951) uses the term in describing the primitive and grotesque dreams of certain patients who were either overtly schizophrenic or largely free of breaks with reality. Ekstein (1955) described the structural changes in a convalescent patient with a "borderline schizophrenia." In neither instance did the author attempt to define this term in any rigorous fashion (cf. Kety et al., 1968, p. 352) nor was there allusion to a familial factor.

Rado and the Border between Normal and Abnormal: The Schizotypal Patient

Although Rado did not use the term "borderline" in any technical sense, he clearly had an awareness of a collection of disorders intermediate between the "neuroses" and the "psychoses." In a 1950 address at the New York Academy of Medicine he discussed the "border region between the normal and the abnormal," outlining four broad types (1956, pp. 324–331). These included the depressive, the extractive, the paranoid, and the schizotype. The depressive, paranoid, and schizotype, he noted, could exist, for reasons unclear to Rado, both in a neurotic and in a psychotic form. Here, incidentally, is a "spectrum" concept in embryo form.

The "extractive" person Rado defined in terms that overlapped considerably with those ordinarily used to portray psychopathic behavior. Thus, the extractive type was impatient, intolerant of frustration, prone to rage outbursts, irresponsible, excitable, parasitic, and hedonistic. Extractive behavior departed from that of the classical psychopath in that one also saw depressive spells and "affect hunger" (David Levy's term for insatiable yearning for affection). Translated into contemporary parlance, Rado's description would, if I understand him correctly, be equated with a borderline person (in Kernberg's sense) with narcissistic and antisocial features—in whom a mild admixture of depressive features was also present. Since Rado regarded the "extractive" patient as extremely resistant to any psychotherapeutic efforts, he probably had in mind persons in whom the antisocial aspects far outweighed the depressive.

In his 1953 paper read before the American Psychiatric Association, Rado expanded on his concept of the *schizotypal* disorder (see Rado, 1962). Choosing the term "schizotype" to designate the phenotype answering to the hereditary predisposition to schizophrenia, Rado expressed the belief that clinical observation would permit the careful observer to detect this phenotype even in those who (*a*) never develop the full-blown psychosis (1956, p. 274) or (*b*) have not as yet manifested it. An inherent incapacity to experience pleasure was one important feature, for Rado, that characterized the schizotype. In addition one encountered in persons of this type a pervasive and continual engulfment in "emergency emotions" (fear, rage, and so on). The intensity of fear in the schizotype led some observers to employ the term "existential Angst." Sexual organization is usually rudimentary, lacking in genuine love and tenderness in the schizotype; in addition, he experiences himself as cut off from and different from the people around him. There is a tendency to lean heavily on external support as a means of reducing the effects of the inherited defects.

Whereas we now tend to see the various forms of schizotypal adjustment as expressions of varying degrees of genetic loading and of modifying influences, Rado spoke of *stages,* as though the less severe forms led into the more severe. He recognized, however, that "in favorable circumstances, the schizotype may . . . go through life without ever suffering a breakdown" (Rado, 1956, p. 278). The stages consisted of:

1. *Compensated schizoadaptation*—The schizoid person who never breaks down is viewed as a "well-compensated" schizotype.
2. *Decompensated schizoadaptation*—This stage is precipitated by panic and is soon accompanied by signs of "proprioceptive disorder" (with distorted awareness of the bodily self) and then of thought disorder. Rado equates this stage with Hoch and Polatin's "pseudoneurotic schizophrenia."
3. *Schizotypal disintegration*—This is "open schizophrenic psychosis."

Rado's concept of a borderline schizophrenia may be understood as a forerunner of the geneticists' adoption of this notion (see Kety et al., 1968, p. 352).

Robert P. Knight: Further Popularization of the Term "Borderline"

Robert P. Knight (1954), affiliated with the Menninger Foundation until he joined the staff of Austin Riggs, worked with hospitalized young adults receiving intensive psychotherapy. After Stern, he was the next to both recommend the term "borderline" and define it in a methodical fashion.

Borderline, for Knight, referred to a band of the psychopathological spectrum between neurosis and psychosis—where diagnosis is "often difficult, and equally often obscured behind a show of dramatic symptoms." The latter may be hysterical, phobic, obsessive, ritualistic, or what have you, but the more important locus of illness is the regressive position of the "ego forces." Knight used the analogy of a retreating army: the superficial clinical picture (the obsessions, phobias, and so on) constituted a "holding operation" in the forward position; the main ego forces, meantime, have regressed "far behind these lines" (1954, p. 101). Traditional diagnostic criteria, relating to reality testing, libido theory, and the supposed exclusiveness of neurosis versus psychosis, are "insufficient and misleading" in these cases which Knight now termed *borderline*. Adopting a more ego-psychological approach than some of his predecessors, Knight emphasized the severe *weakening* in borderline cases of many ego functions, including (1) secondary process thinking, (2) realistic planning, and (3) defenses against primitive impulses. Neutral functions like memory and calculation were preserved.

Knight also drew attention to the utility of the psychiatric interview in eliciting certain aspects of borderline pathology: the patient will tend to be evasive, and will deny or minimize in relation to conflictual material, and may even exhibit occasional blocking or peculiarities of word usage. He may remain oblivious to obvious implications of what is being said. (This is an allusion to the frequency with which "splitting" is encountered, such that contradictory attitudes exist side by side in the patient's mind.) Inappropriate affect and suspiciousness may be revealed at times. Other diagnostic hints include a history of lack of achievement. During a *free-associational* interview, the borderline patient is "more likely to show in bolder relief the various microscopic and macroscopic signs of schizophrenic illness" (1954, p. 104; italics mine). Furthermore, the Rorschach responses are often suggestive of a schizophrenic disorder, just as the word-association test frequently reveals loosening of associations. Knight thus defined "borderline" in a manner that overlaps greatly with at least the less dramatic cases of *schizophrenia*. Still, it does not appear that Knight was merely describing a kind of subclinical schizophrenia. Although his theoretical model is much more a part of what we would call the *spectrum concept* of schizophrenia, the actual cases Knight outlined (there are four in the original article) are somewhat mixed. By contemporary standards, two would be considered chronically schizophrenic; one, (an evenly divided) schizoaffective; and one, a severe hysterical character disorder with panic attacks and globus hystericus. Knight did not call these patients "borderline schizophrenics," and it is clear he wished to utilize a term divorced from the central concept of schizophrenia. Yet, as we shall see, Knight's borderline cases are nearer the schizophrenic end of the psychotic spectrum than are the borderlines of Grinker and Kernberg, though not at all as solidly schizophrenic as the borderline cases of the psychogeneticists Kety, Rosenthal, et al. (1968, pp. 345 ff.).

Bychowki's "Latent Psychosis"

In 1953 Gustav Bychowski expanded on the concept of *latent psychosis*, giving it more precise borders than Federn did. Bleuler (1950) had mentioned in the 1911 monograph that certain persons who are "irritable, odd, moody, withdrawn or exaggeratedly punctual" raise in us the suspicion of being schizophrenic. Since one often discovered concealed catatonic or paranoid symptoms in these persons, Bleuler felt justified in referring to the course of their schizophrenia as "latent." Bychowski introduced this notion with respect to the depressive psychoses also, though admitting that depressive "disposition" is less sharply defined in descriptive psychiatry than is schizophrenic disposition. There were five clinical situations Bychowski believed would justify the term "latent psychosis": (1) character neuroses of a sort that, under stress, burst into psychosis, (2) neurotic symptoms with the same outcome, (3) socially deviant behavior (perversion, addiction, delinquency), (4) an "arrested" psychosis destined later on to reveal its true nature, and (5) psychosis provoked by psychoanalysis. Respecting the last group, Bychowski mentions certain analysands who seemed to betray excessive communication between mental systems, such that primary processes spilled over too easily into their speech and thought. Scattering, condensation, and excessive use of allusions might be seen. Ego-boundary disturbances were noted in other cases, along with vulnerability to minor stresses. Some patients would become depressed over slight irregularities in the course of their analysis (a session that started ten minutes late, or whatever); such attitudes Bychowski thought bespoke a "depressive disposition." Bychowski also underlined the importance of the Rorschach as detecting schizophrenic disposition and mentioned that psychological tests per se do not differentiate between active and latent psychosis, a point with which I am very much in agreement.

The cases Bychowski used to illustrate his remarks consisted of three males and one female patient, all very gifted intellectually, who exhibited paranoid tendencies, splitting, severe narcissistic features, and peculiar somatic complaints, behind a facade of good functioning. One was a man of forty who only bathed once a year for fear he would die from the water and who feared the FBI would apprehend him because of communist sympathies he had some years earlier. Another was an analytic candidate who had an acute schizophrenic psychosis in the midst of her analysis. All these patients happened to be within the realm of schizophrenia, if defined to include "trait." All were initially "in between" with respect to neurosis and psychosis. I suspect their high intelligence operated to provide them with a better grasp of reality, such that their distortions fell short of delusion and hence fell short of easy diagnostic categorization.

Frosch and the "Psychotic Character"

Beginning in the mid-fifties John Frosch made a number of contributions to psychoanalytic theory regarding (*a*) impulsive character deformations and (*b*) a group of conditions in the intermediate range of severity, similar to what is currently being called "borderline" within the analytic community. Some features of the latter (including heightened impulsivity) were present in the impulse disorders Frosch described, though the two types of disorder are distinct in many ways.

Disorders of Impulse Control

Impulse disorders were the theme of a 1954 paper by Frosch and Wortis, refined later by Frosch (1977), who discussed the relation between *acting out* in the transference situation and disorders of impulse control, with which the phrase "acting out" was sometimes confused. The taxonomy of impulse disorders advocated in the 1977 paper was based on a division into *symptom* impulse disorders and *character* impulse disorders. The former involved impulsive acts that could be isolated or recurring and included such entities as kleptomania, voyeurism, and examples of intermittent explosive behavior secondary, in some instances, to temporal lobe epilepsy, drugs, or other factors affecting the central nervous system.

Character impulse disorders ("impulse-ridden characters" as they were called earlier by Wilhelm Reich) could also be divided into an organic and a nonorganic group. In either, chronic impulsivity "permeates character structure as a pathognomonic feature [and] is not limited to any one type of impulsive act" (1977, p. 298). The nonorganic cases needed to be distinguished from psychopathic (antisocial) personalities and from some instances of impulsive "acting out."

A good many patients with the impulse disorders depicted by Frosch would, I suspect, satisfy the criteria for a borderline condition as defined by Kernberg or Gunderson (see Chapter 9) or as described under the rubric "psychotic character" by Frosch himself in another series of papers (see below).

A number of factors may contribute to the development of an impulse disorder, their intensity and mixture varying from case to case. Hereditary factors might include genetic liability to a manic disorder. Bipolar patients are characteristically "driven" and are often impulsive, quick-tempered and irritable from birth (see Chapter 7). Action oriented by nature, they are more than ordinarily prone to acting out (in the strict sense) should they undergo psychoanalytic therapy. Psychosocial factors may also play an important role, as underlined by Frosch (1966) in a paper stressing the significance of interference (by parents or others) with the child's capacity to delay gratification. Severe frustration (or overgratification) may foster impulsivity even in the absence of constitutional or neurological factors. As examples: an engulfing mother might minimize frustration in a child to the point where proper delay patterns do not develop; a frustrating mother might contribute to the fostering of ungovernable wishes and faulty impulse control. The "as if" character was said to illustrate the former; the impulsive character, the latter. Fenichel, in this connection, saw a relationship between impulsive character and certain depressive reactions, because of fear, common to both, of loss of supplies (Kanzer, 1957, p. 138).

The organic factors noted in a proportion of impulse-ridden characters were sometimes accompanied by electroencephalographic abnormalities. Frosch also considered the possibility of a constitutional factor, acknowledging Fries's work on differences in infant motility patterns. Some infants show a hyperexcitability derived from abnormality of the neuromuscular system "as a result of inheritance, intrauterine life and birth" (1954, p. 136).

Psychotic Character

In a series of articles (1960, 1964, 1966, 1970) Frosch outlined the features of a group of patients in the intermediate range of psychopathology. Frosch proposed the term *psychotic character* as a replacement for conditions hitherto known by such labels as "borderline," "pseudoneurotic schizophrenia," "ambulatory schizophrenia," and "latent psychosis." The qualities shared by these various types of intermediate-level disturbance, and which made Frosch feel justified in gathering them under one title, were (1) preservation of reality testing, (2) infantile object relations that were nonetheless superior to those seen in overt psychotics, (3) a capacity for "reversibility," that is, for recovering quickly from a psychotic episode (should one occur), such that the patient's usual level of adaptation was at least fair, and (4) primitive defensive operations.

With respect to etiology, Frosch offered the following view (1964):

> When we use the term borderline, we are obviously referring to conditions which are borderline to psychosis. . . . If [such patients] do decompensate and become psychotic, they may reveal a recognizable clinical syndrome such as schizophrenia. On the other hand, the psychotic picture in decompensation may run the gamut of all known psychoses, paranoid, manic-depressive, and the rest. (p. 82)

Frosch's remarks are some of the few detailed comments by anyone writing on borderline or related syndromes, until recently, that attempt to include a biological-constitutional abnormality in the theoretical framework.

Writing mainly from the ego-psychological and object-relational frames of reference, Frosch emphasized that the person with "psychotic character" may go all his life without decompensating into overt psychosis, just as the "neurotic character" may go on all his life without showing a symptom neurosis. Frosch's awareness that at least transient psychotic periods do occur in many patients with psychotic character makes it clear that he was in tune with the concept of vulnerability, though he did not use the language of the psychogeneticists. His term also suggests acceptance of the spectrum concept, in the sense that the psychotic character is, in essence, a schizophrenic, or manic-depressive, and so on, *sine* (overt) psychosis.

Frosch made meticulous distinctions regarding the kind of reality break seen among patients with psychotic character, in contrast to those with full-blown psychoses:

> In examining the position of the ego and its functions toward reality, there are three areas which must be differentiated. . . . These are the *relationship with reality*, the *feeling of reality*, and the *capacity to test reality*. (1964, p. 84)

Disturbances in the *relationship with reality* may manifest themselves as hallucinations, illusions, or as bizarre deviations in social amenities, and so forth. In the psychotic character, any such disturbances tend to be transient or reversible. The same is true for abnormalities in the *feeling of reality*, of which transitory depersonalization before a therapist's vacation might be an example. In full-blown psychosis, not only are there more serious and enduring disturbances in both these functions but the capacity to *test* reality is likewise seriously impaired. In the *psychotic character*, however, this capacity is preserved. Our verbal interventions are more likely to bring about improvement in the patient's reality sense, since it is possible for us to convince him with logical argument that certain unrealistic perceptions, impressions about himself or others, and so on, were indeed unrealistic. Kernberg's indebtedness to Frosch's ideas on reality testing will be apparent when we examine in greater detail his point concerning the response to confrontation in (psychostructurally) borderline versus psychiatric patients (Chapter 9).

The psychotic character exhibits a level of function intermediate between psychosis and neurosis: this level represents the final common pathway for heterogeneous etiological factors. These factors, as Frosch indicated, include schizophrenia, manic-depression, and chaotic early environment. Other psychotic characters showed evidence of minimal brain damage. The latter often stemmed from the perinatal period, a seizure disorder was sometimes present, and in a few cases head trauma in childhood seemed to play a significant role. In this respect Frosch's psychotic characters resembled the patients with severe psychiatric disorders often mimicking schizophrenia that Bellak (1976) and also Quitkin, Rifkin, and Klein (1976) have recently described.

As with most descriptions of borderline patients, regardless of the particular term and author, mention is also made of the multiple and various presenting symptoms. Frosch alludes to "phobias, conversion phenomena, compulsive traits, paranoid features, depression, and anxiety," a catalog similar to that noted among Hoch and Polatin's "pseudoneurotic" patients.

Jacobson and Her Colleagues: An Inchoate Notion of Borderline Affective Disorders

A generation ago, the prevailing approach to the classification of depressive disorders emphasized a categorical distinction between the "endogenous" (or biologically based) and the "exogenous" (or psychologically based) varieties. Examples of depressive disorders where some vegetative signs were present, that nevertheless did not include (or progress to) psychotic symptoms, were therefore regarded as puzzling. Jacobson (1953) gives voice to this uneasiness in her paper on "cyclothymic depression." Impressed by the likelihood that constitution or hereditary predisposition played a key role in the more severe cases, she was also aware that "many cases of simple depression are without psychotic symptoms, yet belong to the manic-depressive group" (1953, p. 50). Since these cases were easily mistaken for psychoneuroses, they were often—and unwisely—referred for psychoanalysis. Jacobson believed that such patients were sometimes amenable to analysis anyhow, so long as the analyst took cognizance of the underlying predisposition. The patients themselves would at times speak of their affective symptoms as something foreign to their nature ("like a fog settling down on my brain"). This was particularly true of what Jacobson called the *psychosomatic* features (e.g., retardation versus the keyed-up state) as opposed to the *endogenous* features proper (e.g., anorexia and insomnia). Elsewhere she drew attention to the tendency of the psychotic patient to seek solution of his psychosexual conflicts through regressive escape "because of the inherited constitution or the emotional deprivation or instinctual overstimulation" (1953, p. 62). Furthermore, in the *prepsychotic* personality (including that of the cyclothymic-depressed patient), inner representations of the self and of objects (i.e., of other persons) were not sharply separated. Similar notions of poor self-versus-object differentiation are reflected in Erikson's concept of ego diffusion (1951) or in Kernberg's allusion (as a criterion for borderline personality organization) to poor integration in one's sense of identity (1967). In a like vein, *lowered anxiety tolerance* (one of Kernberg's "nonspecific" criteria for borderline organization) carries forward Jacobson's point about the cyclothymic patient's "remarkable vulnerability, and intolerance of frustration, hurt or disappointment" (1953, p. 66).

From these remarks it seems clear that Jacobson was receptive to the idea that some of the milder instances of depression and hypomania belonged within the province of the manic-depressive disorders, just as surely as certain "schizotypal" cases were appreciated, even in the 1940s and 1950s, as affiliated in some way with the more striking cases of "core" schizophrenia. This means that Jacobson was alive to the dimensional as well as to the category-based aspects of diagnosis and could envision certain patients as "borderline" with respect to the manic-depressive psychoses (see Stone, 1978). In her discussion of Chodoff's paper on the depressive personality (1973), Jacobson gives a clinical example of three generations of manic-depressives, some of whom suffered severe disorders, others mild.

Like most of the psychoanalysts of her day, Jacobson was, however, rather linear in her conception of causality, relying heavily on distinctions concerning the level of psychosexual development. She saw the manic-depressive as having "reached a higher level of differentiation than the schizophrenic; consequently, the acute regressive process doesn't go so far as in schizophrenia" (1973, p. 65). This linearity is reflected in the papers of the other authors who contributed to Greenacre's book (1953) on affective disorders. Gero (1953) described a young woman with depression and severe anorexia nervosa, presaging the work of Cantwell et al. (1977) and others on the relationship of some cases of anorexia nervosa to the primary affective disorders. But Gero does not mention a constitutional factor, stressing instead "early oral conflicts." He does allude to the mechanism of *splitting* in his patient, as when the young woman spoke of her mother in two contradictory ways: mother's body was seen as magically powerful from one point of view but also as a "destroyed bloody mess," from another (1953, p. 126). By contemporary criteria Gero's patient probably exhibited *borderline* personality organization and, at the same time, a kinship to the affective disorders.

Katan (1953), meantime, sought to understand manic symptoms as an attempt at restitution. He admits (1953, p. 149) that he could find no particular "central conflict" as relevant to the manic cases he had encountered nor could he elaborate any convincing psychological explanation for the switch from mania to depression. This phenomenon is now viewed predominantly in biological terms (see Bunney et al., 1972). The shortcomings of the purely psychodynamic explanations of mania and of severe depressive disorders seem obvious a quarter century after Greenacre's book. But at the time, beyond Jacobson, Rado, Frosch, and a few others, not many were receptive to a multidimensional theory of causality for borderline conditions.

The Hysteroid Patient of Easser and Lesser

Still basing their theoretical conceptions upon a psychodynamic model, Easser and Lesser (1965) drew attention to a group of patients who were hysterical in their outward manifestations yet somehow more deeply disturbed than their classically psychoneurotic counterparts. The more mature and better integrated hysterical patients, according to the traditional psychoanalytic teaching, had a fixation point in their psychosexual development in the genital stage. But the sicker group of hysterical patients appeared, according to the authors, to have pregenital (particularly, early oral stage) fixation points. These patients, some of whom had psychotic features, and others of whom were elsewhere called "borderline," the researchers wished to reclassify "hysteroid."

The "hysteroid" patient they described as "a caricature of the hysteric" (1965, p. 399): some features were (1) irresponsibility, (2) erratic work history, (3) chaotic and unfulfilling relationships that never become profound or lasting (in contrast to the profound, lasting but turbulent relationships of her hysterical cousin), (4) an early childhood history of emotional problems and disturbed habit patterns (enuresis until a late age, for example), and (5) chaotic sexuality often with promiscuity and frigidity combined.

Easser and Lesser also make mention of marked primitivity of defenses in the hysteroid patient, along with starkness in their dream imagery, much of which was violent and repugnant. Disappointingly, in the authors' case descriptions (consisting of six women) there is no mention of premenstrual phenomena, even though emotionally ill women tend to experience an increase in their distress the week or so before their menses—as was appreciated by Hippocrates, and amply documented by countless psychiatrists over the past century (see Diamond et al, 1976; Schukit et al., 1975). This "premenstrual" factor is quite important in many so-called borderline women, a good many of whom stop appearing borderline as soon as this matter is rectified through appropriate medication.

Easser and Lesser also made no mention of any psychiatric abnormalities in the families of their hysteroid patients, except for one uninformative allusion to a mother who also seemed hysteroid.

The term "hysteroid" is of interest in that it represents an effort to grapple with the situation, that seemed paradoxical at the time, where a "healthy" character type (the hysteric) could somehow manifest itself in a patient whose function fell distinctly short of the neurotic level. *Hysteroid* is in reality a two-dimensional concept (character type and level of function). Recently it has become incorporated in the even more elaborate notion of the *hysteroid dysphoric* (of which, more below; see also Klein and Davis, 1969), a three-dimensional concept relating to character type, level of function, and also constitutional predisposition.

Grinker, Werble, and Drye: The Borderline Patient

In the early 1960s a group at the Chicago Psychoanalytic Institute sought to outline the characteristics most commonly encountered in patients accorded the borderline label. The following were singled out for special attention: (1) marked lowering of self-esteem, (2) hypersensitivity to criticism and rejection, (3) suspiciousness, (4) extreme fearfulness, (5) fears of *aggression* (whether of their own or of others), of *closeness,* of *responsibility,* and of *change,* (6) tenuousness in interpersonal relations, (7) deficiency in reality orientation, and (8) heightened use of primitive defenses (*denial* and *projection*). The Chicago group further noted that these borderline features were to be seen over a fairly broad band of psychopathology, spanning the narcissistic character disorders to conditions they described as "near the psychoses."

The Chicago outline was later used as a guide in the diagnosis of the borderline patients studied extensively by Grinker, Werble, and Drye (1968). These investigators pursued an ego-psychological approach, studying ninety-three observable variables in some five dozen hospitalized patients. Their choice of focusing on ego functions was dictated by an understandable disillusionment with the current psychodynamic formulations, inasmuch as apparent "fixation points" in almost all very disturbed patients are much alike, no matter whether one is dealing with schizophrenics or manic-depressives or even these so-called borderline cases. Cluster analysis of their data yielded four subgroups. The first, which they called the *psychotic border,* consisted of patients exhibiting inappropriate negative behavior, poor grooming, rage outbursts, and depression. The second, or "core borderline" group, was composed of patients with pervasive negative affect, little involvement with others, a tendency to act impulsively and self-destructively, and an awareness of their own identity side by side with behavior that was inconsistent with this identity. Group III contained "as if" patients, who tended to copy the identities of others. The last group, rather near the psychoneuroses, consisted of patients with "anaclitic" depression.

In Table 1–1 (adapted from Perry and Klerman, 1978) the characteristics of the four groups are spelled out in greater detail. The importance of Grinker's contribution stems from the fact that he and his colleagues were the first investigators who tried to objectify the diagnosis of borderline in some methodical fashion. They did not, however, carry their work to the point of establishing definite inclusion and exclusion criteria or weighted rating scales. Though less precise in these respects than the more recent criterion sets of Gunderson, Kernberg, Klein, or Spitzer (see Chapter 9), Grinker's group represents an important advance over their predecessors.

TABLE 1–1

Criteria of Grinker et al. for Borderline Syndrome

I. *Common Characteristics*
   - A. Anger is main or only affect
   - B. Defect in affectional (interpersonal) relations
   - C. Absence of consistent self-identity
   - D. Depression characterizes life

II. *Characteristics of the Four Subtypes*
   - A. Type I: The Psychotic Border
     1. Behavior inappropriate, nonadaptive
     2. Self-identity and reality sense deficient
     3. Negative behavior and anger expressed
     4. Depression
   - B. Type II: The Core Borderline Syndrome
     1. Vacillating involvement with others
     2. Anger acted out
     3. Depression
     4. Self-identity not consistent
   - C. Type III: The Adaptive, Affectless, Defended, "As if" Persons
     1. Behavior adaptive, appropriate
     2. Complementary relationships
     3. Little affect; spontaneity lacking
     4. Defenses of withdrawal and intellectualization
   - D. Type IV: The Border with the Neuroses
     1. Anaclitic depression
     2. Anxiety
     3. Resemblance to neurotic, narcissistic character

SOURCE: Adapted from Perry and Klerman (1978), *Archives of General Psychiatry,* 35:141–150. Copyright 1978, American Medical Association. Reprinted by permission.

Little attention was paid in the Grinker monograph to the question of hereditary predisposition to the major psychoses.[3] The borderline syndromes were felt to be distinct from schizophrenia; only a tiny percentage of the original patients had developed, at follow-up, a clear-cut schizophrenic illness. Certainly the borderline patients of the Grinker study are distinct, symptomatically, from chronic (core) schizophrenia. Less clear is the degree of distinction from the concept of schizophrenic *vulnerability* (see Chapter 5). As it happens, the definitions of the four subgroups emphasize *depressive affect* in three (I, II, and IV). Others besides myself have wondered whether these subgroups of Grinker are not borderline (in terms of predisposition) to the *primary affective disorders,* especially to unipolar depression (see D. F. Klein, 1975, and Chapter 9). At least some patients with severe schizoid/narcissistic character disorders would be included in the Type III subgroup.

With respect to the evolution of ideas, Grinker's work may be viewed as a stage in advance of Stern and Knight, one that has been carried forward in the work of Gunderson and his collaborators (Chapter 9).

Other Recent Commentators

The preceding survey cannot of course do justice to all the competing formulations of borderline psychopathology that exist in the literature. Other relevant articles on the subject have been reviewed recently in the thoughtful paper of Liebowitz (1978).

Some of the points made by other psychoanalytic commentators on the borderline syndrome include the following.

Modell (1963) speaks of schizophrenia as a symptom conglomeration and not as a disease, analogizing the current usage of the term to that of dropsy in the nineteenth century, that is, a term seems at first to denote one malady but as time passes is seen to include a number of etiologically separable entities. The borderline patient Modell believes is sometimes a schizophrenic manqué: eccentric, withdrawn—but without the full-blown psychosis. But others to whom the label "borderline" is applied are, as Modell mentions (1963, p. 283), "depressed, or addicted, or perverted, or any combination thereof" (including withdrawn and eccentric). Modell alludes to the subtle destruction in the sense of reality which is reminiscent of fully developed schizophrenia. From an object-relations viewpoint Modell

[3]This topic receives little attention even in the more recent monograph (Grinker and Werble, 1977), where only two of the references allude to psychogenetic studies. It is clear that if one's bias is against a spectrum concept with respect to the major psychoses, many borderline cases will strike the observer as an entity apart. Those endorsing such a concept will see many borderline cases as dilute forms of the classical psychoses: Grinker and Werble's case 16 (p. 94), for example, resembles my case 20, one that I consider in the penumbra of manic-depression.

makes the interesting observation that borderline patients make a transference which is "transitional" in the analytic encounter. The therapist, for example, is viewed as *outside* the self (a failure in this would indicate psychosis), yet the therapist is not fully recognized as existing as a separate individual (the capacity to grasp which would be compatible with the healthier neurotic organization). In his attempt to find a psychodynamic explanation for this intermediate type of relationship, Modell makes reference to arrest in ego development from possible failure in maternal care, a formulation in harmony with that of Mahler and her colleagues. My own objection to this line of thought lies chiefly in its unidimensionality. There may indeed be a proportion of patients diagnosed according to one set of criteria or another as borderline who indeed suffered the sort of ego-rigidifying early environment Modell refers to. But I hope to make the point clear in subsequent chapters of this book that many persons who exhibit the sicker forms of psychic organization (borderline or psychotic) come by their frailty via strong biologically based predisposition and would function at no better than a borderline level (by any definition) irrespective of the quality of mothering, and other influences, in their formative years. In this regard the elegant adoption studies of Kety and his co-workers (where children whose fathers were schizophrenic are reared by normal adopting parents) are particularly convincing (see Chapter 8).

The Swiss investigator Benedetti (1965) spoke of borderline psychoses (*Grenz-psychosen*), which he believed exhibited three main clinical characteristics. This symptom triad consisted of hypochondriasis, ideas of reference, and depersonalization. Benedetti, whose borderline concept is, after Kernberg's, the most widely accepted in Norway (Stone and Oestberg, 1979), was strongly influenced by Hoch and Polatin; his definition is thus primarily related to the realm of schizophrenic disorders.

Lewis (1968) offered a formulation stressing the ego-function defects common to the class of patients called "borderline." Less emphasis is placed on specific symptom clusters. The chief ego defects, in Lewis's view, involve the sense of boundary and the sense of identity: the psychopathology is in the area of perception of the self. Again, one cannot quarrel with this formulation as far as it goes: Impairment in the integration of the self is central to most if not all metapsychological constructions of the borderline state. But these constructions tend to hang in midair for want of grounding to the genetic and biological foundations relevant to the bulk of these cases.

Zetzel (1971) indicates how the course of analytic psychotherapy differs in borderline versus schizophrenic patients, insofar as the borderline patient will gradually become able, even without medication, to acknowledge and later to relinquish magical expectations of the therapist, whereas the schizophrenic remains mired in this form of primitive extractiveness. The doctor-patient relationship, as it evolves, becomes in and of itself a diagnostic tool in Zetzel's model. Those who do intensive psychotherapy with borderline and psychotic patients do, of course, regard this kind of difference as a criterion of diagnosis—as a validation later on, perhaps—but only those criteria can be called truly diagnostic that we distinguish when the patient is first seen. We will have more to say on this matter in the chapter on diagnostic criteria (Chapter 8).

Pfeiffer (1974), from the Duke Medical Center, at least attempts to offer a set of initial diagnostic elements that set apart the borderline patient. In his opinion no clear pattern emerges in the borderline group with respect either to psychological testing or to etiological factors (I agree with the heterogeneity he is hinting at, but I think we can already delineate specific etiology-based syndromes to a certain extent; Pfeiffer seems too pessimistic here). The *clinical* pattern Pfeiffer refers to includes (*a*) a limited range of affects, especially limited to anxiety and anger, (*b*) deficits in affective relationships, (*c*) proneness to periods of "depressed loneliness," and (*d*) lack of integration of the total personality. The kinship between Pfeiffer's formulation and the more well-delineated criteria of Grinker and Gunderson is apparent.

In a similar vein Cary (1972), from the Hershey Medical Center in Pennsylvania, outlined a number of differential-diagnostic points said to distinguish borderline patients from those with similar conditions. It is Cary's contention that this differentiation can be accomplished through use of a (psycho-) structural-dynamic analysis alone. According to his model, the schizoid patient, for example, shows resignation in the face of frustration, in contrast to the borderline patient, who in this situation exhibits rage. From the standpoint of psychic development, the borderline is seen as fixated at a pre-Oedipal level of identification of ego with object, in such a way that he struggles between distancing and fusion; that is, "between experiencing threatening emotions as a *separate* individual versus identifying with the behavior of others" (p. 35; italics mine) as a protection against overwhelming experiences. Cary also mentions the dilemma in borderline states characterized by fear of losing both a sense of identity and a sense of relatedness to others. This Cary sees as conspiring to promote contradictory wishes to fuse with and separate from the object. Finally Cary attempts to distinguish the borderline patient's sense of futility and pervasive feeling of loneliness and isolation from the guilt, self-derogation, anxiety, conscious expectation of help, and self-critical preoccupation with thoughts about others that are found in neurotic depression. Regarding the latter, "angry rageful demands after exaggerated bids for attention" and "childlike narcissistic needs" are more what one encounters among borderline patients. To my way of thinking, Cary is describing in this last point an intersection between borderline structure, as Kernberg conceives it, and narcissistic character type. But a predominantly narcissistic character is not a prerequisite to borderline structure (though this character type is overrepresented in the borderline realm): any character type can predominate in a given borderline patient. Furthermore the point about the oscillation between fusion and distancing is seen so generally in sicker patients, including those with psychotic structure (see Burnham on the "need-fear" dilemma in schizophrenia, 1969), that I doubt it can reliably differentiate patients with, versus patients without, borderline organization. In general I think the diagnostic model Cary proposed, lying entirely within the psychoanalytic framework, would still gather in a group of persons heterogeneous with respect to genetic and constitutional factors, even to the point where prognostic and treatment implications would become blurred. A similar point has been made recently by Meissner (1978), who commented that attempts to establish borderline pathology, using psychoanalytic models, as distinct from the neurotic and psychotic have led to formulations of the borderline personality as having quite stable defensive and object-relational characteristics. But Meissner warns that "This unifying . . . trend may be overreaching itself in . . . providing a . . . unified account of an underlying diagnostic *heterogeneity*" (p. 309; italics mine). About the two cases Cary describes (both college women) in some detail, not enough symptomatological and family data are mentioned to permit assignment of patients or relatives to areas within the standard nosology.

Moving much more in the multidimensional direction advocated here are the views expressed by Dickes (1974) from the Downstate Department of Psychiatry in Brooklyn. Dickes is dissatisfied with the old continuum concept "psychosis-borderline-neurosis" because he finds evidence within the group of borderline conditions of a multiplicity of syndromes—of differing etiologies. Dickes makes some reference to work in the biological sphere: to studies of children at high risk for schizophrenia, to recent work with lithium in the manic-depressive illnesses, and so on. At the end of Dickes's article is an interesting example of a patient whose initial productions made her physicians think in terms of a phobic disorder but who subsequently gave clear evidence of delusional thinking in the area of phobic avoidance. There is a difference, of course, between a subtle and initially misdiagnosed schizophrenic patient and one who is borderline (in the sense of having *no* delusional ideation but poor ego integration). Dickes finds that the purely psychological formulations of his predecessors leave much to be desired, but he does not go as far as would now seem feasible in building the necessary bridges between the psychological and biological aspects of borderline disorders.

CHAPTER 2

Two- and Three-Dimensional Diagrams Useful in Defining Borderline Conditions

The Diagnosis Cube

As we have seen there have been many usages of the term "borderline" in psychiatry; if one includes terms not containing the word "borderline" but which designate a condition in the intermediate range of severity, the list swells even further. Some of the terms have already fallen into desuetude (e.g., "incipient schizophrenia"); some enjoy only local popularity (e.g., "pseudoneurotic schizophrenia"); others are beginning to gain a wider audience (e.g., "hysteroid dysphoria"). Terms embodying the word "borderline" answer to a variety of criterion sets, some more precise, some less so.

In part this variety is a reflection of differences among prominent clinicians, each of whom has popularized a particular definition. These definitions, in turn, will reflect the peculiarities of the patient population with which each of these prominent clinicians is especially familiar. Differences in degree of genetic loading, in socioeconomic status, intellectual endowment, and level of organicity will make one "borderline" patient sample strikingly dissimilar to another.

Figure 2–1. The Diagnosis Cube

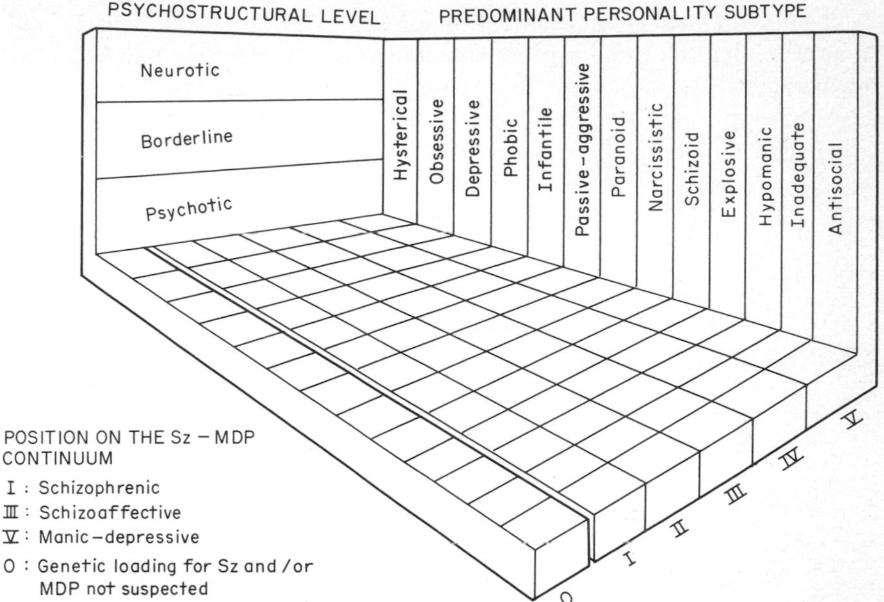

NOTE: Three important dimensions of psychiatric diagnosis—constitutional type, usual adaptational level, and predominant personality subtype—may be portrayed, for didactic purposes, as sides of a cube.

The floor of the cube has been divided into a number of tracks that are of relevance to borderline conditions. These represent arbitrary divisions of a phenotypic continuum ranging from "pure" schizophrenic (I) to predominantly schizophrenic schizoaffective (II) to the pure-type affective disorders (V). An additional track (O) has been added for those patients in whom no predisposition to any form of classical psychosis is discernible.

One wall is divided into three regions designating the three types of personality organization or structure: neurotic, borderline, and psychotic (as defined by Kernberg). The height reached by a person, at any given time, with respect to this wall, may be said to define the current level of adaptation or "coping."

Paradoxically, there are important areas of agreement where one might least expect it. The usages of Kernberg, Grinker, Gunderson, and Spitzer derive from different theoretical orientations and different patient populations from four large communities across the United States, yet there is a strong tendency for a patient, called "borderline" by the adherents of one of their systems, to be so considered by adherents of the other three. Because borderline cases defy traditional categories, one is often at a loss on how to diagnose them within the framework of our standard nomenclature. Yet if one attempts to assess each such case with respect to its constitutional, adaptational (coping), and characterological aspects, even if one must hazard a guess about the constitutional factors, some sense can often be made of an otherwise baffling clinical picture.

The three-dimensional diagram of Figure 2–1 shows the author's method of representing the three aspects simultaneously. Borderline patients who are thought to be capable of benefiting from psychoanalytically oriented psychotherapy can, using this method, be represented as occupying a specific region within this three-dimensional space (Figure 2–3). The remaining diagrams demonstrate areas of overlap and distinctness among some of the more important usages of the borderline concept.

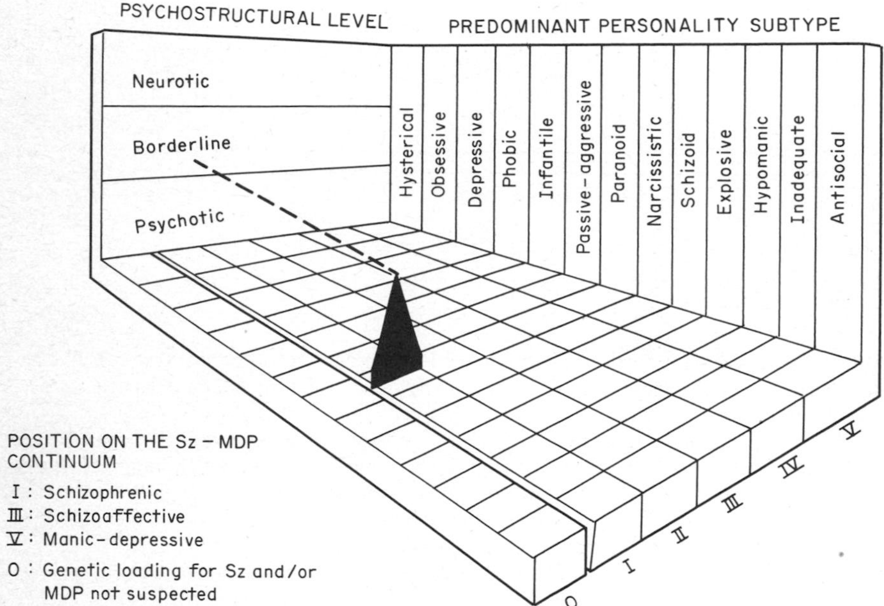

Figure 2–2. The Diagnosis Cube: Illustrative Example

Region of Optimal Response to Analytically Oriented Psychotherapy

The advantage of the Diagnosis Cube (Figures 2-1 and 2-2) lies in its permitting simultaneous diagnosis according to all three frames of reference. Thus, a patient with a paranoid personality functioning at a borderline level, and showing schizophrenic stigmata, can be represented by a single marker (1) overlying the schizophrenia track, (2) at the height of borderline structure, and (3) opposite the compartment for paranoid personality. This situation is portrayed in Figure 2–2.

The second wall in Figure 2–2 is divided arbitrarily into small sections, each representing a personality type in the traditional or in the psychoanalytic nomenclature. While it is not possible to well-order these types from sickest to healthiest, there is a way of ordering them in relation to responsiveness—or lack of it—to modified psychoanalytic method. Generally speaking, persons with predominantly antisocial, explosive, or hypomanic personalities respond poorly or not at all to psychoanalytic approaches. This is reflected in Figure 2–3. The personality types are examined in detail in Chapter 10.

Figure 2–3. The Diagnosis Cube: Region of Optimal Response to Analytically Oriented Psychotherapy

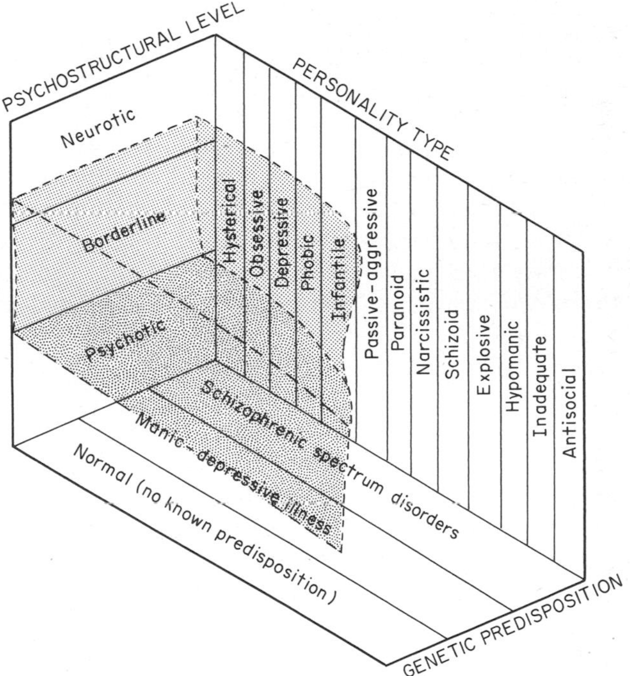

NOTE: The volume outlined within the diagnosis cube delineates a territory within which "intensive" or "expressive" psychotherapy (analytically oriented psychotherapy) is generally thought to be useful.

The territory includes the borderline region, plus the lower end of the neurotic level (where certain severe phobics might be represented, for example) and the highest part of the psychotic level. The territory includes most of the "healthier" character types but begins to collapse in the region of the narcissistic and schizoid characters (the less responsive groups), vanishing altogether in the region of the nonresponsive hypomanic and antisocial characters.

The Sz-MDP Continuum Diagram

Persons with the various borderline syndromes may be, according to one definition, borderline with respect to one of the major or classical "psychoses." The borderline schizophrenia of Kety et al. (1968) is an example (this syndrome is more precisely defined in Chapter 7). They may, according to another definition, be in the borderland between the "pure" types, that is, in the broad region of "schizoaffective" disorders, loosely defined. Finally, there is a group of definitions (Bergeret, Grinker, Gunderson, Kernberg, and Masterson) where the term "borderline" is used to depict a clinical syndrome; no relationship to the major psychoses is implied. I have contended (Stone, 1977a) that many of the cases embraced by these latter images are related to the major psychoses, after all. Further remarks about possible genetic factors are to be found in Chapter 7. In any event, I have found it useful, when evaluating a new patient or in recording the evolution of a patient whose illness began some time ago, to envision a continuum of outward manifestation, among severe psychiatric disorders, stretching from undisputed schizophrenia at one end to undisputed affective illness at the other. In between is a whole host of "mixed" conditions, whose symptoms may be predominantly schizophrenic, or predominantly affective (manic-depressive), or rather evenly divided between these two. For convenience, one may then make three divisions in this "schizoaffective" region. With the two "extremes," schizophrenic (Sz) and manic-depressive (MDP), a five-region Sz-MDP continuum is generated. These are the same regions (where I designates "pure" schizophrenic or schizotypal disorders and V, pure affective) on the floor of the Diagnostic Cube.

The Sz-MDP (phenotypic) Continuum Diagram is shown in Figure 2–4. Severity of illness may be indicated along the vertical axis. Since very mild cases seldom show any obvious affiliation to the major psychoses, for practical purposes, the diagram includes cases of high and *intermediate* severity. Thus, the upper half of the oblong may be used for patients with psychotic structure; the lower half, for those with borderline structure or level of function. Florid examples of schizophrenia would be positioned in the cell on the upper left. Borderline schizophrenics would be placed in the lower left cell. The two cells on the far right are used for primary affective disorders, functioning at the psychotic or borderline levels. The six cells in between remain for schizoaffective disorders. In actual practice, some of these cells will be sparsely populated. Deciding on the proper locus of any given patient at any particular moment in his clinical course can be approached in two ways: by clinical intuition (preferably, the shared intuition of two or more raters working independently of one another) or by use of a weighted rating scale for "schizophrenic" versus "affective" symptoms. Such a scale is described in Chapter 8. The weighted scale permits the rater to establish a numerical ratio of schizophrenic to affective signs

Figure 2–4. Phenotypic Continuum of Schizophrenic and Manic-Depressive (Primary Affective) Disorders

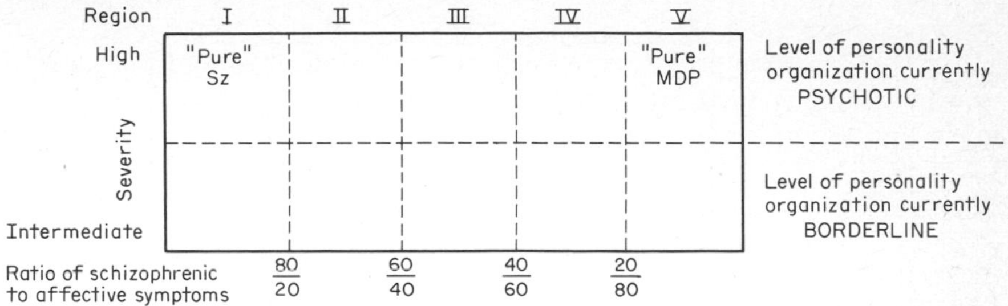

KEY: *Region I:* Schizophrenic syndromes without any features of affective disorder. At this (as at the opposite) end of the continuum, the clinical picture is distinctive, permitting the notion of a separate category.

Region II: A region of apparently schizophrenic disorders, where there are sufficient degrees of affective (manic, depressive) symptoms to incline one away from the diagnosis of unequivocal schizophrenia and toward a schizoaffective disorder.

Region III: Schizophrenic and affective stigmata are here rather evenly divided. This region comprises the conditions which are most justifiably labeled *schizoaffective* without qualifying adjectives.

Region IV: A region of disorders with predominantly affective (manic and/or depressive) symptoms, but where there are signs and symptoms usually associated with schizophrenia sufficient to incline one away from a purely manic-depressive diagnosis.

Region V: The pure affective disorders, free of any schizophenic symptoms. Unipolar depression, bipolar-I and -II disorders, and so on, would be placed here. Severity may range from psychotic (manic-depressive psychoses proper) to borderline (spectrum MDP conditions).

and symptoms. The five regions of the diagram represent different ranges of this ratio (indicated at the bottom of the continuum). Raters in either situation may place a dot somewhere on the diagram if they think the patient has, in core or borderline form, an illness within the Sz-MDP continuum. Conditions seemingly unrelated to this universe of cases are simply rated as "outside." It must be emphasized that one is evaluating outward manifestation or phenotype here. Whether any correspondence exists between this external picture and inner genotype, we can only guess at; validation would require not only elaborate study (namely, of relatives of patients in various cells of the diagram) but the ability to test for biochemical and other "reliable" markers—which are not as yet available even in the "purest" examples of the classical psychoses (see Chapter 8).

Good reliability can be achieved among raters for either the intuitive or numerical localization of cases within the Sz-MDP Continuum Diagram. For purposes of illustration, the averaged loci (three to four raters) of the first twenty-seven patients admitted to one of the long-term units of the New York Hospital, Westchester Division, between January and June,

Figure 2–5. Loci of Twenty-seven Consecutive Admissions within the Sz-MDP Continuum Diagram

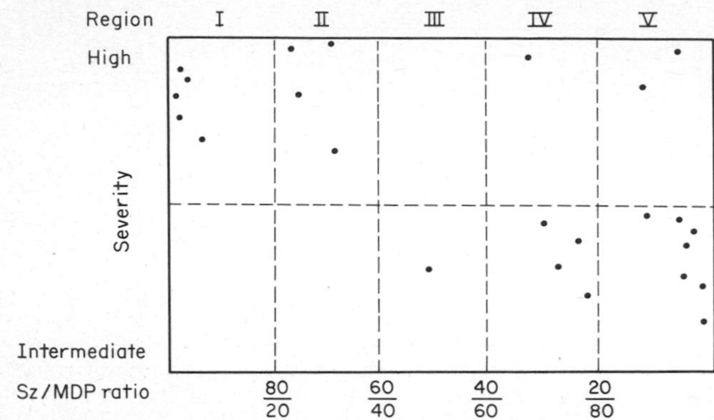

NOTE: By consensus of three to four raters, the number of patients whose conditions were considered to lie outside this continuum was three; one patient (who had two first-degree relatives with major depressive illness) could not be accurately placed and two borderline patients had conditions not relevant to this continuum.

1978, are shown in Figure 2–5. In the introduction to Part IV (case illustrations) of this book, the loci of the twenty-nine cases are similarly outlined.

The Sz-MDP Continuum Diagram, if accompanied by a separate space for conditions that have no apparent connection to the major psychoses, may be used as a large "universe" of all moderately to very serious functional psychiatric disorders. Onto this large universe, one may then map the smaller domains occupied by the various syndromes and other nosological entities under examination in this book. It would be of interest, for example, to compare the location of all patients to whom the label of "pseudoneurotic schizophrenia" would apply, with the location of Kasanin's "schizoaffectives." Figures 2–6 through 2–8 represent my attempt to make this sort of mapping for some of the earlier borderline and related labels (Figure 2–6), for some of the more etiologically specific modern terms (Figure 2–7), and for some of the broader usages (Figure 2–8). The procedure used was the same as in the preparation of the table in Chapter 7, reflecting the history of borderline and related terms. Detailed case descriptions by the different authors and investigators were analyzed according to modern research diagnostic criteria; cases not classifiable in this manner were diagnosed impressionistically and also according to the weighted rating scale mentioned above (see Chapter 8). One must tolerate a certain degree of imprecision in an attempt of this sort to specify the area on the "universe" described here—occupied by one or another borderline term. It is a useful exercise, nevertheless, since close comparison of one

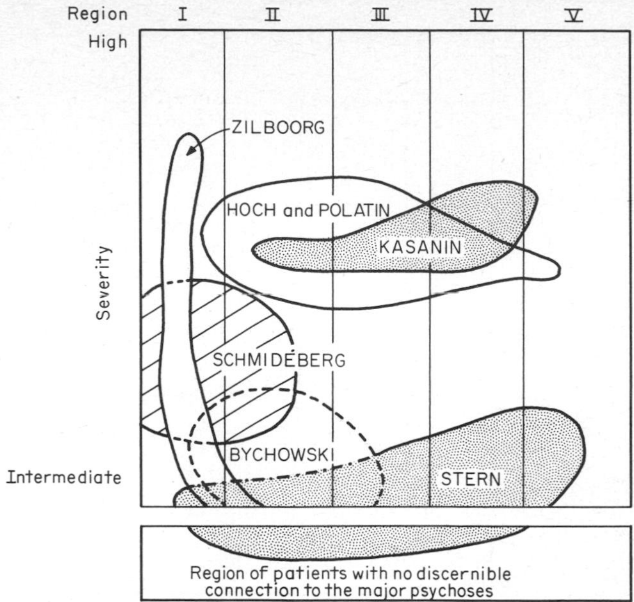

Figure 2–6. Mappings of Some Earlier Borderline and Related Terms onto the Sz-MDP Diagram

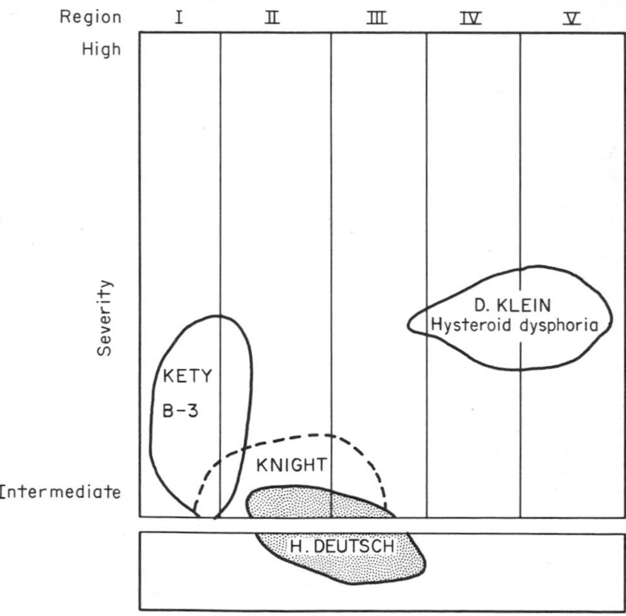

Figure 2–7. Mappings of Several Borderline and Related Terms onto the Sz-MDP Diagram

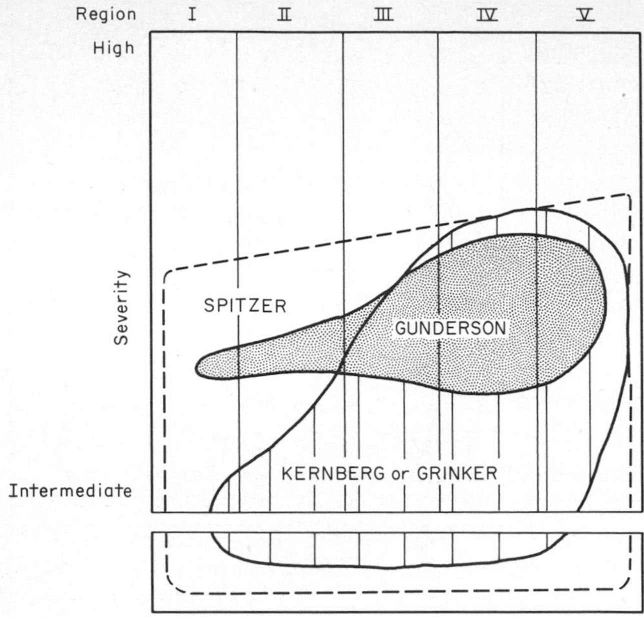

Figure 2–8. Mappings of Some Recent Borderline Domains onto the Sz-MDP Diagram

author's cases with another's will often allow the kind of differentiation that clears up the confusion stemming from using roughly equivalent labels to describe rather different samples of patients. In Figure 2–6, for instance (assuming my assignment of regions is not too far off the mark), Zilboorg's "ambulatory schizophrenics" will be seen to designate a sample quite different from Hoch and Polatin's pseudoneurotic schizophrenia. But the latter overlaps considerably with the earlier sample of Kasanin. Stern's use of the term "borderline" (1938) was fairly broad, from an etiologic standpoint; some of his patients probably were not at particular genetic risk for a major psychosis—for which reason a portion of the Stern region extends into the nongenetic realm of the diagram.

In Figure 2–7 the mappings of four syndromes are displayed. Kety's "borderline schizophrenia" (type B-3) represents an effort to describe the dilute manifestations of genetic loading for schizophrenia. Cases meeting this description fall, as would be expected, almost entirely within the first two regions of the continuum but toward the lower end of a severity scale. The population is fairly homogeneous; clinically, schizotypal. The "map" of this syndrome is therefore rather compact.

Similarly compact, but occupying a space at the affective pole (Regions IV and V), is Donald Klein's "hysteroid dysphoria." A few of these cases have enough schizotypal features (paranoid ideation with ideas of reference, magical thinking, and so forth) to have led some clinicians toward a pseudoneurotic schizophrenia diagnosis, hence the small "tail" into Region III. Other syndromes genetically borderline to the primary affective disorders are discussed further in Chapters 7 and 9.

The less precise definitions of Knight and Helene Deutsch ("as if" personality, from the 1942 paper) require a broader area on the diagram (Figure 2-7); several of Deutsch's cases seemed to have no predisposition to a disorder within the Sz-MDP axis.

Figure 2–8 depicts the areas occupied by several contemporary usages of the term "borderline," namely, those of Grinker, Gunderson, Kernberg, and Spitzer. These are broad definitions, etiologically; some schizotypal patients are included, more so in the Gunderson system than in Kernberg's. Possible explanations for this overlapping are offered in Chapters 7 and 9.

Spitzer and his colleagues have attempted to capture what is common to the currently popular definitions; their view does not, as a result, represent a particular school of thought. Rather, they hope to have achieved a synthesis stemming from several competing schools of thought. As such the borderline personality of Spitzer et al. is the broadest definition of the term "borderline" and maps out an area that embraces the others.

The territory occupied by Frosch's "psychotic personality" (1964), though less precisely defined than the Spitzer or Gunderson domains, would probably be coextensive (or nearly so) with the Gunderson domain.

PART II

Genetic Factors in the Major Psychoses and in Borderline Conditions

I figured that when you go back enough generations, everyone stems from thousands of forebears, and from each of them he has inherited some trait. By day, this is nothing more than a passing thought, but at night it becomes terribly relevant and even scary. Tsutsik, you write about dybbuks. The past generations are our dybbuks. They sit within us and usually remain silent. But suddenly one of them cries out. . . . A person is literally a cemetery where multitudes of living corpses are buried.

Isaac Bashevis Singer, *Shosha*

Part II is devoted to discussion of the genetic aspects of both the major psychoses and "borderline" conditions. Older theories are reviewed. The most recent models for transmission either of the single-major-locus type or of the polygenic type are also presented, along with an attempt to synthesize contemporary theories and clinical observations as they may relate to borderline conditions. The spotlight shifts from schizophrenia in Chapter 3 to the schizoaffective disorders in Chapter 4 and to the affective disorders in Chapter 6. Conceptually it may be easier to appreciate the nuances of the schizoaffective disorders, having already encountered the more easily distinguishable conditions at either extreme; namely, schizophrenia and the primary affective disorders. But because there is, from the standpoint of symptomatology, a kind of natural continuum—in which the schizoaffective disorders occupy an intermediate region—the genetic aspects of the schizoaffective disorders (Chapter 4) are presented between the chapters devoted to the "pure" conditions (Chapters 3, 5, and 6). Following these is a discussion of genetic factors in the borderline states (Chapter 7).

In the earlier chapters we observed, given a "nuclear" case to begin with, what borderline conditions might be found in close relatives. When examining the genetic factors in the borderline conditions, we will assess, using the milder cases as our starting point, what kinds of conditions, nuclear or borderline, we are likely to encounter in the family.

In an Afterword (pp. 155–160) I offer a hypothetical model predicated upon the possibility of heightened genetic risk, in at least certain patients, for both schizophrenic and affective disorders. There is in this section also a diagram which I hope will facilitate grasp of the interaction between (*a*) genetic factors *specific* for either major psychosis and (*b*) the host of nonspecific factors that affect the impact upon behavior of whatever complement of specific genes one may carry.

CHAPTER 3

Genetic Aspects of Schizophrenia

Historical Overview through the Beginning of the Twentieth Century

Statistical analysis of data is not encountered in the area of clinical psychiatry before the nineteenth century. In the second volume of Esquirol's classic textbook of psychiatry (1838), some rudimentary statistics are offered regarding the incidence of suicide in France and other countries.

Belief in a hereditary influence operating in certain cases of mental disorder was widespread even before the era of Esquirol: the notion that "degenerate" parents beget more than their share of "degenerate" offspring goes back very far, even into antiquity.[1] Morel is given credit for fathering the term "démence précoce," the forerunner of Kraepelin's dementia praecox, although the phrase was added almost as an afterthought in his 1860 description of a boy who showed deterioration of habit

[1]For further details on some of the early writers, one should consult Tourney's chapter on the history of the schizophrenic concept (1971).

and intellect beginning from around age fourteen. Morel considered the boy's case as exemplifying some form of hereditary degeneration, inasmuch as the boy's father was a severe alcoholic. As Zilboorg (1941a) has mentioned, Morel's case resembled the patients described a decade later by Hecker (1871) under the new term "hebephrenia."

Moreau (1852) postulated that the mental and physical aspects of a person were inherited from the parents in a mutually exclusive fashion, such that if the child *resembled* a mentally ill parent with regard to physical features, he was apt to be *free* of the mental illness (and vice versa).

Perhaps the earliest *systematic* effort to approach these issues was that of Baillarger (1850), who examined the family histories in 660 hospitalized patients. He was attempting to answer such questions as (1) "Is madness in the mother more frequently transmitted to the child than is madness in the father?" (2) "Is the disease of the mother transmitted to a greater number of children than a similar malady in the father?" and (3) "Is madness more often transmitted from mother to her *daughters,* and from father to his *sons?*"

Baillarger concluded that because 271 of 453 insane persons examined had become so "through the mother" and only 182 "through the father," the majority of mental illness *did* pass from the maternal side. He likewise believed that an affected mother gave rise to a higher proportion of mentally ill children (one-fourth) than would occur if the father had been ill (one-sixth) and that an ill mother had more ill daughters, an ill father more ill sons (by factors of about 3:2).

Assertion of hereditary influences within the realm of the psychoses could have had no other status than that of an educated guess until two lines of investigation converged in the latter two decades of the nineteenth century: that of the geneticist Mendel (died 1884) and that of the great psychiatric systematizer, Kraepelin. Kraepelin, although he began to unify many hitherto seemingly unrelated cases under the rubric of dementia praecox, was more interested in pursuing neuroanatomical than genetic avenues in his search for an etiology. In his ample case descriptions (1905), for example, he generally mentions the status of the family members, though seldom in any detail. Often enough the parents of his paranoid, catatonic, or other praecox cases are characterized briefly as depressed *(schwermutig).* The causative factor was rarely placed on heredity.[2]

Those who did begin to explore the psychoses from the standpoint of

[2]Kraepelin believed heredity played some role in psychopathology, but he saw no regularity in its working. He once commented, "We must regard the statistics of heredity in insanity as facts of experience, without finding in them the expression of a 'law' " (cited by Rosanoff and Orr, 1911, p. 222).

genetics had, of course, to work within the confines of the limited theories then available. It is easy for us to assume that the status of heritability in human psychoses would be many times more complex than what obtained for color variations in Mendel's peas. Yet there were few theoretical constructs available to the geneticists in Kraepelin's time except for those of straightforward dominance and recessiveness. If statistical data about psychoses in relatives of dementia praecox patients did not conform to those classical constructs, it was hard to justify the assertion of a heritable factor. It should not surprise us that the first investigators lucky enough to find strong evidence of a heritable factor in what we now call schizophrenia were those who worked with the most severely ill patients. In such patients the heritable factor, even in the light of the much more stringent and cautious studies of our own day, does indeed seem impressive: so much so as almost to approach the kind of percentages one would expect to see in a true recessive disorder. Many of the figures emerging from the early studies seem the product, in part, of certain biases in the research protocols, and, as such, exaggeratedly high.

Other early systematic studies of the heredity factor in psychosis include those of Sandy (1910) and McGaffin (1911) who dealt primarily with "manic-depressive insanity." The most thorough study was that of Rosanoff and Orr (1911), who analyzed 206 matings and the resultant 1,097 offspring, collected in connection with their work at the Kings Park State Hospital in New York. They attempted, after establishment of a genealogy of "neuropathic conditions" for each index case, to fit their observations into one of the six molds yielded by simple Mendelian laws for one-trait situations. As an example, a crossing of a person heterozygous for a neuropathic condition with a "recessive" spouse should give rise to 50 percent normal "carriers" and 50 percent recessive neuropaths amongst their children. Since the discrepancies between expected and observed percentages did not seem very great, for any of the six situations, these authors believed they had demonstrated that neuropathic conditions were indeed the products of recessive traits.[3] Their findings have been criticized, and correctly so, on the basis of using diagnostic criteria that were too broad, and starting out with the sickest and most chronic cases.

Rosanoff and Orr were aware that "neuropathy," as the term was used in their time, was not likely to be a unitary clinical entity but a catchall term (similar to our notion of "psychiatric disorder") that comprised a variety

[3]They found, for example, that fifty-four of sixty-four offspring were affected where *both* parents were ill and the remaining offspring still young. Where *one* parent was ill, forty percent of the offspring were affected. The bias in their study that led to such high figures consisted in using chronic patients and very broad diagnostic criteria.

of separable clusters. They paid homage to Kraepelin for having seen the red thread that united frank mania with certain depressive conditions, certain cases of alcoholism, and suicide, all under the rubic "manic-depressive illness." Likewise Kraepelin's "dementia praecox" united the formerly unrelated-appearing catatonias and hebephrenias, and so on. Rosanoff and Orr expanded this notion to the less obviously affected family members of the clear-cut index cases. We see here, in embryo, the idea of a *spectrum* of related disorders.

Rosanoff and Orr singled out three such clusters for special attention: manic-depressive insanity, dementia praecox, and epilepsy. As they characterized them:

> Thus in families of patients suffering from manic-depressive insanity, we find not only subjects clearly recognized as insane, but also subjects described as follows: high-strung, excitable, dictatorial, abnormally selfish, awful temper, periodic drinker, a demon when drunk, committed suicide, had severe blue-spells.
>
> In the pedigrees of cases of dementia praecox we find . . . relatives described in the following terms: cranky, stubborn, worries over nothing, religious crank, nervous, queer, suspicious of friends and relatives.
>
> And in the families of epileptics we find, besides cases of actual epilepsy . . . also cases of hemicrania, of . . . fainting spells, nervous fidgety make-up, and the like. (1911, p. 234)

Rosanoff and Orr accounted for these phenomena as expressions of "varying degress of recessiveness," a departure from the black-or-white model of inheritance, which they realized was simplistic.

It is of interest that the Japanese psychogeneticists of our day picture psychopathology in terms of three similar circles (see Mitsuda, 1967, and Chapter 6).

Meanwhile, Rosanoff's intuitive sense of a possible shading, from overt dementia praecox into subtler conditions of litigiousness and querulousness, corresponds fairly well with current notions about dilute or borderline conditions within the areas of the major psychoses.

Schizophrenic Disorders: The Data before 1960

After the pioneering work of Rosanoff and Orr, a number of genetic investigators began to concentrate their attention on one special form of psychosis.

Rüdin (1916), working in Munich, analyzed family patterns of psychosis in dementia praecox patients. He used stricter diagnostic criteria than were incorporated in the earlier American study and also used the Weinberg correction[4] for age of onset. Examining 701 sibships of dementia praecox probands, Rüdin noted that 4½ percent of siblings older than seventeen had the same psychosis; another 4 percent had other psychoses. Where one parent had dementia praecox, the same illness was found in 6.18 percent of their children (10 percent of whom had other psychoses). Since an ordinary Mendelian recessive condition would not be expected to yield these figures, given one homozygous affected parent, Rüdin's data did not support the earlier notion that dementia praecox was inherited as a simple recessive trait. There was the possibility, however, that one was dealing with two recessive genes operating independently, both necessary to the evolution of manifest psychosis. In the situation of two parents, each heterozygous for each locus, one might expect an incidence of affected offspring in the range of 6 percent (¼ × ¼ or 6.25 percent), a figure close to Rüdin's findings.[5] This was, in any case, the theory Rüdin favored. As Gottesman and Shields mention (1972), Rüdin and his Munich school were "to establish the essential genetic independence of *typical* schizophrenia and *typical* manic-depressive psychosis" (p. 20; italics mine).

Also working in Munich, Luxenburger published in 1928 the first twin study devoted to the genetics of three major psychotic conditions; namely, "dementia praecox, manic-depressive insanity, and epilepsy" (1928, p.

[4]The short form of the Weinberg correction is expressed in the formula:

$$m = \frac{\Sigma(z)}{\Sigma(n \cdot r)}$$

where m = morbidity-risk estimate
z = affected (in this instance, schizophrenic subjects)
n = total subjects in the sample
r = amount of risk completed

With respect to schizophrenia, the age of risk is usually considered to span the years fifteen to forty-five. As Rosenthal (1970, pp. 40–42) explains, "Every relative in this age range is counted as half a subject" ($r = 0.5$). Relatives younger than fifteen are not counted, and those over forty-five are counted as full risk-completed subjects ($r = 1.0$). Since in any large sample of relatives, some individuals will be under forty-five, overall r will be less than 1.0; m will therefore be elevated above what it would be if one merely divided the number in the total sample by the number affected.

[5]In light of the current interest in schizophrenialike conditions precipitated by minimal brain damage (see Bellak, 1976, and Quitkin et al., 1976), it is of interest to note that as Schulz (1932) discovered from reexamination of Rüdin's material, this 6+ percent risk to siblings of schizophrenic index cases reduced to approximately 3 percent in those families where the proband's "schizophrenia" followed head injury. Since even a three percent incidence of schizophrenia in a group of siblings is higher than what one would find in the general population, the revised figures indicate simultaneously that (1) many of the probands had inherited schizophrenic vulnerability, head injury or no (perhaps the organic insult "exposed" the latent schizophrenia in some instances) and (2) some of the head-injury probands may have been "phenocopies" or simulated cases whose sibs would not be at greater risk for the "true" condition.

299). Luxenburger's research had the virtue of relying on a systematic sampling of psychiatric patients rather than upon collection of isolated cases. In 9,531 cases with any of the three major conditions were 163 patients who were one of a twin pair: 106 with schizophrenia ("dementia praecox"), 38 with "manic-depressive insanity," and 19 with epilepsy. Restricting ourselves for the moment to schizophrenia, the results showed a concordance rate in monozygotic (MZ) twins of 67 percent. This figure, which would be considered high by contemporary standards, may have been a reflection of including only comparatively severe cases (whose concordance rate is generally higher than for less ill probands). At the time, however, Luxenburger believed his concordance rate was, if anything, too low. Elsewhere Luxenburger expressed disagreement with Rüdin's theory of recessive inheritance for dementia praecox.

Several years after the Luxenburger twin study came that of Rosanoff (1934) and his colleagues, based on a larger number of twin pairs (142) where one or both members were schizophrenic. Of the latter, 41 were classified as monozygotic. The concordance rates noted by these observers were 68 percent in the MZ twins and 15 percent in the DZ pairs, figures very much in keeping with those of the earlier studies. Rosanoff concluded that heredity played an important part in the etiology of schizophrenia, but because hereditary factors in and of themselves seemed to be "inadequate . . . to produce the psychosis," they were therefore "not essential in the etiology of . . . schizophrenic psychoses" (1934, p. 283). These investigators were impressed with what they believed to be the heterogeneity of the illnesses labeled *dementia praecox* or *schizophrenia;* perhaps the particular syndrome that exhibited the high concordance rate was one special form of an otherwise etiologically diverse condition. They were also impressed by the frequency with which earlier and initially asymptomatic trauma seemed to play a causative role in some cases of schizophrenia, especially in males, while psychological disturbances in the sexual realm were common among the female cases.

The results of a twin study based on records of 10,000 patients admitted to certain Swedish mental hospitals over a selected time span were published by Essen-Möller in 1941. Scrutiny of these records yielded sixty-nine pairs of like sex, of which twenty-one were MZ. Seven of the probands were "markedly" schizophrenic. Initially Essen-Möller related that "in none of them was there a pronounced schizophrenia in the other twin, although one may be regarded as a borderland case" (1941, p. 192). Four of the co-twins *did* have a psychosis. Ironically, this psychosis appeared to be of a different type, namely, depressive. These psychoses were to some extent "reactive" (i.e., following strong psychological stresses) and remitted with no residual symptoms. Three of these four co-twins also had certain stigmata of schizophrenia—not enough for a "hard" diagnosis—and these symptoms also disappeared when the depressive symptoms subsided.

Essen-Möller drew attention to another group of four index cases whose psychoses were not "classically" schizophrenic but worthy of being "included in the sphere of psychoses hereditarily related to schizophrenia." One such patient was, for example, querulous and given to ideas of reference. Actually Essen-Möller was more impressed by the nature of the symptoms in the healthier co-twins who, even though they did not exhibit the same psychosis as the clearly schizophrenic index cases, did exhibit psychological abnormalities that seemed closely related to those of the more disabled probands. Thus full-blown delusions in an index case might crop up only as occasional referential thinking in the co-twin.

At thirty-year follow-up Essen-Möller (1974) was to report that of the seven certain and four doubtful schizophrenic MZ probands, seven co-twins had by this time become concordant (if one includes strongly suggestive as well as unmistakable criteria for schizophrenic diagnosis). This yeilds an MZ concordance rate of 65 percent (which contrasts with his DZ concordance rate of 15 percent).

Franz Kallmann, who began his investigations in Germany and continued them later in the United States, collected an enormous series of twin pairs between 1937 and 1945 in which at least one member had a psychotic illness. Of 1,232 such pairs, 953 were schizophrenic, 75 manic-depressive, and the remainder had involutional or senile psychoses.

Kallmann's system for diagnostic classification was such that his "schizophrenia" cases included a number that were schizoaffective or "pseudoneurotic," that is, less seriously disturbed. This might tend to inflate the percentage of concordance, and indeed Kallmann's concordance rate was very high. Among "definite" cases (where the index case had unequivocal schizophrenia), concordance was 59 percent, but 69 percent if the "pseudoneurotic" cases were included. As Gottesman and Shields (1972) mention, age correction of these figures yields the much quoted concordance rate of 86 percent (for DZ pairs, 15 percent). Curiously, despite the relative looseness of diagnostic criteria, affected relatives and co-twins from Kallman's sample always had a diagnosis within the same category as their index twins; manic-depressives were not found in the families of schizophrenics and vice versa. Such perfection in data regarding the "breeding true" among the psychotic disorders seems too good to be true; this has not been the experience of other investigators (see Ødegaard, 1963). To some extent this exaggerated picture of purity of type within families may have resulted from the diagnostic assessments which were not done in "blind" fashion; another factor may have been the severity of the psychoses encountered in the large state hospitals where the index cases were collected. In severely ill hospitalized schizophrenics there has been a consistent tendency toward higher concordance rates among MZ twins and toward less admixture in their families with other categories of psychotic disorders. In Kallmann's earlier work, for example, at the Herzberge Hospital in Berlin (1938), over a thousand schizophrenic patients were selected from among some 15,000 admissions. In this fashion he may have collected a group of particularly severe cases. At all events, their 8,000 parents and sibs were studied, along with their 3,000 children. Among the offspring 11 percent were overtly schizophrenic and another 33 percent "schizoid," making for over 40 percent who showed abnormalities seemingly related to schizophrenic heredity. The offspring of two schizophrenic parents almost all succumbed: 63 percent with overt schizophrenia and 32 percent with some lesser form of schizophrenic tendency, usually a "schizoid personality." The latter was felt to be an outward manifestation of the schizotype (schizophrenic genotype) or, as it was often called, *schizoidia*.

In a study of risk not involving twins, Böök (1953) examined families of nearly 100 schizophrenic persons in rural Sweden. A fifth of this group had never been hospitalized so that Böök's patient population on the whole was somewhat less severely affected than the patients who were studied by Kallmann. Böök found that the risk to siblings of the index cases varied in accordance with the degree of schizoidia in their parents: if neither parent was schizophrenic, only one sibling in twelve fell ill (by age sixty); where one parent was schizophrenic, the risk increased to about one in five. Where both parents of a schizophrenic index case were also schizophrenic, one sib in three eventually developed a schizophrenic disorder.

Another important twin study (Slater, 1953), was based in London and involved pairs in which at least one member was hospitalized. In this fashion forty-one MZ pairs, where the proband was schizophrenic, were collected. The concordance rate (uncorrected for age) was 68 percent. Among the thirteen discordant pairs, three may, according to Gottesman and Shields (1966), have been "organic" cases to begin with and not instances of true schizophrenia. Others in the discordant group were often relatively mildly affected and came from families less heavily saturated with other clear-cut schizophrenics than was true among the concordant pairs. Slater noted the same tendency for schizophrenia remarked upon by his predecessors to "breed true," though (unlike Kallmann) he did draw attention to certain pedigrees where manic-depressive illness was found in families of schizophrenic index cases (and vice versa).

Those interested in reading further on the contributions made before 1960 should also consult the comprehensive reviews of Zerbin-Rüdin (1967, 1971).

Schizophrenia: Contemporary Data

Research on the genetic factor in schizophrenia has broadened during the last two decades to include not only further epidemiological studies, such as those introduced by Rosanoff at the turn of the century, and twin studies, such as inaugurated by Luxenburger, but also a number of adoption studies, where the adopted-away offspring of a schizophrenic parent(s) are systematically followed as they enter the age of risk for schizophrenic decompensation.

The most jarring note among the twin studies was registered by the Finnish investigator Tienari (1963), whose study of psychiatrically ill male twins born throughout a large region of his country during the 1920s initially revealed a concordance rate of zero (!) in sixteen MZ pairs. Since he was not beginning with hospitalized probands, the twin group as a whole was more representative of the population at large and not apt to be slanted toward the very ill. Accepting less rigid criteria would have permitted a concordance rate of 19 percent, since three of the co-twins were regarded as borderline. Many of the remaining were considered schizoid. Gottesman and Shields mention that eight years later, Tienari's co-twins now contained at least one schizoaffective case and four borderline cases, yielding (after two pairs were dropped because of suspected organic etiology) a concordance rate of 36 percent.[6] And Shields (1968) expressed the opinion that, if the schizoid personalities were included as reflections of the "schizotype," Tienari's concordance rate would be 75 percent.

One of the most impressive twin studies was that of Kringlen (1968), who made use of the national registry of psychoses maintained by the Norwegian government. Kringlen was able to examine the records of some 50,000 Norwegian twins born in their country between 1901 and 1930. This survey yielded 342 pairs containing at least one schizophrenic whose zygosity was then determined by blood type. From this emerged 75 MZ pairs (37 male, 38 female) and 257 DZ pairs (with approximately the expected ratio of ¼ both male, ¼ both female, and ½ mixed).

When a strict definition of schizophrenia was used, the MZ concordance rate was 24 percent (as against 12 percent for the DZ pairs). When diagnosis was made by Kringlen in a personal interview (this applied to four-fifths of the twin population under study) and when "schizophreniform" cases were included as positive, the rate of concordance rose in the MZ group to 38 percent and remained at about 10 percent in the DZs. Unlike Slater who noted a higher concordance in female MZ pairs, Kringlen found no such difference between the sexes.

Apart from these findings, no clear-cut correlations could be established in relation to severity: in some pairs, for example, a co-twin appeared normal even when the index case was a severely affected schizophrenic; in others, the more "normal" of a twin set in childhood was the one to succumb to schizophrenia in adult life.

With regard to specificity at the clinical level in Kringlen's studies, over

[6]Another study of the early 1960s showing a concordance rate in this range is that of Inouye (1961): 36 percent by strict diagnostic criteria, 60 percent if borderline co-twins were also included.

90 percent of the concordant pairs shared the same schizophrenic subtypes, whether hebephrenic, catatonic, paranoid, or mixed. In the borderline realm of schizophreniform psychoses, three concordant twin pairs each consisted of two schizophreniform twins.

Preliminary results of another large twin study carried out at the National Institute of Mental Health (NIMH) by Pollin and his group were reported in 1969. The sample was taken from all pairs of white male twins born between 1917 and 1927 who served in the U.S. Armed Forces from the time of World War II through the Korean War. The 15,909 pairs of the original survey yielded 338 pairs in which one or both twins had been given a diagnosis of schizophrenia. Zygosity could be established definitely in 226 pairs, and in these the MZ concordance was 15½ percent as against 4.4 percent for the DZ pairs. The incidence of schizophrenia in the entire twin sample was 1.14 percent, quite in keeping with percent-incidence figures for schizophrenia in the general population. The NIMH investigators also noted that the *heritability*[7] for schizophrenia was significantly higher than that noted for several other conditions they studied, including ulcers, diabetes, and affective disorders.

Pollin (1969) and his colleagues present a table of figures (p. 604) outlining the MZ/DZ ratios of the major studies of schizophrenia preceding and including theirs: these range from 1.2 (for Tienari, 1963) to 6.1 (Rosanoff et al., 1934), the average ratio being just over 4.[8] This ratio contrasts with the MZ/DZ concordance ratio in psychoneurosis, where the average in seven separate studies was not quite 1½. This is an important point of comparison, because it argues strongly for a genetic factor in schizophrenia and against the presence of any particularly strong genetic underpinning in the neurotic conditions.

The low MZ concordance in Pollin's study may be a reflection of relatively low severity of illness in schizophrenic Army inductees as compared with a hospital population, as well as of the nonrigorous diagnostic standards used in the armed services. The investigators of Pollin's group were, meantime, intrigued with the high discordance rate in their sample and carried out further studies directed at elucidating the nature of this discordance. Stabenau and Pollin (1969) described their search for differentiating

[7]Heritability (H) is defined in terms of "excess" MZ concordance compared to DZ concordance according to the following formula:

$$H = \frac{\text{Conc. (MZ)} - \text{Conc. (DZ)}}{1 - \text{Conc. (DZ)}}$$

[8]More recent figures are beginning to converge around a MZ/DZ ratio of 3. An updated version of Tienari's own figures also suggests a ratio in the range of 35 percent to 13 percent (Gottesman and Shields, 1976, p. 373, table 4).

characteristics that might help explain how the nonschizophrenic co-twins of the schizophrenic MZ index cases escaped decompensation. A number of variables were pursued in this regard, including birth weight, birth order, perinatal complications, and certain personality traits such as sensitivity, submissiveness, stubborness, shyness, and the like. In twelve of the sixteen MZ pairs studied, the schizophrenic twin was significantly lighter at birth.[9] The affected twins tended also to be more submissive and more sensitive in childhood than their healthier co-twins, but such traits may themselves be seen as the products of complex interactions among many biological and psychological factors, which, however "early" with respect to the immediate precipitants of "schizophrenia" before actual breakdown, are nonetheless rather late manifestations compared with the still earlier conditions and events of the fertilized ovum.

Conducted along lines comparable to the Norwegian twin study of Kringlen is the study of Fischer (1969) and her co-workers, who utilized the Danish national twin register (for the half century beginning 1870). They located twenty-one MZ pairs where at least one was schizophrenic by strict criteria. Four of the pairs were concordant (24 percent) by similarly strict diagnosis. Concordance in forty-one DZ pairs was 10 percent. When diagnostic criteria were stretched to include borderline cases ("schizophreniform," "paranoid," or "atypical"), the MZ concordance jumped to 48 percent (and 19 percent in the DZ group) by pairs, or 56 percent (and 26 percent) by probands. Stretching still further to include persons who were odd or eccentric but without signs *strongly* suggesting schizophrenia, the MZ concordance (by probands) rose to 64 percent. This situation is represented in Figure 3-1, where the concordance rate can be compared, at a glance, for MZ versus DZ pairs and according to the strictness or laxity of diagnostic standards. It should be noted that Fischer's study yields generally higher concordance than was found in Pollin's but a lower degree of heritability, owing to the comparatively high DZ rates. These figures should be compared with those generated by Slater who showed, corroborating Gottesman and Shields' earlier data, that using "middle-of-the-road" diagnostic criteria for schizophrenia—neither too strict nor too lax—gave the best discrimination between MZ and DZ concordance rates. As Zerbin-Rüdin cites (1974, p. 251), heritability will then be at the 50 percent level in the MZ group (and only 9 percent in the DZs), suggesting a powerful genetic factor in schizophrenia.

[9]More recently Gottesman and Shields (1977) have reexamined the data relating to birth weight and schizophrenia. Their own twin study and that of Kringlen do not support the contention that, in discordant MZ pairs, the lighter twin was more likely to be the schizophrenic. The earlier reports, according to these authors, probably reflected unrepresentative samples. *Ultra*low birth weight, may, however, constitute a significant risk factor.

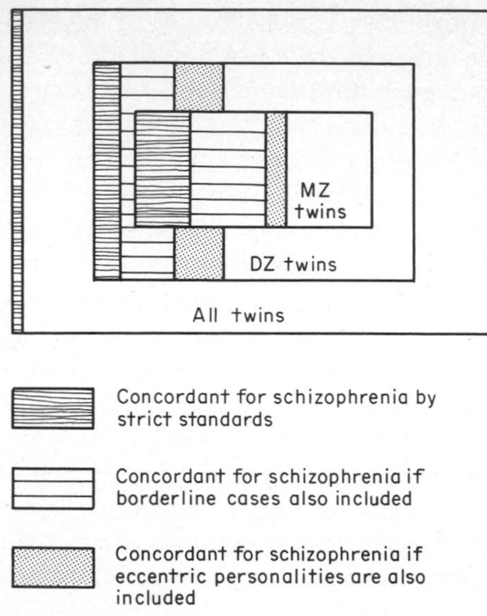

Figure 3–1. Concordance for Schizophrenia in MZ *vs.* DZ Twins

A number of recent studies on the heritable factor in schizophrenia have focused not so much on its sheer dimensions as on the qualitative aspects of what is inherited: are the classical subtypes of schizophrenia themselves genetically directed? are certain personality traits understandable as *formes frustes* of the relevant genetic factor(s)? and so on. Much information on these issues did arise out of the research on twins, but often as by-products of the investigative work. Alongside them various clinical and epidemiological studies have sought to elucidate these questions more directly.

A book appeared in 1963, edited by Rosenthal, that addressed the issue of subtype heritability using as a springboard for discussion the unusual finding of a set of quadruplets concordant for schizophrenia (the so-called Genain quadruplets). Of the four girls, three were hospitalized because of psychotic decompensation, but all four had catatonic symptoms; in three, these were admixed with hebephrenic features (the healthiest quad was free of hebephrenic features). The age at breakdown was roughly equal for the three (twenty-two, twenty-two, twenty-four). Of interest, the sickest had been the lightest at birth (4 pounds) and the healthiest had been the heaviest (6 pounds, 4 ounces).

Despite the apparent homogeneity of their clinical state, the parents both had paranoid personalities. Their mother was the more ill parent, also presenting some autistic traits.

Rosenthal reviewed the earlier data bearing on subtype heritability, mentioning Kallmann's impressions of 1938 that (1) there was a higher rate of schizophrenia (20 percent) in offspring of either hebephrenic or catatonic parents as compared with offspring of paranoid parents (where 11½ percent of the children succumb) and that (2) there was a strong tendency for hebephrenia and catatonia to breed true (61 percent of schizophrenic offspring of hebephrenic parents were specifically hebephrenic and 60 percent of schizophrenic offspring of catatonic parents were specifically catatonic, but only 36 percent of the affected children with paranoid parents were also paranoid). As matters stood, reanalysis of Kallmann's figures by Slater ten years later no longer revealed significant correlations. Zehnder (1940) somewhat earlier expressed the opinion that there was interchangeability of subtypes. Paradoxically reanalysis of Zehnder's data, also by Slater, suggested that the Kraepelinian subtypes in sib pairs *were* highly associated with, and perhaps under the influence of, common "modifying genes" (Rosenthal, 1963, p. 517). Perhaps the most compelling comment on this subject came from Elsässer whose 1952 report noted heterogeneity of subtype even in the affected children of two schizophrenic parents who were *alike* in subtype. Surely, if the schizophrenic offspring of such a dual mating were not of their parents' subtype, heritability of subtype could not be very impressive. From such conflicting data, no straightforward answers emerge. Subsequent chapters of Part II address the issue in greater detail.

A number of other investigators also attempted to get a clearer view of *what* is inherited in mental disorder. The tendency of family histories to contain relatives with the same type of psychosis (or even [as in the case of schizophrenia] the same Kraepelinian subtype), particularly in the first-degree relatives of an index case, has been noted by Mitsuda (1967) in Japan and by Ødegaard (1963) in Scandanavia. Both authors noted that the correlations in these pedigrees were not so near perfect that they established genetic factors as the only operative element. Mitsuda observed that in nuclear cases of the different psychoses, close and affected relatives were of the same type in four out of the five cases, whereas in more borderline or "peripheral" disorders, family histories were more often mixed. Likewise Ødegaard concluded that, while the Kraepelinian classification had a clear hereditary background, only about a half of affected first-degree relatives were of like diagnosis; this finding militated against any "simple effect of specific genes" (Ødegaard, 1963). These discrepancies were interpreted by Mitsuda as arguing in favor of genetic heterogeneity in each group of endogenous psychoses (schizophrenia, manic-depressive illness, epilepsy) and by Ødegaard as exemplifying a "multifactorial inheritance . . . with a high degree of intra-familial and individual variability."

Seeking to clarify these issues further, Tsuang (1967) undertook a study of pairs of siblings who were both hospitalized for any mental disorder over a period of some time. Seventy-one pairs of full sibs were isolated for statistical analysis. Whereas chance would have predicted (from their initial diagnostic evaluations) that fourteen pairs of sibs would both have the same diagnosis, actually twenty-two such pairs were observed, a finding that is statistically highly significant. In addition it was recorded whether certain diagnoses were *ever* made during the course of the subject's illness. Regarding *schizophrenia,* only nine sib pairs had the same independent diagnosis (a correlation not statistically significant), though thirteen had a similar *final* diagnosis and twenty-eight pairs were alike, if one included *ever*-diagnosed schizophrenics. The latter two correlations were considered significant.

Data regarding resemblance in symptoms were less impressive in Tsuang's study. Significant correlations were reached with respect to suicidal depression and manic-depressive features. Intrapair resemblances in thought disorder, delusions, and hallucinations among the schizophrenic group were not close enough to be considered significant. In contrast to Essen-Möller who believed genetic factors contributed to symptom-similarity even more than to diagnosis-similarity, Tsuang favored the hypothesis that overall diagnosis was the clinical entity more closely related to inherited factors than were specific symptoms.

Later McCabe, Fowler, et al. (1972) offered, in support of Tsuang's impressions, evidence from their family studies of psychotic disorders. McCabe et al. noted that if one restricted one's attention to poor-prognosis schizophrenics, there was a particularly impressive percentage of schizophrenic first-degree relatives (15 percent). This was three times as high a rate as noted among similar relatives of their "good-prognosis" schizophrenic index cases. Here again, the disease (more than the symptoms) was what the inherited factors apparently predisposed to.

A contrasting view emerges from the work of Rosenthal and Van Dyke (1970) in their analysis of MZ twins discordant for schizophrenia. Their impressions were in line with those of Essen-Möller, who emphasized that MZ pairs were not usually concordant in clinical picture (despite the earlier studies of Luxenburger, Kallmann, and Slater, who concluded that schizophrenia itself was the inherited entity). Rosenthal even adds that none of Essen-Möller's co-twins would, if strict criteria for schizophrenic diagnosis were applied, have been accepted in Scandinavia as a proper index case in a study of schizophrenia. But many of the Swedish co-twins had personality abnormalities which, as Rosenthal and Van Dyke speculate, could be taken to represent a "core pattern of traits" which are inherited and which compose the personality anlage that may exacerbate into clinical schizophrenia.

Rosenthal and Van Dyke, working with the same eleven MZ twins (discordant for schizophrenia) whom Pollin, Stabenau, and Tupin had discussed earlier (1965), submitted the twins to a battery of psychological tests, paying particular attention to intrapair variations in subtest scores. It is noteworthy that the schizophrenic twins showed a reduced level of performance, in general, compared with their healthier co-twins. This should be kept in mind in evaluating the observations of Offord and Cross (1969) on the intelligence factor in schizophrenia (see below). On some of the subtests, both twin groups achieved essentially the same scores (e.g., block design), whereas on others—in a *selective* rather than pervasive fashion—the affected twins' performance was inferior (digit symbol, picture completion).

Though none of their findings could be said to have discovered a reliable psychological "marker" for schizophrenia, the *pattern* of subtest score responses was strikingly similar within each pair. In general, arithmetic, picture completion, and object assembly (and to a lesser extent, digit symbol) were the weak spots in both groups; only the schizophrenic twins did even worse on these subtests than the co-twins. It was this similarity of performance pattern even in the healthier twins that led Rosenthal and Van Dyke to speculate that this pattern was itself an aspect of the charactero-logical defect proposed a generation earlier by Essen-Möller.

Somewhat different were the impressions of Marget Fischer (1973) in her study of schizophrenic twins and their families. This investigator had access to the Danish Central Psychiatric Register and the Danish national twin register, from which she was able to collect a fairly complete and representative sample. She addressed herself to the issue of whether there were an etiological difference between "strict" schizophrenia and the borderline conditions: "schizophreniform psychosis" and "paranoid psychosis." Like her predecessors she noted a significantly higher concordance rate for MZ as against DZ probands, arguing for the presence of a genetic factor. This belief was further reinforced by the interesting finding that the nonschizophrenic MZ co-twins of schizophrenic twins had "the same percentage of schizophrenic children as the probands" (1973, p. 70). She could find no clinical or hereditary difference between concordant and discordant probands, nor could her data support the speculation that "concordant" schizophrenia was a different disease from "discordant" schizophrenia. In this respect her conclusions resemble those of Kringlen and Luxenburger. Fischer also noted that intrapair similarity between MZ and DZ concordant pairs suggested that schizophrenic *subtype* and *age of onset* were mostly under genetic control. *Severity of illness,* on the other hand, varied enough among the concordant pairs to indicate the preponderance of "environmental" or at least nonhereditary influences. The fact that the lightest of the Genain quadruplets (at birth) turned out to be the most severely affected might serve as an illustration (though by no means a proof) of this line of reasoning.

Offord and Cross (1969), in their paper on behavioral antecedents of adult schizophrenia, also reviewed evidence relating to contributions of hereditary versus environmental factors in the development of clinical schizophrenia. They mention, for example, that in the *preschizophrenic* twin of a pair eventually to be labeled *discordant,* a number of physical traits are characteristically found. These include: (1) childhood history of a central nervous system illness, (2) birth complications, (3) neonatal asphyxia, (4) physical weakness, (5) light weight at birth, and (6) shortness. Apart from shortness, these traits are often found in children with "minimal brain damage."

A surprising finding from their retrospective studies concerned the relatively low incidence of schizophrenia in adults who had once been shy children (0.6 percent), whereas the rate was almost double (1.1 percent) among those who had been childhood extroverts. This would make one cautious about the rather common tendency to pay a great deal of attention to *shyness* as a characterological trait associated with the predisposition to schizophrenia. Some of the high MZ concordance rates in schizophrenia reported by the earlier investigators may have been an outgrowth of the assumption that shyness could be taken as an expression of "schizoidia." Qualities that were more impressive in preschizophrenic children were inability to relate to others (peers, in particular), poor capacity to form a stable sense of identity, and being considered peculiar or odd by others. The preschizophrenics also had a tendency toward antisocial and aggressive behavior (though not so marked as in those who became sociopaths in adult life).

Although the majority of shy children do not go on to develop schizophrenia in adult life, Offord and Cross did find several studies showing the high frequency of shyness, introversion, or "shut-in" personality in the school records of schizophrenics as compared with a control population (1969, p. 273). Other noteworthy points in their review related to the *wide* range of personality types found among those who later became schizophrenic (as noted also by Bellak, 1976) and to the frequency with which preschizophrenic children had lower childhood IQs than their unaffected siblings. Chronic schizophrenics, nevertheless, gave "no evidence of a decline of I.Q. even after ten years on the back wards," their retest IQs being virtually identical with their first hospital test scores. The observations of Pollack (1960) were also mentioned in connection with that author's study of IQ in relation to recovery in schizophrenic patients: half of his "unimproved" group had IQs below 90, whereas the "much improved" group tended to have higher than average IQs. Many of these patients seemed less unequivocally "schizophrenic" to begin with. Weingarten and Korn (1967) had also alluded to the higher than average IQs in "pseudoneurotic" schizophrenics when compared with test scores in the "core" group. We seem to be dealing here with something akin to a self-fulfilling prophecy: the higher the intelligence, the better the coping capacity and the better the operation of internal feedback mechanisms monitoring reality sense. Hence (in many instances) the less pronounced and long lasting the delusions (or other "psychotic" symptoms) and the less clear-cut the schizophrenic signs and symptoms in such a person. Apropos the role of intelligence as a modifier of expressivity of the schizophrenic genotype, Offord was later, in cooperation with M. B. Jones (1975), to offer evidence that IQ and schizophrenia are transmitted independently (see also Gottesman and Shields, 1972).

In the end Offord and Cross wonder if schizophrenic patients ought not to be divided into two major groups: those who have difficulty in childhood before the onset of an overt schizophrenic illness, and those who do not. The authors hope the answer might be forthcoming in a prospective study of children at "high risk" (the product of one or two schizophrenic parents), in whom subtle antecedents of adult schizophrenia might be detected, if appropriate tests were done during their childhood. Clearly the results of prospective studies, such as are now underway in Erlenmeyer-Kimling's group (1975) at the New York State Psychiatric Institute, would help define what are the phenotypic boundaries of the schizophrenic genotype, what childhood symptoms appear as stigmata of "schizoidia" (like shyness), yet may not be, and what constellation of symptoms may deserve to be spoken of as "borderline schizophrenia." If there is validity to the concept of borderline schizophrenia, does it comprise persons of heavy genetic loading who have high social and intellectual assets, or persons of mild loading with average assets? Or might either sort of person emerge as a "borderline" schizophrenic? We will attempt to answer these questions later in Chapters 5 and 7.

High-risk studies,[10] prospective in their design, offer a way around some of the biases encountered in the older retrospective studies. They are, nevertheless, not without particular biases of their own. Most people who become diagnosed schizophrenic in adult life do not have a parent who has been hospitalized for a similar condition. That is, from a genetic standpoint, the ordinary case appears to arise *de novo,* where there may be at most some neurotic or eccentric relatives. On the other hand, the "schizophrenia" seen in patients who do have overtly schizophrenic parents might, as some have contended, be a special breed not altogether typical of schizophrenia in general. Recently, the continuity of such studies, once initiated, is quite vulnerable to the ever-increasing divorce rate (here I am referring to projects undertaken in the United States), which greatly hampers follow-up and evaluation of family members. Erlenmeyer-Kimling (1968) has pointed out that over a third of children born to *two* schizophrenic parents are given up for adoption. Controls for children from such chaotic homes are hard to come by. This investigator also assessed the morbidity in children of two schizophrenic parents and noted it to be in the range of 35 to

[10]The risk of developing schizophrenia in children of *one* schizophrenic parent is in the range of one in six to one in ten, depending upon the study (see Stevenson et al., 1970).

44 percent (higher in Kallmann's series; lower in Elsässer's 1952 study), figures dependent in turn upon the mathematical factors used in correcting for the "age of risk." For schizophrenia, the age of risk is traditionally taken to be fifteen to forty-five, although certain authors, notably Garrone (1962), believe some "new" cases of schizophrenia crop up even during the sixth and seventh decades of life.[11]

If the high morbidity figures in children of two schizophrenic parents have withstood the test of time, the same cannot be said regarding risk estimates in close relatives of schizophrenic index cases. While the range of 10 to 15 percent for parents, children, or sibs was regarded as accurate by the earlier generation of investigators, this estimate has been challenged in a number of recent studies. Thus Winokur et al. (1972) reported a risk for schizophrenia in first-degree relatives of schizophrenic patients of just over 2 percent, and at the same time noted a higher risk, actually, for affective illness in these relatives (5½ percent). This latter figure, since it is similar to published risks for affective disorder in the general population, may reflect a "background noise" not related to the relatives' heightened schizophrenia predisposition. In the Winokur study the strict criteria for diagnosis developed by the St. Louis School were adhered to. Not long afterwards Karlsson (1973) reported a similarly low risk (2.7 percent) for schizophrenia among the parents of "core" schizophrenics, adding that another 13 percent did show "other functional psychoses." In Karlsson's opinion, earlier workers may have lumped all such disorders into the category of schizophrenia, thus inadvertently inflating the degree of risk in the parents and other relatives.

Contemporary use of strict research criteria for diagnosis has lowered the apparent degree of risk in close relatives of schizophrenics, an impression foreshadowed by Kety and his co-workers' finding of only moderate risk in first-degree biological relatives of schizophrenics who were adopted in childhood (1968 and see below).

How best to interpret the newer data is not an easy matter. One could adopt a hard-line attitude, claiming simply that the risk figures from the forties and fifties were grossly exaggerated and that the heritability of schizophrenia, though far from negligible, is not as great as was once thought. One could equally well defend the position that while we must curb our notion of high risk for *full-blown* schizophrenia in the relatives, the risk for a milder form of the illness is still considerably high. The relationship between risk in the close relatives and the severity of illness in the probands

[11]To claim a psychosis in a patient of, say, sixty-five or seventy, was a "first break" of schizophrenia, one would have to rule out a "phenocopy" due to senile brain changes, and so forth—not an easy claim to substantiate. Taylor and Abrams (1975, p. 1278) raise a similar objection.

was highlighted by McCabe (1972). If one concentrated on the "process" or "poor prognosis" schizophrenic probands, McCabe et al. (1971, 1972) found that the schizophrenia risk in their first-degree relatives was three times that noted among similar relatives of "good prognosis" probands (15 percent, as against 5 percent in the latter). Like Winokur, McCabe also noted a fairly high incidence of manic-depressive disorders among the relatives, especially in the good-prognosis group (20 percent, as against 4 percent in the "process" patients).

In general, adherence to strict diagnostic criteria will reduce to half or less the schizophrenia-risk estimate of almost any correlation one is investigating. Gottesman and Shields (1966) demonstrated a 42 percent concordance (in twenty-four MZ pairs) according to the criteria "hospitalized for schizophrenia." This figure is doubled (79 percent) if hospitalizations for "other" psychoses plus co-twins treated as outpatients are included. By the same token Belmaker, Pollin, et al. (1974), in their follow-up of seventeen MZ pairs discordant for schizophrenia from the NIMH sample, reported a new concordance rate of 8.3 percent eight years later—if strict criteria were adhered to. Using looser criteria, this figure would rise to 25 percent. Twin pair 4, for example, contained a co-twin with vagueness, anhedonia, and two hospitalizations who was considered a "borderline schizophrenic" by the authors, as well as a case creating a "possible new concordant pair" (p. 221).

The importance of Gottesman and Shield's results will be dwelt on more fully in the discussion of contemporary concordance figures and their validity at the end of this chapter.

Other recent commentators on schizophrenia risk include Sartorius and his colleagues (1975), who noted that (in comparison to discordant MZ pairs) more "concordant" schizophrenic twins showed Schneider's "first-rank symptoms" of schizophrenia. Also, more concordant pairs were male; the discordant females had more available "affect," leading one to wonder whether or not femaleness may predispose both to the retention of appropriate affect and to relative mildness of disorder (see Chapter 4).

Interestingly, Wahl (1976) in his study of MZ twins discordant for schizophrenia believed there was a higher degree of concordance among female pairs and concluded that the *dis*cordant females were of special importance from the standpoint of genetic analysis. This author hypothesized that certain "environmental" differences account for discordance and that these must occur early in life, perhaps even in that special *Zwischenland* between heredity and environment occupied by the period of intrauterine life.

Though not directly related to the topic of schizophrenia, the pioneering work of Mirsky in the fifties and sixties on genetic factors in gastric pepsinogen levels helped greatly to promote a more sophisticated approach to "causality" in biological systems. Mirsky's experiments enabled us to see that certain persons with constitutionally high pepsinogen levels—the tendency to which ran in families—were the ones who *sometimes* got ulcers (1958). Their high levels in combination with unfavorable psychological factors (of which the intrusive mother was occasionally an example) might in time interact to stimulate the formation of an ulcer. If psychological factors remained favorable, even in these *vulnerable* people, the ulcer would usually not develop. An exception might occur in those few persons whose enzyme activity was so grossly exaggerated that it conduced to ulceration even in the absence of adverse emotional factors.

These studies helped replace the "either/or" notion of causality (e.g., *either* genes *or* environment) prevalent before Mirsky's time, with an *interactional* viewpoint, in which the importance of multiple contributing forces is taken into account and possible interactions are evaluated. In an interactional model one also tries to assess the relative weights of the various etiological factors and to order them, where feasible, according to the time sequence in which they exert their maximum impact. This more sophisticated model is of relevance not only to schizophrenia but to the affective disorders as well, and to the in-between and borderline versions of both (see Chapter 5).

Acceptance of a hereditary factor in the classical psychoses and their milder variants was also enhanced by the advent of specific psychopharmacological agents during the 1950s. These agents helped reduce the aura of hopelessness which had surrounded schizophrenia especially, against which the psychoanalytic community had reacted by denying genetic influences (Don Jackson, 1960) and by stressing the efficacy of purely psychological therapies (John Rosen, 1947; Sechèhaye, 1956).

Beginning in the 1960s, a series of investigations using adopted-away offspring of schizophrenic parents shed light on the hereditary factor in schizophrenia in a manner not possible before even with the twin studies. Earlier, the claims of the geneticists had always been open to the criticism that the affected offspring of a schizophrenic parent had been exposed to the psychological environment created by that parent and that this exposure might just as well be the "causative agent" as the complement of genes inherited from that parent.

The first of the adoption studies was Heston's (1966) concerning psychiatric disorders in foster-home-reared children. Heston collected forty-seven subjects for examination who had been born to schizophrenic mothers and had then been adopted out within the first few weeks of life to foster parents, neither of whom was schizophrenic. To these subjects were matched fifty control subjects (adoptees born to biologically normal mothers). At the time of Heston's investigation, the average age for the entire group was thirty-five, that is, about two-thirds the way through the age of risk for schizophrenia. None of the control group was clinically schizophrenic, whereas five (10.6 percent) of the adoptees born to an affected mother were. Despite their having been raised in rather unexceptional homes, and apart from having a distorted biological parent, the experimental group was also heavily studded with other forms of severe psychopathology, including mental deficiency, sociopathy, and criminal behavior. These manifestations were present, along with schizophrenia, in twenty-five subjects (53 percent), but in the control group, only in four (8 percent). An interesting by-product of Heston's study was the observation that many of the nonpsychiatrically ill members of the experimental group were imaginative, artistic, and successful people; these attributes were scarcely to be found among their counterparts in the control group. In this respect Heston's work mirrors that of the Icelandic investigator Karlsson, in whose papers (1968, 1974) are also references to possible advantages to the individual from *milder* degrees of schizophrenic genetic legacy (again, usually in the form of artistic creativity).

In another adoption study, reported by Kety, Rosenthal, Wender, and Schulsinger (1968), emphasis was laid on the biological relatives of adoptees who later became schizophrenic. As with many of the twin studies, a Scandinavian country (Denmark, in this instance) was chosen as the locus, taking advantage of the excellent registries of mentally ill persons and of adoptees. Five thousand of the latter were screened, from which thirty-three schizophrenics were collected. They had some 463 relatives available for diagnostic evaluation. While there were hardly any schizophrenics among the relatives of the adopting parents, there was a significant number among the biological relatives of the adopted schizophrenics. Comparison of the two relative groups showed about *six times* as many schizophrenics in the biological, as compared with the adoptive, relatives. This argues for the presence of some factor predisposing to schizophrenia, already present at the time of adoption. Although it was assumed this factor was genetic, the study design did not permit ruling out other distal but postgenetic factors, such as perinatal traumata of various sorts.

As with Heston's study, Kety's also helped clarify questions relating to the other mental disorders, short of obvious schizophrenia, that were noted in the pedigrees of the index cases. Precisely because the biological mother of an adoptee is different from his psychological mother, the phenotypic sequelae of different hereditary endowments stand out in bolder relief in adoption studies. Dilute forms of supposed schizophrenia, schizoid, and other personality disturbances, as well as other conditions discernible in the penumbra surrounding nuclear cases, can be evaluated more carefully and hence assigned with greater precision *to*—or separated with greater conviction *from*—the core condition. Kety used a diagnostic classification (in assessing the adoptees' relatives) ranging from "*not schizophrenic*" (A) through disorders affiliated with schizophrenia, at least in appearance—

core schizophrenia (B-1), *acute* schizophrenic reaction[12] (B-2), and *borderline states*[13] (B-3)—to *inadequate personality* (C). The features of Kety's "B-3" borderline schizophrenia are outlined in Chapter 9.

In analyzing their data, Kety and his co-workers found that the pattern of schizophrenia-related disorders in the biological families of the adoptees was the same for those index cases diagnosed "core" or chronic schizophrenia (B-1) as for cases with "borderline" schizophrenia (B-3). This lent weight to the argument that the "borderline" patients belonged genetically to the same group as their less equivocally schizophrenic sample mates.[14] By contrast the seven index adoptees with "acute schizophrenic reactions" (B-2) had no schizophrenia-related disorders in their biological relatives, raising, as Kety put it, "some question regarding the relationship of that state to schizophrenia" (1968, p. 361). If anything, the data could be viewed as reinforcing the opinion of the Scandinavian and Japanese schools that "acute schizophrenia" is a disorder *sui generis*[15] (Kety, Rosenthal, et al, 1968, p. 357), as Kety elsewhere mentions.

Apparently outside the penumbra of core schizophrenia were a number of other disorders noted with approximately equal frequency among the biological relatives of the schizophrenic adoptees as well as among relatives of the controls. Even here there was a slight imbalance, not reaching statistical significance, in which psychopathy, character disorder, and suicide were seen rather more often in the schizophrenics' relatives. Affective disorders, organic psychoses, and retardation were seen more often in the control relatives. This observation led the authors to speculate that character disorder and psychopathy (and even suicide) could represent outermost phenotypic extensions of the schizophrenic genotype. Their conception of "true" schizophrenia, and its milder variants, and how this differs from conditions that mimic the spectrum disorders can be portrayed as in Figure 3-2, where the outer shell of the true schizophrenias consists of the questionable layer "character disorder-psychopathy-suicide."

It should be kept in mind that while the biological parents of schizophrenic adoptees demonstrated a considerable amount of serious mental disorders, this was not so of the adopting parents (see Wender, Rosenthal, and Kety, 1968), again supportive of the theory of *genetic* transmission in schizophrenia.

Rosenthal, who also endorses the notion of a "subpsychotic" form of

[12]This category consisted of conditions often called schizoaffective, acute undifferentiated schizophrenia, or acute paranoid reaction.

[13]A category that included pseudoneurotic schizophrenia, ambulatory schizophrenia, and psychotic character.

[14]Of the B-3 adoptees, their thirty-eight biological relatives had six schizophrenic spectrum conditions.

[15]Mitsuda (1965) has been particularly emphatic in hypothesizing independence for the "atypical psychoses."

Figure 3–2. Spectra Associated with Schizophrenic Disorders

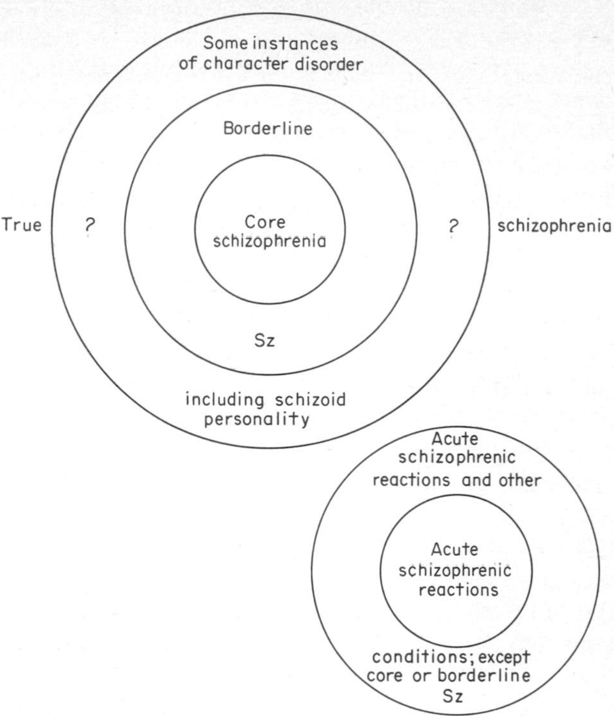

SOURCE: Adapted from Kety et al. (1968).

schizophrenia because of its frequency in the biological relatives of adopted-away schizophrenics, reported (1972) on the schizophrenic disorders of adoptees, each of whom had a *known schizophrenic parent* (seventy-six such index cases were found, belonging to the 11,000 biological parents screened from the Danish registries). Biological parents with no known psychiatric history, who had given a child up for adoption, were used as a control group: psychiatric morbidity in these adoptees was then compared with that of the adoptees with a schizophrenic parent. Schizophrenia spectrum disorders were twice as frequent in the affected parent group (32 percent) as in the control adoptees (18 percent). Of the twelve affected *children* from core (B-1) schizophrenic parents, only three were also "core" schizophrenics, and only one was hospitalized. In general these adoptees were sicker than the "spectrum" adoptees from "normal" biological parents; in the latter adoptee group, there were only borderline cases. Furthermore, it is probably fair to say that even the "control" cases of children given up for adoption by allegedly normal parents may not be coming from such healthy stock, after all. Horn, Green, Carney, and Erikson (1975) administered Minnesota Multiphasic Personality Inventory (MMPI) tests to a general group of unwed mothers and found considerable psychopathology even in the "nonpsychotic" ones. Their impression was that the "control" mothers, because they were less healthy emotionally than might otherwise be thought, might constitute a genetic pool not typical of the population at large and more apt to give birth to children who later on would develop a schizophrenic disorder. This in turn would introduce a bias against the genetic hypothesis: the "controls" used in modern psychogenetic investigations might be nearer to the experimental group with respect to mental illness.[16]

A particularly compelling piece of evidence for the genetic transmission of schizophrenia, also arising from the Danish adoption study, involved the finding that the (biological) paternal half siblings of schizophrenic adoptees showed a considerably greater number of schizophrenia-spectrum disorders than did the paternal half sibs of the control adoptees (Kety, 1976).[17] The ratio was 7:1, there being fourteen spectrum diagnoses among the sixty-three paternal half sibs of the index cases but only two in sixty-four paternal half sibs of the control group. What makes this observation so impressive, of course, is the fact that an adopted person's paternal half sibs have had a different mother, a different intrauterine and perinatal environment, and do not even grow up in the same household. They are similar only insofar as they are legatees (to a certain degree) of a father's genetic endowment.

Bearing on the issue about *mode* of transmission was the additional finding that the cases of schizophrenia located among the biological relatives of the schizophrenic probands were distributed in a rather lopsided fashion. The twenty-four schizophrenic relatives belonged to only seventeen of the

[16]If Horn's assumptions are correct, the statistics reported by Kety and Rosenthal might have been even more dramatic, had a more representative control group been available. Even Horn's study, however, is not free of complications: his was an American project based in the Southwest, and it is not clear to what extent parents who give children up for adoption in the United States are—or are not—comparable to their Scandinavian counterparts. It may well be that in the current generation, especially with improved facilities for legally permitted abortions, mothers who still give their babies up for adoption are very unrepresentative indeed. On top of all this, adoptive rearing may "reduce the rate of schizophrenia requiring hospitalization among children with a schizophrenic parent, and may reduce the rate of diagnosed [hence of countable] schizophrenia among them as well" (Rosenthal, 1972, p. 74). These points merely underline the complexities inherent in designing a good adoption study and illustrate how the genetic factor emerges as something impressive, despite the negative biases with which the cautious studies of the last decade were beset. Problems in general relating to the design of adoption studies are discussed further in other papers by Rosenthal (1971); Rosenthal, Wender, Kety et al. (1971); and Gottesman and Shields (1976).

[17]For further comments and criticisms on the issue of paternal half sibs, incidences expected in this group according to the single major locus and to the polygenic models, and so forth, one should consult the paper of Gottesman and Shields (1976) and the reply of Matthysse (1976).

probands; the biological families of the other sixteen adoptees did not contain any schizophrenia-spectrum members (Kety, 1976, p. 28). Such data make it tempting to speculate that there are two different "brands" of schizophrenia, one with a pronounced capacity to predispose its carriers to clinical illness, another without such capacity. This, in turn, might be understood as an example of genetic heterogeneity, the merits of which we will examine more closely in Chapter 5.

Afterword

We have noted up to this point that the concordance rate for schizophrenia in MZ twins had been estimated by the earlier investigators at about 60 to 80 percent, a level generally four times the DZ concordance rate from the same studies. More recently the estimates have hovered around 40 percent if borderline schizophrenia cases are included (ranging from 36 percent in Tienari's study to 48 percent in Kringlen's). The MZ/DZ ratio has ranged between 2 and 4 among the contemporary studies. What figures should one use, then, for the current "standard" in this area? Clearly there is a subjective element here, inasmuch as clinicians from various countries will feel more sympathetic to one line of investigation than to another, depending upon the degree to which the investigators' concept of schizophrenia overlaps with that of the clinician. A certain amount of chauvinism and insularity is bound to creep into one's judgment.

Figures emanating from the twin studies of Gottesman and Shields (1972) are probably the most compelling currently available, owing to the particular elegance of their methodology. The diagnosis of schizophrenia in their studies was based on evaluation by blind ratings, made by six experienced raters from three different countries (U.S.A., England, and Japan). Case review of this sort lends an atmosphere of authenticity to the resulting diagnoses not easily matched by most of the other twin studies. *The pairwise*[18] *concordance of twenty-four MZ sets was 42 percent; of their thirty-three DZ sets, 9 percent*. These figures represent a conservative estimate, arrived at by as scrupulous a methodology as one will find in any of the studies over the past six decades. If borderline or "questionable" schizophrenia cases were included in the reckoning, the concordance rate would be elevated to approximately 50 percent MZ and 10 percent DZ (1972, p. 304).

In summary, an MZ schizophrenia concordance rate in the mid 40 percent range, as suggested by Gottesman and Shield's most conservative estimate, may be taken as our current standard. As we shall see in Chapter 5, Matthysse and Kidd use this kind of standard in estimating the goodness

[18]That is, the proportion of pairs in which both twins are affected, as opposed to *probandwise,* the proportion of index cases with an affected co-twin.

of fit between observed and expected data in relation to a single-major-locus model of schizophrenic inheritance.

One should, at the same time, avoid the tendency to think that schizophrenia is "40 percent inherited and 60 percent environmental." A more prudent view would insist that there exists a large subset within the set "phenotypic schizophrenia," where a genetic factor acts as a necessary but not sufficient cause, engendering a manifestational rate (of *overt* schizophrenic illness) in MZ twins of 40 percent concordant.

One would want to add that this concordance will be even higher if borderline (nonpsychotic) co-twins are included. Some of these will be subtle enough to be included also in the group of patients who exhibit borderline psychic structure (according to the criteria of Kernberg). If one accepts these assumptions, one is accepting a *spectrum* concept of schizophrenia. If in addition one accepts Zerbin-Rüdin's estimate (1974) that in the general population phenocopiers of schizophrenia (frontal lobe tumors, certain endocrine disturbances, and so on) may constitute only one or a few percent of all conditions that receive a diagnosis of schizophrenia, then our remarks apply to a very large subset indeed, perhaps one embracing 95 percent or more of what is called "schizophrenia."

Chapter 4

Genetic Aspects of the Schizoaffective Disorders

There is fairly good reliability to the diagnosis of "process" schizophrenia and of florid mania. Isolation of a homogeneous patient sample is therefore relatively feasible; this in turn permits a meaningful family study to be carried out. With the schizoaffective disorders, diagnosis is a more treacherous matter, and variability in patient samples given this label is often so marked from one institution to another that investigators attempting to probe these conditions are saddled with a serious problem in communication. Psychogenetic studies in this area, since they are dependent on accuracy and translatability of diagnosis, are necessarily affected by this confusion.

A problem arises when one tries to decide whether schizoaffective illness represents (1) an entity (or group of entities) distinct from "true" schizophrenia, (2) a variant of schizophrenia, perhaps characterized by less severe genetic loading for schizophrenia, (3) a variety of affective disorder in which some of the clinical findings mimic "true" schizophrenia, or (4) a variety of severe emotional disorder in which at least a modest degree of genetic loading exists for *both* schizophrenia and manic-depressive illness.

Angst (1966) also drew attention to diagnostic problems relating to the time factor. Patients initially given a diagnosis of schizoaffective disorder tend to go in several different directions over the course of their illness. In some, one sees episodic attacks characterized by a mixture of classically "manic" and "schizophrenic" symptoms (see Chapter 8). A few have eventual relapses of a clearly schizophrenic type, while others change to a manic-depressive course (case illustration 4; see also Vaillant, 1963 and 1963a).

Early Family Studies

The Scandinavian family studies of Astrup and Noreik (1966) established that psychotic patients who proved to have a poor prognosis had a significantly larger share of schizophrenics among their mentally ill relatives than did the good-prognosis group.

Some authors believed that relatives of index cases with a schizoaffective disorder are, to the extent that they may also have succumbed to a psychosis, also diagnosable as "schizoaffective" (see Mitsuda, 1967; McCabe, 1975; Ødegaard, 1963). Here the implication is that schizoaffective illness, or in the term these authors prefer, *atypical psychosis,* is a separate disease that tends to "breed true."

Vaillant (1963, 1963a) followed up a number of patients admitted with "schizophrenia" fifty years before his study. Those with a remitting course had a higher incidence of manic-depressive disorders among their relatives than did the chronically ill patients. Some of the original cases "changed tracks" and manifested manic symptoms during subsequent psychotic episodes. Welner and Strömgren (1958) found that the ill relatives of seventy-two "schizophreniform" patients were primarily of an affective type. These findings are admittedly in contrast to those of Mitsuda (1962), who observed that his patients with atypical schizophreniform psychoses did tend to "breed true" and had ill relatives with the same sort of psychosis—a finding that appeared to corroborate the earlier work of Leonhard (1934).

The results of Winokur and his colleagues supported those of Welner and Strömgren.

Winokur (1974), equating "acute schizophrenia," "good-prognosis schizophrenia," and "schizoaffective illness" as roughly synonymous, believed this group of disorders could be differentiated from chronic schizophrenia on the basis of affective symptoms, confusional symptoms, and acuteness of onset. Patients in the "acute" category had significantly less affect blunting, while, as a group, they had significantly more perceptual disorder, catatonic traits, dysphoria, sleep disturbances, flight of ideas, agitation (or retardation), euphoria, and pushed speech. Winokur thought "acute schizophrenia" was not only distinguishable by the presence of affective symptoms but carried a much better prognosis (61 percent were well at one to two years, compared with 8 percent of process schizophrenics). Furthermore, in studies by his colleagues, nine ill family members of thirty-nine schizoaffective index cases were documented, and of these, eight had "clear depression or mania" and the ninth was a process schizophrenic (Clayton, Rodin, and Winokur, 1968). This argued against the notion, according to this author, of a third group of major psychoses ("schizoaffective illness"), since there seemed to be the absence of "breeding true." Indeed, the ill relatives could for the most part be categorized simply as suffering from manic-depressive illness.

In the large study of Army-veteran twins, on the other hand, MZ concordance was actually higher in pairs where the index twin had been diagnosed schizoaffective (50 percent) than the rate noted for manic-depressive psychosis (39 percent) or clear-cut schizophrenia (24 percent). These findings suggested that schizoaffectives might be genetically distinct (Cohen, Allen, Pollin, et al., 1972), a notion shared by the Japanese and Scandinavian investigators.

Elsässer[1] (1952) favored a two-psychosis theory. He did not find an increase in "schizoaffective" psychoses in his admittedly small series of mixed (manic × schizophrenic) matings. Instead he found either pure schizophrenics or pure manics among the offspring. His case descriptions, however, provided very few details, leaving one at the mercy of whatever diagnostic criteria Elsässer was applying. It is by no means clear whether contemporary diagnosticians would have arrived at the same diagnoses nor was Elsässer's sample necessarily comparable to those upon which subsequent reports are based. Case illustration 29, by way of contrast, concerns a mixed mating that nevertheless yielded three schizoaffective children.

The studies cited above, along with several others mentioned in a review by Procci (1976), have yielded inconsistent results, for which inconsistency of diagnosis appeared to be the chief factor. There does, however, appear to be general agreement that, phenotypically, the mentally ill relatives of schizoaffective probands—regardless of whose definition of schizoaffective one starts with—inclined more toward the affective pole of the endogenous psychoses (for example, Clayton et al., 1968; McCabe et al., 1971). Whether these relatives incline so far toward this pole as to warrant reclassification within the manic-depressive realm seems to be more a function of variation in initial patient sampling.

[1]Collecting nineteen matings of a schizophrenic parent with a manic-depressive spouse, this investigator showed that of their nineteen psychotic offspring, eight were schizophrenic, eight manic-depressive, only one "atypical," and two of "uncertain" diagnosis.

Varieties of Family Background

Patients labeled with any of the related terms—schizoaffective, pseudoneurotic, atypical, reactive, and so on—tend, as Procci mentions, to be young, and to have had an acute onset with identifiable external precipitants and a good premorbid history regarding work and friendships. Superficially at least, these features are quite dissimilar to what one ordinarily encounters in less problematical cases of schizophrenia.

Whether schizoaffective disorders are a dilute variety of true schizophrenia is in any case more complex than it seems on the surface. One can envision the possibility that the greater affectivity in some of these patients (especially those without gross mania) may be an expression of a kind of escape phenomenon in which a milder genetic loading simply allowed more of the person's ordinary affectivity to remain intact. Here the hypothesis would be that severe affective blunting represents an important phenotypic expression of *strong* genetic loading for "schizophrenia" whereas in cases of *mild* loading, little or no impairment of affectivity need develop. If this were so, the good "affectivity" would belong to that portion of the patient's personality not dragged down by the schizophrenic process; one wouldn't have to invoke participation in an entirely different disorder (namely, manic-depressive illness). There are individual family pedigrees in which a "schizoaffective" index case has close relatives—of normal affectivity—who are free of either schizophrenic or manic-depressive illnesses (see case illustration 8).

There are, to be sure, still other pedigrees in which a schizoaffective disorder is found nestled in the midst of numerous relatives with unmistakable affective psychoses, where the subsequent course of the index case ceases to resemble schizophrenia, taking on more and more the features of an affective psychosis (see case illustration 4). Cases of this sort tend to support the impressions of Winokur. Nevertheless, side by side with those pedigrees are others, known to the author, in which a "schizoaffective" patient is a person (usually a woman in her early twenties) from a family in which there are first-degree relatives with unequivocal schizophrenia, along with other relatives who exhibit clear-cut affective psychoses (see case illustrations 2, 5, 9, and 29). Families of this sort run counter to the experience of Elsässer.

If one were to judge by still other pedigrees (rather uncommon ones, in the author's experience) where the psychotic relatives of a schizoaffective patient were themselves schizoaffective, one would of course incline toward acceptance of the idea of a third major psychosis. We have already noted how the Scandinavian school had been particularly interested in a group of disorders designated "reactive psychoses" (RP): some authors, most notably the Danish investigator Strömgren, believe that genetic data warrant the singling out of the "reactive psychoses" as a separate category. McCabe and Strömgren (1975) found, for example, that siblings of "reactive" probands had significantly more reactive psychosis and manic-depressive psychosis. Reactive psychosis seemed more separable from schizophrenia. These authors describe three main clinical forms: acute paranoid reactions, reactive confusions, and syndromes consisting of reactive depressions and excitations (the latter not dissimilar to the "hysteroid unstable" group of D. F. Klein, 1969).

The reactive psychoses are said to occur in persons with a prior history of neurosis or character disorder, are generally short-lived, and follow severe "understandable" trauma. The patient retains good emotional contact, with "preservation" of the personality, and no more than transient thought disorder. If delusions or hallucinations are present (namely, in the acute paranoid form), they also tend to be "understandable and related to the trauma."

Whereas Strömgren has selected a group of patients so low in family incidence of schizophrenia and so free of conventional schizophrenic symptoms that his "reactive psychosis" scarcely overlaps with schizophrenia in any sense of the term, others have described patient populations where such neat distinctions are not so readily made. Two typical situations are encountered instead. In the first, certain young patients are diagnosed "schizophrenic" during their first episode, only to make an excellent recovery, perhaps succumbing later on to a clearly manic-depressive illness. This was the case with many of Vaillant's (1963, 1963a) "recovered" schizophrenics.

The more recent case described by Pope (1976) is illustrative. It concerns a fifty-seven-year-old man initially diagnosed as schizophrenic. He presented a mostly manic picture years later, albeit with some hallucinations and delusions (of a sort that made Pope concerned about the validity of the more recent diagnosis). This man responded well to lithium, having failed to improve on phenothiazines. More and more such cases are found in the current literature; in the case illustration section are four patients, each initially diagnosed schizophrenic, whose course subsequently "changed" to manic-depressive (see case illustrations 1, 4, 7, and 11).

A second situation concerns patients whose psychosis occurred in the wake of some severe life trauma (hence "reactive") but was characterized by elements of a more schizophrenic stamp than is typical of Strömgren's RP cases and by a family history quite positive for unequivocal schizophrenia. These patients often have such a relatively benign clinical course, even while retaining some schizophrenic stigmata, that one would not be inclined to reassign them to a different diagnostic category. With this group of patients, an original diagnosis of schizoaffective disorder is often made, and it seems to remain valid over time.

Other Theoretical Views: Modifying Factors

Some researchers have expressed the view that schizoaffective disorders belong to the "true" schizophrenias (Hoch and Polatin, 1949; Kolb, 1973).[2] This concept is implied by some of the labels favored by these researchers: schizoaffective schizophrenia, pseudoneurotic schizophrenia, borderline schizophrenia, and the like. Proponents of this view have suggested that the clinical features represent a schizophrenic predisposition softened by certain favorable attributes.

High intelligence may be the most important of these independent factors (Jones and Offord, 1975); schizophrenics with lower intelligence tend to run a more chronic course and to have an earlier onset. Shields et al. (1975) mention that schizophrenics tend to have lower IQs than their nonschizophrenic siblings (p. 180). Weingarten and Korn (1967), alluding to psychological test findings, report that a "pseudoneurotic group had higher I.Q.'s on the average than did 'core' patients." It is difficult to generalize on this point; clinicians see occasional schizoaffective cases with low IQ (see case illustration 2), and of course there are many unmistakable (especially paranoid) schizophrenics with high IQ (see case illustration 23). Probably it is fairer to say that there are many instances where high intelligence appears to exert a modifying and ameliorative influence on the schizophrenic vulnerability, to the point where the clinical manifestations emerge as less *process*like. On the other hand, to claim high intelligence can always protect against process schizophrenia would be a serious mistake. Occasionally one encounters even hebephrenic schizophrenics whose premorbid intelligence has been in the superior range. The progressive downhill course of the adolescent paranoid schizophrenic described by Kestenbaum (1977, case 3) also occurred in the face of superior intelligence.

In a model constructed around interaction between genetic and environmental influences, it is perfectly possible to envision whole families where for several generations genetic loading for schizophrenia is modified by the same set of favorable factors, such that all the ill members over successive generations appear as cases of "reactive psychosis." McCabe and Ström-

[2]A similar stand has been adopted by Welner, Croughan, et al. (1977) as an outgrowth of their follow-up study of 114 schizoaffective patients. Of this sample, 71 percent showed a chronic course and four-fifths of the latter also exhibited deterioration (namely, in marital or occupational status). The deteriorating course in turn was regarded as arguing in favor of an essentially schizophrenic process. As in all such studies, the question is not "how accurate were the results?" (they were most likely quite accurate) but "how representative a sample?"—of all that is currently being subsumed under the schizoaffective label. A family study, using the same group of probands, revealed that five out of six ill first-degree relatives also had a chronic course with both schizophrenic and affective symptoms (Welner, Welner, and Fishman, 1979). These authors, again emphasizing the deteriorating course, concluded that the ill relatives, like the probands, suffered a disorder that would most properly be considered schizophrenic in nature (p. 24).

gren (1975) may be correct in citing the similarity of psychoses in these families, but one need not invoke a third type of inherited illness to account for this phenomenon. We may very well be talking about a social-class factor here, contributing to differences in the *manifestation* of genetic liability.

Another important variable is the sex of the patient. In a study of 100 consecutive admissions to the New York Psychiatric Institue (Stone, 1975), seven patients were considered schizoaffective: six were female, one was male. Since the completion of that study, three more patients were given that diagnosis, and all were female. The patient population at the Institute of course differs in certain respects from that of other psychiatric hospitals, but within that population it has been true for many years that "schizoaffective disorder" is a diagnosis only occasionally applied to a male patient.

One of the disadvantages in the many brief articles on schizoaffective disorders lies in the impossibility of describing cases in great detail. McCabe has been able to make up for this deficit, partially, in a monograph on the reactive psychoses (1975). Even so, the reader is not always able to gather enough information to make a firm diagnosis of his or her own. It is hoped that the comparatively lengthy case illustrations at the end of this book transmit enough clinical information that the reader may be able with greater conviction to agree or disagree with my diagnostic impressions.

Category versus Continuum in the Schizoaffective Realm

Recently Kendell and Gourlay (1970) tried to come to grips with the problem of how best to categorize this intermediate group of patients. Using discriminant function analysis with extensive questionnaires, they attempted to distinguish a schizophrenic from a manic-depressive group. They found that at a clinical level, there were many patients who might well have received either diagnosis. They concluded that these disorders could be pictured as stretched out along a continuum. They saw this as arguing in favor of a heterogeneous inheritance rather than an inheritance which always stemmed from a common source. Diagramatically their findings were represented as shown in Figure 4–1.

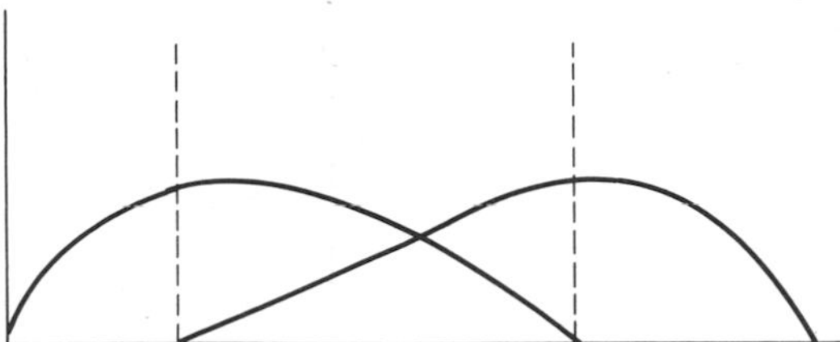

Figure 4–1. Symptom Overlap in Cases of Schizophrenia and Manic-Depression

The questions addressed to the patients studied by these authors showed an area of overlap so significant that schizophrenia did not distinguish itself territorially from manic-depressive illness. The ideal situation would have been a mapping like the one shown in Figure 4–2, which would have spoken for the possibility of isolating two absolutely distinct conditions.

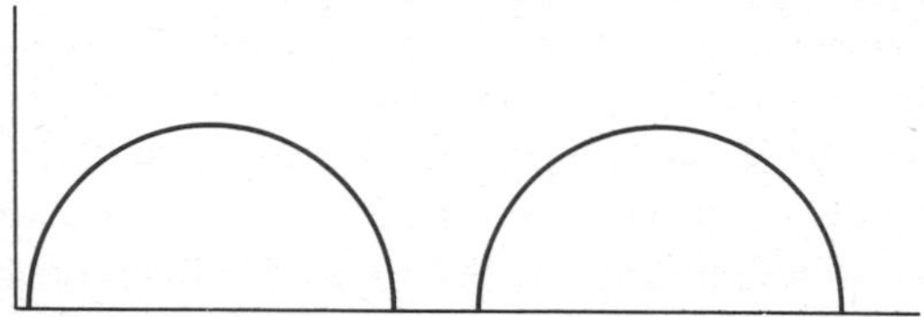

Figure 4–2. Nonoverlap of Symptoms in Hypothetical Ideal Situation when Schizophrenia and Manic-Depression Are Totally Distinct Categories

My views and those of Kendell and also Walter Reich (1975) embody the notion of a continuum of disorders from schizophrenic to manic-depressive. Our impressions are in turn similar to the earlier observations of Ødegaard. Although he noted a tendency for diagnoses in relatives to be similar to those of their respective schizophrenic, manic-depressive, or "reactive" probands, Ødegaard (1963) still thought that there was:

> . . . a gradual transition between [the] schizoaffective group and the remaining nuclear group. . . . Actually we seem to deal with a continuum without natural borderlines, but with a gradual series of transitions from the extreme schizophrenic to the affective pole. (p. 102)

More recently Reiser and Willett (1976), in their description of a schizoaffective father-son pair, both lithium responders, also expressed the opinion that there are "practical advantages to considering schizophrenia and manic-depressive psychosis on a continuum." The authors point out that, among other advantages, this view permits decision making regarding the use of lithium on a quantitative basis (i.e., on clinical impression of "manicness"), thus obviating the usual "either/or" dilemma experienced by the clinician who is locked into a diagnostic system composed only of discrete categories.

The opposite view, in which only catgories are emphasized, is embodied in the study of Taylor and Abrams (1975). These investigators examined two groups of patients, one initially diagnosed "schizoaffective, manic type," and the other "manic disorder." The schizoaffective/manic group had to have, in addition to manic symptoms, at least one Schneiderian first-rank symptom. No differences were noted between the two groups on psychopathological, demographic, family-history, or treatment-response parameters. The schizoaffective/manic group was quite small ($n = 10$) in comparison to the manic-disorder patients, of whom there were seventy-eight. The absence of schizophrenic relatives in both groups makes them seem more "alike," but one could easily envision a run of schizoaffective patients in subsequent admissions who did have schizophrenic relatives. Much larger numbers of schizoaffective probands would be required to settle this point. And one would like to have known whether there were relatives with schizophrenia-spectrum disorders in which research diagnostic criteria were not quite fulfilled. Adherence to category-based thinking may have allowed valuable information about subtle differences to slip through unnoticed, which might have been captured through simultaneous use of dimensional methods.

Like Abrams and Taylor, Sovner and McHugh (1976), as well as Tsuang and Dempsey (1976), have also emphasized the manic-depressive side of many cases bearing the schizoaffective label. There is a parallel here to the trend I mentioned in connection with borderline conditions. Before the early 1950s, especially before Robert Knight's papers, many psychoanalysts were using the term "borderline" to designate an "almost schizophrenic" group of patients. In recent years the term has been applied most often to patients with illnesses akin to the affective disorders. The earlier usage of "schizoaffective," likewise, was applied mostly to patients who were at least thought to be fundamentally schizophrenic. Since the advent of lithium, many such cases are being reappraised, and the current tendency is to consider "schizoaffective" a dilute or unusual form of manic-depressive illness.

Overview

The term "schizoaffective" has been used more loosely than its parent categories, schizophrenia and affective disorder. Even where there has been a consistent usage at one center, at another center the label is used to denote a somewhat different kind of condition. Sample homogeneity has been especially difficult to achieve *between* institutions. For these reasons, family studies of the schizoaffective disorders have yielded rather conflicting results over the years. Regarding etiology, every claim that could be made has been made. "Schizoaffective" has been considered, as we have noted, a brand of schizophrenia, a brand of manic-depressive psychosis (Himmelhoch et al., 1976), an illness *sui generis* (Leonhard's "cycloid psychosis," Strömgren's "reactive psychosis," Mitsuda's "atypical psychosis"), or a blend of the two polar conditions (my own view, in relation to selected instances of Sz and MDP mating).

One is faced with the choice of coining new terms to accommodate the myriad clinical subgroups within this realm, as though each constituted a syndrome worthy of separate study. Phenomenologically at least, it seems more parsimonious, if not more prudent, to speak of two clinical spectra (a schizophrenic continuum, "Sz", and a continuum for affective disorders, "MDP"), both of which are relevant to all but the "pure" cases of Sz or MDP. In such a schema, all combinations of both main tendencies would be possible throughout the broad segment that bridges the extreme (and unmixed) types. Figure 2-4, depicting an *Sz-MDP continuum,* represents such a model. The rectangular block of Figure 4–3 contains phenotypically pure Sz and MDP cases at either end, and all possible mixtures in between. Depending on where the block is "sliced," any type of blend can be generated. The slice at *A,* for example, singles out a region of predominantly schizophrenic symptomatology (namely, "pseudoneurotic schizophrenia"). A slice at *B* isolates a subgroup in which affective symptoms clearly predominate. In clinical discussions I prefer to restrict the term "schizoaffective" for the more evenly divided mixtures (see Chapter 8). Though cumbersome, a term such as "predominantly affective schizoaffective"

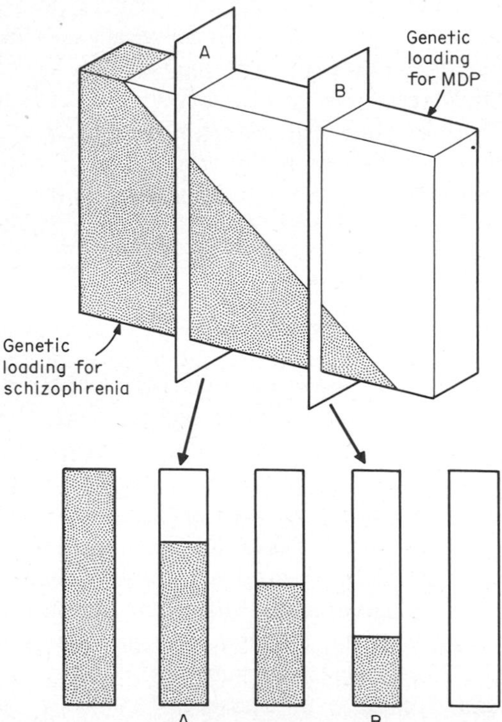

Figure 4–3. Hypothetical Complementary Series of Genotypes Related to Schizoaffective Disorders

might be more appropriate for a patient sample such as that studied by Sovner and McHugh.

As long as one specifies the mixture—in speaking of single cases or of particular samples—in semiquantitative fashion, more effective communication can take place. One can then compare more meaningfully mental illness in relatives of probands occupying specific regions within the realm of severe but "impure" disorders.

Fuller representation of the underlying factors in the various "schizoaffective" subtypes (in the broad sense of the term) would of course require a more complex model than the one suggested in Figure 4–3. One would want to take into account severity of the genetic loading of either schizophrenia or MDP (or both), even though we cannot yet measure such liability directly. A number of independent factors (intelligence, sex, social class, type of early environment, and so on) must also be weighed in the balance. Thus far I have the impression that a disorder somewhere in the broad realm of schizoaffective illness may eventuate in such situations as:

1. *High* genetic loading for both Sz and MDP in the presence of favorable independent factors
2. Moderate genetic loading for Sz, with less favorable independent factors, especially in female patients
3. Modest genetic loading for Sz, mild loading for MDP
4. Mild genetic liability but pronounced *un*favorable independent factors
5. Moderate to high loading for MDP, with perhaps none for Sz; unfavorable independent factors, all leading to an acute "schizophreniform" psychosis in young adult life, followed by episodes more clearly affective in nature

Other combinations would be possible as well. Situation 5 might be valid for the type of schizoaffective case referred to by those authors who believe they are dealing essentially with an affective disorder.

One advantageous aspect of the term "schizoaffective" consists in its not containing (though often implying) "psychosis." To those of us who embrace the notion of genetic underpinning for the bulk of severe emotional disorders, those labels are more welcome which allow a *range* of manifestation spanning psychotic and borderline (at times, even neurotic). The surplus meaning in the phrase "manic-depressive psychosis" is unfortunate because many relatives of MDP probands have similar illnesses but never show faulty reality testing. The same is true in the realm of schizophrenia, and also in the in-between "schizoaffective" realm. I have used "MDP" in many places throughout this book as a kind of shorthand and because of its historical importance, well aware that the less prejudicial term "affective disorder" is taking its place. With this thought in mind, one can approach patients with borderline structure in a new way. Many may have come by their conditions as an outgrowth of genetic liability to an affective disorder, to schizophrenia, or, in certain instances, to both. The final expression of this predisposition (or *vulnerability,* as it is more often called—see the next chapter) will of course be shaped by whatever combination of independent factors is operative in any given case. Most patients for whom the label "schizoaffective" has ever been appropriate will have at best a *borderline* structure (case illustrations 9, 10, and 16), but may have as many relatives with significant psychiatric disorders as do certain more frequently *psychotic* schizoaffective persons (case illustrations 2 and 5).

CHAPTER 5

Genetics of Schizophrenia:

Theoretical Considerations

Analogies with Classical Models

In medicine, sharply circumscribed borders can seldom be drawn around putative clinical entities until the discovery of some reliable sign. This may come in the form of a characteristic observation in physical diagnosis or, more often, in the form of a laboratory test result or a "highly suspicious" radiographic abnormality. The clinician's dream is to find a distinguishing mark of perfect reliability—the pathognomonic sign—but this hope is seldom realized. Nevertheless, it is often possible in the realm of infectious disease to isolate offending bacteria or viruses, which then satisfy the clinician as having demonstrated a necessary (though not sufficient) *cause* of his patient's ailment. By the same token, in the instance of illnesses with a strong familial tendency, diagnostic impressions become immensely sharpened after the development of a readily confirmable test for some abnormality—more often than not, a biochemical one—which thereupon becomes known as the endophenotype of a disorder (whose boundaries will usually be redrawn to include persons with a "positive" test). Benign discoid lupus can now be distinguished from disseminated lupus erythematosus by means of a biochemical test—which thus serves to resolve doubt in uncertain or "borderline" cases.

In general, as laboratory technology has progressed, the conceptual space occupied by many disease labels has shrunk to the point of enveloping only a "core" condition, characterized by the inclusion of a "positive test" from a frame of reference outside the clinical-descriptive.

It may be that where schizophrenia is concerned, we are today where clinicians were a century ago in talking about "consumption." There can be no rigid definition of what schizophrenia "is," since we have not yet found its "Koch's bacillus." (It may be arrogance and ignorance combined even to assume that so neat a correlation awaits discovery.) There can only be a series of trial-and-error *preliminary* definitions, which we then subject to various methods of measurement and relate to certain external frames of reference. If some psychological test response crops up in nine out of ten cases we are *initially* calling schizophrenia, we tend to redefine "schizophrenia" for the future as a condition in which that sign is found. Meehl (1972) has mentioned this sort of phenomenon, in discussing what he and others have called *psychometric drift* in diagnoses. Such shifts are inevitable as one attempts to move from crude to refined methods of diagnosis, but there is always the danger of leaning too heavily on a new and not yet validated test finding. This in turn will incline toward excessive narrowing or skewing of one's conception of a diagnostic entity. In the case of schizophrenia this would involve rejecting a certain number of cases that might very well have been included, if at some later date, for example, a still "truer" test of the condition were to prove positive in the given instance. Currently we seem to be swinging away from the tendency toward overinclusiveness (and its false positives) of the 1940s and 1950s to *under*inclusiveness and the creation of false negatives.

A state of dynamic equilibrium exists between clinical and research diagnoses of schizophrenia. Suspecting that heredity plays an important role in this condition, we examine the families of patients to whom we apply this label. Our findings (along with other findings in psychology and psychopharmacology, and elsewhere) lead to a modified labeling process. A new "brand" of schizophrenia is created, somewhat different from and more sharply delineated than the old.

MacMahon (1968) has drawn our attention to the *order* in which the various etiological components of a disease were discovered. This may shape our impressions regarding a given disease as "primarily dependent on genetic factors but modified by the environment" or "primarily dependent on environmental stressors, only modified by genetic influences." MacMahon went so far as to state that in the light of a more sophisticated approach that respects *all* the relevant factors and their interactions, the supposed quantitative estimates of "heritability," as well as other comparisons of the "relative importance of genes versus environment," may be nonsensical. One could, in fact, envision a continuum of diseases, at one end of which were conditions whose "heritability" was dramatic and self-evident (Huntington's chorea, hemophilia, and so on). At the other end one could place conditions for which the genetic factor was subtle and rather in the background (tuberculosis, malaria, and so forth). For heuristic purposes we have tended to designate one end of this continuum "hereditary disorders," the other end, "nonhereditary disorders." This is erroneous, if we are speaking *strictly; loosely* speaking, such categorization has a certain utility. In the middle of such a continuum we might place idiopathic schizophrenia, and even here one would have to add the qualifier (see Erlenmeyer-Kimling, 1968, p. 74) that a hereditary component is in all likelihood an indispensable element—a necessary though not sufficient "cause" of the illness. Rather than claim, because the MZ concordance in schizophrenia is about 40 percent, that heredity accounts for "40 percent" of the variance, it is more reasonable simply to assert that the illness becomes manifest only in a percentage of its "carriers."

There are other reasons why it may be simplistic to think along the lines of percentage heritability where schizophrenia is concerned. Between the most distal etiology of genetic abnormality and more proximal (but still early) ones in the causal chain (such as postnatal environment, mother-child interaction, and so on) stand a row of intrauterine factors so similar in their impact to the strictly genetic ones that they are scarcely separable. In the case of phenylketonuria (PKU), for example, there are a few recorded instances where a pregnant woman with unrecognized PKU—because her abnormally high levels of blood phenylalanine so readily cross the placental barrier—gave birth to a (heterozygous) child with mental retardation (and other overt manifestations of the PKU syndrome ordinarily only seen in the homozygous offspring). MacMahon cites this occurrence as exemplifying a defect "virtually independent of the genotype of the affected individual [the fetus in this situation] but highly dependent on the genotype of another person, who is providing the 'environment' of the affected person" (1968, p. 397).

One cannot of course claim that certain manifest schizophrenics have become so by virtue of being bathed in the schizophrenic juices of an affected mother. In our ignorance of what the schizophrenia genotype actually consists in, we cannot show that a particular person is free of it. Our current level of understanding here is much less than holds true for a number of monogenic metabolic disorders like PKU. Analogous disturbances *may* be involved with certain examples of "schizophrenia." We already have hints of other intrauterine events and disturbances that seem to predispose toward schizophrenic decompensation later in life.

Anthony (1968) has implicated constitutionally small size and strength, noting that the prepsychotic child, within a given sibship, was often the most puny at birth. Perinatal hypoxemia has similarly been implicated as an early (but postgenetic) causative factor. This was hinted at by Eisenberg (1968) when he drew attention to the increased incidence of neurological "soft signs" in adolescent patients admitted with a diagnosis of schizophrenia. Many of these young people seemed to have suffered various perinatal complications of a sort temporarily compromising oxygenation. In some instances these "schizophrenics" have quite normal parents and relatives and come from reasonably healthy home environments, so that it is not easy to claim a genetic factor in addition. In others, unfavorable genetic antecedents do appear to have underlain the schizophrenic breakdown; in these cases one tends to speak of the perinatal morbidity as having "exposed" the preexisting genetic defect. The latter might (one could argue) have remained dormant or undetected, had it not been for the central nervous system damage provoked at birth.

Preliminary Remarks on the Diathesis-Stress Theory

The foregoing remarks lead us into consideration of one of the more prominent theories respecting the transmission of schizophrenia, the diathesis-stress theory, espoused by Gottesman (1968), Kety et al. (1968), Anthony (1968), Eisenberg (1968), and others.

Proponents of this theory hypothecate the presence of an inborn (genetic) predisposition, or "diathesis" in persons who ultimately exhibit clinical schizophrenia. This diathesis is activated by various stressors subsequent to the moment of conception (and including the usual environmental stresses of extrauterine life). The class of *precipitant* stresses is ordinarily thought to include events and conditions *after* birth. This division is somewhat arbitrary, since certain links in the middle part of the causal chain can be viewed in two ways. Perinatal hypoxemia, if this indeed does contribute to some instances of schizophrenic decompensation, could be seen as a stressor, because it occurs long after fertilization, but also as part of diathesis, since it occurs so long before overt psychosis. As we have touched on briefly elsewhere, not all investigators are in agreement regarding the significance of the alleged diathesis: Erlenmeyer-Kimling assumes genetic errors underlie all true cases of schizophrenia (1968, p. 74), whereas Tienari (1975) wonders whether what is inherited is not the schizophrenic syndrome at all but a particular personality disturbance. The latter view is one Tienari shares with many of the Scandinavian school, including his predecessor, Essen-Möller, and is supported (less passionately) by Rosenthal and Van Dyke (1970) and opposed by Tsuang (1967) and Tsuang and Winokur (1973). Tsuang, for example, not only emphasizes the separateness of schizophrenia from the manic-depressive group of disorders (see also Rosenthal, 1975a, and Shields, 1972) but mentions that he has yet to hear of an MZ pair anywhere in the world where one twin is schizophrenic and the other, manic.

The vulnerability concept in schizophrenia seems simultaneously incontestable yet elusive (see pp. 93–95). Meehl (1972) and Zerbin-Rüdin (1972) have alluded to both features of this paradoxical situation. The chief reason underlying the paradox is that the twin and adoption studies leave no doubt of the strong genetic factor, while shedding only a dim light on its nature. Patterns of transmission do not appear to fit neatly into simple monogenic or two-gene models, so that the classical Mendelian rules do not readily apply. Even about this there is some controversy, however, as we shall examine later in more detail. At all events, since we do not know precisely what is inherited, we cannot precisely measure it or assay its influence in a manner uncontaminated by a host of other influences. The "high-risk" studies may help answer some of these questions. Anthony (1968, 1972) has examined and followed children, some between five and ten, others between ten and fifteen, one or both of whose parents were schizophrenic. He postulated that among the various children of all these parents some 10 to 20 percent would harbor a "strong" diathesis; 20 to 30 percent, a weaker diathesis; and 30 to 50 percent would be genotypically normal or perhaps even (in some instances) specially gifted and creative (see Heston, 1966; Karlsson, 1972). Respecting the children with a strong diathesis, Anthony estimates that half are schizoid and shy; half appear initially normal. The weak-diathesis group contains some children who go on to exhibit neurotic and other personality disturbances. I suspect some children in this group would develop milder clinical pictures that would place them in a borderline category, even by psychostructural standards.

On Gene-Environment Interplay

As Gottesman (1968) has pictured it, diathesis without stress does not lead to schizophrenia and stress without the specific diathesis also doesn't lead to schizophrenia. The situation with schizophrenia is probably not so simple as with certain monogenic conditions like galactosemia. Eisenberg (1968), for example, has put forward the notion that a genotypically "normal" child exposed to an "abysmal" home might develop a schizophrenia-like syndrome, here a *phenocopy,* due to a crushing environment. Some of Anthony's (1972) "parapsychotic" children (who have grown up around a grossly psychotic parent and have adopted some of his or her bizarre views) may be genotypically free of schizophrenic diathesis. This does not refute the diathesis-stress model but rather appends to it the footnote that very special and prolonged stresses may culminate in a clinical disorder that is hard to distinguish from "true" schizophrenia, even when borne by persons free of the diathesis. Until we are in a better position to detect the schizophrenic vulnerability objectively and early in life, there must remain of course a speculative air to any discussion about this model of transmission. Eisenberg provided a useful guide for orienting one's thinking about the manner in which diathesis and stress may combine to induce psychosis. Table 5–1 depicts the chances of various individuals succumbing to overt schizophrenia using Eisenberg's guide.

TABLE 5–1

Family Life × Genetic Studies

	Family Life		
	Optimal	*Average*	*Abysmal*
GENETIC STATUS			
Carrier	±	+++	++++
Normal	0	±	+++

NOTE: 0 represents no chance of developing clinical shizophrenia; ±, slight chance; and ++++, very great chance.

SOURCE: After Eisenberg (1968).

According to this schema, the optimal environment protects most "carriers"; the abysmal home induces phenocopying even in those without hereditary predisposition. One might revise this schema by taking into consideration that genetic loading, where schizophrenia is concerned, is not an on-off matter, but may vary along a gradient (see Table 5–2). This schema embodies the hypothesis that very high degrees of loading may make the development of schizophrenia at some stage of life all but inevitable. Noting an increase in fetal deaths among conceptuses of schizophrenic mothers compared with a carefully matched control group, Rieder, Rosenthal, and

TABLE 5–2

Environmental Factors × Genetic Loading

	Environmental Factors		
	Optimal	*Average*	*Abysmal*
GENETIC LOADING			
Very High	++	+++	++++
Moderate	±	++	++++
None	0	±	++

Wender (1975) even speculate that particularly high loading for schizophrenia may constitute a "lethal gene" whose possessors succumb long before they could demonstrate characteristic psychological abnormalities. These schemata also make more readily understandable the need felt by psychogeneticists to concentrate their attention upon persons situated in the middle rather than at the extremes of environmental and genetic variability. For example, persons reared in particularly chaotic homes by grossly psychotic parent(s) would constitute a group too contaminated by nongenuine cases of "schizophrenia" to permit methodical research. Borderline cases migh crop up, meanwhile, in persons with marked loading protected by optimal home environment or in those with more modest degrees of diathesis reared in average to mildly turbulent environments. Children with modest "loading" and nonturbulent homes may of course escape the illness to which their predisposition would seem to consign them. This illustrates the point of Zerbin-Rüdin (1972) that heredity need *not* mean predetermination. Schulsinger and Mednick (1975) are impressed by the impact not only of perinatal complications but also of parental separation upon children at high risk for schizophrenia. These authors also allude to the higher than expected incidence of schizophrenia in urban slum areas where "parental separation, social stresses and insufficient obstetrical service [are] present" (1975, p. 41), a point similar to that raised by Kohn (1973) in his article on social class and schizophrenia. Kohn advocates an interactive model that would integrate genetic predisposition, stress, and the conditions of life associated with social class.

Organic "stressors" that can produce conditions mimicking schizophrenia include frontal lobe tumors (Belfer and d'Autremont, 1971), basal ganglia degeneration (West, 1973), and disseminated lupus. The list is actually much longer, although Zerbin-Rüdin (1972) estimates that phenocopying from these sources is low, perhaps on the order of 1 percent of all cases of clinical schizophrenia. Turner (1979), in writing on patients *hospitalized* with the diagnosis, has estimated the percentage of phenocopies to be as high as 15 percent.

Vulnerability

The concept of *vulnerability* has begun to have a wide impact in the field of biometrics as well as in psychogenetics.

Zubin (1976), synthesizing material from a number of interrelated areas in psychiatry, reached conclusions similar to those of Gottesman, Shields, and Rosenthal that vulnerability may well be the common denominator uniting various contrasting theories about the evolution of schizophrenia (see also Zubin and Spring, 1977). Clinically overt schizophrenic episodes Zubin views as the recurrent manifestations of a chronic (lifelong) vulnerability. The latter becomes the essence of what it is to be schizophrenic, not the presence of overt characteristic symptoms (the "disorder"). Between episodes the patient reverts to his premorbid level, which, in the case of persons with schizophrenic vulnerability, is usually distinguishable from the normal. One seldom sees the *restitutio ad integrum* said (by Kraepelin and many others) to characterize the interpsychotic phases in manic-depressive patients. Only a few schizophrenic persons, it would seem, are so severerely affected as never to enjoy periods of return to their premorbid level: Manfred Bleuler, for example, has followed a number of schizophrenics over many years and has noted that only about 10 percent remain continuously ill—while half have remained "usually well." Zubin offers the analogy of a weight attached to a suspended string. The organism (the suspended string) must cope with a certain measure of internal and external life stress (the weight). As the weight increases, nothing happens until a critical point is reached, when suddenly a catastrophe occurs: the string's intermolecular forces are overcome and breakage follows. In the analogy, a patient's coping capacities are swamped and psychosis supervenes. These phenomena may be illustrated graphically. Zubin's diagram (Figure 5–1) resembles the chart of Eisenberg just alluded to (Tables 5–1 and 5–2).

Figure 5–1. Relationship between Schizophrenic Diathesis and Symptom Outbreak

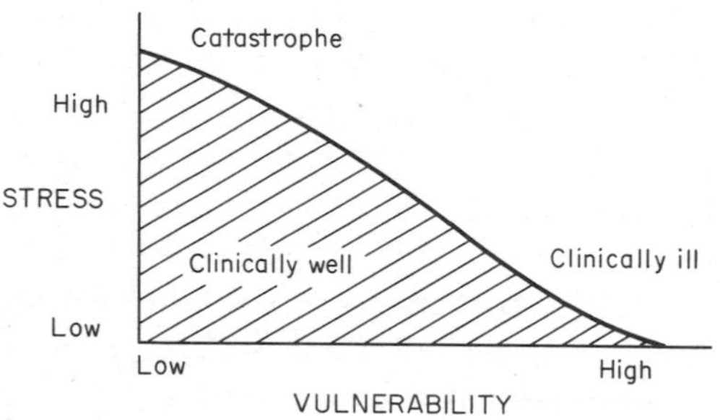

SOURCE: Adapted from Zubin and Spring (1977).

The concept of vulnerability, however compelling, still rests to an uncomfortably large degree upon intuition. An outgrowth of certain established facts (about MZ concordance, and so on), this concept awaits validation through newer data stemming from future investigations along a broad front. It is worth noting what steps have already been taken in an effort to quantify this notion and to what degree these efforts have borne fruit.

Salzinger, Portnoy, and Feldman (1964), to cite one such study, have transcribed speech samples of schizophrenic patients from which every fifth word is then deleted. The doctored transcriptions are then examined (by college students, in this particular experiment) with the object of determining to what degree the missing words can be filled in correctly by a stranger. Later, they made the observation (1966) that patients with the greatest comprehensibility (i.e., whose missing words strangers found it easiest to guess) had the best prognosis. Efforts are underway to examine the clinically well relatives of these patients. Should some of these relatives exhibit the same kind of incomprehensibility as the probands, one might be entitled to claim a degree of inherited vulnerability. Furthermore, this vulnerability can be said to exist independent of whether the relative is well or ill. Some of Zubin's colleagues have made progress in establishing a possible neurophysiological marker for schizophrenia involving pupillary reactivity (Hakarem and Lidsky, 1975).[1]

As Hakarem and Lidsky (1975) observed, eyelid shutting was less frequent and briefer in duration in schizophrenics than in normals, and interestingly, normal control subjects with the least amount of eyelid shutting could still be distinguished from the schizophrenic subjects with the most eyelid shutting. Their finding that pupillary reaction time was abnormal in chronic schizophrenics who had made some degree of recovery suggested that this "marker" remained detectable beyond the acute or more overt phases of the illness.

Comparisons might be drawn between the concept of vulnerability and "catastrophe theory"—elaborated by the French mathematician Thom and summarized by Zeeman (1976). This theory provides a comprehensible framework for the conceptualization of dramatic shifts of state occurring suddenly in what can be seen in retrospect to have been *critical* points.

The analogy to catastrophe theory is intriguing, although, as Kolata (1977) cautions, this theory is not yet equipped to refine clinical intuition mathematically. The subject, as it relates to schizophrenia, is discussed further in my paper on turning points in therapy (Stone, 1978a).

The "Essence" of Schizophrenia and the Search for Biological Indicators

Schizophrenia research is in the paradoxical position of having established beyond reasonable doubt the operation (in most cases) of a strong genetic factor as a primordial causative element, without being able to declare *which* cases this factor applies to, what the factor consists in, or what neurological, biochemical, or other abnormalities may justifiably be said to relate directly *to* the genetic factor. These are some of the questions underlying the intense effort in contemporary psychiatry to define and diag-

[1]Contraction to light was not as great in chronic schizophrenics as in controls. The authors speculated that this phenomenon reflected the schizophrenic's attempt to cope with sensory "overload" via delayed response.

nose schizophrenia in the most reliable manner, to validate the diagnoses via tests from external frame(s) of reference, and to discover biochemical, electrophysiological, and other abnormalities that will be *unique* for (this more sharply defined) schizophrenia. The isolation of such a unique and valid laboratory finding would constitute the establishment of a biological *marker*.[2] This marker, in turn, would presumably be more directly related to the essential genetic factor than the classical clinical findings have been. If there were pathognomonic signs of schizophrenia at the clinical level, one could have perhaps relaxed in the search for such a marker. But, as Carpenter, Strauss, and Muleh (1973) have demonstrated, there are no such signs that *include* all that is schizophrenia and *exclude* all that is not. What we have instead are certain suggestive signs, like loosening of the associations, which are relatively far removed from the more distal links in the etiological chain.

Our contemporary system of classification—which remains in what Fink (1974) has called a pre-Linnaean stage of development—is built on the same framework that suggested itself to physicians of two and a half millennia ago: We speak of mental retardation in all its many forms (*stultitia* and *amentia* in the older nosologies)—mood disorders (mania, melancholia); characterological disorders (hysteria, plus much of what was included in Theophrastus's writings—see Chapter 10); and loss of the mental faculties from illness, arteriosclerosis, and so on, in previously well persons (dementia). Finally, we have cases of marked eccentricity and peculiar idiosyncratic thought that we now tend to subsume under the rubric "schizophrenia" (vesania). It is precisely the quality of eccentricity, of "weirdness," that alerts us to the presence of schizophrenia or to the presence of some stable disorder of mental life whose most striking feature is this eccentricity—whether one chooses to call it vesania, or dementia praecox (as Kraepelin [1905] did), or schizophrenia (for those of us who prefer Bleuler's term), or by some other term as yet unaccepted or undreamed of.

For Kraepelin the essence of this illness was the deterioration of the mental faculties, beginning relatively early in life (hence, *dementia praecox*). The reasoning faculty was the one primarily affected, not memory and orientation. Kraepelin's great achievement lay in seeing the red thread underlying a variety of cases, collected by his predecessors, Kahlbaum, Hecker, Sommers, and others under the labels catatonia, hebephrenia, and "simple" dementia, all of which Kraepelin brought together, along with paranoia, under the umbrella "dementia praecox."

It is understandable why a deteriorating course became a criterion for diagnosis because, while more subtle than the criteria for madness

[2]Concerning the usage of the term "biological marker" or "indicator" versus the more specific term "genetic marker"—often used incorrectly in reference to schizophrenia—the reader should consult the definitions provided by Gottesman and Shields (1976, p. 380).

employed by the ancients, it is still easy to observe and record. Like all criteria, unless validated by a cross-check with another frame of reference (anatomical, biochemical, and so forth), this criterion settled into a self-fulfilling prophecy (*if* deterioration, *then* dementia praecox).

Bleuler's reworking of the Kraepelinian classification represents a refinement of diagnosis as well as a new hypothesis regarding the *essence* of the term he coined, schizophrenia. In his 1911 monograph Bleuler (1950) drew attention to the features *autism, ambivalence, loosening of associations,* and *inappropriateness of affect* as shared by the patients heretofore labeled "dementia praecox." One could add *anhedonia*[3] to this list of features Bleuler considered most important to the diagnoses.

Both loosening of association and inappropriateness of affect, meantime, create the effect of bizarreness or eccentricity. These qualities, when present in a psychiatric patient, probably alert the clinician to a schizophrenic diagnosis more readily than would ambivalence (which is almost universal in severe mental illness of whatever sort) or anhedonia (the detection of which may require knowing the patient over a longer time span than is necessary to register incongruity of thought and affect).

Further from the self-evident is the concept of schizophrenia as a disorder characterized, at the clinical level, by "ego weakening" (Alias, 1974). Basing his ideas on the work of Bellak and Loeb (1969), Alias emphasizes the loss of ego boundaries and the weakening of the integrative and executive functions as the essence of schizophrenic psychopathology. Ever since Tausk (1919) elaborated his notion of ego boundary,[4] many investigators have been drawn to this concept in their search for what is essential in schizophrenia. Most of the eleven "first-rank" symptoms of Schneider, codified in the 1940s and 1950s, involve abnormalities of ego boundary (namely, broadcast of thought, insertion into one's mind of someone else's thoughts or feelings, thought aloud and at a distance from oneself [hallucinations], and so on). The patient of Arieti (1970) who reported "I'm growing my father's hair" betrays at once an elemental confusion of ego boundary and an eccentricity arising out of this bizarre confusion—both of which we identify strongly as schizophrenic.

Returning to a more Kraepelinian model, Langfeldt (1937) warned that

[3]Meehl (1972, p. 414) believes the "hedonic deficit" in schizophrenia emphasized earlier by Rado is of central importance. Stein and Wise (1971) speculate that the schizophrenic's "inherently deficient pleasure-resources" may stem from dysfunction of noradrenergic pathways in the central nervous system. Here one of the classic "fundamental" symptoms is seen as the expression of a particular neurological (limbic system) abnormality.

[4]"Attention may now be called to a symptom in schizophrenia, which I have named 'loss of ego boundaries.' This symptom is a complaint that everyone knows the patient's thought. That his thoughts are not enclosed in his own head, but are spread throughout the world and occur simultaneously in the heads of all persons. The patient seems no longer to realize he is a separate psychical entity." (Tausk, 1919, p. 45)

psychosis in the absence of primary or "process" symptoms should not be labeled *schizophrenia*. Later he expressed the view (1969) that typical schizophrenia exhibited an unfavorable response to treatment and a lack of spontaneous remission. For Langfeldt, the essence of schizophrenia might be seen as a combination of process symptoms in conjunction with a chronic or even a downhill course. Persons with "schizophrenic" symptoms who remitted spontaneously and who showed a favorable treatment response were considered "atypical" ("schizophreniform") by Langfeldt, perhaps not a part of the central concept of schizophrenia at all. A number of contemporary investigators, especially among the Scandinavians, share Langfeldt's opinions, including Astrup, Fossum, and Holmboe (1962), who regard the presence of depression or confusion as part of an acute schizophrenic psychosis meriting a shift in diagnosis to a "reactive" group that may not actually be associated with "true" schizophrenia. These views are also shared by Angst (1966) and Serban and Gidynski (1975). There is of course no exit from the labyrinth created by these postulates, without access to a frame of reference outside the clinical.

Trait versus State

If one considers the syndrome of *process* schizophrenia as the *core* condition, psychotic persons who fail to exhibit the syndrome (or *state*) will appear "outside," even though some biological tags might point to their being inside. If one considers, along with Meehl (1972), certain characterological traits as central to schizophrenia (e.g., some combination like shyness and eccentricity), then the "process" cases will be seen as full-blown examples of trait inheritance. In this model, many persons with milder degrees of the trait will also be counted as *within* the concept "schizophrenia." Some "atypical" cases would be included if one accepted this theory. As Meehl points out, researchers tend to focus first on the full-blown cases, on the grounds that information about biochemical and other abnormalities in them may later be demonstrated (to a milder degree perhaps) in more subtle cases. For the moment, it is most likely premature to exclude entirely the schizoaffective and reactive patients from the central concept of schizophrenia: the bathwater of the "atypical" cases may contain the baby after all.

There is a strong inclination to "see" as the essence of schizophrenia some factor that, as if by strange coincidence, lies exactly within the province of one's own subspecialty. Biochemists have favored one or another biochemical model. Among the psychologists, for instance, Broen (1968) is impressed by the importance in schizophrenia of a central inhibitory defect, leaving the person with this vulnerability more open to being swamped by internal and external stimuli. This theory has become incorporated into other theories related to the mode of action of chlorpromazine and other neuroleptic drugs that appear to act as a filter in the central nervous system

(CNS), reducing the impact of such stimuli. More recently, these theories have been connected to still more microscopic frames of reference, as one moves from the macroscopic clinical and psychological realms down to the neurological and biochemical. In particular, the role of the dopaminergic pathways in the CNS and their relationship to this hypothecated CNS-inhibitory defect has been explored by numerous investigators (Malek-Ahmadi and Fried, 1976, and others). Other psychological models have been propounded, including that of Watson (1973) who noted that abstract thinking was particularly deficient in "process" schizophrenics, whereas autistic preoccupations were more characteristic of the thought patterns of patients labeled "reactive." By itself such a distinction cannot settle the issue whether reactives with their autism are a breed apart from the process patients, or just a less aggressive manifestation of the same disorder.

Before we examine further some of the interrelated biochemical and neurophysiological models, we should stress once again the importance of these new conceptualizations because of their impact on theory and diagnosis. As one's personal theory of schizophrenia becomes modified through assimilation of new data about the "essence" of the disease, one's diagnostic standards inevitably change. We alluded before to "psychometric drift" in diagnosis, as clinicians of the preceding generation began to reorient their diagnostic machinery in line with the results of the Rorschach test, the MMPI, and so on. Currently the various research diagnostic criteria proposed for schizophrenia (see Chapter 8) are exerting a similar impact.

The research design of "high-risk studies" requires awareness of both trait and state models, inasmuch as one is searching—among children of parents diagnosed schizophrenic because of manifesting the "state"—for subtle traits that may earmark certain children as likely to develop clinically recognizable schizophrenia at a later date. Apart from the small number of childhood schizophrenics that clinicians have been able to recognize,[5] most children one could have called preschizophrenic *in retrospect* betray nothing like the fully developed schizophrenic *state*.

In connection with Erlenmeyer-Kimling's High-Risk Project (at the New York State Psychiatric Institute), Kestenbaum and Bird (1978) reported some preliminary observations on a number of latency-age children born to a schizophrenic parent. They found that the global assessment scores (i.e., of overall functioning) were uniformly lower than scores accorded a control group with healthy parents. No one trait has emerged that the high-risk children share as a whole. Thus far, the commonest abnormality noted (by raters who were blind to the diagnosis of the parents) was poor relatedness to others.

[5]The diagnosis of childhood schizophrenia in its various forms has recently been reviewed by Kestenbaum (1977).

Possible Biological Markers of Schizophrenia

The past quarter century has witnessed an intense search for consistent abnormalities—on the microscopic as opposed to the macroscopic level—that would predict the presence of a schizophrenic disorder or even of the more subtle entity, schizophrenic vulnerability. This time period coincides fairly closely with the development of effective antipsychotic medications. Chlorpromazine had come into widespread clinical use by the mid-1950s, and there seemed good reason to hope that elucidation of its site and mode of action would carry us a giant step nearer the biochemical derangement supposedly underlying schizophrenia itself.

To the extent that a gene encodes and governs the manufacture of a particular enzyme, the ideal marker—from a practical standpoint—would consist of a significant abnormality in the activity of a particular enzyme (as measured by abnormality in a chemical reaction under the control of that enzyme). Since a disease of the mind is—ultimately—a disease of the brain, the logical place to look for such markers is within the central nervous system. In humans this is possible only to a limited extent, because of obvious ethical considerations relating to experimentation with the brain. Yet in animals, as Snyder et al. have pointed out (1974), no strictly comparable analogue of human schizophrenia occurs in the state of nature—nor can one be induced so far in the laboratory. Even the "model" psychosis induced (in animal or human subjects) by such psychotomimetic agents as lysergic acid diethylamide (LSD) or the amphetamines provoke mental aberrations more typical of the acute phase of a schizophrenic reaction than of the chronic condition whose presence we more confidently label "schizophrenia." Or, viewed from a different angle, the "model" psychosis may, as the one resulting from amphetamine administration, resemble *one* form of schizophrenia (in this case, the paranoid form) but not others.

The tendency has been, for readily understandable reasons, to search for markers from within a pooling of paradigmatic cases of schizophrenia. Enough promising leads have failed even with this restriction; inclusion of doubtful cases at the outset would most likely have led to even more fruitless investigations. When a promising lead is found, application of the related laboratory test is spread out to include more equivocal cases; at times, the close relatives of the probands as well.

The markers thus far proposed for schizophrenia have mainly been biochemical; in recent years a number of other possible markers have been investigated that represent abnormalities one or two steps further along in the causal chain. This chain is sketched in Figure 5–2. Underneath each link in the chain an illustrative example, or suggested example, is provided.

Before looking at data relevant to schizophrenia in greater detail, it should be noted that the need to identify biological markers goes well

Figure 5–2. Causal Chain in Schizophrenia

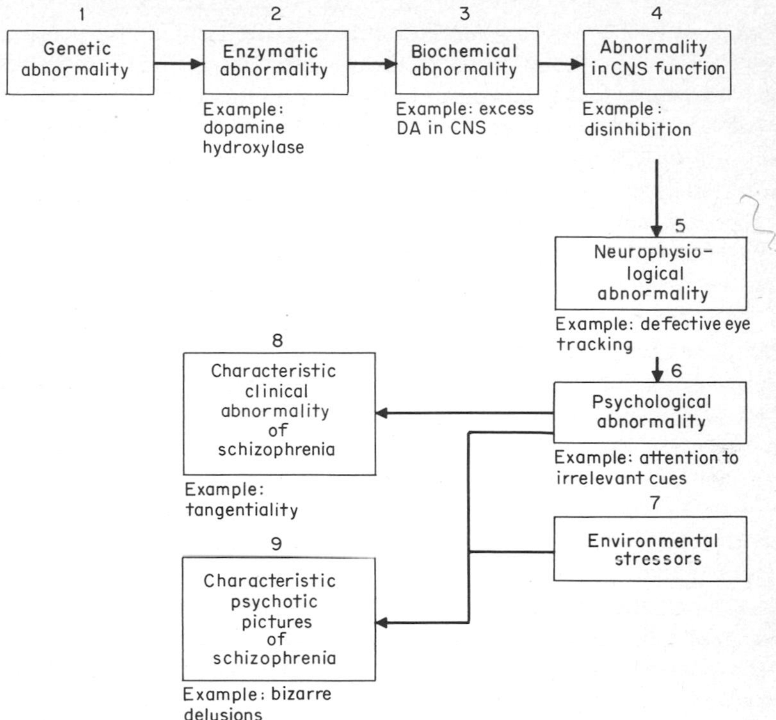

NOTE: Many of the abnormalities relating to steps 5, 6, and 8 are to be found in quiescent schizophrenia (interpsychotic phases). Step 9—representing fulminant schizophrenic psychosis—is visualized as the result of interaction between the genetic abnormality and various stressors (usually environmental but may be internal as well). The environment, as in Kety's view, does not create schizophrenia *de novo* but triggers its manifestation under certain circumstances in predisposed persons.

beyond the issue of improved psychodiagnosis. The discovery of such a marker would inevitably have a profound impact on treatment and prevention. Our awareness of the genetic factors underlying a whole host of medical—as well as psychiatric—conditions is now growing so rapidly it has given birth to a new subspecialty: predictive medicine (Pines, 1976). The capabilities of this new branch relate to determining who is at greatest risk for what, and to recommending measures either for circumventing the birth of those whose lives would be irremediably bleak (as in the case of Down's syndrome) or for circumventing the most crippling effects of an illness so that the predisposed person can lead a productive and comfortable life.

Certain inborn errors of metabolism and diseases resulting from parental blood-group incompatibility can already be detected by means of body-fluid tests of the parents (to determine the likelihood of having a child with Rh sensitization), the mother (amniocentesis, to determine the presence of Tay-Sachs disease in the fetus), or the newborn (to detect those vulnerable to galactosemia, PKU, and so on). These conditions are for the most part autosomal one gene-one enzyme disturbances that obey relatively simple laws of dominance or recessivity. Where schizophrenia is concerned we are not at all near being able to detect markers in this fashion, nor does the situation governing its inheritance seem so simple (see pp. 113–123).

With this word of caution, we may review the existing evidence. Proposed markers for schizophrenia fall predominantly into two categories: biochemical and neurophysiological. These, along with their principal proponents, are outlined in Table 5–3.

Because of the presumed priority of biochemical abnormalities in the causal chain, as depicted in Figure 5–2, the biochemical theories are presented ahead of the others. This portrayal is in keeping with the model of Meehl (1972),[6] involving genic error(s)—to biochemical endophenotype—to neurophysiological endophenotype (such as "synaptic slippage")—to an abnormal behavioral disposition—and thence to the ultimate learned (and abnormal) behavior we label "schizophrenia." As B. Fish (1975) mentions, "clinical" schizophrenia cannot in and of itself be inherited, because it contains components on the behavioral level that are learned. It makes more sense to think of what *is* inherited, in the opinion of Meehl and Fish, as a "subtle neurointegrative defect." Meehl labels this defect *schizotaxia* and postulates that the schizotaxic person (one could think of this as a shorthand for "person vulnerable to clinical schizophrenia") develops a "schizotypic" personality organization. If environmental factors are favorable and if other constitutional-hereditary factors governing intelligence, artistic talent, and so on, are also favorable, the affected person could remain well (as a *compensated* schizotype) but would probably exhibit throughout life faint signs of "cognitive slippage" along with certain neurological abnormalities.

Biochemical Markers

As Malek-Ahmadi and Fried (1976) mention in their recent review, the search for biochemical correlates goes back to the time of Kraepelin. The great Munich clinician, along with others at the turn of the century (Bleuler

[6]Meehl's position is analogous to that of Gottesman and Shields, Rosenthal, and Zubin (see above); my own model is closely related to theirs, and I rather like Meehl's suggested terminology. *Schizoidia,* the term of the previous generation, signifying vulnerability to schizophrenia in certain distinctive personality types, does not lend itself to the making of an adjective quite as well as Meehl's term. From "schizotaxia," for example, the adjective "schizotaxic" readily derives (and with minimal assault on the English language).

TABLE 5–3

Proposed Markers of Relevance to Schizophrenia

Category A (BIOCHEMICAL)	*Category B* (NEUROPHYSIOLOGICAL)	*Category C* (EMBRYOGENIC)
1. Excessive O-methylation (abnormal methylation of norepinephrine; Osmond and Smythies, 1952)	1. Abnormal eyelid shutting (Zubin, 1976)	1. Increased visualization score in nailfold capillary plexus (Maricq, 1975; Maricq and Jones, 1976)
2. Disturbed N-methylation (Fischer, 1960)	2. Abnormal amplitude of pupillary contraction to photic stimulation (Rubin and Barry, 1976)	
3. Adrenochrome (Hoffer, 1954)	3. Abnormal eye tracking (Holzman et al., 1973, 1974; Shagass et al., 1974)	
4. Catechol-O-methyltransferase (Matthysse and Baldessarini, 1972; Shein, 1975; Buchsbaum, 1975)	4. Abnormal cortical evoked response (Buchsbaum, 1975)	
5. Abnormal lactate/pyruvate ratio (Pollin et al., 1965; Abelin, 1972)	5. Abnormal EEG/evoked response correlations (Shagass, 1976)	
6. Dopamine-beta-hydroxylase deficiency (Stein and Wise, 1971; Snyder, 1974; Kety, 1976)	6. Abnormal galvanic skin response (Mednick and Schulsinger, 1968)	
7. Monoamine oxidase deficiency (Murphy and Wyatt, 1972; Wyatt et al., 1973, 1975)		

included), believed that some cases of dementia praecox might be the result of "autointoxication."

Little headway was made in Kraepelin's day in this area, nor was his neurologist, the celebrated Alzheimer, much more successful in the pursuit of neuroanatomical correlates of the major psychoses.

In our own era Osmond and Smythies (1952) were among the first to formulate a biochemical hypothesis of schizophrenia, postulating a disturbance of O-methylation in which (CNS) norepinephrine is converted to an abnormal compound (4-methoxy or 3,4-dimethoxyphenylethanolamine) similar in structure to the psychotomimetic agent mescaline (3,4,5-trimethoxyphenyl-ethanolamine). These investigators concluded that the excessive O-methylation brought on the symptoms of schizophrenia by means of these mescalinelike compounds. As such, theirs was a hypothesis related more to the "state" of (acute) schizophrenia and not necessarily to the trait that presumably underlies this condition. At all events, further investigation regarding catecholamine metabolism[7] was spurred by Osmond's work. This includes the work of Axelrod on catecholamines and their related enzymes (namely, catecholamine O-methyltransferase [COMT]). It is now fairly well established that alterations in catecholamine and indoleamine neurotransmitters in CNS synapses are "of importance in the pathophysiology of affective as well as schizophrenic disorders" (Shein, 1975).

With respect to indoleamines, E. Fischer (1960) developed a hypothesis similar to Osmond's, only involving the N-methylation of the indoleamine *serotonin* to form bufotenine, another potentially psychotomimetic compound. Hall and his co-workers (1969) demonstrated exacerbation of symptoms in four schizophrenic patients following administration of COMT and expressed the view that there may be a genetic defect in schizophrenia leading to abnormal methylation in critical neurotransmitter metabolic pathways.

A theory of schizophrenogenesis similar to that of Osmond's was enunciated by Hoffer et al. in 1954, that is, the "adrenochome hypothesis," which is based on the observation that under certain circumstances epinephrine could be oxidized to adrenochrome, a psychotomimetic compound. This theory has not found wide acceptance and may have even been based on an artifact of the laboratory.

Thus far we have been concerned with the search for a genetic marker that represented an abnormal compound capable of inducing schizophrenia from *within,* and related (presumably) to an abnormal gene. Biochemists interested in schizophrenia focused their attention on this kind of autointoxication model until the early 1960s. More recently, as Barchas et al. (1975) mention, the emphasis has shifted to research on the "regulation of normal processes which relate to behavior and, at some time in some individuals, may result in alterations which could change behavior" (1975, p. 51). Norepinephrine and dopamine, for example, are normal compounds, each acting as a neurotransmitter within particular areas and pathways in the CNS. At least six dopaminergic neuronal tracts have thus far been identified (Meltzer and Stahl, 1976). Two of these, the mesolimbic (with termi-

[7]Catecholamines are a class of compounds that includes epinephrine, norepinephrine, and dopamine. These compounds appear to behave as circulating hormones peripherally, but in the CNS as neurotransmitters (Barchas et al., 1975). For a comprehensive account of the neurotransmitters relevant to psychiatric disorders, the excellent review of Cohen and Young (1977) should be consulted.

nals in the limbic forebrain) and the mesocortical (with terminals in the limbic cortex), have been implicated in schizophrenia.

There is, according to Meltzer and Stahl, "circumstantial evidence that the limbic system mediates various autonomic, neuroendocrine, memory, learning, affective and behavioral functions," and may also control or mediate certain varieties of stereotyped motor behavior. The mesolimbic may be the relevant dopaminergic tract for amphetamine psychosis.

Many patients with tumors in the area of the limbic structures have originally been misdiagnosed as schizophrenic (Melamud, 1967). The similarity between some of the symptoms common to temporal lobe ("psychomotor") epilepsy and schizophrenia has also lent weight to the hypothesis that clinical schizophrenia may be related to specific types of limbic system malfunction. Regarding the mesocortical dopaminergic tract, some evidence has begun to accumulate suggesting that the disturbances of thinking and symbolic processes characteristic of schizophrenia may be based on dysfunction of mesocortical DA neurons with cerebral cortical terminals (Meltzer and Stahl, 1976, p. 24).

Meantime Stein and Wise (1971) have found a parallel between the functions of the norepinephrine-dependent dorsal "noradrenergic" pathway (innervating the cerebral cortex and hippocampus) and the anhedonia emphasized by Rado as crucial to the psychopathology of schizophrenia. This pathway appears to mediate reward-and-goal-oriented behavior, and may somehow be bound up in what at the experiential level we speak of as "pleasure sense." The connection here to the "dopamine hypothesis" lies in the reduced activity noted by these investigators—of dopamine-beta-hydroxylase (DBH) in the CNS of schizophrenic patients. This enzyme is necessary in the conversion of dopamine to norepinephrine. Stein and Wise postulate an inherent reduction in DBH as a basic defect in schizophrenia. How such a deficit may conspire to provoke the symptoms we know collectively as schizophrenia is not entirely clear but may be related to the ensuing accumulation of DA in selected areas of the brain and of a purportedly psychotoxic compound 6-hydroxy-DA. A number of authors feel that the DBH-deficiency hypothesis offers more promise than any of the competing biochemical models (Malek-Ahmadi and Fried, 1976; Kety, 1975; Meltzer and Stahl, 1976). Another advantage of this model has to do with its ability to integrate the action of the antischizophrenic phenothiazines (Snyder, 1976; Wise and Stein, 1973). Chlorpromazine, for example, protects the postsynaptic receptors (of the reward-or-"pleasure" system) by blocking the uptake of endogenously produced 6-OH-DA so that its alleged psychotoxic properties are not exerted. This dopamine-receptor blockade has come to be taken as the measure of a drug's antischizophrenic properties; Snyder (1976) and his colleagues have shown that only those phenothiazines (for example, chlorpromazine and thioridazine) which block DA-receptors are truly antipsychotic.

Despite these interesting correlations, Davis (1976) has warned against the assumption that the DA-hypothesis is by itself sufficient to account for the clinical manifestations of schizophrenia and has stressed an interactional model involving (also) other neurotransmitters, other enzymes, and other pathways. Similarly Reis (1974) has drawn attention to the difficulty in making linkages between the various neurotransmitters and behavior and has expressed doubt whether a single behavior is subserved by a single transmitter. Davis (1976) has actually advanced a two-tiered neurophysiological model as possibly operative in the majority of schizophrenic patients. In this model, schizophrenia, in its manifest form, may be mediated by factor(s) unrelated to DA levels. Collectively (since more than one neurophysiological or psychological factor may make up this first tier) these make up the "first" factor, which excess DA levels (the "second" factor) then aggravate. By counteracting this excess, the antischizophrenic drugs may reverse this aggravation enough to permit normal reparative processes to gain the upper hand.

Whatever the biochemical correlates of idiopathic schizophrenia turn out to be, it is obvious that the relevant biochemical abnormalities cannot be assayed directly on human brain tissue except in the rarest of circumstances. One is therefore at the mercy of indirect measurements; namely, of by-products of the relevant enzymes, and so on, or of activity in cognate enzymes located in tissues whose assay poses no threat to the patient.[8]

On the basis of indirect or postmortem assay, a number of studies have converged on the theory of excess CNS dopamine in schizophrenia. Dopamine levels in the brain could, for example, build up as a consequence of lowered DBH activity. According to Wise, Baden, and Stein (1974) the activity of that enzyme was lowered in the postmortem schizophrenic brain, although, as Snyder, Banerjee et al. (1974, p. 1250) point out, the expected deficiency in brain norepinephrine was not found by other investigators. Affective disorders, on the other hand, were not associated with changes in (plasma) DBH activity (Levitt and Mendlewicz, 1975).

In an analogous fashion, underactivity of brain monoamine oxidase (MAO) might also lead to excess CNS concentration of dopamine. Here one has looked chiefly to platelet-MAO determinations, in the hope that any abnormality in the platelet enzyme might reflect a similar abnormality in the activity of brain MAO. Several years ago Murphy and Wyatt (1972) indeed reported a reduction of MAO activity in the blood platelets of chronic schizophrenics. Even more impressive was this group's later report that platelet MAO was reduced even in the nonschizophrenic co-twins of schizophrenic MZ twins (Wyatt, Murphy, Belmaker, et al., 1973). Thirteen

[8]Several studies with cerebrospinal fluid in reactive versus chronic schizophrenics have been performed recently (Rimon et al., 1971; Post et al., 1975; Biederman et al., 1977), but these have not yielded consistent differences from their control groups.

discordant pairs were studied. Although activity was lowest in the affected twins, and still reduced in the co-twins, the ranges of enzyme activity showed considerable overlap. Despite the overlap, here was an intriguing piece of evidence that lowered MAO activity might be a marker of schizophrenic vulnerability in an otherwise healthy person and not merely an aftereffect of overt schizophrenic illness (Snyder, Banerjee, et al., 1974). Subsequently, however, others have shown normal platelet-MAO activity in acute schizophrenia, suggesting that reduced activity may be associated only with the chronic form of schizophrenia (Carpenter, Murphy, Wyatt, 1975). Still more recently Owen, Bourne, Crow, et al. (1976) have called into question the whole issue of platelet-MAO activity in schizophrenia, since they could find no significant differences in levels between a chronic and drug-free schizophrenic sample and their normal controls.

Owen's observations notwithstanding, Murphy and his colleagues continue to defend their original assertion of reduced platelet-MAO activity in chronic schizophrenia (Murphy, Donnelly, et al., 1976), admitting however that this reduction is noted only in a percentage of chronic schizophrenics (Wyatt, Belmaker, and Murphy, 1975) irrespective of clinical subtype. Search for altered MAO activity in schizophrenic brain tissue has been less promising in any case: Most postmortem studies report no difference in levels between schizophrenics and normals (Wyatt and Murphy, 1975).

To summarize, there is good reason to believe that abnormalities in neurotransmitter-related enzymes play an important role, though perhaps not a primary or a simple role, in unleashing the neurophysiological chain of events leading to manifest schizophrenia. In this regard the MAO and DBH systems seem the most likely candidates. Catecholamine O-methyltransferase (COMT) activity in erythrocytes of schizophrenics, on the other hand, does not appear to be abnormal,[9] according to a number of studies, and in autopsy brain samples the results are equivocal (Murphy and Wyatt, 1975). For further comments on the importance of the individual's *state* prior to administration of an antipsychotic drug and on the puzzling manner in which amine-neurotransmitter abnormalities may underlie, under certain circumstances, depressive psychosis and under others, schizophrenia, the reader should consult the review of Halaris and Freedman (1975).

While at the time of this writing no reliable biochemical marker exists that can distinguish schizophrenia from its imitators, immunochemical, biochemical, and endocrinological technics may soon lead to a breakthrough in our grasp of the organic correlates of this "mental" disease (Kety, 1975).

[9]Matthysse and Baldessarini (1972), while mentioning that no statistically significant differences in erythrocyte-COMT were found between a group of schizophrenics and controls, found the highest values were all among the schizophrenics. Sampling according to different diagnostic or other criteria might have singled out a more homogeneous schizophrenic sample, in which significant COMT elevation could be shown.

At that time it may also be possible to detect vulnerability in currently well-functioning persons and to identify those *borderline* patients with a genuine kinship to schizophrenia. Thus far the neuroendocrinological technics pioneered by Sachar (Sachar, Finkelstein, and Hellman, 1971) have proved more fruitful in the realm of the affective disorders than in schizophrenia (Sachar, 1975).

Proposed Neurophysiological Markers for Schizophrenia

A number of neurophysiological tests can be performed without much difficulty and are suitable for surveying a borderline as well as a schizophrenic population. Pupillary reaction time was, according to Zubin and his colleagues, abnormal even in "recovered" schizophrenics. In many instances borderline patients have not been evaluated by these tests, because investigators have preferred to begin with chronic, unmistakable schizophrenics and their close relatives.

Among the neurophysiological phenomena, abnormalities of which have been considered potential markers for schizophrenic vulnerability, are the already mentioned eyelid shutting (Zubin and p. 92 of this chapter), amplitude of pupillary contraction, eye tracking, galvanic skin response, and evoked cortical response to various stimuli.

Pupillary contraction as a function of intensity of illumination was measured by Rubin and Barry (1976) in schizophrenics and controls. Their patient sample consisted of thirty rather severely ill paranoid and "chronic undifferentiated" schizophrenics, along with smaller numbers of patients with schizoaffective disorders and acute schizophrenic reactions. In the control group a linear relationship was found between amplitude of pupil contraction and logarithm of light intensity. The patient group showed two kinds of deviations: one (accounting for 35 percent of their number) manifested the same pupillomotor threshold as the normals, but as the light intensity was increased, amplitude and rate of pupil contraction fell below that evidenced by the controls. A larger group (65 percent) showed an abnormal threshold and required a higher intensity of illumination before the first pupillary contraction could be recorded.

Of particular interest among proposed neurophysiological indicators of schizophrenia is that of abnormal eye tracking. In their original report Holzman, Proctor, and Hughes (1973) described impairments of smooth pursuit eye movements they believed were specific to schizophrenic patients. Subsequently Holzman, Proctor, et al. (1974) showed that deviant eye tracking was not only exhibited by half their "recent" and seven-eighths of their "chronic" schizophrenic subgroups but in almost half of the (not psychiatrically ill) *relatives* of their schizophrenic patients. Holzman also compared eye-tracking abnormalities in patients diagnosed schizophrenic according to clinical criteria versus psychological test criteria. Patients meeting test criteria of "bizarre and contaminated thinking" showed a somewhat higher percentage of eye-tracking abnormality than did the hospital-diagnosed schizophrenics (Holzman, 1975). High incidence of deviant tracking in relatives of schizophrenics suggested the possibility that one was dealing with a useful tag for schizophrenia.

In further but still preliminary study of first-degree relatives of schizophrenics, one of Holzman's colleagues noted that in a group of thirteen probands, all thirteen had at least one parent with deviant eye tracking (Holzman, 1975, p. 223).

Although Holzman had speculated that the eye-tracking dysfunction might constitute the long-awaited endophenotype for schizophrenia, Shagass, Amadeo, and Overton (1974) found that similar abnormalities were noted also in a group of psychotically depressed patients (to a degree greater than that observed by Holzman in the few psychotic depressives he studied). Shagass also emphasized the need for carefully matched controls with respect to age, since older subjects show more tracking deviation than younger ones. Both Shagass and Holzman (in the latter's 1975 article) make reference to the *nonspecificity* of eye-tracking dysfunction, inasmuch as it may be noted in a variety of neurological disorders including general paresis and Parkinson's disease. Holzman originally thought that there might be some relationship between the peculiarities of perception (and thinking) in schizophrenics and their jagged pattern of eye tracking, but he later modified his views on any such isomorphism. Since many clinically well relatives of schizophrenics show the same abnormal tracking pattern, no simple connection can be made between this pattern and the phenomenology of overt schizophrenia.

Recently, Březinová and Kendell (1977) have even suggested that the eye-tracking abnormality in chronic schizophrenia was a factor of the impaired attention and heightened distractibility characteristic of this condition. They found, for example, that in normal subjects during experiments designed to distract attention or produce lowered states of arousal, eye tracking was impaired in a manner indistinguishable from patterns observed in the schizophrenics. As a result these investigators postulated that the tracking phenomenon may be of no greater etiological significance than other psychomotor-task abnormalities encountered with regularity in chronic schizophrenia.

As with any proposed biological indicator, the eye-tracking phenomenon will have to be studied more extensively in those populations that shade off from the unequivocal core of schizophrenia. The kinds of groups this may involve are sketched in Figure 5–3, where core schizophrenia is visualized as an area of overlap among such universes as "schizophrenia—schizoaffective—affective," "schizophrenia—borderline schizophrenia," and "schizophrenia—healthy relative (of a schizophrenic proband)." Investigations of this sort are already underway at a number of centers.

Another fruitful area of neurophysiological research relevant to schizo-

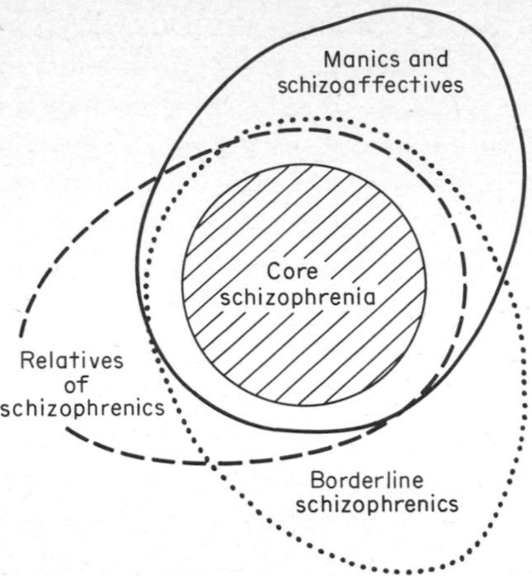

Figure 5–3. Populations Shading Away from Core Schizophrenics in Which Proposed Genetic Markers Must Be Tested

phrenia concerns the measurement of evoked cortical responses to a variety of stimuli (Buchsbaum, 1975; Shagass, 1976). Applications of evoked response (ER) technics to the affective disorders have been described by the same investigators and are discussed in Chapter 6.

Buchsbaum has demonstrated that chronic schizophrenics respond to increasing intensities of illumination with reduction in ER amplitude. In this sense they are called *reducers,* a quality they share with unipolar depressives. Thus reduction is not a phenomenon *specific* to schizophrenia. When the results of ER testing were analyzed in conjunction with platelet MAO, however, multivariate discriminant analysis permitted reasonably good discrimination among different diagnostic groups. Possible relationships between the ER-reducing effect in chronic schizophrenia and the apparent hypersensitivity in schizophrenia to sensory "overload" are discussed by Buchsbaum (1975), who is in sympathy with Broen, Venables, and others in their assumption that the "basic defect in schizophrenia consits of a low threshold for disorganization under increasing stimulus input" (p. 139).

In his 1976 review Shagass also refers to the greater power of multiple neurophysiological tests (including the electroencephalogram) to generate results (in the form of *patterns*) of a kind that allow distinctions among diagnostic subgroups. Thus far, these methods have not been discriminating to such an extent that testing "borderline schizophrenics" would be likely to yield positive results, so it is not yet possible to utilize these tests as indicators of lesser degrees of schizophrenic vulnerability. Nevertheless some beginnings have been made in this area. A number of investigators (including Shagass) have recently evaluated not only the customary severe and chronic patients with respect to various neurophysiological and other assays but have also used in a number of instances less severely affected populations as a starting point. Several of these new approaches and their results are outlined below.

Embryogenic and Other Markers

An embryogenic effect said to be found frequently in association with schizophrenia concerns an abnormal picture in the morphology of the fingernail-fold capillaries, characterized by immature formation of a primitive network of vessels. Reported in the late 1940s by Hauptmann (Abelin, 1972), this phenomenon has been investigated in recent years by Maricq (1975) and Maricq and Jones (1976) in both chronic schizophrenics and their relatives. The abnormalities observed by Maricq are not specific to schizophrenia, however, nor have they been replicated by other investigators.

Still further along the causal chain relevant to schizophrenia lies a collection of phenomena too distantly related to the responsible gene(s) to offer much promise as a biological indicator. Among these phenomena are certain psychological correlates; namely, the deviations in speech patterns studied by Chapman or Gottschalk (in both clear-cut and borderline schizophrenic subjects) and the characteristically abnormal patterns of family interaction, such as those recently reported by J. E. Jones et al. (1977). A number of these phenomena are examined in some detail elsewhere in this text.

Other Markers of Possible Relevance to the Detection of Borderline Schizophrenia and of Schizoaffective Disorders

Differential morbidities for psychosis in relatives of "good" versus "bad" prognosis schizophrenics were noted by Garver and his colleagues (1977). They found that risk for *affective disorders* in first-degree relatives of the "good-prognosis" probands was 10 percent (as against 3.3 percent for schizophrenia) but only 1½ percent in the "bad-prognosis" probands. Using a neuroendocrine strategy of the sort pioneered by Sachar et al. (1971), Garver et al. (1977; see also Pandey, Garver, et al., 1977) administered the dopamine receptor agonist, apomorphine, to both groups of patients: "interaction of apomorphine with those dopamine receptors associated with the growth-hormone (GH) system caused release of GH in quantities presumably proportional to dopamine-receptor sensitivity." Following the apomorphine challenge, peak GH responses in the good-prognosis patients were significantly higher (28.4 ± 5.4 nanogm/ml) than those observed in the bad-prognosis group (10.2 ± 2.2 nanogm/ml). Garver speculated that "there may be a group of schizophrenialike patients diagnosable as *Schizophrenia of Good Prognosis,* who show indirect evidence of postsynaptic dopamine-receptor hypersensitivity" (italics mine). Studies of the first-degree relatives themselves have not as yet been carried out. Such studies might help clarify more precisely whether certain good-prognosis patients with schizophrenialike episodes indeed have greater natural kinship to the affective disorders. Schizotypal patients exhibiting borderline personality organization would, of course, also be of interest to study from this vantage point.

Although the milder schizophrenic syndromes are not associated with distinctive abnormalities on tests of cortical evoked response, some recent refinements in testing and sampling have begun to show promise of differentiating the borderline case from the normal. Shagass et al. (1977) have demonstrated that the wave pattern of evoked potential in chronic schizophrenics often shows a sharp "dip" (*N*, or negativity) at about 60 milliseconds after stimulation (Figure 5–4). This pronounced "*N*-60" pattern is not usually seen in normals nor in episodic or latent schizophrenia. Shagass has, however, noted a tendency in latent schizophrenics with known family histories of schizophrenic psychoses to exhibit pattern abnormalities resembling those of chronic cases. Latent schizophrenics without this positive family history usually have patterns indistinguishable from the normal. How much overlap there may be between Shagass's latent schizophrenia and the schizotypal patient with borderline structure is not clear. But it may be that the more sophisticated neurophysiological technics will soon be able to detect characteristic abnormalities at least in those borderline schizophrenics where the evidence for genetic loading seems most convincing. Shagass believes a relationship may exist between the evoked response pattern in chronic schizophrenia and the deficiencies in *modulation* and *filtering* (of response to stimuli) many regard as primary abnormalities in schizophrenia.

Figure 5–4. Cortical Evoked Responses

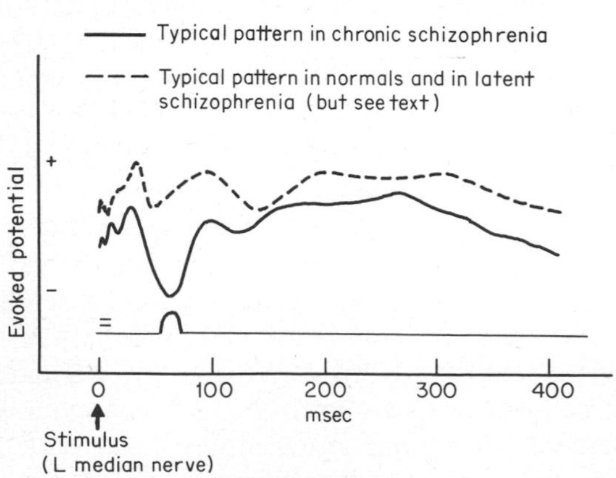

SOURCE: After Shagass et al. (1977).

A number of investigators believed that response to galvanic skin stimulation might be a distinguishing factor in determining normal children from those at high risk for schizophrenia (Mednick and Schulsinger, 1968; Schulsinger and Mednick, 1975). Latency in the galvanic skin response (GSR) was reported *briefer* in the high-risk group. Schizophrenia was seen as characterized by "greater volatility of the autonomic nervous system," a viewpoint criticized by Planansky (1972). At all events, other investigators have not corroborated the earlier reported GSR differences in their high-risk children (Erlenmeyer-Kimling, personal communication; also Van Dyke, cited by S. Kety in Wolf and Berle, 1976, p. 78).

It will become apparent to the reader that within the entire realm of conditions bearing the label "schizophrenia"—with whatever accuracy—there is a bewildering array of tests that can be applied. If this realm is extended to include the close relatives of schizophrenic persons, a number of combinations of test abnormalities will be encountered. These combinations include the "nuclear" schizophrenic with perhaps several detectable enzymatic abnormalities, markedly abnormal psychological test responses, highly deviant speech patterns, and so on. Related to such a patient may be family members with abnormal enzyme or neurophysiological patterns but fairly normal responses on the Rorschach and other tests. "Reactive" schizophrenics will be encountered: those in whom psychological testing is highly suggestive, yet whose enzyme patterns, and so on, are quite within normal limits. If, in the latter instance, the family history is "negative," it is often difficult to distinguish a "genuine" schizophrenic whose enzymatic and physiological abnormalities are too subtle to be detected by contemporary methods from a "phenocopy" whose abnormalities originate from organic or other factors. Despite the impressive advances in our understanding of the biological correlates of schizophrenia over the past two decades, the practitioner will often continue to puzzle about "borderline schizophrenic" or "schizotypic borderline" patients whose classification cannot as yet be improved by the markers we have been referring to (see Shields, Heston, and Gottesman, 1975). In Part III of this book, focusing on the hard and soft clinical signs of the major psychoses and of the borderline syndromes, we shall see how diagnosis of these conditions may be sharpened even in the absence of reliable markers.

Theories of Transmission of Schizophrenia

Since the beginning of the century, theories about the genetic factor(s) in schizophrenia have grown not only in number but in complexity. Early theories centered on the notion of simple Mendelian dominance. Single-major-locus (SML) models were proposed by Böök (1953), Slater (1958), and Garrone (1962). Kallmann (1938) postulated a one-major-gene model in which the pathogenic gene operated as a recessive rather than as a dominant factor. Abelin (1972) favored a monogenic model with "intermediateness." Heston's adoption studies also led him originally to endorse a single-dominant-gene model (1966). Planansky's (1972) position is similar, as is that of Holzman and his colleagues (1974), whose eye-tracking studies in relatives of schizophrenics appeared to them compatible with SML models.

More complex schemata have been elaborated by Rüdin (1916), Karlsson (1968, 1972), and Maricq (1975), each of whom favors a two-gene theory in which one of the genes may, under certain circumstances, confer useful rather than disadvantageous properties.

In recent years a number of psychogeneticists have interpreted family-study data as compatible with a polygenic mode of inheritance (Gottesman and Shields, 1972; Ødegaard, 1972; Stephens, Atkinson, et al., 1975).

Evidence for a polygenic system seemed more impressive within the realm of schizophrenia than in that of the affective disorders, according to Cavalli-Sforza and Bodmer (1971); Carter (1973, p. 206) also speaks of schizophrenia as exemplifying polygenic transmission, which, if validated, would make schizophrenia the analogue, among psychriatric disorders, to diabetes or to cleft lip among the "somatic" conditions where polygenic systems are now strongly suspected. Kringlen (1975, p. 42) expresses support for a multifactorial model consisting of a polygenic system influenced by a variety of environmental factors including social class. The importance of some kind of interaction between genetic and independent factors (the latter involving both environmental factors plus genes not directly concerned with schizophrenia per se) has, of course, been apparent to all contemporary investigators, since, as Kringlen mentions, an MZ co-twin of a schizophrenic proband has about a 60 percent chance of escaping overt schizophrenic psychosis. Zerbin-Rübin (1974) has drawn attention to the popularity of a polygenic model for schizophrenia. Whereas an SML model would foster intensified search for a discrete enzymatic defect, "assumption of polygenes," she mentions, "will result in the endeavor to single out several basic characteristics, for example, errors in perception, inclination to anxiety reactions, or quantitative [rather than] qualitative [abnormalities] of common metabolites" (p. 253). Zerbin-Rüdin also makes the point that the polygenic model, where schizophrenia is concerned, is at once so complex and so flexible that it cannot be refuted.

A positive family history for schizophrenia will tend to put the observer more at ease with the notion of a heritable factor in this illness, but what if it is not present? This could be interpreted as arguing for genetic heterogeneity (Erlenmeyer-Kimling and Nichol, 1969; Erlenmeyer-Kimling and Paradowski, 1971), where one envisions one or more family-history-positive strains and a family-history-negative one. But chance and new mutations could also account for these discrepancies. Severity as a factor also enters in, especially within the context of a polygenic model—where there would tend to be a higher family incidence of overt schizophrenia—if one begins with a severely affected proband rather than one only mildly ill.

Mitsuda (1972) argues strongly for heterogeneity among the schizophrenias, which would then be united more by common phenotypic expression than by commonality of genic error(s). Shields accepts the notion of genetic heterogeneity as relevant to schizophrenia, though he thinks it may be less important here than among the affective disorders (1972). The views of Venables (1964) regarding psychological test differences between "process" versus "reactive" and paranoid schizophrenics are also consistent with heterogeneity. In Venables's opinion input dysfunctions in the realm of schizophrenia are too diverse to be easily relegated to a one-gene or one-genic-system disorder. The process or chronic patients, for instance, seem to suffer a restriction in the attentional field, whereas the reactive and paranoid patients react as though overwhelmed by sensory input from all quarters and behave as though all items in the attentional field have equal importance.

The concept of *heterogeneity* in schizophrenia does not exclude the other models mentioned above. It is quite possible that among the heterogeneous genetic routes to manifest clinical schizophrenia, several genic systems can be implicated: one system may depend on a single major locus, another on a polygenic system.

The criteria by which schizophrenia and similar conditions are diagnosed is a matter of tremendous importance in deciding on a most likely model of transmission. If certain personality disorders, schizoid character types, and so on, are counted as valid phenotypes of the schizophrenic geneotype(s), the apparent risk (as measured in twins of families) may almost double (Inouye, 1972) and in so doing tend to lend more support to an autosomal single-dominant-gene theory (Planansky, 1972). Similarly, in Heston's adoptee study (1966), among the offspring of the schizophrenic biological mothers were a large number of sociopathic and other severe character disorders. The total number of "affected" offspring was so high as to be compatible with a one-gene model. But others have questioned whether the "related" conditions were really related and have pointed out that the fathers of the adopted-away children were a relatively unknown quantity: how much responsibility they bore, rather than the mothers, for some of the sociopathy in the offspring is hard to estimate.

One recent family study showed that the parents and sibs of chronic schizophrenics were at high risk for schizophrenia itself and for "nonneurotic personality disorders" but not for ordinary psychoneuroses (Stephens, Atkinson, Kay, et al., 1975, p. 104).[10] The nonneurotic personality

[10]Other investigators, such as Bender (1975), include within the spectrum schizoid, sociopathic, and also neurotic personalities.

disorders in this study were either psychopathic, paranoid, or schizoid; many of these people would be considered borderline by most of the current schemata.

With a partially dominant gene, whose manifestation rate was reduced in the heterozygote (Slater's model), we might expect that some of the close relatives of schizophrenics would show psychopathological conditions with markedly schizoid features suggestive of "incomplete or abortive forms of schizophrenia." In the latter situation we would expect, ideally, at least one parent to be affected in each family; the ratio of spectrum disorders (including obvious schizophrenia) to unaffected persons should approximate 1:1. Some of the proponents of SML models have reported figures in this range (see Heston, 1970), but the problem arises, Is it justifiable to count severe alcoholics, for example, in families of schizophrenics *in* or *out?* If such a person were examined in some psychiatric setting outside the context of a psychogenetic study, he might not be regarded as exemplifying "schizoidia." If seen within such a study, the temptation is strong to count him in, as among the less severe expressions of the schizophrenic genotype. Stephens, pursuing a more conservative approach, tends to exclude such cases, and partly for this reason believes a polygenic model has more merit than a single-gene model. The kind of schizophrenia spectrum he envisions, however, can accommodate the schizotypic borderline patient as one valid expression of the underlying genic abnormality.

At the present time one cannot decide between an SML and a polygenic model on clinical grounds alone, and still lacking a reliable endophenotype, one must resort to statistical methods based on large surveys in order to bolster one or another theory.

Observed versus Expected Risk in Relatives of Schizophrenics: Measuring Compatibility with Different Models of Transmission

One method of gaining insight into the mode of inheritance of a given condition relies on the comparison of observed incidence in relatives of various degrees of closeness, with the percentages that would be predicted by theory.[11]

[11]In the case of single-gene dominant conditions, for example, one expects a 50 percent incidence in both siblings and children; among second-degree relatives (uncles, nephews, and so on), a 25 percent incidence, with each further degree of relatedness diminishing the risk to one-half that for the preceding degree.

Because only the homozygote has the manifest condition in recessive conditions, the risk is 25 percent in siblings but is markedly reduced in the children, except where the affected person marries (*a*) another *homozygous* person—in which case, the risk to their children is 100 percent—or (*b*) a heterozygous person—in which case (assuming the heterozygous state is asymptomatic and that there was complete penetrance) the risk to their children would be 50 percent.

Matthysse and Kidd (1976) have drawn attention to some of the ambiguities and limitations besetting the concept of heritability, upon which many previous estimates of risk for schizophrenia have rested. They mention the need to define a trait in quantitative terms, if heritability is to be meaningfully measured, but such definition has not yet become possible where schizophrenia is concerned. Heritability calculations depend on merely additive contributions to the trait, by genetic and environmental factors, but in schizophrenia there appears to be interaction between these factors (Zerbin-Rüdin, 1974).

To circumvent these obstacles, Matthysse and Kidd began with a single-major-locus (SML) model and a polygenic model as givens, and then determined the degree to which available data for the relevant parameters fitted or failed to fit these models. The best current estimates of risk were utilized in their equations.

The SML Model Calculations for the SML model depend on four unknowns: (1) the frequency in the general population of the (presumed) pathogenic allele predisposing to schizophrenia (= "q"), (2) the frequency of phenocopies: genetically normal persons who at some time have a phenotypically schizophrenic illness (= f_0), (3) the frequency of manifest schizophrenia in those with one pathogenic allele; that is, the heterozygotes (= f_1), and (4) the frequency of schizophrenia among homozygotes (= f_2).[12]

These frequencies cannot all be calculated directly but can be estimated from the incidences established (with more or less accuracy) for schizophrenia in (*a*) monozygotic twins (= 47 percent), (*b*) children of two schizophrenic parents (= 39 percent), (*c*) children of one schizophrenic parent (= 12 percent), (*d*) sibs of schizophrenics (= 8.7 percent), and (*e*) the general population (= 0.87 percent). Since both the SML and the polygenic models require that the risk for offspring not exceed that of sibs, the authors averaged (*c*) and (*d*) to yield an incidence of 10.4 percent for both.

Matthysse and Kidd (1976) demonstrate that q, the population frequency of the pathogenic allele (in an SML model), can vary from 0.3 percent to 2.2 percent; the other three parameters are affected by the q-value chosen. If one assumes the lowest q value (0.3 percent) to be correct, the corresponding values for f_0 = 0.5 percent (the probability of a genetically normal person becoming schizophrenic), for f_1 = 50.3 percent, and for f_2 = 100 percent. With this q, the probabilities of a given "schizophrenic" being homozygous = 0.1 percent, heterozygous = 38.7 percent, and free of the pathogenic allele = 61.2 percent. In this situation, the homozygote is *rare*

[12]"Recessiveness" describes the situation where the heterozygote is unaffected: $f_1 = f_0$. "Dominance" is characterized by both heterozygotes and homozygotes exhibiting the trait: $f_1 = f_2$. If having only one pathogenic allele leads to effects only half as severe as the "double dose," one speaks not of dominance or recessivity but of "intermediateness" (see Abelin, 1972).

but always clinically schizophrenic. Depending on *q,* the probability (f_2) that a homozygote will exhibit schizophrenia varies from 100 percent down to just below 40 percent. The implication is that "according to some versions of the SML model, genes play an extremely important role when they are present in double dose; but such individuals are very rare, even among schizophrenics" (1976, p. 189). In other SML versions, the genetic contribution in homozygotes appears less striking.

A most important by-product of Matthysse and Kidd's approach is the observation that homozygotes, in a random population of schizophrenics, would not exceed (were an SML theory valid) 1 in 45. The authors speculate that these may become the patients, nevertheless, in whom some enzyme abnormality might be detectable peripherally. If so, biochemical study even of fairly large numbers of schizophrenics would be quite likely to turn up *nothing,* since the heterozygotes and phenocopies, who would crowd the rest of the sample, would prevent any significant deviations from becoming demonstrable; results would closely approximate those of the controls. This creates a heavy bias *against* significant findings turning up in studies of the various proposed markers we reviewed in the preceding section (pp. 108–113). To complicate matters, one cannot rely on severity of illness to separate out possible homozygotes, since at least some heterozygotes (those with the worst "independent factors") might also be severely affected. To "enrich" the percentage of homozygotes in a schizophrenic sample, one might seek children of *two* schizophrenic parents: in them Matthysse and Kidd calculated the likelihood of homozygosity to range between 20 and 50 percent.

One difficulty with the SML model is that it predicts, in any of its versions, risk in both MZ co-twins and offspring of two schizophrenics at 20 percent, and this is substantially lower than the observed rates (47 percent and 39 percent, respectively). Heterogeneity is predicted by the SML model: some schizophrenics would be homozygotes, some heterozygous, and some genetically normal.

Polygenic Model Vulnerability, in a polygenic model, depends on the contributions of a large number of genes, each contributing a small amount to overall risk. In the example provided by C. O. Carter (1973), for heuristic purposes, we are asked to suppose that there are ten "risk genes" for some "polygenic" conditions. Suppose further that affected persons possess nine of these, while only five are typically present in the general population. First-degree relatives sharing only half their genes with the affected person will tend to have a number of risk genes midway between these two levels, in this instance, seven.

Predicted patterns of incidence among relatives of various degrees may be represented graphically, as in Figure 5–5. To pick a number of risk genes arbitrarily, again for illustrative purposes, suppose that the mean in the general population is four risk genes, but twelve in affected individuals.

Figure 5–5. Polygenic Model of Transmission

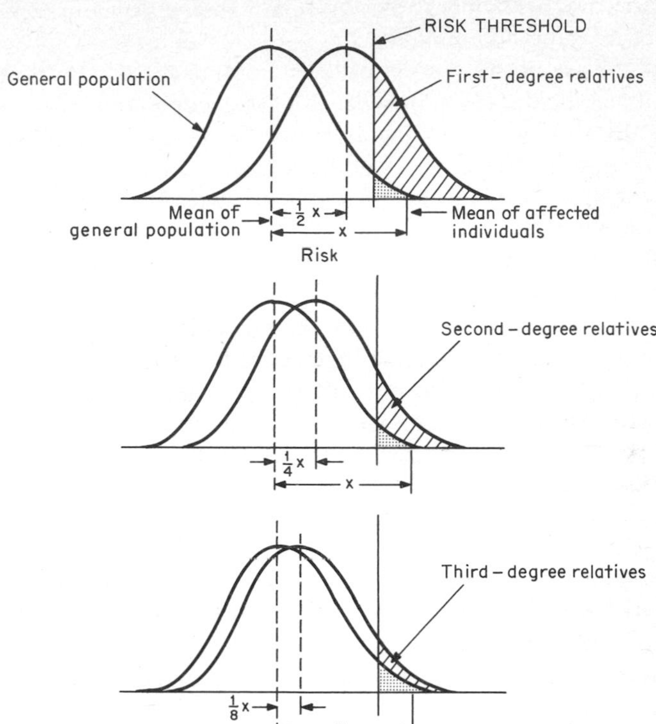

SOURCE: After C. O. Carter (1973).

The distribution of numbers in a large sample will vary so that a "bell-shaped" curve is described. The curve for first-degree relatives is skewed to the right (in the direction of greater risk) to an extent halfway between the mean for the general population and the mean for affected individuals. In this example, their mean number of risk genes will be eight; a higher percentage of these relatives will be beyond the *threshold* for the condition and will thus exhibit it (their proportion is represented by the *hatched area,* whereas the much smaller proportion of affected individuals in the general population is represented by the dotted area).

Second-degree relatives, in this model, will have, on the average, an extra number of risk genes equal to only ¼ the difference between the two means; that is, they will have four plus two or six such genes, and will exhibit an incidence of the condition as shown in the middle diagram of Figure 5–5. Their risk, as noted in the figure, is substantially less than that for first-degree relatives.

Third-degree relatives (e.g., cousins) will have only five risk genes on the average [4 + ⅛(8)]; as the lowest diagram of Figure 5–5 shows, their bell curve is shifted only slightly to the right, and their risk is not much greater than that of the general population.

Through the use of this theoretical construct, one is in a position to compare the actual incidences observed in a large population with those predicted by the theory. Using the example of congenital hip dislocation, believed to be an example of a multifactorial condition, Carter shows that the *expected* incidences in the three classes of relatives are 13 percent, 5 percent, and 3 percent, respectively. The *observed* values are 23 percent, 3½ percent, and 2½ percent, which constitute a reasonably good, though by no means perfect, fit.

Other features predicted by a polygenic model include: (1) the more individuals in a given family who are affected, the higher the risk component in the family[13] (including that for new offspring born into the family) and (2) the risk varies directly with the severity of the index case; more severe cases are presumed to carry relatively more risk genes. In schizophrenia the risk about doubles where two first-degree relatives are affected (C. O. Carter, 1973, p. 206), a finding in line with a polygenic model.

Matthysse and Kidd have estimated the goodness of fit of a polygenic model by a different method based on the supposition that a scale for vulnerability to schizophrenia can be constructed comparable to the one commonly employed in the measurement of IQ. Although there is as yet no test for the "schizophrenic quotient" (SQ), one can analogize to the situation with intelligence and assume that a certain SQ is associated with a 50 percent risk for ever developing schizophrenia and that another higher value of SQ is associated with almost certain development of the illness. An SQ of 148, in Matthysse and Kidd's model, is correlated with 99 percent risk of schizophrenia and corresponds (in Carter's model) to having nearly all, or perhaps all, the "risk genes," however many there might be. Their model also predicts an MZ concordance of 61 percent, somewhat higher than the best available figure of 47 percent, and a risk in offspring of two schizophrenic parents of 54 percent (again, somewhat higher than the observed 39 percent). According to these authors, a multifactorial model fits the data so closely that, like the SML model with "intermediateness," it cannot be rejected in the light of available data. Another interesting aspect of the multifactorial model is that it predicts about 9 percent of a schizophrenic sample will be made up of persons with an SQ so high that their risk would be 99 percent or more. In this subgroup, in other words,

[13]Ødegaard has submitted evidence for this feature (1972), having observed that among 320 schizophrenic probands, those with *no* psychotics in their parental generation had 6.8 percent schizophrenic *siblings,* those with one such relative had 10.6 percent Sz sibs, and those with two or more such relatives had 15.8 percent Sz sibs. This finding was not replicated, however, in a similar study by Essen-Möller (1977).

schizophrenia is almost completely genetically determined and an almost inevitable consequence of the high genetic loading. As with the homozygotes of the SML model, these high-SQ schizophrenics may be the ones, if only there were a way of identifying them, in whom the sought-for biochemical marker might be identifiable. There is a kind of heterogeneity implicit in a polygenic model also, inasmuch as some schizophrenics would have no risk genes (the phenocopiers), some would have intermediate levels of risk, and 9 or 10 percent would be the "inevitable" schizophrenics just mentioned.

Important contributions to the polygenic model in schizophrenia have been made by Gottesman and Shields (1972). Certain views they express offer the possibility of integrating "spectrum disorders" or *borderline* types of schizophrenia into the main theory.

Gottesman and Shields elaborate a *diathesis-stress* model to account for the unfolding of schizophrenia (i.e., of the clinical manifestations we call schizophrenia) over the life course of the person. Overt illness is seen as a precipitate brought about by a stress of sufficient magnitude acting upon a diathesis or predisposition of a certain intensity (as might be represented by various SQ levels in the Matthysse and Kidd model). In Figure 5–6, adapted from Gottesman and Shields (1972, p. 334), the life course is plotted along the horizontal axis and the combined genetic and environmental liability along the vertical axis. When these two quantities exceed the threshold for manifest schizophrenia, schizophrenic psychosis develops. This schizophrenic psychosis may be short-lived, as in a recompensating patient, or it may last from the first moment of appearance until death. Although a two-threshold model is adumbrated in their book, it was not developed there as fully as it is in Gershon's more recent model for transmission of affective disorders (see Chapter 6).

The bottom of the "zone of Sz spectrum disorders" in Figure 5–6 may, nevertheless, be understood as a lower threshold for, namely, less-than-psychotic types of schizophrenia (or for whatever seems most justifiable to include as a "spectrum" disorder emanating from genetic loading for schizophrenia). As shown in Figure 5–6, one of two MZ twins succumbs briefly to a schizophrenic illness and then goes on to remain identifiable as suffering from some type of spectrum disorder (namely, schizoid personality). The discordant co-twin, in this example, because of more favorable environmental factors, escapes overt schizophrenic psychosis or spectrum disorder, remaining throughout life just below the lower threshold. Still another person, with initially less genetic loading (though still above the general population average) ends up a "borderline schizophrenic," never succumbing to full-blown psychosis. As we shall see in Chapter 6, a similar mechanism may operate in the realm of serious affective disorders so that a sizable proportion of structurally *borderline* patients may come by their particular symptoms, fragility, and so forth, via substantial (but, for the

Figure 5–6. Polygenic System in Schizophrenia: Diathesis-stress Model

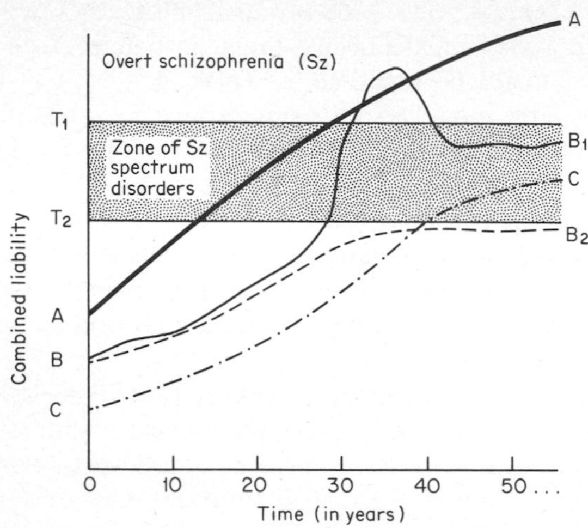

NOTE: Time is plotted along the x-axis from birth; liability is plotted along the y-axis. The genetic component of liability is not often so high that it exceeds the threshold (T_1) for psychosis, although in the multifactorial model of Matthysse and Kidd, 9 percent of schizophrenics are "obligatory" schizophrenics of this sort. Such persons would eventually become overtly schizophrenic in no matter how favorable an environment they were reared. Example *A* concerns a person with high genetic liability who goes on to exhibit, say, withdrawal and eccentricity during adolescence (having crossed the lower threshold for a spectrum disorder, T_2) and then becomes, and remains, psychotic several years later. Example *B* involves a discordant MZ pair: B_1 has an acute psychotic episode but remains impaired after recompensation. Twin B_2, because of more favorable environmental factors, never develops sufficient liability to push him even into a spectrum disorder, although his level stays very close to the lower threshold. Example *C* involves an individual in whom intermediate genetic liability conspires with an unfavorable environmental component to bring about a "borderline" schizophrenia-spectrum disorder, in which overt psychosis never occurs (T_1 is never crossed).

SOURCE: Adapted from Gottesman and Shields (1972).

most part, intermediate) genetic predisposition to one or another—or even to both—of the major "functional psychoses." Zubin, Salzinger, et al. (1975) in their comments on schizophrenia (which could apply with equal cogency to the affective disorders) have stated:

> The inheritance of schizophrenia, though undeniable, is no longer specific, but lies along a continuum, spreading from genotypes whose phenotype is quite normal to those [whose phenotype is] schizoid, and [finally] to the more severely afflicted. (p. 659)

Recently, Stabenau (1977) has advocated a polygenic model not only for schizophrenia but for primary affective disorders as well:

> . . . two separate gene pools of polygenic nature may relate to the development of schizophrenia and manic-depressive illness . . . ; *schizoaffective illness may result from genetic transmission from each of these separate gene pools* (italics mine). The hypothetical model for each psychosis proposes that polygenic inheritance affects different CNS neuroanatomical sites . . . which are in homeostasis as to catecholamine neurotransmitter regulation of the psyche. With sufficient environmental stress, an "imbalance" occurs in the neural integrative systems which produces phenotypically the three separate psychotic behavioral syndromes of schizophrenia, manic-depressive psychosis and schizoaffective psychosis. (p. 149)

Cerebral Asymmetry: A Possible Influence on the Schizophrenic Genotype

Split-brain research has begun to suggest correlations among schizophrenia, dream phenomena, and the nondominant hemisphere. Some of this work has direct bearing on borderline syndromes, at least those that exist within the pale of schizophrenia.

The subject of differential development of the two cerebral hemispheres has been reviewed by Galin (1974). Evidence has been accumulating rapidly to support the contention that while the "dominant" hemisphere (usually the left even in many left-handed persons) specializes in language and logic functions, the right or "nondominant" hemisphere develops a superior capacity for pattern comprehension and recognition of emotion (Bogen and Bogen, 1969). There is also evidence that dreaming during rapid-eye-movement (REM) sleep depends for its visual imagery and surrealistic quality upon right-hemisphere activity, which itself seems to be increased during this phase of sleep (Bakan, 1975). The right brain appears to be the dreamer (Baken, 1975; Stone, 1977), although activity is still registered in the left hemisphere as well during dreaming (but with diminished interhemispheric cross-talk in terms of electrical activity measured in the corpus callosum).

Recently a number of investigators have submitted evidence pointing to a disorder in interhemispheric communication in schizophrenics (Roemer, 1977; Eaton, 1977) as well as a disorder in left-hemisphere function (Eaton, 1977) characterized by slower and more variable reaction times to verbal stimuli presented to the left (but not to the right) hemisphere. Flor-Henry (1969) has noted that temporal lobe epileptics, when they become psychotic, tend to have "affective" symptoms when the epileptic focus is on the nondominant side, whereas a left-sided focus is usually associated with "schizophrenic" symptoms. In the intriguing study of Boklage (1977), *discordance* for schizophrenia in MZ twins was found more often in those pairs where one or both twins were *not* right-handed. In the concordant pairs, the twins were usually both right-handed. The tendency for the one- or two- non-right-handed pairs to exhibit milder disorders—of the "non-nuclear" or borderline schizophrenic type—led Boklage to speculate that left-handedness or mixed laterality may be associated with a higher degree of brain plasticity in those functions most frequently disturbed in schizophrenia (1977, p. 29). It is important to note that among viable MZ twin pairs, 30 percent separate before, and about 70 percent *after,* the commitment to the differentiation of the inner-cell mass from the chorionic trophoblast; that is, unpredictable events in early embryonic life may affect the handedness even of genetically "identical" twins. If Boklage is correct, these differences in handedness may play a role in determining which twin succumbs clinically (years later) to the schizophrenic illness to which his (presumed) extra load of risk genes predisposed him. Handedness, or more correctly, the balance between the cerebral hemispheres, may have to be added to the list of modifying influences, like intelligence, that affect the degree to which schizophrenic predisposition exerts itself. Some "borderline schizophrenics" may be just those in whom the influence of risk genes has been softened by a favorable situation with regard to cerebral dominance.

CHAPTER 6

Genetic Aspects of Manic-Depressive Disorders

Early Observations

Baillarger (1854) described a circular form of insanity a generation before Kraepelin, under the heading *folie à double forme,* but Kraepelin (1921) usually receives the credit for having, in 1896, classified manic-depressive psychosis (MDP) as a unitary form of mental illness.

An early American description of a family pedigree replete with manic-depressive individuals is that of McGaffin (1911).

In his 1921 monograph Kraepelin estimated the occurrence of hereditary taint in "manic-depressive insanity" as approximately 75 percent but expressed no opinion on the kind of transmission that might be involved. He also noted a lopsidedness to the sex ratio in manic-depressive illness, 70 percent of his cases being women. He felt strongly that the processes of sexual life played a part, inasmuch as bouts of affective disorder sometimes occurred just after the menarche, and many attacks (especially of depression) occurred during the climacterium. The different forms of MDP were, for Kraepelin, distinctive clinically but not genetically. Many now regard mania and recurrent depression as genetically distinct as well, although, as we shall see, some investigators now postulate a model of transmission in which the differing clinical forms are unified once again.

Pooled data from a number of studies in the 1920s and 1930s (Luxenburger, Schulz, Slater, and others) suggested that manic-depressive psychosis occurred in about 0.5 percent of the general population (see Kallmann, 1954). This contrasts with the oft-quoted figure of 0.85 percent for the worldwide incidence of schizophrenia.

The association of alcoholism with the affective disorders was suspected for some time. Winokur, Clayton, and Reich mention (1969, p. 30) the high rate of alcoholism among parents of manic-depressive probands; in a like vein, Kraepelin observed long ago (1921, p. 178) that 25 percent of male manic-depressives were alcoholic.

Early Theories of Transmission

Rüdin's Observations

A portion of Ernst Rüdin's 1923 review on the inheritance of mental illness is devoted to the manic-depressive disorders (pp. 463–468). While some of his data argued for straightforward Mendelian inheritance, the smaller percentage of affected children (6 percent) of MDP probands—compared with affected sibs (25 percent)—suggested recessivity. Rüdin speculated that the mode of inheritance depended on three elements (a "Trimerie," 1923, p. 465): two recessive and one dominant factor. He did not, as Winokur mentions, take into account the disproportionality of incidence between the sexes.

The Findings of Rosanoff and His Co-workers

Access to over 1000 pairs of twins with mental disorders allowed Rosanoff, Handy, and Plesset (1935) to probe the genetic aspects of manic-depressive disorders in a much more sophisticated fashion than was possible for their predecessors. Ninety pairs of twins at least one of whom suffered a serious affective disorder were extracted from the larger sample. These investigators found among their MZ twins a concordance rate of 69.6 percent, a rate higher than that noted in their series of schizophrenic twins (61 percent) or epileptic twins (52 percent). These figures, they believed, justified the widespread impression that the manic-depressive psychoses were the "most hereditary" of the common psychotic conditions.

A higher incidence of MDP was noted among women (slightly over 2:1 in their series), but analysis of sex ratios among the subtypes of MDP was not undertaken. Rosanoff's findings did tend to confirm Kraepelin's impression about the distinctness of the two major psychoses, inasmuch as no MZ pairs were found where one twin was manic-depressive and the other, schizophrenic.

Though cautious in his appraisal of the hereditary factor in MDP, Rosanoff gives us one unusually compelling piece of evidence attesting to its power in his first clinical example. This concerned an MZ pair separated almost at birth because of economic reasons—one boy being raised in poverty, the other in affluence some two hundred miles away. Despite their having almost no contact with one another and despite the great differences in their environments, both twins at twenty-one suffered manic decompensations of the same sort, unbeknownst to each other, within a space of three months!

Rosanoff's emphasis on the role of loss as the psychological stressor that may precipitate manic-depressive psychosis presages my own efforts (Stone, 1975) to quantify this phenomenon. He said his co-workers also recognized the possibility that MDP could manifest itself in youth: 0.5 percent of their cases were under age fifteen; 5 percent were between ages fifteen and twenty. These figures, it should be emphasized, relate to hospitalized cases. Presumably the frequency of subtler manifestations of manic-depressive predisposition even in this age bracket would be significantly higher. Yet the psychiatric community had somehow forgotten this fact until the quite recent work of Berg, Hullin, et al. (1974), McKnew, Cytryn, and White (1974), Von Greiff, McHugh, and Stokes (1975), and Carlson and Strober (1978).

To account for the female "preponderance" in MDP, a mode of transmission was postulated that involved two "factors," one "autosomal," predisposing to cyclothymia, and the other an "activating" factor located presumably on the X chromosome. An intricate schema was then elaborated to account for the distribution of MDP-related temperaments (see Chapter 10). Closer to the more modern notions of polygenic inheritance in the functional psychoses, Rosanoff's hypothesis was better able to account for the fine gradations in psychopathology and for the existence of "latent" disorders than were the theoretical formulations of the previous generation.

Slater's Findings

Selecting cases with a first attack before age fifty and with a clear-cut manic or depressive course, Slater (1938a) was able to isolate a diagnostically purer sample than had previously been collected.

The incidence of MDP in parents of Slater's probands was 11 percent; of their children, 22 percent; and if suicides were included as suspected MDP cases, these figures rose to 17 percent and 26 percent respectively. This represents a thirty- to sixtyfold increase in expectancy over what would be found in the general population.

The sex ratio in Slater's series was, as in previous studies, approximately two females to one male, but access to other large surveys (namely, Weinberg and Lobstein, 1936) led Slater to conclude that the sex ratio "in nature" was nearer unity, some artifact being responsible for the ratio usually cited. Slater was not at this time impressed by advocates of a sex-linked factor in the transmission of manic-depressive disorders, and thus disagreed with Rosanoff. Absence of father-son transmission would be required of such a hypothesis. Although the number of relevant cases was small in Slater's material, father-son transmission not only occurred but did so proportionally as often as father-daughter transmission.

Kallmann's Findings

Kallmann (1954) reported on a series of twins collected from state hospitals in New York. The rates observed for manic-depressive psychoses of one form or another ranged from 16 percent in half sibs and 23 percent in full sibs to 26 percent in dizygotic co-twins and *100 percent in MZ co-twins*. Among parents of index cases, the MDP rate was 23 percent. To the remarkable finding of perfect concordance in MDP monozygotic twins, Kallmann adds the caveat that his series was composed of hospitalized cases, thus representing the most severe end of the affective spectrum. As Kallmann mentioned, "Beyond question, there are many mild cyclic cases requiring no hospitalization" (p. 6). "Cycloid" personality types (characterized by periodic but relatively mild tendency to emotional instability) were observed by all psychogeneticists, among family members of MDP probands. Many such cases remain disguised under various psychoneurotic and psychosomatic labels (see Stone, 1978), making accurate tabulation of MDP-related illnesses in the families no easy matter.

In discussing probable mode of transmission, Kallmann favored the notion of a single dominant gene, rejecting the more complex and sex-linked model of Rosanoff. The phenotypic expression of this factor, which Kallmann regarded as an *abnormal* gene, involved "the recurring ability to exceed the normal range of emotional responses, with extreme but self-limited mood alterations" which, in turn, could not in his opinion "be considered a part of a person's normal biological equipment" (p. 19). Nonetheless the abnormality underlying the MDP family of mental disturbances was taken as a kind of indirect evidence for a regulatory mechanism, also gene controlled, in normals, one that ordinarily serves to protect a person's emotional life from the harmful extremes of affective responses.

Leonhard's Findings

Impressed by Kretschmer's observation that abnormal temperaments were often seen in family members of psychotic manic-depressives, Leonhard, Korff, and Schulz (1962) in Berlin searched for possible correlations between particular temperaments (the "hypomanic," the "subdepressive," and the "cyclothymic") and particular variants of full-blown manic-depressive illness. Ideally one might expect that MDP variants exhibiting deviations in only one affective direction (for which he and his group coined the term "monopolar") might be accompanied in family pedigrees by the corresponding temperament: hypomanic temperament going with monopolar manic psychoses, and so on. To a large extent this is the direction in which Leonhard's findings eventually pointed. Within the realm of psychoses characterized by mood swings in either direction, that is, the "bipolar" manic-depressives, one finds among the *nonpsychotic* relatives with temperamental abnormalities, predominantly cyclothymics. The relationship was not exclusive, however: a small percentage of "subdepressive temperaments" was also noted in the first-degree relatives of some bipolar index cases.

The risk of serious disorders was significantly higher for close relatives of bipolar probands than was noted in the realm of unipolar depression. Leonhard believed this finding supported his contention that bipolar and unipolar diseases were genetically distinct.

Findings of the Scandinavian Studies

Stenstedt The Swedish investigator Stenstedt (1952) reported that in 5 out of 6 (of his 288) cases, the first attack in manic-depressive psychosis was a depression. A few schizophrenialike characteristics were noted in 18 percent of his cases, but only 10 percent showed "deviating personality traits." There was only a modest excess of female patients. Endorsing a single autosomal dominance hypothesis, Stenstedt found similar risk levels (15 percent) for siblings, parents, and children of the index cases. The relative purity of the sample may be gauged by the low morbidity risk in relatives for schizophrenia: 1.2 percent. Stenstedt postulated that unfavorable environmental factors played a definite role in the precipitation of overt psychosis on the basis of his observation that in a subgroup of siblings defined as having "unfavorable" environments, the risk was 31 percent. In the favorable-environment subgroup the morbidity risk to siblings of index cases was only 10 percent.

Perris Perris, from the University Clinic-Umeå, in Sweden, sought to verify Leonhard's model of affective-disorder taxonomy. He was struck by the frequency with which the term "endogeneous depression" was used by many diagnosticians interchangeably with "manic-depressive psychosis." Furthermore there was a tendency among his predecessors (namely, Stenstedt) to include as examples of MDP a number of patients with exclusively depressive episodes. Here Perris was touching indirectly on the seemingly paradoxical situation that patients with recurrent depression and those with manic *and* depressive episodes may all be "homogeneous" with respect to the concept of *affective disturbance* (they are equally distinct from the concept of schizophrenia) while being heterogeneous with respect to the direction of their mood swings. Whether one chooses to speak of the different forms of affective illnesses as similar or distinct would depend on the specific topic under discussion. Evidence of distinctness was offered via the results of Perris's observations on a number of genetic, constitutional, social, clinical, neurophysiological, and prognostic factors (see Table 6–1).

TABLE 6–1

Positive Findings in Perris's Study of MDP

RESULTS OF INVESTIGATION CONCERNING	*Bipolar Illness*	*Unipolar Illness*
Genetics	Mentally ill relatives mostly bipolar; risk in relatives—20%	Mentally ill relatives mostly unipolar; risk in relatives—14½%
Personality traits	Predominantly "syntonic" patterns	Predominantly "asthenic" types
Median age of onset	30	45
Course	Somewhat shorter episodes, more frequent relapses	Somewhat longer episodes, less frequent relapses

SOURCE: Perris (1966, p. 186).

Because the ill relatives of bipolars were usually bipolar (and vice versa, with unipolars), Perris thought it would be reasonable to assume that one inherits partly a specific tendency to disease—which determines the form and course of the illness—and partly a particular biological substratum—which "determines personality qualities . . . and the type of reaction in various test situations" (1966, p. 187).

Angst Similar findings were to emerge from investigation of a Swiss population by Angst (Angst and Perris, 1968). An important difference, however, lay in the fact that relatives with an affective disorder, of Angst's bipolar probands, showed more depressive than cyclical disturbances. Both Angst and Perris thought this apparent discrepancy might be accounted for by the briefer period of follow-up in the Swiss series (giving less time for possible, future manic episodes to be recorded).

Of particular interest, differentiation into bipolar and unipolar groups led to the discovery that the female "excess" reported earlier for MDP was confined to the recurrent depressive patients. Among bipolars there was numerical parity between the sexes (Angst and Perris, 1968, p. 381). In retrospect one could better understand the confusion and debate over sex distribution in MDP: depressives (especially if the involutional group is included) outnumber the cyclical patients. There would tend as a result to be a female excess in any sample of patients with "affective psychoses" (where all the subtypes were lumped together).

Views of the Japanese Psychogeneticists

Mitsuda The theoretical models of transmission elaborated by the Japanese school are of considerable relevance to discussion of borderline syndromes. Mitsuda (1967) envisions a universe of endogenous psychoses inhabited by three dense regions corresponding to typical schizophrenia, typical MDP, and idiopathic epilepsy. The "pure strain" (that is, those exhibiting homotypy) tend to breed true. But in the ill-defined spaces between these central concepts (see Figure 6–1) are "atypical" or "intermediate" conditions, whose nature is in some instances shaped by an admixture of tendencies to two neighboring "pure" conditions. Schizoaffective psychoses thus occupy the region between schizophrenia and MDP. "Atypical" cases of MDP (those containing at least a few features of schizophrenia or, at times, of epilepsy) had briefer psychotic episodes than typical cases, showed considerable manifestational variation, and also tended to breed true.

Figure 6–1. Mitsuda's Model of Relationships among the Endogenous Psychoses

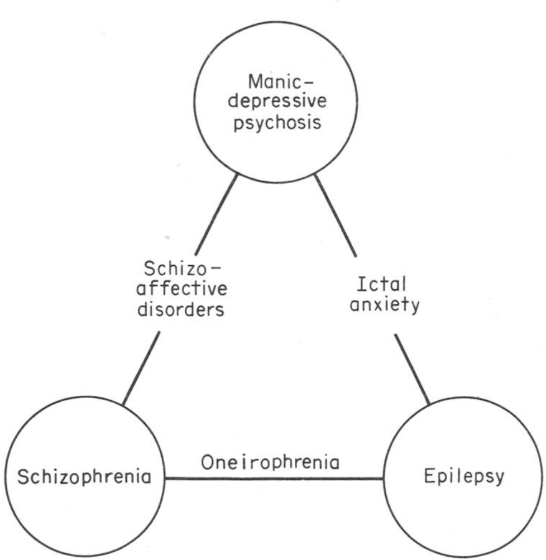

SOURCE: Mitsuda (1967, p. 12).

As mentioned in Chapter 4, Mitsuda eventually concluded that the atypical psychoses were separate forms of mental illness. Pauleikhoff (1974) agrees with Mitsuda in principle and sees the atypical psychoses as distinct from MDP as they are from schizophrenia. He believes a whole new classification of the endogenous psychoses is now warranted, to get around the Kraepelinian dichotomies (*either* schizophrenia *or* MDP) that have for so long dominated the field.

According to Mitsuda's compilations, mental illness among family members of "atypical schizophrenics" (those with favorable outcome) was quite variable in its clinical form, although fully half consisted also of recovered schizophrenics. A few relatives (one-seventh) were chronic, "typical" schizophrenics, and about a fourth manic-depressive. These atypical cases were in a borderland between schizophrenia and MDP, and were perhaps also in a borderland between psychosis and normal neuroticism. Zerbin-Rüdin (1974) cautions that it is not easy to know how some of Mitsuda's cases might be regarded by Western observers, because of the linguistic and cultural differences that separate us. Mitsuda has been willing to claim, however, that "intrafamilial psychotics [other than typical schizophrenics] in families of atypical schizophrenic index cases should not be regarded as possessing a genotype different from the [index cases]. . . . This phenomenon must be regarded instead as multiform phenotypical manifestations of the same gene [such that] MDP may be displayed in one instance; epilepsy, in another" (1967, p. 7). The mode of inheritance Mitsuda regarded as probably recessive, albeit with perhaps some dominant strains in certain pedigrees.[1]

Asano Asano's analysis of mental illness in relatives of 160 patients with schizophrenic stigmata (1967) revealed that probands with "typical MDP" had ill relatives whose clinical diagnoses were entirely within the realm of typical MDP. There was a morbidity risk of 17 percent (similar to the figures of Angst and of Perris). Risk was less (6½ percent) in the "atypical" group, and there was greater diagnostic spread: a few schizophrenic and epileptic relatives were noted. Because no atypical (schizoaffective, as others might call them) relatives were found among the kindred of the typ-

[1]Mitsuda's efforts to interpose new categories in between the traditional categories represent one way around the rigidity of the old system. If one begins to see in nature a "multiplicity" of *genotypes,* however, may this not be in itself an indication that we are dealing with a complex and continuumlike system of genotypic variation (rather than with a system comprising only a few genotypes each quite distinct from the other)? Also, it is not yet clear, as Childs and Der Kaloustian (1968) point out, how much of the clinical variability noted among the functional psychoses can legitimately be understood as *(a)* phenotypic heterogeneity—stemming from genetic heterogeneity—as opposed to *(b)* clinical heterogeneity stemming from other factors.

ical MDP probands, Asano was led to the same hypothesis promulgated by Mitsuda, namely, that the atypical psychoses constituted a third entity in the realm of the endogenous psychoses, alongside schizophrenia and MDP.

Although Asano advocated a tripartite model of the endogenous psychoses, he was nevertheless aware of Kraepelin's sensitivity to what were in essence *borderline* examples of MDP. In 1896 and again in 1905 Kraepelin alluded to subtle affective disturbances in progressively milder versions of the major disorders. The passage, which presages contemporary notions of a spectrum concept in the affective disorders, deserves repetition here:

> Manic-depressive insanity embraces on the one hand the whole realm of so-called periodic and circular psychoses, and on the other hand, simple mania; also the bulk of clinical syndromes described under the rubric "melancholia," not to mention a significant number of amentia cases. Finally we must include in the reckoning certain mild, at times extremely mild, sometimes periodic, at other times, continuous, examples of mood alteration—which may on the one hand constitute the first stage of what is to become a more serious disorder, or which on the other hand may cross over into the realm of personality attributes and talents. (Kraepelin, 1896, cited by Asano, 1967, p. 262)

Résumé of Twin Studies up to 1970

Figure 6–2 illustrates the progress of twin studies within the realm of affective disorders in the forty-year span between 1930 and 1970. The more recent average, as may be gathered from the dotted line in the figure (the

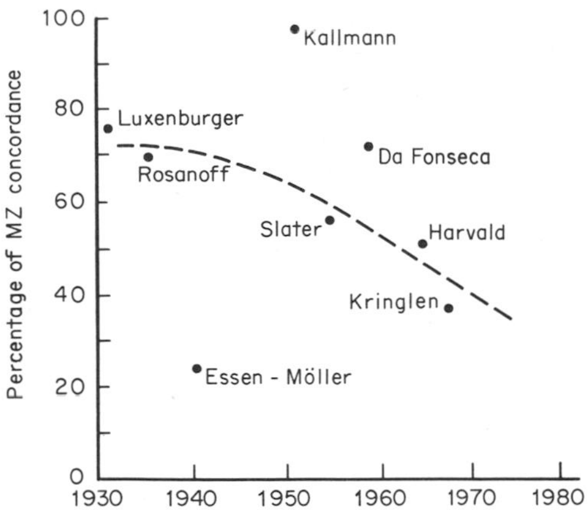

Figure 6–2. MZ Twin Concordance for Manic-Depressive Psychosis

most likely resulting curve if one discards the highest and lowest estimates), is between 40 and 50 percent.[2]

Evidence up through 1970 suggested that a small percentage (probably about 25 percent) of MZ twins concordant for an affective psychosis do show a "split," where one is unipolar and the other bipolar. Few pairs, however, have been followed all the way through the age of risk, so that some affected twins regarded thus far as recurrent depressives may yet develop a manic episode. In the meantime it is probably quite legitimate to call a pair concordant even if the psychotic subtypes are dissimilar.

The Findings of Winokur and His Co-workers

Winokur and his colleagues at the Washington University School of Medicine in St. Louis studied the relatives of 61 manic (bipolar) probands. Of the 122 parents, 36 had a primary affective disorder (Winokur, Clayton, and Reich, 1969) and in only a quarter of these were manic episodes noted. Further analysis of the data yielded a number of interesting results. The 62 parents with some diagnosible psychiatric disorder manifested a variety of conditions, mostly of an affective flavor. One encountered the following clinical pictures: (*a*) depression only (3 fathers, 25 mothers), (*b*) mania only (six instances), (*c*) alcoholism only (9 fathers, 1 mother), (*d*) depression and mania (two instances), and (*e*) alcoholism and depression (two instances). Note the preponderance of *male* alcoholics and *female* depressives.

The 61 manic probands had 33 affectively ill sibs: 12 brothers and 21 sisters. The imbalance in the sex ratio stemmed, as with the parents, from the larger number of females with recurrent depression.

Winokur's results tended to confirm the impression of his predecessors (see Kraepelin, 1921, p. 165) that alcoholism as well as severe affective disorders turned up with great frequency in the families of "manic-depressives." In fact, the variety of conditions in MDP families spread out not only horizontally with respect to form but vertically with respect to severity. Taken together these variants constituted a manic-depressive spectrum of illnesses as impressive in its own way as the "schizophrenia spectrum" championed by Rosenthal and Kety.

The independence of the two polar concepts, schizophrenia and manic-depressive psychosis, was further bolstered by a later observation (Winokur, Morrison, Clancy, and Crowe, 1972) that suicide was more fre-

[2]Though the more recent figures tend toward the lower estimate, the pooled data, including the earlier studies, would yield an MZ concordance of 68 percent in MDP twins (see also Zerbin-Rüdin, 1968). The pooled DZ concordance is about 23 percent. A dozen cases of monozygotic MDP twins reared apart were collected from the world's literature by Price, who noted a 67 percent concordance (Cadoret and Winokur, 1972, p. 160).

quently noted in the relatives of affectively ill probands than in the families of (clear-cut) schizophrenics.

Winokur was not only impressed by the preponderance of females among cases of unipolar depression but also noted, in his original sample, a virtual absence of father-to-son transmission in his bipolar probands. The latter led him to postulate an X-linked gene as fundamental to bipolar illness (which would, if validated, render this form genetically distinct from unipolar illness). Further on in this chapter we shall examine the merits of Winokur's hypothesis.

Theoretical Aspects: Recent Data

Introduction

Eccentricity being the hallmark of schizophrenia, this form of psychosis is relatively easy to detect and isolate for purposes of study.[3] Mania has very characteristic features, but depression is so widespread a phenomenon, and blends by degrees into the "normal" population, that it has been more difficult to define which depressive syndromes would be the most promising to segregate for genetic analysis. Even the older method of classification, emphasizing endogenous versus reactive depression, did not prove reliable as a method of separating a group highly predisposed genetically from a group in whom heritable factors were negligible (Price, 1975). In this connection it is probably fair to say that "endogenous" depression (severe to psychotic depression with either no or minor environmental precipitant) retains a fairly high scientific mortgage even today. But as we now realize, there are so many "reactive" depressions that (1) later on turn out to be the first in a chain of recurrent depressions or (2) occur in persons with a strong family history of major affective disorders (see case illustration 28) that the diagnostic and prognostic utility of this label is compromised (see also Chapter 9, D. Klein).

In the past fewer biochemical markers had been proposed as relevant to MDP in comparison to the number suggested for schizophrenia; this too may be an expression of the comparative proximity of mood swings to the vicissitudes of normal life (Price, 1972).

Bipolar versus Unipolar Illness

It has been difficult to draw appropriate boundaries between depressive disease (the presumed organically based vulnerability to incapacitating depression), neurotic depression, and the "reasonable" depression of

[3]Relative, that is, to most other psychiatric conditions. Ollerenshaw (1973), Carpenter, Strauss, and Muleh (1973), Pope and Lipinski (1978), and others make clear how difficult it can sometimes be, especially in acute episodes or in young subjects, to distinguish between schizophrenia and mania.

abysmal life circumstances, especially since Perris, Angst, and Winokur demonstrated in their separate studies that milder forms of depressive "disease" exist within the spectrum of affective disorders. Against this background the magnitude of Leonhard's breakthrough—finding two clinically, perhaps even genetically, separable groups in the realm of affective illness—can be better appreciated. Psychogeneticists have been able, after Leonhard, to work with more homogeneous populations (Cadoret and Winokur, 1972).

By now it has become widely accepted that what was once called manic-depressive psychosis consists of two intertwining sets of conditions whose genotypes may or may not be distinct but whose phenotypes have at least suggested such distinctiveness. Reclassification (bipolar, unipolar) has led to the greater recognition of "borderline" and milder forms, hence our turning more and more away from the old label. It is obvious that many recurrent depressives, hypomanic relatives of full-blown manics, and so on, manage to avoid psychotic decompensation throughout life. The term "affective disorder," free of any surplus meaning having to do with psychosis, is a much more acceptable substitute.

Although in making the distinction between bipolar and unipolar cases reliance on family history and clinical data was initially strong (Hopkinson and Ley, 1969), in recent years, biological data (D. W. Goodwin, Schulsinger, et al., 1973; Dunner, Goodwin, Gershon, et al., 1972) and pharmacological data (F. K. Goodwin, Murphy, Brodie, et al., 1970; Baron, Gershon, et al., 1975) have come to play an increasingly important role (see lithium response, pp. 138–141).

Other characteristics helpful in distinguishing bipolar from unipolar groups include those derived from clinical studies such as the recent one by Mendlewicz on affective "equivalents."[4] He found, for example, that the suicide rate was higher in the bipolar group, as was the incidence of episodic alcoholism. Chronic alcoholism was found more frequently among those with unipolar depression. Both bipolar patients and their relatives showed a heightened tendency to peptic ulcer (as much as 13 percent among probands), whereas this correlation was not found among recurrent depressives and their relatives. Young patients with borderline structure and peptic ulcer may be particularly prone later on to show more clearly recognizable signs of bipolar illness (Stone, 1978; case illustration 28).

[4]A term used earlier by Da Fonseca (1963) in referring to certain inpatients with affective disorders; namely, asthmatic attacks, peptic ulcer, and certain dermatoses. Although Da Fonseca regarded these as "alternative modes of manifestation of the basic diencephalic disturbance which we suppose to underlie the mood changes of endogenous affective disorders," many would nowadays dispute his idea of there being a true interrelationship, except perhaps in the case of peptic ulcer. The frequency of ulcer in affective-disorder patients does seem sufficiently great to warrant further search for a possible interconnectedness between the two phenomena.

Another distinguishing feature suggested by several authors concerned the heightened vulnerability of bipolar females and their affectively ill female relatives to psychotic episodes in the postpartum period. Women with recurrent depression did not seem to be at greater than average risk in this connection (Cadoret and Winokur, 1972).

Finally, a number of investigators have drawn attention to differences in age of onset between the two major groups of affective illness. Although the total age range in each is quite similar (roughly twenty-five to sixty), Mendlewicz (1974) noted that the age of onset was significantly earlier in bipolar illness (31.8, as against 43.7). Cadoret and Winokur give the median-age figures 28 for bipolar patients and 36 for unipolars (Sperber and Jarvik, 1976, p. 69).

The Controversy over X Linkage

The apparent absence of father-to-son transmission in bipolar illness reported by Winokur and Tanna in the late sixties spurred a number of investigators to examine pedigrees of bipolar probands. Confirmation of Winokur's finding would strongly suggest that bipolar illness was under the influence of a gene on the X chromosome. Patients and relatives were also examined for other X-linked traits such as red-green color blindness (Stone, 1971) and $X_g{}^a$ antigen Mendlewicz, Fleiss, and Fieve, 1972). Evidence for linkage[5] at first seemed strong (Fieve, Mendlewicz, et al., 1975), although nine instances of father-son transmissions were noted among 120 probands studied by Fieve. Winokur and Tanna's data, while failing to support an X-linked model in an absolute sense, still suggested that an X-linked dominant mode was operative at least in some MDP pedigrees.

What is lacking in the studies just cited is any correction for ascertainment bias. Gershon and Matthysse (1978), warning that sampling procedures may under- or overrepresent certain classes of pedigrees, have recently described a method for reducing this bias, using the traits of color blindness and bipolar illness in their formulae. Were corrections for ascertainment bias made, the apparent evidence for linkage would have been weakened considerably, the more so if certain noninformative pedigrees had been excluded from the final tabulations.

Investigators from other centers also began contributing results that questioned the universality of the X-linked theory. Father-son transmission, for example, was reported simultaneously in a number of centers: by James and Chapman from New Zealand (1975), by Goetzl and his co-workers at Dartmouth (1974), by Loranger (1975) from Cornell in White Plains, and by the Canadian investigator Hays (1976).

[5]"Linkage" refers to the presence on the same chromosome of two genes, each responsible for a separate trait and located near enough to each other that, despite crossing over, they assort in a *dependent* fashion (Cadoret and Winokur, 1972, p. 171).

Helzer and Winokur (1974), on the other hand, continued to find a relative absence of father-son transmission—only one instance among thirty male bipolar probands and their first-degree relatives. Several explanations were offered that might account for their results, since Helzer and Winokur were now advocating what in the light of other recent studies was becoming a minority position. Possible differences in the patient cohorts might play a role; nor could "fortuitous associations of certain genes in isolated populations" be ruled out (Gershon, Dunner, and Goodwin, 1971). Differing diagnostic criteria for the two forms of affective illness may also have contributed to the disharmony in results (1974, p. 77). But more important than all these factors may have been sample bias which resulted from the manner in which the study patients were collected. Certainly the St. Louis studies do not have the elegance or the authenticity of a large random population survey, nor can they match the breadth and comparative freedom from bias of a sample assembled from a national registry, as was available to Kringlen in Norway.

The question of X linkage has been reexamined thoroughly in the excellent article by Gershon and Bunney (1976). They submit evidence that color blindness, for example, is associated with affective illness *across* pedigrees rather than *within* individual pedigrees. This finding suggests not chromosomal linkage but that color-blind individuals tend to have a higher incidence of affective illness than the general population. Furthermore, their analysis of the data did not confirm the earlier reports that suggested close linkage between bipolar illness and both the X_g blood group and protan or deutan color blindness ($CB_{p/d}$). The map distance between the X_g locus and the $CB_{p/d}$ region of the X chromosome is, according to evidence Gershon and Bunney mentioned, too great to be compatible with the linkage hypothesis.

In summary, the bulk of recent work has not supported the contention that bipolar affective illness emanates from a gene located on the X chromosome and closely linked spatially to the X_g locus. This failure, in itself, does not disprove a single-major-locus (SML) postulate for bipolar illness, though it suggests that the initial enthusiasm for an SML involving the X chromosome was not warranted.

Lithium Response as Diagnostic Aid and Biological Marker

One of the most dramatic features of manic-depressive disorders, especially the bipolar varieties, is *periodicity*. When present, this feature aids greatly in the exclusion of schizophrenia, although as the "wavelength" increases, periodicity becomes harder to diagnose. This subject becomes all the more intriguing when one takes into account the vicissitudes in psychological state common in many women through their menstrual life, a topic adumbrated below in Chapter 8. Even normal women will tend to show mild but measurable increases in depression or anxiety the week before (or in some instances, the week of) the period (Beaumont, Richards, and Gelder, 1975).

The question arises, Are we describing a clinical syndrome that crosses paths with the manic-depressive disorders phenomenologically, or are the very severe premenstrual syndromes, themselves, one manifestation of the genetically predisposed biochemical alterations (see Bunney et al., 1972) of true affective illness? My own impression is that the periodic aspects of both manic-depressive disease and the severe (including psychotic) premenstrual disorders are interrelated. They may in some instances be the expressions of the same or of highly overlapping combinations of genes. Likewise, periodic maladies occurring in the same family may present different clinical pictures in affected males from what is observed in the affected females, but this too may relate to phenotypic variation stemming from a common genetic source.

Even in men, monthly attacks of psychotic depression are not unknown; recently I reported on such a patient, whose attacks, spaced twenty-eight days apart, coincided with the full moon (Stone, 1976). This man responded dramatically to lithium.

The whole issue of interrelationships among bipolar affective disorders, severe premenstrual syndromes, and the phenomenon of periodicity is highlighted in the burgeoning literature on lithium salts.[6] Lithium, as it turns out, is one of the very few compounds capable of altering the rhythmicity of the "biologic clock" (Palmer, 1975) and can do so in plants as well as in animals. Its usefulness in minifying the mood swings of bipolar patients, especially, is by now well established (Johnson, Gershon, et al., 1971; Mendlewicz and Stallone, 1975; Fieve, 1975). A number of authors have also reported the greater effectiveness of lithium in bipolar as compared with unipolar conditions (Goodwin, Murphy, et al., 1972; Baron, Gershon, Rudy, et al., 1975), although some benefit apparently occurs in selected unipolar patients (Fieve, Kumbaraci, and Dunner, 1976). Bipolar patients are symptomatically not always so easy to differentiate from unipolars and, in addition, often experience varying degrees of depressive symptoms even in the midst of their "highs" (Murphy and Beigel, 1974).

Certain investigators have even suggested that lithium response might be used as a diagnostic aid. Thus Forssman and Wålinder, from the Psychiatric Research Centre of Gothenburg University (Sweden), gave two detailed descriptions of initially puzzling cases where a positive response to lithium helped solidify their eventual conviction that bipolar MDP was the correct diagnosis. One patient had had symptoms since he was seven (phobias, severe obsessive preoccupations); he threatened suicide at fourteen and was diagnosed as "schizophrenic." He was afraid he could kill people with

[6]Women with unipolar illness are by no means free of premenstrual symptom aggravation (see case illustration 17).

"thought waves" and was tormented by pseudophilosophical questions about "What is nothing?" "What is free will?" In later adolescence "thought control" and feelings of unreality were experienced, but at twenty-one, he had periods of hilarious mirth, overspending, and hyperactivity. Lithium was given at this time, and he made an excellent recovery.

Others allude to a sliding scale of lithium response, bipolars profiting the most and unipolars the least (Johnson, Gershon, et al., 1971; Goodwin, Murphy, et al., 1972), with certain schizoaffectives (namely, those with racing thoughts and early awakening) somewhere in between (Glassman, 1974). Mendlewicz, Fieve, and Stallone (1973) reported evidence that bipolar patients with a positive family history for bipolar illness responded even better to lithium than those without such histories. Differential drug response between certain groups of patients may argue for genetic heterogeneity (Winokur, 1975, but see pp. 144–145 in this chapter).

Although I agree strongly with Kendell's warning (1975a) against incorporation of drug response into one's diagnostic method (drug response constituting a frame of reference external to clinical diagnosis, of use only as a means of validation in the future), I can sympathize with those who are enthusiastic about lithium response in differential diagnosis. The atypical patient of case illustration 11, for example, responded to lithium in a way that seemed to carry diagnostic significance.

The idea that lithium might be able to correct the mood fluctuations and extreme irritability in women with the most severe forms of premenstrual tension has won support from the work of Sletten and Gershon (1966). The two patients they discussed in detail both became rather edematous the week before the period (weight gains of five to six pounds). No information was included about possible relatives with mental illness; whether their cases have some kinship to the manic-depressive disorders or are merely "phenocopies" is not clear.

Not long after Sletten's article appeared, McClure, Reich, and Wetzel (1971) submitted a brief report on fifty-six women who made phone calls to a suicide prevention center. Several had clear-cut affective disorders, usually bipolar; one had a manic family member, though she herself had not been manic. The majority of the calls were made during or just before the menses (Wetzel, Reich, and McClure, 1971). Earlier reports, including that of Coppen (1965), emphasized the frequency of premenstrual *depression,* particularly in women with affective disorders. About a fourth of McClure's patients reported euphoria or even some hypomanic symptoms premenstrually (at times preceded by more typical premenstrual depressive symptoms). Some of D. Klein's hysteroid dysphoric patients exhibit premenstrual exacerbations of affective symptoms. Since a number of them are known to me as having been so diagnosed by Klein personally, and by Kernberg as showing borderline structure, they may exemplify a patient group where borderline structure, bipolar (and at times unipolar) disease, and "hysteroid dysphoria" meet. Some of the more flamboyant cases are also lithium responders.

A Comment on Anorexia Nervosa The subject of lithium response in manic-depressive conditions cannot be closed without reference to the fascinating case of Berg, Hullin, Allsopp, et al. (1974) about a girl of only fourteen who developed a florid bipolar psychosis. Her psychosis had been preceded by *anorexia nervosa.* "School phobia" and suicide gestures were also noted (as in many of the severely anoretic girls admitted for intensive therapy to the Psychiatric Institute in New York City over the past fifteen years). She became hypomanic after a small amount of Elavil. Ultimately she responded to lithium but only in supranormal doses (2.4 grams/day). Her father, also a bipolar manic-depressive, likewise required two to three times the usual daily lithium maintenance. In her prepsychotic state the daughter probably exhibited many features of borderline structure, by Kernberg's definition; almost certainly she was borderline by the clinical criteria of Gunderson. Like most anorexia cases, hyperactivity was present, along with the false cheer or mild hypomania so often displayed by these young women, even as they approach alarming levels of cachexia. I have often been struck by the similarity between certain cases of anorexia nervosa, for these reasons, and the bipolar affective disorders. It is as though anorexia nervosa may, in these instances, be regarded as a *forme fruste* of manic-depressive illness. The family history is often positive for affective disorders. Since the syndrome usually occurs in adolescent girls, the age of risk for MDP has barely been entered, so it is no easy matter to say, confronted with the young patient, what her subsequent course will be. Berg's case is exceptional in that a borderline prodromal state was quickly followed by affective psychosis before the patient had even reached fifteen. Almost all severely anoretic girls admitted to a hospital unit are *borderline* structurally and clinically. A tiny minority are overtly schizophrenic. How many go on to develop obvious manic-depressive conditions in their twenties and thirties is not clear. But it will be intriguing to see whether or not, in the future, genetic and biochemical bridges can be built spanning the affective psychoses and a subgroup of anorexia nervosa.[7] Case illustration 9 concerns a young woman with anorexia in adolescence,

[7]A similar viewpoint has also been adopted independently by Cantwell et al. (1977). They found a large number of primary affective disorders among the close relatives (especially the mothers) of a group of anorexia probands, many of whom themselves had exhibited severe dysphoric mood and other symptoms associated with depression. Favorable response to lithium was reported by Barcai (1977) in two adult women with anorexia nervosa, who also exhibited maniclike symptoms (restlessness, mood instability, pressured speech, irritability). Children of lithium responders have also been noted to show hyperactivity, decreased attention span, sulkiness, irritability, and explosive temper (Dyson and Barcai, 1970).

who then suffered a nervous breakdown of ill-defined type in her early twenties, only to succumb to full-blown mania several years thereafter (responsive to lithium).

Mode of Inheritance

The mode of inheritance of affective disorders is, with respect to borderline syndromes, more than just an academic issue. We want to ascertain whether the milder affective disorders, certain severe character disorders, "impulse" disorders (with rage attacks, alcoholism, other drug abuse, and so on), severe premenstrual disorders, and perhaps even anorexia/bulimia cases—occurring among relatives of affective-psychosis probands—are genetically related to the major disorders. We want to know whether the phenotypic "continuum" that stretches between the severe and the mild cases rests on a foundation of related and graded genetic liability or whether the nonpsychotic cases and structurally borderline individuals became ill through factors independent of the gene(s) responsible for the psychotic cases.

On the surface it would seem quite difficult to account for a spectrum of related conditions, mild to severe, on the basis of simple Mendelian mechanisms, such as that of autosomal dominance. In the past the concept of *incomplete penetrance* was invoked (Slater, and again, Kallmann) to account for the lower-than-expected risk figures and comparative mildness of illness in some of the relatives. Gottesman and Shields (1972) speak of *modifying influences*—some genetic but unrelated to the disorder in question, some environmental—that may affect the expressivity of a postulated major single gene (or of a polygenic system). These influences correspond to what Gershon, Baron, and Leckman (1975) refer to as "independent factors," in their discussion of *multiple-threshold* models in the transmission of affective disorders. The comprehensive study of Gershon and his colleagues—to be further discussed in this chapter—helps resolve some of the problems encountered in the earlier models.

At one time or another most of the common modes of inheritance have been implicated in the affective psychoses. Earlier in this chapter we noted how Slater (1938a) and Kallmann (1954) advocated a *monogenic-autosomal-dominant theory*. Two kinds of biases that would tend to bolster such a model are (*a*) beginning with severely ill probands and (*b*) inclusion of cycloid temperament and other mild ("borderline") cases, making the risk in first-degree relatives begin to approach 50 percent. To account for the gap between this expected morbidity and the 15 percent (Slater) or 25 percent (Kallmann) levels they observed, the notion of incomplete penetrance was invoked. Contemporary thinking, however, has leaned away from this model of transmission, particularly since Leonhard suggested that MDP was an umbrella term covering two genetically distinct varieties of affective disorder, bipolar and unipolar (see Gershon et al. [1975] for a model compatible with a single gene plus thresholds).

The merits and criticisms concerning an *X-linkage model* have been discussed above. Most investigators, including Fieve and Dunner (see Gershon, Dunner, et al., 1973; Dunner, Fleiss, et al., 1976) now incline toward the view that X-linked dominance may be the mode of transmission in a minority of bipolar families. Taylor and Abrams go a step further and suggest that in bipolar probands with onset before age thirty, family distributions of affective illness are compatible with X linkage, in contrast to distributions in the *late-onset* cases, which were not compatible with X linkage. Furthermore Hays (1976) thought that the evidence for a heritable factor in the late-onset bipolar group was very weak to begin with, and he also agreed that evidence was accumulating against X-linked transmission as a *general* theory.

A *two-gene theory,* such as Rosanoff and his co-workers originally promulgated (1935), has been espoused more recently by Winokur and Reich (1970) for bipolar illness. They envision a "disease factor" composed of an X-linked dominant gene and a second factor, responsible for mania per se, which may be operative in affectively ill relatives (of bipolar probands) who actually have manic episodes. Many of the relatives, as has been universally observed, will suffer from recurrent depression only. Alcoholism, seen frequently in families of bipolar patients, appears to have a heritable component also, but one that evolves independently of the affective disorder. Winokur and Reich speculated that (1) alcoholism may be "one way in which such a second factor may manifest itself in the absence of primary X-linked dominant contribution" (1970, p. 98) and that (2) mania (rather than simply depression or alcoholism) may appear in the clinical picture "when the two factors coexist in the same person." The question of heritability of alcoholism is a complicated subject in itself, one that will not be discussed at length here. The strongest evidence for a genetic component comes in the form of a twin-concordance rate that is higher in the MZ pairs than in DZ pairs. Also impressive was the finding that a third of males reared apart from alcoholic parent(s) eventually developed alcoholism themselves (D. W. Goodwin, Schulsinger, Hermansen, et al., 1973). The reader should also consult the article of Omenn (1975), who postulates a variety of transmission mechanisms within the realm of alcoholism (genetic heterogeneity). Returning to the two-gene theory of Winokur and Reich, this model may be a possibility within some bipolar pedigrees, but it has not received much support as a likely model for the majority of cases.

Several theoreticians have begun to postulate the existence of a *polygenic system* as the most likely mode of transmission in the affective disorders (Price, 1975; James and Chapman, 1975; Von Greiff, McHugh, and Stokes, 1975). For data to be compatible with a polygenic model, a number of elements should be present. Heritability, as defined by Falconer (1965),[8] should be between zero and one. Also, there should be (1) a consistency for heritability between the sexes, (2) a consistency for heritability among relatives of the same degree, and (3) a consistency between relatives of differing degrees. These criteria were satisfied (except in item 2, where the numbers were too small to draw valid conclusions) in the series of James and Chapman. Their heritability figures, for example, were 0.83 for all bipolar male relatives and 0.80 for all bipolar female relatives. These authors ascribed the higher incidence of females in affective disorders, in general, to a lower threshold in females rather than to X-linked inheritance.

Price (1975) likens the situation in affective disease to that presumably present in schizophrenia and diabetes:

> Probably the most likely method of transmission is polygenic, the action of innumerable genes determining a continuum of predisposition, either with a discrete threshold or with the chances of manifestation increasing as the genetic predisposition increases. (1975, p. 70)

There is at this time less solid evidence for polygenic inheritance in the affective disorders than in schizophrenia (Cavalli-Sforza and Bodmer, 1971), though the evidence may be more impressive than seemed the case a few years ago (Gershon et al., 1975).

There are certain clinical conditions, exemplifying genetic *heterogeneity,* whose external form represents the end product of more than one type of genetic abnormality. Genes at different loci and operating through different mechanisms of transmission may thus manifest themselves as indistinguishable or scarcely distinguishable phenotypes. McKusick (1973) cites the example of the neurological condition *peroneal muscular atrophy* (Charcot-Marie-Tooth's disease) which can arise in some families as an autosomal dominant disorder, in others as an autosomal recessive condition, and in still others, on an X-linked recessive basis. To the extent that heterogeneity might be relevant to the affective disorders, we should have to speak of the "family" or the "group" of affective psychoses, much as Bleuler spoke of the "group of schizophrenias." Many geneticists interested in the affective disorders have invoked the concept of heterogeneity over the past quarter century. Once Leonhard's division into bipolar and unipolar disorders won wide acceptance, it was noticed that more than half the first-degree relatives of bipolar probands suffered from depressions alone (Goetzl, Green, Whybrow, and Jackson, 1974), a finding investigators interpreted as evidence of genetic heterogeneity. One must of course be cau-

[8]In his formula h^2 = heritability $- b/r$, where b = the difference between the population rate for the condition in question and the morbidity risk in relatives of probands and r = the degree of relationship (first-degree relatives = ½; second, ¼; and so on).

tious about settling for such an interpretation. Variable expressivity would have to be considered, that is, both recurrent depression and manic-depression stemming from a common genetic abnormality and differentiating outwardly because of other interacting factors (see also Gershon et al., 1975). James and Chapman (1975) warn about the problematic nature of the "unipolar diagnosis" in any case: How can one be sure in a relatively young patient that an attack of mania is not still a part of his psychopathological destiny?[9] If an X-linked model is valid for even a few bipolar families, this too would argue for heterogeneity (Sperber and Jarvik, 1976; Hays, 1976; Taylor and Abrams, 1973, 1975a; Mendlewicz, Fleiss, and Fieve, 1975; Von Greiff, McHugh, and Stokes, 1975).

Heterogeneity and polygenic inheritance are, incidentally, not mutually exclusive mechanisms. One could envision, for sake of illustration, a clinical universe in which four different sets of genes were each capable of predisposing to clinically similar affective disorders. This would be heterogeneity. We could then imagine that of the four sets, one involved an autosomal dominant factor; the second, an X-linked gene; and the last two, a pair of different polygenic systems, each composed of a dozen or so separate genes (one set not overlapping with the other). By now we would have both heterogeneity and polygenic systems. This kind of model can be made to fit reasonably well with the evidence available to us at the moment. Whether we need to resort to so complex a schema, however, is another matter. If Gershon is correct, for example, one model (or a series of closely related models) may suffice to explain much of the apparent diversity in these conditions. Before examining this model in more detail, we need first to look briefly at some special difficulties that beset the researcher interested in "purely" depressive disorders.

Heritable Factors and Phenocopying in the Depressive Disorders

Not many people go through life without experiencing at least a brief period of depression. The dividing line between "exogenous" or "secondary" or "reactive" depression and the variant of manic-depressive illness, which we speak of as recurrent depression, can often be difficult to draw, much more so than in the case of schizophrenia or mania whose characteristic features are less a part of common experience. Though depression is experienced as painful and ego-alien, it appears to have some raison d'être

[9]Dunner, Fleiss, and Fieve (1976) have recently shed some light on this important question. Mania, when it was to occur at all, usually occurred early in the course of bipolar illness (80 percent of bipolar conditions begin with a manic episode). In the smaller group of eventually bipolar patients admitted initially for depression, the first manic attack almost always occurred (*a*) within ten years of the initial depressive episode and (*b*) *before* the patient experienced three subsequent depressive episodes. Only about 5 percent of "unipolar depressives" change later to bipolars.

in the overall scheme of human behavior, especially in relation to such matters as social ranking and pair-bond disruption. The ethology of depression (and mania) is discussed at length by Price (1972, 1975).

Depressions of psychotic proportions do, of course, occur and far exceed in intensity the apparent environmental stimulus; severe depressive states may occur periodically and without recognizable stimuli (as in case illustration 11). When individuals with either type of depressive condition also have close relatives with similar conditions, one feels justified in claiming to have moved into a special territory on the map of depressive ailments, where heritable factors operate. If severe depressive episodes occur repeatedly, especially within the context of a "positive" family history, the term "unipolar depression" tends to be utilized. Heterogeneity appears to exist in this realm. Cadoret and Winokur (1972), for example, speak of (1) *depressive disease,* in which affected relatives of probands themselves suffer only from depressions and (2) *depressive spectrum disease,* where close relatives also turn up with sociopathy or alcoholism. The pure depressive disease group tends to have later age of onset and more homogeneity of expression in affected relatives (that is, little or no alcoholism or sociopathy). Baker, Dorzab, et al. (1972), from Winokur's group, have submitted evidence that unipolar depressive disorders (either type) may be manifestations of polygenic rather than (single-) dominant-gene abnormalities.

Some recent work by D. W. Goodwin et al. (1977) bears testimony to the ease with which environmentally induced and genetically predisposed depression may be confused with one another. The risk of developing alcoholism in sons reared apart from their alcoholic fathers remained considerably heightened, Goodwin noted, although the risk for depression was not. Daughters reared apart from alcoholic fathers became neither alcoholic nor depressed. But daughters reared with alcoholic fathers, while not more at risk for alcoholism, did show a greater incidence of depression. This would suggest their depression was more a product of exposure to an unfavorable environment than of genetic factors. Before Goodwin's study it would have been assumed by many that the daughter's depression was primarily a genetic matter—one manifestation of "depressive spectrum disease," of which the son's alcoholism was another.

Comprehensive Models for Affective-Disorder Transmission

At the time of this writing there would appear to be two comprehensive models for integrating existing information on heritable factors in the affective disorders.

The first model emphasizes heterogeneity, in that unipolar (UP) and bipolar (BP) forms are treated as genetically distinct.

Many of the data reviewed in the preceding sections are incorporated here, along with even more recent material such as the twin studies of Allen

(1976) and Bertelsen et al. (1977). According to Allen's calculations, the MZ concordance rates for BP cases is greater than that of UP cases (72 percent as against 40 percent), suggesting not only genetic distinctness but also the importance of heritable factors in BP rather than in UP disorders (see also Angst and Perris, 1968). Pairwise concordance in Bertelsen's Danish twin study was 58 percent by strict criteria but 84 percent if schizoaffective psychoses, "cycloid" personalities, and suicides were also included.

Some have theorized that *bipolar* illness is characterized by (1) transmission via a dominant, single major gene, (2) early onset, (3) better response to lithium, and (4) more mania in first-degree relatives, in contrast to *unipolar* illness, seen as (1) transmitted via a polygenic system, (2) with a later age of onset, (3) with worse response to lithium, and (4) with fewer manic first-degree relatives (Rainer, 1977, personal communication; Angst and Perris, 1968).

The first model is represented in Figure 6–3 and embodies the formula-

Figure 6–3. A Model for the Transmission of Affective Disorders in Which Unipolar and Bipolar Forms Are Genetically Distinct

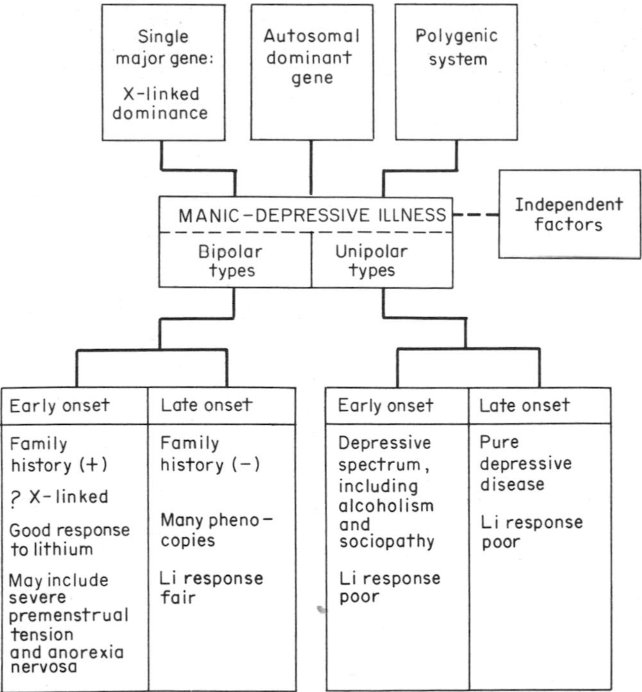

SOURCE: Based in part on Cadoret and Winokur (Sperber and Jarvik, 1976, pp. 67, 69).

tions of Cadoret and Winokur (Chapter 4 in Sperber and Jarvik, 1976), as well as my own synthesis of earlier models up to, but not including, that of Gershon et al. (1975). The heterogeneity is seen as involving several different gene pools, represented arbitrarily as the three "genotypes" at the top of the diagram. Space is provided at the side of the figure for *independent factors* (environmental, modifying-gene related, and so on), which not only influence the manifestations of the various genotypes (if indeed there is more than one) but under certain circumstances may suffice to "cause" serious depression in and of themselves.

A second comprehensive model has been elaborated recently by Gershon, Baron, and Leckman (1975). Their schema is built on threshold models of genetic factors in all-or-none disease states elaborated by Falconer, T. Reich, Kidd, Matthysse, and others (see Reich, Cloninger, and Guze, 1975; Matthysse and Kidd, 1976).

In a threshold model, "a variable liability to a disorder is postulated, to which genetic and independent factors may contribute. If the net liability crosses a threshold, the disorder becomes manifest" (Gershon et al., 1975, p. 301). How such a model might operate in the case of the affective disorders is illustrated in Figure 6–4, which was designed originally to accommodate a single-major-gene theory. In this model, the mean liability for the homozygous normal individual (M_{AA}, as it touches the [horizontal] liability axis) is well beneath that associated with the threshold (T_{aff}) for even mild affective disorder. Between this lower threshold and a second threshold for bipolar disorders (T_{bp}) is the liability region associated with recurrent depression and other varieties of unipolar disorder. A small percentage of each kind of homozygote and a large percentage of heterozygotes occupy this region. Similarly, the few heterozygotes whose overall liability exceeds the threshold for bipolar illness will have a bipolar rather than unipolar disorder. Note how this two-threshold model could be made to accommodate the situation where bipolar probands often have a few unipolar relatives and vice versa. This has customarily been ascribed to heterogeneity. The Kidd model, on the other hand, is the outgrowth of a theory in which unipolar and bipolar illnesses represent positions on a continuum of liability. Greater liability tends to manifest itself as a bipolar disorder, lesser liability as a unipolar disorder. Since "independent factors" include certain genes unrelated to the gene(s) responsible for affective disorder, plus various environmental influences, differences in their quantitative strength from one person to another will help account for why some "recessive" individuals are only mildly ill or why certain heterozygotes are severely (and bipolarly) affected.

Gershon and his colleagues applied their formulae to data derived from analysis of the relatives of seventy affective (BP and UP) patients and of seventy-five normal controls. Using a two-threshold solution, as exempli-

Figure 6–4. Parameters of a Single-Major-Locus Model of Affective-Disorder Transmission

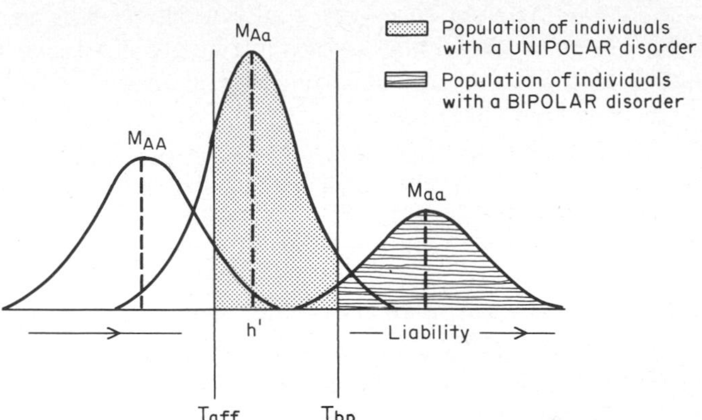

M_{AA} = mean liability value for the homozygous normal
M_{Aa} = mean liability value for the heterozygote
M_{aa} = mean liability value for the homozygous affected
T_{aff} = threshold for all affective disorder (i.e., least amount of liability that will still induce manifest affective disorder)
T_{bp} = threshold for bipolar disorders (i.e., liability at or above this level will induce an affective disorder of the bipolar type)
h' = the liability value associated with the mean of the heterozygote group

SOURCE: Adapted from the modification of Kidd's model by Gershon et al. (1975).

fied by Figure 6–4, a recessive single-major-gene theory could be accommodated. If a third threshold for "related disorders" was added, results were suggestive of a partially dominant gene. The "related disorders" included persons with cyclothymic personality, moderate depression, or certain hard-to-classify conditions to which Gershon applied the label "undiagnosed major psychiatric disorder" (see Welner et al., 1973). I suspect that many of these "related disorders" are to be found in patients with borderline structure. If so, the genetic models under discussion may prove to have explanatory value not only in relation to mild forms of depression, and so on, in families of BP or UP probands but also in the realm of patients with borderline structure (a good many of whom have large numbers of relatives with major affective disorders: see Chapter 2).

Gershon et al. (1975) further analyzed their data with regard to how well these data fit with the expected prevalences predicted by a polygenic system (with both two and three thresholds). When the prevalences of UP and

BP disorders in sibs, parents, and children of UP and BP probands were set beside the prevalences expected in a single-major-locus (SML) model or in a multifactorial (MD) model, agreement was satisfactory in most particulars. The upshot of the Gershon study was that, at least at the time, neither an SML or a polygenic model could be ruled out:

> Multifactorial or single major locus models of inheritance can acount for the family history differences of probands with BP and UP disorders, and for the prevalence of related disorders in the same families, without [having to invoke] separate genetic diathesis [i.e., heterogeneity]. (1975, p. 311)

When one sifts through available evidence from other quarters, in an effort to decide which model is more likely to be correct, still neither one emerges as clearly superior. The above-mentioned observation (that a two-threshold SML solution presented a *recessive* gene) favors a polygenic model. If this were so, BP and UP probands would have an "a-a" genotype and "would be expected to have the same proportion of BP and UP disorders in their relatives" (Gershon et al., 1975, p. 311). But as Gershon mentions, most reports have shown different prevalences of BP and UP relatives of the two types of probands.

Since no firm choice between these modes of inheritance can be made on the basis of family studies alone—until huge and systematic regional surveys can be carried out—one must look to biochemical and neurophysiological studies for support of one or another hypothesis. In the following section, data on a number of proposed "markers," relevant to the models in question, are summarized.

Biochemical and Neurophysiological Markers in Affective Disorders

In the two comprehensive schemata for affective-disorder inheritance, we have noted that the earlier model pictured depression and mania as moving in opposite directions from some neutral starting point. The Gershon model pictures unipolar depression as corresponding to intermediate levels of combined genetic/environmental liability (i.e., between the threshold for "all" affective disorders and that for bipolar) and bipolar depression as occurring at higher levels of liability. This unidirectional view of the affective disorders has certain advantages at the clinical level, whatever its merits from a genetic/biochemical standpoint. Agitated depression, for example, is seen usually in a unipolar rather than bipolar population, yet the restlessness and irritability are reminiscent of mania. Accompanying full-blown mania is often dysphoria (rather than the euphoria of lesser degrees of mania), which begins to remind one of the depressive. Gershon's model can accommodate these apparently paradoxical observations more readily than a model in which depression and mania are seen only as opposites.

It is at this point that one looks to evidence from external sources for support. A number of "markers" have been proposed, mostly over the past ten years, as of relevance to various taxonomic problems posed by the affective disorders. Several in each category are enumerated in Table 6–2, which offers a representative, though not exhaustive, sampling. Some of the proposed markers yield data compatible with Gershon's monotonic theory; others tend to favor the earlier "dichotomous" model. Gershon's own work with others of his colleagues at the National Institute for Mental Health (namely, Murphy et al., 1971) has, for example, shown that administration of L-dopa provokes hypomania if given to bipolar-I patients; this does not occur with unipolar patients, but a bipolar-II group shows an intermediate response. These outcomes suggest that the three forms are all on a continuum. A similar impression emerges from the work of Bunney, Goodwin, et al. (1972) on the "switch process" (from one state to another) in manic-depressive illness. Excretion of certain catecholamine metabolites (namely, 3-methoxy 4-hydroxyphenylglycol—MHPG) also appeared to

TABLE 6–2

Proposed Markers in the Affective Disorders

	Findings in	
	Unipolar Patients	*Bipolar Patients*
A. NEUROPHYSIOLOGICAL		
1. Visually evoked cortical response (Buchsbaum et al., 1971)	Reduction	Augmentation
2*a*. REM latency during EEG sleep study (Kupfer, 1967)	Shortened	Shortened
2*b*. Time spent asleep (Kupfer and Foster, 1972)	Discontinuous or decreased in unipolar depressives	Unchanged or increased in bipolar depressives
B. DRUG RESPONSE		
1. Antidepressant effect of lithium (F. K. Goodwin et al., 1971)	In 40%	In 80%
2. Manic response to L-dopa administration (Murphy et al., 1971)	None	Marked

TABLE 6–2 **(Cont.)**

Proposed Markers in the Affective Disorders

	Findings in	
	Unipolar Patients	*Bipolar Patients*
C. BIOCHEMICAL		
1. 17-OH corticosteroid excretion (Dunner et al., 1972)	Normal	Diminished
2. Dopamine turnover after probenecid, as measured via homovanillic acid excretion (Dunner, 1971)	Mildly increased	Moderately to markedly increased
3. Erythrocyte catecholamine O-methyltransferase activity (Cohn et al., 1970)*	Reduced (females only)	Only mildly reduced (females only)
4. Growth hormone secretion after insulin-induced hypoglycemia (Garver et al., 1975)	—	Diminished
5. Excretion of 3-methoxy 4-hydroxyphenylglycol (MHPG) (Schildkraut, 1965; Maas et al., 1968; Himwich, 1971; DeLeon-Jones et al., 1975)	Diminished	Slightly more diminished than in UPs
6. Platelet-monoamine-oxidase activity (Murphy and Weiss, 1972)	Normal	Diminished

*In a Jerusalem-based study, Belmaker and Ebstein (1977) noted that erythrocyte COMT was increased in manic patients rather than decreased, as in Cohn's study.

Dunner, Levitt, et al. (1977) have, however, questioned the previous reports of altered COMT activity in affectively ill patients. In their study no overall differences were noted in mean activity between affective-disorder patients and controls; no significant differences were noted between the sexes. The authors believed their findings (1) reflected variation in patient samples and (2) suggested that COMT could not be considered a reliable marker in primary affective illness.

NOTE: Of the nearly one dozen markers mentioned in the table, not all are of equal promise as potential discriminators between affective and nonaffective disorders (or between different forms of affective disorders). At the time of this writing the most reliable and valid discriminator in the realm of depressive disorders is *decreased REM latency* (time from onset of sleep to onset of the first REM period) in depressed patients. Other findings stemming from electroencephalographic sleep studies in depressed subjects include decreased sleep time, reduced sleep efficiency, and prolonged sleep latency (Spiker, Coble, et al., 1978). These neurophysiological tests have not been applied in any systematic way to the various types of borderline patients.

vary monotonically: lower than normal in UP patients and still more diminished in BP patients (DeLeon-Jones et al., 1975; bipolar II's, however, were not studied). MHPG has been considered particularly promising as an index of brain catecholamine metabolism. This compound has been identified as a major metabolite, specifically of norepinephrine (NE) and normetanephrine (NM). Over half of brain NE and NM appears to be metabolized as MHPG (Maas, Fawcett, et al., 1968; Schildkraut, 1971). Although lowered MHPG excretion could come about from changes in the body pool of NE, this finding in depressed persons has been taken as supportive of the catecholamine hypothesis of the affective disorders as elaborated by Schildkraut (1965). The particularly pronounced decrease in MHPG excretion among bipolar patients has inspired some optimism that assay of this metabolite may help distinguish those depressed patients who will ultimately have—but have not as yet had—their first manic episode from a ("true") UP group not destined to have manic episodes.

In 1972 Murphy and Weiss reported their results from a study of platelet-monoamine-oxidase (MAO) activity in depressed patients. Whereas unipolar patients exhibited values similar to the controls, average activity in their twenty-three bipolar patients was reduced. Five of the bipolar patients showed values lower than the lowest noted in any of the controls or unipolar patients. It is still too early to say, as the authors noted, whether this test can reliably discriminate between the two types of depressive illness, whether MAO reduction is secondary to other psychobiological differences, or whether it represents a difference of primary etiological significance. One needs also to consider the possibility, raised by Matthysse (1977), that the five patients with the extremely low MAO activity exemplify genetic *heterogeneity*—in the sense that reduced activity of MAO may be of primary significance in a specific subgroup of severely depressed patients but not in the group as a whole (see the work of Buchsbaum, p. 154).

More equivocal are the results of 17-OH corticosteroid excretion (Dunner, Goodwin, Gershon, et al., 1972), where bipolars tended to show diminished levels, unipolars normal levels, and bipolar-II patients levels that were either normal (in males) or higher than normal (in females).

Average cortical responses evoked by photic stimulation, on the other hand, tended to move in opposite directions (Buchsbaum, Goodwin, et al., 1971). Bipolar patients, in either phase of their illness, showed *augmentation,* that is, greater rates of average evoked response (AER) amplitude with increasing light intensity. Unipolar patients often showed *reduction* (decreasing amplitude of AER).

At this stage of our knowledge one cannot determine which of several competing theories of affective-disorder transmission is valid, or, if more than one is valid, which covers the greatest number of clinical situations.

Part of the controversy hinges on the views of "lumpers" versus those of "splitters" (see McKusick, 1973). The model of Cadoret and Winokur envisions an array of genetically separable disorders: UP versus BP forms, early versus late onset types in each compartment, and so on. The model of Gershon, Baron, and Leckman (1975) is a unifying theory capable of embracing most of the variety in affective disorders, with only minimal dependence on heterogeneity, and so forth, to account for disorders not otherwise integrated into their models. All existing theories, however, show promise of being able to demonstrate true kinship between at least some, and perhaps a good deal, of what is now diagnosed as *borderline* (structurally or phenomenologically) and the more serious and easily categorized "psychoses." It may soon be possible to test borderline patients with some of the suggested markers in Table 6–2. This will of course be easier to do with the hospitalized patients; the ambulatory borderline patients, especially those in intensive psychotherapy, are not readily approached for the requisite laboratory tests.

Some of the markers mentioned in Table 6–2 have been investigated enough (or almost enough) to permit concentration on the borderline or even on the unsuspected case, from which one can try to work backwards toward the more severe forms of illness. Such, at any rate, is the ingenious strategy of Buchsbaum (1977), who tested platelet MAO in 400 college students not initially known to suffer from emotional disturbances. MAO activity values formed a "normal" bell curve. Subjects with the lowest 10 percent and highest 10 percent of all values were then recalled for further testing. MMPI material was obtained, analysis of which revealed that subjects with *more* than three MMPI subscores in the range of 70 or above were distributed almost exclusively in the *lower* platelet-MAO group (eight out of thirty-seven) whereas only one out of thirty-two *high*-platelet-MAO subjects had MMPIs with that degree of abnormality. Upon further questioning it turned out that several of the low-MAO, abnormal-MMPI subjects had already sought psychotherapy and one had made a suicide attempt. Even more intriguing: when those same students were considered as probands in a family study, their close relatives had a higher rate of suicide attempts (3.56 percent) than did relatives of the high-MAO students (0.31 percent). Evoked cortical response testing of the low-MAO probands whose relatives had made suicide attempts indicated that these probands were for the most part "augmenters." Analysis of personality organization of these vulnerable students was not made, so we do not know whether any were borderline according to structural criteria. Also much time will have to elapse before it becomes clear which of these high-risk individuals go on to develop full-blown affective disorders, which become borderline patients of the "cycloid" variety, and which remain relatively healthy despite their apparent manic-depressive diathesis.

Afterword: Toward a Synthesis of the Data on the Genetic Factor in the Major Psychoses

It would appear, from the data we have reviewed, that both the schizophrenias and the group of affective psychoses, in their clinically most unambiguous forms, are manifestations of two distinct sets of genetic influences. These influences in and of themselves are seldom capable of altering the nervous system in such a way that eventual psychosis becomes inevitable. Presumably, in the absence of such influences the same stresses which precipitate specific psychoses in the vulnerable will either be handled adequately or may set in motion a psychiatric disorder of a different type.

Earlier models of transmission—in both the schizophrenic and the affective realm—were based on the notion of one, or at most a few, abnormal genes whose presence acted as a necessary but not sufficient cause of eventual decompensation. There was a tendency to speak of genetic and environmental influences in such a manner that their respective percentages "added up" to 100. Their relative importance was equated with the degree to which MZ twins, as a group, were either concordant or discordant. While available data are compatible, for both types of psychosis, with either a single-major-locus (SML) or a polygenic model, most investigators would now regard the "additive" approach, emphasizing genetic *versus* environmental, as simplistic. Instead, as Cancro (1975) has underlined, it is more meaningful to speak of both genetic and environmental influences as essential, simultaneously. Certain combinations of these—for the most part separate—streams of influence conspire to precipitate the illnesses to which we affix one or another of the traditional labels.

The more "correct" an SML model turned out to be (for either or both conditions), the more analogous would that condition be to the inborn errors of metabolism encountered in traditional medicine, and the more rewarding would be the search for a reliable genetic marker. As we have seen, there is still much ambiguity in this area: many markers have been called; few have been chosen. One cannot even say whether our most sophisticated theories have thus far not been crowned by discovery of the relevant endophenotype—because the theories themselves are pitifully oversimplified (or wide of the mark) or because we can as yet assay only distantly related materials (blood, urine, cerebrospinal fluid [CSF]) where the truth of the theories remains obscured in equivocal results.

If, on the other hand, a polygenic model were to emerge as valid, we would be inclined to reorient our thinking about the psychoses, viewing them as stemming from accumulations of liability, beyond a particular threshold, in persons who already began life as *predisposed* by virtue of possessing more risk genes than would be found in the majority of the population. Depending on the combination of interacting genetic and independent factors specific for each given individual, some persons with excessive risk genes would remain clinically "normal," and some would soon begin to exhibit behavior that deviated in the direction of either (or both) major psychoses. Cancro's remark (1975, p. 357) that the polygenic approach "makes the phenotypic characteristics continuous and not dichotomous" may be correct in the main, but as we have seen from the work of Matthysse and Kidd, there would probably be a small percentage of individuals so burdened with risk genes that psychosis is inevitable. Such individuals would inhabit a region of a "continuum" where it would be correct, from a practical if not from a semantic standpoint, to speak of a dichotomy.

If a polygenic system were composed of genes no one of which could provoke serious illness by itself, we would have a situation where the necessary but not sufficient genetic factor harked back to an aggregate of genes belonging nonetheless to a system that was otherwise part of normal endowment. In such a model "normal" behavior might be the end product of several combinations: (*a*) the possession of very few "risk" genes plus a nurturing or only mildly disadvantageous environment, (*b*) a moderate number of risk genes and a highly favorable environment, and so on. Conditions characterized by borderline psychic organization could arise from a complementary series of interacting factors, namely, (*a*) moderate loading with risk genes plus mildly to moderately unfavorable environment in the presence of average intelligence or (*b*) fairly severe genetic loading, high intelligence, moderately unfavorable environment, and so on.

Inasmuch as healthy adaptation depends on relative normality of mood and of those mental functions related to synthesis (the "synthetic function"), boundary sense, and the like, it would seem fair to assume that ordinary people harbor genes related to both these broad systems. One system, when it goes awry, underlies schizophrenia; the other—in its highly deviant states—the affective psychoses. For the sake of convenience we might label one system "S"—for synthesis[10]—and the other "M"—for mood.[11] We usually regard the psychoses from the sick end of the spectrum. Normality, scarcely visible from this vantage point, like a distant star, is experienced as a thing apart—no more kindred to the psychoses than the star is, in our commonsensical impressions, to the vast

[10]While I have advocated the notion that disturbances in boundary sense and mental synthesis constitute the essence of schizophrenia, I hope I have given a fair hearing to other (often closely related) hypotheses, such as that espoused by Cancro, who stresses an *attentional* defect:

> "In my clinical judgment, the critical phenotypes (for schizophrenia) can be conceptualized best as parameters of attention. Those traits which can be thought of as regulating attention, I expect, will be the ones which are involved in the vulnerability to a schizophrenic disorder" (1975, p. 358).

[11]Again, one could have chosen the notion of energy regulation or of *responsivity* to stimuli.

expanse of intervening space. But if one views behavior from the normal end of the spectrum, schizophrenia, the affective psychoses, their borderline variants, and their mixed states will appear comprehensibly related to ordinary behavior, just as the erstwhile dissimilar entities—star, cosmic dust, and space—can be understood as thicker or thinner collections of small particles.

Since nature has no vested interest in whether we view some of her manifestations from a differential or from an integrative standpoint, we cannot speak here so much of absolute truth—as of utility. It will be clear to any reader who has persevered with me to this point that I find it eminently practical in many clinical situations to understand borderline psychopathology as occupying (1) a region within the continuum of system S, (2) a region within the continuum M, and (3) a region where S and M intersect. The latter relates to individuals, some (but not all) of whom probably have moderately high loading in both systems. This may be one of the avenues leading to the so-called schizoaffective disorders (see Chapter 5).

To illustrate these viewpoints I have constructed a diagram (Figure 6–5) in which the S and M spectra are combined, allowing the representation of

Figure 6–5. A Hypothetical Genotypic Continuum (of Tendencies to Schizophrenic and Affective Psychoses)

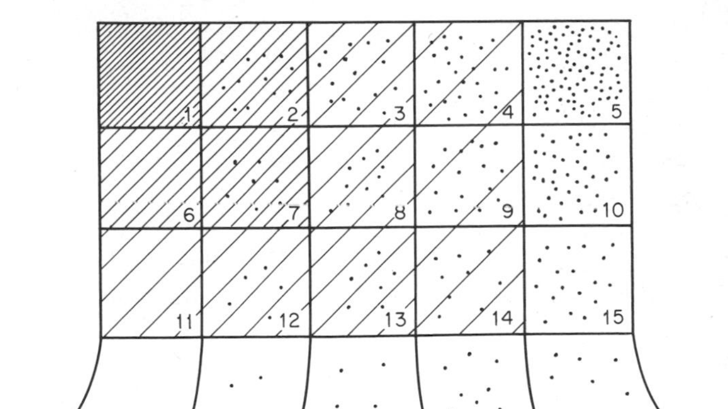

Relative strength of the tendency toward a schizophrenic psychosis

Relative strength of the tendency toward an affective psychosis

EXAMPLES: Region 1—High loading for schizophrenia only
Region 3—High loading for both schizophrenic and affective disorders
Region 5—High loading for an affective psychosis only

all possible "pure" states of either system as well as all degrees of admixture. The diagram, emphasizing genotypes, assumes, for the purposes of simplification, that S and M are both polygenic systems.[12]

Loading above a certain threshold may be associated with severely disturbed and continuously psychotic individuals. Loading just under that threshold may be expressed in adult life with a borderline syndrome of schizophrenic flavor ("schizotypic" borderline), or of affective coloration, as the case may be. Beneath still another threshold—one serving to demarcate the normal from the deviant population—one no longer speaks of psychopathology at all. Here, both polygenic systems are compatible with normal adaptation.

Persons in whom one system is compatible with normality may develop symptoms because of marked abnormality in the other. In this case, the clinical manifestation may be a "pure" disorder of one type or the other. No extra load of risk genes in M, coupled with strong abnormalities in S, may predispose strongly to pure schizophrenic psychoses free of any appreciable affective signs and symptoms (apart from those considered quite in keeping with schizophrenia, such as flattening of affect). This situation is represented by the first square in Figure 6–5.

Squarc 5 represents high excess in M without abnormality in S. This situation is associated with strong predisposition to a severe affective illness without any schizophrenic coloration.

When both systems are severely out of line, a severe schizoaffective disorder may result. Square 3 contains the universe of such individuals.

Squares 6 through 10 represent intermediate examples of the same phenomena. Square 6, for instance, might contain the borderline schizophrenics of Rosenthal and Kety: persons with an abnormal S—but a normal M—system, hence no discernible mood disorder.

The next lower level, squares 11 to 15, representing barely perceptible deviations of either system, would contain persons who would seldom have psychotic episodes but who might display severe character disorders.

Beneath this structure is a foundation composed of the majority of the population; that is, persons with very little in the way of extra risk genes of either system. What had been inherited predisposition to psychopathology above this level has here melted away into the general population.

This diagram, it will be noted, is analogous to the Sz-MDP Continuum (of phenotypes) presented in Chapter 2. Figure 6–5 is designed to show more graphically the abnormal states of the two systems. Degrees of severity are indicated along the vertical dimension (with greatest severity along the top row); degrees of admixture of risk genes of the two systems are

[12]In this chapter we have seen how Gershon could account for a continuum of affective disorders even within the context of a two-threshold, single-major-locus model of transmission.

shown along the horizontal dimension. The normal system S and its abnormal counterpart, schizophrenia, occupy the left side of the diagram; M and its abnormal counterpart, the affective disorders, the right side.

Patients with *borderline structure* will have genic combinations that for the most part will map onto regions 7 through 15. Of course, those patients whose borderline structure is the end product of largely nongenetic influences (minimal brain damage, brutalizing early environment, and so on) would be located in the unnumbered, genetically "normal" region of the diagram.

In the final diagram of this synopsis (Figure 6–6) I have attempted to portray the complexities of interaction between specific genetic factors and independent (environmental plus nonspecific genetic) factors. Cancro underlined the fact that "a given genotype has the potential for a number of possible phenotypic outcomes (phenoptions)" (1975), as exemplified by identical twins discordant for, say, schizophrenia. Discordant twins are, to use other terms, isogenic but not isophenic. Such a pair might be represented in Figure 6–6 by Route A—which can branch off into obvious schiz-

Figure 6–6. Interaction of Genetic and Nongenetic Factors

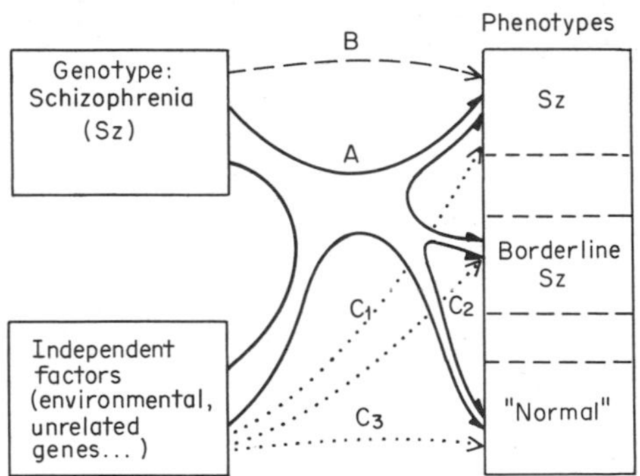

NOTE: *Route A:* The ordinary situation in which schizophrenia (Sz) results from interaction of specific adverse genetic loading plus sufficient adverse independent factors to push the combined liability above the Sz threshold (upper right limb). Less severe combinations are associated with borderline or even asymptomatic states.

Route B: Risk genes are so abundant that risk for Sz is 99%; eventual breakdown is inevitable even in the midst of high intelligence, good environment, and so on: independent factors are largely irrelevant.

Route C: Independent factors are so abysmal or "somatic" illness is of such a type (CNS tumor, lupus cerebritis, and so on) that a phenocopy of Sz arises (route C_1). There is no extra burden of risk genes. If these nonspecific factors are less severe, milder conditions may ensue (route C_2) or the phenotypic derivative may be symptom free (route C_3).

ophrenia, or, given different environmental and other factors, into a borderline realm (or even into quasinormality). The converse of this situation is the common one in which isophenic individuals are shown to be not necessarily isogenic. The diagram contains, for example, three routes to overt schizophrenia. Two of these (A and B) relate to individuals with excess risk genes for this particular psychosis. But Route C designates a phenocopy. The diagram happens, again for reasons of simplicity, to concentrate on schizophrenia, but could have served as well to illustrate the situation of the affective disorders. Clinical mania, to cite one instance, can stem from high loading for bipolar illness but can also represent a manifestation of tertiary lues.

CHAPTER 7

Genetic Factors in Borderline Conditions

Sincc psychogenetic research has customarily concentrated on paradigmatic cases of whatever disorder is under study, most reports have dealt with severe and mild conditions present in relatives of comparatively ill index cases. There is not much material on the relatives of "borderline" cases, since the homogeneity of the proband group would be problematical at best. In addition the frequency and intensity of illness in their relatives might very well be too low to permit good detection of all those in whom genetic predisposition might, under ideal circumstances, be demonstrable. Despite these difficulties, some investigations have been carried out, working backwards, as it were, from the borderline cases to the paradigm cases they might belong to.

Some of the earlier "borderline" concepts did, as we have seen, define a small area quite within the realm of schizophrenia. That was so with Zilboorg's, Federn's, and Bychowski's particular variety of borderline cases. Information about the close relatives of their cases was spotty and not very detailed, although they sometimes made passing references to schizophrenic or psychotic individuals in the families. Whether meticulous and blind ratings of these relatives would have turned up individuals with disorders confined mostly to the schizophrenic realm is an unanswerable question.

Kasanin's "schizoaffective" patients may have been a mixed group with respect to the major psychoses: one had two manic-depressed relatives and was himself (in my opinion) much nearer the manic-depressive end of the psychosis spectrum (clinically speaking) than to the schizophrenic. That patient had depression with periods of manic excitement; during the latter he had delusions about God and experiences of thought insertion. Another two of Kasanin's patients had hebephrenic or paranoid-schizophrenic relatives.

Stern, whose 1938 article does not offer case histories, mentions only that some of the mothers of his borderline patients were "neurotic or psychotic." Depression or melancholia was noted in so many of Stern's patients that his borderline group seemed nearer the depressive pole than Kasanin's patients.

Four of Deutsch's five "as if" cases had psychotic relatives, none described in detail. One patient had a "catatonic" brother.

Grinker and his colleagues (1968), seemingly unimpressed by the possibility of a strong genetic factor in borderline conditions, offered little data about family pedigrees in their monograph.

Apart from the psychogeneticists, investigators who have contributed to elucidation of the borderline realm have cast their nets wide, capturing a rather heterogeneous population. Small wonder that they have not been impressed by the issue of hereditary predisposition. Those who have believed themselves to be describing variants of schizophrenia (Zilboorg, Kasanin, H. Deutsch, and so on) have been more attentive to this element. The earlier psychoanalytic writers were more methodical about clinical description and family history than their colleagues of the 1950s and 1960s.

Quite recently Procci has reviewed the family and genetic studies of patients labeled "schizoaffective." Over the past ten years about a dozen such reports have all inclined toward the impression that patients with a poor outcome have a higher proportion of relatives with schizophrenia than with affective illness and that the opposite is true with the good-outcome group (see also Chapter 5).

With respect to genetic studies on patients who have been categorized as "borderline," whether according to the definitions of Knight, Kernberg, Grinker, or Gunderson, little material has thus far been collected systematically—a preliminary report of my own (Stone, 1977a) and the excellent review of Siever and Gunderson (1978).

Before discussing contemporary data in detail, it will be helpful to show what correspondence exists, in a rough and general way, between the various terms denoting "borderline" conditions and the factors of hereditary or constitutional predisposition. Table 7–1 is based on case descriptions by twenty-nine different investigators, listed chronologically. I assessed the nature and relative strengths of the antecedent factors on the basis of the more complete case presentations, especially those where comments about psychiatrically ill family members were included in the anamnesis. Cases were then assigned to the schizophrenic cell (Sz) or to the affective (MDP) according to the degree to which modern diagnostic criteria would have been satisfied or closely approximated.

It will be noted that, despite the close kinship of Knight's cases to the schizophrenia spectrum disorders, Knight wished to divest the term "borderline" of its associations with the diagnosis of schizophrenia. Interestingly, as can be seen from Table 7–1, the trend in usage among clinicians since his 1954 paper has been to define "borderline" in such a way that it ends up in the penumbra of the manic-depressive disorders. Still, the heterogeneity of the underlying factors will be readily apparent with respect to the modern usages of "borderline." It is probably no coincidence that the popularity of this term, and its uncoupling from the concept of schizophrenia, began shortly after the introduction of the potent neuroleptic drugs: over the past two decades these agents have done much both to restore equilibrium to psychotic patients and to attenuate the symptoms by which they were once so easily categorized.

Because the term "borderline" is used in a variety of ways, rational discussion of any genetic factor requires that we specify carefully at the outset the taxonomic boundaries of the particular "borderline" condition we are evaluating. "Borderline schizophrenia," as used by Kety, Rosenthal, et al. (1968), describes a very different patient sample from that covered by Kernberg's "borderline personality organization." The relative positions of the more important borderline regions, with respect to the Sz-

TABLE 7–1

Underlying Factors in Borderline Cases

Author	*Date*	*Term Proposed*	*Contributing Factors*			
			Heredity		*Other*	
			Sz	*MDP*	*Env.*	*Org.*
Clark	1919	Borderland neurosis	+	+		
Moore	1921	Borderline; parataxis		+		
Wilhelm Reich	1925	Impulsive character	+		+	
Oberndorf	1930	Borderline	+	+		
Glover	1932	Incipient schizophrenia	+			
Kasanin	1933	Schizoaffective	+	+	+*	
Stern	1938	Borderline	?	+	+	
Zilboorg	1941	Ambulatory schizophrenia	+			

TABLE 7–1 **(Cont.)**

Underlying Factors in Borderline Cases

Author	Date	Term Proposed	*Contributing Factors*			
			Heredity		*Other*	
			Sz	*MDP*	*Env.*	*Org.*
H. Deutsch	1942	"As if" personality	+		+	
Rapaport, Gill, and Schafer	1945	Preschizophrenic	+			
Schmideberg	1947	Borderline	+			
Federn	1947	Latent psychosis	+			
Hoch and Polatin	1949	Pseudoneurotic schizophrenia	+	±		
Bychowski	1953	Latent schizophrenia	+			
Knight	1954	Borderline	+		+	
J. Frosch	1954	Psychotic character		+?	+	+
Ekstein	1955	Borderline schizophrenia	+			
Rado	1956	Mood cyclic or "depressive"; schizotypal	+	+		
Beck	1959	Nonpsychotic schizophrenia	+			
Easser and Lesser	1965	Hysteroid		?+		
Mitsuda	1965	Atypical psychosis	+	+		
Kernberg	1967	Borderline structure	rare	+	+	
Grinker et al.	1968	Borderline	±	+		
Kety et al.	1968	Borderline schizophrenia	+			
D. Klein	1969	Hysteroid dysphoria		+		+
Mahler	1971	Borderline	?			+†
Aarkrog	1973	Borderline psychosis	+			
Gunderson	1975	Borderline personality disorder	±	+		
Spitzer, Endicott, and Gibbons	1979	Schizotypal borderline personality	+			
		Unstable borderline personality		+		

Key: Sz = schizophrenia
MDP = manic-depressive psychosis
Env. = adverse environment (namely, death of a parent, chaotic home, parental neglect, parental brutality, and so on)
Org. = minimal brain damage or other organic factors
\+ = case histories strongly suggest this factor has played an etiological role
± = evidence from review of cases only slightly positive for this factor
? = only questionable evidence this factor played an etiological role
* = "severe situational stress"
† = developmental arrest

MDP continuum, are portrayed in Chapter 2; the criteria of the currently popular usages are set forth in Chapter 9. Methodical family studies have not been done for every variety of borderline condition—in fact, only for a few. Preliminary surveys have been done for some of the others. We will examine this material in relation to two broad bands of usage: "borderline" as a dilute form of a more serious condition with well-established genetic underpinnings (schizophrenia, primary affective disorder) and "borderline" as the label for a clinical syndrome, as defined by a number of investigators (Gunderson, Kernberg, and so forth).

Borderline Schizophrenia

Kety, Rosenthal, and Wender, in cooperation with Schulsinger and his co-workers at Kommune-Hospitalet in Copenhagen, completed a study of mental illness in the biological and adoptive families of adoptive schizophrenics (1968). Since they needed to use rigid research criteria for the diagnosis of schizophrenia for their index cases, in order to maximize the homogeneity of their starting group, they realized that "a system of classification with finer gradations would be needed . . . in making diagnostic evaluations of the relatives" (p. 352); this system allowed the researchers to classify in some fashion every relative with a record of mental illness or behavioral aberration, without having to reject those not fitting already existing categories.

Eventually Kety et al. were able to evaluate the ill relatives of those index cases who just failed to meet research diagnostic criteria for schizophrenia, from which investigation they came to "recognize the existence of a group similar in quality to the borderline schizophrenic but of considerably less intensity." This group came closest in form to the "inadequate personality" of the standard nomenclature.

Two varieties of "borderline" were acknowledged: an *acute* (as opposed to chronic) schizophrenic reaction and a *borderline* state.

Characteristics of the first group included (1) relatively good premorbid adjustment, (2) rapid onset of illness with clear-cut precipitants, (3) Bleulerian signs in the relative absence of productive signs (i.e., absence of hallucinations or delusions), (4) a good posthospital course, (5) preservation of affect or even presence of affective symptoms, and (6) brevity of episode with good drug response. This was their "B-2" type of borderline patient, which corresponded to various phrases already in use such as "acute undifferentiated schizophrenic reaction," "schizoaffective psychosis," and so on. The similarity of this group to Kasanin's cases will be readily apparent.

Kety's "B-3" (borderline state) cases were more chronically ill. Here the clinical picture resembled the descriptions of pseudoneurotic schizophrenia, ambulatory schizophrenia, "psychotic character," severe schizoid state, or the "stably unstable" borderline of Schmideberg. The characteristics of the B-3 borderline schizophrenic are outlined in Table 7–2. Kety and his colleagues did not specify how many items from which subgroups were necessary in order to establish the diagnosis of (B-3) borderline schizophrenia; the diagnosis rested on clinical judgment. More recently, Spitzer and his collaborators, in conjunction with Kety, have attempted to objectify this diagnosis in a more precise fashion (see Chapter 9 for the features of Spitzer's "schizotypal borderline personality").

TABLE 7–2

Clinical Features of the Borderline Schizophrenic (B-3 Type)

1. THINKING:	Strange or atypical mentation; thoughts show tendency to ignore reality, logic, and experience. . . . Fuzzy, murky, vague speech.
2. EXPERIENCE:	Brief episodes of cognitive distortion*; feelings of depersonalization, of strangeness or unfamiliarity with or toward the familiar; micropsychosis.
3. AFFECTIVE:	Anhedonia; no deep or intense involvement with anyone.
4. INTERPERSONAL BEHAVIOR:	May appear poised but lacking in depth ("as if" personality); sexual adjustment characterized by chaotic fluctuation, mixture of hetero- and homosexuality.
5. PSYCHOPATHOLOGY:	Multiple neurotic manifestations which shift frequently (obsessive concerns, phobias, conversion, psychosomatic symptoms, and so on); severe widespread anxiety.

*Sometimes resembling the "overvalued ideas" of Hoch and Polatin (1949) or Kernberg (1967).

SOURCE: From Kety, Rosenthal, Wender, and Schulsinger (1968, p. 352).

In their 1968 paper, Kety et al. reported on findings in the biological and adoptive relatives (parents and sibs) of thirty-three schizophrenic adoptees and a like number of controls. The breakdown of their results is shown in Table 7–3.

From Table 7–3, it is clear that both the chronic (B-1) and borderline (B-3) probands had a fair number of borderline schizophrenics among their close biological relatives. This number, if one included uncertain cases plus

TABLE 7–3

Affected Biological Relatives of Thirty-three Schizophrenic Adoptees

Diagnosis in the Index Cases	*N =*	*Number of Biological Relatives*	*Diagnosis in Affected Biological Relatives*					
			B-1	*B-2*	*B-3*	*C*	*D-1*	*D-3*
B-1 (chronic)Sz	16	82	1	0	3	1	0	3
B-2 (acute)Sz	7	30	0	0	0	0	0	0
B-3 (borderline)Sz	10	38	0	0	3	1	1	0

Key: C = inadequate personality
D-1 = uncertain chronic schizophrenia
D-3 = uncertain borderline schizophrenia

SOURCE: From Kety, Rosenthal, Wender, and Schulsinger (1968, pp. 354–355).

"inadequate personality," was significantly greater (twelve) than that observed among the adoptive relatives (two) or among the control group's biological (three) or adoptive (three) relatives. No such excess of B-1 and B-3 schizophrenia was observed among the biological relatives of the seven "acute schizophrenic" probands. The authors felt justified in concluding that borderline schizophrenia, as they were defining it, belonged quite properly in the penumbra of unequivocal "chronic" schizophrenia. The presence of either in an index case predicted an excess of either in the close relatives. This homogeneity did not extend to the B-2 type, "acute" schizophrenia. The latter, not accompanied by an excess of B-1 or B-3 relatives, appeared genetically unrelated to "true" schizophrenia.

The question arises, How far out does the schizophrenic spectrum extend? Beyond borderline schizophrenia, for example, is a still more shadowy area where one encounters character disorders, delinquency, and suicides. All were found in excess of the expected among the relatives of the B-1/B-3 index cases. In Heston's study (1966), it will be recalled (Chapter 3), there was a distinct excess of "neurotic personalities" among the adopted-away offspring of schizophrenic mothers as compared with the offspring of normal mothers. Should the schizophrenic spectrum be stretched to include the psychoneuroses? Probably it is wisest to use borderline schizophrenia as the cutoff point, lest one inflate both the experimental and the control groups with false positives. Allen (1976) has drawn attention to a possible cultural factor: genetic vulnerability to schizophrenia seemed to express itself phenotypically as "borderline schizophrenia" in the Danish studies, whereas comparable American studies turned up larger numbers of delinquents.

One of the drawbacks of the otherwise elegant adoption strategy is that, even with the help a national registry, one must settle for relatively small numbers. Certain correlations that might be valid, were larger numbers available, remain undiscovered or unconfirmed. The chronic schizophrenic probands of the Kety study, for example, had among their relatives both chronic and borderline schizophrenics—but only *one* chronic (B-1) individual. The B-3 probands had B-3 relatives but no B-1 relatives. As Siever and Gunderson have argued (1978), from the sample of B-3s *alone,* there was no evidence for genetic relatedness to chronic schizophrenia; the likelihood of such relatedness was supported only by the mixed B-1 and B-3 relatives of the B-1 probands. One could claim that "borderline schizophrenia" breeds true and is a separate entity—or perhaps that *heterogeneity* was involved—and only a percentage of B-3s are genetically related to chronic schizophrenia. Kety's results could be interpreted as (faint and only suggestive) evidence for a *severity factor:* the more "chronic" the probands, the more chronic schizophrenic relatives turn up, and vice versa. But the sample size was not large enough to permit a convincing statement to this effect. In a companion study beginning with schizophrenic parents (whose adopted-away offspring were then evaluated diagnostically), however, Rosenthal, Wender, Kety, and Schulsinger (1968) submitted evidence that did suggest such a severity factor. Though the samples were again rather small, chronic schizophrenic parents had a greater than expected number of chronic schizophrenic (B-1) children and an even larger number of B-3 children. The four B-3 parents, however, had no B-1 children, but two of the four had a B-3 child. As Siever and Gunderson mention, the results of the Rosenthal study "confirm common genetic factors in the etiology of borderline and chronic schizophrenia, but also suggest these factors are weaker in the case of the (B-3) borderlines" (p. 69).

Up till this point, psychogeneticists and family specialists have focused on chronic schizophrenia, later tallying how often "borderline" schizophrenia occurred among the relatives (namely, Lidz, Fleck, and Cornelison, 1965). Though as many as 20 percent of first-degree relatives (of chronic schizophrenics) have been considered borderline (B-3) (see Alanen, 1966), the reverse strategy—using B-3's as index cases—has been carried out only to a limited extent.

The best available evidence to date tempts one strongly to see a connection between the less equivocal ("core," "chronic," "process" and so on) form of schizophrenia and the borderline variant (as described by Kety or more recently by Spitzer et al.—see Chapter 9), at least when the borderline cases occur in close relatives of a core schizophrenic. Since a few of Gunderson's borderline (-personality disorder—see Chapter 9) cases are schizotypal clinically, some of these may also be genetically akin to core schizophrenia. But the data at hand allow for a certain latitude of interpretation—all the way from the hypothesis that B-3s and B-1s are kindred entities to the conservative viewpoint expressed by Siever and Gunderson (1979). The latter contend that persons with schizotypal (B-3-like features "may have neither a strong nor necessarily even a specific relationship to chronic schizophrenics." And one must always keep in mind that the diagnosis even of chronic schizophrenia is still a treacherous business: "most so-called schizophrenic symptoms . . . have remarkably little, if any, demonstrated validity in determining diagnosis, or prognosis" (Pope and Lipinski, 1978, p. 811). Overdiagnosis of schizophrenia and corresponding underdiagnosis of manic-depressive disorders, especially in "first-break" patients in their teens and twenties, is still a serious problem (especially in the United States: Ollerenshaw, 1973; Edwards, 1972; Cooper, Kendell, et al., 1972; Pope and Lipinski, 1978). This complicates the task of accumulating samples of diagnostically "pure" schizophrenics for genetic studies, a task that becomes even more formidable if one attempts to isolate a group of unequivocally (!) borderline schizophrenics as one's starting point.

Borderline Affective Disorder

The concept of borderline schizophrenia arose out of the attempt to describe an outer shell of conditions that were softer in their manifestation but tantalizingly similar to their more flamboyant counterparts at the core. A body of research, particularly the adoption studies we have just examined, has already begun to give some sense of definition and boundary to this otherwise hazy concept. One would suppose that, surrounding the core of bipolar and unipolar affective illness, an analogous shell of "borderline"affective disorders exists and that it would have become the object of independent study. But this has seldom been the case; the phrase "borderline affective disorder" has no currency. Instead one finds only passing references in articles not primarily devoted to this outer shell but rather to the core conditions themselves.[1] Apart from some recent remarks by David Rosenthal (1975) about a "spectrum" in the affective realm, unifying labels like "borderline" or "spectrum" affective disorder have rarely been suggested.

Yet there are many allusions in the literature to conditions that could meaningfully be viewed (from a genetic standpoint) as "borderline" with respect to primary affective illness. We have encountered several in the

[1]Recently Akiskal and his co-workers have submitted evidence that cyclothymic personality is a less rare phenomenon than was formerly thought and, furthermore, that cyclothymia could well be considered an attenuated (read *borderline*) form of manic-depression. Data were marshaled from family studies, follow-up, and (manic) response to tricyclics in support of this contention (Akiskal, Bitar, et al., 1978; Akiskal, Djenderedjian, Bollinger, et al., 1978).

In an interesting but less systematic study from Thailand, Ionescu-Tongyonk (1978) concluded that the borderline syndrome is "only the mask of atypical endogenous depression" (p. 76).

chapter devoted to the genetic aspects of manic-depressive disorders (Chapter 6). To recount these briefly: Kraepelin referred as early as 1896 to mild conditions, and later he also spoke of certain abnormal temperaments which were either the first stage of a more serious (affective) disorder or else personality disorders related, but not destined to become, "psychotic"; Kallmann spoke of "mild cyclic cases" among the relatives of manic-depressives; Kretschmer used the term "cycloid" in referring to mild instances of manic-depression; Slater believed suicides among such relatives might be included, at least tentatively, in the reckoning of concordance ratio; Winokur thought alcoholism was a spectrum affective condition. More recently, Bertelson estimated MZ concordance in the affective realm at 58 percent but added that the figure would increase to 84 percent if "schizoaffectives, cycloid personalities and suicides were also included." Cantwell and Barcai independently presented evidence that suggested a kinship between some cases of anorexia nervosa and primary affective disorder. Gershon mentioned "cyclothymic personality" and certain cases of moderate depression as worthy of inclusion within the spectrum of affective illness. He speculated that some of Welner's "undiagnosed major psychiatric disorder" cases were within the affective spectrum, a supposition later confirmed by Fard and Welner. Buchsbaum carried the notion of a "borderline" area in the affective realm to even greater levels of subtlety in drawing attention to the frequency of depression among low-platelet MAO "outliers" of a "normal" population and to the heightened risk of suicide attempts among the relatives of these outliers. Spitzer's "unstable borderline personality" seems, in large part, to describe a group of patients borderline to the primary affective disorders; the same is true for D. Klein's "hysteroid dysphoria." These entities, and their relationship to other usages of "borderline," are described in Chapter 9.

In a preliminary consanguinity study of hysteroid dysphoric (HD) probands, a high percentage of these patients were found to have first-degree relatives with serious unipolar or bipolar affective disorders (Stone, 1979a). In this study eight HD probands were culled from thirty-four consecutive borderline patients treated by the author; two additional HD patients showed neurotic structure when first seen. Nine of the probands were female. Information about first-degree relatives (of whom there were forty-four) was obtained from personal interview or anecdotal material (a "blind" technic was not carried out with this sample). Primary affective disorders were noted in eight relatives,[2] belonging to six of the probands; a seventh proband had a schizophrenic parent. There were also five alcoholic relatives; in two instances an HD proband had at least one alcoholic relative but none with unipolar or bipolar illness. If these cases were included

[2]Of the eight, six were unipolar and two, bipolar.

as "spectrum" or borderline affective disorders, then eight of the probands would have had at least one core or borderline affectively ill relative. In addition, seven of these dysphoric patients had an abnormal temperament, as defined in Chapter 10, within the affective realm (i.e., depressive, irritable, cyclothymic, or manic). None were schizoid or paranoid. These data suggest that patients satisfying D. Klein's "HD" criteria (see Chapter 9) may, in most instances, be considered borderline with respect to primary affective illness from a family-study as well as from a psychostructural viewpoint. This hypothesis will have to be further tested by means of a more controlled study using "blind" diagnosis, and so on.

One of the few reports in the literature beginning with a "borderline" affective disorder, where diagnoses of psychiatrically ill relatives were then methodically evaluated, is that of Akiskal, Djenderedjian, et al. (1977). The "borderline" condition (not referred to as such in their paper) in the probands was cyclothymic personality. Among the close relatives, a higher percentage of bipolar disorders was noted than among the controls. The authors did mention that some of the index cases had been considered "borderline" by clinical criteria (see also Akiskal, Bitar, et al., 1978).

Borderline Personality Organization

Since investigators of the genetic factor in psychiatric conditions have concentrated on the major psychoses and their (presumed) borderline variants, there has been a dearth of information bearing on the question, What kinship, if any, may exist between the psychoanalytic and clinical uses of the term "borderline" and the major entities of schizophrenia and manic-depression?

In an effort to rectify this deficiency, I undertook to examine the pedigrees of psychostructurally borderline (according to the criteria of Kernberg) patients, using patients with psychotic and neurotic structure (see Kernberg, 1967) as reference groups on either side. The results of this pilot study were analyzed for a hospitalized and a nonhospitalized group.

Hospitalized Borderline Patients

In this project, structural diagnosis was determined via consensus among three raters. Hospitalized patients are seldom neurotic in structure; the main distinction, therefore, was between borderline and psychotic. The patients had all been admitted to a unit specializing in long-term intensive psychotherapy. At any given time, about half the patients were considered borderline; forty-six consecutive admissions were used to establish the sample. There were twenty-three borderline patients; the twenty-three psychotic-structure patients served as the comparison group.

Patients in both categories were also diagnosed according to the canons of traditional classification. Relatively few fit research diagnostic criteria for schizophrenia or manic-depression, except among the psychotic-structure patients (most of whom were schizophrenic). Some of the borderline patients could also be classified as unipolar depressives; two even went on to experience their first manic episodes (within two years after initial evaluation) and were rediagnosed as bipolar. Simultaneously, a dimensional approach was also employed, using a modified version of the Cohen weighted rating scale for schizoaffective disorders (see Chapter 8). Compartmentalization into five regions, according to the Sz-MDP Continuum Diagram (see Chapter 2), was done routinely. Actually a sixth "region" (No Known Relationship to a Major Psychosis, designated "0") was also utilized; this region was occupied by two of the borderline patients. The results of this compartmentalization are shown in Table 7–4.

TABLE 7–4

Loci of Patients with Borderline and Psychotic Structures in the Sz-MDP Continuum Diagram

	Sz-MDP Region					
	I	*II*	*III*	*IV*	*V*	*0*
Psychotic patients (N = 23)	9	10	3	1	—	—
Borderline patients (N = 23)	—	—	2	3	16	2

NOTE: For explanation and definitions, see Chapter 3.

The borderline patients, as can be seen from Table 7–4, had conditions which were for the most part either classical or "spectrum" affective disorders. These were usually depressive and only rarely bipolar. The psychotic patients were mostly classical schizophrenics or else had predominantly schizophrenic schizoaffective disorders.

The two groups were comparable with respect to age, sex, and so on, as is depicted in the demographic data of Table 7–5.

Psychiatric disorders in the relatives were evaluated by a combined personal-interview/anecdotal method. Since none of the probands had children older than fifteen, the first-degree relatives consisted entirely of parents and sibs; most were available for interview. The interviews were conducted by second-year psychiatric residents who did not know the structural diagnosis of the probands. The nature of the interviews was semistructured: a list of signs and symptoms was used to insure inclusion of relevant data (the Genetic Data Sheet,[3] Figure 7–1). Affected relatives were then analyzed

[3]This form combines features of that used by Winokur et al. (1969) and Spitzer et al. (1971).

TABLE 7–5

Demographic and Family-Study Data concerning the Probands

	Structural Diagnosis	
	Psychotic	*Borderline*
N	23	23
Age range	15–29	15–35
Male:female	7:16	9:14
Socioeconomic status range*	I–III	I–III
Total number of first-degree relatives	75	91
Number of probands with at least one affected first-degree relative	15	15
Total number of affected first-degree relatives	19	23
Percentage of first-degree relatives with serious psychiatric disorders	25.3	25.3

*According to Hollingshead and Redlich (1958) and Spitzer et al. (1971).

with respect to Sz-MDP regions. Since there were hardly any schizoaffective relatives, Regions II, III, and IV were lumped together. Another category was used to include those with alcoholism or psychoses of unknown type. The numbers and percentages of these psychiatrically ill relatives are also given in Table 7–5. In each group, fifteen probands had at least one affected relative; eight did not. That is, two out of three patients in either group had at least one close relative with a serious psychiatric illness. The percentage of affected relatives compared to the total number of relatives was also the same for each group; approximately one in four was psychiatrically ill.

Allocation of affected relatives to the four categories just mentioned yielded the results shown in Table 7–6. If the relatives with alcoholism or psychoses of unknown type are put to one side for the moment and if, furthermore, the one schizoaffective relative is grouped with the affectively ill (Region V), the borderline and psychotic groups compare in the following manner: the borderline probands had no schizophrenic and eighteen affectively ill relatives; the psychotic probands had five schizophrenic and ten affectively ill relatives. This tendency for the patients with borderline structure to have fewer schizophrenic relatives (and more affectively ill relatives) appeared significant at the $p < 0.01$ level ($\chi^2 = 6.92$). This relationship held up, even if one grouped the schizoaffective relative with the Region I relatives ($\chi^2 = 4.71$; $p < 0.05$).

Figure 7–1. Genetic Data Sheet

Patient ____________ Hosp. Dx. ____________ Date of Adm. ____________ Age ______

Hosp. Ident. #____________ Sex ______ Identical Twin?: Yes ______ No ______ Birthdate ____________

Informant: ____________ Relationship to Pt.: ____________

CODE:

01 adopted
02 was hospitalized
03 had psychotherapy
04 received psychotropic drugs
05 suicided
06 made suicide attempts
07 ever incapacitated for psychiatric illness
08 affect blunting
09 agitation
10 alcoholism
11 angry affect, intense
12 anorexia nervosa
13 anxiety, marked or chronic
14 appetite poor
15 assaultive acts
16 asthma

RELATIVE	AGE	SEX	CODED ITEMS THAT APPLY	DIAGNOSIS* I	II	III	°/C
MOTHER		F					
MAT. G-M		F					
MAT. G-F		M					
MAT. SIB							
MAT. SIB							
MAT. SIB							
MAT. SIB							
OTHER MAT. RELATIVES							
FATHER		M					
PAT. G-M		F					
PAT. G-F		M					
PAT. SIB							
PAT. SIB							
PAT. SIB							
PAT. SIB							
OTHER PAT. RELATIVES							
SIBLING							
SIBLING							
SIBLING							
SIBLING							
OTHER							
OTHER							

41 hypertension
42 hypochondriasis
43 ideas of reference
44 identity disturbance
45 illusions
46 impulsivity
47 inappropriate affect
48 insight lacking
49 insomnia
50 intolerance of being alone
51 introversion
52 irritability
53 lability of affect
54 magical thinking
55 mannerisms
56 melancholia
57 memory decreased
58 obsessions
59 odd communications
60 overtalkative
61 paranoid
62 passivity feelings

17 attacks, spells
18 bulimia
19 colitis
20 compulsions
21 concentration poor
22 conversion symptoms
23 delusions
24 depressed mood
25 disoriented
26 diurnal mood variation
27 drug abuse
28 eccentric behavior or thought
29 emptiness, chronic
30 epilepsy
31 euphoria, elation
32 extraversion
33 fatigue, chronic
34 flight of ideas
35 grandiosity
36 guilt feelings (excessive)
37 hallucinations
38 hostility, pervasive
39 hyperactivity
40 hypersensitivity to criticism

*Diagnostic Code

CATEGORY I:

01:schiz. undiff'd.
02:schiz. paranoid
03:schiz. hebephr.
04:schiz. catatonic
05:schiz. latent
06:schiz. residual
07:schizoaffective
08:manic, bipolar-I
09:manic, bipolar-II
10:mania only
11:unipolar depres.
12:retardation
13:sociopathy
14:org. mental syndr.
15:alcoholism
16:other drug abuse

CATEGORY II (CHAR. TYPE):

As = Antisocial; Cy = Cyclothymic; DM = Depressive/Masochistic; Ex = Explosive; HM = Hypomanic; Hy = Hysteric; If = Infantile; In = Inadequate; Na = Narcissistic; Ob = Obsessive; PA = Passive/Aggressive; Pr = Paranoid; Sz = Schizoid

CAT. III (LEVEL/FUNCTION):

N = Normal/Neurotic
B = Borderline
P = Psychotic

63 phobias
64 premenstrual tension, severe
65 querulousness
66 reality sense altered (viz., depersonalization)
67 relatedness poor
68 restlessness
69 self-damaging acts
70 sex interest decreased
71 sex interest increased
72 social isolation
73 somatic complaints
74 speech bizarre
75 speech pushed
76 speech slowed
77 suspiciousness
78 tearfulness
79 thoughts racing
80 thoughts slowed
81 ulcer, peptic
82 withdrawn
83 work (or school) capacity impaired
84 other(s) specify
a.
b.
c.

Note: If relative dead, give age at death.
°/C = Degree of Certainty. Grade: #1. uncertain; #2. fairly certain; #3. certain.

TABLE 7–6

Diagnoses by Sz-MDP Regions in the Affected First-degree Relatives of the Hospitalized Patients

			I	*II, III, IV*	*V*	*Alcoholism or Psychosis of Unknown Type*
Diagnoses by Sz-MDP regions of the twenty-three psychotic-structure probands	I	(*N* = 9)	2	0	2	2
	II	(*N* = 10)	3	0	5	1
	III	(*N* = 3)	0	0	2	1
	IV	(*N* = 1)	0	0	1	0
Diagnoses by Sz-MDP regions of the twenty-three borderline-structure probands	III	(*N* = 2)	0	0	1	0
	IV	(*N* = 3)	0	0	4	1
	V	(*N* = 16)	0	1	12	3
	0	(*N* = 2)	0	0	0	1

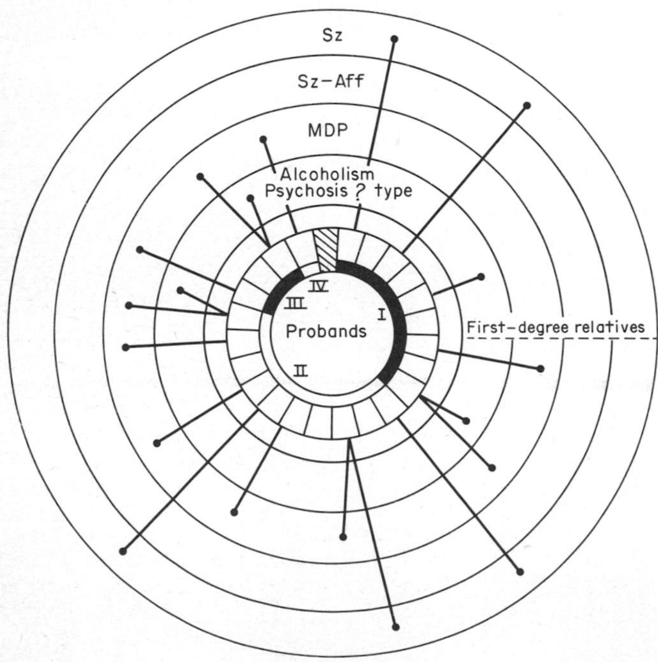

Figure 7–2*a*. Mental Illness in First-degree Relatives of Probands with Psychotic Structure (*N* = 23)

It should be noted that this separability of ill-relative profiles between the two groups occurred even though the patients with "psychotic structure" were not, in this sample, deteriorated schizophrenics. They were, like their borderline counterparts, young and intellectually gifted (average IQ in both groups = 122); they were considered amenable for the most part to intensive psychotherapy. The distribution of relatives is shown in another way in Figures 7–2*a* and 7–2*b*. From these diagrams it will be clear that some probands had as many as three psychiatrically ill relatives.

The numbers of affected first-degree relatives should be considered a conservative estimate, inasmuch as the probands (both groups together) had seventy-four siblings, and most of the latter were no more than a third of the way through the ages of risk for either a manic-depressive or a schizophrenic illness. The probands themselves included many adolescents whose clinical picture was often elusive by research-diagnostic standards.

Since borderline patients are distributed in both outpatient and inpatient realms, efforts were also made to evaluate mental illness in the families of a somewhat healthier group of borderline cases that were ambulatory, at least when first seen. To this end the author surveyed some fifty-three

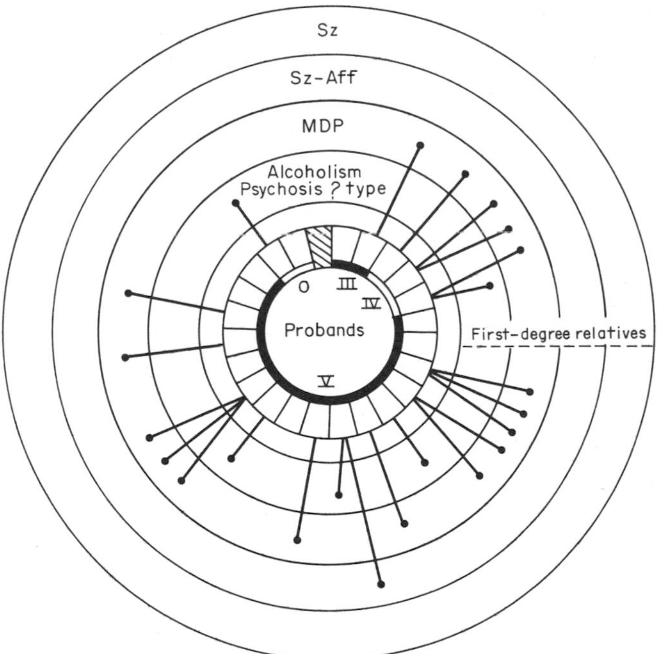

Figure 7–2*b*. Mental Illness in First-degree Relatives of Probands with Borderline Structure (N = 23)

patients and their families. This permitted comparison of borderline with neurotic patients and their relatives, a comparison not possible in the hospital, where it is rare to see a patient with neurotic structure.

Table 7–7 presents the findings in the borderline and neurotic groups. The figures referred to in this table are derived from analysis by the author of all patients seen in treatment during ten years of private practice, on whom sufficient data could be gathered from diagnostic interviews and other contacts with relatives of the patients. In this fashion twenty-five neurotic patient-family units were studied along with twenty-eight borderline index cases and their families. Borderline diagnosis was made at first

TABLE 7–7

Diagnoses by Sz-MDP Regions in Affected First-degree Relatives of Neurotic and Borderline Office Patients

Psychic structure in Probands	No. Sibs	No. Children > Age 15	Total No. 1° Relatives	Core Conditions (by region) No. c̄ Sz (I)	No. c̄ Sz-Aff (II-IV)	No. c̄ MDP (V)	% c̄ Core Conditions	No. c̄ Alcoholism
1. Neurotic (*N* = 25)	50	4	104	2	0	4	*5.8*	2
2. Borderline (*N* = 28)	53	3	112	10	2	14	*23.2*	2
2a. Ever hospitalized borderlines (*N* = 9)	18	—	36	2	2	4	*22.2*	1

on clinical grounds, rechecked according to Kernberg's structural criteria, and rechecked again, using Spitzer's borderline checklist. Only patients with six or more positive items on the checklist were included. Four patients considered "borderline" had only five positive items and were not included in the study. These cases were reclassified as "transitional," situated as they were at the interface between neurotic and borderline structures.

Sex ratio in the neurotic group was quite even: 13M:12F. Among the borderline patients, there was a female preponderance (7M:21F); the nine borderline patients who were eventually hospitalized were all female.

An attempt was made to assess the degree of genetic loading for any kind of major functional psychosis by evaluation of all available first-degree relatives. Relatives with schizophrenia, any form of manic-depressive disorder, severe alcoholism, or psychosis of equivocal type but necessitating hospitalization were counted for the two groups. It was found that of twenty-five neurotic patients nineteen had pedigrees free of such disorders, whereas only ten of twenty-eight borderline patients had no ill relatives. The tendency of borderline office patients to have ill relatives in a higher percentage of cases than noted among neurotic patients appeared significant: $p < 0.01$.

In this borderline sample there were 1.0 ill first-degree relatives per index case, as compared with 0.32 ill relatives per neurotic proband.

Among the eight ill relatives of the neurotic patients, two were schizophrenic, four had unipolar or other serious and distinctly depressive disorders, and two were alcoholic. The twenty-eight ill relatives of the borderline group were distributed as follows: ten schizophrenic, two schizoaffective, fourteen primary affective, and two alcoholic. The rather large number of schizophrenic relatives contrasts with the near absence of schizophrenia in the relatives of the hospitalized borderline patients referred to on p. 172.

The number of first-degree relatives per patient was the same for both groups of office patients (4.1), as shown in Table 7–7. Like the patients in the hospital-based study, this was a young population, mostly in the twenties; only a few had children who had entered the age of risk for the major functional psychoses. Inspection of Table 7–7 reveals the marked excess of relatives with "core" conditions (23.2 percent of the total number of first-degree relatives), compared with their counterparts in the neurotic group (5.8 percent). Separate analysis of the nine borderline patients who were eventually hospitalized during the course of psychotherapy showed figures in the same range as the borderline group as a whole (Table 7–7, 2*a*). There was no significant difference in the percentage of first-degree relatives who were psychiatrically ill between the hospital-based borderlines and the (initially) ambulatory borderlines (25.3 percent and 29.0 percent respectively, if the two alcoholic relatives of the latter group are included). Similarly, two out of three probands in both the hospital-based and office samples had at least one affected first-degree relative.

It seems paradoxical that there were no instances of schizophrenia and only one of a schizoaffective disorder among the relatives of the hospital-based borderline patients (Table 7-6), whereas there were ten schizophrenic and two schizoaffective relatives in the office borderline group (in percentages: 1 percent as compared with 10.7 percent). Although etiological heterogeneity was apparent in both borderline samples, the preponderance of affective illness in the probands (and relatives) of the hospital-based group may be a reflection of the frequency with which structurally borderline patients with serious depressive (or at times bipolar) tendencies show impulsivity of a self-destructive nature.

Suicide attempts, dramatic gestures with wrist cutting, dangerous driving, and the like, were common in these mood-disordered patients. Hospitalization was mandatory as a lifesaving (as opposed to custodial) measure; despite the flamboyance of the symptoms, the long-range outlook was rather good (see pp. 181–184). The nine originally ambulatory borderline patients who later were briefly hospitalized all had affective disorders (schizoaffective in three instances). Presenting symptoms were suicide gestures (five cases), suicidal ruminations (one), phobic/panic reactions (two), and premenstrual rage outbursts and depression (one). Of the remaining nineteen ambulatory borderline patients, however, ten had *schizoid personalities* (such as were seldom noted in the hospital-based sample). Many of these were chronic "underachievers," led marginal existences, and were "loners," social eccentrics, and so on. None, despite the seriousness of their disabilities, toyed with suicide or indulged in other forms of self-destructive behavior (apart from mild abuse of marijuana in two instances).

I do not know how representative either of my samples is of other ever- versus never-hospitalized patients with borderline structure. But it may be that there is a subgroup of marginal, schizoid borderlines (many would be like Kety's B-3 borderline schizophrenics or Spitzer's schizotypal borderline personalities) whom one seldom encounters in the hospital setting because of their relative freedom from impulsive, self-injurious behavior. Such a phenomenon might help account for the differential distribution observed here. Various selection factors, operative at different institutions, could also affect the ratio of affectively ill to schizotypal borderline patients.

Hospitals participating in the Boston-based project devoted to intensive psychotherapy of schizophrenics (of which Alfred Stanton is the principal investigator) tend to select patients from the healthier end of the schizophrenic spectrum, that is, "schizotypal borderlines." Some of these patients satisfy Gunderson's criteria but just fail to satisfy Kernberg's (because of poor reality testing in the interpersonal realm: see Chapter 9). Gunderson, in turn, is one of the more prominent investigators connected with the Boston project. The Kernberg criteria, as suggested in Chapter 9, tend to select a population slanted toward the affective pole.

In both of my borderline samples, ill relatives usually suffered from a primary affective disorder if the index case (1) was affectively ill also or (2) was only moderately ill, even if schizotypal. Schizophrenic relatives were associated, for the most part, with either schizophrenic probands or with those whose illness, regardless of form, was more severe.

The sex distribution of ill relatives of the ambulatory borderline patients was as follows: *males,* eleven (fathers, nine; brothers, two; sons, zero) and *females,* seventeen (mothers, eleven; sisters, five; daughters, one). No excess of ill mothers over ill fathers was noted. The role of "abnormal mothering" as a psychogenic factor in the etiology of borderline conditions must be assessed in the light of these observations. This topic is discussed in Chapter 9 in connection with the theories of Mahler, Masterson, and Rinsley.

Prognosis in Various Types of Borderline Conditions

No simple statement regarding prognosis in borderline conditions seems possible, partly as a reflection of their etiological diversity. To the extent these conditions are distinguishable from the chronically psychotic, they might be nonetheless expected to have outcomes intermediate between those typical of neurotic or psychotic individuals. By and large this is true, although there are exceptions. A borderline patient with antisocial tendencies will tend, for example, to have a poorer outcome than certain schizophrenic and chronically psychotic persons with high assets, good social functioning, and conventional mores.

Systematic studies of outcome in borderlines are scarce, being restricted to those of Grinker and Kernberg. These are based on relatively small numbers and represent particular patient populations including only some of all the many borderline "species" mentioned in the literature.

Before these studies there were only anecdotal reports, most of which were based on samples of less than a dozen patients.

Several of Kasanin's schizoaffective patients improved dramatically and remained relapse free for at least six years. Their treatment had been minimal and modern psychotropic drugs were not available to them.

But clinicians whose "borderline" cases were situated nearer the schizophrenic end of the diagnostic spectrum were less optimistic about outcome. Schmideberg's borderlines were a "stably unstable" group, many of whom led only a marginal existence. Bychowksi's "latent psychotics" contained a number of very gifted individuals with schizophrenic symptoms (some cases eventually developed "secondary symptoms"), who were able to maintain a fairly satisfactory extrainstitutional life. Zilboorg's "ambulatory schizophrenics," by contrast, included several murderers, as well as others with less violent antisocial tendencies. One may assume that social recovery was poor to nonexistent in this group.

The pseudoneurotic schizophrenics of Hoch and Polatin occasionally had subsequent rehospitalizations for one of the more recognized forms of schizophrenia. More often they pursued their own stably unstable course but sometimes made dramatic improvements with intensive psychotherapy. The more affect retained by the patients, the better the prognosis; most of the successful cases were in women.

Grinker, Werble, and Drye (1968) followed fifty-one initially hospitalized borderline patients for one to three and a half years. Two patients had undergone schizophrenic decompensation. Most had been and had remained socially isolated. Three-fifths of the group were considered to have had a good outcome as measured by work history (nineteen regularly employed, twelve fairly regularly employed but with frequent job changes).

Kernberg, as director of the Menninger Foundation's Psychotherapy Research Project of the late 1960s, reported on the project's sample of forty-two adult outpatients and hospital patients in whom diagnoses of neurotic conditions, borderline conditions, latent psychosis, or characterological disturbances were made (Kernberg, Burstein, et al., 1972). Patients with organic mental syndromes, mental retardation, or overt psychosis were not included in the study. The forty-two patients underwent treatment within the framework of psychoanalytic theory, ranging from supportive to classically analytic psychotherapy. Results of the project showed that borderline patients, as defined by the study, did improve, and did so optimally if they had received an expressive psychoanalytically oriented psychotherapy with special attention to negative transference—and in which the transference was not resolved through interpretation alone (1972, p. 173). The project did not set out to compare outcome in borderline versus psychotic patients.

Some patients given the label "borderline" have been young people at high risk for one of the major functional psychoses. Their prognosis is influenced to a great extent by the nature of the illness to which they seem predisposed. Aarkrog (1973), for example, recently discussed prognosis in a small number of adolescents who were, in his terminology, borderline as children. Although the adolescent breakdown in these patients was of a decidedly schizophrenic stamp (formal thought disorder, delusions, eccentricity, and so forth), because a less severe borderline psychosis had been present in childhood (usually of a symbiotic type), this Danish investigator preferred to reclassify the cases as "borderline." Aarkrog adheres to the Scandinavian school of diagnosis, where borderline or "reactive" psychoses are understood as a third major entity. Yet one of his three patients had a schizophrenic mother. I suspect the burden of proof is on the clinician to show why an adolescent who meets Research Diagnostic Criteria for schizophrenia, and who has a likewise affected parent, should be placed in a third category just by virtue of having had a not yet readily classifiable illness in childhood. One of Aarkrog's cases appeared to have mild genetic loading, for example, but subnormal intelligence, and wound up with the rigidities of personality so typical of a borderline group. Another had high genetic loading and high intelligence—again, a "borderline" picture, yet one with a better prognosis.

Prognosis is dependent on so many factors besides clinical picture and genetic loading that any taxonomy based on outcome alone is bound to generate more confusion than it dispels.

Meaningful discussion of outcome requires that one begin with a well-defined clinical syndrome and a well-matched control group.

The patients of the General Clinical Service of the Psychiatric Institute (up to the time of its discontinuance in 1976) constituted a high genetic loading, high asset group. Application of Kernberg's criteria for borderline versus psychotic structure permitted division into these two subgroups in a reliable manner. Since it is in the nature of manic-depressive illnesses to remit, usually with good interpsychotic function, it is understandable that those patients with "psychotic structure" are at the same time almost all chronic schizophrenics.

In a follow-up study of these subgroups, all forty-five patients admitted to the service during the calendar year 1974 were reevaluated in October of 1976. This population was homogeneous with respect to age, ethnic background, and educational experience. Average verbal IQ in both the borderline and psychotic subgroups was approximately 120. Patients in both groups had on the average two first- or second-degree relatives with a serious emotional disorder (some had no such relatives; a few had as many as five). Outcome at two to three years was rated by various members of the hospital staff still in contact with the patients, according to a nine-point scale. The points ranged from 4+ (dramatic improvement in social and occupational function) through 0 (no change) to 4− (suicide). The distribution of the twenty-seven patients initially diagnosed *borderline* in structure (via consensus among three raters) and the eighteen initially diagnosed *psychotic* is shown in Table 7–8. If one arbitrarily considers "1+" or "slight" improvement as equivalent to no change, one may separate two subgroups within the borderline and psychotic patients: those experiencing substantial

TABLE 7–8

Outcome at Two to Three Years in Inpatients with Borderline and Psychotic Structures

STRUCTURAL DIAGNOSIS	*Degree of Change*								
	−4	*−3*	*−2*	*−1*	*0*	*+1*	*+2*	*+3*	*+4*
Borderline (*N* = 27)	—	—	2	—	2	3*	9*	6	5
Psychotic (*N* = 18)	2	2	1	1	5	3	4	—	—

Key: −4 = suicidal
−3 to −1 = severe, moderate, or mild worsening
0 = no change
1+ = slight improvement
2+ = definite but moderate improvement
3+, 4+ = greatly to dramatically improved (such as a 20- to 30-point increase in global assessment score)

*Four borderline patients showed schizotypal features: one was rated as "1+" improved, three as "2+" improved.

(moderate to dramatic) improvement versus those who remained the same or got worse. Table 7–9 shows the distribution of patients after this simplification is made. Category I signifies substantially improved; category II, not substantially improved. Substantial improvement was seen much more often in the borderline group; the figures are significant at the $p < 0.01$ level by the χ^2 test.

TABLE 7–9

Outcome in Borderline and Psychotic Inpatients Analyzed for Two Categories: Substantial versus Lack of Substantial Improvement

	Structural Diagnosis	
CATEGORY	*Borderline*	*Psychotic*
I. Substantial improvement (2+, 3+, or 4+)	20	4
II. No substantial improvement (−4, −3, −2, −1, 0, or 1+)	7	14

Of interest, the two borderline patients who were substantially worse on follow-up both had severe character disorders with antisocial features and abuse of illicit drugs.

These preliminary data strongly suggest that methodical usage of the term "borderline," as defined by Kernberg, is capable of sorting out a good-prognosis from a poor-prognosis group. The purity of the division could be enhanced by exclusion of the antisocial and heavy-drug-use members of the borderline group.

It should be emphasized that these results do not consitute an endorsement for a particular method of treatment. Borderline patients, whether defined according to the criteria of Kernberg, Gunderson, or Spitzer, constitute diverse groups with respect to distal etiology and to syndrome type. Included were severe anorexia nervosa patients who improved with a behavior-modification approach. Others were bipolar-II manic-depressives with hysterical character disorders (D. Klein's "hysteroid dysphorics"), and they improved with a combined antidepressant and psychotherapy approach. Still others improved with expressive psychotherapy without medication. The main point is that the presence of borderline personality organization on initial evaluation predicted substantially better prognosis than psychotic personality organization (the latter diagnosis overlapping greatly with clinically manifest schizophrenia).

PART III

Diagnosis of the Major Psychoses, of Borderline Conditions, and of Personality Type

Part III of this book is divided into three main sections. The first (Chapter 8) deals with conventional psychiatric diagnosis: the criteria are set forth, both contemporary and past, for diagnosis of the unequivocal types of the major psychoses, and their dilute, mixed, or borderline counterparts are discussed. Methods of assessing these otherwise "undiagnosable" conditions in dimensional terms are presented. Several small sections are devoted to review of multiaxial models of diagnosis and to the presentation of multiaxial models advocated by the author. The assumption that hereditary factors play an important, often crucial, role in fostering schizophrenic and affective disorders serves as an organizing principle throughout. It is essential to be steeped in the psychodiagnostic criteria for the major psychoses, because many borderline patients, especially those selected for expressive psychotherapy, present clinical pictures closely akin to those of the classic "psychoses." The author endorses the notion of two spectra of illnesses, one having "process" schizophrenia as an extreme, the other having some form of manic-depressive psychosis as its extreme. As one travels along either continuum, one encounters cases where grossly faulty reality testing ("psychosis") is no longer present. For this reason the older term "manic-depressive psychosis" is giving way to a less prejudicial term "affective disorder," some forms of which are characterized by (frequent) psychotic periods, and some not. Many patients diagnosed borderline either in structural or clinical terms suffer nonpsychotic affective disorders. A few appear to have non- (or rarely) psychotic schizophrenic conditions.

Criteria for the diagnosis of these subtle borderline conditions are set forth in Chapter 9. The special problems experienced in diagnosing disturbed adolescents are also discussed, particularly the problem that an adolescent is just entering the age of risk for either major "psychosis."

Subtle forms of thought disorder are touched on, including those that can be regarded as dilute versions of classical schizophrenia, and others that appear to derive from nonhereditary factors. Examples are given of confrontations with patients functioning at each of the three levels of personality organization. The manner in which the pressure of confrontation required to evoke genuine material (i.e., to break through the resistances) may be used as a gauge of structural level is discussed separately.

The closing chapter, Chapter 10, is devoted to the analysis of personality elements, both characterological and temperamental. Special attention is given to the Kraepelinian temperament types seen in families of manic-depressives and schizophrenics. A method of estimating the strength of various character tendencies is proposed by the author. This "dimensional" approach to characterology rests on the assumption that elements of many character subtypes are present in most patients and that it is useful to quantify these elements because of their prognostic import in regard to both advisability of intensive psychotherapy and ultimate outcome.

CHAPTER 8

Criteria of Diagnosis:

The Major Functional Psychoses

Category versus Dimension

Systems in psychiatric diagnosis have been organized traditionally around categories. Ideally categories represent compartmentalizations of some universe of discourse into discrete "packets" of meaning, with sharp boundaries and absolute criteria of exclusion and inclusion. Even the most ardent proponents of various category-based systems in psychiatry admit difficulty in defining many categories so well that firm criteria of exclusion and inclusion can be drawn up. Categorical definitions of schizophrenia, for example, often can take comfort in the *exclusion* element of elation, but it is not so easy to find an element absolutely *inclusive* for schizophrenia alone. Loosening of associations may be seen in delirioid states, manics can have paranoid delusions, and "thought disorder" may occur in depression (Braff and Beck, 1974).

Certain continuously varying functions, such as height and intelligence, are not now conceptualized solely in categorical terms. Rather, as Kendell has pointed out (1975, p. 119), we think of a *continuum* (or a *dimension* or a *spectrum*, depending on the function) made up of (potentially) infinite points or bands capable of being well-ordered from "most" to "least." The development of an adequate measuring device permits such dimensional thinking: before the Binet test, people could only be "categorized" as dull or brilliant, and so forth, but *after* Binet, fine gradations could be detected and represented numerically.

One would suppose on the face of it that anything as complex—anything as dependent on multiple interacting but independently variable factors as mental functioning—would vary along a continuum, no matter what function one used as a reference point. In psychiatry we inhabit a universe where there are *both* continua and categories. Whether it makes more sense to draw attention to one or to the other depends on a number of factors: the size of a patient sample, the flagrancy or subtlety of the cases, or whether the subject under discussion is one symptom ("flight of ideas" was either present or absent) or a whole disorder. How well we know a patient is another factor, as is the factor of severity.

With respect to familiarity, psychoanalysts are often castigated for being poor diagnosticians, when in fact (*a*) most of their cases are free of flagrant signs of any well-established diagnostic category and (*b*) in any case they are soon swamped by acquaintance with hundreds of variables. This compels them to see each patient as a unique individual, "defying" neat categorization. Categories are easiest to defend in the presence of flagrant deviation from the norm. This may account for there being a dozen entities, in Feighner's system, among the severe conditions, but only three in the neurotic realm (hysteria, anxiety neurosis, and phobic neurosis). Although certain categorical diagnoses permit fairly reliable agreement among raters, and have been fairly well validated over time regarding homogeneity of treatment response or outcome, there are no absolutes. Mania does not always respond to lithium. Schizophrenics with several Schneiderian first-rank symptoms do not, as Carpenter, Strauss, and Muleh (1973) mentioned, always do poorly (see also Serban and Gidynski, 1975). Yet Kendell and Gourlay (1970) cast doubt on whether there is any "natural discontinuity between schizophrenia and the affective psychoses," though there seem to be areas in which "the chances of demonstrating discontinuity are the highest." Two simple ways of illustrating this point follow.

First, consider the function "psychostructural diagnosis" (meaning "psychotic" [P] or "borderline" [B] or "neurotic" [N]). In relatively small samples (see Figure 8–1), one may discern trimodality with regard, say, to a variable like Global Assessment Score (GAS).

When the sample becomes enlarged to thirty or forty patients, a picture like the one in Figure 8–2 emerges, if diagnostic criteria are rather loose and intuitive.

The shaded regions in Figure 8–2 indicate zones or bands where diag-

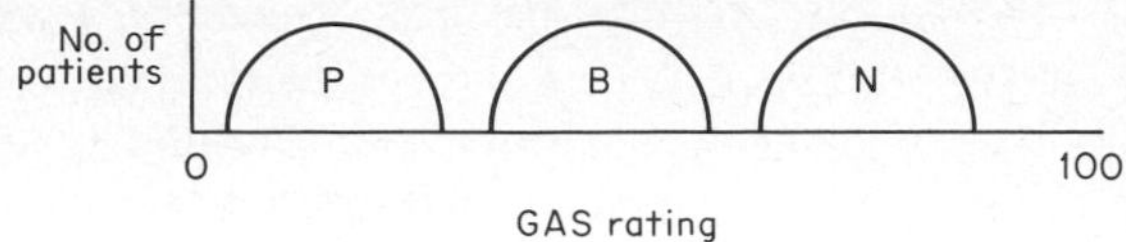

Figure 8–1. Category versus Dimension

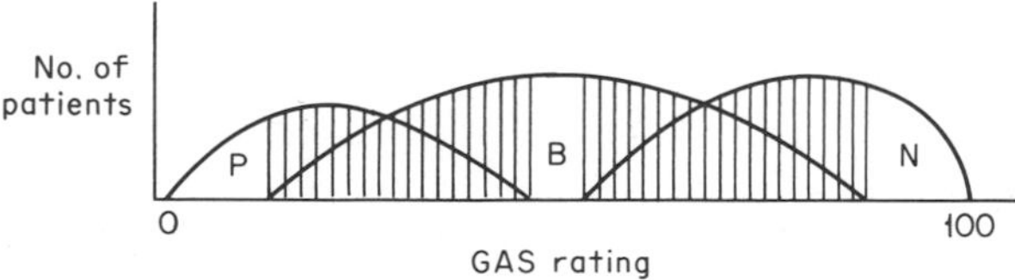

Figure 8–2. Category versus Dimension

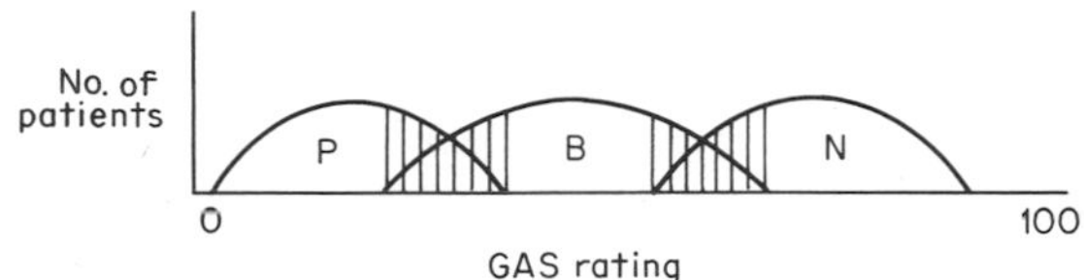

Figure 8–3. Category versus Dimension

nostic confusion occurs. By adherence to stricter criteria, such as those outlined by Kernberg, the *width* of the confusion bands can be narrowed (see Figure 8–3).

The unshaded regions of these diagrams, it should be noted, constitute the areas where various raters agree without hestitation or exception. *These are the areas where it makes sense to speak of categories.*

Second, the same picture emerges when one considers the so-called schizoaffective disorders. As in my phenotypic continuum diagram (see Chapter 2), there are unequivocal regions where the diagnostic categories of schizophrenia and manic-depressive psychosis hold up very well. There is the midregion where the label "schizoaffective," at least as a name for a phenotype, seems justifiable. But no definition of the functional psychoses with which I am acquainted permits perfect trimodality. One is left instead with alternatives like (1) measuring "schizotypia" and "degree of mood dysregulation" (as one measure IQ or height) and (2) assigning scores for each patient, representing this mixture visually as in the continuum diagram. A method for this dimensional approach is outlined later in this chapter. I prefer to resort for the time being to diagrams in order to portray the dimensional aspects, because an accepted numerical system is not yet available (much less validated). This method obviates the proliferation of new diagnostic terms that often worsen the confusion they were to resolve. Whoever would look deeper into the realm of borderline syndromes would be better equipped for carrying along a dimensional as well as a category-based approach, just as the physicist needs to be able to picture light both as wave *or* corpuscle, depending upon the particular nature of an experiment.

Kendell (1975a) has rightly drawn attention to the medical model in psychiatry as fostering (or maintaining) adherence to categories and, *pari passu,* to the rejection of a dimensional model. I think one should also emphasize, however, that as natural as it seems to be for our patients to spread themselves out along dimensions, it is natural for us—as human beings—to think first in categories. There is a parallel in ordinary human ontogenesis: children learn categories (good guys—bad guys) long before they grasp continua (a basically good man but with certain shortcomings; a crook with a heart of gold, and so on). Almost all trainees in psychiatry learn archetypes (the "pure" obsessive, the "pure" hysteric, the "core" schizophrenic, and so on) and only *then* the shades of gray.

It is the careful and reasoned manipulation of both the categorical and dimensional aspects of psychopathology, rigorously and systematically evaluated, that will permit the clinician the deepest understanding of his patients, as their conditions unfold over time. Refinement of diagnosis in this fashion should contribute to refinement of therapeutic strategies. Many of the case illustrations reflect the need for this kind of flexibility (such as cases 3, 6, and 14).

On Nosological Revision along Genetic Lines

As we have noted (Chapter 7), many families of borderline patients contain at least one affected close relative. On the strength of this observation, one could claim that revision of our nosology in accordance with the type of mental illness in the family might have as much—or more—to offer as revision in accordance with drug response. Genetic makeup, after all, answers to something fundamental about an organism; drug response, while often intimately linked to enzymatic activity, discrete biochemical abnormalities, and the like (hence, linked to genetic makeup), is under many circumstances influenced by any number of extraneous ("noise") factors not directly related to genetic endowment. This has led certain investigators to invest more hope in genes than in drugs, as when Rainer (1972) speculated:

> . . . whether explicitly acknowledged or not, the future state of psychiatric nosology depends ultimately on the genetic model. (p. 39)

Although mentioning that pharmacogenetics has turned out to be a "possibly productive field in helping predict response to drugs in various psychiatric illness," Winokur (1975) has also been struck by the similarity of mental illness in close relatives of psychotic patients. Here he referred to the Iowa-500 studies in which he and his collaborators evaluated the primary and extended families of 200 schizophrenics, 100 manics, and 225 depressives (all diagnosed according to strict criteria). His group (Morrison, Winokur, Crowe, and Clancy, 1973) found that the risk of schizophrenia in parents and sibs of their schizophrenic probands was 2.1 percent but only 0.6 percent in the parents and sibs of patients with an affective disorder. The reverse of this threefold difference was found when affective disorders in close relatives were tabulated: relatives of manics and depressives showed a risk of 13.5 percent but the relatives of the schizophrenics had a risk of only 5.5 percent for an affective disorder.

Data of this sort make it alluring, from a statistical standpoint, to nudge a diagnostically confusing patient into the category to which his ill relatives (if he has several) belong (see case illustrations 11, 14, and 27). Nevertheless one must attend to Kendell's admonition against using prognosis and treatment response as part of the defining criteria of a diagnostic category (1975, p. 132). As Kendell points out: "If diagnosis is to be of any use in determining treatment, it must be based on information available *prior to the institution of treatment* [italics mine] . . . and it is in any case illegitimate to use as a defining characteristic something which is also being used as a criterion of validity" (1975, p. 132). By implication, diagnosis via family history should be avoided just as stringently, since the genetic aspects of the patient's background constitute a frame of reference by which we hope to validate our original clinical diagnosis. Similarly, "recovery" does not invalidate a diagnosis of schizophrenia; it simply enlarges one's storehouse of information regarding the fate of persons so diagnosed. Bleuler's correction of Kraepelin's equation (schizophrenia means deterioration) exemplifies this point.

What I do think is justifiable, where the subject of mental illness in relatives is concerned, is this: In those instances where one or more close relatives exhibit a fairly pronounced and readily classifiable disorder, the clinician is entitled to the supposition that his patient (especially a hard-to-diagnose patient) has in *forme fruste*—or may eventually develop in more recognizable form—a similar illness. The clinician makes an educated guess on behalf of his patient. The researcher and the clinician have rather different tasks in this regard. Certain subtle cues the researcher may choose, for the purity of his investigation, to ignore or eliminate, the clinician must at times seize upon and integrate as best he can. Eysenck and Eysenck (1969), whose enthusiasm for explanation via heredity is strong, have also underlined the fact that *genotype* is invisible to us: "Any measurement we take is always of phenotype, never of genotype" (p. 57).

Mental Set and Most Favored Theory

Validation of any diagnostic model is dependent upon demonstration of its ability to be mapped onto an external and already accepted set of criteria. One explains something in terms of something *else*. Many of the purely psychological theories of personality diagnosis have turned out to be cleverly concealed tautologies (concealed even from their authors). The simple is explained via the abstruse—but still within the same universe of discourse.[1] This pitfall is avoided in various ways.

With respect to the borderline syndromes, Kernberg has sought to map the (more visible) clinical phenomena onto a (less visible) psychostructural, object-relations-oriented frame of reference. Such a mapping is, in part, a reflection of Kernberg's special areas of interest and training. The attempt of D. Klein, Fieve, and others to redefine certain diagnostic areas in terms of drug response represents another effort arising, at least in part, out of their interest and expertise in psychopharmacology. Gunderson and Singer (1975) have made reference to certain differences on psychological tests[2] which they believe are characteristic of patients with (clinically) borderline features. Gunderson has also drawn attention to certain clinical parameters that are useful in distinguishing between neurosis and overt schizophrenia—and the "borderline personality disorder." Each of these mappings has its particular utility. My own sympathies are with Eysenck and Kretschmer in espousing a genetically based external frame of reference as providing the greatest promise of "explaining" certain phenomena in (many) borderline patients.

Recently Rieder (1974) has voiced a similar sentiment in his examination of our current confusion about schizophrenia:

> The best information we have about the etiology of schizophrenia is from a set of studies on relatives of schizophrenics, by Rosenthal, Kety, Heston and others. Among these we find borderline schizophrenics, psychopaths, and character disorders as well as typical schizophrenics. If there is a common inherited biological cause for some patients now classified under these diverse

[1]Peterfreund (1971) has properly inveighed against this tendency. "Ego weakness," for example, may get hypothecated on the "basis" of flooding of "chaotic id-impulses." But this is not an explanation; this is a *redefinition* through a language in the same universe of discourse (the psychological) and at the same level of abstraction.

[2]Psychological tests are often useful but do not appear to have reached that level of sophistication necessary to distinguish reliably between borderline and psychotic (despite claims to the contrary). The unstructured tests, particularly, dive so deep below the surface that they tap "schizoidia" even in the presence of relatively good clinical functioning. And some very bright schizophrenics (see case 3) can turn in perfect records on the structured areas of the standard batteries—a feat alleged to distinguish borderlines (whose records do show this quality) from psychotics (whose records supposedly are contaminated to a degree, even in the more structured subtests).

> headings, we may end up grouping, under a meaningfully defined etiological classification, patients who are carefully differentiated from each other at the present time. (p. 207)

At this time it may be that the most defensible "model" for explaining the borderline syndromes is a flexible and complex one, embracing most of the models I have mentioned.[3]

Various Dimensional Models

Dimensional models in psychiatry, though they are not widely taught, have existed for a number of decades. Kretschmer (1948), for example, did not consider schizophrenia and manic-depressive illness qualitatively different from normal mental states but merely as extremes of a continuum.

The diagram that I have evolved to relate normal integration and normal mood regulation (the exaggerations of which become known, beyond a certain threshold, as "schizophrenia" and manic-depressive illness respectively) to the functional psychoses is shown in Figure 8–4.

The similarity of my diagram will at once be noted to the much earlier diagram of Kretschmer (see Figure 8–5). Kretschmer's diagram constitutes a bell-shaped curve, in which the extreme ends are marked off to designate (clinically recognizable) schizophrenics or manic-depressives. His "borderline" regions consist of the *schizoids* and the *cycloids*. These regions, in turn, shade into the general population of clinically well individuals who (characterologically) are either on the shy, ill-at-ease side ("dystonics") or on the outgoing side ("syntonics"). Although conceptually easier to grasp than my diagram, I believe Kretschmer's diagram suffers when trying to come to grips with persons who show simultaneously (1) shyness and eccentricity and also (2) abnormal mood swings (the extreme examples of which are the schizoaffectives).

In the material that follows, a number of other multidimensional models are examined.

Eysenck's Model

Eysenck has been shaping and refining a multidimensional model of personality over the past thirty years. Impressed by certain striking differences between the psychoneuroses and psychotic disorders, he expressed the view (1947, p. 42) that "psychoneuroses relate to types of reaction to the environment," whereas psychosis "involves changes in the whole personality of the subject in whom it appears." Only a *part* of the personality is

[3]Division of "borderline" cases into two groups, one with a probable hereditary factor and one without, would be a useful step, similar to Goldfarb's (1961) division of "childhood schizophrenia" into organic and functional groups.

Figure 8–4. Three-dimensional Representation of the Whole Population with Regard to Loading for Schizophrenia and/or MDP

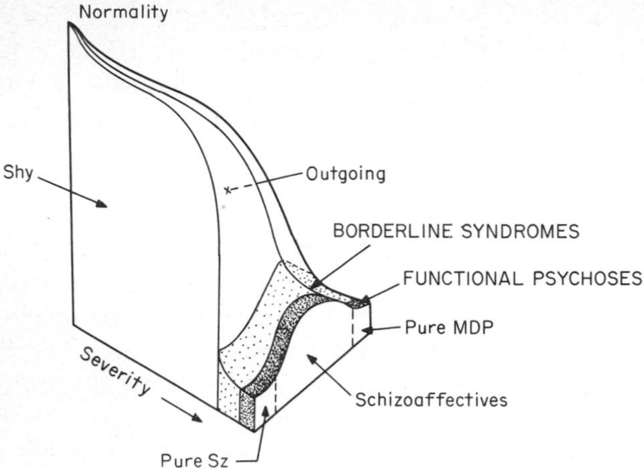

NOTE: Normal people, in my three-dimensional diagram, may be placed at the apex and along the ridge in the *middle* of the two outermost (*shy* versus *outgoing*) vertical planes. The normal person will be neither excessively shy nor compulsively extraverted. If he is emotionally healthy but inclined toward shyness, self-consciousness in social situations, and so on, his "dot" may be placed still at the apex, but toward the outer wall for shyness.

The lightly shaded area (whose volume corresponds to the "volume" of borderline or clearly emotionally disturbed persons in the whole culture) represents a sicker population, some of whose members will be "borderline" manic-depressives; namely, Klein's hysteroid dysphorics, my protomanic personalities (Stone, 1978).

The darkly shaded area represents psychotic persons. Notice that in cross section this area reduplicates my phenotypic continuum diagram: "pure" schizophrenia on one side, "pure" MDP on the other, schizoaffectives in the middle.

Figure 8–5. Major Dimensions of Personality

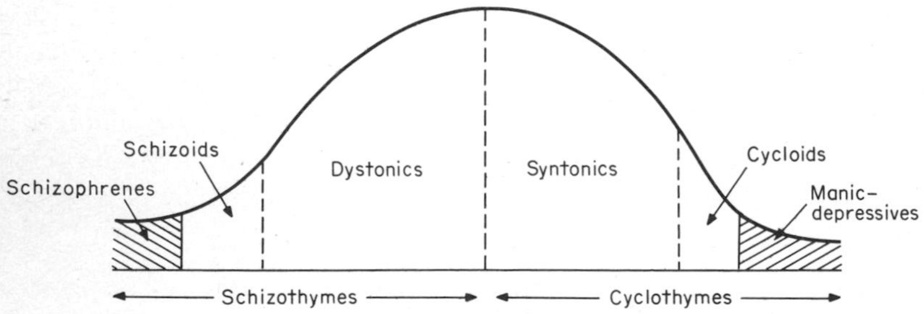

Schizoids
Schizophrenes
Dystonics
Syntonics
Cycloids
Manic-depressives
← Schizothymes → ← Cyclothymes →

SOURCE: According to Kretschmer (1948).

affected in neurotic conditions. Eysenck developed a questionnaire (1947, p. 65) designed to measure and encode neurotic traits; from its use with large numbers of people—in the general as well as psychiatrically ill population—he was led to postulate "neuroticism" as an overall dimension (with "emotionality" at the opposite end of this spectrum) of personality.

Distinct from *neuroticism-emotionality,* according to Eysenck, was another dimension—that of *extraversion versus introversion.* The extraversion-introversion dimension is closely analogous with Kretschmer's schizothymia-cyclothymia dimension (and corresponds to the schizophrenia-MDP spectrum of my phenotypic continuum diagram).

Plotting the various traits of extraversion (namely, sociability, impulsiveness, liveliness, activity, and excitability) and introversion as they occur among individuals with various traits of neuroticism or (healthy) emotionality can be represented graphically, the axes positioned horizontally and vertically. One such graph (based on Eysenck, 1960) is presented in Figure 8–6.

Figure 8–6. Diagram Depicting Various Groups on Two Main Personality Dimensions as Diagnosed by the Minnesota Multiphasic Personality Inventory

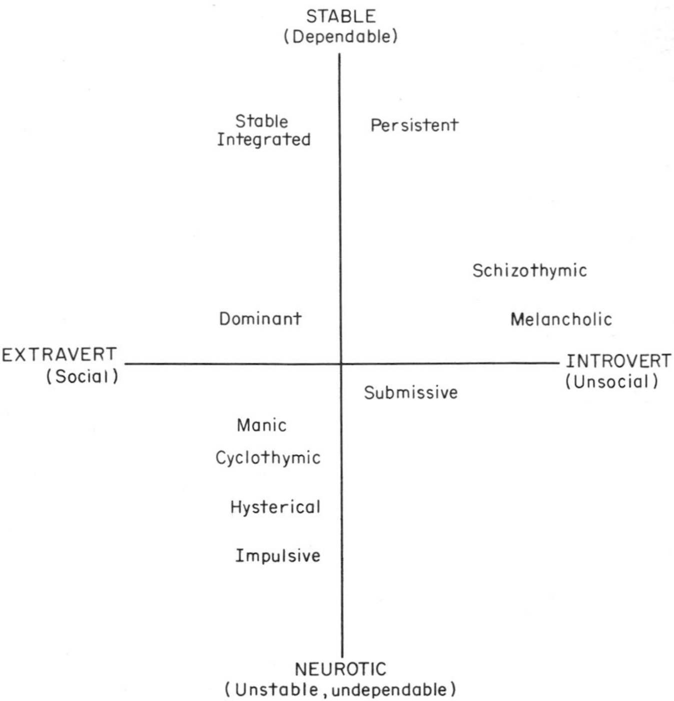

SOURCE: Adapted from Eysenck (1960, p. 19, and 1969, p. 46).

Eysenck has elsewhere speculated that one could regard as a third personality dimension, independent of neuroticism, a dimension called *psychoticism* (1967, p. 223). Psychoticism he believes is also inherited according to a polygenic model "very much as are the other two [dimensions]." In Eysenck's opinion, experimental work with psychotic subjects has found it "easier to measure what all psychotics have in common [which he then abstracts as this "psychoticism"] than what differentiates one [clinical] type from another." Here he cites the investigations of several psychologists who evaluated *thought disorder* among various types of psychotic patients (namely, Payne and Hewlett, 1960). Eysenck is at pains to make clear his belief that the neuroses are "not just psychotic disorders writ small."

In my opinion this view may place excessive reliance on psychological tests as criteria of validity. Certainly it has been the clinical experience of many that (1) patients with acute psychoses of whatever clinical type do indeed show many similarities on a number of psychological test responses, especially the Rorschach, and (2) even some chronically psychotic patients of one type may give responses that can be confused with those ordinarily belonging to another type. A constricted paranoid schizophrenia with depressive features may, for example, test out as a psychotic depression (F. Schwartz, personal communication). To compound the confusion, patients with "mixed" psychotic pictures (see case 14) may have "schizophrenic" responses and a clinical course eventually steering closer to MDP. I do not take this to signify, however, that the psychotic labels are useless and should be boiled down to "psychoticism: present or absent." I take this to signify that the classical psychotic types have much in common and much *not* in common and that psychological testing happens not to be the most successful way of differentiating the types.

The Strauss-Carpenter Model

In a number of recent studies Strauss and Carpenter (1972, 1974) have called into question the original Kraepelinian view that dementia praecox showed a deteriorating course and manic-depression a nondeteriorating course. Their earlier report focused on the schizophrenic *symptoms* and concluded that these have only limited prognostic significance. The later report emphasized the importance of *good social relations* as a predictor of good outcome, irrespective of the specific syndromes exhibited by the patients initially.

The latter factor is of course the counterpart in their schema of *"quality of object relations"* in Kernberg's schema.

These observations led Strauss and Carpenter (1975) to fashion a three-dimensional model with special applicability to the major functional psychoses.[4] They also visualize psychotic *symptoms* as capable of being described on a continuum from schizophrenic to affective. Their dimension for clinical *course* has "continuously psychotic" at one extreme, "single brief episode" at the other. The third dimension, *social relationships,* varies from "relates well" to "relates poorly."

Figure 8–7. Revised View of Relationships among Diagnostic Axes

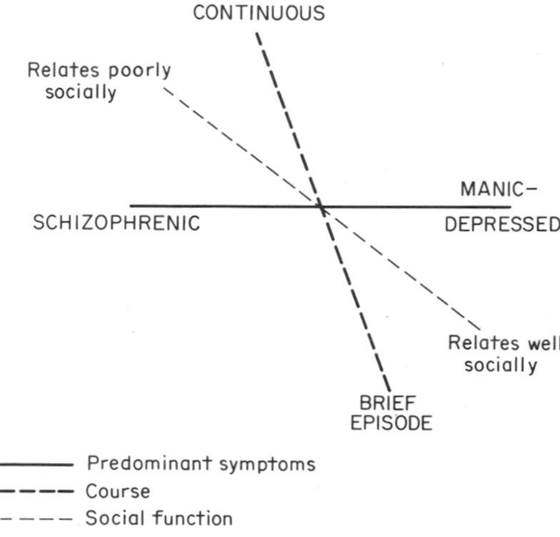

SOURCE: Adapted from Strauss and Carpenter (1975, p. 16), "The key clinical dimensions of the functional psychoses." In D. X. Freedman (ed.), *Biology of the Major Psychoses.* Copyright 1975. Reprinted by permission of Raven Press, New York.

As noted in Figure 8–7, they have chosen to depict their model upon a plane rather than as a cube. Therefore three points (one on each axis) must be established for the patient being evaluated. Strauss and Carpenter incline, furthermore, to the hypothesis that there is a significant *but only partial* (italics mine) relationship among the three axes. Such a relationship "can best be understood using the systems-theory model of open-linked

[4]Their position is opposite to that suggested by the more category-oriented Taylor, who concluded in his 1972 report that hospitalized patients *without* Schneider's first-rank symptoms and with "good" prognostic signs, although admitted as schizophrenic, were suffering from other, nonschizophrenic illnesses. It is not clear whether this subgroup really was not schizophrenic to begin with (by a more powerful criterion than outcome) or whether he simply recategorized them as nonschizophrenic later, the better to fit his theory.

systems. . . . Each of the three axes, although interacting with the others, would be considered as a representation of a separate 'system' with its own determinants" (1975, p. 15). The authors express the hope that attention to all three axes will facilitate future correlations with external (biological and psychological) variables: "abnormal levels of a particular enzyme may be found only in patients who are at an extreme for all three axes, or . . . who relate only to one of the axes."

By way of illustrating the utility of the Strauss-Carpenter model, the clinical vignettes 7, 11, and (to a lesser extent) 21 concern patients who showed one form or another of manic-depressive illness (some "schizophrenic" symptoms also being present in 21), yet who exhibited *chronicity*.

Other Models

Pull, Pichot, et al. (1976) have constructed a three-dimensional model for portraying various dimensions of psychopathology. The three primary discriminant functions consist of "f_1" (predominance of thought disorder, "f_2" (excitation versus withdrawal or inhibition), and "f_3" (hostility or its absence). This model is of greater use in general psychiatry than in the realm of borderline syndromes per se.

Another three-dimensional model is that of Freides (1976), also better suited to the broader population of psychiatric patients than to the borderline group.

The Importance of Drug History

Over the past twenty years there has been a phenomenal increase in the use of both legitimate and illicit drugs for altering mental state. Furthermore, the rate of manifestational change seems to have accelerated greatly since the development of potent neuroleptic drugs and since the use of cannabis, LSD, Dexedrine, and their congeners, has become widespread.

Some investigators, impressed by manifestational changes, have been led to question the applicability of the classical schizophrenic subtypes (paranoid, schizoaffective, catatonic, hebephrenic, and simple). Carpenter, Bartko, Carpenter, and Strauss (1976) thought that use of cluster-analysis technics suggested a subgrouping of a different kind. They offered the terms "usual," "flagrant," "insightful," and "hypochondriacal" as more appropriate than the traditional subtypes for the 600 schizophrenics they evaluted.

Added to the kinds of symptomatological shifts Carpenter et al. were attempting to characterize are the at times even more impressive muting of delusional and hallucinatory symptoms that results from the use of phenothiazines. Apart from those who work in emergency rooms, research units (where drugs may be withheld temporarily for diagnostic purposes), or chronic-care wards, few psychiatrists see flamboyantly psychotic schizophrenics. What one sees, instead, are patients who have undergone an acute decompensation, whose outward form (and often enough, whose inner essence) is schizophrenic, and who have received psychotropic drugs soon after the crisis. Usually the grosser disturbances of reality testing will have subsided in a matter of days, leaving a patient whose speech is much more coherent and who has recaptured whatever was his premorbid ability to relate. The "first-rank" symptoms of Schneider (1959) or any of the contemporary research diagnostic criteria can no longer be elicited in many instances. What will be still visible are certain behavioral eccentricities, and such signs as aloofness, anhedonia, magical thinking, and constriction of affect, which create a picture no longer satisfying "hard" diagnostic criteria.

Many of us who work in this area have had the experience of treating a patient whom a colleague had previously treated—quite adequately—for a schizophrenic break, whose clinical signs are no longer suggestive of schizophrenia. Sometimes they are referred to, or soon rediagnosed as, "borderline." In a loose sense of the term, they might be so labeled—especially by those for whom only "Kraepelinian" schizophrenia is schizophrenic. But it is just this loose sense of the term "borderline" that causes so much confusion. If evaluated according to the standards of Kernberg or Gunderson, these patients will usually betray some deficit in reality testing that is enough to disqualify the borderline diagnosis. In the rare instances where even these methods will not alert one to the psychotic process (and these rare instances do exist), time will often make the diagnosis in a harsher fashion! This point is illustrated in the following vignette.

A young woman had been studying abroad for two years. Shortly before she was due to return, she developed a secret love for one of her professors, whom she began to imagine was reciprocating her feelings and attempting to reveal them via cryptic signs nestled in homework assignments. Within a short time her behavior became erratic, and her roommates eventually were obliged to arrange a return home ahead of time, so that she could be hospitalized. She was grossly delusional and negativistic when first admitted, but two weeks later she had become much more realistic and composed, partly through the use of phenothiazines in high doses. She was considered well enough to be discharged.

By this time her speech was coherent and no longer betrayed evidence of unrealistic preoccupations. She did, however, feel apprehensive in social settings, such as she had never done before, and was in addition quite weepy, shedding tears with very little provocation. Although her tearfulness was not, strictly speaking, suggestive of inappropriateness of affect, it had a noticeably indiscriminate quality. She would cry not only in relation to themes of sadness and loneliness but at the merest mention of any topic (especially sexual) that she would have preferred not to discuss.

Her progress was sufficiently rapid that she was able, a month after leaving the hospital, to go to a different city, where she intended to find a job. She was still taking Thorazine, 100 milligrams, twice daily as "maintenance," and she began twice-weekly psychotherapy. Rational, engaging, and psychologically astute, she no longer presented a picture reminiscent of psychosis, especially to the new psychiatrist, who had heard the details of her hospitalization only by report.

Only two signs of fragility remained visible: her tearfulness and a tendency to dream in stark and primitive images in which transference themes emerged in unmistakable fashion much earlier in the course of treatment than would be the norm with better integrated patients. After the fifth session, for example, she reported to her analyst a dream in which "I see your penis on top of a hill; it seems huge—like a tall building. I'm at the bottom of the hill, groping toward the top."

After five months of treatment, she was able to work and maintain herself in an apartment. Her medication was tapered, partly in response to her insistence, and during the seventh month of treatment was discontinued.

The psychiatrist was aware that the patient's father had been hospitalized several times during her childhood for schizophrenic episodes and was still functioning only marginally. He also considered the patient herself to be somehow "schizophrenic," although clinical evidence was now lacking.

One month after discontinuance of phenothiazines, and two days before the psychiatrist's summer vacation, the patient began speaking in a bizarre fashion about an obscure religious cult to which she suddenly felt drawn. She felt God had appointed her part of a group elected to proselytize the unfaithful, of whom she saw her doctor as particularly in need of conversion. Toward the end of the hour, she became agitated, hostile, and combative, hurling books all over the office. Immediate hospitalization was necessary.

Reinstitution of antipsychotic medication led to rapid reintegration. Her eventual course was quite satisfactory. Throughout this period, however, small amounts of phenothiazines (Thorazine, 100–150 milligrams/day) were maintained. This appeared to contribute to the smoother course she now followed: stresses were handled effectively, and easy tearfulness was no longer apparent.

The clinical course of this patient demonstrates how a combined psychotherapeutic-psychopharmacological[5] approach in certain schizophrenic patients may be so effective that (1) the patient is elevated to a level of function and freedom of symptoms where the classical diagnoses can no longer be made with ease and (2) the practitioner is lulled into a false sense of security about the resiliency of the patient. In the enthusiasm of the moment, one forgets the patient's vulnerability.

This vignette may also be taken as an illustration of a point made by Strauss, Carpenter, and Bartko (1974, p. 68) that the "positive" symptoms of schizophrenia (hallucinations and delusions) seem to have less (and less ominous) prognostic import, dramatic as they may be, than the "negative" symptoms (namely, blunting of affect) or what the researchers refer to as "disordered relationships." This woman exhibited only the first type of abnormality.

Drug-Related Psychotic Reactions

If effective psychotropic medication has contributed, as one of its side effects, to a certain measure of diagnostic confusion, this confusion is still

[5]Those interested in the theoretical and clinical aspects of maintenance therapy in schizophrenia should consult the article of Ayd (1970).

relatively mild in comparison to that brought about by the widespread and indiscriminate use of illicit drugs over the past fifteen years. This abuse is of course more prominent among adolescents and young adults, if for no other reason than that their sense of identity is still unsolidified and hence more susceptible to the "psychotomimetic" properties of the commonly misused drugs. Young people are also, of course, just entering the ages of risk for schizophrenia and the manic-depressive disorders, so that it is not always easy to discern whether a particular psychotic reaction represents the first break along lines of heredofamilial predisposition (a break which might have occurred at around the same time irrespective of drug abuse) or whether one is dealing with a reaction *mimicking* the classical psychoses, induced by the drug(s) in a person free—as best one can tell—of such predisposition. Elsewhere I have dwelt at some length on the complexities of this issue (Stone, 1973).

These complexities are further compounded when one takes into consideration the likelihood that chronic, heavy abuse of certain drugs (marijuana and, at times, LSD) can, apparently in and of itself, induce permanent or semipermanent CNS alterations of a sort manifesting themselves as personality deterioration (even in previously well persons not suspected of harboring genetic loading for a classical psychosis).

Puzzling Diagnostic Pictures Associated with Drug Abuse

Among emergency-room patients and inpatients, one can recognize acute psychotic reactions related to drugs, presenting somewhat different clinical signs than are typical of schizophrenia or mania in an acute stage. Even in the absence of information concerning recent drug ingestion, the correct diagnosis can often be suspected on the basis of bizarre and shifting visual hallucinations, or, still more suggestive, reports of "mixed" hallucinations—where sounds were "seen" and images were "heard." Not only is lability of affect common in these conditions, but lability in the form assumed by the psychosis. Paranoid delusions with ideas of reference may be noted one day; clang associations, pushed speech, and hyperexcitability the next; tearfulness and suicidal ruminations the day following.

In less severe but more chronic hospitalized cases, drug abuse had apparently led to, or at least fostered, social withdrawal, negativism, and deterioration in intellectual functioning, grooming, and motivation for help of any kind. The combination of contemptuousness, grandiosity, and aloofness—in the face of serious social and occupational handicaps—has been especially prominent in this group. Many of these patients show not only the nonspecific borderline features mentioned by Kernberg but also the syndrome of "identity diffusion" or *poor ego integration*. All this in the face of relatively well-preserved reality testing and primitive defenses goes to establish a *borderline personality organization*. Here the problem is, What would the patient's personality organization have been in the absence of drug abuse? In cases of very heavy and chronic hashish ingestion, another diagnostic problem will sometimes arise: If the drug is discontinued for a period of months and a borderline syndrome persists, is this now a reliable indicator of the patient's premorbid level, or is one witnessing a *drug-induced,* hence artificial, type of borderline pathology?

These questions are often difficult to answer; sometimes one is fortunate in seeing a very ominous-looking clinical picture reverse itself after cessation of drug abuse, to the point where the life course appears to have resumed its natural path. If so, personality organization later on may fall convincingly within the neurotic level on reexamination. This point is illustrated by the following vignette.

A college student of twenty was referred for consultation because of a serious decline in his academic performance, combined with social withdrawal and loss of motivation for work of any kind. He dropped out of college in midsemester and had gone back to live with his parents. Toward them he was sullen and negativistic. Most of the day he spent watching television in his room, seldom venturing out except for his thrice-weekly sessions with a psychoanalyst whom he had been seeing for two years. He had sought help originally because of a depressive reaction mobilized by the death of a close relative. There did not appear to have been any progress. He had not mentioned anything to his analyst about his use of marijuana.

He had begun smoking marijuana at sixteen; his use of it had grown to the level of three "joints" a day, every day. Apart from having taken LSD on two occasions at college, he did not use other illicit drugs.

During the consultation, he was noted to have a haughty demeanor, which contrasted sharply with his unkempt appearance. He was markedly obsessive, isolated, and antagonistic toward those in authority.

No abnormalities of thought or speech were noted.

He spoke of aspirations to become a great jazz musician, although he had only begun lessons recently, and seldom practiced his instrument. The incongruity of this did not strike him; he claimed that as long as one had "soul," practice was irrelevant.

Both parents were professionals. There were no first- or second-degree relatives with any significant psychiatric disorder.

A psychological test battery, done in conjunction with the consultation, revealed an IQ in the superior range (136 full scale; a verbal 139). Signs commonly associated with schizophrenic reactions were not noted on the Rorschach, nor was the Bender Visual Motor Gestalt Test suggestive of organicity.

The patient was eventually persuaded to stop smoking marijuana. Within six weeks he was no longer negativistic and apathetic; he found summer employment and was able to return to college in the fall.

Information-Theory Aspects of Category Diagnosis

Diagnosis by category depends upon the unequivocal presence of certain signs and symptoms and, often, upon the absence of others. The more flamboyant the symptoms, the easier it is to hazard a particular diagnostic impression. This state of affairs usually coincides with the communication—from the patient's speech and behavior or from the reports of those familiar with him—of relatively few "bits" (or units) of information. When we are led to conclude that the diagnosis of a given patient is "hazy," we are alluding to a situation where many bits of information have been communicated, none of which manages to trip the on-off switch specific for the category we are evaluating.

In acute psychosis, every sentence uttered by the patient may convey information capable of steering the interviewer toward a particular diagnostic category, or at least toward a specific level of function. The first three words of the patient in case illustration 1, "I'm an actress," do not establish a level of function. For all that the interviewer knew, she could actually have been an actress. But the next four, "I have five faces," narrow down the possibilities drastically: she is either poetic or psychotic. And by the time she has uttered her twenty-fourth word (" . . . you're my son"), even the possibility of her being poetic has vanished. One could add that the diagnosis of level of function here does not even require a trained observer. Contrast this case with the last three, where there is nothing to suggest psychosis even in a speech sample of many hundreds of words.

The first task in psychodiagnosis, generally, is to test for the presence of psychosis. In case 1, the task was accomplished speedily, after a minimum of informational exchange. But in case 27, even after a lengthy interchange with the patient, one could only say, "No evidence yet" (actually, evidence was gradually building up that psychosis was absent).

Many clinicians who were familiar with the patient in case 1 assumed that their spot diagnosis of "schizophrenia," based on the presence of hallucinations, delusions, constricted (though not flattened) affect, feelings of passivity, and loosening of associations, was unassailable. But over the seventeen years the patient has now been followed, the cyclical nature of her psychosis, the pressured speech, her good interpsychotic function, and her (in recent years) infectious warmth and good humor have inclined most clinicians to swing toward bipolar-I MDP in their assessment of diagnostic *category*. With respect to the *type* of psychosis, the case was no longer flagrant but actually rather problematic; some years (and mountains of informational bits) were required to place the patient in the manic category.

The borderline syndromes are by definition more subtle entities, since their diagnosis rests on ruling psychosis *out*. As one ascends the adaptational level, the informational load necessary for diagnosis becomes much greater: the presence of seriously faulty ego integration must be ruled out to qualify for a neurotic diagnosis. This, in turn, requires the often lengthy assessment of the quality of object relations. Several hours of interviewing by an astute and well-trained clinician will not always suffice for this task.

Ideal categories have validated inclusion and exclusion criteria and are, hence, programmable.

Clinicians have their own mental logic tree in this regard, though they are not usually in the habit of displaying it on paper. Figure 8–8 depicts a

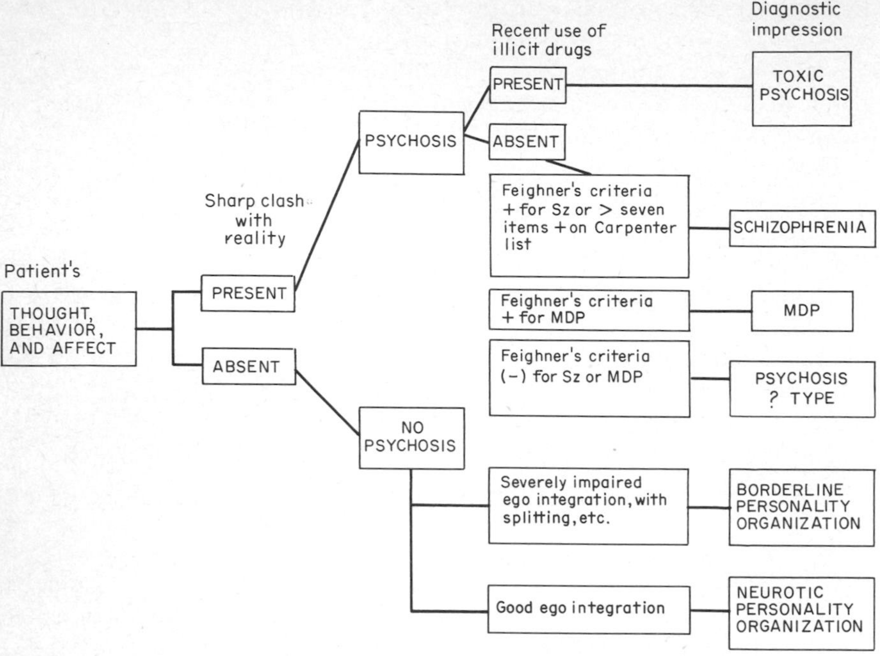

Figure 8–8. Logic Tree for General Psychiatric Diagnosis

logic tree relevant to the assessment of several diagnostic categories. This diagram is intended only as an example and is by no means complete: clinicians who work with patients many of whom have neurological abnormalities would of course require "branches" that deal with factors relating to the organic psychoses, and so on.

Although a logic tree is necessarily a linear, step-by-step representation of a mental process, events in the mind of a diagnostician do not usually proceed in a manner that rigidly linear. One may indeed, confronted with a very disturbed patient, begin to assess first for signs of psychosis and then for signs suggestive of certain varieties of "psychotic" illnesses (schizophrenia, mania, and so forth). But it seems equally defensible to suggest that in certain instances evaluation about level of function (psychotic, not psychotic) *and* type of illness proceed simultaneously. However this may be, many more informational bits are required, at a minimum, to establish the niceties of subtype and character. Hence to refine diagnosis down to those levels requires passage from a category-based realm of thought to a dimensional realm. There is simply no litmus paper to provide instant determination of a character type in the way simple assessments of reality testing give quick answers to the question of psychosis.

Information-Theory Aspects of Dimensional Diagnosis

Diagnosis by category stands in relation to a digital computer as diagnosis by dimension does to the analog computer. The first depends upon on-off decisions; the latter, on placement along a continuum.

The ruler and sextant are simple "analog computers" of height, with which everyone is familiar. The Stanford-Binet and the Wechsler tests may be seen as analog computers of intelligence. The IQ, as a number, bears a statistically reliable relationship to the person tested (he will tend to achieve a similar number on repeated testing) and to the group of persons within a culture who achieve that "score" (there are certain tasks which all of them can accomplish with roughly the same proficiency).

Patients diagnosed as "borderline" may be further evaluated with respect to schizophrenia and manic-depressive illness. Here one attempts to measure (1) the degree to which such patients resemble the paradigm cases of those categories and (2) the place, along a continuum of schizophrenic versus manic-depressive signs, best suited to each patient's clinical picture.

This procedure requires a considerable amount of information; the information, furthermore, reflects data collected on many variables, some of which are themselves evaluated, of necessity, along a dimension and by means of trained raters, whose average score becomes the analog-computer "reading" of any particular variable.

To do justice to the immense number of combinations that have clinical interest, a new and lengthy vocabulary would have to be created. The alternative is to devise appropriate dimensional scales, test them for reliability among raters, and validate them to genetic and other frames of references. This process will generate numbers and ratios which, in time, will convey meaning, to all clinicians schooled in such a method, about the relative degree to which a given patient is "schizotypic" or affectively ill or both. Mention of the coordinates on a commonly accepted graph will evoke the same fairly precise understanding that mention of an IQ figure now evokes in regard to intelligence.

Category and Dimension: The Need for a Dual Approach in Borderline Conditions

By definition the borderline syndromes do not fit comfortably into existing psychodiagnostic categories, or they would cease at once to be "borderline." Many clinicians and investigators are nonetheless heavily invested philosophically in adherence to a category-based model. Those adopting this outlook are interested in assessing how closely borderline cases resemble already existing categories. Welner et al. (1973), as mentioned earlier, has proposed the category "undiagnosed patient" for cases defying inclusion in the commonly accepted categories.

Others prefer a dimensional or a combined model in dealing with borderline cases. Grinker (1968) may be taken as an example, insofar as "borderline" for him represents an intermediate position between psychosis and neurosis; also the four subtypes his study generated range from a near-to-the-psychotic to an almost-neurotic variety.

I have for some time been impressed by the utility of a simultaneous categorical/dimensional model for the borderline syndromes. Carpenter, Gunderson, and Strauss (1976) also advocate a dual approach:

> A third model for classification [of the borderline syndromes] combines the properties of the continuum and typological approaches. Such a combined . . . model provides the means for integrating the conflicting data presently available. . . .

These authors emphasize the point that such a model allows for (1) allocation of the psychopathology noted in any given case to some point on a continuum and (2) designation of cases deviant beyond a certain arbitrarily defined locus as belonging to a (perhaps newly proposed) category.

The variables I consider of most importance in assaying potential borderline conditions are, as mentioned in Chapter 9, constitutional predisposition, level of adaptation (psychotic-borderline-neurotic), and the personality type. Thus a three-dimensional model will usually suffice and has distinct advantages if it is used not as a mathematical construct but as a heuristic device. Use of such a device may, for example, ensure attention to diagnostic parameters that might otherwise be overlooked. Also, categorical and dimensional impressions may be recorded simultaneously. Patients who have been grossly psychotic in the recent past but whose partial recovery has obliterated the "hard" signs of mania or of schizophrenia will still occupy a certain position within my three-dimensional model. The model emphasizes constitutional type (in essence, the kind of condition to which the patient is *vulnerable*) rather than manifest psychosis. Furthermore, all gradations of schizoaffective illness, from the predominantly schizophrenic to the predominantly affective, can be designated by shifting the marker to the left or right on the "floor" of the cube. Modifications may be introduced, according to the requirements of the case or the patient sample. For certain patient samples, it may be necessary to enlarge the "floor" of the cube to include a *track* for organic conditions as well as for the schizophrenia-MDP continuum. One wall of the cube is ordinarily used to record three levels of function (psychotic, borderline, and neurotic). The marker, in this situation, can only have three heights (corresponding to the different levels). But if it were important to record serial scores of global function at brief time intervals, the "level-of-function" wall could be converted into the 100-point scale of the Global Assessment Score. It is often useful to arrange the cube in this way when following the progress of hospitalized patients during periods of rapid change. The wall ordinarily used for personality type can, in this instance, be changed into a time scale, marked out for the appropriate intervals. Examples of this are provided in the case illustration section. Patients occupying the same small region within the cube may be meaningfully lumped together and studied with respect to other variables, so that their similarity or lack of similarity can be further tested and documented.

Criteria Used in Evaluation of Borderline Cases

Precisely because the phrases "borderline syndrome" or "borderline case" imply failure to fit within categories, it becomes important to understand just what these categories involve in a detailed way.

Thus far more attention has been paid to the business of differentiating borderline states from schizophrenia than from the manic-depressive disorders. The historical reasons for this I hope I made clear in Chapters 1 and 7. I have also mentioned (Chapter 6) that depression blends more easily into the normal population than does schizophrenia, hence in certain depressive individuals it may be particularly difficult to select an appropriate line dividing the borderline from the neurotic.

In the sections immediately following, I am going to concentrate on the manner in which "borderline" is set off from (or compared with) the schizophrenias. It should be understood that the task of distinguishing borderline from MDP is no less important. Both tasks proceed in a similar fashion, and what I will be presenting in regard to schizophrenia is in every way analogous to the situation with the manic-depressive disorders.

At the time of this writing there are already a fairly large number of systems for diagnosing and classifying schizophrenia. After the formulations of Kraepelin and Bleuler, not many were added to the literature beyond those of Schneider (1959) and Langfeldt (1969) until the past decade. The recent proliferation of research diagnostic categories include those of Feighner (1972), Astrachan et al. (1972), Taylor and Abrams (1975), and Carpenter, Strauss, and Bartko (1973). The last mentioned emanates from the International Pilot Study of Schizophrenia (IPSS). The IPSS is sponsored by the World Health Organization (WHO) and is a transcultural investigation of some 1200 patients in nine countries. An outline of IPSS schizophrenia taxonomy, as described by Sartorius, Shapiro, and Kimura (1975), is provided below. Other classifications include those of Spitzer and his group (Spitzer, Endicott, and Robins, 1975) in connection with the Diagnostic and Statistical Manual of the American Psychiatric

Association (DSM), and that of Helmchen (1975), who has reported on a study relating to the eighth revision of the International Classification of Diseases (ICD-8).

None of these classifications represents the "last word" on what is (or is not) schizophrenia. But many embody improvements over some of the earlier systems. To take but one example: Langfeldt believed patients with his "characteristic" symptoms of schizophrenia (see pp. 214–215) had uniformly poor outcomes, but in the study of Hawk, Carpenter, and Strauss (1975) it was noted that these symptoms do not define a "poor outcome group" nearly as well as Langfeldt predicted. The classification system of Carpenter was thus constructed in such a way that less reliance is placed on some of the original Langfeldt items as "discriminating" for schizophrenia.

A more reasonable approach than aligning oneself behind one or another advocate of some particular method is thus to keep *all* of them in mind, extracting from each something that may be of special value in assessing a borderline case. Since some of the methods are more lax and others more stringent, it is even possible to well-order them from loose to rigorous. Having done so, each diagnostician may pass the clinical picture of a case under consideration through a series of graded filters, where the relevant classification systems are set up as coarser or finer "filters" of schizophrenia. Such a process is pictorialized in Figure 8–9. This diagram should be

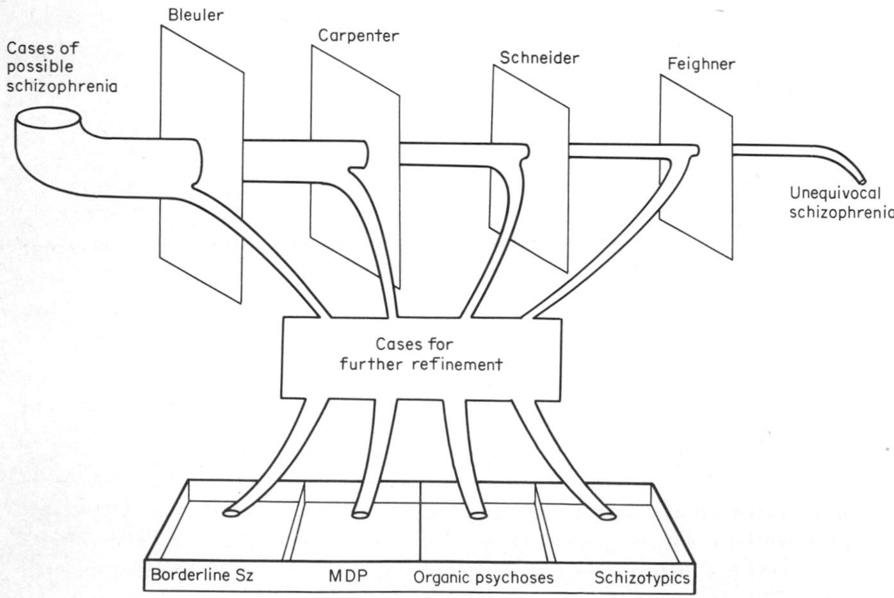

Figure 8–9. Diagnostic Filter for Schizophrenia

understood as a schema only; it makes no pretense to completeness. Some systems, in addition, are so similar that they screen out roughly the same patients and thus could not be aligned in so strictly linear a progression.[6]

Schemata for Schizophrenia

Systems of Diagnosis at the Turn of the Century through 1960

The most influential classificatory systems for schizophrenia in the early part of this century were those of Kraepelin and Bleuler. Jung wrote extensively on the subject as well, but his contributions were mainly concerned with the psychodynamics, apart from the observation that the premorbid personality in dementia praecox was typically one of "introversion." Adolf Meyer, besides espousing a psychodynamic viewpoint in conceptualizing schizophrenic breakdown, was even more widely known for his emphasis on multiple interacting factors as causative of what he came to call the schizophrenic *reactions*. He joined Bleuler in criticizing Kraepelin's pessimism, a deteriorating course having (originally) seemed to the latter an inevitable consequence of dementia praecox. Further aspects of Jung's and Meyer's work may be gleaned from the valuable historical review of Tourney (Chapter 1 in Tourney and Gottlieb, 1971).

Kraepelin's Criteria (for Dementia Praecox) Although Kraepelin's diagnostic criteria were not tabulated in the point-by-point manner to which we have become accustomed in the recent research-diagnostic formulations, Kraepelin made clear the main features of dementia praecox in his 1896 text and again in his 1925 monograph. Kraepelin's observations regarding the causation, course, and diagnosis of this condition are enumerated in Table 8–1.

From Table 8–1 it can be appreciated that Kraepelin emphasized the more drastic aspects of what have at various times since been included within the concept of schizophrenia. As such the Kraepelinian criteria constitute a rather fine filter, through which only the more serious cases might be expected to pass. Among the cases illustrated in this book, 3 and 6 would have met many of the criteria, but not that of deteriorating course;

[6]Strauss and Gift (1977) have recently demonstrated the interrelationships and relative stringencies of some of the popular diagnostic concepts of schizophrenia. These include the New Haven Index, the IPSS Flexible System, the Research Diagnostic Criteria, Feighner's criteria, and so forth (see pp. 217–223). The authors recommend an "orientation toward using these approaches . . . that permits employing several approaches simultaneously"—to provide the greatest chance for determining important relationships among diagnostic, clinical, and research variables. Such an approach allows the clinician to make sense out of a case failing to meet Feighner's criteria (one of the most stringent)—hence "undiagnosable" in the St. Louis system—but which fulfilled the New Haven criteria for schizophrenia.

Familiarity with all the "borderline" syndromes and concepts allows, in a similar fashion, for a more rational approach to a prospective "borderline" case (see Chapter 9).

TABLE 8–1

Kraepelin: Observations on Dementia Praecox

1. *Causation*
   - *a.* Defective heredity, resulting in—
   - *b.* (an assumed but never proved) Autointoxication
2. *Course*
   - *a.* Onset usually in adolescence or young adult life
   - *b.* Progressive, usually with deterioration of intellectual and social capacities
3. *Diagnostic Elements*
   - *a.* Loose or wandering ("desultory") thought
   - *b.* Discrepancy between thoughts expressed and emotions displayed
   - *c.* Negativism
   - *d.* Stereotyped behavior
   - *e.* Delusions
   - *f.* Hallucinations
   - *g.* (eventual) Mental deterioration

SOURCE: Based on Kraepelin (1896, 1925).

in case 10 there was lability but not inappropriateness of affect, and eventual recovery. Such patients would be screened out by a filter of this sort, and would emerge as "borderline" with respect to Kraepelin's criteria. As we shall see, they all would fit easily within Bleuler's criteria.

Bleuler's Criteria (for Schizophrenia) In his great monograph of 1911, Bleuler advocated that the condition Kraepelin was calling "dementia praecox" be renamed "schizophrenia," emphasizing the split in intellectual versus emotional function. The new name was of course also selected in order to deemphasize the notion of deterioration implied in the word "dementia," since Bleuler did not agree with his predecessor about the importance of this factor. In Bleuler's experience many schizophrenic patients pursued a level course, never deteriorating and never becoming asymptomatic. Some even enjoyed excellent recoveries, as he mentions in his chapter on the course of the illness:

> I know schizophrenics who, after their illness, have been able to carry on complicated business transactions at a high level; I know another who, after two catatonic decompensations about seven years apart, remains capable of doing good scientific work . . . a heboidophrenic of Professor Hess' is [now] a university professor. Schumann [the composer] . . . was a schizophrenic. . . . These examples should serve to demonstrate that we must not turn our eyes away from cases with a favorable outcome. (p. 210, my translation)

TABLE 8–2

Bleuler's Diagnostic Criteria for Schizophrenia

1A. Primary Symptoms (Simple)
- *a.* Disturbance in the associational aspect of thought
- *b.* Split between affect and intellect
- *c.* Ambivalence

1B. Primary Symptoms (Compound)
- *a.* Autism

2. Secondary (Accessory) Symptoms
- *a.* Delusions and illusions
- *b.* Hallucinations
- *c.* The catatonic symptoms
  - (1) Catalepsy (with "waxy flexibility" of the facies and body, or, more rarely, complete rigidity)
  - (2) Stupor
  - (3) Hyperkinesis
  - (4) Stereotypy
  - (5) Mannerisms
  - (6) Negativism
  - (7) Echopraxia

SOURCE: Abstracted from Bleuler (1950, pp. 14 ff., 94 ff. and 180 ff.).

As is well known, Bleuler divided schizophrenic symptomatology into two subdivisions, "primary" and "secondary," as outlined in Table 8–2.

In addition, "melancholic" and "manic" forms of acute schizophrenia are described—the former characterized by the triad of depressive affect, inhibition of thinking, and inhibition of action, the latter by euphoria, flight of ideas, and pressured activity. Bleuler also described other secondary forms, in which confusion, mental clouding over (*Benommenheit*), delirium, or certain dreamlike states ("twilight" states) dominated the clinical picture.

From this it should be clear that, for our purposes, Bleuler's criteria constitute a "coarser" filter than those of Kraepelin. Many acute schizoaffective psychoses, for example (cases 4, 6, and 8), will pass Bleuler's criteria (retaining the schizophrenic label) only to be reclassified borderline or manic-depressive in relation to Kraepelinian nosology. Similarly, patients with mild thought disorder, displaying little affective disturbance (in the sense of mania or depression), will nowadays be "Bleuler-positive" schizophrenics but will not meet research diagnostic criteria unless Bleuler's "secondary" signs (especially delusions and hallucinations) are also present.

Langfeldt's Criteria Whereas Bleuler's attention to phenomenology led to a broadening of the concept of schizophrenia (to include nondeteriorating cases with thought disorder similar in kind but less intense than seen in flagrant cases, and so forth), the Norwegian investigator Langfeldt (1937) gave precedence to outcome and divided the field into "process" and "reactive" schizophrenia. He preferred to label as schizophrenic only those patients with a deteriorating course. This deterioration, furthermore, tended to occur, in Langfeldt's impression, in the absence of acute precipitating factors and in patients with a schizoid premorbid personality. This, in contrast to what he called *schizophreniform* or *reactive* psychoses, where affective symptoms and clear-cut precipitants were customarily noted.

As mentioned earlier (Chapter 4), Langfeldt and his followers, including McCabe and Strömgren (1975), see the realm of functional psychoses as tripartite: schizophrenia, reactive psychosis, and the manic-depressive psychoses.

In Table 8–3 the various diagnostic criteria by which these three categories may be distinguished are presented in outline form.

For Langfeldt the essential ingredients of schizophrenia were (1) a serious disturbance of ego boundary, (2) a defect in the chain of associations, and (3) the sensation that the world around one had changed in some drastic way. Although he used the terms "depersonalization" and "derealization" to describe this last abnormality, he meant by them something more cataclysmic and pervasive than what these words usually convey to a contemporary clinician.

Although the reactive psychoses seemed to constitute a separate entity, the statistics of Langfeldt and his co-workers may be read either way. Welner and Strömgren (1958), for example, studied 106 patients presenting with an acute "schizophreniform" picture and noted on follow-up (1½ to 20 years later) that 72 were "cured" or suffering from some "nonschizophrenic mental disorder" (whereas their initially schizophrenic group had a much higher rate of recidivism and marginal adjustment). On the other hand 30 of the 106 index cases *were* considered "chronic schizophrenics" on follow-up.

Since Langfeldt's criteria for "schizophrenia" are constructed to capture chronic cases with poor outcomes, they serve as a fine-gauge filter, above which are trapped "borderline" cases—a good many of which (one-third?) are dilute forms of schizophrenia.

Schneider's Criteria Schneider (1959) has been influential, particularly in Europe, in reshaping the diagnostic criteria used for selection of schizophrenic subjects. Rejecting the Bleulerian classification as too broad, he proposed a set of distinguishing symptoms considered "pathognomonic" for schizophrenia. Furthermore, as pointed out by Carpenter, Strauss, and Muleh (1973, p. 847), the symptoms Schneider set apart were readily

TABLE 8–3

Langfeldt's Criteria for Schizophrenia, Reactive Psychosis, and the Manic-Depressive Psychoses

Schizophrenia	*Reactive Psychosis*	*Manic-Depressive Psychoses*
1. Severe derealization	1. Affective symptoms	1. Depressive or manic symptoms
2. Severe depersonalization	2. Normal motor activity	2. Altered motor activity
3. Somatic hallucinations	3. Mood follows no distinct pattern	3. Diurnal variation, with depression worse in the morning
4. Delusions of passivity		
a. Thoughts broadcast		
b. One's will under external control		
c. One's movements under control of an external force		
d. Verbalizations under external control		
e. Impulses and feelings under external control		
5. Clear consciousness	4. Clouded consciousness	4. No associational defect
6. Associational defect	5. Associational defect	5. Course independent of external events
7. Poor outcome	6. Course dependent on external events, outcome usually good	6. Premorbid personality depressive or cyclothymic
8. Premorbid personality schizoid	7. Premorbid personality neurotic	7. No apparent prior traumata
9. Poor empathy with interviewer	8. Good rapport	
10. No obvious precipitants	9. Clear-cut precipitants	8. Family history of mania or depression
11. Family history of schizophrenia	10. Heredity uncertain	

SOURCE: Langfeldt (1937, 1969), Eitinger, Laane, and Langfeldt (1958), Tourney and Gottlieb (1971), and Hawk, Carpenter, and Strauss (1975).

observable by the average clinician, whereas Bleuler's "ambivalence" depends on a much more subjective, hence questionable, evaluation.

Schneider's criteria are set forth in Table 8–4. The items listed are Schneider's "first-rank symptoms" (FRS) and, as can be seen, overlap with certain symptoms Bleuler regarded as of only "secondary importance."

TABLE 8–4

Schneider's "Pathognomonic" Symptoms of Schizophrenia

A. *Hallucinatory*

1. Patient hears hallucinatory voices speaking his thoughts aloud.
2. Patient experiences himself as the subject about whom hallucinatory voices are arguing or discussing.
3. Patient hears hallucinatory voices describing his activity as it takes place.

B. *Delusional*

4. A normal perception is followed by a delusional interpretation of a highly personalized significance.

C. *Pertaining to Ego Boundary*

5. The patient is a passive and reluctant recipient of bodily sensation imposed from the outside. (*Somatic Passivity*)
6. The experience of one's own thoughts as though they were put in one's mind by an external force. (*Thought Insertion*)
7. Patient believes his thoughts are being removed from his mind by some external agency. (*Thought Withdrawal*)
8. The experience of one's thoughts being magically transmitted to others. (*Thought Broadcast*)
9. Affects experienced as controlled externally.
10. Impulses experienced as controlled externally.
11. Motor activity experienced as controlled externally.

NOTE: The presence of one or more FRS, with a clear sensorium, is "pathognomonic" of schizophrenia.

The high hopes of Schneiderian FRS as promising a perfect means of discriminating schizophrenia from its imitators have not withstood the systematic appraisal of other investigators in recent years. Assessing the frequency of FRS in patients given a careful clinical diagnosis of schizophrenia, Carpenter, Strauss, and Muleh (1973) found no significant relationship between the initial presence of FRS and either duration or outcome of illness. More importantly, FRS were noted in a quarter of another cohort of patients in whom a manic-depressive psychosis was diagnosed. This is a high percentage of false positives for a purportedly "pathognomonic" symptom list. Furthermore, FRS may be detected rather often in acute psychoses of whatever sort, as well as in "chronic" schizophrenia. Hence the boundaries between "acute" and "chronic," good outcome and poor outcome, schizophrenia and manic-depressive psychoses cannot be drawn with great precision, relying only on Schneiderian criteria. One or more FRS were present at one time or another, for example, in cases 1 through 6, 11, and 13. Yet these patients present a range of clinical diagnoses from "pure" schizophrenia through the intermediate schizoaffective disorders to "pure" mania.

Recent Systems of Diagnosing Schizophrenia

Most of the recent sets of research diagnostic criteria for schizophrenia, including the one bearing that label (RDC), have been summarized in the excellent review of Endicott et al. (1976).

Renewed interest in psychodiagnosis has by now grown so intense as to dominate our meetings and our journals throughout the current decade. The confluence of factors responsible for this welcome reexamination must surely include the advent of lithium, improvements in computer technology, and refinements in psychogenetics. Lithium rendered the distinction between primary mood versus primary thought disorders of more than academic interest. Computer designs are now capable of making the kinds of multiple correlations between symptoms and diagnoses that would have overwhelmed the resources of investigators only a decade ago. Finally, the important adoption studies of Kety and Rosenthal, and the elegant twin studies of Gottesman and Shields, have stifled arguments against the notion of a heritable factor in schizophrenia. This in turn has solidified the concept of schizophrenia as an independent disease (albeit with various phenocopiers), manifesting itself in both a "core" and a "borderline" variety.

The contemporary diagnostic systems are arranged in a language better disposed to computer evaluation and thus obviate some of the pitfalls inherent in the earlier systems. With Bleuler's criteria, for example, much was left to the discretion of each clinician in regard to how many items need be present, and how much of each, to warrant the diagnosis of schizophrenia. One consequence of this ambiguity was that too much weight was given by some practitioners to *ambivalence,* even though the latter may be found in rather extreme form in very ill patients all across the diagnostic spectrum.

The new systems having arisen almost simultaneously, it seems both reasonable and equitable to present them in alphabetic order.

Astrachan's Criteria Combining certain features of Bleuler's, Langfeldt's, and Schneider's formulations (see pp. 212–217), Astrachan and his co-workers at Yale (1972) devised a checklist, the so-called New Haven Schizophrenia Index, whose items are recorded in Table 8–5. The Yale investigators have assigned different weights to different symptoms, in

TABLE 8–5

The New Haven Schizophrenia Index

1*a*. Delusions (other than depressive) (2 points)
b. Hallucinations (auditory)
c. Hallucinations (visual) (2 points for *b, c,* or *d*)
d. Hallucinations (other)

2*a*. Bizarre thinking
b. Autism or grossly unrealistic private thoughts
c. Looseness of association, illogical thinking, overinclusion (2 points for *a, b,* or *c*)

2*d*. Blocking
e. Concreteness (2 points for *d* or *e**)

2*f*. Derealization
g. Depersonalization (1 point *each* for *f* and *g*)

3. Inappropriate affect (1 point)
4. Confusion (1 point)
5. Paranoid ideation (ideas of reference, suspiciousness) (1 point)
6. Catatonic behavior: (*a*) excitement, (*b*) stupor, (*c*) waxy flexibility, (*d*) negativism, (*e*) mutism, (*f*) echolalia, or (*g*) stereotyped motor activity (1 point for any one of *a* through *g*)

*Where the fourth point necessary for diagnosis of schizophrenia is provided by 2*d* or 2*e*, these symptoms are not scored.

NOTE: Minimum of four points necessary for diagnosis of schizophrenia.

SOURCE: Astrachan, Harrow, Adler, Bauer, Schwartz, Schwartz, and Tucker (1972).

accordance with the discriminating capability of each. This method allows for many symptom combinations, any of which can generate the necessary four points for inclusion as "schizophrenic." Such an approach more nearly approximates nature, in the sense that clinical diagnosis depends on not one but a variety of patterns. As a result, however, some rather "weak" combinations emerge as positive alongside the stronger ones (the combination 2*f*, 2*g*, 4, and 6*d*, for example, would constitute a rather unimpressive rationale for diagnosing schizophrenia). Endicott also raises the criticism that affective syndromes are not eliminated by the New Haven Index, to which one could add that certain drug-abuse syndromes might also be falsely included. Other patients, with only one (but very dramatic) symptom on the checklist would be falsely excluded: Case 23 was strikingly paranoid, and had poor rapport—the latter not being reflected among the New Haven items. Nonetheless, the checklist has permitted high interrater agreement and led to inclusion—that is, positive according to the New Haven criteria—in 88 percent of clinically diagnosed schizophrenics. From the standpoint of filtering, the Yale checklist may be viewed as finer than Bleuler's but coarser than Feighner's or Taylor's.

Carpenter, Strauss, and Bartko: The IPSS Criteria The World Health Organization has sponsored an International Pilot Study of Schizophrenia (IPSS), with nine countries participating. In an analysis of which clinical criteria were most widely used throughout the world in arriving at a diagnosis of schizophrenia, material from 1,202 patients was analyzed: "Twelve signs and symptoms were found to be especially discriminating between schizophrenia and other psychiatric disorder" (Carpenter, Strauss, and Bartko, 1973, p. 1275). The twelve items (of which three are exclusion items) are listed in Table 8–6. The Carpenter criteria constitute a flexible system for diagnosis, inasmuch as various scores yield a diagnosis with varying levels of certainty. Almost all (91 percent) patients thought clinically to be schizophrenic had at least four positive items—but so did about a third of clinically nonschizophrenic psychotic and borderline patients in the original survey. Most of the false-positive cases had one or another form of manic-depressive disorder. By the time one narrows down to eight or more positive items, "false-positive" patients were completely eliminated—but only a fifth to a fourth of clinically diagnosed schizophren-

TABLE 8–6

IPSS Criteria of Carpenter, Strauss, and Bartko

1. Restricted affect
2. Poor insight
3. Thoughts aloud (thought broadcast, auditory hallucinations)
4. Poor rapport
5. Widespread delusions (several areas of the patient's life are interpreted delusionally)
6. Bizarre delusions
7. Nihilistic delusions (patient feels he is dead, or decaying, or that part of the body is missing)
8. Incoherent speech
9. Unreliable information
10. *Absence* of early awakening
11. *Absence* of a depressed facies
12. *Absence* of elation

NOTE: Minimum of four positive items needed for diagnosis of schizophrenia.

SOURCE: Carpenter, Strauss, and Bartko (1973).

ics were included. The IPSS criteria, in other words, can be adjusted to create a coarse or a superfine filter.

Another group of investigators also connected with the IPSS, Sartorius, Shapiro, and Kimura, mention (1975) that the most *prominent* symptoms in the schizophrenic group (some 811 patients) were lack of insight (97 percent), suspiciousness, poor rapport, ideas and delusions of reference and persecution (60 percent), and also flatness of affect and hallucinations. The "catatonic" symptoms were noted only on rare occasions.

When symptom profiles of individual schizophrenic patients were compared with a set of ideal subtype categories (CATEGO, fashioned by Dr. J. K. Wing), computer analysis was able to identify two groups of patients: one in which clinical and CATEGO diagnoses were concordant and a (smaller) group where this was not the case. Most of the "concordant" patients were of the subtypes "paranoid," "acute," or "hebephrenic"; among them was a significantly higher proportion of young single males. This finding would be in keeping with the observations of many clinicians, including myself, that schizophrenia often stands out more clearly in this population; so many otherwise schizophrenic female patients show either well-preserved or flamboyantly disordered affect that the schizophrenic diagnosis becomes pulled toward the schizoaffective, or thrown out altogether. This is particularly true in the less seriously ill "borderline" group, which is "overpopulated" by females: here, the traditional 1:1 male-female ratio for schizophrenia does not seem to hold. The reasons for this have been discussed elsewhere in this book.

As with all the new diagnostic systems, the criteria employed are "intended to enhance, not replace, clinical diagnosis, which should utilize all available information" (Carpenter, Strauss, and Bartko, 1973, p. 1277).

Feighner's Criteria Feighner is the senior author of the paper published in 1972 outlining diagnostic criteria, for use in psychiatric research, of some fourteen conditions where it was thought such criteria could be set forth in programmable fashion. His co-workers are for the most part connected with the Washington University School of Medicine in St. Louis, for which reason their criteria are also known as the "St. Louis Criteria." Those for schizophrenia are to be found in Table 8–7. Of special interest is their item C-3 ("Family history of schizophrenia"), the only item honoring the importance of the genetic factor in schizophrenia to be found in any of the diagnostic schemata.

Because the St. Louis criteria require chronicity as well as the absence of affective symptoms, they tend to single out a sicker population than would Astrachan's criteria.

Spitzer's Criteria: The "RDC" Spitzer, Endicott, and their co-workers at the New York State Psychiatric Institute have developed a set of research diagnostic criteria (their "RDC") for a number of major disorders,

TABLE 8–7

Feighner's Criteria for Schizophrenia

A. *(Both of the following are necessary)*
   1. A chronic illness with at least six months of symptoms prior to the index evaluation without return to premorbid level of adjustment.
   2. Absence of depressive or manic symptoms sufficient to qualify for probable or certain affective disorder.

B. *(At least one of the following)*
   1. Delusions or hallucinations without perplexity.
   2. Verbal production that makes communication difficult.

C. *(At least three of the following for "definite," two, for "probable," schizophrenia)*
   1. Single.
   2. Poor premorbid social adjustment or work history.
   3. Family history of schizophrenia.
   4. Absence of alcoholism or drug abuse during the year before onset of psychosis.
   5. Onset of illness before age forty.

SOURCE: Adapted from Feighner et al. (1972), *Archives of General Psychiatry,* 26:57–63.

including schizophrenia, schizoaffective disorder, and major depressive disorder or manic disorder.

The Spitzer checklist for schizophrenia (presented *in extenso* in Table 8–8) has been designed to navigate a course between the chronic deteriorating ("Kraepelinian") type of schizophrenia and less severe syndromes (such as Kety-type borderline schizophrenia, brief hysterical or situational psychoses, and borderline syndromes in the usage of Kernberg or Gunderson).

Advantages of the Spitzer criteria include (1) allowance for estimating degrees of diagnostic certainty and (2) the ease with which they can be modified to create a new set of criteria for the related category "schizoaffective" (see pp. 239–241).

Taylor and Abrams's Criteria Similar to the criteria of the St. Louis group, those elaborated by Taylor and Abrams are the most stringent of all the systems examined in this text. As can be seen from Table 8–9, their criteria contain the requirement of an illness of *greater* than (as opposed to "at least") six months duration. In addition, stress is placed not on restriction of affect but upon absence of a broad affect. This last requirement would probably exclude a number of chronic undifferentiated schizophren-

TABLE 8–8

Spitzer's Research Diagnostic Criteria for the Diagnosis of Schizophrenia

(A through C are required for the period of illness being considered)

A. (At least two for "definite," one, for "probable." If symptoms occur in the context of drug or alcohol abuse, do *not* score.)
1. Thought broadcast, insertion, or withdrawal.*
2. Delusions of being controlled or influenced; bizarre or multiple delusions.*
3. Delusions other than persecutory or jealousy, lasting at least one week.
4. Delusions of any type if accompanied by hallucinations of any type for at least a week.
5. Auditory hallucinations in which either a voice keeps up a running conversation on the subject's behaviors or thoughts as they occur, or two or more voices converse with each other.
6. Nonaffective verbal hallucinations spoken to the subject.*
7. Hallucinations of any type throughout the day for several days, or intermittently for at least one month.
8. Definite instances of marked formal thought disorder,* accompanied either by blunted or inappropriate affect, delusions, or hallucinations of any type or by grossly disorganized behavior.

B. (Either 1 or 2)
1. The current period of illness has lasted at least two weeks from the onset of a noticeable change in the subject's usual condition.
2. The subject has had a previous period of illness lasting at least two weeks in which he met the criteria *and* residual signs of the illness have remained; for example, extreme social withdrawal, blunted or inappropriate affect, formal thought disorder, or unusual thoughts or perceptual experiences.

C. At no time during the active period of illness being considered did the subject meet the criteria for either probable or definite manic or depressive syndrome to such a degree that it was a prominent part of the illness.

*As defined in the manual of explanations prepared by Spitzer et al. (1978).

NOTE: Further subtyping is done for *course* (acute, subacute, subchronic, chronic) and for clinical phenomenology (paranoid, catatonic, undifferentiated, and so forth).

SOURCE: Spitzer et al. (1978), *Archives of General Psychiatry,* 35:773–782. Copyright 1978, American Medical Association. Reprinted by permission.

ics in a recuperating phase of their illness, in whom items A, B, C, E, F, and G would be present but whose affective range might be fairly broad and not inappropriate (as might be exemplified by case illustration 3, shortly after admission).

Taylor and Abrams (1975) justify the exacting nature of their criteria on the grounds that the next most stringent set, those of Feighner, did not

TABLE 8–9

Taylor and Abrams's Modified Research Criteria for Schizophrenia

(All the following must be present for a diagnosis of schizophrenia)

A. Duration of episode greater than six months
B. Clear consciousness
C. Presence of either delusions, hallucinations, or formal thought disorder*
D. Absence of a broad affect
E. Absence of signs and symptoms sufficient to make a diagnosis of affective disease
F. Absence of alcoholism or drug abuse within one year of the index admission
G. Absence of clinical focal signs and symptoms of coarse brain disease or major medical illness known to produce significant behavioral changes

*Namely, verbigeration, non sequiturs, word approximations, neologisms, blocking, and derailment.

SOURCE: Taylor and Abrams (1975), *The American Journal of Psychiatry,* 132:1276–1280. Copyright 1975, the American Psychiatric Association. Reprinted by permission.

always differentiate manic from schizophrenic patients (at least, not in Taylor's patient sample). As they noted:

> . . . the presence of delusions, hallucinations, or lack of understandable speech; being single; or having a poor premorbid adjustment—were equally frequent in manic and schizophrenic patients. (p. 1278)

One does encounter puzzling cases on occasion that would bear out this point (e.g., case 11).

Elsewhere these authors (Abrams, Taylor, and Gaztanaga, 1974) allude to another source of diagnostic confusion: many acutely psychotic patients with paranoid symptoms are given a clinical diagnosis of schizophrenia. But in their sample, only a few of these patients met their criteria for schizophrenia, while about half could be considered manic by equally exacting criteria, and were so rediagnosed by the authors. This startling finding, even if somewhat exaggerated, does demonstrate the powerful "surplus meaning" of *paranoid*. In the minds of most clinicians, "paranoid" signals "schizophrenic," probably because "paranoid" is one of the classic subtypes of schizophrenia, outlined by Bleuler and others half a century ago, and is taught to every psychiatric resident during his first weeks of training. This points up the problems generated by confusing universes of discourse. Schizophrenia and mania are underlying conditions: "paranoid" describes a type of temperament or character, which may occur with *any* underlying psychiatric condition (see cases 7 and 11), including toxic psychosis.

Fine versus Coarse Diagnostic Filters

One could arbitrarily divide the diagnostic schemata just examined into "coarse" (Bleuler), "medium-fine" (Astrachan, Spitzer) or "fine" (Kraepelin, Langfeldt, Schneider, Feighner, Taylor) filters of schizophrenia. The IPSS index (Carpenter) is flexible, depending on the number of positive items demanded. Endicott, Forman, and Spitzer (1976) noted that of sixteen patients in a certain sample, regarded as schizophrenic by the New Haven criteria, only five remained so labeled by the St. Louis criteria. The realm of "borderline" schizophrenia would expand or contract in accordance with the scheme utilized.

Although the Spitzer RDC can separate "acute" from "chronic" cases, the New Haven criteria do not; neither do Langfeldt's or Schneider's FRS really: many acute psychoses exhibit FRS and are soon followed by excellent recovery. Which "acute schizophrenic episodes" go on to become chronic schizophrenia and which are succeeded by recovery or by "change" to manic-depressive illness is still difficult to predict (see Serban and Gidynski, 1975; case illustrations 1 and 4).

Before examining the schizoaffective and manic-depressive categories in greater detail, we may review briefly the evolution of diagnostic standards in schizophrenia.

Nearly a hundred years have passed since the classic papers of Kahlbaum on catatonia and of his pupil, Hecker, on hebephrenia. Both men were describing groups of symptoms; their respective syndromes were based essentially on clinical-phenomenological observations. Though both were originally assumed to be separate entities, Fink drew attention in 1880, as Scharfetter mentions (1975), to cases with "mixed" catatonic and hebephrenic features.

From this era of *nosography,* that is, of a taxonomy based on observation of symptoms alone, we pass to Kraepelin, who added the notion of a common *outcome* as the ingredient capable of unifying many hitherto discrete syndromes. Bleuler substituted for emphasis on course, his emphasis on certain signs—some of them rather subtle—of illness that could take a variety of courses. "Trait" took precedence over "state." Furthermore, Bleuler adopted Freud's view that schizophrenic psychopathology could be understood in psychodynamic terms. Craziness was not so "crazy" if one looked underneath to the level of motivation and symbolization. This led to a maximal broadening of the concept of schizophrenia to include patients whose developmental fixation points seemed to be in the same early oral phase, as had been noted among more classical cases of schizophrenia. A psychological approach to the diagnosis of schizophrenia took its place side by side with the older phenomenological approach. This tendency was more prominent in the United States than in Europe, and more prevalent among office-based psychiatrists than among their colleagues in the hospitals. Elsewhere, however, contracting forces were at work. Schneider and Langfeldt, as we have seen, turned once more to what the observer could detect with the naked eye. Helmchen (1975) makes the point nicely when he quotes the German psychiatrist Neumann as having said, in *1843:* "Recognition of a disease is not recognition of the essence, but rather recognition of phenomena" (p. 10) and then, in the next breath, cites Cooper et al. in *1972:* "The actual object of the diagnosis is . . . concrete, visible symptomatology" (p. 10).

We find ourselves in the 1970s reverting to phenomenology. In this respect we have come full circle with our predecessors of the 1870s, only this time armed with biometric instruments, an ever-increasing storehouse of genetic data, and the computer. Meantime, those who adhere to a category-based taxonomy are reluctant to use the label "schizophrenic" except in the most flagrant cases. This in turn swells the ranks of the borderline syndromes; it will be some years before we know whether this shift represents prudence or mere conservatism. As we move toward the diagnostic habits typical of the European continent and of England (see Cooper et al., 1972; Cooper, 1975; Edwards, 1972), we have begun to see what one might call "biometric" drift. Analogous to the psychometric drift of which Meehl spoke, this shift in diagnostic standards is toward the criteria embodied in the recent research systems for establishing diagnosis in psychiatry.

The problems under discussion here have been nicely highlighted in the recent work of Strauss and his colleagues (Strauss, Gabriel, et al., 1979). In their study of the fit between actual patients and archetypal patients (the latter derived from stereotyped concepts of schizophrenia, mania, neurotic and psychotic depression), they found that "the vast majority of patients fall between these syndromes, having characteristics of several of them" (p. 105). Criticizing our current archetypes as providing insufficient diagnostic coverage for our patient population, Strauss et al. expressed the opinion that the problem lies not so much in the inadequacy of our rating scales or of our diagnostic skills as in the inappropriateness of our contemporary diagnostic system to represent real patients accurately (p. 112). As a partial solution they advocate a multiaxial approach, such as we have been emphasizing throughout this book.

The Subtleties of Schizophrenic Symptomatology

It is not always self-evident when a particular sign or symptom of schizophrenia is present, let alone when the "critical mass" of symptoms is present that would, taken collectively, confirm the diagnosis. Frank Fish, for example, has drawn attention to the manner in which schizophrenic symptoms can be distributed into the compartments of *emotion, perception, thinking,* and *motor behavior* (1975, p. 4). But, "If flattening or incongruity of affect are clearly present, then schizophrenia may be diagnosed, but minor degrees of these signs are not diagnostic'' (p. 4). A similar observation was made earlier by Eva Johanson (1964) in relation to ''minor delusions.'' Only six of her fifty-two cases satisfied enough other criteria to be called schizophrenic (all were male); the families' histories presented a varied picture, and the patients themselves showed various combinations of disorders from alcoholism or minor brain injuries to severe character disorders or depression. Cultural differences affect the way in which clinical signs are perceived, as when Fish gives the example, ''A continental psychiatrist might believe that a depressed upper-class Englishman with a 'stiff upper lip' had flattening of affect'' (p. 4). Temporal lobe epilepsy may mimic paranoid schizophrenia, but electroencephalographic evidence is not always available or conclusive. When the pronounced jealousy of an otherwise unclassifiable ''borderline'' patient crosses a certain line and becomes the delusional jealousy of a schizophrenic, again, is not always easy to demonstrate.

The hallucinosis of LSD and other catechol and indoleamine hallucinogens can be differentiated from schizophrenia, according to Meares and Horvath (1973), by psychophysiological studies of habituation rate, but at the clinical level this distinction may sometimes be very difficult (Stone, 1973). Borderline patients with abnormal sensitivity to such drugs are not always easy to tell apart from ''true'' schizophrenics whose first break was precipitated by drugs.

Certain signs, taken one by one, may each be quite compatible with a schizophrenic diagnosis but may, if viewed in context, suggest a different syndrome. Lilliston (1973), studying ninety hospitalized average-IQ male patients, attempted to quantify the degree of CNS damage as reflected in a battery of psychological tests. He noted that the higher the likelihood of organicity, the more the supposed schizophrenic patient was apt to show (rather gross) perceptual abnormality, sluggishness, and apathy about his illness. In contrast, the schizophrenics with low likelihood of CNS damage were more anxious and had more affect and greater concern about their problems. Lilliston believed his results argued for the view of schizophrenia as a nonhomogeneous entity, even when one begins with a sample labeled ''schizophrenic.'' It often remains a matter of clinical judgment whether a high-organicity ''schizophrenic'' patient becomes reclassified a borderline (or psychotic) phenocopy or a ''genuine'' schizophrenic whose illness is exaggerated by CNS damage.

Although all systems for classifying schizophrenia emphasize verbal production that makes communication difficult, there is a range of speech and thought disorder from mild to gross and from nonspecific to paradigmatic. *In fact every symptom considered important in the diagnosis of the major psychoses can be viewed as varying in intensity in continuous fashion; ''categorical'' diagnosis rests upon extremes of many different continuous functions.* Regarding verbal production, a number of technics have been elaborated in recent years to evaluate purported schizophrenic speech in more quantitative fashion. Looseness of associations has been studied by Reilly et al. (1975), who propose a classification ranging from "L-1" (mild shift within a sentence) to "L-6" (drastic shift within a sentence). Gaps in communication, vagueness of ideas, and blocking were also recorded in a sample of fifty-one acute psychiatric patients (twenty-six of whom were considered schizophrenic). The latter abnormalities were much more common in the schizophrenic group. Private meanings (including neologisms) and perseveration were even more typical of the schizophrenics. Whereas many types of looseness of association were noted in 80 percent of the schizophrenic patients, only half exhibited *blocking* (as against only 8 percent in the nonschizophrenics). Certain forms of speech abnormality (namely, perseveration) were recorded only from what appeared to be a particular subgroup of schizophrenics whose course was chronic and downhill. Such abnormalities might help in distinguishing dilute (borderline, in Kety's sense) schizophrenia from the more aggressive forms. Other important contributions to the quantitative analysis of schizophrenic speech have been made by Gottschalk and his co-workers (1961) and by Chapman and Chapman (1973). Familiarity with the more recent studies should serve to underline the cautionary note expressed by Salzman et al. (1966) that cognitive disruption may be a common feature of all severe psychiatric illness, whether schizophrenic, manic-depressive, or organic. This impression has been seconded more recently by Braff and Beck (1974) in connection with depressive disorders and by Breakey and Goodell (1972), who found thought disorder prominent in manic as well as in schizophrenic disorders. Diagnosis, if based on observations at only one moment in time, emerges as a shaky practice indeed: phenomenology alone is simply not that reliable a guide. This state of affairs has even led Skodol, Buckley, and Salamon (1976) to suggest that the "so-called schizophrenic symptoms are protean in origin and not in and of themselves sufficient to make a diagnosis" (p. 512). These authors, in sympathy perhaps with Adolf Meyer, recommend abandonment of "Bleulerian reliance" on symptoms[7] for diagnosis in favor of paying heed to the longitudinal course, the outcome, the family genetics, and the drug responsiveness. Van Praag (1976) and Ollerenshaw (1973) have also warned against equating the presence of "schizophrenic" signs and symptoms with the disease "schizophrenia," inasmuch as clinical *syndrome*—especially the one we often label "acute schizophrenia"—can occur in what eventually is recognized as mania (see case illustration 1), depression, drug reactions, and even hysteria.

[7]Actually, as David Raskin (1975) has recently mentioned, Bleuler did *not* rely as much upon his "4 A's" for diagnosis as is commonly supposed. Though he thought loosening of associations, as well as thought broadcast, was pathognomonic, Bleuler placed much more emphasis on the *intensity* and *extensiveness* of a symptom than on its individual nature.

Multidimensional Systems for Schizophrenia

Besides the multidimensional systems mentioned earlier (pp. 195–200) for general psychiatric diagnosis, or for borderline syndromes, there remain several others of particular use in schizophrenia.

Grinker and Holzman

Recognizing the difficulty in confirming the diagnosis of schizophrenia in certain young adult patients, Grinker and Holzman (1973) proposed a schema designed to aid in distinguishing schizophrenic from non-schizophrenic.

Five parameters were chosen, each to be graded on a scale from zero to six. Their "schizophrenia-state inventory" dealt with (1) language abnormalities, (2) anxiety, (3) capacity to experience pleasure, (4) integration versus lack of integration of the self, and (5) inconsistency of thought, affect, and perception. Notice the position of importance given to pleasure capacity, a point not mentioned in the various research schemata (as it is often confused with depression and thus does not lend itself to the achievement of interrater reliability). Rado (1962), it will be recalled, gave anhedonia a place of great importance in his diagnostic schema for schizophrenia.

The most relevant features of the young schizophrenic were, in the opinion of Grinker and Holzman (1973, pp. 170–171):

a. The presence of a disorder of thinking, even though it is subtly present

b. A striking quality of diminished capacity to experience pleasure, particularly in interpersonal relationships

c. A strong characterological dependency on other people

d. A noteworthy impairment in competence (as judged by school or work performance)

e. An exquisitely vulnerable sense of self-regard

Patients with borderline syndromes of whatever etiology frequently exhibit items *c, d,* and *e*. If scores on *a* and *b* are equivocal, one can see how difficult it can be at times to differentiate a borderline case without schizophrenic underpinnings from a case of "borderline" (mild) schizophrenia. The authors provide a small collection of clinical vignettes, depicting acute schizophrenia, paranoid schizophrenia, schizoaffective psychosis, and so on. These should be compared with case illustrations 6, 8, and 10.

Helmchen

Recently Helmchen (1975) analyzed which symptoms were noted with significantly increased frequency in the eight schizophrenic subtypes recognized in the International Classification of Diseases, 8th revision (ICD-8). His findings are presented in Table 8–10. Note that in this table the "+" indicates the occurrence of a symptom in a given subtype significantly higher in frequency than the occurrence of that symptom among the other subtypes. There are no symptoms found exclusively in only one of the recognized subtypes, and none that were *particularly associated* with "latent" schizophrenia.

Helmchen's "schizoaffective" schizophrenia referred to a subtype characterized by "simultaneous manifestation of pronounced depressive or manic features intermingled with schizophrenic features, . . . with an inter-

TABLE 8–10

Prominent Symptoms in Various Subtypes of Schizophrenia

	ICD-8 Subtype							
SIGNS AND SYMPTOMS	*295.1*	*295.2*	*295.3*	*295.4*	*295.5*	*295.6*	*295.7*	*295.8*
Disturbance of comprehension		+						
Disturbance of concentration						+		
Thought blocking		+						
Thought slowing; circumstantial						+		
Paralogia or incoherence	+							
Flight of ideas								+
Delusion of persecution or of reference			+					
Delusion of guilt		+						
Hearing voices			+					
Autism	+							
Flattening of affect						+		
Depressive; suicidal tendency							+	
Anxious				+				
Elated	+							
Lamenting						+		
Fatuity	+							
Inadequate affect	+							
Rigidity of affect		+						
Impulse poverty						+		
Impulse blocking, stupor, mutism, negativism, or stereotypy		+						
Lack of insight	+							

Key: 295.1 = schizophrenia, hebephrenic
295.2 = Schizophrenia, catatonic
295.3 = schizophrenia, paranoid
295.4 = schizophrenia, acute episode
295.5 = schizophrenia, latent
295.6 = schizophrenia, residual
295.7 = schizophrenia, schizoaffective
295.8 = schizophrenia, other

SOURCE: Adapted from Helmchen (1975).

mittent course [remissions without defect]'' (1975, p. 15). Although *Zwischenfälle* (in-between cases) were considered rare by Schneider, they made up 8½ percent of the 432 schizophrenic admissions evaluated by Helmchen.

Overlapping occurrences of various symptoms among all the subtypes were the rule. Flattened affect, for example, while prominent in ''residual'' schizophrenia, was never noted in less than a fourth of the patients in any of the eight subtypes. Very little reliability could be achieved among the various subtypes; this led Helmchen to suggest standardization of diagnosis through use of biometric instruments, videotapes, and the like. Furthermore he proposed a *multiaxial* coding system, whose axes include (*a*) symptomatology, (*b*) ''etiology,'' and (*c*) time, along with two others, intensity and degree of certainty. When considering *etiology,* Helmchen recommends attention to familial disposition, personality type, psychological factors, somatic illnesses, social factors, and any untoward side effects of prior treatment. The *time* axis requires consideration of age and speed of onset, course (intermittent versus chronic), duration, and outcome.

Van Praag

Similar to the multiaxial system of Helmchen, the three-dimensional system of Van Praag (1976) is based on three criteria: symptomatology, etiology, and course. Van Praag advocates this method of classifying the schizophrenic psychoses, because, as he put it, ''one word diagnoses, such as neurosis, depression and schizophrenia, are futile. . . . either they suggest something about symptomatology, etiology and course simultaneously, but not explicitly, giving these concepts the diagnostic depth-of-focus of a poor photograph . . . or they are used sometimes in the symptomatologic and at other times in the etiologic sense, thus creating chaos rather than diagnostic order'' (1976, p. 491).

Van Praag's symptom dimension includes evaluation of patients in regard to (*a*) level of consciousness, (*b*) delusions, (*c*) hallucinations, (*d*) emotional flattening, (*e*) abnormal motor activity, (*f*) inertia (namely, loss of initiative), and (*g*) incoherent train of thought.

Acknowledging the commonly held position that schizophrenia and manic-depressive psychoses are fundamentally different illnesses, Van Praag believes the family-history factor should be regarded as *positive* if there are first- or second-degree relatives with (present or past) schizophrenic psychoses and as *negative* if the only ill relatives are manic-depressive.

Bellak and the Ego-Function Profile

For many years Bellak has espoused a *multiple-factor psychosomatic theory of schizophrenia* (1949; Bellak and Loeb, 1969). Regarding what clinicians insist on labeling ''schizophrenia'' as hardly unitary but rather as the "shared common path of a variety of etiologic factors," Bellak has roundly criticized the tendency for so many investigators to search for the *one* factor operative in all cases accorded the schizophrenic label (1969, pp. 8–9). The schizophrenic *syndrome* is seen, instead, as stemming from the interaction of several factors, no one of which may be significant in and of itself.

Bellak stresses the need to assess simultaneously the genetic endowment, the family constellation, possible organic predisposing factors (namely, "minimal brain damage" of certain varieties: Bellak, 1976), and a possible serum factor.

This multifactorial model has been further embellished by elaborate scales for assessing a number of ego strengths considered highly related to schizophrenic vulnerability. In effect this is therefore a *dimensional* model, one of considerable relevance to the borderline syndromes—inasmuch as it is possible to capture all manner of shadings and gradations with these measuring devices. The model proposed in Bellak's 1969 book is tilted very far in the direction of a dimensional view only. The chapter on diagnosis, written by Thomas Freeman, goes so far as to state that "the patient who suffers from a schizophrenic psychosis presents manifestations which are not fixed . . . after the manner of some physical diseases. . . . The phenomena are present one day and not the others; revealed to one examiner and not the other"; and "the changing nature of the symptomatology. . . does not carry implications for etiology beyond underlining the sensitivity of the schizophrenic patient to his physical and psychological milieu" (Bellak and Loeb, 1969, p. 338). Finally, Freeman concludes, "The diagnosis must . . . depend almost entirely on the psychiatrist's conception of schizophrenia" (pp. 337–338).

In my opinion Freeman's conceptions would lead to a solipsistic world in which all attempts at meaningful diagnosis are thrown to the winds.

At all events, the *ego-function profile* of Bellak can be quite valuable, especially in the assessment of patients who fail to meet the criteria for category diagnosis, that is, patients with borderline conditions. In Table 8–11 the eleven ego functions routinely measured in Bellak's system are outlined. Each function, in actual practice, is appraised according to a 13-point scale (Bellak and Loeb, 1969, p. 790), as well as by appropriate psychological tests.

The psychoanalytic orientation of the Ego-Function Profile (and the accompanying Id and Super-Ego Scales) (1969, pp. 817 and 825) differentiates Bellak's approach from the others we have just been inspecting. Although several of the items (reality testing, thought processes, stimulus barrier) are especially suited to the evaluation of a possibly schizophrenic group of patients, the items in general will be appropriate to patients at all levels of functioning, but particularly the borderline. There are important similarities and differences between this profile and that utilized by Kern-

TABLE 8–11

Bellak's Ego-Function Profile

Ego Functions to Be Assessed	
1. Reality testing	7. Adaptive regression in the service of the ego; free association
2. Judgment	8. Defensive functioning
3. Sense of reality	9. Stimulus barrier
4. Regulation and control of drives	10. Autonomous functioning
5. Object relations	11. Synthetic-integrative functioning
6. Thought processes	

SOURCE: Bellak and Loeb (1969, p. 790).

berg and his associates. These will be discussed below when we examine criteria for borderline organization in greater detail. Apart from the phrase "borderline schizophrenic" in Schniewind's chapter, "Group Therapy of Schizophrenics", the term "borderline," it should be noted, does not appear in Bellak's book.

Wing's "Nuclear Syndrome"

John Wing has been closely connected with the International Pilot Study of Schizophrenia (IPSS) and has been particularly concerned with the establishment of clearer boundaries for the concept of schizophrenia. He mentioned (Wing and Nixon, 1975) that we apply the label upon recognition in a patient of one of several "schizophrenic syndromes." Recently, Wing set out to sharpen the definition of the symptom clusters that would best discriminate between schizophrenia and nonschizophrenia. A 360-item questionnaire was administered to the 1200 patients in the IPSS study; of these, some 17 items were isolated which captured most of the Schneiderian FRS (see p. 216). Wing telescoped these 17 items into five clusters to be then included in the CATEGO computerized system of classification. The presence of any one of the five symptom-groups (such as insertion, broadcast, or withdrawal of thought) indicated the presence of the *nuclear syndrome*.

The nuclear syndrome (NS) was noted in almost *half* of all IPSS patients accorded a *clinical* diagnosis of schizophrenia (432 out of 878). Of the 469 examples of NS in the total patient sample, 446 had received a diagnosis of either schizophrenic or "paranoid" psychosis. This meant that 95 percent of "NS +" patients were thought to be schizophrenic clinically—a very high concordance between computer and clinician. The other 23 *non*-schizophrenic "NS +" patients were considered "discrepant positive" cases (all but one were manic-depressive). Wing makes a special point of using the term "discrepant-positive" rather than "false-positive" and criticizes Carpenter's use of the latter in similar contexts because the label "false-positive" assumes the clinical diagnosis is correct. Wing wishes to avoid this circularity and thus resorts to a more even-handed approach where neither the clinician nor the computer is regarded as "correct" until the diagnosis is validated in the future.

Other remarks of Wing and Nixon (1975) or of Wing (1976) make it clear that a dual approach is embraced, including category and dimension, toward diagnosis—despite identification primarily with interest in improving category diagnosis. Categories enable the practitioner to "count heads" and to make quick decisions about treatment, but, as Wing states, it is the ability to switch from the categorical to the dimensional type of thinking that marks the most highly creative scientist.

Recognizing that the FRS occur in less than half of what is currently being called "schizophrenia," Wing also pays respect to the efforts of Gottesman and Shields and of Kety to "investigate the associations between the central syndrome and a penumbra of less and less precisely defined phenomena" (Wing and Nixon, 1975, p. 858) (i.e., the "borderline schizophrenic" and related groups). The importance of the whole clinical picture was stressed by Schneider himself, as Wing mentions; Carpenter, Sacks, et al. (1976) have also recently remarked on the superiority of collecting data from multiple sources, over longer periods of time, to any existing questionnaire for diagnosing schizophrenia.

Walter Reich and the Spectrum Concept of Schizophrenia

Walter Reich (1975) has recently commented on the spectrum concept of schizophrenia, cautioning against the adverse side effects of adopting such a concept lest a large number of patients, currently labeled in other ways, come to be stigmatized as schizophrenic even though their conditions are much milder than those meeting category criteria. Meanwhile Reich does assert that a genetic model for schizophrenia, utilizing a spectrum (i.e., dimensional) concept, is "particularly attractive . . . from a theoretical point of view, since it provides not only a relatively parsimonious and unifying etiological theory but also, through its research, a method of delimiting the outer boundaries of the genetic spectrum, and of testing whether or not specific clinical states hypothesized as lying within those boundaries do in fact do so" (1975, p. 490). While I clearly have no quarrel with this line of reasoning, I do take exception to Reich's warning about the "dangers" of overdiagnosis. The problems of a treating psychiatrist are often very different from those of the investigator. There are numerous instances when awareness of a "positive" family history serves as a useful guide in orienting the practitioner's diagnostic thinking. This is especially true when all other diagnostic efforts have seemed to lead nowhere. The family history *in no way establishes* the diagnosis. But in practice it frequently helps organize otherwise elusive cues and symptoms, no one of which is decisive, into a diagnostic "hunch" of great value to the patient (see case illustration 27).

Reich, further on, contrasts the overdiagnosis of schizophrenia in America, based on a psychodynamic model, with the Russian overdiagnosis of schizophrenia, based on the concept of a genetic spectrum. The latter, he believes, is the more dangerous, because there is less tendency for a clinician to modify his diagnosis in the light of subsequent events if diagnosis rests more on a hereditary than on an environmental foundation. The result may be a therapeutic nihilism. The Russian school, he adds, inclines toward the belief that initially milder forms of schizophrenic and "subschizophrenic" disorders (see Nadzharov, 1972) may progress to the more severe forms, in a rather fluid fashion, reminiscent of a similar notion held by the psychodynamic school here in the 1940s (see Zilboorg, 1941). At least some Russian investigators, however, use "borderline" in a manner similar to the definitions of Gunderson or Kernberg. With Shakhmatova-Pavlova, for example, the label "schizophrenic" was reserved for those with severe outward manifestations (akin to Wing's "nuclear syndrome") while "borderline schizophrenic" was used in a spectrum sense to designate patients whose less obvious psychopathology was *probably* set in motion by genetic predisposition to the major disorder.

If one accepts a *spectrum* concept in schizophrenia, then one will be obliged at times to register an initial impression that (*a*) a particular patient is not clinically "schizophrenic" by any of the category definitions in current use, because (*b*) he is not "psychotic" (i.e., reality testing is essentially preserved), yet (*c*) he does show enough of the less crucial signs of schizophrenic disorders to warrant a "spectrum" diagnosis (namely, "borderline" schizophrenia; see the "schizotypal" patients of case illustrations 10 and 23).

Schizoaffective Illness: Criteria for Diagnosis

The focus in this section is on disorders in which at least a few of the features of the two major psychoses appear, irrespective of whether the disorder tilts toward classical schizophrenia, toward the affective disorders, or is evenly balanced.

As the British psychiatrist De Alarcon (1975) has mentioned, the many studies of schizoaffective disorders may be grouped according to whether the author conceives of schizoaffective illness as an independent entity (see Mitsuda, 1965; McCabe and Strömgren, 1975), a variety of affective disorder (Clayton, Rodin, and Winokur, 1968), a true mixed state (A. T. Beck, 1967), or a variety of schizophrenia (Kasanin, 1933). The more one is wedded to a diagnostic system based on categories, the harder it will be to live comfortably with these in-between cases. In Britain, De Alarcon states, "the use of schizoaffective disorder as a category is . . . frowned upon," adding that the main British textbooks recommend that one should "endeavor to decide . . . for either one or the other, schizophrenia or affective disorder" (1975, p. 138).

The either/or approach to the problems posed by these intermediate cases has the virtue of simplicity but the serious drawback that it does violence to nature. The more even the mixture of schizophrenic and manic-depressive symptoms, the more there will be to ignore, if one is compelled to settle for an either/or diagnosis.

There is one drawback to the term "schizoaffective" I readily acknowledge: The word is so constructed as to emphasize schizophrenia (to be sure, Kasanin originally thought he was describing a variant of schizophrenia). This is not so bad for the cases where symptoms are, as best one can quantify, more than half schizophrenic in flavor. But when the balance is tipped the other way, one grows impatient with the label and wishes there were some convenient term to designate a more-than-fifty-percent-affective disorder. There is none, however. The English language rests comfortably with "schizoaffective" or even "schizomanic" (a term that once enjoyed some popularity) but recoils at "manoschizic" or at any other adjective where the affective component comes first.[8]

In the most recent edition of the American Psychiatric Association diagnostic manual (DSM-3), there is an improved method for classifying schizoaffective disorders: one may now refer to them as predominantly depressive, predominantly manic, or mixed. Ideally one would also want to characterize them as predominantly schizophrenic, evenly divided, or as predominantly affective (see Sz-MDP Continuum Diagram; also Cohen's weighted scale, pp. 240–244).

Before we look at the criteria in common use for schizoaffective disorders, it is important to keep in mind that schizoaffective disorders in which schizophrenic symptoms are fairly prominent account for at least 8 (Helmchen, 1975) to 10 (De Alarcon, 1975) percent of large samples of schizophrenic patients.

Welner's Criteria for Schizoaffective Psychoses

Welner, Croughan, and Robins (1974), colleagues of Feighner and Guze in St. Louis, have presented a methodical approach to the schizoaffective psychoses, acknowledging the importance of achieving reliability in diagnosis. They mention at the outset some twenty-four labels by which these disorders have been known—a tribute both to the thoroughness of the authors and to the thoroughness of the confusion in the psychiatric literature devoted to this topic. A patient meeting Welner's criteria will be in the

[8]Leonhard's "cycloid psychosis" is used to some extent in Europe; it has never been popular in the United States.

"borderland" between schizophrenia and manic-depressive psychosis (viewed as "categories"); if usually psychotic, he will of course *not* be *borderline* in Kernberg's terminology. Some patients appear to exhibit less flagrant symptoms in both the schizophrenic and affective areas, in conjunction with a personality organization that does appear to meet Kernberg's criteria (see case illustration 16). The method proposed by Welner et al. for diagnosing schizoaffective psychoses is outlined in Table 8–12.

An alternative method suggested by Welner et al. for satisfying their *first* criterion (concerning depression or mania) would simply require *any six* of the seventeen symptoms represented by Table 8–12: Part 2, A-1*a*, 1*b* (items 1 through 8), A-2*a* (1), 2*a* (2), and 2*b* (items 1 through 6). I find this method more useful because it circumvents the requirement of satisfying *either* depressive *or* manic criteria before the schizoaffective label can be applied. Clearly some patients have several symptoms in both categories, without having enough to meet criteria for either one alone.

Schizoaffective Psychoses: Most Frequently Encountered Symptoms

In the article of Helmchen's referred to on p. 228 is a table listing the common symptoms of schizophrenic psychoses, showing frequencies for each among the eight subtypes recognized by the ICD-8 (International

TABLE 8–12

A Proposed Method for Diagnosis of Schizoaffective and Related Psychoses

Part 1

A. Patient should have enough severe affective manifestation to meet criteria for mania or depression (see Part 2, A).

and

B. Patient should have sufficient signs of thought disorder and of behavior disorder, *different* from those associated with affective disorder, to render an affective diagnosis unlikely; these nonaffective manifestations may or may not be sufficient to meet criteria for schizophrenia (see Part 2, B).

and

C. At least one of the following
   1. Acute onset
   2. Episodic course
   3. Pronounced perplexity or confusion

and

D. The psychosis must not be due to, or associated with, alcohol, drug abuse, or a known organic brain disease.

Part 2

A. Specific Items for Diagnosis of Depression or Mania

1. Depression (*a* plus *b* plus *c* required)
   - *a*. Dysphoric mood (for details, see pp. 250–253, Feighner's criteria for depression)
   - *b*. Five out of eight for "definite;" four for "probable"
     - (1) Poor appetite or weight loss (> 2 lbs/wk; > 10 lbs/year when not dieting)
     - (2) Sleep difficulties (insomnia or hypersomnia)
     - (3) Loss of energy
     - (4) Agitation or retardation
     - (5) Loss of interest in usual activities or in sex
     - (6) Feelings (including *delusional*) of self-reproach or guilt
     - (7) Difficulty with concentration; slow or mixed-up thoughts
     - (8) Recurrent thoughts of death or suicide
   - *c*. A psychiatric illness lasting at least one month
2. Mania (*a* plus *b* plus *c* required)
   - *a*. (1) Euphoria or
     (2) Irritability
   - *b*. At least three
     - (1) Hyperactivity (motor, social, sexual)
     - (2) Pushed speech
     - (3) Flight of ideas
     - (4) Grandiosity (may be delusional)
     - (5) Decreased need for sleep
     - (6) Distractibility
   - *c*. A psychiatric illness lasting at least two weeks

B. Specific Items for Schizophrenic Psychopathology (two out of five required for consideration of schizoaffective disorder)

1. Delusion, any type
2. Hallucination, any type
3. Formal thought disorder—including any of the following
   - *a*. Tangential speech
   - *b*. Loose associations
   - *c*. Blocking
   - *d*. Neologisms
   - *e*. Word salad
   - *f*. Echolalia
   - *g*. Clang associations

   but *not* including circumstantial speech or flight of ideas associated with pushed speech
4. Abnormal thought disorder—manifested by inability to communicate in a logical manner (i.e., autistic or dereistic thinking)
5. Bizarre or strikingly inappropriate behavior

SOURCE: Welner, Croughan, and Robins (1974), *Archives of General Psychiatry,* 32:628–631.

TABLE 8–13

Symptoms Found with High Frequency in Schizoaffective Schizophrenia

(ICD 295.7)

	Percent
Disturbance of concentration	70
Depressive	62
Thought narrowing	46
Anxious	44
Thought slowing	43
Disturbance of comprehension	41
Rigidity of affect	38
Agitation	38
Suicidal tendencies*	32
Impulse poverty	32
Feeling of insufficiency	32
Flight of ideas	30
Disturbance of memory	30
Lack of insight	27
Incoherence	27
Circumstantiality	24
Feelings of guilt	22
Delusional idea	19
Hearing voices	11

*It should be noted (see De Alarcon, 1975) that the incidence of suicide in the schizoaffective group is remarkably high—fifty times greater than in the normal population.

NOTE: Based on percentage noted in thirty-seven patients.

SOURCE: Adapted from Helmchen (1975, p. 13).

Classification of Disease, 8th revision). Table 8–13 shows the frequencies with which certain symptoms commonly encountered in schizoaffective patients were actually noted in Helmchen's study of 427 schizophrenic patients of all types. A number of symptoms occurred significantly more frequently in the schizoaffective than in any other subtype: these included suicidal tendencies, depression, and guilt feelings.

Sovner and McHugh

Sovner and McHugh (1976) reviewed twenty-seven patients given a schizoaffective diagnosis. A bipolar course was noted in thirteen; the remainder exhibited an evolution more in keeping with unipolar depression. In the bipolar group, five actually met Feighner's criteria for a primary affective illness (see pp. 250–251)—three of the seven excited (manic) patients and two of the six bipolar depressed patients. No patient in the sample met research criteria for both affective and schizophrenic disorders simultaneously, a point tending to confirm Welner's impression that "schizoaffective" patients often have a wide variety of serious symptoms but not always ordered in such a way as to fulfill RDC for any one classical entity.

Three-fourths of the Westchester patients were depressed on admission. Those with a bipolar course had received their first psychiatric treatment at an earlier age (twenty-one) than the depressed-only group (twenty-six). A deteriorating course was rarely seen, occurring only in one "bipolar" patient. There was only a modest preponderance of females (17:10).

Symptoms customarily associated with schizophrenia were seen more often among the "unipolar depressed" schizoaffectives; thought disorder, blunted affect, or delusions were noted most frequently. The suicidal thoughts and preoccupation with death, observed in a third of Helmchen's cases, were recorded in 26 percent of Sovner and McHugh's patients.

These authors were sufficiently struck by the closeness of the symptom constellations to those of unequivocal depression or bipolar MDP to recommend, in the presence of a bipolar course, giving precedence to the diagnosis of *manic-depressive illness* rather than to schizophrenia. Lithium appeared to be effective in seven of the "bipolar" patients (five predominantly excited, two predominantly depressed). I suspect many of these patients would fit into Region IV of my schizophrenic-MDP continuum; that is, in between evenly divided schizoaffective illness and pure MDP. Here, of course, a dimensional approach obviates the problem of having to choose between MDP and schizophrenia. There is as much to be lost by giving diagnostic "pride of place" to MDP, ignoring to some extent the schizophrenic elements, as there is in the more widespread habit of focusing on the schizophrenic aspects to the neglect of the affective.

Schizoaffective Disorders: The Research Diagnostic Criteria of Spitzer's Group

Spitzer, Endicott, and Robins (1975) have formulated a set of RDC for schizoaffective disorders as an outgrowth of their methods for diagnosing schizophrenia and the major affective disorders. Two prototypic forms are recognized: a manic type and a depressed type. Though their schema is category oriented, they have introduced various complexities and stipulations to allow for the tendency of these disorders to shift manifestionally from one episode to another. Similarly, they acknowledge a number of subtypes with respect to severity and duration: acute, subacute, and so on. The details for all these components are included in their Schedule for Affective Disorders and Schizophrenia ("SADS"). The booklet is the work of Spitzer and Endicott (1975); it is quite rich in clinical examples of the different varieties of formal thought disorder. A section is devoted to "borderline features" (SADS-Lifetime Version, 1975, p. 36).

In Figure 8–10 I have tried to represent via a flow diagram the procedure for evaluating a prospective "schizoaffective" case according to SADS.

The criteria of Spitzer's groupings are somewhat stricter than those of Welner's.

The Research Diagnostic Criteria require the occurrence, for a week or more at some time in the past, of hallucinations or delusions (as described in the forms). The "significant"—but not definitive—signs of schizophrenia listed under "E" of Figure 8–10, if present in the here and now, are by themselves insufficient for confirming the schizophrenic component of this disorder. Thus the eccentric and severely withdrawn patient with some manic episodes, recently or in the past, could not receive the RDC diagnosis of schizoaffective unless there were a positive history for productive signs.[9]

The efforts of both Welner and Spitzer and their co-workers have done much to restore respectability to what was often a "wastebasket" diagnosis. But it is my impression that many patients, especially ambulatory patients, might be meaningfully diagnosed as "schizoaffective," especially those whose day-to-day function over time is consistently at the borderline level (in Kernberg's or Gunderson's definitions). Never having had hallucinations or delusions, they would not meet RDC standards for this category (see case illustration 16). One way in which they might be accommodated is described in the section immediately following.

A Weighted Scale for Schizoaffective Disorders

In connection with the National Institute of Mental Health Army twin study (see Chapter 3) Cohen et al. (1972) devised a rating scale for semiquantitative evaluation of hospital records of MZ twins at least one of whom was diagnosed as having a functional psychosis. The diagnoses had been made clinically on the basis of symptomatology in both affective and schizophrenic categories. In some instances, for example, "flattened affect, autistic thinking, loose associations, cognitive disorganization, and ambivalence [were] present even when the twin was not depressed or psychotic" (1972, p. 540). Chronicity and a deteriorating course were often noted, but these elements were not required for application of the schizoaffective label.

By way of achieving a more accurate comparison of the degrees to which

[9]A *partially recovered* schizoaffective patient, however, may still exhibit nonproductive signs of schizophrenia (namely, any one of the three itemized, either singly or in combination); the absence of hallucinations or delusions in this instance does not militate against the diagnosis (Spitzer, 1977, personal communication).

Figure 8–10. Research Diagnostic Criteria for Schizoaffective Disorders: Spitzer and Endicott

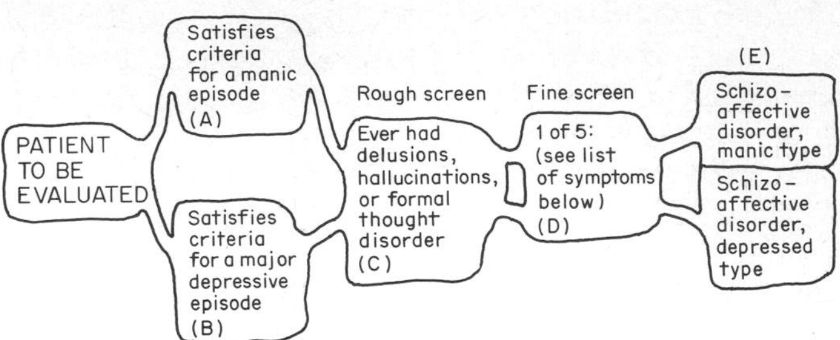

KEY:

(A) Manic Episode:

Elevated mood

or

Irritability

+

Two of Seven:

a. Hyperactivity
b. Pushed speech
c. Thought racing
d. Grandiosity
e. Decreased need for sleep
f. Trouble concentrating
g. Reckless behavior

+

Above mentioned symptoms do *not* occur in relation to alcohol or drugs.

(B) Episode of Major Depressive Syndrome:

1 or > periods of dysphoria

or

sought help for dysphoric episode, etc.*

or

3 (if past) or 4 (if current):

a. Weight change; ↓ Appetite
b. Insomnia
c. Loss of energy
d. Decreased interest in sex
e. Feelings of guilt or low self-esteem
f. Trouble concentrating
g. Preoccupation with suicide
h. Agitation or retardation

(C) Formal Thought Disorder:

a. Incoherence
b. Loosening of the associations
c. Illogical thinking
d. Poverty of thought
e. Delusions involving von Domarus's principle

(D) One of Five Present:

a. Delusion of influence broadcast
b. Nonaffective hallucinations
c. Auditory hallucinations, namely, voices talk about patient
d. Delusions or hallucinations without affective symptoms, for at least one week
e. Formal thought disorder without affective symptoms

(E) May Still Show One of Three:

a. Social withdrawal
b. Eccentric behavior
c. Unusual thoughts or perceputal experiences

SOURCE: Text adapted from Spitzer and Endicott (1975).

the psychotic twins resembled each of the classical disorders, the NIMH group devised a scale composed of affective and of schizophrenic items, to which different numbers were assigned. These values reflected the importance they attached to each (intuitively) in establishing a diagnosis of either MDP or schizophrenia. Scores are to be given for items which have *ever* (now or in the past) *been present.*

In the affective portion of Cohen's scale, fifteen points were assigned to an item, "Became psychotic when separated from twin." For use in general psychiatry, some revision would be necessary. Table 8–14 represents my attempt at such a revision. Though affective-disordered patients are often exquisitely sensitive to separation (Stone, 1975), this sensitivity does not constitute a diagnostic item per se. I redistributed the fifteen points proportionally over the remaining items of the affective scale. This may be

TABLE 8–14

A Semiquantitative Scale for the Assessment of Possible Schizoaffective Cases

Symptoms Usually Considered Schizophrenic	*Weighted Score*	*Symptoms Usually Considered Affective*	*Weighted Score*
1. Disorganized thinking or ambivalence	1	1. Somatic complaints	1
2. Mute (catatonic)	4	2. Insomnia	2
3. Mannerisms or bizarre behavior	10	3. Weight loss	2
4. Flat or blunted affect, or apathy	10	4. Self-depreciation	2
5. Delusions of grandeur or persecutions; or autistic thinking	15	5. Flight of ideas	3
6. Hallucinations (auditory or visual)	20	6. Tearfulness	6
7. Chronicity	30	7. Retardation, psychomotor	6
8. Inappropriate affect	10	8. Agitation	12
		9. Suicide attempts	12
		9*a*. Suicide gestures	6
		10. Euphoria	12
		11. Repeated episodes with good remission phases	17
		12. Depressive affect	25
	100		100

SOURCE: Adapted from Cohen et al. (1972), *Archives of General Psychiatry,* 26:539–545.

mathematically inelegant but does permit one to utilize the scale for the majority of the population. Further refinements may well be necessary in the future.

Analysis of the symptom scores among three groups of psychotic twins (and co-twins) in Cohen's study revealed means of 54.9 affective versus 27.5 schizophrenic in the manic-depressives. Those with a clinical diagnosis of schizophrenia showed mean scores in a ratio of 29.1:55.2, tilted toward the "schizophrenic." The schizoaffectives were quite evenly balanced: 51.5:53.2 (with the affective score always given first). As can be seen, the scores in this relatively small sample (thirty-three individuals) suggest that patients clinically diagnosed schizoaffective resemble classical schizophrenics (schizophrenia scores in the low 50s) as well as cases of MDP (affective scores in the low 50s). Of interest, the age of onset of schizoaffective illness was younger (about twenty)—like that for the schizophrenics—than that noted for MDP (about twenty-six).

As the authors remarked, their findings do not help resolve the question whether schizoaffective disorders are a part of the two classical psychoses or a *third entity* of their own. Nor could they claim definitely that these disorders are on a continuum between schizophrenia and MDP. They even offer the possibility that genetic loading for both types of psychosis may be present. In these respects their speculations are very similar to mine; validation will require, among other things, systematic study of close relatives.

The use of the weighted scale may be demonstrated by its application to several cases described in this book. The affective predominance in the borderline patient of case illustration 29 is 78:19 (= 80/20). The schizoaffective patient of illustration 6 would be scored 51:70 or "42:58" (although the thirty-point item "chronicity" was not so striking in her as, say, in illustration 2).

At this time the scale should be reserved for patients who have had at least one psychotic episode. To rate the balance between mood and boundary disturbances in less ill patients, a revision would be needed that included, and gave greater weight to, the less dramatic symptoms of MDP or schizophrenia. If there is validity to the hypothesis that *spectra* exist for both forms of mental illness, then we would want to measure both "schizotypia" and "manic-depressiveness" in their subtle and nonpsychotic aspects as well as in their psychotic aspects.

Since the "schizophrenic" and "affective" items are not pathognomonic for their respective categories, the resultant scores must be interpreted with caution. *Chronicity* (a "schizophrenia" item), for example, should only be scored when there have been persistent and severe symptoms and not merely the persistence of personality traits that interfere with social adjustment. The latter type of chronicity has been noted even in bipolar manic-depressive patients (Welner, Welner, and Leonard, 1977).

By the same token, the rating scale usually cannot be used effectively in young patients during their first psychotic episode: they will not have gone far enough in their course to demonstrate either "chronicity" or "good remissions between episodes."

In any event, the methodology of the NIMH group is useful in attempting to objectify and quantify clinical impressions within this realm of psychiatric disorder. At the New York Hospital–Westchester Division we are currently engaged in a reliability study of the modified scale (Table 8–14) on a personally interviewed hospitalized patient sample.

Afterword on the Category Diagnosis of Schizoaffective Disorders

We have reviewed some of the more important category-based methods for approaching the schizoaffective disorders and one (Cohen et al., 1972) dimensionally oriented method. In the light of these standards one may speculate that the "reactive" psychoses (see McCabe and Strömgren, 1975; also Chapter 4), rather than representing a new illness, are more often understandable as (*a*) predominantly affective schizoaffective psychoses or (*b*) milder but similar conditions accompanied by borderline rather than psychotic personality organization.

At the end of their article, Cohen et al. pose the rhetorical question, Can schizoaffective disorders arise from loading for *both* classical psychoses? My own belief is that they can. But I would have to qualify this by adding that what we are labeling *schizoaffective* may represent the final common pathway for several combinations of "causal" factors, of which dual heredity is one example. *Mild* loading for schizophrenia may provide another example, if found in a patient whose normal (or somewhat labile) affectivity remained "intact," escaping the affect-constricting influence of schizophrenic endowment. Certain biological and sociocultural factors may be at work that foster this preservation of affect more in *women* than in men. Whatever biological factors predispose to the 2:1 female surplus in major depressive disorders may be related to this phenomenon. Exacerbation of symptoms premenstrually has been long noted in many conditions that get called "schizoaffective," "borderline," "manic-depressive," "hysteroid dysphoric," and so on. The wrist slashers reported on by Grunebaum and Klerman (1967) or by Graff and Mallin (1967) were, for example, almost all young women whose symptom picture, in the light of contemporary diagnostic standards, would have to be seen as *formes frustes* of manic-depressive illness (less often, of schizophrenia). Many function at a borderline level, and premenstrual outbursts of self-destructive behavior are a regular feature in this group. Female excess representation among the depressions and anorexia nervosa and the exclusively female premenstrual disorders (see pp. 256–259) speak for a strong biological underpinning in these conditions. These factors, however, may have more to do with genes governing hormonal regulation and sexuality than with genes affecting "mood" in any primary way. Many "borderline" patients are women between the ages of fifteen and thirty-five with one of the syndromes mentioned. In my practice and hospital experience, premenstrual symptom outbreak is the rule rather than the exception. Even better-integrated (neurotic) female patients often complain of rather severe premenstrual tension; careful charting will often demonstrate what was hitherto an unnoticed correlation. Some women seem "borderline for the day" a few days before the period and if seen in diagnostic consultation during those moments, might be viewed in a quite different light from how they would be seen during the rest of the cycle.

What we must face, then, in theorizing about the schizoaffective disorders is not so much a nature-nurture problem as a problem involving two facets of "nature": genetic control of the mood "thermostat" and control (by a different, though possibly overlapping, set of genes) of hormones and biological rhythms related to the reproductive cycle.

We have seen how the category-based methodologies bring *specificity* to diagnosis, but at the expense of *coverage* (some cases remain outside as "undiagnosed"). A dimensional method can accommodate many of the otherwise undiagnosed cases—but at the expense of specificity. Ideal diagnosis would provide maxima for both important elements.[10] The dynamic tension between these two needs has been explicated in the excellent article of Blashfield (1973). Addition of a dimensional approach, such as that advocated by Cohen, has the advantage of cutting through casuistical arguments about whether "schizoaffective" is "really" part of schizophrenia or of mania. Medications may also be prescribed more rationally—in accordance with the extent to which a patient resembles the various categorical archetypes. Having made a diagnosis of "schizoaffective disorder," one is now freed of any prejudice toward use of a phenothiazine (because of the "schizo-" prefix). If manic symptoms overshadow others, a trial of lithium may prove quite justified.

As a guide to rational usage of the various psychoactive drugs, the following diagram (Figure 8–11) may be useful. As schizophrenic cases depart from the pure type and move toward the affective pole, there is a divergence into "mainly depressive," "mixed," and "mainly manic" varieties of schizoaffective disorders. This is observable within each subdivision (predominantly affective) of the schizoaffective realm. This situation is most easily pictured via a triangle, with schizophrenic cases at one end, radiating out into the different balances of depressive versus manic symp-

[10]Spitzer, Endicott, and Robins (1978) have recently expanded RDC terminology in the schizoaffective realm to include the phrase "predominantly schizophrenic" and (predominantly) "affective." These correspond to Regions II and IV of my Sz-MDP continuum. The addition of these two categories alleviates much of the difficulty with the previous three-category system.

Figure 8–11. Sz-MDP Continuum: Emphasizing Balance between Depressive and Manic Symptoms

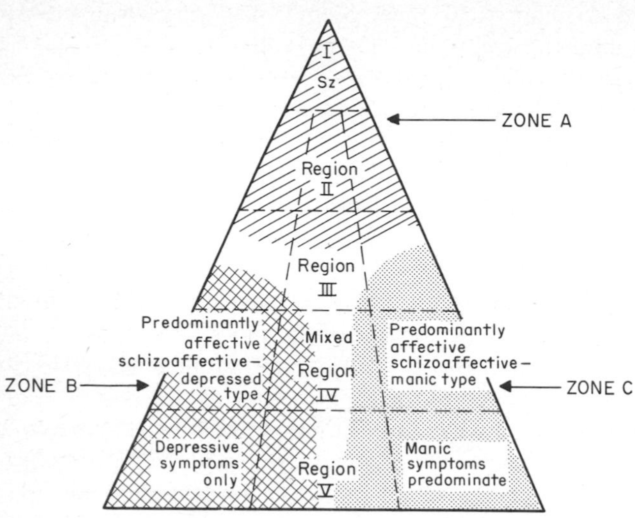

NOTE: The diagram depicts the universe of schizophrenic (Sz) to affective cases. This is the same realm as depicted in the Sz-MDP continuum diagram, only here portrayed as a triangle. At the apex is Region I or pure schizophrenia. Just below are the three schizoaffective realms: Region II (predominantly schizophrenic schizoaffective), Region III (cases with evenly divided symptom pictures), and Region IV (predominantly affective). Each of these latter regions, along with Region V (purely affective), is divided again into three areas. In the left-hand area depressive symptoms predominate; in the middle area affective symptoms are evenly divided between the depressive and the manic; and in the right-hand area manic symptoms (with respect to the affective component) predominate.

Zone A denotes a territory where phenothiazine or other neuroleptic drugs would be the most efficacious.

In Zone B, antidepressants would exert their maximum benefit.

In Zone C, lithium would have its greatest chance of being effective.

The unshaded zone denotes a region of such evenly divided symptom pictures that decisions about the drug of choice are not easily made.

toms (among the schizoaffective cases). Careful assessment of a given patient's diagnostic "locale" on this diagram may help in the selection of the most useful medication. Such a procedure is outlined in the note accompanying Figure 8–11.

On the Diagnosis of Manic-Depressive Disorders

A borderline condition cannot be diagnosed without a manic-depressive psychosis (as well as a schizophrenic psychosis) being ruled out. Manic disorders are often easier to diagnose than schizophrenia; there seem to be fewer phenocopiers of mania than of schizophrenia. Guze et al. (1971) concluded that "secondary" mania does not exist, although some have contested this (Rickarby, 1977; Wiesert and Hendrie, 1977). Episodes of mania sometimes occur so closely in conjunction with life trauma (usually a separation or loss, Stone, 1975) as to confer a "secondary" quality to the case, even though the primary etiological factors are still hereditary/biological. Mania secondary to entirely different sources (lues, tumors) is quite rare. The difficulty often encountered in distinguishing recurrent, "endogenous" depression from "reactive" depression has been touched on in Chapter 6 (see also Winokur, Clayton, and Reich, 1969, chapter 2). Some depressions apparently triggered by acute situations will be seen in retrospect years later as the first of many recurrent episodes in someone with a strong family history of depression. The older endogenous/exogenous classification turns out to have only limited utility and poor discriminating ability.

Since many patients with familial depressive illness (namely, "unipolar") function at a borderline level, it will be easy for the clinician to ignore one or the other facet of the patient's total diagnostic configuration. Those whose training leans toward the biological will see the unipolar depression and pay little attention to the underlying structure. Instead the patient makes only a partial recovery, because his serious personality disturbances are left largely unattended. Those whose training leans toward the psychoanalytic are often better attuned to the borderline structure, but not so well to the heredofamilial aspect. They may be slow in adding antidepressants to the therapeutic regimen, for want of appreciation of the (in this case, truly) "endogenous" nature of the depression. Case illustration 15 provides an example of initial mistreatment of a borderline patient, based on this narrow, unidimensional method of diagnosis. Optimal diagnosis will of course depend on proper attention to both the biological and psychological factors whenever both are present.

Manic-Depressive Illness: Earlier Definitions

The modern conception of manic and depressive psychoses constituting a unitary group of disorders ("single morbid process") we attribute to Kraepelin (1921). The nineteenth century antecedents of Kraepelin's synthesis have been noted in Chapter 6.

Clifford Beers's celebrated description of his own case of insanity (1908) would appear to be that of a manic-depressive (alternating or "bipolar") psychosis.

The main symptoms found in manic-depressive psychosis (MDP) according to Kraepelin are outlined in Table 8–15. The manner in which those symptoms (namely, hallucinations and delusions) otherwise mistakable for schizophrenia are to be differentiated from the latter are explained at length

TABLE 8–15

Symptoms of Manic-Depressive Psychosis as Emphasized by Kraepelin

SYMPTOM	*Mania*	*(Psychotic) Depression*
a. Alterations of perception	+	–
b. Distractibility	++	–
c. Hallucinations	+*	
d. Flight of ideas	+++	±
e. Diffusiveness of associations	++	
f. Delusions	Grandiose	Self-denigratory
g. Ideas of sinfulness	–	++
h. Mood disturbance	Exalted	Gloomy
i. Activity	Pressured	Inhibited†
j. Speech	Pressured	Retarded

*Tend, in mania, to be isolated and closely connected with the patient's train of thought and mood. *Illusions* may be reported, where stray noises are interpreted in a personalized manner (the clock says, "You dog! you're still here! you're the devil!").

†Except in instances of *agitated depression* where anxious excitement replaces motor retardation.

in Chapter One of the 1921 monograph. The essence of the difference relates to the linkage in MDP of productive signs with the *mood* of the patient, whereas in schizophrenia these signs when present tend to reflect disturbances in ego boundary and identity.

Despite Kraepelin's efforts to define as well as to distinguish from one another the two major psychoses, manic-depressive disorders remained for some quite easily confused with schizophrenia. In the United States, particularly, schizophrenia became the focus of everyone's attention; MDP was relegated somehow to the periphery and was regarded as diagnosable more by exclusion than by inclusion criteria. This echoes Bleuler's comment of a generation earlier, but Lewis and Piotrowski (1954) went so far as to say that the diagnosis of manic-depressive psychosis can be made only by elimination of schizophrenia (p. 37). For these writers "even a trace of schizophrenia is schizophrenia"; they claimed that many patients with few and mild schizophrenic signs and with a strong affective element fail to improve and spend years in institutions. These statements would strike the clinician of today as almost fanciful, were they not uttered by a diagnostician of Nolan Lewis's prestige. The ten signs Lewis and Piotrowski considered so *inclusive* of schizophrenia as to exclude MDP are outlined in Table 8–16.

Their faith in the presence of paranoid signs (cases 2 and 3) as pathognomonic for schizophrenia contrasts sharply with the more recent impres-

TABLE 8–16

Discriminating Signs of Schizophrenia Useful in Excluding MDP

1. Physical sensation with dissociation (e.g., "There is a steel plate in my forehead" or "I have the skin of a monkey and am going to be turned into an animal.")
2. Delusions regarding others
3. Delusions regarding physical objects
4. Feeling of physical isolation and personal unreality (e.g., "I am living in a world of my own; everything stands still.")
5. Inability to concentrate
6. Feeling of having changed (e.g., "Something has slipped in my mind; some nerve jumped.")
7. Speech disturbance and intellectual blocking
8. Uncontrolled repeated interrupting, anxious thoughts (including auditory or visual hallucinations telling the patient about horrible experiences which are awaiting him)
9. Ideas of reference and/or feeling of being controlled by inimical outside forces
10. Seclusiveness (maintained or increased while in the hospital)

SOURCE: Adapted from Lewis and Piotrowski (1954).

sions of Abrams, Taylor, and Gaztanaga (1974), who demonstrated that many patients admitted as paranoid schizophrenics had to be rediagnosed as manic-depressives in the light of more careful evaluation.

Modern Diagnostic Criteria for Manic-Depressive Disorders

As we noted in Chapter 7, many patients with borderline structure have one or more first-degree relatives with either a full-blown or moderately severe form of manic-depressive illness. Many patients who have had psychotic episodes, of either manic or depressive type, are not only well interpsychotically but may exhibit neurotic structure except during those brief episodes. A few (as in case illustration 7) will show psychotic structure even when in a relatively quiescent phase. Others (case illustrations 14 and 15) have a borderline structure in and around their psychotic episodes. The last group is of special interest to us, since it is composed of patients who can often be helped materially by expressive psychotherapy, provided one remains aware of their vulnerability to a severe affective disorder. The depressively inclined patients outnumber those who tend toward mania and are ordinarily more accessible to analytically oriented psychotherapy than those whose psychotic episodes are predominantly *manic* (regardless of whether the character structure is hypomanic or merely obsessive-compulsive).

Research Criteria for Primary Affective Disorders

A number of contemporary investigators have been concerned with diagnosing manic-depressive conditions by *inclusion* rather than by exclusion criteria.

By virtue of recent family studies, the older term "manic-depressive psychosis" is becoming replaced by the term "primary affective disorder" (see Winokur, 1976, p. 8). This in turn constitutes a group of conditions, based on relative homogeneity of familial mental illness, namely, "manic-depressive disease" and "depressive disease." The St. Louis investigators have established several sets of working criteria for these states, as shown in Table 8–17.

Bipolar conditions are often subdivided into two groups: a bipolar-I type (mood swings are in both directions and of equal amplitude) and a bipolar-II type (characterized by depressions which are considerably *deeper* than the elations are high; i.e., depressions plus *hypo*mania). Depressive disease may be analyzed into several subgroups, the most important of which is an early-onset illness mostly in females (= "depression spectrum disease"). Not mentioned in Winokur's 1976 paper is the rare variant of "pure mania," where episodic mania occurs in the absence of depressive mood swings. A convenient way of representing the main variants is illustrated in Figure 8–12. The sine curve stands for recurrent mood alterations. If one imagines this undulating curve intersected by different horizontal "baselines," different conditions can be depicted. With the baseline (of neutral mood or *euthymia*) at position IV, the curve is either just touching or well *below* the baseline. This is the situation in *unipolar depression*. As the imaginary baseline is lowered to positions I, II, or III, the other MDP variants are generated.

In their study of lithium response in depression, Baron, Gershon, et al. (1975) used a checklist different in certain respects from the criteria of the St. Louis group. Besides "depressed mood," they required four of the following fifteen items: (*a*) hopelessness, (*b*) low self-esteem, (*c*) guilt or self-reproach, (*d*) anorexia, (*e*) weight loss, (*f*) crying spells, (*g*) suicidal thoughts, (*h*) sleeplessness, (*i*) loss of energy and interest, (*j*) restlessness, (*k*) loss of sexual interest, (*l*) constipation, (*m*) slowed-down thoughts, (*n*) inability to concentrate, and (*o*) suicide attempts.

Pointing out that the usefulness of a classification system is limited by its reliability, Spitzer, Endicott, and Robins (1975a) analyzed the sources of unreliability in contemporary psychodiagnosis into several components. The patient may present different conditions at different times (occasion variance); clinicians evaluating the same case may rely on different sources of information (information variance); clinicians may differ in what they choose to notice while witnessing the same patient (observation variance);

TABLE 8–17

Diagnostic Criteria for Primary Affective Disorders

---

*I. Manic Type (A + B + C required)**

A. Euphoria or irritability

B. Three of the following six

1. Hyperactivity (motor, social, or sexual)
2. Pushed (pressured) speech
3. Flight of ideas
4. Grandiosity (whether or not delusional)
5. Decreased sleep
6. (Easy) distractibility

C. A psychiatric illness lasting at least two weeks, with no preexisting psychiatric conditions (including schizophrenia, organic mental syndrome, etc.)

II. Depressive Type (A + B + C required)

A. Dysphoric mood (patient reports feeling depressed, sad, blue, despondent, hopeless, down in the dumps, irritable, fearful, worried, or discouraged)

B. Five for "definite," four for "probable"

1. Poor appetite or weight loss (more than two pounds/week or ten pounds/year when not dieting)
2. Sleep difficulty (insomnia or hypersomnia)
3. Loss of energy (easy fatigability)
4. Agitation or retardation
5. Loss of interest in usual activities (including sex)
6. Feelings of self-reproach or guilt (either may be of delusional proportions)
7. Diminished ability to think or concentrate
8. Recurrent thoughts of death or suicide

C. A psychiatric illness lasting at least a month without preexisting psychiatric illnesses, and in the absence of a truly life-threatening or incapacitating physical illness

---

*If the following criteria are satisfied but are also accompanied by massive or peculiar alteration of perception or thinking, the patient should be considered to have a *schizophreniform* or *atypical* psychosis.

SOURCE: After Feighner et al. (1972), *Archives of General Psychiatry,* 26:57–63. Copyright 1972, American Medical Association. Reprinted by permission.

and, finally, disagreements may exist regarding inclusion and exclusion criteria for specified conditions (criterion variance).

In primary affective disorders, "occasion variance" is an important source of potential error, since the bipolar forms in particular may exhibit dramatic changes in outward appearance over relatively short periods of time. Observation variance will be affected not only by the competence of

Figure 8–12. Varieties of Mood Swing in Primary Affective Disorders

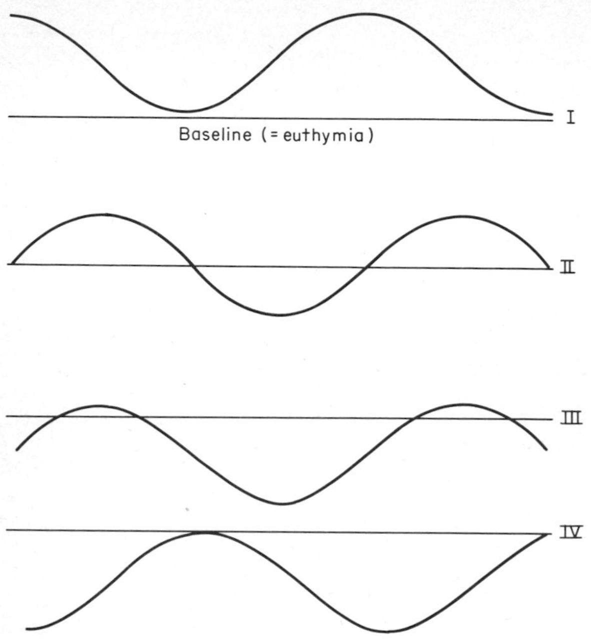

KEY:

I	("pure mania")	Fluctuations of mood are only *above* baseline
II	(bipolar-I MDP)	Amplitude of the "highs" about the same as for the "lows"
III	(bipolar-II MDP)	Mood varies from mild "highs" to marked "lows"
IV	(unipolar depression)	Mood varies from euthymic baseline to marked "lows"

the clinician but also by his mental set (largely the product of his training). A patient's digression may strike one interviewer as insignificant; another, with schizophrenia on his mind, may hear tangentiality.

The chief thrust of Spitzer's efforts has been to improve reliability through reduction of criterion variance. The Research Diagnostic Criteria (RDC) of Spitzer and his collaborators embody, where affective disorders are concerned, expansion and modification of the St. Louis criteria in order to accommodate less severe and less easily subtyped cases.

Criteria for a "Major Depressive Disorder" in the RDC classification are, in their first two sections, the same as those mentioned in Table 8–17, section 2 (Depressive Type), parts A and B. The remaining sections include a time factor (dysphoric features more than two weeks for *definite,* between one and two weeks for *probable*) different from Feighner's, plus two sections relating to social disability and to the absence of certain "schizophrenic" features. (Presence of the latter would necessitate diagnostic revision to "schizoaffective, depressed type.")

The New Approach to the Diagnosis of Affective Disorders: Some Practical Considerations

Diagnostic criteria for affective disorders have changed in two important ways since the emergence of advanced biometric technics for their appraisal. The most obvious change is the greater precision in diagnostic standards. Inclusion criteria are now spelled out with as much clarity as were exclusion criteria a generation ago. The second change involves the conceptual base itself upon which diagnosis rests.

The Kraepelinian taxonomy emphasized the presence or absence of a break with reality: manic-depressive *psychosis*. There was even a tendency to assume that an "endogenous" affective disorder implied psychosis (past or current). But the genetic and biochemical studies of Kraepelin's day had not yet advanced to the point where classification could be revamped, as Leonhard proposed (1963), along heredofamilial lines. The newer model rests on just such a foundation, as explicated with considerable clarity in the articles of Gershon, Dunner, and Goodwin (1971) or F. K. Goodwin, Murphy, et al. (1972). In the latter, response to lithium (better in bipolar than in unipolar depression) is also considered of diagnostic relevance.

Guze, Woodruff, and Clayton (1975) have also questioned the utility of the old psychotic-neurotic dichotomy in affective disorders. These authors divided groups of bipolar and unipolar depressed patients into those with psychotic features (hallucinations, delusions, ideas of reference) and those without. Although psychotic features were somewhat more frequently noted (at some point in the course of the illness) in the bipolar group, in other respects no demographic, family history, or other variables (apart from frequency of hospitalizations) were detected that could distinguish the neurotic from the (ever) psychotic samples. For this reason the authors believed it made much better sense to link the two samples by virtue of common symptomatic and family-history findings rather than to set them apart because some had never had a psychotic episode.

These changes have in and of themselves introduced the need for a combined categorical/dimensional approach, since nonpsychotic though still serious affective disorders are now united, conceptually, with their psychotic counterparts. Borderline, while used as a category by Kernberg, with respect to structure, becomes a dimensional term (for "intermediate severity") when applied to primary affective disorders. In addition, a fair proportion of hospitalized patients with borderline structure would also receive a "spectrum" diagnosis among the primary affective disorders, according to RDC standards. Gershon, Dunner, and Goodwin (1971, p. 6) present similar evidence. They noted, for instance, that the morbid risk for affective disorders in a sample of hospitalized "neurotic depressive reactions" was higher (3½ percent in Stenstedt's study) than in the general population, though not as high as in families of more clear-cut affective disorders. Similarly Kallmann (1950, 1954) found a considerably increased incidence (by a factor of 20 to 30) of what he called *cycloid* personalities (patients with mild affective disturbances and related personality traits) in the relatives of probands with manic-depressive psychosis.

Mania or Schizophrenia?: Other Views

In the borderland between obvious schizophrenia and unequivocal manic psychoses, one encounters psychotic episodes, especially in an *acute* stage, that either defy classification or invite misdiagnosis.

Paranoid reactions are so regularly associated with schizophrenia that the presence of the former establishes a mental "set" from which many clinicians do not easily extricate themselves. Yet many patients with mania (as their illness is eventually recognized to be) are irritable, hostile, and markedly (even delusionally) paranoid during the acute phase. The premorbid personality will often have been paranoid as well. Lipkin, Dyrud, and Meyer (1970) pointed out the high incidence of delusions and hallucinations (15 to 25 percent) in "manic-depressive patients" (i.e., in bipolar primary affective disorders with psychotic episodes) and mentioned how often acute mania may be mistaken for acute paranoid (schizophrenic) reactions, as Abrams, Taylor, and Gaztanaga (1974) later corroborated. The hostile aggression and haughtiness of many manic patients were also symptoms that led to diagnostic confusion. Case illustration 7 typifies this kind of confusion: the patient in question was written off as an obvious schizophrenic for seventeen years because of her aggressively paranoid qualities.

The premorbid history will be of aid in making the proper diagnostic distinctions. Successful interpersonal relationships in the past should raise suspicion about an affective rather than schizophrenic illness. As is noted in case illustration 1, the manic patient may at times be annoying or hostile, but this may alternate with periods of humor and warmth that the hospital staff will often call "infectious." Such humor is much less often available in schizophrenics. Lipkin et al. mention that certain manics, including those diagnosed schizophrenic at the height of their illness, will have demonstrated a cyclothymic personality beforehand. Aloofness and withdrawal are seldom part of the premorbid picture. Not all cyclothymic personalities experience manic or depressive psychoses, nor are eventually psychotic affective disorders necessarily preceded by a personality that gives a hint of what is to follow. Many manics, in retrospect, were ordinary obsessive-compulsives or hysterics (Stone, 1978).

Carlson and Goodwin (1973) draw attention to how easily mania could be confused with schizophrenia if one relied only on a cross-sectional view at the time of acute decompensation. These investigators studied twenty manic patients over the whole course of hospitalization and beyond, into a follow-up period when euthymia had been restored. Their patients had their first psychotic episode at an average age of twenty-eight (range seventeen to fifty-seven); they had experienced about four manic and two depressive episodes by the time of inclusion in the study. *Three out of four* had a family history positive for serious affective disorder in a first-degree relative. Evolution of full-blown mania proceeded in a stepwise fashion that Carlson and Goodwin found convenient to divide into three "stages."

The first stage was characterized by (1) an increased rate of speech and of physical activity, (2) euphoria (with some irritability if the patient's demands were not met), (3) expansiveness, grandiosity, and overconfidence, (4) incoherence (with perhaps some tangentiality at times), (5) increased preoccupation with sex, religion, or certain public or business affairs, and (6) increased telephone use, letter writing, smoking, and spending.

By the second stage, euphoria had given way to anger and irritability. Behavior that was still under control in the initial stage had by now become explosive or at times assaultive. Flight of ideas and increasing cognitive disorganization supervened. Their former preoccupations were taking on the shape of paranoid or grandiose delusions. Observers unfamiliar with the patient's prior course often made the diagnosis of schizophrenia at this time.

About two out of three patients progressed to a "final" stage (stage III); here the mood was distinctly dysphoric and was accompanied by terror, panic, and hopelessness.

Of special interest to us in the evaluation of borderline syndromes is the list of classical and "atypical" symptoms observed at various times in the sample of manic patients. Besides the classical ones of hyperactivity, verbosity, and manipulativeness (seen in all their patients) were other symptoms either easily confusable with schizophrenia (loosening of association, religious preoccupation and, less often, hallucinations and ideas of reference) or rather subtle and easily overlooked (namely, intrusiveness). In any bipolar group such as this, severe premenstrual depression or irritability may, as in the study of McClure, Reich, and Wetzel (1971), serve as an indicator of primary affective disorder.

Before returning to the connection between affective illness and premenstrual (or, more abstractly, endocrinological) dysregulation, a final point about thought disorder is in order.

Like "paranoid," the expression "thought disorder" has long been weighted down with surplus meaning that connotes schizophrenia. At the same time we have seen how recent investigators, reexamining this concept in the light of more sophisticated diagnostic methods, have introduced doubts about the pathognomonicity of this symptom: Braff and Beck (1974) noted thought disorder in severe depressions; Breakey and Goodell (1972), in mania. Harrow and Quinlan (1977) have carried this work one step forward. These authors studied some two hundred acutely ill psychiatric patients with respect to different varieties of "thought disorder" (by means of a battery of psychological tests including the Rorschach and the object-sorting test). Their sample, carefully diagnosed according to the research criteria used at Yale, included fifty-five schizophrenics and a larger number of manic-depressive and "borderline" patients. Thought disorder was analyzed into such components as idiosyncratic thought, vagueness, looseness, illogicality, boundary fluidity, concreteness, impoverishment, autism, and confusion. In addition a graded scale of severity was also applied.

What emerged was the detection of at least mild to moderate degrees of thought disorder, not only among the acute schizophrenic patients but also in many of the psychotic depressive, borderline, organic, and disturbed personality-disorder groups. The same was true in their small subsample of (predominantly) manic patients. Of special interest was their finding that concreteness and impoverishment of thought did *not* strongly differentiate *acutely* ill schizophrenic and nonschizophrenic patients (although these abnormalities did become more manifest in later phases of the schizophrenic illness). In line with the modern emphasis on boundary disturbance as central to the idea of schizophrenia, those varieties of thought disorder exemplifying boundary confusion *were* more prominent in the schizophrenic population (namely, deviant, bizarre, autistic responses). Nevertheless in the phase of partial recovery, distinctions in type and severity of thought disorder between schizophrenic and nonschizophrenic patients became less marked. Harrow and Quinlan postulate a *continuum* of thinking disorder stretching from the normal to grossly bizarre. Milder levels of abnormality are noted in people who are acutely upset for whatever reason, irrespective of diagnosis. Since organic and other less well-known factors may also predispose to certain types of thought disorder, one must be careful not to jump to conclusions about "schizophrenia" the minute one elicits signs of a subtle thought disorder.

Among the case illustrations, examples of obvious thought disorder occur in 1, 2, and 7; subtle abnormalities will be found in 8, 10, 22, and 25, among others; all regions of the psychosis continuum are represented, as are the structural levels—"psychotic" and "borderline."

The Premenstrual Syndrome and Affective Disorder

Various references have been made throughout this text to a premenstrual factor in certain women with primary affective disorders.

Complaints of depressed mood, irritability, headache, and a bloated feeling often accompanied by actual swelling of the feet and a weight gain of more than two pounds—occurring within the week before the menses—constitute the syndrome of "premenstrual tension." Moyer (1974) has collected a number of demographic studies bearing on this issue, including one that showed a 52 percent incidence of the syndrome among 1,100 wives of graduate students at a large university. Other estimates suggested that 25 percent of all women experience moderate to severe forms of the syndrome; two reports included figures as high as 90 percent if milder variations of the syndrome were included. In certain women the irritability is accompanied by overt hostility and on occasion assaultive acts. Most crimes of passion and violence that women commit occur in the premenstrual phase. Moyer also mentions that in France very severe premenstrual tension is sometimes placed in the category of "temporary insanity" (p. 360). Tonks (1968) reported figures similar to Moyer's: 73 percent of a sample of student nurses suffered from varying degrees of the syndrome, considered in 5 percent to be "severe." These percentages are all in line with others mentioned recently by Schuckit et al. (1975) and Weissman and Klerman (1977), who also found good evidence from around the world for the often touted 2:1 female-to-male ratio in *depressive* illnesses. Whereas Moyer believed there was rather general agreement that "the symptoms are associated with a fall in the progesterone (P) level and a relatively greater amount of estrogen (E) in the E/P ratio," in Weissman and Klerman's opinion the endocrinological evidence was not yet sufficiently clear-cut to permit definite conclusions about the actual role of hormonal changes or even about which hormones might be implicated. They do suggest, however, that since a substantial number of women experience the premenstrual syndrome on a regular basis, this could account for some of the excess of female depressives (1977, p. 104).

The crucial factor may involve an interaction between "manic-depressive heredity" (the nonspecific component) and the biological elements underlying the menstrual cycle (the necessary but not sufficient component). Particularly in a population of women who seek help for psychiatric disorders, premenstrual exaggeration of symptoms is the rule rather than the exception. This is true among office patients as well as among those admitted to a hospital. Whereas the majority of women, even in these situations, experience only a mild exacerbation of their underlying condition, or else an otherwise unexplainable tearfulness or irritability the week before the menses, there are a few whose personality undergoes a drastic change. This change may be so pronounced as to defy ordinary psychodiagnostic classification. The psychostructural organizations, for example, are thought of as characteristic over time for each individual. But one will occasionally encounter a woman who, before adequate treatment, seems to exist in two unrelated states: her usual self two-thirds of the time and an impulsive, hostile, or grotesquely self-destructive self the remaining third. The two vignettes that follow illustrate the disjointed existence of some female patients with especially severe premenstrual syndromes. Case illustration 29 provides another example.

Borderline Structure with Premenstrual Psychotic Depressions

A twenty-three-year-old woman had been admitted to a psychiatric hospital because of a serious suicide attempt. She had been a fine-arts major at a local college and had become depressed over the breakup of a romantic relationship. In the hospital she made another suicide attempt several days after arrival. Three days later, without medication, she was in excellent spirits, making sketches and being helpful with the other patients. After three weeks in this euthymic state, her mood suddenly plummeted for no ostensible reason, and she tried to cut her wrists with some bits of concealed glass. It was noted that her period was due shortly. Two days later her menses came, and within hours her mood brightened as if nothing had happened. A careful graphing of her mood and weight was initiated. This revealed that within forty-eight hours of her period a psychotic depression would abruptly come on, and just as abruptly turn off within hours after the beginning of menstrual flow. Premenstrual weight gain was in the range of two to five pounds. Alerted to this correlation, the hospital staff was able to rescue her from several near-fatal suicide attempts. A course of lithium was instituted because of the cyclical nature of her illness. She did not respond to lithium but did respond to a combination of an MAO inhibitor plus diuretics.

In her now-stabilized condition it became possible to evaluate her personality resources more accurately. She had a borderline structure with severe ''splitting'' involving conflicts around her identity as a woman. Expressive therapy was now possible, and she made considerable strides in resolving these conflicts; social and occupational adaptation also showed excellent improvement.

Of interest: her mother had suffered from moderately severe depressions since her early twenties. Her father had been treated with ECT for ''psychotic depressions'' on two occasions.

The case is noteworthy with respect to the extreme gravity of her premenstrual psychosis. Had not strict attention been paid to this factor, she would almost certainly, despite her many personality assets, have succumbed to a suicide attempt before one or another menstrual period.

Borderline Structure with Premenstrual Rage Attacks

A forty-year-old married woman was seen for psychotherapy because of marital problems and depression. Some years earlier she had had a moderately severe problem with episodic drinking but had maintained sobriety for over two years.

Her father was a manic-depressive, mostly with ''highs''; a brother and a paternal aunt were alcoholic; a maternal aunt had been hospitalized because of a severe depression and a suicide attempt.

Initially the patient was tearful, clinging, and at times panicky, making frequent calls to her psychiatrist. There was a crescendo effect to her symptoms, which intensified within a week to include recurrent nightmares, suicidal ruminations, and outbursts of rage directed against her husband. Although a woman of considerable wealth and refinement, during the attacks of rage she would hurl both objects and verbal abuse at her husband, following very minor provocations.

Eventually it was noted that her episodes of rage and panic occurred approximately a week before her menses. During this stretch of time she would be delusionally jealous, but after the menses would quickly settle down into a placid demeanor, regaining her usual charm and self-confidence.

She responded well to a combination of diuretics and antidepressant (tricyclic) medication. Focus in psychotherapy on her unrealistic self-image and equally unrealistic perception of her husband's personality led to greater tolerance and a solidification of her improved status.

Primary Affective Disorders: Dimensional Aspects in Diagnosis

Depressive and bipolar disorders can be quite difficult to diagnose either in their incipient stages (in those patients who eventually go on to develop clearly recognizable conditions) or in their *formes frustes* (in other patients, who may seek help but who never become seriously ill).

Recently I drew attention to a group of patients, referred initially for psychoanalysis, who ultimately experienced full-blown manic episodes. The character structure was for the most part obsessive-compulsive; only a few hypomanic features were present in one case (Stone, 1978). One patient had had an acute depressive episode in the past; another had had a solitary panic attack. None had had episodes at all suggestive of mania, so that when the manic psychosis occurred, it seemed to have come "out of the blue." Some hints, not noticed at the time, but which in retrospect might have alerted a clinician to the possibility of such an outcome, were provided in the form of subtle symptoms of a "manic-depressive" flavor. These symptoms and signs are listed in Table 8–18. No one symptom by

TABLE 8–18

Signs and Symptoms That May Aid in the Detection of Early or Subtle Bipolar Affective Disorders

1. Denial of illness; denial of impending or actual loss; a poor degree of psychological aptitude despite good intelligence
2. Rigidity of character
3. Marked insensitivity to the feelings of others
4. Narcissistic personality features
5. Boastfulness; "know-it-all" quality
6. Intensity
7. Drivenness
8. Ambition; publicity seeking
9. Impatience
10. Social awkwardness
11. Overfamiliarity or intrusiveness
12. Externalization of problems and conflicts
13. Primitive dreams
14. Extraversion
15. Social abrasiveness
16. Satyriasis
17. Explosive temper
18. History of brief hospitalization for panic or depression
19. Compulsive talking; frequent interrupting
20. Prodigality
21. Alcoholism or other substance abuse
22. Exaggerated interest in punning; compulsive witticism

SOURCE: Adapted from Stone (1978).

itself carries sufficient weight to steer one's diagnostic thinking in the proper direction. Of the four patients mentioned in my article, one had only five of the twenty-two items in the table, while one had as many as nineteen.

The similarity between many of the items of Table 8–18 and the "hard" criteria for mania formulated by Feighner et al. will be at once apparent. Compulsive talking or interrupting can be seen as a mild form of pushed speech. Boastfulness, publicity seeking, prodigality, and narcissistic personality may end up as manic grandiosity. Extraversion is a few steps away from hypomania; impatience and an ill-tempered nature may suddenly progress to the extreme irritability of the manic. The concurrence of half a dozen or more of these symptoms in someone who is not clearly cyclothymic or hypomanic may nonetheless communicate to the clinician the potential for eventual manic decompensation (if not the existence in the here and now of a mild bipolar disorder that just fails to meet "hard" diagnostic criteria). The presence of half a dozen of the items from Table 8–18 may constitute a "manic temperament" (see Chapter 10 below; Stone, 1978c). Many patients in the borderland between outward normality and overt bipolar illness will also exhibit borderline structure (see Stone, 1978, cases 1 and 2).

Analogous to the above-mentioned study of personality characteristics noted in eventual bipolar patients is the study of Wittenborn and Maurer (1977) in which initial descriptions of 190 depressed women were compared with descriptions at follow-up one year later. A number of personality attributes were found to have a traitlike stability, in that they tended to persist over time—even after the dysphoric symptoms were alleviated with appropriate treatment. Petulance, lack of self-confidence, irritability, and a tendency to worry over trifles were some of the characteristics that resisted change. It will be interesting to determine whether, among the close relatives of unipolar depressed patients, there is an "excess" of persons exhibiting some of the traits mentioned by Wittenborn and Maurer.

Temperament disturbances found in association with the affective disorders are examined in greater detail in Chapter 10.

CHAPTER 9

Diagnosis of the Borderline Syndromes:

Contemporary Definitions

In the preceding chapter we concentrated on two main entities, schizophrenia and the group of primary affective disorders. We examined in some detail criteria for diagnosing full-blown as well as dilute forms of either entity and also for detecting clinical states that represent mixtures of the two fundamental tendencies, again, either in full-blown (severe schizoaffective disorder) or milder versions. Since the two extreme disorders (chronic schizophrenia; manic-depressive psychosis) may well exist as gross exaggerations, genetically induced, of attributes detectable in all human beings (relating to self-other boundary and psychointegration, or to drive intensity and energy level), one may assume with some justification that in making these two distinctions, nature has truly been carved at her joints.[1]

When we come to examine the diagnostic criteria for the various borderline syndromes in current use, we enter a realm where genetic and consti-

[1]Schizoaffective patients constitute a kind of exception: they have such marked difficulties in both departments that any notion of a "joint" between schizophrenic and affective trends is defied.

tutional differences are not uniformly relevant, as in the major psychoses, and are more difficult to discern when present. Even so, genetic constitutional factors are important to the development of "borderline" conditions, no matter how defined, in many, perhaps even in a majority of, instances. How much this is so will depend on the patient sample. Also, there will be less specificity than is customary among the classical psychoses: some borderline patients appear to have schizophrenic "loading"; more still, loading for some form of affective disorder; a few seem to have loading for both; others, for neither.

The borderline designation, in psychoanalytic parlance, relates primarily to object relations, treatment methodology, and prognosis. It is not so much nature as the profession of psychiatry which is being carved at the joints. Bergeret (1974), for example, has emphasized the predominance in borderline conditions of pregenital conflicts and primitive qualities in ego and superego development. From the standpoint of object relations, Bergeret conceives of the borderline structure as a *category apart* from either neurotic or psychotic structures. This viewpoint is expressed also by Kernberg (1975). But it is precisely because the distinctions these investigators make exist within a psychological more than within a biological world that the niceties of structural diagnosis appear so elusive and, often enough, irrelevant, to those without a psychoanalytic background.

In the sections that follow, we will examine current definitions of "borderline," some emphasizing structural criteria and others based more on material from direct observation. We will concentrate (in alphabetical order) on the systems of Bergeret, Gunderson, Kernberg, D. Klein, and Spitzer. The advantages and drawbacks of each will be outlined, as will their points of overlap and points of dissimilarity. The reader should also consult the excellent review of Perry and Klerman (1978) in which two contemporary systems (Gunderson and Kernberg) and two somewhat older systems (Knight and Grinker) are analyzed and compared.

Bergeret's Metapsychology of Borderline States

The Lyonnaise analyst Bergeret (1974) has recently presented a psychoanalytic model of psychic structures, to which he is indebted partly to Kernberg, partly to earlier theoreticians including Melanie Klein. Bergeret conceives of the various nosological entities—the psychoses, the neuroses, and the borderline states—as stemming from traumata that impeded maturation at certain points in individual development. His schema for the differential diagnosis of the three structural states is outlined in Table 9–1. The chief anxiety at work is different at each level: in the psychotic, fear of fragmentation; in the borderline, fear of loss of the object; in the neurotic, fear of castration. While I think the distinction between "borderline" and "psychotic" on these grounds is somewhat artificial (depressive psychotics

TABLE 9–1

Bergeret's Structural Schema

Characteristics of the Three Types

	Symptoms	*Anxiety*	*Object Relations*	*Defense*
PSYCHOTIC STRUCTURE	Depersonalization Delusion	Fragmentation Death	Fusional (merging)	Denial Splitting of self-image
BORDERLINE STRUCTURE	Depression	Fear of loss of the object	Anaclitic	Disavowal Splitting of images of the object
NEUROTIC STRUCTURE	Hysterical or obsessional symptoms	Fear of castration	Genital	Repression and other high-level defenses

SOURCE: Bergeret (1974).

are not always worried about fragmentation but are routinely worried about loss of the object), on the whole his scheme is useful.

Bergeret also speaks of neurotics as exhibiting deviations from the ideal state with respect to the evolution of object relations, whereas for borderlines the deviation is in the evolution of feeling about the self, that is, in the *narcissistic* path. Bergeret thus sees narcissistic psychopathology as central to what borderline organization is all about. Bergeret also underlines the symptom of *anaclitic depression* as fundamental in borderline structure: this is, after all, the most "sensible" remedy, in the world of the borderline patient, to his fear of loss of the object.

Another element in the scheme of differential diagnosis employed by Bergeret is that of *psychodynamics*. In the following passage, which I have translated from the 1974 book, Bergeret sets forth his views on dynamic issues which he considers important in the formation of borderline structure:

> One encounters rather often in one's practice patients in whom the ego has developed, without undue burden, beyond the point where frustrations in earliest infancy (had they occurred) could have established fixation points of the entrenched and pathological sort that underlie psychotic structure. At the same time we note that these patients have not, in their subsequent development, regressed to these very early fixation points. Around the time, however, that they would have become immersed in the usual Oedipal conflicts, these individuals are found to have suffered severe [and "disorganizing"; see

> Table 9–2] psychic traumata . . . at a stage when the ego's defenses . . . are still too poorly organized and immature (as by sexual seduction, for example; cf. also: Freud's "Wolf Man"). . . . The individual in this situation will be unable to rely upon the father's love in coping with (eventual) hostile feelings toward the mother, and vice versa. Nor will it be possible to use repression well enough to remove from consciousness the [resulting] excess of sexual or aggressive tension. Instead, the future borderline individual will be obliged to fall back upon mechanisms that approximate much more closely those of the psychotic: denial, projective identification, splitting of object representations, and omnipotent manipulation of the object. (p. 183 ff.)

A résumé of Bergeret's psychodynamic-developmental views is presented in Table 9–2.

Bergeret conceives of borderline development as constituting a distinct "track," but one characterized by less fixity of structure than the psychotic or neurotic paths of development. Severe stress, for example, can cause the borderline individual to swerve, temporarily, onto the psychotic track, at least to outward appearance. The even greater stability of the other two structures is such that even dramatically good or bad circumstances will not induce change in structural type.

Abnormalities in borderline object relations are seen by Bergeret as the product of narcissistic injury in persons who have advanced beyond ego fragmentation but not as far as the mature (genital) object-relations level of the neurotic. In borderline structure there is anaclitic dependence on the "important other." Many phobics, symbiotically attached to their objects, are borderlines "posing" as neurotics, according to this metapsychology—a formulation with which I am very much in agreement. The danger against which the ego is pictured as struggling, in borderline pathology, is *depression*.

As with other purely psychological models, difficulties will be encountered in attempting to explain, using Bergeret's theory, phenomena such as differential vulnerability of children from the same family to key stresses like separation from, or loss of, a parent. Sibships exist with at least one child in each of the three psychostructural categories; one would be hard put to explain such striking differences solely on the basis of differential parental feelings and modes of interaction.[2] In reality many neurotic persons have been exposed to devouring or rejecting mothers, aloof or punitive fathers, and the like, without ever succumbing to the more severe forms of emotional illness. And certain persons with high genetic loading who eventually go on to exhibit borderline or psychotic structure have been reared in harmonious families, to whose vicissitudes and mild tensions they grossly overreact.

[2]Of interest in this regard, four of the eight borderline adoptees hospitalized on the General Clinical Service (New York Psychiatric Institute) between 1964 and 1977 were reared, beginning in the first weeks of their lives, by adopting parents who were emotionally healthy.

TABLE 9–2

Bergeret's Schema

Modes of Development of the Various Structures

	Psychotic Structure	*Borderline Structure*	*Neurotic Structure*
INFANCY	Severe frustration in very early (oral; early anal) stages; maternal overprotection or absence	Normal evolution	Normal evolution
	↓	Precocious disorganizing traumata (namely, in Oedipal stage)	Oedipal conflict of ordinary dimensions
	Anlage of psychotic ego structure	↓	↓
		Precocious pseudolatency	Anlage of neurotic ego structure
LATENCY	↓	↓	↓
ADOLESCENCE	Psychotic ego organization	Borderline structure	Neurotic ego organization
	↓ (Severe stress: borderline structure → psychosis)	↓	↓
MATURITY	Psychosis	Borderline state	Psychoneurosis

SOURCE: After Bergeret (1974).

Gunderson: The Borderline Personality Disorder

A prominent advocate of the *borderline* concept, Gunderson has made a number of important contributions to the refinement of its definition on the basis of meticulous analysis of the literature as well as subsequent clinical observation (Gunderson and Singer, 1975; Gunderson, Carpenter, and Strauss, 1975; Carpenter, Gunderson, and Strauss, 1976). From the systematic examination of the ingredients of the term "borderline"—as utilized by his predecessors—Gunderson has teased out a number of essential features; these, in turn, have become embodied as criteria for the syndrome he proposes: the *borderline personality disorder* (BPD). The manner in which these features were isolated, via discriminant function analysis, is described in a more recent article (Gunderson and Kolb, 1978).

In order to render the diagnosis of *borderline personality disorder* more objective, Gunderson and Kolb (1976) elaborated a semistructured interview (the Diagnostic Interview for Borderlines, or DIB). The DIB contains 123 items, tapping twenty-nine characteristics of borderline patients in five main areas of function: *social adaptation, impulse-action patterns, affects, psychosis,* and *interpersonal relations.*

Correspondences between the Gunderson (G) and Kernberg (K) variables may be drawn up in the following fashion: (1) the *reality-testing* item (K) resembles the section entitled "Psychosis" (G); (2) some of the specific questions in the section "Affect" (G) tap information about *anxiety tolerance* (K); (3) both systems have separate questions or scales relating to impulse control; (4) *sublimatory capacity* (K) can be partially assessed by several of the questions on "Social Adaptation" (G)—namely, number 9, "Do you have any special talents or skills . . . ?" and number 10, "Have there been periods when you were particularly effective in school or work?"; and, finally, (5) some of the questions asked in order to assess "Interpersonal Relations" (G) resemble areas for special attention in the "Structural Interview" (K).

The DIB has thus far been administered chiefly to young (ages sixteen to thirty-five) hospitalized patients with average to better-than-average intelligence and in whom drug or alcohol abuse is not a primary diagnosis. Results suggest that a borderline group can be reliably separated out from a schizophrenic and from a neurotic group.

Discriminating BPD from Schizophrenia

In contrast to the patient with BPD, the schizophrenic (here, in the sense of the *core* schizophrenic) will often have *flattening of affect* and episodes of severe derealization. The schizophrenic is often a *loner;* the borderline patient is clingingly dependent or else manipulative and demanding—but in either case, feels a strong need to be in the company of others. Gunderson found that serious and repeated abuse of illicit drugs was far more common in the borderline group than in either schizophrenics or neurotics (1977a, p. 179). This may reflect patient-sample variation, since this has not been uniformly so in the author's experience: both at New York Psychiatric Institute and at New York Hospital–Westchester Division, mild to moderate abuse of marijuana and hallucinogens is almost universal in hospitalized patients under thirty, irrespective of diagnostic subgroup.

Discriminating BPD from the Neurotic Group

Borderline patients frequently experienced *brief psychotic episodes;* this rarely occurred among the neurotics. *Dysphoria* and *anhedonia* were more common in BPD, as was a *deviant pattern of sexuality*. The latter might include either promiscuity or one of the perversions. *Antisocial patterns* were more frequently noted in the borderlines, who also tended to show *poor achievement or work* records. *Intolerance of being alone* was typical in BPD, yet close relationships were characteristically unstable, dependency alternating with devaluation and exploitation. In the hospital setting, staff were often "split" into two or more groups, each with markedly contrasting responses to the borderline patient.

Impulse-action patterns and interpersonal relationships emerged as the most highly discriminating variables in relation to both schizophrenia and neurosis. Gunderson has summarized his findings in the area of social adaptation with the observation (1977) that (*a*) *borderlines* show *good awareness of social conventions* in contrast to the *schizophrenic* but (*b*) show a *poor work–achievement* record when compared with the *neurotic*.

Diagnostic Criteria for BPD

The most discriminating items from the DIB could, through factor analysis, be condensed into a smaller number of recurring features that now constitute the criteria for Gunderson's borderline personality disorder (Gunderson and Kolb, 1978). These are outlined in Table 9–3, which also includes the results on psychological testing characteristically noted (Gunderson and Singer, 1975) in BPD patients.

Inspection of Table 9–3 will make clear that the Gunderson criteria represent a mixture of clinical-phenomenological items (brief psychotic episodes, rageful affect, and so on), derived primarily from direct observation, and other more abstract items (problems with closeness) derived from anamnesis and from experience with the patient over time.

There is less emphasis on defense mechanisms in the Gunderson criteria than in Kernberg's formulations, though it is obvious that anyone satisfying BPD criteria would have the kind of primitivity in defense structure that Kernberg speaks of. The same may be said for disturbance in identity formation: this is alluded to in the Gunderson schema ("shifting identifications" resembles Deutsch's "as if" personality) but underlined directly in

TABLE 9–3

Gunderson's Borderline Personality Disorder

Diagnostic Criteria

1. *Lowered Achievement* (diminished work capacity)
2. *Impulsivity* (especially drug abuse and promiscuity)
3. *Manipulative Suicidal Threats* (namely, wrist cutting)
4. *Mild or Brief Psychotic Episodes* (often of a paranoid quality and sometimes more sustained in duration, if provoked by abuse of psychotomimetic drugs; but severe depersonalization, or widespread delusions, in absence of drugs, contraindicates the diagnosis)
5. *Good Socialization* (mostly a superficial adaptiveness, beneath which is a disturbed identity camouflaged by rapid and shifting identifications with others)
6. *Disturbances in Close Relationships*
   a. Tendency to be depressive in the presence of the important other, and to be enraged or suicidal should the latter threaten to leave; tendency to have psychotic reactions when alone
   b. In general, a predominance of rageful affect rather than emotional warmth

NOTE: Psychological tests will tend to show good performance on the structured portions of the test and poor performance (with the emergence of primitive ideation) on the unstructured portions. Except for possible temporary lapses, reality testing is preserved.

the Kernberg schema. The occurrence of brief psychotic episodes, on the other hand, is spelled out in so many words as part of the BPD, whereas by Kernberg it is simply acknowledged that these episodes are common and quite compatible with his "borderline personality organization." This difference may be a reflection of a greater affiliation in spirit, on Gunderson's part, to Grinker and to the traditional views of hospital psychiatry, and, on Kernberg's part, to Melanie Klein and Rosenfeld, and to the structuralist/psychoanalytic viewpoint. In connection with this it should be kept in mind that Gunderson, although he mentions parenthetically the generally good reality testing of his BPD sample, does not set up as a criterion the feature so central to Kernberg's schema, namely, preservation of reality testing even in the interpersonal sphere. It is this difference which (in my opinion) accounts for the greater ease with which a schizotypal borderline patient (or "borderline schizophrenic," à la Kety) can meet Gunderson's, in comparison to Kernberg's, criteria. Certain schizotypal borderline patients (but not all) therefore constitute an area of nonoverlap with the Kernberg borderline realm.

Since Gunderson and Kolb's DIB requires a lengthier examination than the Spitzer checklist but a less analytically oriented psychiatric interview than Kernberg's diagnostic procedure, the Gunderson schema may be seen as one of intermediate complexity. Because many alcoholic and other substance-abuse patients show Kernberg's borderline organization, Gunderson's BPD occupies a smaller territory on the total psychodiagnostic map, *mostly* within the Kernberg realm, but less slanted toward the affective pole and, indeed, containing a larger "tail" in the realm of borderline schizophrenia than is exhibited by Kernberg's sample. These relationships are reflected in the Venn diagram of Chapter 2.

Gunderson has expressed the hope that the borderline personality disorder, already a definite syndrome as he and his colleagues have defined it, will be validated as a coherent psychiatric disorder. Gunderson and Kolb mention as external frames of reference, in relation to which their syndrome must be further evaluated, *psychological coherence, treatment response, clinical course,* and *etiology*. With respect to treatment response, BPD already seems to correspond well with the particular set of patients in the intermediate range of function, for whom intensive analytically oriented therapy is best suited. Some patients in the group are schizotypal, clinically if not constitutionally, and are still captured by the Gunderson definition. The Kernberg definition, because it is broader, also includes most of the patients destined to benefit from this mode of treatment. But many substance-abusing and antisocial or otherwise intensely narcissistic patients are borderline in Kernberg's sense (but not in Gunderson's), while a number of "Gunderson-positive" schizotypal borderline patients are "Kernberg-negative" because their reality testing does not improve, initially, on confrontation. It will be interesting to see which definition, as further follow-up studies are performed, more closely overlaps with the set of patients responding well to intensive psychotherapy.

Regarding etiology, I have already expressed my view that both the Gunderson and the Kernberg definitions of borderline embrace a heterogeneous population, with the difference that Gunderson's BPD includes more schizotypal patients—probably with more schizophrenic and borderline-schizophrenic relatives—than does the more affectively tilted Kernberg definition.

As with other definitions of *borderline,* the female-to-male ratio in the Gunderson syndrome is approximately 2:1.

A Note on Psychological Testing in Borderlines

In their 1975 paper, Gunderson and Singer drew attention to a psychological test result they considered characteristic of the "borderline" patient. Typically one observed good performance on the structured portions of the test battery (such as the WAIS or the Bender Visual Motor Gestalt Test) but poor performance on unstructured portions. In the Rorschach, for example, borderline patients might respond in a way that suggested weakening of ego boundaries. Bizarre or highly idiosyncratic responses were common; on some records, confabulation and a preponderance of "minus"-form (*F*−) responses were noted. These were the abnormalities to which McCully (1962) drew attention in his report on the Rorschach findings in "borderline schizophrenia." It is not clear, however, what diagnostic criteria McCully required in using that term, nor to what extent those criteria may coincide with the Gunderson criteria for borderline personality disorder.

In my experience many patients who meet the borderline criteria of either Gunderson or Kernberg show the split in test performance Gunderson and Singer allude to, but so do a number of intellectually gifted patients (usually schizophrenic) with psychotic structure. This split, when present, cannot be understood as inhering exclusively to the realm of borderline conditions.

Psychological testing, as McCully mentions, dives below the surface of ordinary experience, therefore tapping layers of mental functioning not necessarily accessible to the clinician. If one favors the notion that *vulnerability* to schizophrenia may be present, and often suspected, even in the absence of "hard" signs, it should not be surprising to find that some recompensated (but once overt) schizophrenics continue to show bizarre responses on the unstructured portions; likewise certain persons with significant loading for schizophrenia, who have not as yet, or who may never, decompensate, may still betray "characteristic" schizophrenic signs on such testing. Those who do not adhere to the notion of vulnerability may, in contrast, experience as paradoxical the "schizophrenic" responses of certain borderline patients who, here and now at the clinical level, are "not schizophrenic."

Singer (1977) has reported on a number of studies she conducted, some in conjunction with Lyman Wynne, of psychological tests on patients at various levels of illness, and on their relatives. In one such study, the index cases were divided into five groups: normal, neurotic, borderline, remitting schizophrenia, and nonremitting schizophrenia. It was noted that on the Rorschach, borderline patients gave even more flamboyant, elaborate, and peculiarly expressed responses than did the "remitting" schizophrenics.

Clinical evaluation of the relatives of these different groups revealed that one parent was borderline or psychotic in 16 percent of the borderline cases. This figure increased with increasing severity in the index case: 21 percent in the remitting Sz group, 35 percent in the nonremitting group. In addition, both parents were *at least* borderline in 40 percent of the nonremitting cases—whereas no instances of combined illness were noted in parents of the less ill cases. On Rorschach study of the parents, Singer noted that the parents of borderlines gave strikingly more responses with *affective* connotations than did parents in the other categories.

Although Singer states that persons who become labeled "borderline" do not conform to a solitary nosological entity, two relationships are suggested by her observations. First, many borderlines are schizotypal not only in their Rorschach responses but also clinically—and some come from families where there are schizophrenic or schizoid relatives. Second, the affective coloration of responses among the (often emotionally ill) parents of her borderline cases mirrors my finding that a high percentage of parents of borderlines suffer affective illnesses within the manic-depressive fold. It may be that some of the patients Singer is calling borderline are indeed borderline schizophrenics, in Kety's sense, and deserve inclusion within the spectrum of schizophrenia.[3] Another subgroup may consist of patients, such as those making up the majority of my sample, with incipient or spectrum affective disorders. As with all "borderline" samples, Singer, too, alludes to a youthful (age sixteen to forty) group of high socioeconomic class, most of whom have attained college level.

Further study is still required before we know the degree of correlation between clinical diagnosis of a borderline condition and the psychometric data. Until then, information obtained through testing should be set to one side as a potential source of validation (or refutation) of clinical diagnosis.

Kernberg's Borderline Structure and Borderline Personality Organization

Over the past decade Kernberg has been influential both as advocate of the "borderline" concept and as theoretician, redefining the concept (as it took shape in the writings of Knight and Grinker) in a more precise and manageable fashion. Kernberg's description of borderline is from the psychostructural[4] point of view, placing particular reliance on the nature and vicissitudes of internalized representations of the self and of others. Hence his classification, strictly speaking, is one of personality organizations, of which "borderline" represents the intermediate variant between neurotic and psychotic organizations. Though by no means divorced from clinical

[3]Singer mentions, for example, that "we found the borderlines and remitting schizophrenics difficult to differentiate on many [Rorschach] items" (1977, p. 209).

[4]Kernberg's psychostructural theory represents a further stage in the development of traditional psychoanalytic metapsychology. There is a direct chain of evolution beginning with Freud's *topographic* model (1900), stressing "unconscious-preconscious-conscious," and passing through Freud's 1923 revision—the *structural* model, stressing ego, id, and superego, in which certain conflicts could be viewed as tensions between two of these three compartments. A full exposition of structural theory would, of course, require a lengthy book in itself. The interested reader should pay particular attention to the seminal ego-psychological papers of Hartmann (1939) and of Rapaport and Gill (1959). An attempt to encompass schizophrenic phenomenology in structural terms was made by Arlow and Brenner (1964); Kohut (1971) has extended structural theory to embrace narcissistic disorders, a task also undertaken (in my view, more successfully) by Kernberg (1975).

signs and symptoms, Kernberg's model is less dependent on purely observational or phenomenological data than is Grinker's model. The critical points in the diagnostic spectrum, psychostructurally viewed, are *reality testing* and *ego integration*. Reality testing demarcates borderline from psychotic structure. The tradition for this distinction in psychiatry is of course well established. Ego integration, which is well developed in neurotic structures but enfeebled in the borderline, is conceptually less easily defined. A crucial aspect of faulty ego integration is the presence of sharply contradictory attitudes permeating vital sectors of the personality and interfering with everyday life, especially in the area of interpersonal relations.

Kernberg also speaks of certain "nonspecific" signs including lowered anxiety tolerance, poor impulse control, and poor sublimatory capacity. Low anxiety tolerance overlaps considerably with the concept of vulnerability, used by the geneticists, but, like faulty ego integration, is an abstraction derived from a specialized confrontational interview or from long acquaintance with the patient. Neither concept permits of easy appraisal within the realm of readily observable behavior. Interrater reliability has been achieved among several raters present at a "structural" interview (of which more below), but reliability has not yet been tested between interviews of the same patient done blindly by separate interviewers.[5] Faulty ego integration remains in any event the least readily teachable ingredient of Kernberg's model.

The mental mechanism by which contradictory attitudes are maintained side by side—without evoking a sense of contradictoriness in the patient—is called *splitting* (corresponding to *vertical splitting* in Kohut's terminology). Splitting that serves to protect the patient from awareness of his ambivalence is thus an important aspect of borderline personality organization. The same mechanism, protecting this time against *fragmentation* of the ego, is frequently encountered in *psychotic* structure, as Bergeret has pointed out (1974).

It should be kept clear that Kernberg's use of *borderline, neurotic,* and *psychotic* to denote structural levels[6] is divorced from the issue of distal

[5]As advocated, for example, by Lee Robins and R. Cloninger of the Washington University Department of Psychiatry in St. Louis.

[6]Speaking from an object-relational point of view, Kernberg makes some very comprehensible distinctions among the three structural types. If one thinks of a person's mental representations of himself, and again, of others, these may be subdivided, each, into positive aspects and negative aspects (yielding four "species" of inner representations). In schizophrenia (the paradigm case of psychotic structure), distinctions between self and object(s) are blurred: good and bad part representations of self and object are all mixed higgledy-piggledy. There is no firm sense of *self;* therefore, as Kernberg rightly points out, it is hopeless to "explain" the schizophrenic's mental life in ego-id-superego terms. It makes no sense to speak of those structures as having developed in the still psychotic schizophrenic. (With good therapy and time, these structures may begin to take shape.)

etiology. Thus manics and core schizophrenics will equally demonstrate psychotic *structure* on confrontational interview during the acute phase of their illness. "Psychotic structure" is used in a manner analogous to the psychogeneticist's notion of "state," where manic-depressives are concerned. Many manic-depressives, because of their tendency to reorganize to a high level upon subsidence of a psychotic episode, will be seen to fluctuate with respect to internal personality structure. In some, however, their functioning remains at the borderline level even during the interpsychotic phases of their illness. Most unequivocal schizophrenics, in contrast, will exhibit "psychotic structure," as Kernberg defines it, even during the phase of recompensation. This is because of the tendency in this group of patients to maintain highly unrealistic notions in the interpersonal sphere—unrealistic images of themselves and of other people—even when no longer grossly delusional. For this reason, *psychotic structure* has, in the realm of schizophrenia, a *trait*like stability (in the psychogeneticist's sense) not usually noted among the primary affective disorders.

The criteria for the psychostructural diagnosis of borderline personality organization are outlined in Table 9–4.

The other two nonspecific signs, as noted in the table, include *poor impulse control* and *poor sublimatory capacity*. The former is an item mentioned in all schemata for borderline diagnosis, and may include such tendencies as self-destructive or self-mutilative acts, sexual promiscuity, strong tendencies to "act out" transference situations, and the like. The connection between impulsivity, defined in this way, and the driven, impulse-ridden quality to the lives of many bipolar patients (of both full-blown and dilute forms) has been mentioned elsewhere (Stone, 1978b). The presence of marked impulsivity in a borderline patient should alert the clinician to the possibility that he may be dealing with a "spectrum" affective disorder (see pp. 285–287, Klein's "hysteroid dysphoria").

Poor capacity for sublimatory channeling is a common feature in border-

---

In the "borderline," self and object(s) are properly differentiated. But the good and bad aspects of each are not blended; they are somehow held apart, compartmentalized, in such a way that the patient is not consciously aware of his *ambivalence*, that is, of both aspects of self or of both aspects of (the important) other(s). Intensive therapy aims at uniting these polarized views into an integrated set of inner representations, characteristic of the healthier "neurotic" structure.

The neurotic, in other words, has available to him a mature and blended view of himself and of others, and is simultaneously in touch with his—and their—virtues and shortcomings.

From the above it will become clear how it is that Kernberg views his "borderline" level of psychic organization as a category. With respect to *structural* metapsychology, it is defined as a homogeneous entity, with upper and lower boundaries. From the standpoint of *etiology*, as I have stressed repeatedly, the patients embodying this structural level are by no means homogeneous. Many have affective illnesses, some schizophrenic, and so on (a point also made by D. Klein, 1975).

TABLE 9–4

Kernberg's Borderline Structure

Diagnostic Criteria

A. *Specific Signs*
   1. Impaired ego integration (especially: sharply contradictory and unassimilated attitudes about important aspects of the self; pathological internalized object relations)
   2. Adequate capacity to *test* reality (both in the interpersonal and nonpersonal realms)

B. *Nonspecific Signs*
   1. Low "anxiety tolerance" (high vulnerability to stress)
   2. Poor impulse control
   3. Poor sublimatory capacity (usually manifested as a poor record with respect to school, work, or hobbies)

C. *Primitive Defenses* (namely, denial, splitting, projective identification, omnipotent control and devaluation, primitive idealization)

SOURCE: Abstracted from Kernberg (1967).

line patients, though in my experience it is a less regular feature than the other nonspecific signs. One occasionally encounters a highly anxious, impulsive borderline patient who nevertheless retains the ability to pursue hobbies or even to work with a modicum of effectiveness.

Borderline structure is essentially a category diagnosis, especially as utilized by Kernberg, who very methodically defines for it an upper as well as a lower boundary. Nevertheless, for diagnoses of all but the most florid psychotic conditions, one is dependent upon evaluation of quite a few variables, each of which varies continuously over a wide spectrum. This dimensional aspect to an otherwise categorical diagnosis naturally gives rise to a certain amount of disagreement, so that in actual practice, there will occasionally be cases that are not at all readily classified (see case illustrations 16 and 18).

To aid in the objectification of borderline structural diagnosis, Kernberg, Goldstein, and their co-workers have developed anchored rating scales for the variables to which special attention is paid. Each variable is rated on a scale of zero to 100, where zero corresponds to the most extremely pathological state imaginable. A hint of what such descriptions would be like is given in Table 9–5, though the full descriptions of the zero—and the other five to seven points described for each scale (as guideposts)—are not yet available for publication. The exception to this is variable number 10, the Global Assessment Score, a 100-point anchored rating scale developed by

TABLE 9–5

Objectification of Clinically Diagnosed Borderline Structure

Patient Variables to Be Assessed via Anchored Rating Scales

1. Reality testing (zero = chronic pervasive delusions)
2. Identity integration (zero = chronic fragmentation or pervasive depersonalization)
3. Anxiety tolerance (zero = chronic pervasive anxiety overwhelms and cripples the patient)
4. Severity of symptoms (zero = [for example] chronic hallucinosis)
5. Quality of object relations (zero = autistic incapacity to relate to others in any fashion)
6. Impulse control (zero = chronic tendency to immediate carrying out of all impulses)
7. Sublimatory effectiveness (zero = no capacity for pursuing any interest)
8. Primitivity of defenses (zero = extremely primitive forms of splitting and fragmentation of the personality)
9. Antisocial features and superego integration (zero = total incapacity for any loyalty or human values; total ruthlessness)
10. The Global Assessment Score (zero = patient would die if unattended constantly)

NOTE: Full formal discussion of the manner in which all these variables are evaluated is beyond the scope of this book. More detailed definitions and descriptions are to be found in Kernberg's 1975 book. There are, however, many examples among the case illustrations of poor to moderately good function with regard to the relevant variables. The reader may consult the following for the variable in question (numbers refer to case illustrations): *Reality testing* (1); *Identity* (or "ego") *integration* (3, 6, 12); *Anxiety tolerance* (15, 27); *Severity of symptoms* (4, 7, 15); *Quality of object relations* (6 and 7, contrasted with the healthier patients: 25, 28); *Impulse control* (4, 10); *Sublimatory effectiveness* (10, 25); *Primitivity of defenses* (1, 10); and *Antisocial features* (17).

SOURCE: Kernberg and Goldstein (1975).

Endicott and Spitzer and derived from the Menninger Health-Sickness Rating Scale (Luborsky, 1962; see also Part IV).

These scales are not used to *establish* the diagnosis of borderline structure; the diagnosis is made from a special interview developed by Kernberg (1976a) and described in some detail in Kernberg (1977).

The Structural Interview

Kernberg has referred to his interviewing technic as "structural"[7] because it aims at elucidating the patient's psychostructural organization.

[7]The term should not be confused with "structured," as though the interview were structured (like a questionnaire), which it is not.

As in any verbal interview, the patient (whether in or out of the hospital) is first questioned about his reasons for seeking help. But the interviewer pays special attention to *discrepancies* that may emerge in the patient's discourse between his "reality" and reality as experienced by the (presumably better integrated) interviewer. At an appropriate moment the patient may be challenged about one or another of these discrepancies. This is of course a matter of tact, timing, and skill; no laws can be laid down for "when," "which," and "how" in a strictly computerizable fashion. The psychiatrist may act like a "digital" computer when he accumulates demographic data or asks about the presence of olfactory hallucinations ("yes"—"no"), but he functions more like an "analog" computer in appraising a patient's life-style, object relations, defenses, and so on, as being statistically either typical of most ordinary people or, rather, at the trailing edges of the bell curve of human variation (see Peterfreund, 1971). Nevertheless, the technic Kernberg has devised incorporates a style of interviewing that places much emphasis on the cognitive. By this I mean that Kernberg makes an endeavor to speak, if you will, to the conscious of the patient, more so than to the unconscious, constantly testing the patient's capacity to reexamine rationally the contradictions and discrepancies in his perception of himself and of those around him.

Naturally enough, the grossly delusional patient may reveal his (psychotic) structure in the first few sentences of the dialogue. The evasive paranoid patient may keep the interviewer at bay for a longer time, but with such a patient the interviewer's instincts will lead him to probe further with regard to reality testing. This becomes the relevant issue: Does the patient possess an adequate capacity to test reality or has this been lost? The interview may be spent almost entirely on clarifying this crucial point.[8] If reality testing is clearly present, however, the interviewer will turn his attention to more subtle details of psychological functioning: Are the "nonspecific" signs present? How intact is the patient's ego integration? Once the inter-

[8]For further remarks about reality testing in borderlines, see also Frosch (1970, p. 33). Kernberg, like Frosch, tends to speak of this variable in discontinuous terms:

> Loss of reality testing in any one area indicates psychotic functioning. . . . This formulation implies that there is no continuum, no gradual shift from presence to absence of reality testing, and that there are qualitative as well as quantitative differences between the structural organization of borderline and psychotic conditions. [1975, p. 182]

In clinical practice, admittedly, it is easier to discern a dichotomous quality in the area of reality testing than in the area of identity integration. Nonetheless, one occasionally encounters a patient (often, a recovering schizophrenic) whose capacity to test reality is somehow "in between": he *isn't quite sure* if the voices were real, isn't quite sure if his relatives wronged him by having him hospitalized, and so forth. Even reality testing, I believe, exhibits *gradations* in certain circumstances.

viewer has satisfied himself that the patient has a structure healthier than *psychotic*, the distinction between *borderline* and *neurotic* emerges as the crucial point. With an obviously neurotic patient, the interviewer will intend to concentrate on still more subtle aspects of function, such as the nuances of interpersonal relatedness.

It may help in grasping the nature of this interviewing style if one can envision a spectrum of interviewing technics—ranging from the highly intuitive (one "unconscious" speaking to another) approach of Searles, to the analytically oriented style of F. Deutsch and Murphy (1955) that emphasizes key (emotionally laden) words and themes, to Kernberg's "structural" interview and on to the more matter-of-fact technics such as the Gunderson semistructured interview, and finally to a computerizable questionnaire like Spitzer's "SADS." Challenges to the patient's professed statements about reality are more *implicit* in the intuitive interview but more *explicit* as one moves toward the opposite end of the interview spectrum.

Consider the following hypothetical interchange between patient and interviewer. The patient has been regaling the consultant with examples of his mother's saintliness. She is a paragon of virtue and earthly perfection: she is beautiful, kind, loving, generous; she feeds the birds in the winter; and so forth. In the next breath the patient relates that she did not attend his high school graduation because her duties with the Women's Auxiliary kept her busy elsewhere and that she never read bedtime stories because she always locked herself in her own bedroom where she read *The City of God* to enhance her self-purification. Having noticed this kind of contradiction, the consultant might say, "Excuse me, are you talking about the same lady?" Here, there is *implicit* awareness of the patient's split image of his mother and an attempt through subtle cajolery to push the patient into reexamining the glaring discrepancies in his narration. A few patients, jolted by this sort of confrontation, will pause in their tracks a moment and then "put things together." One might hear: "Gee, I've been thinking of her as a saint, but she could be pretty neglectful and rejecting, too!" This style, which if used adroitly can be very powerful in the exposure of relevant *dynamic* issues, is nonetheless too "unspoken" to serve as the backbone of a methodological approach to diagnosis of structure.

In the context of a structural interview, therefore, the consultant's response would be more "spelled out" and might sound something like this (in relation to the example just given):

> "You know, you were just telling me how perfect your mother was, as though neither you nor anyone could harbor any negative feelings toward her. Yet two minutes later you volunteered several examples of what most people would consider very uncaring behavior on her part. Does that not want to make you reconsider the degree of 'perfection' she really demonstrated?"

Because this kind of intervention is more explicit, it is easier for observers (including the interviewer) to rate the patient's response in a more reliable fashion. If the patient becomes all the more vehement in his protestation of mother's perfection or if, indeed, he storms out of the room in indignation, we will tend to conclude that (1) confrontation led to worsening rather than improvement of the patient's momentary state, (2) his *reality testing* about this interpersonal relationship is poor, and (3) he uses primitive defenses like splitting and is unable to form an integrated picture of (in this case) his mother's contradictory attributes. One can begin to appreciate that the results of interchanges of this sort can educate the interviewer about many of the variables listed in Table 9–5. Here, for example, one begins to suspect poor reality testing, poor identity integration, serious abnormalities in the quality of object relations, and primitivity of defenses. If the patient went ahead and stormed out of the room, a further hint about impulse control would have been provided, and perhaps also about anxiety tolerance. The poor reality testing would incline toward the diagnosis of *psychotic* structure. Had the patient agreed with the consultant that maybe he had tended to overlook certain characteristics of his mother—that maybe she wasn't so saintly as he once imagined—this would have exemplified *improvement upon confrontation*. This, in turn, is described by Kernberg as an important feature of *borderline* structure. An unrealistic notion that does not yield to confrontation, in other words, has the quality of an *idée fixe,* of a delusion. One that does yield to confrontation is regarded, instead, as an "overvalued idea" and is typical of *borderline,* as opposed to psychotic, structure. In this connection it will become apparent how *psychotic structure* overlaps conceptually with *schizophrenic* thought disorder to a high degree: each notion, though part of a different universe of discourse, relates to the chronicity (structure tending to be stable over time) and to the delusional element in typical schizophrenia. There are, however, some (recuperating or, often enough, intellectually gifted) patients with "schizotypia" whose unrealistic or magical notions can be confronted with very favorable response.

The use of confrontation as a diagnostic tool (in the interpersonal field between doctor and patient) is so critical to the understanding of borderline structure that I have chosen to offer a number of clinical examples further along in this chapter. They are drawn from interchanges with patients on all three structural levels. The measure of how hard one has to work to get an idea "across" to the patient can be used in a semiquantitative manner in the assessment of structure.

At the present time a systematic effort to diagnose borderline structure is being made, under the direction of Kernberg and Goldstein, at the Westchester Division of Cornell Medical School's Department of Psychiatry. This large-scale project got underway in 1973 at the New York State Psychiatric Institute. Much of the work is still in progress and cannot be presented in detail here. Certain aspects of the work have already been incorporated and explicated in some of the recent articles by Kernberg (1974 to 1976).

Kernberg's criteria for borderline structure do not impart to it the kind of etiological homogeneity that is preserved in Donald Klein's definition of hysteroid dysphoria. Instead, the Kernberg criteria constitute a useful distinction with respect to *level of function.* This is not true for Klein's syndrome. Hysteroid dysphorics, as it happens, usually show (at least initially) a borderline structure. But only a percentage of borderline-structure patients will satisfy Klein's criteria (see pp. 285–287).

The chief value of Kernberg's structural analysis of cases is in its correlations within the realm of psychotherapy and prognosis. Certain patients, for example, regarded from a hereditary-constitutional viewpoint only, may exhibit "depressive psychosis" or "schizophrenia" in mild, subtle form. With this alone in mind, one might be led in the direction of applying standard treatments for those conditions in their more full-blown form (medications, ECT, and so on). Yet these may be borderline patients, viewed *structurally,* in whom medications may be indicated only in certain instances and for brief periods. Many (though not all) will be amenable to expressive psychotherapy (Kernberg, Burstein, et al., 1972). Interestingly, other patients with borderline *structure,* in whom mild stigmata of the classical functional psychoses are *not* detectable, also improve with the same treatment modalities (expressive psychotherapy, and so forth) as recommended for structurally borderline patients in general. Thus there is an important clinical relevance to Kernberg's structural approach, since it yields information and conduces to planning of a sort that might be missed if the patient were viewed from within traditional frameworks only.

It will be useful in this connection to note certain distinctions in Kernberg's use of "borderline" from the usage of Kohut (1971) and his colleagues. Both Kernberg and Kohut have large followings in the psychoanalytic community, so that differences in their use of technical terms inevitably create difficulties in communication when adherents of the two groups meet to exchange views. For Kernberg "borderline" is a *diagnostic* term, with inclusion and exclusion criteria defined in precise terms. For Kohut "borderline" is a term used to describe certain patients undergoing analysis, who, after a time, are seen as not really amenable to the analytic process (even in modified form): "borderline" is thus equated with nonanalyzability. Many patients who satisfy the Kernberg criteria for "borderline" *are* analyzable (usually via a modified technic) and would hence not be called borderline by the Kohut school (where they would tend to be called "narcissistic character disorders"). The Kohut "borderlines" constitute a smaller and sicker patient population within the Kernberg borderline realm.

Borderline as Interpreted by Mahler and Other Proponents of Object-Relations Theory

An important usage of the term "borderline" is that stemming from the work of Margaret Mahler (1968, 1972). In the viewpoint promulgated by Mahler, there is a strong emphasis, as in Kernberg's formulations, on object relations and on internal structures. Mahler and Kernberg have influenced one another considerably; their theories are closely interrelated. Whereas Kernberg's definition of "borderline" is set forth in precise language (permitting evaluation of its merits or deficiencies by a scientific method), the diagnostic criteria of Mahler are less readily objectified.

Recently several authors who have been strongly influenced by Mahler's work have also addressed themselves to issues of diagnosis and treatment in the borderline realm. Rinsley (1978) sees borderline disorders as the outgrowth of a developmental arrest or fixation at the phase (in an infant's psychological evolution) of separation-individuation (Mahler, 1972). This arrest may take place during the early subphase (three to eight months) when the infant is ordinarily beginning to differentiate himself from mother and from significant others or during a later period (sixteen to twenty-six months) which Mahler has labeled the *rapprochement subphase*.

One pathological consequence of this arrest is, according to Mahler, an incomplete differentiation of mental representations of one's *self* from one's mother or other important persons (i.e., from one's "objects"). This is seen as characteristic of the mental life of the (future) borderline person. Another manifestation of this abnormality is, as Kernberg has also mentioned, a persistence of the otherwise normal infantile "splitting" mechanism. A split internalized "bad object" (namely, hostile aspects of mother), à la Fairbairn, is retained by the growing borderline-to-be person. There is some debate about the usual timing when good self- and object representations versus bad self- and object representations are formed (Carter and Rinsley, 1977). At all events, the split internalized bad object, or rather, the persistence of this split into adolescent and adult life, has been viewed by Rinsley and Masterson as "pathognomonic" of the borderline (Rinsley, 1978, p. 46).

The followers of Mahler's metapsychology speak of the borderline's developmental arrest as occurring at the "depressive position" of infant development (in the language, here, of Melanie Klein, 1935). Mahler herself (1968, p. 48) does not overlook possible constitutional factors that may aggravate the tendency in certain vulnerable children to fail at the task of making proper self- and object differentiations at their customary periods. She speaks, in fact, of a complementary series relating to two variables: early traumatization of the infant and constitutional predisposition. If either is especially powerful (even in the near absence of the other), psychological development will presumably be abnormal. But the nature of this constitutional predisposition is not further clarified. Masterson and Rinsley (1975), on the other hand, emphasize purely psychogenic (as against biological) factors:

> Our contention is that the determining cause of the fixation of the borderline individual is to be found in the mother's withdrawal of her libidinal availability (i.e., of his libidinal supplies) as the child makes efforts toward separation-individuation during the rapprochement subphase. (p. 165)

These authors think that the mothers of borderline patients are themselves often borderline, and claim that the patient became ill by virtue of having become, in effect, the legatee of the mother's psychological abnormalities. While I would agree that the mothers (and fathers, too) of borderline patients (by any definition) are often ill,[9] it is the degree to which the future borderline patient has been the recipient of his parents' genetic/constitutional endowment that I see as critical in the majority of instances. The exception (where I would agree with Mahler) is the constitutionally normal (to the extent we can ever *know* of this "normality") child under the impact of overwhelmingly bad parenting (see Chapter 9). Meantime, the adoption studies alluded to in Chapters 4 to 7 do not support the notion of bad mothering as of primary etiological significance in the psychoses. This topic I have discussed elsewhere in greater detail (Stone, 1978c).

These points are not casuistical. It makes a great deal of difference, as one approaches the issue of *therapy,* whether one views "depression" (so common in "borderline" patients of all sorts except Kety's schizotypal "B-3" borderlines) as the derivative of a hypothetical "depressive position" or as the final common pathway of a multifactorial process, one element of which *may* be strong genetic loading for manic-depression. There is a danger connected with the purely (or predominantly) psychogenic theories of causation: one tends not to think of vulnerability to a more serious condition nor to anticipate an outbreak at some later time of a more recognizable clinical entity (see Stone, 1978). The truth of the matter is, in my estimation, much more complex: psychotherapy (without drugs) does suffice for certain borderline patients with or without hereditary predisposition to a classical psychosis; medication is a necessary adjunct to certain borderline states, especially where there is predisposition to bipolar illness (see below, pp. 285–287, D. Klein's hysteroid dysphoria). For similar reasons, I believe the purely psychogenic view would fall short in its attempt to explain anhedonia as the result of a "dearth of neutralized energy associated with the split object-relations unit" bringing about an "arrest of the transformation

*In fact, from the standpoint of overt psychiatric illness (granted, this is not isomorphic with "bad parenting"), borderline patients had about as many ill fathers as ill mothers (see Chapter 7).

of the pleasure ego into the reality ego'' (Rinsley, 1978, p. 48). Impulsivity, by the same token, is seen (in borderline persons) as ''periodic emotional buffetings'' resulting from a failure to ''deinstinctualize'' (roughly, to neutralize) certain affects. In my view this failure might better be understood (in most instances) as an epiphenomenon of an otherwise largely biologically driven impulse dyscontrol in the predisposed, borderline-to-be person. Further comments on the spectrum of explanatory hypotheses (from biological to multifactorial to psychogenic) are to be found in my article on etiological factors in schizophrenia (1978c; see also Kripke, Mullaney, et al., 1978, regarding the biological factors in manic-depressive illness).

Because the diagnostic approach emphasized by Masterson and Rinsley depends so heavily on psychodynamic/developmental issues, the criteria are, as mentioned, more inferential than those stressed in the more quantifiable systems dwelt on in this chapter. For a lucid exposition of the various stages making up the dynamic/developmental continuum, the recent paper of Rinsley (1978a) should be consulted. Figure 9–1 represents a simultaneous view of the infant's progress in development, in the area of self- and object differentiation, and of the psychopathological conditions which, according to this schema, arise from difficulties during these phases. I believe the correspondences between the pathological type (as diagnosed in an adolescent or adult patient) and the degree of self/object differentiation typical of the relevant developmental stage are for the most part accurate as Rinsley has portrayed them. Borderline patients (by any criteria) do, for example, exhibit the kind of splitting in self- and object representations one sees with regularity in the 1½- to 2-year-old child. My disagreement is not with Rinsley's version of object-relations theory per se but with the etiological primacy accorded to early parent-child interactions in the more serious (''borderline'' to ''psychotic'') conditions.

Figure 9–1. Relationships among Developmental Stages, Object-relational Stages, and Types of Psychiatric Disorder: The Psychoanalytic View as Set Forth by Mahler, Masterson, and Rinsley

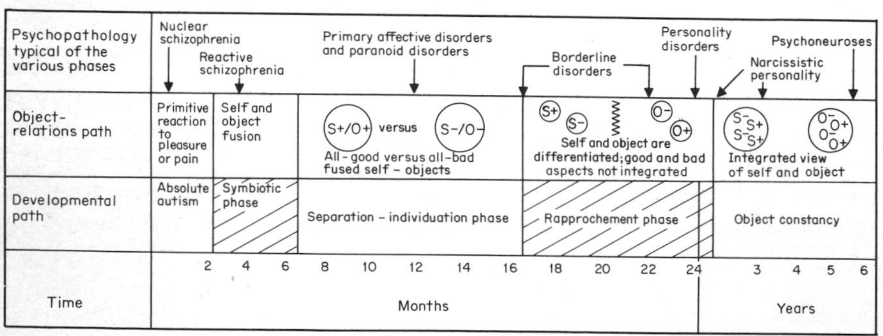

SOURCE: Abstracted from Rinsley (1978a).

Donald Klein's Contributions: Special "Borderline" Depressive Syndromes

In a manner analogous to the work of Kety, Rosenthal, and others on patients borderline with respect to schizophrenia, Donald Klein has been engaged in the careful analysis of disorders within the penumbra of "manic-depressive psychosis." Although Klein does not speak of them as "borderline" affective disorders, many of the concepts and syndromes he has described include patients many of whom are "borderline" (at least in their untreated state) not only with respect to primary affective illness but also within some of the other diagnostic systems (namely, Gunderson, Kernberg). Klein has, in fact, criticized the use of "borderline" as a catchall term for "potential" or symptomatically nonpsychotic instances of the major functional disorders: *borderline* is often used in a way that cannot be proved wrong and may therefore be invoked more to protect the diagnostician than to define his patient (D. Klein, 1975, p. 76).

Noting that many of the cases receiving the "pseudoneurotic schizophrenia" appellation of Hoch and Polatin could also be seen as suffering from severe affective or character disorders, Klein has also cautioned against the too facile assumption that the subtle thinking disorders, autistic life approach, and short-lived psychotic episodes of "pseudoneurotic" patients are necessarily to be understood as milder versions of schizophrenia.[10] Klein (1975, pp. 82 ff.) also drew attention to the prominent affective features in three of Grinker's four borderline subtypes (namely, I, II, and IV; type-III patients have little affect and show schizoid-obsessional character disorders). These remarks highlight a previously overlooked affiliation of many "borderline" conditions with the primary affective disorders, a connection also suggested by my family-study data (see Chapter 7). For this reason, Klein has expressed the opinion that emphasis on *affect* in presumed "borderline" conditions may provide a strategy superior, from a research standpoint, to emphasis on matters of ego structure and identity formation.

Klein and his colleagues have described a number of special syndromes within the affective realm: the *phobic-anxiety reaction,* the *emotionally unstable character disorder,* and *hysteroid dysphoria.* A number of broader concepts have also been outlined: *atypical depression* and *endogenomorphic depression.* These terms have been applied to conditions related to, yet in certain particulars distinct from, the more commonly accepted entities: cyclothymic personality, endogenous depression, or recurrent (unipolar) depression. We have noted (Chapter 6) that severe depressive

[10]According to Klein (1975), perhaps as many as half of patients receiving the diagnosis of "pseudoneurotic schizophrenia" respond favorably to antidepressants, some rather specifically to the MAO inhibitors (Hedberg, Houck, and Glueck, 1971).

phenomena are more widespread in the general population than classical mania and schizophrenia; hence, one encounters greater difficulty in separating those depressive cases that are largely under genetic control from those in which the hereditary factor is minimal or lacking. Klein, like Guze and others of the St. Louis school, is unhappy with the traditional endogenous-reactive dichotomy because there are many depressed patients with strong family histories of affective disorder who nevertheless appear to have been precipitated into serious depression by severe environmental stressors. More recently Quitkin, Rifkin, and Klein (1978) have presented evidence to the effect that "psychotic depression" responds favorably to imipramine just as do the nonpsychotic recurrent cases: one cannot use the presence of (depressive) delusions as a reliable discriminator between "endogenous" and "reactive" cases or between drug-sensitive versus drug-resistant cases. Yet "endogenous" (genetic; constitutional) factors do appear operative in many instances of severe depression, but in a manner that shades, in continuum fashion, into the general population, taking a variety of phenomenological twists and turns along the way. At the clinical level the end results may be a "straightforward" unipolar depressive illness or one of the somewhat rarer syndromes of Klein's nosology.

The importance of these remarks, for our purposes, resides in the high frequency with which the more severe depressive conditions, including those of special interest to Klein, fulfill the criteria for a *borderline* syndrome as defined by the other investigators discussed in this chapter. The dozen patients with hysteroid dysphoria who have come under my care, for example, all began with borderline psychic structure (Kernberg)—though many graduated to neurotic structure after several years of medication and intensive psychotherapy. These patients also met the criteria of Gunderson and of Spitzer (for the "unstable" type of "borderline personality").

Special Syndromes

Phobic-Anxiety Reaction Patients with this syndrome are characteristically anxious, clinging, and (episodically) depressed. In this sense they resemble Grinker's type-IV borderline condition. They are subject to repeated bouts of overwhelming panic, which may be accompanied by "rapid breathing, palpitations, weakness, a feeling of impending death, and occasionally depersonalization" (D. Klein, 1967, p. 121). Despite the frequency of depressive symptoms (namely, sense of futility, profound dysphoria), vegetative signs are customarily absent. Agoraphobic and other severe "neurotic" symptoms may dominate the clinical picture and becloud the underlying depressive diagnosis. Terrifying dreams (e.g., mutilation of the dreamer's body) may occur at the height of the panic attack. Such dreams rarely, if ever, occur in patients with neurotic structure (see pp. 310–316, this chapter). Often borderline in structure, the phobic-anxious patient seldom responds to psychotherapy alone; medication is routinely required, usually imipramine, though MAO inhibitors may also be helpful (Schuyler, Klein, et al., 1977).

Emotionally Unstable Character Disorder (EUCD) This syndrome Donald Klein (1975) likens to Grinker's type-II borderline condition. Though sharing some features of the *hysterical* character disorder, patients with EUCD experience mood swings which "appear to have less relevance to social effect and environmental circumstances" (Klein, 1967). Their lability is not necessarily a response to personal rejection, as is so often the case with the hysteroid dysphoric patient, yet they show a more serious characterological disorder than that found in *cyclothymic* persons. Therapy usually requires psychoactive medication; namely, Mellaril (Rifkin, Levitan, et al., 1972) or lithium (Rifkin, Quitkin, et al., 1972).

Hysteroid Dysphoria (HD) This syndrome, described by Klein and Davis in 1969, bears some resemblance to Grinker's type-I borderline condition (D. Klein, 1975, p. 82).

Exquisitely sensitive to personal rejection, the hysteroid dysphoric patient is nonetheless usually free from anhedonic symptoms; the depressive component can often be alleviated by supportive psychotherapy of a sort aimed at bolstering self-esteem. Praise may even lead to a mild state of giddiness and euphoria. Klein has recently set forth a table of criteria in which the diagnostic features of this syndrome are outlined in a precise fashion (see Table 9–6). Some items overlap with those of Gunderson's borderline personality disorder (suicide gestures, good socialization), but there is more emphasis on histrionic and seductive characterological features and less on rageful affect. The syndrome is to be found almost exclusively in females; heightened premenstrual irritability is common though not universal. Kinship to the major affective disorders is more clearly spelled out in Klein's description of hysteroid dysphoria than is the case with the Kernberg or Gunderson criteria. Some HD patients appear "borderline" with respect to *bipolar* illness; a few even have distinct hypomanic episodes, at times precipitated by antidepressants. HD patients function, when first diagnosed, at the borderline level in most instances. Rarely, mild "schizophrenic" stigmata may be exhibited, amidst the more obvious affective ones, so that the patient emerges in Region IV or even III (see case illustration 16).

Patients with HD are often amenable to intensive psychotherapy; some of my most rewarding experiences with this form of treatment, within the borderline realm, have stemmed from patients with this syndrome. In the beginning phases, however, medication has uniformly been necessary. In Klein's work with this group, he has noted a specificity of drug response, MAO inhibitors appearing to induce a marked improvement not elicited by

TABLE 9–6

Donald Klein's Hysteroid Dysphoria

Diagnostic Criteria

1. Intolerance of personal rejection with particularly severe vulnerability to loss of romantic attachment, as manifest by more than usual difficulty seeking or maintaining intimate relationships or work.
2. A depressive, painful, crashlike reaction to interpersonal rejection.
3. The dysphoric response to rejection is usually associated with either a, b, or c:
   a. Overeating any food or craving for sweets
   b. Oversleeping or spending more time in bed
   c. A sense of extreme fatigue, leaden paralysis, or inertia
4. During the past two years has had at least six periods of depressed mood in response to feeling rejected that were associated with some impairment of daily functioning (i.e., social withdrawal, missing a day of work, neglect of home or appearance, self-medicating with drugs or alcohol). These episodes may or may not have been of sufficient duration to meet the criteria for RDC major or minor depressive disorder, but should occur at a time when a person is not already in a major or minor depressive episode. (Six episodes for definite, four for probable.)
5. Self-esteem is dependent on constant external approval, and markedly diminished by loss of that approval.
6. The rejection-precipitated depressions are usually nonautonomous in that the patient can be brought out of them by well-meaning attention and applause. In an occasional extreme state will be rejecting of help and self-isolating.
7. Normal state is at least one of the following: histrionic, flamboyant, intrusive, seductive, self-centered, demanding, or greatly concerned with appearance (use observational data as well).
8. At least three of the following:
   a. Abuses alcohol, marijuana, or sedatives episodically when depressed
   b. Abuses stimulants on occasion when depressed; may become habituated to them
   c. Normal mood is expansive and active
   d. Chronic dieting is necessary to maintain normal weight
   e. Overidealization of love objects, with poor social judgments
   f. Applause is usually highly stimulating
   g. Usually socially withdrawn when depressed
   h. Makes suicide gestures or threats
   i. Is often physically self-abusing when depressed
9. Above symptoms not due to any other mental disorder such as somatization disorder, schizophrenia, schizoaffective disorder, or cyclothymic disorder.

NOTE: All nine criteria must be met. "Probable" or "definite" is determined by the rating of item 4.

SOURCE: Developed by Donald F. Klein and M. R. Liebowitz (1979, unpublished).

administration of tricyclics.[11] He has postulated that an abnormality of the dopamine precursor phenylethylamine (actively broken down in the CNS by MAO-B) may be operative in HD patients. Others, such as V. Ziegler in St. Louis (1977), question the correlation claimed by Klein, having observed favorable responses to the tricyclics as well. My own experience has been in line with Ziegler's. Those HD patients who have been able to solidify their gains from a combined psychotherapy-antidepressant approach have, after six to eighteen months, continued to remain well without further medication (whereas discontinuance at the height of the illness usually provokes relapse). The question of MAO specificity, still speculative, requires further investigation, such as the double-blind study currently underway at the New York State Psychiatric Institute. Regardless of the outcome, hysteroid dysphoria deserves a place in our nosology, in my opinion, if only because of the high incidence of analogous or identical disorders in close relatives of HD probands (see Chapter 7 and case illustration 29). Furthermore, HD cases are very homogeneous from a clinical standpoint, almost all being concentrated in Region V (pure affective disorders) in the borderline compartment.

A strongly positive family history for serious affective disorders is found in many of the "borderline" affective disorders, not only in HD but also in the other syndromes Klein has described, as well as in the more widely known disorders. Pardue (1975), for example, has offered a five-generation pedigree of persons suffering from unipolar depressive illness and responsive to tricyclic antidepressants. Methodical family studies have not as yet been carried out, however, for some of the affective syndromes (namely, the phobic-anxiety reaction or the EUCD syndrome).

Broader Categories of Depressive Disorders

Endogenomorphic Depression The endogenomorphic variety of depressive disorder is, as Klein defines it, characterized by vegetative signs (including anhedonia for food and sex); some examples appear to be "reactive" to various psychological stresses, but others are not. Some instances

[11] Klein has, in fact, put forward a theoretical model calling for a new nosology more attentive to drug response. The justification for such a revision, he believes, rests on the close link between certain pharmacological agents and the presumed basic biochemical defects underlying the major functional psychoses. In this regard one might call to mind Snyder's work at Johns Hopkins (Snyder et al., 1974; and Snyder, 1976) demonstrating not only the superiority of the phenothiazines to barbiturates or placebos in alleviating schizophrenic symptoms but the high specificity of the phenothiazines in blocking the postsynaptic receptor sites of the dopamine-sensitive neurons in the CNS. Snyder and others have postulated that abnormalities in the CNS dopaminergic neuron tracts may be crucial to the ultimate behavioral manifestations we call "schizophrenia."

of unipolar depression have this endogenouslike or "endogenomorphic" quality. Response to tricyclic antidepressants is generally good, though the degree of homogeneity in this regard has not yet been established. Because of the vegetative signs and the incapacity to experience pleasure in the here and now, endogenomorphic patients often appear sicker, even when they show neurotic structure, than other depressive patients (namely, hysteroid dysphorics) who may function at the borderline level. The endogenomorphic patient's conversation usually reduces to a monotonous litany of self-castigation and pessimism of a sort that often thwarts efforts by a psychotherapist to stimulate any sort of useful dialogue. Supportive psychotherapy will be helpful in sustaining the endogenomorphic patient, but the depression will not usually lift without medication.

Klein has outlined a list of essential features: a decreased capacity to anticipate pleasure in the future, here-and-now anhedonia, loss of interest in one's customary activities, retardation or agitation, and sleep disturbance (usually insomnia). Depression is phasic (episodes must be of at least two weeks duration).

Associated signs include feelings of unworthiness, self-blame, suicidal ruminations, and a diurnal cycle (with mood worse in the morning). Dry mouth, difficulty concentrating, and a history of manic episodes may also be present. Characterologically, the endogenomorphic patient is not usually histrionic.

Atypical Depression The essential features of this variety of depressive disorder overlap with those of the endogenomorphic type in three particulars (decreased anticipation of pleasure, loss of interest in usual activities, phasic nature) and differ in three particulars (the retardation/agitation, here-and-now anhedonia, and insomnia are absent).

Klein has also outlined some fifteen "associated" features (of which six are required for the diagnosis); many of these are the same as those noted for hysteroid dysphoria. The latter is actually a variety of atypical depression. Appetite and weight loss are usually absent.

Affective disorders, as we have noted, are quite common in close relatives of the atypical depressives, just as they are in the families of the endogenomorphic group. In this sense it does not seem rash to speculate that the "atypical" patients suffer "endogenous" disorders, too; they merely happen to lack most of the vegetative signs. Both varieties may be considered as conditions of moderate to high genetic loading for affective disorder. Apparently this loading need not necessarily manifest itself with vegetative signs. Where depressive delusions (of body decay, of being dead, etc.) are lacking, these conditions could be viewed as spectrum or "borderline" variants of primary affective illness (depressed type).

Klein's work has expanded our awareness of the subtle and unusual forms that depressive disorders—those with a strong biological component—may assume. Many of these conditions, especially hysteroid dysphoria, are "borderline" according to all currently popular criteria. Klein's plea to pay attention to underlying etiology as well as to psychic structure, and so on, is well taken, because the presence of a primary depressive disorder usually requires the addition of medication to the therapeutic regimen, at least at the outset.

Spitzer's Unstable and Schizotypal Borderline Personalities

Spitzer and his colleagues at the New York State Psychiatric Institute have recently attempted to clarify and objectify current usage of the term "borderline" through systematic analysis of responses obtained from a questionnaire sent to a large number of psychiatrists with and without psychoanalytic background (Spitzer, Endicott, and Gibbon, 1979). Two main usages were identified: (*a*) a "constellation of relatively enduring personality features of instability and vulnerability which have important treatment and outcome correlates" (as exemplified by the criteria of Gunderson and Kernberg) and (*b*) a set of "psychopathological characteristics which are usually stable over time and are assumed to be genetically related to a spectrum of disorders which includes chronic schizophrenia" (as exemplified by the term "borderline schizophrenia" of Wender, Kety, and Rosenthal; see Chapter 7). Each usage is beset with particular problems: the inconsistency of items among criterion sets of Gunderson, Kernberg, and so on (as mentioned by Perry and Klerman, 1978), and the difficulty in describing the subtle cues upon which the diagnosis of "borderline schizophrenia" has had to rely.

As a first step in devising a questionnaire suitable for discriminating borderline from nonborderline conditions, Spitzer and his colleagues developed and refined two sets of items: one for the *schizotypal* borderline; and one answering to the definitions of Gunderson, Kernberg, and so on, which Spitzer labeled *unstable* borderline.

The final list of *schizotypal* items, distilled from a larger number suggested originally by Wender, Kety, and Rosenthal, is shown in the first part of Table 9–7. The presence of at least three of the eight schizotypal items permitted correct identification of cases diagnosed *clinically* as "borderline schizophrenic" by Wender, Kety, and Rosenthal in thirty out of thirty-six instances (i.e., a *specificity* of 86 percent). Similarly, forty-one of forty-three control cases were correctly weeded out, using this cutoff point of three items (i.e., a *specificity* of 95 percent).

The *unstable personality* items were developed from review of relevant literature, along with consultation with (among others) Drs. Gunderson, Kernberg, Rinsley, Sheehy, and myself. A nine-item set evolved from this collaboration (Table 9–7, Part 2), later modified to an eight-item set by the

TABLE 9–7
Spitzer's Schizotypal and Unstable-Personality Items

Part 1. Schizotypal Personality Items

1. *Odd communication* (*not* gross formal thought disorder) (e.g., speech that is tangential, vague, overelaborate, circumstantial, metaphorical)
2. *Ideas of reference,* self-referential thinking
3. *Suspiciousness or paranoid ideation*
4. *Recurrent illusions,* sensing the presence of a force or person not actually present, depersonalization or derealization (not associated with panic attacks)
5. *Magical thinking* (e.g., superstitiousness, clairvoyance, telepathy, "sixth sense," "Others can feel my feelings")
6. *Inadequate rapport* (e.g., aloof, distant, cold, superficial, histrionic, effusive)
7. *Undue social anxiety* or hypersensitivity to real or imagined criticism
8. *Social isolation* (e.g., no close friends or confidants, social contacts limited to essential everyday tasks)

Part 2. Unstable-Personality Items

1. *Identity disturbance* manifested by uncertainty about several issues related to identity (e.g., self-image, gender identity, long-term goals or career choice, friendship patterns, values, and loyalties)
2. *Unstable and intense interpersonal relationships* (e.g., marked shifts of attitude, idealization, devaluation, manipulation)
3. *Impulsivity* in at least two areas which are potentially self-damaging (spending, sex, gambling, drug or alcohol use, shoplifting, overeating, physically self-damaging acts)
4. *Inappropriate intense anger* or lack of control of anger
5. *Physically self-damaging acts* (e.g., suicidal gestures, self-mutilation, recurrent accidents, or physical fights)
6. *Work history or school achievement below expected**
7. *Affective instability* (e.g., marked shifts from normal mood to depression, irritability, or anxiety, usually lasting hours and only rarely more than a few days, with a return to normal mood)
8. *Chronic feelings of emptiness or boredom*
9. *Problems tolerating being alone* (e.g., frantic efforts to avoid being alone, depressed when alone)

*Not included in the final list as failing to discriminate adequately between borderline and nonborderline.

SOURCE: From Spitzer, Endicott, and Gibbon (1979), *Archives of General Psychiatry,* 36:17–24. Copyright 1979, American Medical Association. Reprinted by permission.

elimination of the item concerning work history. Again, using a cutoff point of at least three positive items led to acceptable levels of sensitivity and specificity, in both the situation of hospitalized "borderline" patients (and their controls) and office "borderline" patients (and their controls).

In a subsequent study, this questionnaire was sent to 4,000 randomly selected members of the American Psychiatric Association. Members were requested to check applicable items for one patient they thought exhibited either borderline personality or borderline schizophrenia and for one moderately ill patient not ever diagnosed as either borderline or psychotic. From this survey 808 usable responses were culled and analyzed. As is customary with other samples of patients considered borderline, no matter by whose criteria, about two-thirds of the borderline group were female; about four-fifths were between the ages of sixteen and thirty-five. Although the schizotypal items were seen less often among the controls than were the unstable items, none of the seventeen items were absent in the controls; the frequency of each item was considerably higher in the borderlines, but none of the items could be considered absolutely discriminating or "pathognomonic." "Recurrent illusions" came closest to this ideal (it was noted in thirty-three borderlines but in only five controls); "undue social anxiety" was the least powerful discriminator (present in eighty-five borderlines but also in sixty controls).

Discriminant-function analysis demonstrated a better capacity of the questionnaire to separate borderlines from the controls (87 percent specificity) than to distinguish between borderline schizophrenics and borderline personality organization (correct classification in 64 percent).

In the survey sample, a cutoff level of four *schizotypal* items led to 89 percent specificity (and 80 percent sensitivity). Use of five *unstable* items led to comparable results (82 percent specificity with 77 percent sensitivity). It would have been most unusual if this large number of randomly selected "borderline" cases exhibited true bimodality and, indeed, half the patients were positive on both scales, at the cutoff levels just mentioned. Eighteen percent were *schizotypal only* and twenty-one percent were *unstable only* (seven percent were positive on neither). Nevertheless, Spitzer believed the data supported the notion of two relatively independent dimensions (schizotypal and unstable) within the borderline realm. If one uses the items from both scales at once, a cutoff level of six positive items satisfactorily distinguishes "borderline" (any type) from control. I have expressed the opinion that the set of items Spitzer has called *unstable* singles out in many instances a group of patients borderline with respect to primary affective illness. I would have been content to call this scale "affective," fully aware, however, that the English language does not offer as many felicitous adjectives to denote "similar to the fully developed affective disorders" as it does for illnesses akin to schizophrenia.

I would also have been happier with a checklist in which the item "identity disturbance" was singled out as an *essential* feature of any condition to be labeled "borderline": it is as regularly encountered among pure schizotypals as among "unstables," and in the mixed types as well. With a regrouping of this sort, a patient would be considered *borderline* if he were positive for this item plus any five of those remaining in the combined list. The special diagnosis *schizotypal borderline* would require the identity item plus four from the "schizotypal" list; the diagnosis of *unstable borderline* would require the identity item plus four from the remaining "unstable" list.[12] With or without such revision, the Spitzer checklist already provides a convenient screening device for borderline conditions (viewed not so much as a "personality" type as a *level of function*). Because schizotypal borderlines are obviously included (a good many of whom still show psychotic structure by Kernberg's criteria), the Spitzer criteria define a *broader* group than Kernberg's (which is actually enveloped within the Spitzer definition, if one were using Venn diagrams). Gunderson's criteria allow inclusion of some patients with schizotypal features but exclude certain alcohol- or drug-abuse patients who might show at least six of the Spitzer items. The Gunderson domain would therefore also be included within the Spitzer realm, occupying more territory toward the schizotypal end than would the Kernberg domain. Klein's hysteroid dysphorics would emerge mainly as "unstable."

The ease with which the Spitzer checklist can be filled out, along with the broadness of the clinically borderline region it defines, make it a highly useful screening instrument in determining a patient's level of function. As Spitzer, Endicott, and Gibbon (1979) point out, validation will have to come through genetic studies and studies of treatment response. These will be necessary to determine either the utility of "borderline" as a diagnostic category or the validity of the division into schizotypal and unstable (affective) subtypes. It should be noted that, at this point, Spitzer is not claiming a strong genetic link between their schizotypal borderline cases and chronic schizophrenia; the apparent genetic relationship is in his view "still controversial" (Spitzer and Endicott, 1979, p. 95) or "suggestive" (p. 98). In a preliminary study of the nine schizotypal borderline patients seen in my

[12]The results of a survey (Stone and Oestberg, 1979) conducted in Norway, using the Spitzer items, yielded similar results. Patients considered "borderline" by the eighty-six clinicians who responded to the questionnaire averaged eleven positive items out of the sixteen in the combined schizotypal/unstable lists. Neurotic patients averaged only three. A cutoff point of five yielded a sensitivity of 82 percent and a specificity of 97 percent (that is, only 3 percent of borderlines had five or fewer items and would thus be confused with neurotics). The Spitzer checklist could serve as a simple screening device to differentiate borderlines from neurotics in the Norway sample as well as in the United States sample. Again "identity disturbance" was the most frequently checked (94.2 percent) item among the borderlines.

office practice since 1966 (all of whom had at least four positive items from the Spitzer schizotypal checklist), there were thirty-two first-degree relatives: of these, four were chronic schizophrenics (three were hospitalized) and one was schizoaffective; four others were schizotypal borderlines themselves, by Spitzer's criteria. One of the two patients who had no ill first-degree relative had an uncle hospitalized for paranoid schizophrenia. This is a small sample and may be unrepresentative, but one in which a genetic relationship between schizotypal borderline and core schizophrenia seems highly likely.

"Borderline" Adolescents

Because adolescents are just entering the age of risk for schizophrenia or manic-depression, emotional disturbances are often extremely difficult to diagnose in this age bracket with respect to the classical psychoses. Illnesses are not fully developed; everything is *in statu nascendi* and often enough only transitory in nature. The psychiatrist who treats adolescents must often make do with a symptomatological taxonomy such as that of Rinsley (1972) or Masterson (1971). Thus one encounters terms like symbiotic psychosis of adolescence (Rinsley) or thought-disorder syndrome (Masterson) or severely handicapped neurotic (Easson, 1969). Anthony (1972) has described "parapsychotic reactions" in certain adolescents who, after years of proximity to an overtly psychotic parent, demonstrate a faulty reality testing that may clear up when the parent is not nearby. Sometimes this folie-à-deux-like situation appears to acquire a kind of permanence. Does one then speak of a psychosis occurring in a child who had high genetic loading anyway? Or can a chronic schizophrenic illness be induced without such biological preparation? This is typical of vexing diagnostic problems that are the everyday fare of psychiatrists who treat adolescents, especially those with a hospital practice. Psychoanalysts working with adolescents have also had to rely upon level of adaptation and upon personality type, in the absence of clear indications of specific hereditary/constitutional factors. When applied to this population the term "borderline" has often been used in a very approximate way to refer to adolescents with too much impulsivity, suicidal ruminations, eating disturbances, and the like, to fit comfortably in a "neurotic" category, yet who give no evidence of delusions or hallucinations (productive signs) or formal thought disorder. Dynamic issues, which are easier to identify in this group, have been stressed instead. Mahler (1971) has focused on abnormalities in the separation-individuation phase of development in the "borderline" adolescent. Since it has not been part of the mental set of many psychoanalysts to pay close attention to mental illness in relatives, one is often left with little evidence on which to base judgment about the nature and strength of the genetic factor. Mahler (1971, p. 417 ff.) cites the example of a young "borderline" patient whose grandiosity, self-denigratory feelings, querulousness, hostility, and inability to feel close to anyone make it quite reasonable to suppose that he did indeed exhibit borderline structure. But the patient was also prone to episodes of depersonalization while on the couch ("I get this floating feeling . . . as if I am floating far away from you into space"). He railed against his mother as "unloving, undemonstrative, impossible to please," and so on. Did she or any close relatives suffer emotional disorders of any significant severity? Did the patient demonstrate, in dimensional terms, soft signs of a functional psychosis? This information is not provided. In Anne Hayman's article on the analysis of an "atypical child" (1972), we are told of the mother's serious depressive illness. Case descriptions of this sort permit us to speculate on the genetic contribution that may be operative in many so-called borderline adolescents. Annemarie Weil's formulations are particularly helpful in this regard. In her 1970 paper on the "basic core," she underlines the importance of the neonate's congenital equipment—genetic heritage plus irreversible perinatal influences—and points out how very early the infant's temperament and patterns of "regulatory stability" manifest themselves. She quotes the comment of Bela Mittelmann, "Heredity goes on," alluding to the manner in which hereditary influences constitute a kind of developmental blueprint. This blueprinting determines the "extent and degree to which each child can withstand later stresses," that is, helps set the level of that individual's "anxiety tolerance" or vulnerability. The basic core Weil speaks of dictates the "nuances of character in healthier persons" and the symptom patterns of our patient population. Weil is in essence arguing for a diagnostic model embracing the same three universes of discourse mentioned throughout this book.

Kernberg (1976) has outlined the various stumbling blocks to reliable diagnosis of borderline organization in adolescence. These consist of (1) the severity of the symptomatic neuroses in some adolescent patients, the disorganizing effects of which can mimic borderline organization in adolescence, (2) rapid shifts in identification that may at times make one suspect poor ego integration and, hence, a borderline condition, (3) severe pathology of object relations, which may be *under*estimated as still compatible with neurotic structure, (4) antisocial behavior that turns out to be part of a "normal" adaptation to an antisocial cultural subgroup, (5) narcissistic reactions, the various forms of which are so common in adolescence that the more malignant types are less readily distinguishable, and (6) the typical emergence of multiple perverse sexual trends in this age bracket, complicating the task of separating occasional homosexual experimentation from an emerging obligatory homosexual pattern. Kernberg cautions that a slowly developing schizophrenic process may surface initially as a severe disorder of object relations, before any ''hard'' signs of schizophrenia appear on the horizon.

The need for a multidimensional diagnostic approach becomes clear in considering the following vignette from Kernberg's paper.

> A girl of eighteen exhibited bizarre sexual thoughts, poor concentration, a sense of estrangement, withdrawal, suspiciousness, vague speech with occasional blocking, and a tendency to mutilate her body secretly and in a bizarre manner. She was at times depressed. So far, one's thinking leans toward schizophrenia, perhaps to the ''schizoaffective.'' Nevertheless, she also showed a capacity for empathizing with others and an ability to integrate, rather than disorganize further, in response to interpretation of her primitive defensive maneuvers. Hallucinations and delusions were absent.

These latter features inclined Kernberg away from the diagnosis of schizophrenia and toward that of borderline structure. According to my own method of formulating such a clinical picture, she would be seen as an example of borderline structure but also as schizotypal in predisposition. The ''schizophrenia'' she did not have is specifically the psychotic form; a milder (borderline in Kety's sense) form does seem to have been present. The precise nature of her affiliation (if any) to ''true'' schizophrenia might require years to become clarified; in the meantime diagnosis can only be tentative. But a diagnosis of ''borderline'' by itself is insufficient and will even steer some clinicians away from the pursuit of evidence that might eventually link the adolescent's condition to one of the classical psychoses. For this reason some prominent clinicians specializing in work with adolescents caution against use of the term ''borderline'' in this age range (P. Dince, 1977).

Welner, who simply prefers the term ''undiagnosed illness'' when criteria for a standard diagnosis are not fulfilled, has reported on the follow-up of twenty-four ''undiagnosed'' adolescent inpatients (Fard, Hudgens, and Welner, 1978). Seven years later, fifteen of these adolescents, many of whom functioned at the borderline level, were still ill. Affective and schizoaffective disorders were now diagnosable in at least five; two others had significant depressive features just short of meeting criteria for unipolar depression.

More instances are coming to light of serious affective disturbances in adolescents, some of whom show borderline organization or Gunderson's borderline personality disorder. McKnew, Cytryn, and White (1974) have described hypomania in a boy of nine. These authors have also begun the search for early precursors of major depressive illness in the younger patient population. Berg, Hullin, et al. (1974) described a father-daughter pair, both of whom had bipolar MDP; onset in the daughter was at age fourteen. Morrison and Minkoff (1975) have described explosive personality as a sequel to the hyperactive-child syndrome, which itself often runs in families, particularly those with manic-depressive proclivities (Goodwin, Schulsinger, et al., 1975). The tendency of certain hyperactive boys to show borderline features (impulsivity, restlessness, concentration difficulty, lowered performance level) twenty to twenty-five years later has been commented upon by Borland and Heckman (1976), who also draw attention to the increased frequency of similar disturbances in the fathers of the hyperactive children. Various depressive and manic symptoms experienced by six adolescents with manic-depressive illness have recently been analyzed by Carlson and Strober (1978).

Kestenbaum (1979), in this regard, has recently suggested a factor that may enhance the likelihood of manic-depressive, rather than schizophrenic, illness being found in association with "borderline" adolescents referred for analytic therapy. The chronicity, gravity of illness, and interpersonal distancing characteristic even of incipient schizophrenia in younger patients will ordinarily suggest to the analyst, during the consultation period, a rather low likelihood of ultimate benefit from expressive psychotherapy. In contrast, the adolescent with predominantly affective symptoms will often be more engaging and seem more "reachable" and more promising as a possible beneficiary of this mode of treatment. It was of interest that all three of Kestenbaum's "control cases" for child psychoanalysis were youngsters with (1) prominent affective symptoms (depressive more than manic) and (2) strong family histories of first-degree relatives with major affective disorders.

a. A nine-year-old girl was referred for four-times-weekly child-psychoanalytic therapy because of marked lability of mood, learning and perceptual difficulties, tantrums, mannerisms, compulsive rituals, and generally "infantile" behavior. Her mother was a bipolar manic-depressive woman who alternated between agitated depressions (usually in connection with loss) and periods of euphoria and pressured speech. In addition her relatedness was impaired and she seldom made eye contact with persons she spoke to. The father had been given several courses of electroshock treatment for depressions.

b. A seven-year-old boy was referred for analytic psychotherapy because of tantrums, inability to get accepted by his schoolmates, and social inappropriateness (tactlessness, gruffness, shrillness, and peculiarity in his wishes and impulses such that he became branded an "oddball"). This boy's father was isolated, friendless, often inappropriate socially, perfectionistic, and unable to relate comfortably to others. A maternal aunt was hospitalized on many occasions for manic episodes and on a few occasions for serious depression, and received either lithium or ECT.

c. A twelve-year-old boy was referred for analytic therapy because of depressed mood, morbid dread of going to sleep, vivid and frightening fantasies, and failure to work up to his potential. His mother had been depressed and emotionally unavailable during the first four years of his life. Three grandparents and a first cousin all suffered from manic-depressive disorders, bipolar in three instances, unipolar depressive in the other.

Confrontational Technics in Evaluating Structural Levels

The Interpersonal Factor

Most of the variables upon which diagnosis of borderline structure rests must be assessed by inferential rather than strictly deductive reasoning. Many borderline patients are masters at appearing to relate, while actually remaining quite aloof. During initial consultations, they will sometimes exhibit what I have, with a flippancy born of exasperation, referred to as the Empty Notebook sign: asked to tell the story of his current emotional crisis, the patient speaks for almost the whole of the session—and the consultant has nothing to show for his efforts except the name and address. That a patient can talk for an hour and reveal of himself nothing of importance is itself a warning signal of deeper psychopathology. But this is a highly inferential sign and not an example of hard evidence, like the admission of hallucinations.

Because one uses oneself as the yardstick with which to measure the patient's capacity for mature object relations, there is a strongly subjective element inescapably built into the diagnostic process, especially where borderline structures are suspected. The consultant, in the manner of Peterfreund's computer model, must monitor the interpersonal field as it becomes established between himself and the patient, meantime scanning his own memory bank for models of appropriate relatedness. The discrepancies between what the patient professes to be true in his interaction with others and what the interviewer senses to be the case, become the data for subsequent evaluation. For this mechanism to yield meaningful results, the interviewer must not only have a firm grasp on reality but must possess unusual empathic skills and a knack for deciphering highly symbolic and allusive speech. Unlike many neurotic patients, the borderline patient often lacks the motivation to speak candidly about his problems; unlike many psychotic patients, he may be able to stave off the interviewer's confrontations very effectively. What finally is revealed by the borderline patient is often more highly dependent on the interviewer's skill than is usually the case with neurotic or psychotic patients. Someone with Harold Searles's intuitive equipment may thus be able to elicit material from a borderline patient that others would fail to obtain. The skilled interviewer may be able to establish facts and make a diagnosis on reasonably convincing evidence, where the average interviewer might have to content himself with skimpy evidence and guesswork.[13]

Other variables which are important in the detection of borderline structure and are also highly dependent on inferential reasoning include *primitivity of defenses* and *identity integration*. It is very hard to prove logically that a patient is denying something, even if it is a matter of a seductive patient claiming not to harbor any sexual feelings or a tremulous and perspiring patient who admits to no anxiety. The distinction between (conscious) disavowal and (unconscious) denial of a feeling state is also difficult; by definition the patient in either state is disclaiming ownership of something the diagnostician—a total stranger, often enough—feels sure is there. Likewise, the distinction between splitting of object representations in a borderline patient and the "logic-tight compartmentalization" of the obsessive neurotic can often be extremely difficult to make.

It is sometimes easier to achieve reliability among raters about such matters as impulse control and antisocial features, since these are abstractions derived from anamnestic data that may be very striking (shoplifting, promiscuity, bulimia, tantrums, and the like are, when present, dramatic indices of these variables).

Confrontational Pressure

Confrontational technics are related to the mechanisms of resistance, the stronger methods being pitted against the more primitive mechanisms—especially *denial*. Instinctively the clinician measures the presence or the strength of denial by the pressure of confrontation necessary to "get through" (i.e., to win some scrap of recognition from the patient that the interviewer was on the right track). In a semiquantitative way, we can say that Kernberg's three psychostructural levels are differentiable in accordance with the required confrontational pressure. There is an inverse relationship with respect to mental health: the neurotic patient responding to gentle confrontation; the psychotic, either not at all or only to intense confrontation. Patients with borderline structure often respond favorably to moderately strong or very strong confrontation, in the sense that their grasp on reality improves.

There will be considerable variation from one interviewer to another in the *styles* of confrontation used even within the context of doing a *structural* interview. In addition, certain patients (those who are more concrete) will force one to spell things out in cumbersome, legalistic fashion. Others will respond to a few carefully chosen words. Given a bright, intuitive

[13]The Kleinian and Sullivanian schools of psychoanalysis have of course stressed the interpersonal factors in interviewing and treatment, especially of less well-integrated patients. In this regard Kernberg has served as a bridge between Sullivanians (with their particular expertise in establishing contact with very sick patients) and the classical Freudians (whose theories and technics have been molded chiefly to those with neurotic personality organization).

patient, a compassionate but blunt confrontation, especially if laced with humor, will, in just a few words, bring the ironies of the patient's conflicting and split-off views of the world into his full view. This may provoke tears of recognition and at the same time a profound appreciation toward the interviewer for having *understood* correctly the patient's dilemma. Harold Searles is a master at this kind of confrontation with psychotic patients. Beginners are often befuddled when a psychotic (usually a schizophrenic; in acute mania, confrontation usually falls flat) patient is empathically "reached." The patient often drops his "crazy facade" and begins to talk in a down-to-earth fashion; the formal thought disorder may clear up in seconds, so that—to all appearances—the schizophrenia goes poof. The underlying condition, or better, the vulnerability to it, of course doesn't go anywhere. If anything goes "poof," it is the constellation of severe symptoms (hallucinations, blocking, negativism, or whatever) that permitted a diagnosis by category in the first place. Now all that is "left" is a history of bizarre experiences and feeling states, or overintense and inordinately rapid transference phenomena. With little remaining on the surface except very weak diagnostic signs (like ambivalence and certain nonspecific peculiarities of thought), the interviewer will find it difficult to convince an onlooker that a schizophrenic disorder is present (see case illustration 6).

Examples of Confrontation as an Instrument of Structural Diagnosis

Confrontation in a Patient with Psychotic Structure In the following instance, moderately intense confrontation led to rigidification of an originally unrealistic stance in a patient with psychotic structure. The example is taken from a case where a schizophrenic reaction was at first ignored in the presence of a pronounced obsessionalism. The patient was actually *psychotic* in the clinical sense (had delusions, in this case), besides exhibiting psychotic structure.

INTERVIEWER: Are you convinced that reversing the order of how you eat your breakfast "caused" your grandfather's death?

PATIENT: Yes. The Force told me something terrible would happen if I made one false move.

INTERVIEWER: This is like saying, in effect, your thoughts could cause someone to die!

PATIENT: Yes.

INTERVIEWER: You see yourself as such a powerful person?

PATIENT: But they're not *my* thoughts! Those are the thoughts put in my head by this Force.

INTERVIEWER: Might it not have been you were annoyed about your grandfather, though? After all, you told me earlier, you had to sleep on a couch in the living room because your parents gave him your room when he came back from the hospital. And he coughed all night and kept you up . . . that could make you angry, couldn't it?

PATIENT: No! Never!

INTERVIEWER: No? You could have had no fleeting fantasy of his dying . . . ?

PATIENT: No! I'm convinced.

A More Subtle Example of Psychotic Structure

C = Consultant P = Patient

C: What led to your coming here?

P: Well, I don't know really. I mean, I made this suicide attempt which I'd been thinking about making for a couple of weeks . . . a month or so, maybe . . . but then, I made an attempt last year and they didn't put me in, so I don't know why they did this time.

C: What did the attempt consist of? . . . I mean, this last one.

P: I tried to hang myself . . . But the cord broke.

C: Oh? *(Pause)*

P: *(Smiling cryptically and looking away from the consultant)*

C: How would you size up this attempt? How serious does it seem to you?

P: Well, ya'know . . . I was planning this for a long time. I really thought I would die. I didn't see any point in going on . . . But then, the cord broke, and I didn't die, and . . . *(smiling cryptically again)* here I am!

C: You say this as though it were not too serious a matter. Yet it seems that only a chance thing saved you: the cord snapping unexpectedly. For me there's a big contrast between your saying, in effect, that it wasn't anything much, and your description of an extremely serious suicide attempt. You were even expressing some surprise that "they" saw fit to hospitalize you.

P: But last year they just let me stay at home. My parents brought me to my therapist . . . I had taken a few sleeping pills . . . and he saw that I was OK, so he said I could go home . . .

C: Your comment suggests to me two things: first, you regard the hanging attempt as no different from taking a few pills, and second, you believe the therapist last year was acting appropriately in not getting too worked up over a suicide attempt. Is that how you see things?

P: Well, I don't know. *(Pause)* I'm OK now. I'm not thinking of suicide now. So I don't know why I'm being asked to remain in the hospital. I'm not thinking of it actively . . .

C: Suicide is still in the back of your mind?

P: Oh, sure. I can't see living beyond the age of . . . *(pause)* So someday I probably will . . . kill myself.

C: Wouldn't that state of mind, if your relatives had any awareness of it, make them want to pursue a conservative course, and have you here for safety's sake?

P: Well, last year, ya'know . . . nobody put me in the hospital then, and . . .

C: *(Interrupting)* You know, I'm not really sure I'm getting through to you. I keep asking you to tell me what *your* impression is about the apparent contradiction between these suicidal feelings you speak of, and how you react in the face of them . . . and you always switch to something else.

P: Well, I just think you're trying to make something out of nothing. . . .

This patient, who did not exhibit a formal thought disorder or any productive signs of psychosis (recently), showed nonetheless a bland unconcern for the gravity of her suicide attempts. Fairly strong confrontation did not break through her denial. Her structure was thus considered psychotic. Clinically, she was thought to have a schizoaffective disorder.

Confrontation with a Borderline Patient

C = Consultant P = Patient

C: What led to your hospitalization?

P: I made a suicide attempt. There was a string of them, over the past few months.

C: I see. And what seemed to prompt them?

P: I was having this intense relationship with a man. It was too intense, I guess. Anyhow, after a year or so of being together, he told me he didn't want to see me anymore.

C: Uh huh.

P: I told him, "I want to die!" I felt worthless. I took an overdose of pills. Three separate times. This last time it was aspirin and some phenobarb.

C: "Some"? Did you take a lot, or . . .

P: No, only a few. I didn't really want to die. I just couldn't go on, though. I wanted him to feel really bad.

C: You were feeling vengeful, in other words?

P: Yes, I felt angry; I couldn't see how else I could make him understand how I felt or what he did to me. I had become so withdrawn after we broke up. The whole world seemed unreal to me . . .

C: How do you mean, "unreal"?

P: I was scared; I felt like an automaton. Just going through the motion of things. I was panicky much of the time. And I felt terribly depressed, though I couldn't say exactly why, at the time. I felt people could see through me, somehow, and just sense what I was feeling, like they could read my mind . . .

C: Did you feel they could do that literally?

P: No, never that far! It was more a question of my hoping, actually, that my friends, especially, could know how I was hurting without my having to repeat the whole story. Without having to say how hurt and angry I was.

C: But what was behind your doing such dramatic things to make your feelings known to your boyfriend or your other friends . . . ?

P: I don't know exactly. But all my life I feel I don't know who *I* am. I idolized this one, I looked up to that one, I worshiped my boyfriend. . . . If one of them let me down, I felt crushed. Like I was no one without *them*. I was so busy being Mr. L.'s daughter and Timothy's sister, and so forth . . . When they go away, I feel there's no "me" anymore . . . no reason to go on.

C: How does that strike you now, as you relate all this to me?

P: I know it doesn't hold up. I mean, I know there's a "me," even though I get so lonely I can't bear to go on. Even when my boyfriend left me, there was still a "me" that was left behind—but it's a "me" I can't stand . . . so empty feeling . . . and helpless . . . I sometimes invent people in my mind, who think I'm fine, talented, and so forth . . . but I know that's only fantasy.

Despite her feeling of helplessness, this patient had functioned quite well at her work for several years. Reality testing was intact, as exemplified by her being able to say that the notion people could "read her mind" was only a fantasy, as was the conjuring up of admirers in her mind's eye. At the same time her sense of identity was very undeveloped. She saw herself and also others as alternately all excellent or all worthless. Her tolerance for stress was low as was her impulse control. Other primitive defenses, denial, projection, and so on, were not present. Psychological testing showed good functioning on both the structured and unstructured portions. Clinically, she exhibited the syndrome of hysteroid dysphoria, manifested the features of Gunderson's borderline personality disorder, and had many of the features of Grinker's healthiest type of borderline patient—the anaclitic-depressed type.

Confrontation with a Neurotic Patient

P = Patient T = Therapist

P: My mother warned me that I'd need a woman to cater to me as far as my asthma was concerned, as a matter of health . . . of safeguarding my health. And I went and told my fiancée the same words my mother told me: what my "needs" were, how I'd have to be "catered to" as if to say, "or else!" I handed her an ultimatum. For no reason! I should have realized she's such a terrific and considerate person, she'd fuss . . . if she had to . . . without my saying anything. Without my yelling about it. I got mad at my mother, but, of course, it was my fault. I didn't *have* to repeat everything she said right back to my fiancée.

T: Mmmm. . . .

P: I notice also that my mother, who's ordinarily very tuned in where other people are concerned . . . , has little interest in my fiancée as a person . . . never asks her about what she's been doing, what her opinions are, etcetera. My mother only talks about her own interests in front of my fiancée. It's weird: I mean, here I am in my twenties, still repeating stuff my mother says like I was a kid. I wound up being very unthoughtful toward Nicole, which I don't want to be. It took some pretty long conversations to patch her feelings, because she was pretty miffed, which I don't blame her. *(Pause)* Why do you think my mother acts so different around Nicole?

T: *(Pause)* You ask that with a very puzzled expression. . . .

P: Yeah, well. . . .

T: . . . is it really beyond your imagining how your mo——?

P: *(Interrupting)* Ah, you think she might be jealous of my fiancée . . . the whole "triangle" business!

T: Never mind what I think! What do *you* think? You're the one who's relaying the facts to me. If you have the facts at your disposal, I have a hunch you can spell out their meaning pretty well.

P: Well . . . put it this way: I like to think of my mother as being above that sort of reaction somehow. Like, I'd be the first husband, maybe, without a mother-in-law daughter-in-law problem. *(Pause)* Then, too, I kinda hoped I'd be completely mature enough so I wouldn't get caught up in crossfires of loyalty and all that sort of thing. I guess I'd have to say we're all of us "mere mortals" . . . a lot more so than I thought.

T: You say that as though it's a bit of a comedown!

P: Well, I try to live my life according to certain ideals; I always hope the people around me try to lead exemplary lives, too . . .

T: But I think the difficulty you have is this: you equate the "good life" with *leading* an exemplary life; for most of us, *trying* to lead an exemplary life is the good life. You allow yourself no room for failure.

P: Yeah . . . I see your point. I guess I'm trying to walk too narrow a tightrope.

T: Mmmmm.

This extract was chosen to illustrate the candor, psychological-mindedness, and flexibility of a well-functioning person with neurotic structure. Integration in the sense of identity was well established; the mechanisms of defense were restricted to those associated with higher levels of personality development. Repression, rationalization, intellectualization, and isolation of affect were the main defenses utilized by this man, whose more noticeable characterological traits were along obsessive lines.

Note how little confrontational pressure was needed to elicit from this man the awareness of "Oedipal" rivalries that were surfacing among himself, his mother, and his fiancée. One had only to ask in a normal conversational tone, "Is it really beyond your imagining how . . . ," and he was quickly able to synthesize the material he had just been presenting. Mother (in all likelihood) resents the prospective daughter-in-law despite all her charms; the patient can be inappropriately loyal to mother's viewpoint, at a time when the main loyalty should be to the fiancée—this came clearly into the patient's view with almost no effort on the part of the therapist.

There is also evidence in the brief extract that the inner world of this man is composed of representations of others and of himself in which both positive and negative qualities are realistically perceived and appropriately integrated. Thus, his picture of himself *includes* awareness of his tendency to be perfectionistic and egocentric. He can see the minor imperfections of his fiancée and his mother's jealousy yet retain a sense of proportion about these negative qualities, that is, they exist, but they are overshadowed by the positive attributes of both individuals.

This encounter with a neurotic patient will serve, it is hoped, as an anchoring point at the healthy end of the continuum of global function. It should not be difficult to see how far short the borderline patients fall from this ideal, and how different is the experience of establishing emotional rapport with borderline- in contrast to (normal-) neurotic persons.

Soft Signs of Thought Disorder

Although delusions are the hallmark of psychosis and overvalued ideas a characteristic of borderline thought disorder, there is a continuum of thought disturbance, making categorical diagnosis not always an easy business. Cultural and educational factors enter into the equation, further complicating the distinction, say, between an overvalued idea and a common superstition. In whom, for example, is preoccupation with astrology a subtle manifestation of psychotic tendencies; in whom is it an innocuous pastime? In an uneducated person from a Levantine country, there would be no diagnostic overtones to such an interest; in a physics professor, one's suspicions would be immediately aroused.

Concrete thinking may also be encountered in people of limited educational background but who show no trace of schizophrenic predisposition.

Apropos concreteness, Watson (1973), in seeking to clarify the nature and range of thinking deficits in schizophrenia, studied the responses to the Gorham Proverbs Test in "process" and "reactive" schizophrenics, who were also compared with normal controls. He concluded that loss of abstracting ability was more characteristic of the process group, but in the reactive group autism was more prominent, even though both had poorer abstracting ability than normals.

One abnormality subsumed under the heading of autistic thinking is persistent magical thinking, certain types of which are encountered in many borderline patients. I suspect this is particularly true of those patients with borderline structure who, in continuum terms, approximate the schizophrenic end of the psychosis spectrum. The following vignettes present a graded series of magical thought, beginning with the overtly delusional.

A married woman of twenty-three, a graduate student, was admitted to the hospital, despite fairly good functioning at home and at the university. It developed that for the past five years she had remained convinced that a professor she once had during her undergraduate days was secretly in love with her. While taking his course, she began to think that the first letters of the words at the top left of the pages he assigned the class to read could be unscrambled in such a way as to spell secret messages to her of a romantic nature. Her preoccupation with this professor grew so intense as to cause problems in her marriage, and ultimately led to her hospitalization.

The following example shows magical thinking of a less grossly delusional sort.

A thirty-five-year-old woman, both of whose parents had been hospitalized at various times for schizophrenic decompensations, had experienced the death of an infant son during the first years of her marriage. Although she held a very responsible position in a publishing firm, she was known to her co-workers as a shy and eccentric woman, who, among other things, was in the habit of wearing dark glasses at all times of day, summer and winter.

Her therapist, with whom she had been in treatment many years, was also struck by her insistence that the shades of the office be drawn and that all but one or two lights be extinguished upon her entering the office. No amount of exploration sufficed to unravel the reasons for this strange custom, until she began, in the seventh year of treatment, to dwell for the first time upon the previously tabooed subject of her first child. It suddenly dawned on the therapist that her meticulous avoidance of bright light—which began around the time of the tragedy—might have arisen as a kind of condensation of the two homonyms, "son" and "sun," which then led her to avoid not only the topic of her dead son but also anything capable of reminding her of the word itself (including the sun, and all manner of bright lights that would make her think of the son-sun).

A man of about forty-five was contacted by phone as part of a follow-up study conducted by the psychiatric facility where he had been hospitalized as a child for multiple phobias. He refused to go back to the hospital for the interview, adding that he had not gone outside a perimeter of three blocks from his apartment for the past twenty-seven years. When he was eighteen and enrolled in college, he chanced to see one of the old "Fox" theaters as he left one morning to go to school. This he immediately associated to "Fucks," which in turn had uncomfortable incestuous overtones for him. To avoid these intolerable obsessive thoughts, he restricted himself to a tiny area around his apartment, thereby obviating ever again seeing the "Fox" theater. His proximity to the schizophrenic pole of psychopathology was further attested by his marked litigiousness, which led him to write innumerable letters to authorities of all sorts.

Still more subtle is the magical thinking exhibited by a woman in her middle twenties hospitalized after a serious suicide attempt. She had a strong tendency to become involved with "father figures," including her boss and a former therapist. Once in the hospital she was assigned a psychiatrist who saw her thrice weekly for about a year and a half in an expressive psychotherapy. She was noted at first to be impulsive, covertly hostile, secretive, and rather fey. Psychic structure was evaluated by three psychiatrists as borderline (according to the criteria both of Gunderson and Kernberg), yet there were some lingering doubts as to whether a psychotic structure might have been overlooked. Some were struck by her preoccupation with obscure Eastern religions, along with her belief that her fate was preordained by the stars. All this was very much out of keeping with her graduate school education. The most compelling evidence of persistent magical thinking, however, concerned her intense idealization of the psychiatrist in charge of the unit to which she was attached. She was interviewed once by this man, early in her stay, and saw him on only a few other occasions, yet she wrote him countless letters requesting special meetings, spoke of him constantly during her therapy hours, related her progress to his good will—or her occasional setbacks to his indifference—treating him in general like the North Star of her existence, while she meantime derogated the efforts of her own therapist. This secret worship was as strong the day she left the hospital as it was when it first developed, and resisted all efforts by therapist and staff to interpret it as a transference manifestation. Although she had among her first-degree relatives two manic-depressives, one would tend to regard her absorption in fantasy and autistic thinking of this sort as in keeping with at least some schizophrenic vulnerability (enough to place her in the "predominantly affective schizoaffective" band of the Sz-MDP continuum).

Milder examples of magical thinking include those where both the element of bizarreness is absent and where the "double awareness" of Sacks et al. (1974) is present. The subject of case illustration 11, for instance, had elaborated an "imaginary companion" for some years. He gave this fantasy figure a name and spoke to him (in his mind, not aloud) about everyday matters. Furthermore he was aware that his "friend" was imaginary, yet he could not readily break this habit of mind. This was therefore double awareness rather than "craziness." As treatment progressed, and as interpretations about his sense of loneliness and friendlessness were made, the imaginary companion of this borderline patient receded from consciousness.

More subtle forms of magical thinking may be noted in persons with neurotic structure. The presence of hysterical character traits is at times accompanied by superstitious thinking beyond the norms of the culture. Certain obsessional men have sexual fears predicated on adolescent fantasies persisting into adulthood. They may continue to feel, for example, that the body contains only a finite amount of semen and that sex must be rationed lest one's strength and substance be prematurely sapped. Phobics fear the symbol as much as or more than what the symbol (snake, elevator, crowds, and so forth) represents. Phobics with neurotic structure tend to fear commonplace objects or places that most people would regard as at most mildly anxiety provoking. Sometimes one can get a hint of deeper disturbance—and of borderline or even psychotic structure—if the phobia concerns something bizarre or remote. A man in his early thirties, as an example, sought psychiatric treatment on account of a phobia about octopuses and scorpions, even though he lived in an area thousands of miles away from the nearest dreaded object. He was a highly intelligent man who sensed his fears were completely irrational but felt almost immobilized by them. Psychostructurally he functioned at the borderline level, but he had had a brief psychotic episode (an acute schizophrenic reaction) in adolescence.

Circumstantiality, which Cohen et al. (1972) spoke of as having little diagnostic significance, may indeed be seen across the spectrum of functional psychoses and at all structural levels. At one time this abnormality was thought to be an expression of schizophrenic psychopathology. The patient in case illustration 21, whose speech is often characterized by circumstantiality, is a borderline woman from a family with both schizophrenic and major depressive disorders. In evaluating the significance of circumstantiality, it is important to note whether the person's subject matter strays rather far from the point, as in case illustration 21, or whether the speech remains on target. Both of these varieties must be distinguished from the circumstantiality of certain "residual" schizophrenics, where the content betrays highly paranoid or other unrealistic elements.

Besides circumstantiality, other subtle forms of thought disorder in persons with schizophrenic vulnerability are encountered. Examples include vague or murky speech, occasional blocking, attention to irrelevancies, and tendency toward tangentiality. Many such patients remain stably at this level for years and never become psychotic. A generation before, such labels as "ambulatory schizophrenia" or "latent schizophrenia" might have been applied. Beck (1959) wrote extensively on this group, under the heading "schizophrenia, type S-3: nonpsychotic schizophrenia." Some of the patients he described were marginally functioning but never hospitalized persons, whose thinking, in addition to the qualities just alluded to, also betrayed *rigidity of attitude, narrowness of interest,* and *stereotyped content.* Thinking was logical and coherent (therefore "nonpsychotic"), but the patients' hold on reality was very rigid. These borderline patients are apt to be "peculiar," "ineffectual," or to "harbor queer ideas." Their affectivity is usually blunted; they appear to others as dull or monotonous.

The excessive tendency to heed various "symbols," imbuing them with great significance—and rather unusual meanings—is typical of schizophrenics, including those with borderline structure who have never decompensated. In the affective disorders, this tendency is seldom encountered except during episodes of florid psychosis.

For another view of early symptoms in schizophrenia, including abnormalities in thinking, the paper of Chapman (1966) should be consulted. Chapman is impressed by the analogy of schizophrenia to temporal lobe epilepsy and other organic conditions.[14] Blocking phenomena, some form of which he noted in 95 percent of a sample of young schizophrenics, he regarded as "transient disturbances in consciousness which develop in association with a failure to exclude irrelevant stimulation from internal and external sources" (1966, p. 24a). Confronted with a nonpsychotic patient who shows either blocking or a sense of detachment from his own

[14]For a discussion of correlations between dominant-hemisphere disturbances in schizophrenia and left temporal lobe epilepsy, see Stone (1978c).

personality, the diagnostician must take pains to exclude clearly organic conditions (see case illustration 19). Chapman mentions several distinguishing points about this depersonalization: when present in psychomotor epilepsy, there is usually clouding of consciousness; the latter does not routinely accompany the depersonalization of the schizophrenic.

On a Subtle Form of Thought Disorder in Patients from Brutalizing Environments

Borderline psychopathology that is born of a harshly repressive environment more than of adverse genetic "loading" will often appear at first blush more reversible psychotherapeutically. One has the impression that the patient, not held down by "incurable" hereditary disadvantage, need only undo the repressive forces and claim his just birthright. But anyone who has attempted to analyze severe obsessional (as they will usually be) disorders growing out of repressive environments knows better than to equate the absence of hereditary "taint" with good prognosis. All of us who work with borderline and psychotic patients can testify to the excellent progress toward emotional warmth and humanization in their life patterns made by certain patients with hereditary predisposition but little in the way of childhood brutalization. And we can equally well testify to the lack of progress made by certain other patients, apparently free of such genetic disadvantage, reared nevertheless in brutal or violent atmospheres.

A kind of "thought disorder" that may occur in this latter setting has been described by Searles (1969) to consist of a curious impoverishment of thought where the emotions are concerned. Feelings are not remembered, or cannot be labeled properly, or are extinguished before they reach a state of conscious recognition. Analysis of patients from this background will often be full of silences, dry spells, and boring verbalizations of trivia. The analyst—in trying to exhume the patient's for all intents and purposes irretrievably buried emotionality—experiences something of the "excruciating torture" to which the patient was once routinely subjected.

This "thought disorder," which is very different from the more properly designated thought disorder of the schizophrenic, does not advertise itself through bizarre or unexpected responses. Instead, the patient claims to have *nothing to report* in circumstances where ordinary folk would be brimming over with fury, lust, indignation, or some other clearly recognizable emotion. It is as though the patient's mind operates like a millipore filter, allowing only the most exiguous drops of mental life to funnel through to consciousness, whilst all the rest—the whole storehouse of memories, feelings, and impressions accumulated over the years—is somehow shunted off and rendered permanently unavailable.

In Searles's patient this disorder seemed to have been induced by a combination of withering ridicule and harsh corporal punishment. Feelings became buried in the process and so did awareness of the sadism (e.g., toward the punitive parents) engendered by this environmental brutality. As the "last nail in the coffin," inability to recall one's dreams, further, and with finality, seals off recollection of the relevant associations.

A patient I had once worked with, reminiscent of Searles's case, was an unmarried man in his late thirties remanded to psychotherapy after arraignment for a solitary episode of indecent exposure. He had held a stable job for many years in engineering but had never been able to achieve any kind of closeness with a woman. There were few sexual contacts apart from isolated experiences with prostitutes, and even with them he had *ejaculatio retardata*. This psychostructurally borderline man was extremely obsessive in character. He sat stiff and motionless in the chair, session after session, rarely initiating conversation but often smiling faintly—around the sides, as it were, of his ill-concealed hostility—in a way that reminded me always of Eichmann. His spiritual kinship to that figure was attested to by his recurrent fantasy of "consigning Negroes to the ovens," as a solution to America's "racial problem." Although he belonged to a "race" whose problems had only recently been "solved" in that fashion in Eastern Europe (where his family had come from), in no way did he experience any irony, let alone horror, in this admission.

The youngest of nine children, he had been infantilized and ridiculed by parents and sibs throughout his life. Typical of the humiliations to which he was subjected was his mother's insistence, when he was seven and had been walking with her in the street, that he urinate between two cars. When he protested at having to expose himself to all the passersby, she yelled, "Go ahead, you got nuthin' to hide!"

His pronounced impoverishment of thought and lack of contact with his deepest feelings I believed could be best attributed to the years of alternating ridicule and neglect; in other words, to primarily psychological "causes." There were no instances of mental illness, even in milder form, throughout his very large family. This suggests, though it does not establish, that genetic factors were not important in his case. He himself did not give evidence of even the more questionable forms of schizophrenic or primary affective disorder.

Sociocultural factors may influence this type of thought impoverishment; one may find it even in patients with neurotic structure. Certain individuals, in and of themselves capable of pleasure, grow up in regions afflicted by a kind of cultural anhedonia, whether based on puritanical mores or grinding poverty. In these regions systematic quashing of children's normal curiosity and pleasure sense is carried out by the older generation as a means of keeping the young ones "in line." A woman in her early thirties, for example, had sought treatment because of difficulties with persons in authority at the publishing house where she worked as an editor. She had been raised in a pietistic farming family in Bavaria, before moving to the United States in her late teens. This patient also experienced considerable difficulty in initiating conversation, in associating to dreams or chance remarks, and in recollecting feelings of any except the most socially sanctioned kind. For a long time she could scarcely comprehend what her analyst was even alluding to when he pointed out these deficits. After many months of bleak sessions, she one day volunteered:

> "I got upset at work several days ago, but I can scarcely recollect what I was really feeling at the time. I can hardly ever acknowledge what I feel about social situations. It's like feelings don't register in my brain at all. I was amazed the other day to see how my three-year-old nephew stood up to my father, who'd come from Germany to visit us for the holidays. He'd been gruff or stern with the child over something, and the boy complained to my sister-in-law, 'Grandpa hurt my feelings.'
>
> "When we were coming up, any manifestations of feelings got stifled decisively after the first appearance. You got a whippin', and that was it, *period!* You knew never to open your mouth about that kind of subject ever again. And there was no use grumbling to anyone else in the family, 'cause they all had the same attitude. So you kept it to yourself, and that was *it*."

In the background of this patient, whose large family was also free of any significant emotional disorders, harsh regimentation rather than ridicule seemed to be the mechanism fostering constriction of thought.

It is important to keep in mind, regarding the "thought disorder" delineated here, that the rather primitive defenses of denial and splitting, the logic-tight compartmentalization of the mind (such that the person does not "know" of his sadistic feelings toward a punitive parent), and the apparent "integrative" disturbance, however typical of schizophrenia, can arise from nongenetic causes. At least it is my contention that severe constriction of thought and affect can develop in response to certain militaristic rearing patterns, without one's having also to invoke a constitutional factor.

Dreams as Diagnostic Clues in Borderline and Psychotic Structures

In neurotic adults, dreams, whatever bizarre or violent elements they may contain, will generally preserve a measure of disguise even when depicting primitive incestuous, incorporative, or sadistic themes. Even the analysand who after years successfully hacks his way through the jungle of his primordial drives to "ultimate" Oedipal strivings does not mate literally with his mother in his dreams. Instead an old schoolteacher from the first grade will be pressed into service, or perhaps the analyst. Nor is the situation reversed in patients with psychotic diagnoses, except *on occasion*. This is the important point. *On occasion,* patients with borderline or psychotic structure will report dreams where intercourse actually takes place with a parent seen as in real life. Or, the patient visualizes his own death.

Or, more characteristically (and more commonly), he will dream of the dismemberment of an important part of his body. One is reminded of the concreteness in schizophrenic thinking. Dead metaphors like "I'm falling apart" or "I'm going to pieces over it . . . " or "She sets me on fire" come alive in the dreams of the more disturbed patient: in his dreams, he really *does* come apart or see himself on fire, and so on.

Certain stark or childlike dreams are still compatible with neurotic structure: violence and goriness when it is visited on *others* may occur in the dreams of neurotics (especially obsessionals); thinly disguised sexual dreams, including those involving animal symbols, will also be encountered. One woman in her twenties reported a dream in which she was in a subway surrounded by the disembodied penises of men she had at one time or another dated; in a subsequent dream, she was rolling amorously on the lawn of her old house with a tiger, while her mother enviously looked on. This was a neurotic patient, hysterical and unsophisticated, but free of deeper pathology. But in a young man with marital difficulties, report of a dream in which his *own* penis was torn off—leaving only a bloody rent in his groin—alerted the therapist to the presence of a serious psychiatric disorder (as it happened, borderline structure in a unipolar depressive).

In listening to patients' dreams for fifteen years, I can recall only one instance where dismemberment, death, or outright incest as dream elements occurred in a patient with neurotic structure. And that patient (who dreamed of his own death) had many subtle temperamental/characterological features of bipolar affective illness (Stone, 1978; see also case 4). Much earlier Kraepelin (1921, p. 123) noted the frequency of "terrifying dreams" in persons with what he called the depressive temperament.

Dreams of this sort have diagnostic import only if they occur in an early phase of treatment with an erstwhile integrated-appearing patient. In this situation the dream may serve as a signal of imminent or actual breakdown. At the very least, it may warn of the likelihood that other manifestations of borderline structure may soon become discernible.

An apparently well-integrated young woman was referred for psychoanalysis because of increasing strain in a romantic relationship. For several weeks she was able to maintain a facade of calmness, and had very little to relate. She began to doubt the need for further treatment. One day she mentioned having had a dream (the first one she remembered since starting analysis) in which she was in a plane crash, hurled to the ground with tremendous force, and smashed literally to bits: she saw one arm in the fields nearby, and her heart half outside her body. The analyst took these primitive concretistic expressions ("I lost my right arm," " . . . brokenhearted . . . ") as providing the first solid evidence of a disorder more serious than "neurotic." Not long afterwards a psychotic depressive episode with suicidal behavior manifested itself, necessitating hospitalization. It was noteworthy that among her first-degree relatives were one unipolar depressive, one paranoid schizophrenic, and one schizoaffective person. Personality organization emerged with greater clarity over time as being distinctly borderline.

The neurotic patient with bipolar "soft signs" who dreamed of his own death, on the other hand, has steadily improved over the course of several years of expressive psychotherapy. For a year and a half at the time of this writing his dreams have no longer contained primitive elements of the type under discussion.

It should be mentioned that these "sick," atypical dreams may occur every so often, even in the absence of intercurrent stress, in patients with these more pathological structures;[15] such dreams may also occur in the phase of recuperation after much intensive psychotherapy. There is an analogy here to the Rorschach test, which may continue to elicit contaminated and otherwise bizarre responses in sicker patients even in periods of quiescence and relatively good function. In this setting the "sick" dream need not be a danger signal but should continue to remind the clinician of the patients' heightened vulnerability.

In the passages that follow, a number of unusual dreams from borderline and psychotic patients are presented.

The following dream occurred in a Southern white homosexual male while in a state of florid psychosis (considered "paranoid schizophrenia" at the time):

> "My mother is encased in concrete in the lithotomy position. A black man is screwing her. My father and I are in an airplane dropping shit on them as we fly over."

The dream is remarkable for its starkly primitive sadistic quality; there is a total absence of disguise of unacceptable incestuous, murderous, and bigoted feelings normally kept under wraps even in dreams. There is no attempt at symbolization. Mother is mother, father is father, and so forth. Although there is no bodily fragmentation or dissolution in this dream, it remains unparalleled in my experience for grotesque display of aggression. Diagnostically it of course told little about the patient that was not already obvious from the rest of his disorganized state.

> "I was eating live gray rats, only I couldn't swallow them because their claws kept grappling at my mouth in their effort to stay outside."

[15]Despite these occasional occurrences, I would agree with the comments of Lesse (1970, p. 66 ff.) to the effect that the worst and most nightmarelike dreams in psychotic patients tend to take place during the acute phase, being replaced in the recovery phase by less sadistic or weird—and by more benign and structured—dreams. One of his patients, while psychotic, dreamed of "shrinking into a shrieking, wriggling mass of shapeless matter" in response to conflicts with his boss. A few weeks later, recompensated, he dreamed of being a "little anxious" because his boss had asked to see him.

The above dream occurred in a hospitalized chronic paranoid schizophrenic patient in his mid-twenties not long after he had been mugged by some boys with knives.

> "I'm in a kitchen. There is a refrigerator with some eggs on top of it, melting and dripping down the side. My brother is there vomiting blood; he seems to be dying. My folks are away, so I have to try to help him as best I can, but I feel I can do nothing."

This dream was reported by a highly intelligent borderline woman of twenty-three hospitalized for a severe anorexia syndrome. Phenotypically, there were schizophrenic features (severe ego-boundary confusion, eccentric speech, constriction of affect) but no productive signs.

> "I was being chased and caught by some pursuers whose identity I can't make out. They catch up with me and kill me. It seemed I was killed. I was dead. . . . Then I awakened in a panic, surprised to see I was still alive."

This dream, one of the few I have encountered where the dreamer pictures his own death, occurred in a borderline but well-functioning young lawyer in whose family were four chronic schizophrenics (two first-degree and two second-degree relatives). The patient himself had a borderline personality organization, with schizotypal features that included affect constriction, rambling and tangential speech that was hard to follow, and moderately pronounced primitivity of defenses (especially externalization/projection).

> "I open the refrigerator door and I see two glasses of water. One of my eyeballs is in each glass staring at me."

One sees in this dream *fragmentation of the body*. This sign comes as close as anything to being pathognomonic of psychopathology severer than neurotic. I have never seen it in anyone (in an adult, that is) who did not show either borderline or psychotic structure and who could not be viewed as either manic-depressive or schizophrenic constitutionally. It should be noted that this rule of thumb does not apply to more benign dreams where a tooth falls out or hair is missing, and so on, which occur from time to time in well-integrated people.

> "I attempt to swim across a narrow river, but before I get to the other side, a shark bites off my leg, and I am stranded and bleeding in the middle of the water."

This dream occurred early in the analysis of a woman in her late twenties, the wife of a busy professional man and the mother of three children.

Her husband's frequent absences from the home provoked in her overwhelming anxiety at times, occasionally accompanied by outbursts of hostility at her children. Personality structure was borderline; heredity, manic-depressive (with three first-degree relatives suffering from serious depressive disorders). This woman's inordinate envy and fear of men are reflected in the imagery of the dream, which she saw as reflecting her terror that in sex she would be (literally) torn apart.

> "I look in the backyard and see three freshly dug graves, one big and two little. I realize they are for my husband and my children—whom I have apparently just killed. A policeman takes me to the morgue to identify the bodies."

This unusually gruesome and undisguised dream was the only one recalled by an extremely guarded, phobic, and obsessive housewife during three years of (attempted) expressive therapy. She had had a severe conversion reaction after the untimely death of her mother. Only after two and a half years of therapy could she begin to express either her murderous feelings toward her family (for making demands she felt inadequate to meet) or her dependency on her mother, with whom she identified to near delusional proportions in her conversion symptom. The dream of this borderline woman (whose family history was free of serious emotional disorders) is reminiscent of those reported by Bradlow (1971) in his paper on murder in the initial dream in psychoanalysis. Of the seven examples he provided, five were in patients who turned out to be treatment failures. Two of his patients had psychosomatic conditions, one was a nonpsychotic schizophrenic (see Beck, 1959), and one was called a borderline character. Several would probably have demonstrated borderline structure, though it is not clear from their descriptions just how many.

The following dream was reported by a girl of thirteen interviewed as part of a large-scale survey of adolescents. The dream occurred not long after a minor accident:

> "I was riding my bike, when suddenly it skidded into a pole, and I died; I was on the ground dead" [she awakened with a sense of surprise at still being alive].

This girl was noted by the interviewer to be an unusually warm, feminine, and affable youngster, who was quite popular at school.

The interviewer, aware that dreams of being dead are not only quite rare but usually found only in persons with serious emotional disorders, felt at a loss to account for this dream—coming from such a wholesome and outwardly normal girl. Either the theory was wrong—and such dreams *can* occur in settings other than those of severe psychopathology—or there was something else going on in this girl that eluded the initial interview.

Further investigation yielded an interesting result: this girl was part of a study of children at "high risk" for schizophrenia (by virtue of having one or two schizophrenic parents). Specifically she was the child of a parent in one of the two control groups ("normal" and "manic-depressive"); her father had been hospitalized earlier for a major depressive disorder. Did this dream occur as an early manifestation of genetic loading for a primary affective disorder (depressed type), in which case she might be a young person still clinically well but "at risk" for depression? There is no way of answering this question at present, but the occurrence is nonetheless intriguing; not only will careful follow-up of her progress be important, but more thorough screening should be done to test whether other apparently normal adolescents (or adults) occasionally experience dreams of being dead. If such dreams could be shown to occur only in those who *eventually* develop serious psychopathology, they would serve prospectively as an important warning signal. If they occurred predominantly or exclusively in those with mental illness in the family, irrespective of whether the dreamer remains normal, this too would establish a subtle "marker" for the presence of genetic loading for a functional psychosis.

It is important to keep in mind that dreams of the mutilation or death of one's own body are not the exclusive preserve of those with schizophrenic liability but also occur in core and "spectrum" affective disorders (Stone, 1979). The more grotesque and bizarre the manifest content, however, the more likely it is that one is dealing with a disorder within the realm of schizophrenia (Carrington, 1971).

The dreams of body fragmentation or death from the preceding examples all occurred in patients who were at the time taking no medications, let alone those known to alter the REM cycle or the relative proportion of stages 3 and 4 sleep to the other sleep phases.

One must be careful not to read too much meaning into certain grotesque and often terrifying dreams that are occasionally experienced during the course of psychotropic drug administration. Certain commonly used drugs suppress REM sleep and augment the proportion of stages 3 and 4 sleep (which is when most nightmares occur) (Kales, 1970); others, such as the MAO inhibitors and barbiturates, suppress REM sleep even more drastically (Kupfer and Bowers, 1972). After a while on these drugs, or after their discontinuance, the total REM time may temporarily increase, as a kind of compensatory phenomenon. Even in the "acute" situation where a relatively high dose of tricyclic antidepressant is taken just before bedtime, stage 4 nightmares may develop. Flemenbaum (1976), in an elegant study of dreams in psychiatric patients receiving either antidepressants or antipsychotics, showed that frightening dreams were far more common in the single-bedtime-dose groups than in those taking their medications in divided doses. These dreams often interrupted sleep and were often accompanied by temporary confusion and disorganization, similar to the syndrome of *pavor nocturnus*.

In the following nightmare, radical change in perception of the dreamer's body occurred in an otherwise stable bipolar patient who had begun taking 200 milligrams of imipramine before retiring. This woman had had two dreams in which fragmentation of the body occurred at the height of her illness, before chemotherapy was instituted. The nightmare described here, however, had been preceded by four months of excellent social and occupational recovery. There has been no "day residue" of the sort commonly associated with disturbing dreams; the preceding day had been unusually pleasant.

> "I see myself lying in bed. Suddenly my body melts, like butter in a pan, into the bed and merges with it. I lost all sense of direction and seemed to be floating dizzily in space."

She awoke from the nightmare highly anxious and momentarily unsure whether it was a dream or reality.

In this setting, no special significance should attach to the body-distortion dream regarding borderline or psychotic structure.

Intelligence: Its Influence on Psychodiagnosis

Intelligence is a key patient variable for two reasons. First, the degree to which an expressive psychotherapy can be accomplished will depend in no small measure upon the intelligence of the patient. If the intelligence is average or better than average, and other factors are positive (motivation, introspectiveness, and so forth), the work may flourish (although brilliant intelligence in the absence of motivation will not conduce to successful psychotherapy).

The second reason intelligence is so important is that it appears to exert a modifying (specifically, a softening) influence on the impact of an otherwise strong genetic loading for schizophrenia. The impact of strong predisposition to affective disorder may also be mollified, but because of the nature of certain classical "schizophrenic" symptoms, intelligence may soften the impact in a manner that also blurs the diagnosis. Sadness will come through as depression regardless of the intelligence of the patient. But delusional tendencies, when filtered through a keen intelligence, have a way of surfacing as "overvalued ideas" (Kernberg) or "double awareness" (Sacks et al., 1974).

This is not to imply that patients recovering from psychotic episodes do not in general, and regardless of their intellectual level, reach a stage where they realize certain thoughts were—or are—"crazy." It is rather that this state of "double awareness" is reached more quickly and more often in those with superior intellectual endowment. To speak metaphorically, they have a swifter and more reliable "reality organ." It is as though they had a feedback loop by which they can more effectively compare their perceptions with those of the people around them. This permits better monitoring of their own speech, so that they may elect to withhold or modify the expression of certain thoughts that would emerge otherwise as "crazy"; that is, out of keeping with the standards of reality in their environment. The *brevity* of the psychotic episodes experienced by certain patients with borderline structure may be a manifestation of this advantage, stemming from high intelligence.

The subgroup of borderline patients to whom expressive psychotherapy is offered, whether in office or in hospital practice, probably does constitute an intellectually gifted sample, as Weingarten and Korn speculated in their 1967 paper on "pseudoneurotic schizophrenia." One also encounters chronic schizophrenic patients with high psychological aptitude, and high intelligence, who make better candidates for analytically oriented psychotherapy than some less well-endowed borderlines. Many of the institutions specializing in the intensive psychotherapy of borderline patients are referral services and, therefore, select a highly skewed sample. At the Psychiatric Institute in New York, the patients on the intensive psychotherapy unit who did best tended to have IQs in the 110 to 140 range, along with borderline structure. Those who did worst had on the average IQs in the 85 to 105 range and psychotic structure.

Ever since Stern introduced the term "borderline" to psychoanalysis in the late thirties, it has been applied, within the analytic community, largely to two groups of patients. In one, there is better than average intelligence along with subtle indications of a depressive or schizophrenic disorder. In the other, average intelligence is combined with severe characterological disturbances but no discernible connection with the endogenous psychoses. One may speculate, with regard to the first group, that superior intelligence has helped them, in the manner I sketched above, convert the "hard signs" of delusions and hallucinations into soft signs (overvalued ideas, milder degrees of magical thinking, and so on), where category diagnosis of psychotic depression or schizophrenia is no longer possible. This is the kind of patient we encounter again and again, whether in Bychowski's descriptions of the latent psychotic or in Hoch and Polatin's "pseudoneurotic schizophrenics" or in their more modern counterparts—the borderline patients of Knight, Kernberg, and Gunderson.

To test this hypothesis concerning a cushioning effect of intelligence, a sociological field survey, comparable to Srole and his co-workers' "Midtown Manhattan" study (1962), might be required. This would permit comparison of measurements obtained from random samples of persons with borderline versus psychotic structure.

TABLE 9–8

Overview of Five Borderline Systems

SCHEMA OF	*1. Syndrome Is Rigorously Defined*	*2. Utility as a Level of Function*	*3. Response to Intensive Psychotherapy*	*4. Utility as a Prognostic Indicator*	*5. Etiological Homogeneity of Sample*	*6. Are Schizotypal Cases Included in Sample?*
Bergeret (borderline)	−	±	+	±	Low	?
Gunderson (borderline personality disorder)	+	−	++	+	Low	Yes
Kernberg (borderline personality organization)	+	+	+	+	Moderate[b]	Rarely
D. Klein (hysteroid dysphoria)	+	−	+[a]	+	High	Very rarely
Spitzer (borderline personality)	+	+	?	±	Low	Yes[c]

[a] If combined with appropriate medication.
[b] Probably more than half have affective illness of one type or another.
[c] One of the two subdivisions of Spitzer's item set is ''schizotypal.''

Overview

In this chapter we have examined in some detail five systems for categorizing a patient as within a borderline realm: four systems employ the word "borderline" in the diagnostic label; the schemata of D. Klein do not, but the hysteroid dysphoria syndrome exists so much within the borderline realm—as defined by the others—that its inclusion is warranted here.

Use of the preceding seven tables of this chapter will facilitate placement of any given patient within one or more of the systems presented.

Table 9–8 provides an overview of the five systems, which are compared here with respect to a number of variables relevant to most clinicians working with patients in this range of psychopathology.

Many of the responses in the table represent educated guesses; in only a few instances have methodical studies, of a sort that would supply definitive answers, already been carried out. As an example, many patients with (Kernberg's) borderline personality organization respond well to intensive psychotherapy, but the definition is quite broad and includes many patients who abuse drugs or alcohol—and whose response to this treatment is notoriously poor. Therefore, on the basis of my clinical impressions, I have recorded only one + in the corresponding space. Gunderson's borderline personality disorder, by virtue of excluding substance-abusing patients, defines a sample more uniformly responsive to intensive psychotherapy; hence the two +'s.

CHAPTER 10

Diagnosis of Personality Type

Early Systems of Personality Type

Although the ancient Greek medical writers are well known for their classification of the more florid mental disorders, the Greeks also paid some attention to comparatively subtle aberrations of personality as well. The most important author in this respect was Theophrastus of Eresos (fourth century B.C.). A pupil of Aristotle's, Theophrastus earned a considerable reputation for his description of personality profiles typical of his day, his so-called "Characters" (1947). The majority of these thirty profiles are actually devoted to rather unpleasant types, for which the Greeks had a rich vocabulary. Theophrastus paid little attention to character typology in the abstract. He neither attempted to depict normal variants and traits nor to extract from the wide assortment of character types a smaller number of "axes" relating to patterns exhibited by all people to one degree or another.

Some of the profiles relate to obnoxious character traits that, to the modern reader, cut across the familiar diagnostic lines. Thus, *aponoia* (laziness) or *akairia* (tactlessness) can be found in conjunction with any of the commonly recognized character disorders or personality-trait disturbances of our current nomenclature. On the other hand, some of Theophrastus' archetypes belong primarily with one particular character disorder as we have nowadays defined them. For example, *mempsimoiria* (querulousness), *apistia* (distrustfulness), and, to a lesser extent, *kakologia* (calumniousness) can be viewed as ingredients of our "paranoid personality." There were no solid links between the Characters of Theophrastus and the attributes we associate with the hysterical personality. The terms *mania* and *melancholia* were in use the century before Theophrastus, but the only allusion to mood disorders in the "Characters" is the description of *dyschereia* (moroseness, peevishness).

For many centuries the predominant schema throughout Western culture for the classification of character types was that of the four "humors"—choleric, sanguine, phlegmatic, and melancholic. This schema also derived from the ancient Greeks. The Hippocratic physicians described these temperaments, which were thought of as corresponding to the four primordial elements, Air, Water, Fire, and Earth. Galen utilized these notions; they were carried forward by the great medieval Semitic physicians Avicenna and Maimonides. The same notions appear in the prescriptions of the sixteenth-century moralist Huarte y Navarro for creating children with the optimal temperament (Stone, 1973a). Both normal and abnormal personalities were depicted in these terms, and where the personality could not be neatly categorized as "pure" choleric, and so forth, the physicians of the time spoke of combinations of these basic qualities. The four types correspond closely to our use of such terms as cheerful or excitable (sanguine), gloomy (melancholic), angry or irritable (choleric), and sluggish or imperturbable (phlegmatic). Mixed terms like sanguineo-choleric were still used to describe temperament or "disposition" by Pinel, Esquirol, and Kraepelin's predecessor, Griesinger. Earlier, George Cheyne, an English physician of the eighteenth century, described his own "phlegmatic" temperament. Samuel Johnson is described by his contemporaries as "saturnine," a term implying moroseness, gravity, sluggishness, and bitterness—not unlike Kraepelin's "depressive temperament" (see pp. 324–329). Johnson might also have been described as a combination of the choleric and phlegmatic types.

Character and temperament constitute the two major subdivisions in the analysis of personality type. In retrospect, Theophrastus may be said to have concentrated on aspects of *character;* that is, on the habitual personality facade and mode of interaction in the presence of others. The schools of Hippocrates and Galen were primarily concerned with *temperament;* that is, with the innate response tendencies of the individual that would be noticeable even outside the context of interpersonal relations. Inevitably there was a degree of overlap. Whereas the "tactlessness" and "snobbishness" mentioned by Theophrastus seem like learned qualities and distinctly characterological, other qualities (namely, moroseness) are more closely linked with temperament. Elsewhere I have commented on these distinctions in greater detail (Stone, 1978b).

Recent Systems

There appeared to be little need, even into the early nineteenth century, to create a complex taxonomy of character types. Until the era of Mesmer and his followers (Stone, 1974) there was little recognition of emotional disorders in noninstitutionalized persons. With the growth of the psychoanalytic movement, this situation changed: the development of psychoanalysis as a treatment method stimulated a more careful scrutiny of character disorders. Some character disorders were noticed to be, for the most part, amenable to analytic treatment; others were highly resistant. Abraham and some of the analytic pioneers advocated a characterology based on Freud's theories of individual evolution, such that ''oral,'' ''anal,'' and ''genital'' characters were recognized. Further subdivisions into oral-sadistic, anal-erotic, anal-sadistic, and so on, were also created.

A certain correspondence was noted between the older character classifications and the one based on the Freudian states. Thus ''obsessive'' character traits were nearly interchangeable with those of ''anality,'' especially those relating to parsimony, obstinacy, and orderliness (or their opposites). The hysteric's emphasis on sexuality led to an initial linkage of this character type to the more mature ''genital'' stage of psychic growth. Nevertheless, the common occurrence of ''oral'' traits in many (especially poorer-functioning) hysterics led others (namely, Easser and Lesser, 1965) to draw attention to the ''paradoxical'' orality (hence, immaturity) of some erstwhile ''genital'' hysterics.

Pierre Janet, a contemporary of Freud's, devoted several long works to obsessional and hysterical conditions in all their many variations. Unfortunately, Janet's failure to appreciate the new conceptions of Freud relegated him to an undeserved obscurity. True, he dismissed the emerging psychodynamic psychology as so much ''quaint theorizing of the German school'' (Raymond and Janet, 1903, p. 367), but his case descriptions remain unsurpassed for their rich detail. His patients come alive for us in the reading, even eighty years later; many seem like textbook examples of borderline structure (namely, case 166 in the 1903 monograph).

Jung (1921) wrote an extensive treatise on psychological types, amplifying his concepts of the ''introvert'' and ''extravert'' mentioned earlier in his work of 1912 on the transformation and symbols of the libido. There, Jung spoke of extraversion and introversion as ''the two fundamental mechanisms of the psyche,'' considering them to a large extent the normal and appropriate ways of reacting to ''complexes''—extraversion as a means of escaping from the complex of reality, introversion as a means of "detaching oneself from external reality through the complex" (1956, vol. I, p. 178).

Earlier (Chapter 8) we saw how these Jungian types became interwoven into Kretschmer's model of the endogenous psychoses: schizophrenia was seen as the logical extension of schizoid personality, itself the charactero-logical equivalent of introversion. The natural opposite was mania—the extension of the "cycloid" personalities and of extraversion. Cesare Lombroso (1876, 1880), the author of a widely read book linking heredity, physiognomy, and criminality in a psychopathic population, was also interested in the constitutional antecedents of certain phobic conditions. Kretschmer's interest in body habitus and personality (schizoid ectomorphs, etc.) was spurred by these nineteenth-century speculations.

The classification we encounter in Wilhelm Reich's *Character Analysis* (1949) adheres to Freud's concept of stages: Reich limns in detail the hysteric, the compulsive (= anal or obsessive), and the phallic-narcissistic (a stage closest to the highest or "genital" level). In addition, another kind of character type is sketched—one that Reich labels "aristocratic" (1949, p. 180), though we would consider it a variant of the narcissistic. Prognostic value was attached to these different character types. Reich, for example, believed that the "phallic-narcissistic" was nearest to emotional health and was the easiest to treat with psychoanalysis. While many analysts would dispute the notion of easy analyzability for this kind of patient, Reich's carefully delineated metapsychology has permitted testable hypotheses.

Following Reich, classifications of character types have tended to diverge along two paths. Psychoanalytic characterologies have continued to embody the series of stages in individual development outlined by Freud and elaborated further by Melanie Klein and her followers. Among the latter, the "depressive" and "paranoid" personalities are seen as related to the corresponding "positions" of early childhood development. Possible biological underpinnings to such personality types are mentioned but not emphasized by this school. The depressive personality, in particular, may stem from a variety of factors; it can arise out of severe parental deprivation or out of strong hereditary predisposition to a primary affective disorder without necessarily having to invoke the particular vicissitudes of mother-infant interaction alluded to by the Kleinians.

The other path, relating more to temperament than to character, attaches more importance to hereditary and constitutional factors and rather less importance to the psychological stages or to the mother's influence. The work of Escalona (1968), for example, unites the neurophysiological concept of an innate stimulus barrier with the notion of innate temperaments—whose outlines are already discernible in newborns. Escalona also postulates that styles of mothering are themselves governed to varying extents by the stable (and inborn) characteristics of infants' behavior. The emphasis in her 1968 monograph is on the quantitative assessment of strength either of the inner or the outer (ego) boundaries. Bridges are not made from temperament to adult character type here, but in the paper of Chess, Thomas, and Birch (1967) possible connections between certain temperaments identifiable in three-month-old infants and the more irritable or withdrawn character types of adult life are hinted at.

The Kraepelinian Temperaments

Both in his 1905 textbook of general psychiatry and in the 1921 monograph on manic-depressive psychoses and paranoia, Kraepelin discussed cases falling in the ''in-between region'' (*Zwischengebiet*)—between full-blown psychosis and normality. He felt it necessary to defend against the reproach leveled by colleagues in other fields that psychiatrists consider all people more or less disturbed emotionally, but admitted that it is by no means always easy to draw a line marking off the transition from normality to mental illness. What makes this task particularly difficult is the occurrence in many well-functioning persons of compartmentalized areas of thought or behavior where ''madness'' or deviancy holds sway. To each major psychotic condition, then, belonged an outer region of ''morbid personalities,'' some of whom went on to develop the more serious disorder and some of whom limped along throughout life with their disability.

Certain forms of what we now label ''antisocial personality'' were described at length by Kraepelin in his chapter on morbid personalities (1905, p. 314 ff.). Kraepelin's views evolved from notions which were taken for granted by most nineteenth-century alienists, namely, that ''degenerate'' personalities were set in motion largely on a hereditary basis.[1] There is a direct line from the ''moral insanity'' cases of Pinel (1806) and Prichard (1835) through the degenerate (*entartet*) personality of Kraepelin to our own ''psychopathic'' (or, more euphemistically, ''antisocial'') personality.

Kraepelin also offered several examples similar to our severe obsessional cases in his description of ''compulsive ideas'' (*Zwangsvorstellungen*) and, elsewhere, examples of various hysterical manifestations. Regarding compulsive ideas (monomania or *idées fixes* in the French nineteenth-century nosology), it is clear that they form part of the psychopathology of many clear-cut schizophrenics, but when present and *unaccompanied* by other symptoms it becomes hazardous to back-diagnose schizophrenia on just this one piece of evidence.

We have also noted earlier that paranoia is not pathognomonic of schizophrenia; many manics (of the more irritable variety) have, as a kind of substrate, paranoid personalities and, likewise, so have certain epileptics, alcoholics, and so forth. Nevertheless, the paranoid personality is one of

[1]For a discussion of the hereditary factor in certain cases of epilepsy, the paper of Vercelletto (1972) should be consulted.

TABLE 10–1

Characteristics of Paranoid Personality according to Kraepelin

A.	Uncertainty, with excessive valuation of the self
B1.	Distrustfulness
2.	Preoccupation with "injustices"
3.	Pronounced jealousy
4.	Faultfinding, querulousness
5.	Suspicions tend to remain vague and unaccompanied by full-scale change in life-style in line with the unrealistic ideas (as would be so in the *delusional* patient)
C.	Often accompanied by (1) irritability, obstinacy, impatience, and a discontented (sour) mood, and/or (2) feelings of superiority, grandiosity

the "sicker" characterological types, since there tends to be a strong measure of denial, externalization, hostility, and other negative features in this condition. One is obliged, when confronted with paranoid symptoms of any significant degree, to probe for other signs of a major "psychotic" condition and for evidence of mental aberrations in the close relatives. The features that may be present in paranoid persons, according to Kraepelin's clinical descriptions, are outlined in Table 10–1.

Among his manic-depressive patients, Kraepelin noted that about half showed aberrations in their premorbid personality. These seemed so deep and lasting as to suggest a kind of inherited predisposition, and, therefore, Kraepelin spoke of "fundamental states" or "temperaments" (see Chess et al., 1959). In the four sections of Table 10–2, I have abstracted the most important features of the temperaments associated with MDP, as mentioned in the vignettes of Kraepelin's monograph.

It is interesting to compare the Kraepelinian temperament descriptions with some of the impressionistic descriptions offered by his predecessors. Benjamin Rush, for example, wrote of certain persons—usually ambulatory—afflicted with what Pinel had called *démence,* for which Rush preferred the term "dissociation." In this disorder there is a flow of unrelated perceptions: "Ideas, collected together without order, frequently constitute a paroxysm of the disease. It is always accompanied by great volubility of speech . . . with a kind of convulsive rapidity. . . . Persons who suffer with it are good-tempered and quarrelsome, malicious and kind, all in the course of the same day" (1812, p. 259 et seq.). Rush cites as an example the celebrated Swiss physiognomist, Johann Lavater (1741–1801), through the words of Lavater's acquaintance, Reverend Hunter:

> "I was detained the whole morning by the strange, wild, eccentric Lavater, in various conversations. When once he is set a going, there is no such thing

TABLE 10–2

Kraepelinian Temperaments Associated with MDP

I. *Depressive Temperament* (noted in at least 12 percent of manic-depressives*)

A. Permanent gloom in all life experiences

B. 1. Joylessness in work, with easy fatigability
2. Self-doubt; self-tormenting
3. Hypochondriasis
4. Irritable, unfriendly, repellent social facade
5. Lack of self-confidence
6. Guilt over minor indiscretions in the remote past
7. Sexual inhibition
8. Sentimentality†
9. Lack of initiative
10. Scrupulosity; excessive precision and orderliness
11. Morbid fear of poverty; exaggerated frugality
12. Indecisiveness
13. Inordinate fear of examinations
14. Suicidal ruminations
15. Psychasthenia; bodily complaints
16. Terrifying dreams

II. *Manic Temperament* (formerly called "constitutional excitement" by Kraepelin; seen in 9 percent of Kraepelin's manic-depressive patients)

1. Distractibility; failure to persevere in learning; excessive pursuit of side interests with resultant superficiality
2. Desultory thought
3. Judgment hasty or shallow
4. Heightened self-confidence; at times: exalted mood
5. Boastfulness
6. Lack of insight into "the morbid imperfection of one's temperament"‡
7. Haughtiness
8. Stubbornness
9. A tendency to tease or ill-use others
10. Gruffness; coarseness (especially following criticism)
11. Restlessness; unsteadiness; "wanderlust"
12. Dilettantism
13. Use of forcible language; raucous laughter
14. Compulsive, at times highly scatological, humor
15. A writing style characterized by bombast, verbosity, prolixity, witticism, personal attacks
16. Insubordinate, antiauthoritarian

17. Truancy; leadership in dyssocial gangs or groups
18. Sexual promiscuity (in either sex)
19. Alcoholism
20. Ambitiousness
21. Fervent advocacy of new movements and causes
22. Professional jokers, town "originals"
23. Overspending
24. Involvement in excessively many and complex business schemes
25. Brilliance or inventiveness that does not come to fruition, for want of perseverance: certain unevenly gifted personalities with artistic inclinations
26. Irascibility
27. Litigiousness
28. Arrogance
29. Ineducability
30. Churlishness

III. *Irritable Temperament* (seen in 12½ percent of Kraepelin's manic-depressive patients)

A. A condition in which some "manic" and some "depressive" traits are commingled

B.
1. Hot-tempered; irascible
2. Irritable
3. Exquisitely sensitive to criticism
4. Abusive
5. Uncompromising; opinionated
6. Jealous
7. Mood labile: often cheerful but periodically ill-humored, anxious, listless
8. Irritability in women increased at the time of menses
9. Paranoid (mild to moderate degree)
10. Impractical; full of extravagant schemes that come to nothing
11. Impulsive

IV. *Cyclothymic Temperament* (seen in 3 to 4 percent of Kraepelin's manic-depressive patients)

A. Oscillation between two opposite poles of mood, sometimes taking on some of the characteristics of the *depressive temperament,* sometimes those of the *manic temperament:* "rejoicing to the skies" or "sad as death" by turns

---

*And in a significant but unknown percentage of their relatives.

†Of the sort that "leads to vegetarianism after a visit to an abattoir."

‡Analogous to my notion of "low psychological aptitude" in the temperament of many bipolar patients.

> as stopping him till he runs himself out of breath. He starts from subject to subject, flies from book to book, from picture to picture; measures your nose, your eyes, your mouth, with a pair of compasses; pours forth a torrent of physiognomy upon you, but will not let you open your lips to propose a difficulty." (1812, p. 261)

The similarity of Lavater's personality and symptoms to the features of Kraepelin's "manic temperament" will be obvious. Lavater's condition might also satisfy research criteria for manic illness.

Modern Systems of Personality Typology

The current diagnostic manual (DSM-III) makes reference to some dozen or more personality disorders. Some are recognized by the psychiatric community as a whole (hysterical, obsessive-compulsive, paranoid, passive-aggressive, schizoid, inadequate, explosive, antisocial, phobic-anxious); others enjoy a popularity more within the psychoanalytic community (depressive-masochistic, narcissistic, infantile). One might expand this list to include the abnormal "temperaments" mentioned by Kraepelin: depressive, (hypo)manic, irritable, and cyclothymic.

Our current nosology, with its overarching concept of *personality* disorder, does not make fine distinctions between disorders of character and those of temperament. Despite a degree of overlap, these concepts need to be differentiated where possible, if only to permit more accurate appraisal of heritability.[2] *Schizoid* and *explosive,* for example, seem to belong more to the realm of temperament than do *hysterical* and *obsessional,* though the latter are not without biological underpinnings (see pp. 329–334). Under certain circumstances, even *antisocial personality* is encountered with high frequency among adoptees of antisocial biological parents (Cadoret, Cunningham, et al., 1976).

The personality disorders we now recognize represent higher levels of abstraction than were to be found in the early Greek characterology. The latter, as we saw, consisted of individual and rather narrowly defined traits, of which some could be subsumed under one of the broader rubrics of our taxonomy. Narcissism is a larger concept, for example, than haughtiness.

Even higher levels of abstraction are of course possible. We noted earlier Eysenck's interest in certain dimensions of human behavior which seem applicable to all people, "normal" as well as ill. Extraversion-introversion can be seen as constituting one "axis," for example: at one end the manic is situated; at the other, the schizoid. One could create a number of other axes uniting various disorders and temperaments into a still smaller number

[2]One would want to test the hypothesis that the more a personality disturbance is a reflection of temperament (rather than of character), the more it would show up in, say, the adopted-away offspring of the original subjects.

of polarities where most people could be placed at some in-between point. Hysterical-obsessive might constitute one such spectrum, with the spontaneous, nonlogical, imaginative "hysteric" at one end and the cautious, self-conscious, hyperrational "obsessive" at the other. Depressive versus paranoid constitutes another pair of opposites (see M. Klein, 1960), as does, in another context, depressive versus manic. "Narcissism" may be seen as the exaggeration of enlightened self-interest, which in turn is midway between egocentricity and its polar opposite altruism. As altruism is not pictured as an aberration of character, it is not to be found in our diagnostic manuals. The same is true for "autonomy" which, though honored in Erikson's schema for normal maturation, is seldom mentioned in our nomenclature as the opposite "extreme" to the well-established entities, "inadequate" or "infantile" personality. Most people can also be rated as occupying some point along a spectrum concerning *passive aggressivity* versus *cooperativeness*. Finally, the *phobic-anxious* character may be the natural opposite to the *explosive* (similar to Kraepelin's "irritable") personality.

Both obsessive and hysterical character types, unlike most of the other personality labels, seem like exaggerations of socially sanctioned attributes in men and women respectively. There may even be subtle differences of cognitive styles in the two sexes predisposing to superior verbal and rhythmic skills in girls and to superior spatial-relational and mathematical skills in boys. According to Hamburg (1974), there is evidence that "lateralization of the (cerebral) hemispheres and functional activity of the language centers occur earlier in girls than in boys" and that parallel early cerebral changes contribute to higher spatial-task proficiency in boys. Eventually a division of roles is fostered, leading to "stereotypes": men are expected to demonstrate independence, objectivity, competitiveness, logical mentality, decisiveness, and ambition; women are expected to be noncompetitive, gentle, warm, empathic, and capable of expressing tender feelings. The relationships that appear to exist between our biological heritage and the norms of characterological differences between the sexes are discussed also from an evolutionary standpoint in Hamburg's excellent chapter. It goes without saying that psychic normality, in the ideal sense, would require the appropriate blending of the characteristics just mentioned. Well-integrated men are capable of expressing tender feelings; well-integrated women are assertive and logical, and so on. The more one encounters stereotypes where such integration has not developed, or where the "normal" qualities are grossly overdeveloped, the more one is entitled to speak of character pathology.

Borderline structure, as Kernberg has emphasized, is often accompanied by character aberrations of a more pathological type *ab initio*. Instead of hysterical or obsessive traits, one may find depressive, paranoid, hypomanic, or antisocial traits—which are not mere exaggerations of normal attributes. Narcissism, as a concept, can be compartmentalized into healthy and abnormal varieties. Because of this continuumlike property, diagnostic problems often arise concerning where healthy self-regard leaves off and pathological narcissism (as a defense against early injury to self-esteem, etc.) begins. This is a complex subject in itself, one that is discussed in great depth by Kernberg (1975) in his treatise on the pathological narcissism of many patients with borderline structure. Structure and character must be diagnosed separately, however, because even the "sicker" character types (schizoid, paranoid, infantile, etc.) can occur alongside neurotic structure. And some patients with psychotic structure show predominantly (and often, grotesque) hysterical or obsessional traits. This is true of many obsessional hand washers, for example. Cornfield and Malen (1979) have recently made the point that "obsessive" character can exist at all levels of function—neurotic, borderline, and psychotic. They even suggest the term "obsessionoid," as a counterpart for "hysteroid," but I suspect it will be more elegant (though more cumbersome) to speak here of the "obsessive person functioning at the borderline level."

Since many of the character diagnoses in current usage represent polarities and spectra that have one end in normal psychic makeup ("antisocial" is one notable exception), it will also be useful to think in *dimensional* terms. It should be possible to locate patients somewhere along a continuum for each character type, as it varies from the most to the least pathological. The manner in which this may be approached is described in the following sections of this chapter.

Toward a Multiaxial Model of Personality Typology

Some of the contemporary taxonomies represent significant advances in abstraction and integration but are not quite broad enough to do justice to the full range of personality types encountered in psychiatric practice, let alone in the population at large. If one collected a large sample of patients with classical psychoneuroses, certain types (hypomanic, schizoid, antisocial) would probably be in short supply, while others (hysteric, depressive, obsessive) would be "overrepresented." A borderline population would contain a disproportionately large percentage of narcissistic, infantile, paranoid types. Still, almost all the commonly recognized personality types can occur at any level of psychic structure.

Hysterical and obsessive traits, if one views them on a more abstract plane, may be expressions, at least in part, of fundamental differences in the organization of the nervous system—something we now refer to as "cognitive style." Research interest in correlations among (1) characterological polarities, (2) biological differences between the sexes, and (3) differential modes of processing in the two cerebral hemispheres is now both active and promising (Stone, 1977a; Dimond, 1972). While it would be simplistic and premature to equate "left"-hemisphere dominance, linear-logical thought, and obsessiveness with maleness (or "nondominant" hemisphere predominance, intuitive-holistic thought, and hysterical traits with femaleness), there may well be validity to the existence of such trends (see also pp. 329–330). In the meantime it may not be stretching the facts too far if we think of "hysterical-obsessive" as a continuum, corresponding roughly to a spectrum with emotionality and imaginativeness at one end, emotional control and logicality at the other.[3] One can then locate a person's general cognitive style somewhere along this continuum. The degree to which a given person partakes of the stereotypes of either the hysterical or the obsessive personality can also be rated on two separate scales, as in Table 10–3.

TABLE 10–3
Traits of the Various Personality Types
Guide to Dimensional Assessment

PERSONALITY TYPE	*Rating*	*Traits*
Hysterical	10	Extremes of such qualities as overdramatic, irresponsible, seductive, promiscuous, childish, overemotional, fantasy-oriented, self-indulgent, noncompliant, exhibitionistic, helpless, chaotic, imitative, unstable, attention-seeking. (Extreme Hysterical will overlap with "Narcissistic.")
	2	Appropriate degrees of such qualities as imaginative, feelingful, empathic, spontaneous, vivacious, sexually responsive.
	0–1	Deficiency or absence of some of the normal attributes of level 2.
Obsessive	10	Extremes of such qualities as moral scrupulosity, overconscientious, perfectionism, overcontrolled, inhibited, conformist, overdetailed, affectively dry or deadened; may show full-blown "obsessive neurosis" with rituals or preoccupations with certain words and phrases; punctilious, obstinate, parsimonious. (Extreme Obsessive may overlap with "Paranoid" or "Passive-Aggressive.") Extremes of such defenses as isolation of affect, rationalization, intellectualization, reaction formation, and of traits like ingratiation.

[3]However this may turn out, I take some comfort from enjoying, in this connection, the company of Sir Francis Bacon (1640, Bk. V., p. 218).

TABLE 10–3 **Traits of the Various Personality Types** *(Cont.)*

Personality Type	*Rating*	*Traits*
Obsessive (*cont.*)	2	Appropriate degrees of tidiness, thrift, orderliness, reserve, conventionality, dutifulness.
	0–1	Deficiency or absence of some of the normal attributes of level 2.
Depressive-Masochistic	10	Extremes of such qualities as joyless, gloomy, pessimistic, self-tormenting, unself-confident, guilt-ridden, preoccupied with thoughts about death. Relationships are ungratifying and show extreme and repetitive self-destructiveness or self-abrogation. (If these traits are found in alternation with those of "Hypomania," the term "cyclothymic" may be appropriate.)
	0	Appropriate self-confidence and optimism; appropriate respect for one's own needs and wishes; capacity for gratifying relationships.
Phobic-Anxious	10	Extremes of such qualities as fearfulness, avoidance of the most harmless objects and situations, clingingly dependent relationships.
	0	Self-sufficiency; capacity to deal with all ordinary things and situations without squeamishness.
Infantile	10	Extremes of such qualities as childlike dependency, dull demeanor, unself-sufficiency, petulance.
	0	Mature, autonomous, responsible, capable of independent and appropriate interdependent relationships.
Passive-Aggressive	10	Extremes of such qualities as obstructionism, pouting, procrastination, stubbornness; covert hostility.
	0	Respectful; able to deal with hostile and aggressive feelings in an appropriate and diplomatic manner; appropriately assertive.
Paranoid	10	Extremes of such qualities as querulousness, suspiciousness, jealousy, hypersensitivity; extreme tendency to blame others for all problems. (Extreme Paranoid will overlap with "Narcissistic" insofar as grandiosity and pomposity may be exhibited, and with "Passive-Aggressive" or "Antisocial" insofar as belligerence may be present. Some

PERSONALITY TYPE	*Rating*	*Traits*
		of the features of Kraepelin's "irritable temperament" will be present.) Religious or political zealousness.
	0	Appropriate capacity to sense others' motives; capacity for trust without undue gullibility.
Narcissistic	10	Extremes of such qualities as contemptuousness, coldness, self-centeredness, vanity, ruthlessness, exploitativeness, manipulativeness, selfishness, egocentricity, grandiosity, pomposity, arrogance; incapacity for deep and meaningful relationships, snobbishness, shallowness. (Extremes of Narcissistic overlap with certain "Antisocial" features.) Thoughts and behavior are dominated by idealized and unrealistic images (whether positive or negative) of self and others.
	2	Appropriate regard for the self as well as for others; accurate self-appraisal and appropriate ambition. "Enlightened self-interest."
	0–1	Extremes of altruism, saintliness, or inability to recognize or assert one's needs; self-effacing.
Schizoid	10	Extremes of such qualities as seclusiveness, shyness, oversensitivity, avoidance of intimacy. Eccentricity, preciosity, peculiarity of thought, inability to express strong feelings. Hermits and other isolates exemplify the extreme degree.
	0	Healthy capacity for interaction with others and for expression of emotions; appropriate balance of logical and imaginative thought.
Explosive	10	Extreme degrees of such qualities as ragefulness, irritability, hyperexcitability; rage outbursts are episodic but violent. (Lesser degrees of Explosive overlap with Kraepelin's "irritable temperament.")
	0	Calm, poised, restrained, able to tolerate high degrees of frustration without "flying off the handle."
Hypomanic	10	Extreme degrees of such qualities as expansiveness, "energy," ambition, extraversion, cheeriness, optimism, giddiness, sleeplessness (diminished need for sleep), flightiness, intrusiveness. (If these traits are found to alternate with "Depres-

TABLE 10–3 **Traits of the Various Personality Types** ***(Cont.)***

Personality Type	*Rating*	*Traits*
Hypomanic (*cont.*)		sive-Masochistic" traits, the term "cyclothymic" may be appropriate.) May overlap with "Explosive."
	0	Calm, measured, euthymic without being euphoric.
Inadequate	10	Extreme degrees of such qualities as markedly ineffectual toward social, emotional, intellectual, physical demands of any kind; inept, unstable, lacking in judgment or stamina (all in the absence of actual mental deficiency).
	0	Capability, adaptiveness, savoir faire, appropriate amount of stamina, perseverance, and enthusiasm for work and leisure activities.
Antisocial	10	Extreme degrees of such qualities as impulsivity, callous disregard for others, selfishness, irresponsibility, shamelessness, incapacity for loyalty. (There is an overlap with "Narcissistic.") The extreme degrees will tend to include criminality, vagrancy, ruthlessness, sadism, etc.
	0	Scrupulous regard for other peoples' lives, feelings, and possessions; trustworthiness, and a high ethical sense which is apparent in behavior as well as thought.

Neither the list of personality "disorders" in the DSM-III nor the characterology generally used within the psychoanalytic community has the coverage necessary to include the full range of normal personality configurations, abnormal traits, pathological types, and so on, that one would like to include in a full typology. In an effort to compensate for this, I have included a larger number of archetypes in the instrument I use in this book for appraisal of this dimension (Figure 10–2). This instrument and its use are described below (pp. 337–340).

Hysterical-obsessive, then, may be thought of as one "axis"; several others may also be extracted from the whole catalog of traits and disorders, so that we are left with a small number of essential "elements" which are of particular relevance to the universe of psychiatric, especially borderline, conditions. These axes are shown in Figure 10–1.

The second axis depicted in the figure begins with the element *depressive*. One continuum develops from the pair of opposites "depressive-par-

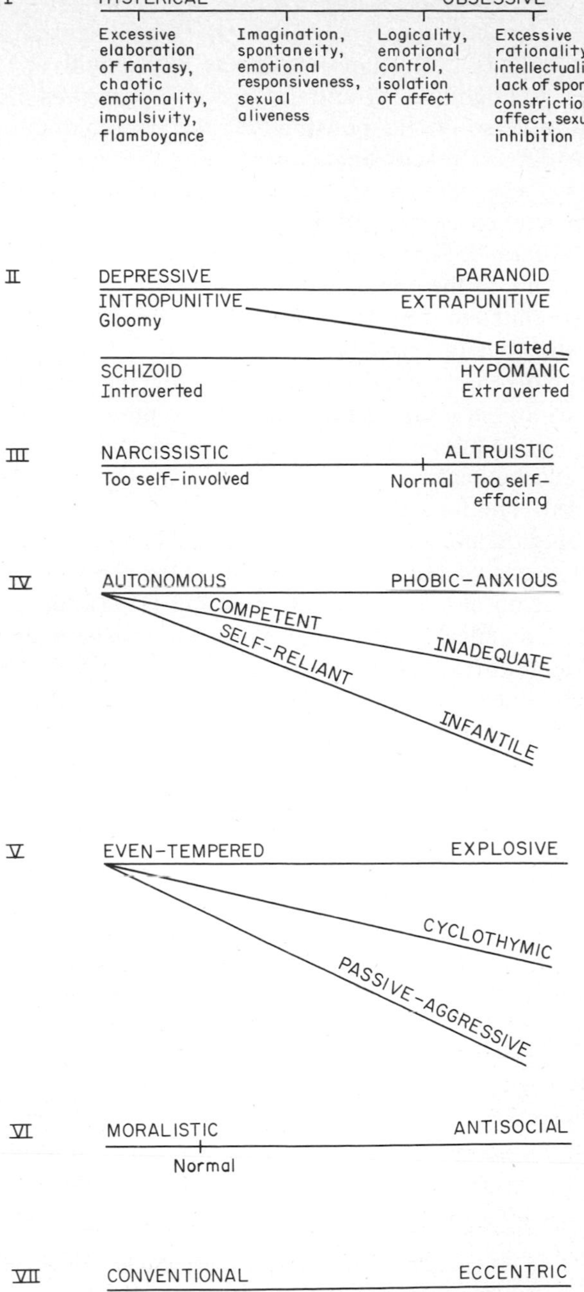

Figure 10–1. A Multiaxial System for Character Typology

anoid''; most people can be located meaningfully at some point on this continuum. The corresponding dimension in the four-dimensional model of Overall et al. (1967) is ''intropunitive versus extrapunitive.'' This also relates, in a way, to cognitive style: the depressive perceives himself as at the center of a universe of ''responsibility''; the paranoid sees everyone else, except himself, as ''responsible.''

But depression, when the spotlight is on *mood* rather than on *thinking,* is also the opposite of *elation.* This gives rise to another continuum, *depression*-(hypo)*mania.* The *hypomanic* person is typically also extraverted and, therefore, at the opposite pole to the introverted *schizoid.*

The third axis relates to object relations. The extreme condition on one side is *narcissistic,* where this label is used in the pathological sense of inordinate overinvolvement with the self and a concomitant incapacity to relate to others except in a superficial way. As one progresses to the opposite end, *altruism,* one passes through an area of normal or healthy narcissism (which would be accompanied by a good capacity for deep involvement with others). The idea that the term ''narcissism'' can refer to the appropriate self-regard and ambition of the normal person, as well as to the pathological variations we have in mind when we use the word as a clinical term, finds expression also in the work of Kohut (1971) and Lichtenberg (1978). These authors speak, for example, of a narcissistic line of (normal) development (Lichtenberg, 1978, p. 435).

The fourth fundamental axis embraces *autonomy* at the ''healthy'' end and, branching off into several directions as one moves toward the pathological, the three character types where autonomy is most noticeably lacking: the *phobic-anxious,*[4] the *infantile,* and the *inadequate.*

The fifth axis concerns irritability. The *explosive,* the *cyclothymic,* and the *passive-aggressive* character types all share the quality of excessive irritability. Their contrasting traits at the healthy pole would be calmness, candidness, and even-temperedness.

The sixth axis has at one extreme the *antisocial* personality and at the other, the moralistic or overscrupulous. The values of the normal person are at neither extreme, although much closer to the moralistic. For this reason, it is difficult to assign a priori a numerical value to the normal ideal: if the extremely psychopathic is ''zero'' on this scale, and the extremely moralistic ''100,'' where does normality fit? Perhaps in the high 80s.[5]

Finally, I have included a seventh axis relating to a group of traits neglected in many typologies. In dealing with borderline patients, either in the structural or genotypic sense, one wants to have a measure of peculi-

[4]As mentioned earlier (see p. 329), *phobic-anxious* could also be viewed, in its sense of timidity, as a natural opposite to the explosive personality

[5]The research scale used by Kernberg and Goldstein for assessing the degree of ''superego integration'' resolved the dilemma in this fashion. I am indebted to them for the idea of placing the healthy-valued person in this region of a spectrum.

arity or eccentricity. This is because eccentricity occupies such an important place in the psychology of *schizophrenia.* As I have mentioned in discussing the search for biological markers, so many symptoms (thought disorder, delusions, hallucinations) have failed the test for pathognomonicity (of schizophrenia), one is often left with this one quality of eccentricity. Often eccentricity is an outgrowth of ego-boundary confusion. The average person tends to regard someone who thinks he *is* Napoleon as "crazy," for example, whereas one who claims superiority to Napoleon in generalship might be regarded as merely grandiose. The boundary confusion that often accompanies extremes of eccentricity has little diagnostic value in acute psychoses. Many acutely psychotic manics think they are some exalted figure from history, but show no such ideation when they have recovered. It is the persistence, even during periods of calm, in such "mix-ups" that pushes one's diagnostic thinking toward schizophrenia (see Rosenthal, 1975; Shakhmatova-Pavlova et al., 1975, on borderline schizophrenic traits; see also pp. 340–344). Since not all schizoid persons are eccentric, I believe it is all the more useful to add this measure to our multiaxial system. The opposite to eccentricity would be *conventionality.*

Personality-Profile Scale

The Personality-Profile Scale (Figure 10–2) represents an effort to appraise personality in a dimensional fashion. This scale consists of a grid with space for the various personality and character types along one axis and for ratings along the other. For the patient population on which this book focuses, I have chosen thirteen types, as shown in the figure. Since it is not possible to arrange them in any natural order (such as the degree to which each is more healthy or pathological), a more arbitrary arrangement was chosen. The character types that are more common in better integrated patients, and more often encountered in classical analysis, are placed on the left; those ordinarily associated with more severe or less analyzable conditions, on the right. It is important to note that this scale should be thought of as *open-ended.* Should it be desirable to add additional types to the scale by way of providing better coverage for a particular patient sample, the scale can be readily adapted to this purpose.

The ratings are to be made on an eleven-point scale along the vertical axis (numbered 0 to 10).

For most of the character types, a rating of zero signifies the absence or virtual absence of traits associated with the type in question; 10 represents the extreme pathological exaggeration of a particular type. Three exceptions to this rule are to be noted—for the "hysterical," "obsessive," and "narcissistic" types where psychopathology exists at either extreme. These are in effect bipolar scales with normality somewhere in the middle; pathology branches off in either direction from the ideal level. I have arbi-

Figure 10–2. Personality-Profile Scale

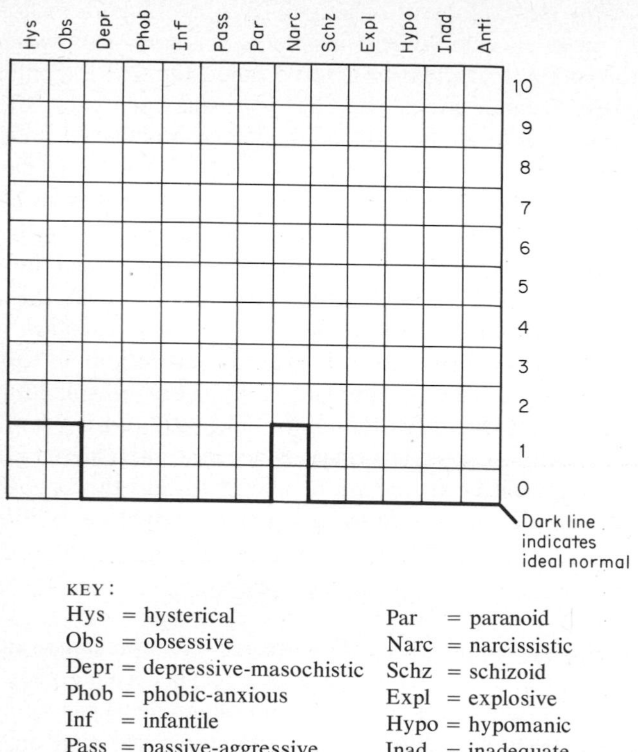

KEY:

Hys	= hysterical	Par	= paranoid
Obs	= obsessive	Narc	= narcissistic
Depr	= depressive-masochistic	Schz	= schizoid
Phob	= phobic-anxious	Expl	= explosive
Inf	= infantile	Hypo	= hypomanic
Pass	= passive-aggressive	Inad	= inadequate

Anti = antisocial

Instructions: Rate subject on each of the thirteen subtypes of the scale with a point from 0 (indicating that the traits of this subtype are absent) to 10 (indicating striking); join the points to make the characterological profile.

trarily chosen the number 2 for the ideal levels of these three types. The clusters of traits associated with each type are outlined in Table 10–3, which also serves as a guide for those using the Personality-Profile Scale.

What will emerge is a profile, made by connecting points placed in the box opposite the rating score for each type. (See Figure IV–3 below for an example.) The profile then serves as the *dimensional* diagnosis of character. The *category* diagnosis of character is given in the terms used either in the DSM-III or in the current psychoanalytic characterology. Ordinarily, the term given for each patient will correspond to the personality type that achieved the highest score. In everyday practice, we use the expression "features" to refer to other noticeable but less striking character aspects. One may speak, for example, of a patient as exhibiting "infantile personality with narcissistic features." These aspects might be reflected in scores of 8 under "infantile" and a 6 under "narcissistic."

The scale may be useful in helping to achieve consensus among a group of raters judging an interview. Character diagnoses in the past have been notoriously imprecise and interrater agreement notoriously poor. Not only is personality diagnosis a "fine point" in comparison to the florid symptoms many borderline patients exhibit, but there are also more to choose from. This in itself may contribute to the poorer level of agreement. Constitutionally, borderline patients will fall within the schizophrenic or manic-depressive spectra (or somewhere in between the polar regions of these two concepts) or else will have arrived at their clinical picture via organic or adverse early environmental factors. Here one is choosing among three or four possibilities. From the standpoint of adaptational level, there is a real triage: neurotic, borderline, or psychotic. But most personality typologies contain at least a dozen elements, at times more.

An additional source of confusion stems from the frequent occurrence of splitting in the borderline patients, whole aspects of whose character may be made manifest to one group of people and concealed to others. Many arguments that take place among hospital staffs regarding the nature of one or another borderline patient can be quickly resolved when information is pooled: the physician staff may be quite correct in describing as "compliant" a particular patient whom the nursing staff, equally correctly, describes as surly and contemptuous. It is probably correct to state that real precision about the personality profile of a patient, especially a hospitalized patient, would almost invariably depend upon ratings of a number of persons who relate to the patient in different roles.

Before using the Personality-Profile Scale, the reader may also wish to refresh his memory about some of the more recent descriptive and family-study papers on the various personality types. Those of Chodoff and Lyons (1958) and Chodoff (1974) on hysteria will be helpful, as will the articles of Cloninger, Reich, and Guze (1975, 1975a) on hysterical and antisocial personalities. The latter discuss the transmission of these traits, hysteria being seen predominantly in women (1975a) and sociopathy predominantly in men (1975). Welner and his co-workers' article (1976) on obsessive-compulsive neurosis points out the degree to which obsessional traits may be noted across all adaptational levels from psychotic to neurotic. The melting away of delusional or catatonic symptoms in schizophrenics, as treatment progresses, and their replacement by obsessional symptoms in many cases has been observed repeatedly (Blacker, 1966). Welner noted that a large sample of patients hospitalized for severe obsessional symptoms was composed primarily of persons with significant depressive disorders (38 percent); others were schizophrenic (9 percent). The remainder were either severe character disorders (in whom soft signs of an endogenous psychosis could not be detected) or patients whose clinical pictures fell short of meeting RDC for schizophrenia. This is a clinically *borderline* group; whether they would also show borderline structure would have to be tested separately. Jablensky's overview (1976) is useful both for its historical survey of character typologies and for its emphasis on the "fit" between the patient sample of interest to a particular diagnostician and the typology he or she fashions to meet his or her needs. The attributes of the narcissistic personality may be gleaned from Kernberg's 1974 paper. There the reader will find descriptions not only of the more commonly encountered qualities of narcissistic persons (namely, haughty grandiosity that may be coupled with shyness and feelings of inferiority, overdependence on external admiration and acclaim, feelings of boredom and emptiness, restless search for wealth, power, and beauty, etc.) but also of more subtle qualities that become apparent in the unfolding of psychoanalytic exploration. Lack of curiosity about the analyst's life is one such quality Kernberg mentions, something I too have been struck by in attempting to analyze highly narcissistic patients.

In actual practice it will be impossible to avoid a certain degree of overlap among the various subscales that make up the Personality-Profile Scale. This becomes more apparent as one moves toward the extremes of each archetype. The extreme obsessive almost always shows some paranoid feature; the extreme hysteric, some narcissistic qualities. Likewise, pathological degrees of narcissism are a regular feature of the antisocial personality. Nevertheless the narcissistic and exploitative aspects of antisocial persons, to take the last example, will not always be at the same levels of intensity. The profile scale should permit teasing apart of these often intertwined qualities, which can then be rated separately.

Personality Traits Reminiscent of Schizophrenia and Personality Abnormalities Noted in Relatives of Schizophrenics

In discussing manic-depressive illness we noted that personality disturbances were often detectable during the quiescent, as well as premorbid, phases and that in many instances relatives of the full-blown cases themselves exhibited some of these abnormalities. Within the realm of schizophrenia, the same situation holds. There are certain unusual traits that turn up frequently in relatives of schizophrenics, but at times also in ambulatory people whose families are not known to include severely ill or hospitalized members. Whereas disorders of *mood* and *irritability* predominated in the abnormal personalities associated with affective illness, the characterological accompaniments and "soft signs" of schizophrenia relate mostly to eccentricity, withdrawal, and emotional impoverishment. One might expect to see shyness, oversensitivity, or aloofness (as soft signs of the basic condition) and grudge holding and reformism (as subtle manifestations of the paranoid variants) as well as touchiness and litigiousness. A paralyzing kind of *indecisiveness* should also be included as a sign of either dilute or incipient schizophrenia.

A woman of twenty-four, exhibiting many of the features of borderline psychic structure, used to pore over menus in restaurants for as much as half an hour, and even then feel helplessly undecided about what to order. She also paid attention to irrelevant details, trying to select foods whose colors "matched," whether or not she enjoyed the items in question. For equally idiosyncratic reasons, she eschewed beets as too "sadistic," because they were red and contained the word "beat." The same indecisiveness immobilized her in front of her wardrobe in the morning. Ultimately she was to succumb to a full-blown schizophrenic episode requiring lengthy hospitalization.

Another quality associated with schizophrenia that is not often mentioned is *preciosity*. This may be taken as one manifestation, however, of the large concept—eccentricity. Preciosity includes attributes like fastidiousness, affectation, and a peculiar sort of artiness in which the schizophrenic's overattention to irrelevant details is exhibited in his or her artistic and literary efforts.

A young woman of nineteen, many of whose first-degree relatives were overtly schizophrenic, prided herself on her artistic productions. She herself had many borderline features: she was clingingly dependent; related to others not as they actually were but in terms of certain "ideal" qualities she superimposed upon them; was exquisitely vulnerable to criticism and even to compliments; was sexually promiscuous; and so on. Her dress was untidy as well as unconventional. She would write many letters to her boyfriend of the moment, always choosing stationery of an exotic color, and she would write around the margins in all directions as well as in the middle of the page. Tiny drawings of a bizarre and inappropriately "suggestive" nature were scattered all over the page. The letters were carefully addressed in such a way that nothing ever appeared where it usually would: the address was put vertically in the extreme left corner, the stamp on the back of the letter; in addition, further comments and poetical excerpts were sprinkled on both sides of the envelope, such that one had to marvel how the letter ever reached its destination at all. She, too, was later hospitalized for several months in a delusional state, following the disruption of a romantic involvement.

Mannered speech was apparent in the father of two adolescent schizophrenics under treatment at the Psychiatric Institute. This man, although a salesman in average circumstances, spoke as though he were an eighteenth-century Oxford don (as he often fancied himself). He combed the dictionary for obscure words, whose meaning he only half grasped, which he then sprung upon his family in various high-sounding but incomprehensible insults. Once he called his wife, for example, a "retromingent bitch." Everyone was properly impressed and mystified until a dictionary large enough to contain the word was finally located. When it was discovered that "retromingent" relates to animals of the cat family that urinate to the rear instead of to the front, the family realized he was talking nonsense. Actually he used speech more as a distancing than as a communicative mechanism, and this too might be taken as a subtle sign of schizophrenic peculiarity. Another way of looking at these characterological quirks—preciosity, eccentricity, and so forth—is to see them as manifestations of autistic thinking, one of Bleuler's essential schizophrenic traits. To speak in polarities, the archetypal schizophrenic inhabits a solipsistic world of his own; the affectively ill person, the world of others (to manipulate or cling to, as the case may be). This may make more understandable the relative conformity of many manic-depressive patients, and the seeming uniqueness of each schizophrenic person. Many town "originals" are within the schizophrenic spectrum, such as the elderly man who for years stood throughout the day, winter and summer, on a certain street corner in New York, clad in Viking costume, complete with spear.

Severity of character pathology in relatives of obvious schizophrenics appears to vary in a continuous rather than in an abrupt fashion. Subtle gradations exist ranging from distinctly abnormal character disorders, of the sort Shakhmatova (1975) mentions, to what Leonhard called "accentuated personalities." The Russian group uses this term for personality disturbances of a milder kind, characterized by one or a few outstanding traits, in persons the remainder of whose personalities are relatively healthy. Such traits, if we are dwelling on the schizophrenia spectrum, may include extremes of secretiveness, unusual degrees of monotonousness in life pattern, and a kind of emotional coolness or imperturbability lacking "either compassion or the capacity to arouse sympathy." Beyond this point, personalities seem to blend into the healthy population and we are no longer entitled even to speculate about the presence of predisposition to schizophrenia.

The faulty integration of mental life so characteristic of schizophrenic vulnerability appears capable of exaggerating various personality traits, in a manner analogous to the exaggerations seen in certain manic-depressives. (In the latter, irritability or "poor impulse control" seemed to be the factor behind these exaggerations.) This may account for the caricatures of obsessives or hysterics seen rather often in schizophrenics or their relatives. Many obsessional hand washers and other persons who are fanatical avoiders of "dirt" are either overtly schizophrenic or "borderline" (at least by the criteria of Kety or Gunderson; a few also by Kernberg's). This is especially true in our culture, whereas in relatively primitive cultures obsessive hand washing need not have such grave significance (Stone, 1970). Closer acquaintance with obsessive hand washers often reveals they are living out a delusion regarding germs, contamination, and so on. The same is true for a certain percentage of anorexia nervosa patients, especially when the symptoms are encased in unusually rigid and therapeutically unyielding character armoring. These patients will show no productive signs (at least initially), no formal thought disorder (though they may have bizarre fantasies about what the food would "do" to them if ingested). But their denial of illness is so profound, their resistance to clinical interventions and their chronicity so great, that the appraisal of psychic structure often has to be revised from borderline, as first seemed the case, to psychotic.

A woman of twenty-three had earned a reputation in her community as an opera singer. She was the only child of a rather passive father and an intensely ambitious mother, herself a singing teacher, who was determined to see her daughter established as one of the "greats." Shortly after a recital that received negative reviews, the patient developed an anorexia syndrome so severe that she required hospitalization (she had lost almost half her body weight, down to seventy-two pounds). Although she exhibited no productive signs or formal thought disorder, it was noted that she was negativistic and compulsive to a remarkable degree. One ritual that developed was a need to remain standing all during the waking day. No amount of persuasion could induce her to sit down. She denied all emotional problems and shortly thereafter signed out of the hospital against advice. Twelve years later she was admitted to a medical unit for realimentation because of profound anorexia and cachexia. Her weight was only sixty-six pounds. The physicians were unaware of her psychiatric hospitalization, but the psychiatric consultant remembered her from before. The denial of illness was as pronounced as ever. Now a teacher of voice, she was "content" to remain at home and had never ventured onto the street for nine or ten years, claiming "there's no need to; my pupils come to see me."

Although this patient had broken off all relationships with the psychiatric community and had never revealed her innermost thoughts to anyone, one feels entitled to speculate that a psychotic process underlay this clinical picture. The patient talked "normally" and professed health, but this assertion flew so violently in the face of reality that it carried her beyond "borderline" structure. She behaved as if responding to the symbolic rather than to the actual meanings of things. There was no real reason she dared not sit down; the act must have had secret and special meanings for her, rendering it "dangerous." An uncommunicative patient, one can only guess at what sitting, eating, venturing out, and other "forbidden" activities may have meant to her. At the same time, she showed no mood disturbance nor symptoms of other psychotic syndromes. Schizophrenia (or a disorder within the schizophrenic spectrum) seems the most likely, if unprovable, diagnosis. It is of interest that she did not even exhibit many of the features of Kety's B-3-type borderline schizophrenia (no vague or murky speech, for example), yet she was sicker than many overtly delusional patients.

Related to the attribute of eccentricity, but combining many other features of schizophrenic symptomatology, is a tendency found among certain ambulatory schizophrenics or relatives of schizophrenics. These persons may at times be referred for psychotherapy, but are largely unmotivated for any kind of change. Diagnostically they usually exhibit borderline structure. This tendency I find hard to describe with one adjective or even a phrase; the best label I can offer at the moment is the "malignant do-gooder." Any or all of the following traits may be present: intrusiveness, illogicality, manipulativeness (on a scale approaching the malicious), ingratitude, hypercriticalness, imperiousness, deviousness, fickleness, and a special kind of grandiosity in which the person fancies himself of tremendous importance to others (who actually regard him as a pest), whose lives he continually schemes, unbidden, to "improve." Since these persons relate to other people almost exclusively in terms of their own fantasies and illusions, their involvements quickly emerge as pseudoinvolvements, motivated by narcissistic interests only. They are completely blind to social cues and perceive themselves and others so unrealistically that they border on the psychotic.

A divorced woman in her late forties made numerous "urgent" calls at all hours of the day to her relatives pressing on them various schemes for improving their home decorations, making money via wild ventures about which she was momentarily enthusiastic, or for getting one relative to influence another behind the other's back. She shuttled back and forth between the east coast and a family estate in Oregon, claiming she was going to settle in one or the other place and get a job. Actually she never worked at all, relying on "allowances" from wealthy relations. She would barely alight in one spot when she would decide she was "needed" in the other, and would pack bag and baggage and return. When her mother died, she persuaded the family to move the coffin, at great expense, to the family plot in Oregon, but only weeks after the complicated manuever was effected she got them to move the coffin back to its original site. Shortly after her brother mentioned in passing that he had purchased a new sofa, she commissioned an artist to make for him an oil painting, the length of the sofa, charging the cost to him, but not apprising him of the arrangement. When a nursing home needed to be selected for an elderly relative, she initially agreed to the one chosen by the family council, but then set about immediately to undermine the choice. She hired Pinkerton men to investigate the nursing-home physician, after he disagreed with some requests of hers; when he got wind of it, he refused to remain responsible for the relative. Later she tried, unsuccessfully, to find a surgeon who was willing to shorten the legs of her son so he would be too short to serve in the armed forces. Throughout life she played the grand dame and fooled many people with her "charm." She was master at playing one faction off against another; those "in the know" were never able to convince the others, who were about to be taken advantage of, until it was too late.

Taken together, this woman's denial, flightiness, manipulativeness, impulsivity, lack of any interests or occupational skills, incapacity to be alone, and tendency to "split" others into opposing camps (representing the two sides of her own inner conflicts and split object-representations) spelled out *borderline* psychic structure. These qualities, even in the presence of her grandiosity and litigiousness, could not serve to establish her as within either the schizophrenic or manic-depressive spectrum. But, in addition, there were no less than six unequivocal schizophrenics in her immediate family (four among the first-degree relatives), many of whom were paranoid, querulous, and markedly eccentric. From a clinical standpoint one feels justified in assigning her to a location within the schizophrenic spectrum as a severe and "schizotypic" character disorder.

Abnormalities of Temperament in Borderline Patients

The following remarks stem from a recent study by the author on abnormalities of temperament in a large group of office patients (Stone, 1978c). One hundred and one patients, of whom thirty-four were borderline by Kernberg's criteria, were evaluated according to a seventy-two-item Temperament Index. The Index (Figure 10–3) is composed of five subscales (Depressive, Manic, Irritable, Paranoid, and Schizoid) plus a "nonspecific" group of four items. The sources of these items were the Kraepelinian descriptions (see above, pp. 324–328) plus the lists of descriptive phrases applying to schizophrenics and their abnormal but nonpsychotic relatives (Wolf and Berle, 1976, p. 18; see also Morgan et al., 1968, on "soft signs" in rehospitalized schizophrenics).

When the 101 patients were rank-ordered by means of their Global Assessment Score (GAS) when first seen, an inverse relationship was noted between this score and the number of Index items applicable to the patient. The average number of items (not broken down as to subscale) for the entire sample was 14.9; the twenty-two psychotic-structure patients averaged 21.5, the borderlines, 17.5, and the forty-five neurotics, 9.7.

A patient was considered *temperament-positive* ("T+") if he showed at least seven "Depressive" items, or six or more "Manic" items, or five or more "Irritable," or four or more "Paranoid," or five or more "Schizoid" items. Many borderline patients were T+ for more than one subscale. None of the healthier neurotic patients—with initial GAS higher than 56—was T+ on any subscale.[6]

Adequate information was available regarding the first-degree relatives in thirty of the thirty-four borderline patients. Of the 115 relatives there were 21 (18.3 percent) with a history of psychosis (7 schizophrenic, 6 schizoaffective, and 8 primary affective) and 18 (15.7 percent) with a borderline condition (4 borderline schizophrenic, one schizoaffective at the borderline level, 13 affective).

In the borderline group there were nineteen T+ patients. Eighteen had at least one affected first-degree relative, whereas among the eleven "T−" patients, only six had an ill relative. This difference (Fisher's test; $p = 0.15$) strongly suggests significance and implies that the presence of a temperament abnormality (as defined above) predicts the presence, in a borderline patient, of a positive family history of mental illness. This relationship was not observed in the neurotic group, where only six of the fourteen T+ patients had an ill relative (as did ten of the twenty-eight T− neurotics).

In the borderline group, although the affective subscales (Depressive, Manic, Irritable) were more often positive than the Paranoid or Schizoid

[6]In order to facilitate factor analysis, the index has recently been revised so that each item is scored on a five-point scale.

Depressive (D)

7 Bodily complaints; hypochrondriasis
13 Dissatisfaction (chronic) or pleasurelessness
15 Dysphoria (sadness, *Weltschmerz,* tearfulness)
16 Easy fatigability
21 Guilt over minor indiscretions
31 Indecisiveness
33 Inordinate examination fear
40 Joylessness in work
42 Lack of initiative
47 Morbid fear of poverty
53 Pessimism
57 Scrupulosity
59 Self-doubt; excessive worrying
60 Sexual inhibition
63 Suicidal ruminations
68 Terrifying dreams

Irritable (I)

1 Abusiveness
23 Heightened premenstrual irritability
29 Impracticality
30 Impulsivity
37 Irascibility
38 Irritability
39 Jealousy
41 Labile mood
46 Mild paranoid features (in a personality that is not *predominantly* paranoid)
48 Opinionated; dogmatic

Manic (M)

2 Alcoholism
3 Ambitiousness
4 Arrogance
6 Boastfulness
8 Bombastic, witty style
9 Brilliance that does not come to fruition; or dilettantism
11 Compulsive gambling
12 Desultory thought (jumping from one topic to another)
14 Distractibility
19 Extraverted; very "outgoing"
24 Heightened self-confidence; overoptimism; mild euphoria
28 Hypersexuality or promiscuity
32 Ineducability
34 Insensitivity or coarseness
35 Insubordinate
36 Intensity
43 Lack of insight
49 Overinvolvement in various schemes
52 Overspending
55 Raucous laughter or scatological humor or inveterate punning
62 Stubbornness
66 Talking too much, too fast, or too loud
67 Teasing others inordinately
71 "Wanderlust" (inability to settle in one place; constant need to travel or roam from one place to another)

Paranoid (P)

5 Blames others
20 Grudge holding; unforgiving
25 Humorless
26 Hypercritical of others
44 Litigious
54 Quarrelsome; querulous
56 Resentful
65 Suspicious (marked)—or—*intense* jealousy

Schizoid (S)

10 Circumstantial
17 Eccentricity
18 Excessively reserved
45 "Loner"
51 Overprecise
58 Self-consciousness (severe)
61 Shyness (moderate to extreme)
64 Superstitious
69 Unsociable
72 Withdrawn

Nonspecific (NS)

22 Haughtiness
27 Hypersensitivity to criticism
50 Oversensitive (in general)
70 Unsympathetic

Figure 10–3. Temperament Index: The Temperament Scales

scales, the "schizoid" items, as a group, were more closely correlated with a positive family history than were those of the remaining scales. Again, this relationship was not noted in the neurotic patients. Of interest, two of the neurotic (and outwardly obsessional) patients had as many as thirteen items on the manic scale: one later developed a full-blown manic psychosis four years after beginning psychoanalysis; the other, a man of twenty-six, had several hypomanic episodes during the course of psychotherapy.

A systematic analysis of temperament in borderline patients, using a questionnaire devised by Eva Kahn for eliciting information about the Index items, is currently underway at the New York Hospital–Westchester Division.

PART IV

Case Illustrations

Part IV of this book consists of a series of case illustrations arranged to constitute a dictionary of psychopathology ranging from the psychotic to the neurotic levels of personality organization. Examples are included of cases intermediate between paradigmatic schizophrenia and manic-depressive illness ("borderline" in the clinical realm) and cases satisfying the intermediate level of psychic organization ("borderline" in the structural sense). Various problem cases are shown: those appearing first as schizophrenia and emerging subsequently as manic-depressive, transitional cases where the nature of the underlying structure could not be stated unequivocally, and cases rendered difficult to diagnose through admixture of a drug-abuse factor.

I have relied on excerpts of interviews, or other examples of the patient's speech, so that the reader would be less biased by my own diagnostic impressions, being left freer to form his own opinions as he goes along. Comments have occasionally been interspersed within these excerpts to clarify the nature of the mood or tone of voice, when either would not be apparent from a written reproduction of someone's speech.

The case illustrations follow in sequence from the lowest Global Assessment Score to the highest. At the end of each case, I have appended some comments about what special points the material exemplified. Diagnostic impressions are divided into two sets: category based (which will include the traditional forms of psychodiagnosis) and dimension based. In some instances the case illustrates a well-known psychiatric syndrome (e.g., anorexia nervosa); if so, the "syndrome diagnosis" is also given. Accompanying the case illustrations is a family pedigree, outlining other instances, if any, of serious mental illness among relatives. The personality dimension is further analyzed for each case via the Personality-Profile Scale (Table

IV–1), which allows for demonstration of other relevant characterological and temperamental features besides the predominant one. Figure IV–6 outlines which items in each case were positive with respect to the contemporary systems for diagnosing borderline conditions.

Some further remarks on the various scales and diagrams used in Part IV are to found below.

The Global Assessment Scale (GAS) The GAS is modeled after the Menninger Health-Sickness Rating Scale (MHSRS) developed by Luborsky (1962). An outgrowth of the biometrics research section of the New York State Psychiatric Institute, the GAS, like the MHSRS, requires the clinician-rater to assign to the subject or patient he has just seen a number from 0 to 100. This number should reflect the total current level of adaptation, specifically, the lowest level at which the subject has functioned in the week just preceding any given assessment. The scale is "anchored" in the sense that both the lower and upper numbers represent absolute extremes (seldom encountered in nature): "zero," for the "absolutely" nonfunctional psychotic institutionalized patient who has ceased caring for himself or may even be relentlessly self-destructive. The "zero" individual would die unless attended constantly. The "100" number would be assigned the hypothetically ideally healthy person who, besides being asymptomatic, has positive features like warmth, integrity, and superior functioning in his areas of endeavor.

The GAS, developed by Endicott, Spitzer, et al. (1978), provides descriptions for each tenth point as guidelines in the scale's use (see Figure IV–1). In use only a few years, the GAS has not had the opportunity to be validated as extensively as the older MHSRS. Nevertheless, there is the advantage that there are no diagnostic hints included in the format. Furthermore, decile descriptions conduce to a greater spread of score assignments, whereas the MHSRS, with written clues at about every twenty-five points, tends to attract numbers on or close to these relatively few guideposts.

The Sz-MDP Continuum Diagram: Further Remarks The Sz-MDP continuum diagram, presented in Chapter 2, may be modified, through the use of the schizoaffective weighted rating scale (Chapter 8), to permit a more quantitative appraisal of the balance between typically schizophrenic and typically affective symptoms. Relative severity of illness may be indicated by placement of the points, chosen to represent the balance between schizophrenic and affective signs, up or down along a vertical axis. In Figure IV–2, the upper regions are set aside for greatest severity, the lower regions for milder cases. The horizontal component is marked off into regions ranging from schizophrenia without affective symptoms ("pure" Sz or 100/0) to "pure" MDP (no schizophrenic signs; 0/100). Arbitrarily I have chosen to place the relative measure of "schizophrenicness" in the numerator part of the ratio; the affective measure, below.

Figure IV–1. Global Assessment Scale (GAS)

Rate the subject's lowest level of functioning in the last week by selecting the lowest range which describes his functioning on a hypothetical continuum of mental health–illness. For example, a subject whose "behavior is considerably influenced by delusions" (range 21–30), should be given a rating in that range even though he has "major impairment in several areas" (range 31–40). *Use intermediary levels when appropriate* (e.g., 35, 58, 62). Rate actual functioning independent of whether or not subject is receiving and may be helped by medication or some other form of treatment.

Name of Patient __________ ID No. __________ Group Code __________
Admission Date __________ Date of Rating __________ Rater __________
GAS Rating: __________

100–91 Superior functioning in a wide range of activities, life's problems never seem to get out of hand, is sought out by others because of his warmth and integrity. No symptoms.

90–81 Good functioning in all areas, many interests, socially effective, generally satisfied with life. There may or may not be transient symptoms and "everyday" worries that only occasionally get out of hand.

80–71 No more than slight impairment in functioning, varying degrees of "everyday" worries and problems that sometimes get out of hand. Minimal symptoms may or may not be present.

70–61 Some mild symptoms (e.g., depressive mood and mild insomnia) OR some difficulty in several areas of functioning, but generally functioning pretty well, has some meaningful interpersonal relationships and most untrained people would not consider him "sick."

61–51 Moderate symptoms OR generally functioning with some difficulty (e.g., few friends and flat affect, depressed mood and pathological self-doubt, euphoric mood and pressure of speech, moderately severe antisocial behavior).

50–41 Any serious symptomatology or impairment in functioning that most clinicians would think obviously requires treatment or attention (e.g., suicidal preoccupation or gesture, severe obsessional rituals, frequent anxiety attacks, serious antisocial behavior, compulsive drinking, mild but definite manic syndrome).

40–31 Major impairment in several areas, such as work, family relations, judgment, thinking or mood (e.g., depressed woman avoids friends, neglects family, unable to do housework), OR some impairment in reality testing or communication (e.g., speech is at times obscure, illogical or irrelevant), OR single suicide attempt.

30–21 Unable to function in almost all areas (e.g., stays in bed all day) OR behavior is considerably influenced by either delusions or hallucinations OR serious impairment in communication (e.g., sometimes incoherent or unresponsive) or judgment (e.g., acts grossly inappropriately).

20–11 Needs some supervision to prevent hurting self or others, or to maintain minimal personal hygiene (e.g., repeated suicide attempts, frequently violent, manic excitement, smears feces), OR gross impairment in communication (e.g., largely incoherent or mute).

10–1 Needs constant supervision for several days to prevent hurting self or others (e.g., requires an intensive care unit with special observation by staff), makes no attempt to maintain minimal personal hygiene, or serious suicide act with clear intent and expectation of death.

SOURCE: Spitzer, Gibbon, and Endicott (1978).

Figure IV–2. The Sz-MDP Continuum

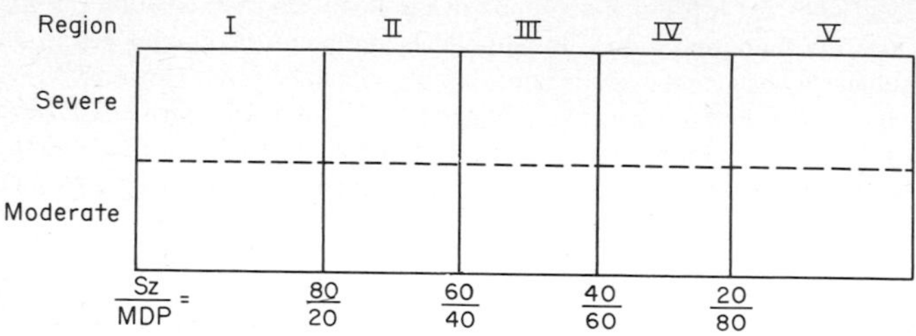

Region I: Clinically "pure" schizophrenic features, without any admixture of affective symptoms.

Region II: Predominantly schizophrenic schizoaffective disorders.

Region III: Schizoaffective disorders with evenly balanced symptom pictures.

Region IV: Predominantly affective schizoaffective disorders.

Region V: Clinically "pure" affective features without admixture of clinical signs and symptoms felt to be characteristic of schizophrenia.

This diagram provides for a dimensional measure, refining (where relevant) the traditional category-based approach to diagnosis. Compartmentalization of the continuum into five broad regions seems justifiable, because clinicians find it both comfortable and natural to subdivide "schizoaffective" into a predominantly schizophrenic group, a predominantly affective group, and a third that is symptomatically evenly divided. Further subdivisions would strain our conventional vocabulary, nor would they (at this time) serve any clear purpose therapeutically.

Personality-Profile Scale Each case illustration is represented, where sufficient information was available, on the Personality-Profile Scale (PPS; Table IV–1) filled out in accordance with the case (see Chapter 10). This form then serves as a *dimensional* measure of the personality ingredients relevant to that particular patient. The *category-based diagnosis* of personality may be said to derive from the latter, inasmuch as the personality type applied to the patient in traditional diagnosis corresponds to the subtype with the highest score on the PPS.

Figure IV–3 demonstrates the manner in which the PPS would be filled out on a hypothetical patient. This patient's most striking features were hysterical, phobic-anxious, infantile, and narcissistic. Since the highest score (8) was for the hysterical subtype, the conventional (category-based) personality diagnosis would read "hysterical personality."

The Family History Outline Accompanying most of the case illustrations is an outline of psychiatric disorders in the family of the patient.

The outlines are organized as follows: *seriously* affected *first-degree* relatives, if any, are described first. The total number of first degree relatives is also given. Next, *second-degree* relatives known to have had serious

TABLE IV–1

Scores on the Personality-Profile Scale for the Case Illustrations

Case number	*Hys*	*Obs*	*Depr*	*Phob*	*Inf*	*Pass*	*Par*	*Nar*	*Sch*	*Expl*	*Hypo*	*Inad*	*Anti*
1	6	1	4	0	2	0	7	8*	0	0	4	4	0
2	3	1	3	4	9*	3	4	3	1	0	0	2	0
3	6	7*	4	1	3	3	4	3	3	0	0	0	0
4	7	1	7	2	8*	7	7	7	5	2	4	2	1
5	5	2	4	1	9*	5	6	5	4	1	0	0	1
6	6	1	6	4	2	2	4	8*	3	0	0	0	0
7	1	2	2	0	0	3	7*	6	1	4	5	0	0
8	2	5	3	1	6	6	5	7*	4	0	0	0	0
9	8*	1	5	1	0	1	2	4	0	0	2	0	0
10	7	5	4	7	8	5	4	9*	3	3	2	0	2
11	2	6	4	5	0	1	7*	4	3	3	2	0	0
12	1	8*	1	2	2	2	4	5	3	0	0	0	0
13	5	2	3	2	1	3	6	8*	5	2	1	0	0
14	0	5	1	1	0	2	6*	5	3	1	0	0	0
15	1	5	2	3	2	5	1	6*	1	2	0	0	0
16	6*	2	2	1	2	2	4	5	2	1	0	0	0
17	7	0	4	1	6	7	5	7	1	2	0	1	8*
18	3	1	7	6	7	3	0	8*	1	0	0	0	0
19	5*	2	1	3	3	4	1	3	0	0	0	0	0
20	1	7	2	2	4	5	2	8*	2	0	0	0	0
21	5	4	7*	1	3	1	3	6	4	1	0	1	0
22†	—	—	—	—	—	—	—	—	—	—	—	—	—
23	0	6	0	0	0	3	9*	7	3	1	0	0	0
24	3	3	4	4	1	8*	2	6	3	0	0	0	1
25	2	2	3	2	0	0	2	1	7*	0	0	0	0
26	3	6	4	5	0	3	7*	2	3	1	0	0	0
27	1	8*	5	7	2	2	0	0	0	0	2	0	0
28	4	3	6*	2	5	4	1	3	1	0	0	0	0
29‡	9*	0	8	2	1	1	2	7	0	1	3	0	0

*The predominating personality feature.
†Data not available.
‡Pattern when first evaluated.

psychiatric disorders are described; their total number is also provided. Finally, brief descriptions are given of more distant relatives (such as cousins, great-grandparents) with serious disorders. Mention is also made in this last section of *less seriously* affected first- and second-degree relatives, ones whose psychiatric disorders do not meet strict diagnostic standards.

Figure IV–3. Personality-Profile Scale

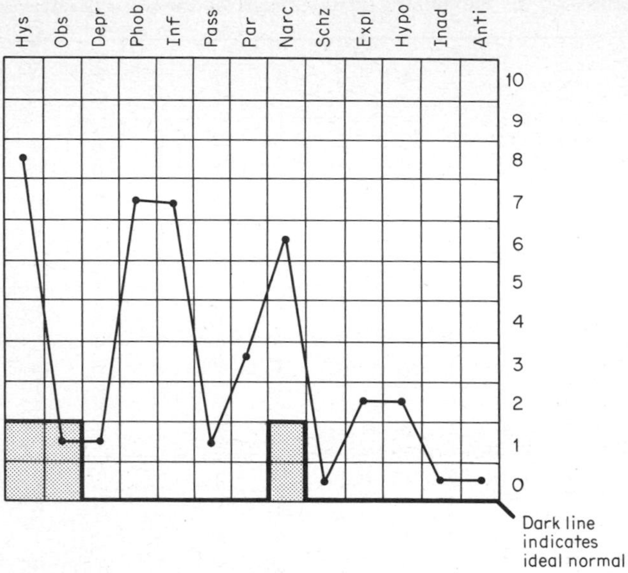

Hys Obs Depr Phob Inf Pass Par Narc Schz Expl Hypo Inad Anti

10 9 8 7 6 5 4 3 2 1 0

Dark line indicates ideal normal

KEY:

Hys	= hysterical	Par	= paranoid
Obs	= obsessive	Narc	= narcissistic
Depr	= depressive-masochistic	Schz	= schizoid
Phob	= phobic-anxious	Expl	= explosive
Inf	= infantile	Hypo	= hypomanic
Pass	= passive-aggressive	Inad	= inadequate

Anti = antisocial

Instructions: Rate subject on each of the thirteen subtypes of the scale with a point from 0 (indicating that the traits of this subtype are absent) to 10 (indicating striking); join the points to make the characterological profile.

Figure IV–4. Rorschach Card I

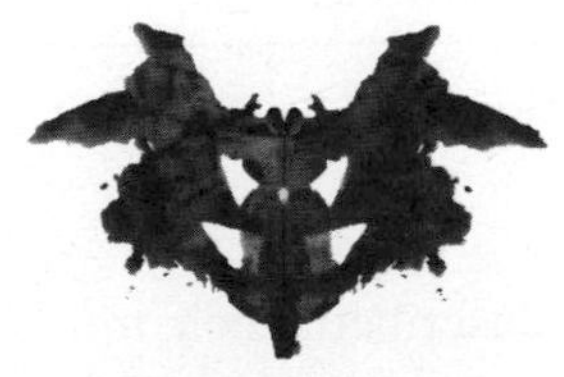

SOURCE: Rorschach (1951).

No total number is given for the relatives in this section, because it represents a mixed group; furthermore, the total number of third-degree relatives is not known for all the cases.

Since the majority of borderline patients are young, they seldom have children, let alone children who have passed part way through the age of risk for affective or schizophrenic illnesses. Hence "first-degree relatives" will almost always represent only the combined number of parents and siblings.

The Rorschach Throughout the case illustrations there are frequent allusions to the patient's percepts in response to the ten Rorschach blots. The first of the ten cards is reproduced here as Figure IV–4.

Category and Dimensional Diagnoses in the Case Illustrations

In most instances the case illustrations consist of clinical material followed by comments and a series of diagnostic impressions. Usually the clinical material consists of an interchange between interviewer and patient. A variety of interviewing styles will be noted, from the straightforward to the psychodynamically oriented to the confrontational. Some highlight the psychopathology in conventional terms; others highlight the resistiveness of the patient to any candid talk about his or her difficulties and focus on the intensity of *denial* or on the severity of *splitting* and other primitive mechanisms. In most instances comments of a sort that would "reveal" diagnosis are left to the end, in order to minimize the degree to which the reader becomes biased or nudged into perfunctory agreement with my own impressions.

The time cube (see Chapter 7) may be utilized to portray changes in the clinical picture as the patient's condition evolves over the course of some months or years. Case illustrations 1, 4, and 29 demonstrate this sort of occasion variance; for case 1 a time cube has been provided for illustrative purposes (see Fig. IV–7).

Diagnostic Syndromes

On occasion the diagnostic impressions outlined just above will not do full justice to the case, because the patient also appears to partake of some well-established psychiatric syndrome.

Generally speaking, these syndrome labels are a shorthand in which impressions from two or even three universes of discourse are telescoped. The term "hysteroid" of Easser and Lesser, for example, is a condensation of hysterical personality and worse-than-neurotic structure. In Donald Klein's "hysteroid dysphoria" the "constitution" dimension is also included (see Chapter 9). "Anorexia nervosa" is a useful term, since it immediately evokes an image of a young woman with severe emotional problems centering on individuation-separation and on acceptance of femininity. The term crisscrosses over the three diagnostic dimensions I use in the book in an unpredictable fashion. Some "anorectics" are obsessional and depressive, others mostly narcissistic, still others "symbiotic" or phobic, and so on. Those sick enough to warrant hospitalization are naturally borderline at best, and some will have psychotic structure. Many anorectics in office practice are neurotic. Because the term "anorexia nervosa" adds something not readily captured in my usual approach, I add it where pertinent to the other diagnostic impressions. For similar reasons I have added other applicable syndrome labels at the end of my diagnostic formulation. Some of the patients in the case illustrations have been called "pseudoneurotic schizophrenic" by Polatin or "hysteroid dysphoric" by Klein or "borderline" in structure by Kernberg. In many instances, therefore, there is authenticity to these labels, although for reasons of confidentiality I have not indicated which patients were so diagnosed by the originators of these various terms.

The Patient Universe of the Case Illustrations: Further Remarks

The bulk of the case illustrations concern patients in the intermediate to high ranges of severity of symptoms (see Figure IV–5). Partly this may reflect my own clinical experience, at least half of which derives from work with hospitalized patients. But in addition it is within this range that some

Figure IV–5. Sz-MDP Loci of Patients in the Case Illustrations

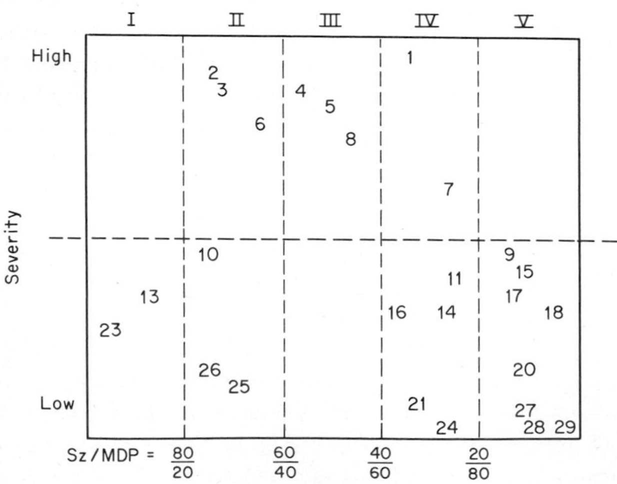

NOTE: Case 12 not relevant to the Sz-MDP continuum; cases 19 and 22 omitted because of insufficient information.

of the more challenging diagnostic problems are encountered, and it was upon these that I wished to focus my attention. All the patients in the illustrative cases spent at least a brief period in the hospital except for cases 19, 21, 22, 23, 25, 26, 27, and 28.

For the most part the interviews were geared to reveal psychic structure (via response to confrontation, etc.), characterological fine points, and the degree and type of relatedness. One will not find questions of the sort, "Did you hear voices?" even though these are crucial questions in determining the presence and variety of a possible psychosis. These questions were asked on separate occasions and the results usually related in a summary of anamnestic data. Instead, even in patients with psychotic structure, the material reflects the efforts made to establish meaningful emotional contact. Usually it was possible to establish a structural diagnosis, though occasions arose where this was indeterminate.

As a group the patients were brighter than average, in some cases considerably so. None had below-average intelligence. Wechsler Adult Intelligence Scale (WAIS) scores were available for all but three. The verbal IQ was in the 90 to 110 range in four instances (cases 1, 2, 16, and 18) and was in the very superior range (greater than 130) in another five (cases 8, 12, 14, 20, and 24). Scores in the remainder were in the 111 to 130 range. The *average* verbal IQ was 116 (the average full-scale IQ was 111.5, since performance IQ was lowered considerably in some patients, apparently in connection with severe anxiety). In average verbal IQ the eight patients with psychotic structure did not differ significantly from those in the borderline group.

Lest the reader object to this sample as being unrepresentative of the population at large (which it surely is), it may be worth pointing out that the average verbal IQ in over 300 patients on whom the tests were performed—during ten years of admissions to the General Clinical Service at New York State Psychiatric Institute—was 122. These 300 patients were selected on clinical grounds as being likely to benefit from intensive, analytically oriented psychotherapy. A similar mixture of borderline and psychotic structures was present in this larger sample.

It seems very likely that the "borderline" patient of interest to the analyst does enjoy better-than-average intellectual, especially verbal, capacities. The experience at the McLean Hospital in Belmont, Massachusetts, compared closely with the findings just mentioned.

For pedagogical purposes the clinical vignettes were chosen in many instances not only because they illustrate some of the subtleties of diagnosis well, but because they do so in a dramatic or poignant, hence easily remembered, way. But case illustrations do not exist only in psychiatric annals. Often examples are to be found in literature, superior in impact and even in "clinical" thoroughness to anything one is likely to read in a psychiatric text. Few case descriptions of the obsessive personality, for example, can be compared in detail, let alone readability, with Goncharov's *Oblomov*. Similarly, nothing can be found in this book to compare with the figure of Charlotte in Joan Didion's novel *A Book of Common Prayer* (1977) for portrayal of what would seem to be a borderline individual with narcissistic personality features.

Before examining the case material, it should be noted that a number of modifications and devices were used to safeguard the confidentiality of the patients from whom this material was derived. Names have been fictional-

Figure IV–6. The Case Illustrations: Positive Items according to Various Borderline Criterion Sets

		Kernberg items						Gunderson items								Spitzer Schizotypal unstable items														
Case	Str.	1	2	3	4	5	6	1	2	3	4	5	6	7	8	1	2	3	4	5	6	7	8	9	10	11	12	13	14	15
1	P		X	X	X	X	X	X	X			X		X	?	X		X		X	X	X			X			X		
2	P		X	X		X	X	X					X					X		X				X					X	X
3	P		X	X	X		X	X	X		X		X	X	X	X	X	X		X	X	X	X	X	X	X			X	
4	P		X	X	X	X	X	X	X					X		X	X	X		X		X	X	X	X	X		X	X	X
5	P		X	X	X	X	X	X	X	X			X	X		X		X	X	X	X	X	X	X	X	X	X	X	X	X
6	P		X	X	X	X	X	X	X	X		X	X	X		X		X	X	X	X	X	X	X	X	X	X	X	X	X
7	P		X	X	X	X	X	X	X				X	X		X	X	X		X	X			X	X	X		X		
8	P		X	X			X	X					X							X		X	X						X	X
9	B	X	X	X	X	X	X	X	X	X	X	X	X	X	X									X	X	X	X	X	X	X
10	B	X	X	X	X		X	X	X	X	X	X	X	X	X	X		X		X	X	X	X	X	X	X	X	X	X	X
11	B	X	X	X	X	X	X	X	X	X	X	X	X	X	?				X	X		X	X			X	X	X		X
12	B	X	X	X			X		X			X		X	(1)						X	X	X			X				
13	B	(2)	X	X	X		X	X	X		X	X		X		X	X	X		X	X	X	X	X		X			X	
14	B	X	X	X	X	X	X	X	X	X	X	X		X	X						X	X	X			X	X		X	
15	B	X	X	X	X		X	X	X	X	X	X	X												X	X	X	X		
16		(3)	X	X	X	X	X	X	X	X	X	+	X	X	(4)					X		X	X	X	X	X	X	X	X	X
17	B	X	X	X	X	X	X	X	X	X	X		X	X	X			X			X	X	X	X	X	X	X	X	X	X
18	B	X	X	X			X	X				X	X		X								X	X				X	X	X
20	B	X	X	X	X	X	X	X	X	X	X	X		X	X					X	X	X					X		X	
21	B	X	X	X		X	X	X			X	X	X	X	?	X	X	X				X	X			X		X	X	
23	P		X	X			X	X						X	X			X			X	X	X			X				
24	B	X	X	X	X	X	X	X	X		X	X	X		X	‡			X	X	X			X	X			X		
25	B→N	X		X				X		(5)	X	X	X	X	?	X		‡				X	X			X				
26	B	X	X	X			X				X	X	X	X	?		X	X		X	X	X	X			X			X	
27	N	X		X			X								?							X						X		X
28	B→N	X		X			X					X	X	X								X				X	X			X
29	B→N (a)	X	X	X	X	X	X	X	X	X	X	X	X	X	?		X				X	X		X	X	X	X	X	X	X
	(b)	X		X								X	X									X							X	

KEY:

Kernberg Items:

1. Reality testing intact
2. Poor ego integration
3. Lowered anxiety tolerance
4. Poor impulse control
5. Poor capacity for sublimatory channeling
6. Primitive defenses

ized; allusions to specific places and incidents have been changed; pec locutions that might constitute a "signature" of a particular person ha been replaced by remarks of a comparable sort that are no longer identi able. Many of the case descriptions are derived from two or three very similar patients—their initial GAS scores were identical—such that the psychological test data reflect the responses of a patient different in identity from the patient alluded to in the dialogue. The family pedigrees have been altered so as to contain the same number of disorders within the same degrees of relatedness but, in many instances, assigned to different family

Gunderson Items:

1. Lowered achievement
2. Impulsivity
3. Manipulative suicide gestures
4. Brief psychotic episodes
5. Good socialization
6. Depressive affect
7. Rageful affect
8. Psychological tests characterized by good performance on the structured portions and impaired performance on the unstructured portions

Spitzer Items (1–8, "schizotypal"; 9–15, "unstable"):

1. Odd communication
2. Ideas of reference
3. Suspiciousness or paranoid ideation
4. Illusions
5. Magical thinking
6. Diminished rapport
7. Exaggerated social anxiety or hypersensitivity to criticism
8. Social isolation
9. Unstable relationships
10. Impulsivity in at least two areas
11. Inappropriate, intense anger
12. Self-damaging acts
13. Affective instability
14. Emptiness or boredom
15. Problems tolerating being alone

Explanatory Notes:

(1) Intact on both structured and unstructured portions.
(2) At time of interview, but not intially.
(3) Variable over time.
(4) Not intact on the structured portions.
(5) In the past only; none recent.
(*a*) Initially.
(*b*) At follow-up.

According to the Spitzer schema, the patients could be partitioned into five groups: (*a*) schizotypal (23, 26), (*b*) predominantly schizotypal (12, 13, 21, 25), (*c*) mixed (10, 11, 14, 17, 20, and 24), (*d*) predominantly unstable (16, 29), and (*e*) unstable (9, 15, 18, 28). All the patients with psychotic and borderline structures were positive with respect to the item "identity disturbance"; this item was omitted (as taken for granted) from the table.

members from those who actually exhibited these conditions. The case illustrations are thus pastiches, reworked so as to preserve as much clinical freshness as possible, while obscuring the actual identities of the patients.

From Figure IV–6 the reader can quickly determine which patients satisfied the criteria of which important system for diagnosing borderline conditions. Furthermore, it will be apparent that a few patients (13, 23, 26) were almost exclusively "schizotypal," and one (9) was predominantly "unstable," according to the criteria of Spitzer et al. (1979). The majority, as is true with borderline patients in general, showed a clinical picture that was mixed with respect to the two factors embodied in the Spitzer schema.

Cases

Case Illustration 1

Patient = P   Doctor = D   GAS = 7

P: I'm an actress . . . I have *five* faces: the Devil, El diablo, Satan, Lucifer . . . *(blocked)*.

D: And who is the fifth?

P: Ray Milland. I can see through you, doctor . . . you're my son. . . . I feel old enough to be your mother. I accomplished a great deal on "7": I cleared out the whole seventh floor. I did it all by myself. Just let me out now: If I can do anything for this hospital let me know . . . money, anything. I've been through five hells . . . that's right . . . I've died . . . lived through death . . . five times.

D: Whose voices did you hear?

P: Eichmann, Castro, Diablo, the Russians . . . I need new glasses, doctor. . . . My vision is blurred. . . . Things look different than they did . . . I was born . . . Adam and Eve . . . at age four . . . innocence . . .

I had every sin . . . every evil. . . . Why else would God punish me by giving me a mother that didn't show love or affection, and a brutal father? *(tears)* . . . It's warm in here . . . I want to get out . . . home *(smiled)*.

D: How did you feel about your baby brother?

P: I wanted to kill him, hurt him, beat him, hit him. . . . I'm a genius, supergenius . . . Jesus Christ. . . . I hate myself because I can cry. . . . I couldn't cry [when I was young] because I was evil . . . the voice [of God] told me to be good. . . . Mrs. Ephraim and I want out! She'll kill herself. . . . I can't live through another death . . . I want to see my son . . . I'm an Egyptian! . . . I'm all wrapped up like a mummy . . . I don't want to be a mummy, I want to be a mommy! I'm Spanish, Negro, Jewish, Scotch . . . I know I'm Scotch, because I like to drink Scotch . . . with *ice!*

Throughout this interchange, the patient spoke with some pressure, paced the floor, opening and closing her hospital gown in a seductive manner. There was some affective display, rather labile, and either inappropriate to the examiner's question, or "appropriate" to some inner feeling state about which the interviewer had only an imperfect idea.

Anamnestic Data

The patient was a twenty-six-year-old married woman with two young children. A year before her first hospitalization (from which the material in the case illustration is derived), she had felt under increasing "pressure" from her family, including her parents, because of extra responsibilities and conflicting loyalties. Until just before admission, no abnormalities were noted, apart from argumentativeness and irritability. But immediately after a visit with some relatives, she became overactive, garrulous, and preoccupied with strange ideas about religion and philosophy. She felt she was a "saint" inspired to lead others to the True Way, and felt her thoughts were broadcast over the radio as soon as they occurred in her mind. Self-depreciatory delusions existed side by side with the grandiose ones. Voices commanding her to save the world were also experienced. After creating a disturbance on a street corner, she was taken to a psychiatric receiving hospital, where the diagnostic impression of "acute schizophrenic reaction" was recorded. Treatment with large amounts of phenothiazines led to control of her symptoms within five weeks.

Subsequent Course

A year later, also following a visit to relatives, the patient again required hospitalization. Pushed speech and hyperactivity were noted, along with suicidal ruminations and command hallucinations (voices now instructing her to make a sacrifice of herself to save others). She was hospitalized for two months; diagnosis and treatment were the same as on the original admission.

Two similar hospitalizations had to be arranged for similar psychotic episodes over the next two years. Bizarre delusions were present for several months at a time on each occasion. The hostility, grandiosity, and seductiveness noted earlier were especially marked during the fourth admission. Nevertheless, at intervals when she was under better control, the hospital staff found her outgoing and friendly.

The following year, she was readmitted for an episode of hyperactivity and pacing, along with the productive signs present on other occasions. The diagnostic impression had now shifted to that of manic-depressive illness, and she was given a trial of lithium, to which she responded favorably. In between hospitalizations she functioned reasonably well, and was more often depressed than elated. She actually preferred the depressed state to the hypomanic one.

A sixth admission a year later was for a similar outbreak, although there was now a less marked degree of thought disorganization.

The last admission, again preceded by quarrels within the family, was accompanied by religiosity, hyperactivity, deterioration in grooming, and a delusion consisting of the belief she could read other peoples' minds. This last state would alternate with a more lucid one in which she no longer claimed these special powers. Lability of affect with occasional inappropriate giggling was more apparent than in some of the earlier episodes. After treatment with lithium led to relief of her symptoms, she was able to relate that she had stopped taking this medication the month before her last episode, on the assumption that she was well and could afford to dispense with it.

The varying diagnostic impressions registered about this patient (who has been well-controlled on lithium and quite comfortable for the past ten years) in the earlier part of her course are depicted in a time cube diagram (Figure IV–7). No periodicity involving season was noted throughout her course.

Comments

This patient has been followed for almost twenty years and is of special interest because her first decompensation occurred just a few years before lithium began to be used at teaching centers in this country.

Thorazine had already been available for some six or seven years. The original diagnosis of "acute schizophrenic reaction" is thus only in part a reflection of certain "schizophrenic" features in her psychological profile at that time. Thought broadcast, inappropriateness of affect, poor rapport, and command hallucinations are all more reminiscent of schizophrenia than of manic psychosis, though all can occur in the florid state of either. The other important factor leading to the schizophrenic diagnosis was the men-

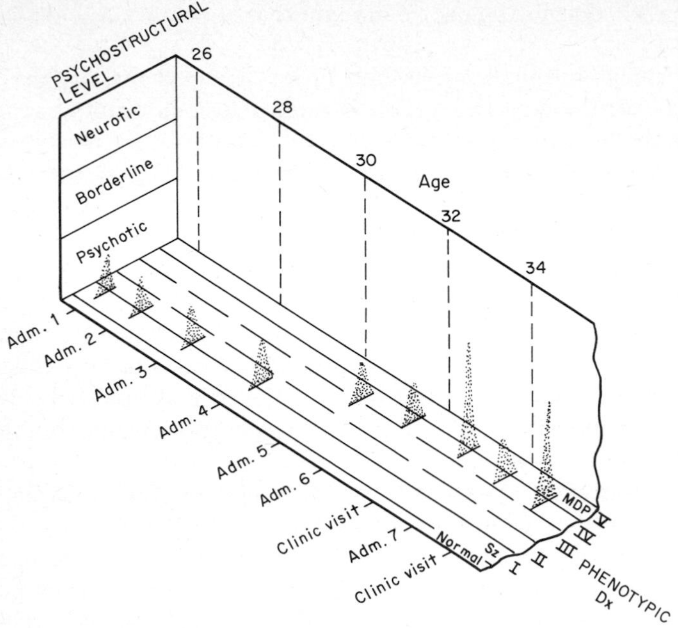

Figure IV–7. Time-Cube Diagram for Case Illustration 1

tal set of American clinicians of that era. The category of schizophrenia seemed much more attractive a choice, given the totality of her symptoms, than did mania, which simply loomed less large in everyone's consciousness at that time. So the patient's pushed speech, hyperactivity, and flight of ideas were relatively ignored or else construed as epiphenomena of a certain variety of schizophrenia.

When lithium came into wider use, and the manic-depressive disorders were back on the diagnostic map, the physicians who came in contact with this patient over the ensuing years began to construe the manifestations of her psychotic episodes (which were more alike than different over the years) as more in keeping with a bipolar manic-depressive disorder. The shift in base (for constitutional factors) in the time-cube diagram reflects the shift in clinical diagnoses made during her successive hospitalizations. Presumably her true constitutional underpinnings remained the same throughout, and were merely misperceived at the outset. In this respect she resembles the case reported by Harrison Pope (1976), who also commented on a shift in diagnosis from schizophrenia to MDP as having arisen more out of "changing awareness of the psychiatric profession" than out of a change in symptoms. Like many manic-depressives, the patient sprang back to rather *good* interpsychotic function, even though she was grossly incapacitated ("GAS" only 7) when first seen.

When one reviews this patient's course and symptoms over the many years she has been followed, one is struck by the fact that even bipolar MDP—as a category—does not do perfect justice to the case, even though she has "settled" for over a decade into this region of the spectrum. Even when well, some eccentricity of thought is present, and the bizarreness of thought when ill has always been easier to fit into a schizophrenic than into a manic-depressive mold. The family history is positive for major disorders in a parent (manic-depressive in type) and a sib (more schizophrenic in character, but less is known about his symptom picture). Phenotypically, at least, it seems appropriate to place the patient in the schizoaffective portion of the Sz-MDP continuum *nearer* to MDP but not in the region of "pure" MDP. From a psychostructural standpoint, this patient has shifted over time from "psychotic" to "borderline": she still shows Kernberg's nonspecific features, along with faulty ego integration, even during her stable state. Since improvement, in her particular case, is more owing to good pharmacological control than to having reached a higher level of adaptation via psychotherapy, her vulnerability to decompensation—when off drugs—is still high.

Final Diagnostic Impressions

A. Categorical diagnoses
   1. Manic-depressive disorder, bipolar-I type
   2. Currently recompensated
   3. Narcissistic personality with hysterical features
B. Dimensional assessments
   1. Region IV on Sz-MDP continuum
   2. Originally, psychotic personality organization; GAS = 7
      Currently, borderline organization; GAS = 50
   3. Personality profile as shown in Table IV–1

Case Illustration 2

Patient = P Doctor = D GAS = 17

The patient, a woman in her early twenties, came into the consulting office at the hospital where she had recently been admitted. She walked in very slowly, apprehensively, and spoke in an almost inaudible monotone throughout the interview.

D: You seem extraordinarily reluctant to shake my hand . . .
P: I am.
D: . . . Let's hear what comes to mind about that.
P: I didn't want to get you filthy and I didn't want to get filthy.
D: Uh-huh. *(Pause)* Which of us do you think was more at risk?
P: *(Long pause)* I am.
D: You are just being gracious or that's how you feel? You see yourself as

filthier than I am *(very, very long pause)*. Yet there is some concern that a little filth could have rubbed off from me onto you. Let me hear about that.

P: Everybody is filthy to me *(long pause)*.

D: But again, you're saying that, not to single me out as being particularly filthy? You don't have feelings that certain people are particularly filthy?

P: Certain people are dirtier than others.

D: Who shall go nameless? *(Very long pause)*.

P: I can't explain why I feel that way, but I do.

D: Well, who do you see as high up on your dirty list or whatever?

P: My father.

D: Do you think of him in a sense as a dirty old man, so to speak?

P: No.

D: No? *(Long pause)* You're making . . .

P: I don't know what he's like.

D: You don't . . . but you kind of assume that he would be rather filthy; somewhat more so than most people? *(Long pause)*

P: I used to think um . . . that I had discovered . . . that I had discovered something that nobody else had discovered about the truth of the filth in the world but I realize now that . . . that . . . that it's not true and I realize that to other people *(pause)* the filth that I feel isn't true, but . . . *(long pause)*.

D But what?

P: But I still believe it.

P: *(Long pause)* I've never done anything that I considered really terrible, but I feel like my . . . feelings of filth come from a feeling inside and come out in my pores, and . . . and when you menstruate, things are going on inside your body. I really . . . I really . . . I don't know. . . . *(Pause)* I mean the feeling of being filthy is always there but it does get intensified at certain times.

D: *(Interrupting)* Well, when was the very first time you can recall having had feelings of being extra dirty?

P: I don't remember having feelings of my . . . way back, of myself being extremely dirty but I stopped touching things, uh, glue, things that you can be creative with.

D: You're a little afraid of *creativity,* are you?

P: I don't know if I'm afraid of being a success or a failure.

D: You ever pondered what it would be like to have a baby?[1] *(Long pause)*

[1]The interviewer wonders whether she is referring indirectly to sexual organs—as "things you can be creative with."

P: Yes . . . *(nervous laugh)* I feel I can't touch babies.
D: Oh really?
P: I feel like I have that little smirk on my face that I get so often.
D: What is it about touching babies?
P: *(Pause)* I guess it has to do with *caring (pause)*.
D: I'm not sure what you're referring to, exactly.
P: *(Silence)*
D: *They* seem a little extra dirty, also, or what?
P: Well. *(Pause)* I have this feeling when I sweat and stuff, that it's not really just *sweat*. It's urine and stuff, and babies do, ya know . . .
D: Do what?
P: Do urinate in diapers or without diapers. And *(pause)* I mean I'm . . . very aware of my symptoms but as to where they came from or why they're there *(pause)* or what to do to get rid of them *(pause)* . . .

D: Have there been times when you *feel* confused as to who you are?
P: Yes *(long pause)*.
D: Uncomfortably confused or just confused?
P: Uncomfortably.
D: Uh-huh. *(Very long pause)*
P: I'd remember being in a restaurant and a woman was talking to herself and my family was laughing at her *(pause)* and . . . my mother . . . who had said she must be a crazy woman *(pause)* and that it was sad and yet I remember them laughing.
D: Uh-huh. *(Long pause)*
P: I think I was eating steamed clams—funny *(laughs) I never go near them now*. *(Pause)* I can't eat with my hands.
D: But the fear is that you might wind up like that lady?
P: No.
D: Sounds to me like that scene made a big impression on you, as if you could see yourself being laughed at by some people at a next table. *(Long pause)*
P: I don't feel like . . . I'll wind up like that woman.
D: How do you feel you'll wind up?
P: Sometimes I feel completely hopeless . . . *(long pause)* and sometimes I feel like there's just gotta be a way.
D: Well, do you really think there's a "way," since you say you're worried that you could wind up *(pause)* dying by your own hands someday . . . *(Long pause)*
P: It's nice to think about.
D: Is it?! In what way? *(Long pause)*
P: I guess what is always coming to my mind when I think of suicide is that, um, the bugs won't even wanna eat me 'cause of my filth.

D: Therefore, you'll be in a high state of preservation? *(Long pause)* You will not decompose, like the *rest* of us? *(Long pause)*

P: I'll just rot. *(Long pause)* When I . . . I used to think of cremation *(pause)* and then that people used to make ashes; *soap* from people's ashes. *(Pause)* Ya know, all soap is, *is* animal fat. *(Long pause)*

D: Are there moments when you feel some hopefulness about the future?

P: *(Pause)* Yes.

D: What do you see yourself doing, under those circumstances?

P: As an occupation?

D: For example.

P: Getting married.

D: And having babies *(long pause)*. It doesn't seem all too messy to you; babies? *(Long pause)*

P: Not if I'm with somebody who cares about me.

Psychological Test Data

Full-scale IQ = 95 (verbal = 100, performance = 92). There was considerable scatter in subtest scores, ranging from 5 (picture arrangement) to 13 (similarities). No evidence of organicity was found. Facial expression was noted to be blank; the voice, expressionless.

Contact with reality seemed variable, within the structured portions of the test battery: some of the difficult "similarities" were done correctly, while the easier ones were missed; picture-completion performance was below average.

Impairment in reality testing was noted in the unstructured tests, as well as a high degree of personalized responses. Loss of distance from the test stimuli was manifest, for example, in one of the TAT responses: "That's my mother when she had her hysterectomy, and they're cutting her open—and they're taking out a fetus from the abortion she once had."

Many images of death and decay appear, or living creatures are seen as "crushed," "lifeless," "torn apart," and so on. To the sentence completion question, "I get most depressed when I . . . ," the response was, ". . . looked in the mirror and saw it was me."

The Rorschach percepts were often idiosyncratic, with many *F*− responses; on card II a "face that's all dirty" was visualized and then "explained" with the comment, ". . . that's how I look when I come back from my boyfriend's."

The diagnostic impression to emerge from the test data was that of a "schizoaffective disorder, depressed type."

Comments

The patient's extreme preoccupation with the theme of dirtiness, coupled with her inability to distinguish (1) actual dirt from figurative "dirt" (forbidden thoughts, shameful acts, etc.) or (2) her "dirtiness" from that of anyone near her constitute a breakdown of ego boundary as well as an *idée fixe* of delusional proportions. She experiences similar confusion between sweat and urine; symbol and the thing symbolized are equated rather than merely analogized. In other contexts she loses touch with the nature of her real fears (having babies) and is conscious only of fears related symbolically (artistic creativity, paste used by artists, etc.). The primitivity of defenses—denial and projection—is so great that at first she is willing to talk only on a symbolic plane; she gives the impression that, without prodding, she would never get down to the fundamental issues that precipitated her hospitalization: depression, suicide gestures, difficulties with her family, and so on. The level of psychostructural organization is thus psychotic. Toward the end of the interview there is an example of loosening of associations: "cremation—soap—all soap is animal fat. . . ."

The constitutional factor appears to involve a mixture of schizophrenic symptoms (bizarre boundary confusion, flatness of affect, a formal thought disorder with loosening of associations, illogicality) and depressive symptoms (suicidal ruminations and gestures, self-depreciation). There is a strong family history of severe psychiatric disorders, mostly affective but in at least one well-documented instance, schizoaffective. In the patient, the schizophrenic elements predominated over the affective, on the order of 80/20 (according to the modified Cohen rating scale).

Though paranoid, phobic, and hysterical traits were readily apparent, they were overshadowed by infantile features.

Final Diagnostic Impressions

A. Categorical diagnoses
   1. Schizoaffective disorder, depressed type
   2. Psychotic structure
   3. Infantile personality with paranoid and phobic features

B. Dimensional assessments
   1. Region II of the Sz-MDP continuum
   2. GAS = 17
   3. Personality profile as shown in Table IV–1

FAMILY HISTORY

First-degree relatives =	3 (parents, plus 1 sib)
affected member:	(1) father (bipolar-II manic-depressive illness, treated with lithium and imipramine)
Second-degree relatives =	5
affected members:	(1) maternal aunt (severe depression)
	(2) paternal grandfather (hospitalized for depression)

Third-degree relatives affected members:	(precise number unknown) (1) maternal female cousin (schizoaffective psychosis, hospitalized) (2) paternal great-aunt (hospitalized for depression) (3) paternal great-uncle (suicidal)
Other relatives affected members:	(1) paternal great-great aunt (suicided) (2) paternal great-great grandfather (suicided)

Case Illustration 3

Patient = P Doctor = D GAS = 23

The patient, who entered the consultation room looking very anxious, described her conviction that the people around her, nurses and patients alike, are angry with her and that the nursing staff in particular would most likely not regard her as an adult.

D: I'm puzzled what you meant when you said you were afraid we would not treat you as an adult. I've heard, for instance, you'd done some things one might regard as somewhat childish.
P: For instance?
D: Well, hiding in back of the piano, being silent for days on end . . .
P: I still do that . . .
D: . . . things, in other words, that would place strain on whoever would try to treat you on an adult level. *(Pause; the patient remains silent)*
D: I'm wondering how you square your wish to be treated as an adult with that sort of behavior?
P: Well, those *are* the very things which I hope will . . . it's just that everything about my behavior is so bad, childish, disgusting—that if I manifest it somebody will be able to . . . *(blocks)* it just occurred to me that my saying it automatically makes everyone think of me as a child; in other words, this is one more manifestation of that impulsive bad childish behavior that I just think about wanting to be treated on an adult level, that a person can never *say* something like that: they have to *do* it. They have to show they are capable, in fact, of interacting that way . . . and they . . . they'll be treated in kind, but, uh, what I was saying that—in the *beginning,* no matter how I behaved, I behaved in such a way as to show how *unfeminine* I was . . .
D: "Unfeminine"?
P: Yes.

The patient began to explain how overt expression of anger is a prerogative, and therefore virtually a manifestation, of being male.

P: I feel anger all the time, when I try to *control* myself *(said almost inaudibly)*.
D: Huh?
P: I said, "I feel anger all the time, when I try to control myself."
D: Like *now?*
P: Not so much now, but when I *leave* here, I will, I suppose. I'll become very angry because it's a lost opportunity.
D: You also indicated before you were angry at *me* for sitting in judgment!
P: Yes. Umm. . . .
D: Is that still smouldering in you?
P: It'll come back *(nervous laugh)*.
D: It'll come back?
P: I feel angry *(pause)* . . . whenever I'm in a new test . . . which anybody else . . . could do, instead of *wanting to do it*. The task is something I see somebody else can do, and he's doing it "against" me, so instead of wanting to learn how to do the task, when I imagine myself wanting to learn it, I become incredibly angry with self-hatred. Particularly self-hatred. Having self-hate has always been my anger—when I imagine having to control myself and not do the things I want to do. I can't do anything else. I can't enjoy anything else, and I feel incredibly angry. I can appreciate certain songs. Certain music that has notes that I may have once liked . . . might have once pleased me; but I feel completely *controlled* . . .
D: By whom? Or by what?
P: Myself . . .
D: Have you at times felt controlled by people or things *outside* you?
P: They're always *inside* me . . . but it depends on the extent I identify with whatever was controlling me . . . inside of me . . . whether I identified with the controller, or the person *being* controlled. And what'd happen was, I wouldn't identify with *either* of them, so that . . .
D: The "person being controlled"?
P: In other words . . . *both* of them are *me:* the person controlling and the one controlled are both me, and I didn't identify with *either* of them.
D: Like there's a third "me" in back of both.
P: A "third" me in back of both, yes . . . there's a person who's *controlling,* that I look upon as some sort of stereotype of sterility . . . there's a person who's being controlled, which I look upon as a stereotype of repulsiveness.
D: And then there's a third "real" you in back of all that . . .
P: Um-humm . . .
D: . . . and what is *she* up to?
P: Oh, she dreams, she used to think . . .
D: What sort of stuff?

P: Well, now I dream about complicated scenes with lots of action, many characters, and I always . . . (*looks* sad, *suddenly*).
D: You looked sad, I thought, as you talked of this "real" you . . .
P: She never comes out *(said sotto voce, and very poignantly)*.
D: Never!
P: *(Pause)* No . . . and yet that's the way I could enjoy. . . . If I could be the real "me" . . .

The patient goes on to describe a relationship with a man who found her attractive and interesting.

P: I felt straitjacketed because I felt that a woman had to behave a certain way. She had to be dumb and docile. Either that or she had to be cruel and biting or sharp, and I always felt that if I *were* cruel and sharp . . . and the sharpness was so spread out, I mean . . . this constant idea of a woman as sharp and cruel—was so complete that I wouldn't . . . I refused to buy costume jewelry with pins—pointed objects—because I looked upon them as a *symbol* . . .
D: Of "pointiness"?
P: Yeah.
D: Well, is the real "you"—who hardly ever makes an appearance . . .
P: For you? No! *(laughs)*.
D: . . . witchy or docile or housewifely or what?
P: No she's just . . . *real*. She's just *real,* I don't know how to describe it: I had all the feelings a person is supposed to have . . . uhh . . . I guess I never sat in judgment . . .
D: Well, what is it that makes the coming forward of the real "you" so difficult?
P: Well, when I think about it when I'm awake, I feel that I don't have the strength to bring across the complexity of . . . I feel that I'm too completely sterile and lacking in imagination to get it across . . . I feel that it's so *big,* I can't get it acr——
D: What's so big?
P: Intricate! The real me. I suppose one way I could get it out would be in speaking of . . . or in dreams . . . The only thing I can say about it is during my entire waking life I'm constantly faced with a mirror . . .
D: A mirror?
P: Yeah: The way I think other people see me and how I behave as a result . . . it just goes back and forth, back and forth, and . . . I feel I don't *have* any sense of self. Except for this mirror.

Psychological Test Data

Full-scale IQ = 122 (verbal = 126, performance = 116). All subtest scores were in the same range. There were no indications of organicity and no signs of disturbance (in the WAIS) in cognitive processes, despite numerous personal and idiosyncratic side remarks to the examiner during the testing.

Integrative functions appeared impaired, however, on the unstructured portions of the test battery. She gave excessive responses to the Rorschach blots, and almost none of them were "popular responses." There were no "human" responses to the blots, but instead the percepts centered on strange creatures surrealistically envisioned: to card III, " . . . two female armadillos with opposum-heads connected by a streak of blood going from the brain of one to the brain of the other. . . ." A number of confabulatory responses, considered highly suggestive of schizophrenia, were made in which ordinarily disparate areas of a blot are fused: card IX, " . . . two pink bears are hauling the corpse of a walrus over a snow bank, with their feet propped up on a giant grasshopper . . ."

Loss of distance (fluidity of ego boundary) was suggested by the patient's remarking that the inkblots seemed about to leap out of their cards and jump on her. Many of the TAT and Sentence Completion test responses centered on themes of self-mutilation or suicide; intense and primitive/aggressive destructive feelings were expressed in the choice of animals seen in the blots: tarantulas, wolves, piranha fish.

Comments

The patient of this vignette, an unmarried woman of twenty-two, exhibits fragmentation of the self. She once spoke of herself as populated by half a dozen "selves," and even has some awareness that this strange feeling state may have arisen out of strong identifications with various people around her. A pronomial reversal in her speech is connected with this fragmentation: when she says "I . . . ," she is usually referring to some aspect of the self that had been taken over, quite unassimilated, from some of "them." But she refers to her "real" self, with whom she is scarcely in touch, as "she. . . ." Sharply contradictory views are held in the realm of interpersonal life, as when she spoke of women as *either* cruel *or* docile. Her behavior is, in certain instances, at the mercy of these impressions, as when she avoids buying pointed objects of feminine apparel. Psychic structure, for all these reasons (but especially because of the lack of any stable sense of personal identity), is at the psychotic level. From the standpoint of research diagnostic criteria, there might be some question about the presence of a major functional psychosis: although her pattern of communication is hard to follow, there are no "productive signs" *per se*. She is aware, for example, of the contradictoriness of her views about the different selves; she is also aware of the symbolic nature of her reasoning about the costume jewelry with pins. This gives some of these otherwise illogical assertions the quality of an "overvalued idea" or what Sacks and his co-workers (1974) referred to as "double awareness."

The patient is unusually intelligent and verbally facile. These attributes may account for her ability to rescue herself—most of the time—from the deluded state into which she could otherwise have so easily slipped. In one portion of the interview, she was less well able to preserve adequate reality testing: she imagined that to become whole, she must incorporate the personality of some normal, well-functioning person. But such a person, according to her logic, would look down on her or even wish to destroy her. Therefore (again, in her own private logic) to incorporate such a "self" would provoke self-destructive urges. The alternative: to remain fragmented and without any strong (borrowed) self.

Insofar as her affect was usually only moderately constricted—at times, actually, she was capable of a wide range of feelings—her clinical picture would fail to meet the Taylor and Abrams criteria for schizophrenia (which require the absence of a "broad affect"). Her affect toward the end of the interview was depressed; initially, it was constricted but not inappropriate.

The Sz/MDP ratio in this patient was 71/29, that is, preponderantly but not exclusively schizophrenic.

Characterologically the most noticeable traits were the obsessive (intellectualization, attention to tiny details, isolation of affect). Self-depreciation and suicidal ruminations were prominent among the depressive traits.

There were no signs of disturbance in cognitive processes on the *structured* portions of the psychological tests, despite her (1) having psychotic structure at the clinical level and (2) showing many signs of primary-process thinking on the *unstructured* portions. This type of split in overall performance on the psychological tests has been said (Gunderson and Singer, 1975) to be characteristic of the borderline patient. But here the same result is seen in the presence of an acute schizoaffective illness—in a patient with very superior intelligence.

Final Diagnostic Impressions

A. Categorical diagnoses
   1. Schizoaffective disorder, depressed type
   2. Psychotic structure
   3. Obsessive personality (with depressive and hysterical features)

B. Dimensional assessments
   1. Region II of the Sz-MDP continuum
   2. GAS = 23
   3. Personality profile as shown in Table IV–1

FAMILY HISTORY

First-degree relatives = 5 (parents, plus 3 sibs)
(none affected)

Second-degree relatives =	6
affected member:	(1) maternal uncle (with moderate depression; treated with medication, but no hospitalization)
Third-degree relatives	(precise number unknown)
affected member:	(1) maternal cousin (considered schizophrenic—with productive signs; also made suicide attempts)

Case Illustration 4

Patient = P Therapist = T GAS = 25

T: (*Toward the end of a session that occurred several days after a joint meeting with her parents and a social worker, in the hospital*) I notice you haven't said much . . . haven't said *anything* about your family session. You hadn't seen your folks in over three months. I imagine the visit must have stirred up a lot of feelings.

P: I didn't feel anything.

T: No?

P: No. So there's nothing to say. *(Pause)* I'm not feeling anything anymore. I'm not getting any better here. What's happened to me? *(Pause)* I used to feel feelings. Not any more. Something's gone out of me.

T: What's that?

P: Something's gone out of me. The *electricity's* gone out of me . . .

T: You say that like you mean "electricity" quite literally.

P: *(Ignoring the question)* . . . someone pulled out the plug on me *(said in such an earnest and anxious manner as to make it quite believable that she saw herself as a piece of complicated machinery suddenly cut off from its source of energy).*

T: You keep talking as though you've lost not just certain feelings, but some vital substance . . . vital juices . . .

P: I have: I don't know what they are. I know I don't have a "plug." But something is gone from me. Drained away somewhere. I didn't even care about my parents when I saw them. The feelings were gone. When Larry *(a recently discharged patient on her unit, with whom she had been quite friendly)* left last week, I didn't feel anything either. I should have, but didn't, and he had nowheres to go.

T: Like yourself? Is that how you see it with yourself when you'll be discharged: that you'll have "nowheres to go?"

P: *(Becoming tearful)* Dr. Byron, are you throwing me out? Can't you see I'm not any better? I can't *do* anything! I forgot how to make change, at the bookstore . . . I don't know how to dial the phone anymore . . . I . . .

T: Look . . . wait a minute . . . you're telling me, "You can't make me leave this place; I'm only three years old." Now the point is, you're not "three years old," and also . . . we're not throwing you out. You can be here at least four months more, if you need to be. But Larry's going got you all shook up. And it's not that you "can't" do anything, it's that you're afraid to let it be seen that you *can* do—what you always used to do—for fear we'll discharge you before you're ready! It's that you're *scared,* that . . .

P: *(Interrupting)* No! It's not *like* that! Something *has* happened to me. Something has gone out of me. I'm not the *same*. I'm not the same person.

Comments

This material was taken from a phase in this patient's course when her speech no longer gave repeated evidence of psychosis according to categorical criteria. Instead, one encountered more muted evidence of psychotic structure, in the form of concretizations about her feelings as though they were the manifestation of some *élan vital* (electricity, as she referred to it) once present in abundance, now mysteriously drained from her body. On this point, her capacity to *test* reality (see Frosch, 1970) remains poor, although she is not so delusional as to insist she was *literally* unplugged.

The therapist is trying to move her from her world of hardened metaphors ("I *am* a baby: I *can't* do anything") into the real world ("I feel as helpless as a baby, as if I can't even manage the chores of daily life") but is unsuccessful. Her denial is still so strong that it does not permit incursions of this kind, let alone cooperative exploration of the relevant feelings.

The predominant characterological tone to assert itself during this phase of her illness is the *infantile*. She sees herself as a baby, and is clingingly dependent.

Background

The patient was a young woman of twenty-three, who had worked as an assistant editor of a magazine upon graduation from college. Her behavior had become progressively more bizarre at work, such that her co-workers urged psychiatric consultation. She complained of belonging to a foreign race from a different planet, felt her bones were "turning to jelly," alternated between imagining herself as either Satan or the Virgin Mary. Her behavior at home had also become eccentric; her sleep-wake cycle was reversed, she wandered about the house complaining of confusion and mentioned hearing her grandmother's voice "in her ear" castigating her for sexual indiscretions. She began to expound theories purporting to cure cancer and rid the world of evil. At the urging of her parents, she was hospitalized—following four nights of almost no sleep. By the time of admission, her speech was somewhat pressured and she paced a good deal on the admission unit.

Two years earlier she had been treated on an outpatient basis for "depression" with psychotherapy; medications had not been prescribed.

As a child, the patient exhibited severe problems in handling separation and was noted to be highly irritable and impatient. Tantrums were frequent till age eight. She had only one friend throughout adolescence. During musical performances, her "stage fright" was at times incapacitating.

Mental Status on Admission

Notable for the following features: marked anxiety and restlessness; circumstantial, evasive, tangential, and pressured speech; bizarre associations; somatic delusions (of melting away, turning to jelly); incomplete hallucinations (voice at the edge of the ear); ideas of reference (that people regarded her as a sorceress or as a "Lilith"); affect that was at times constricted, at times depressive.

Admitting Diagnosis

"Acute paranoid schizophrenia."

Psychological Test Data

Highlights consist of (1) marked split in verbal/performance levels (120/83; full-scale IQ = 103) with much intra- and intertest variability, (2) evidence of faulty judgment and impulse control (If you saw smoke in a theater, you would . . . "scream fire!"), (3) immaturity of figure drawings and absence of sexual differentiation, (4) general paucity of responses on the Rorschach, with some exceptions in the form of highly unusual percepts (a "vagina" on card II), many suggesting hostile, anal-sadistic imagery, and (5) preoccupation on the TAT cards with loneliness and suicide. In general, the Rorschach showed "little indication of ego impairment and fairly well-integrated responses, though at the expense of considerable constriction and rigidity." No diagnosis was offered; only the impression of "having begun to recover from a more acute disturbance."

Subsequent Course

This patient remained in the hospital for ten months; her treatment consisted of twice weekly psychotherapy and neuroleptic medications (Mellaril, 1000 mgm/day). Psychotherapy was supportive at first; later an attempt was made to shift toward a more expressive mode, though this was not well utilized by the patient. Instead she formed an intensely eroticized and clinging relationship throughout her stay and after. During this phase of her illness, her affect was constricted and at times inappropriate.

She resumed work upon discharge, though on a half-time basis, and continued working with the same therapist. A year later, during his vacation, she became acutely manic. Mellaril was reinstituted, and her manic symptoms (pacing, pushed speech, early awakening, irritability, grandiosity) abated. During this psychotic episode there was no evidence of delusions such as had characterized her initial decompensation. She discontinued the Mellaril on her own and quit coming to her sessions. A month later a manic psychosis was again apparent, and on this occasion she was hospitalized and given lithium. Flight of ideas, euphoria, hyperactivity, and early awakening were her major symptoms, but on this occasion she also had delusions of influence. She felt she could read peoples' minds and that they could read hers. There was a chronicity to her illness, though partly this was self-imposed, inasmuch as the grandiose elements in her character led her to belittle treatment and reject her therapist's recommendations.

As her course unfolded, the original diagnosis of schizophrenia seemed less tenable. Repeated episodes were mainly of an affective variety, though tinged with some of the earlier "schizophrenic" signs and symptoms.

Final Diagnostic Impressions

A. Categorical diagnoses
   1. Schizoaffective illness (manic type) with paranoid features
   2. Psychotic structure
   3. Infantile personality with narcissistic features

B. Dimensional assessments
   1. Region III of Sz-MDP continuum
   2. GAS = 25 (first admission)
   3. Personality profile as shown in Table IV–1

FAMILY HISTORY

First-degree relatives =	3 (parents, plus 1 sib)
affected members:	(1) father (episodic depressions of moderate severity treated with medications, not hospitalized; described as having a paranoid personality)
	(2) sister, age twenty-six (severe character disorder—schizoid, with narcissistic features)
Second-degree relatives =	6
affected members:	(1) maternal aunt (hospitalized with "involutional melancholia")
	(2) paternal uncle ("nervous breakdown," hospitalized, with eccentric behavior)
Other (including less seriously affected) members:	(1) maternal first cousin once removed (hospitalized in adolescence for a nervous breakdown characterized by delusions and ideas of reference)
	(2) paternal first cousin once removed ("nervous breakdown" with hallucinations)
	(3) mother (described as "severely neurotic," with hypomanic temperament, given to rage outbursts)

NOTE: Affective and schizophrenic illnesses appear in both maternal and paternal lines.

Case Illustration 5

Patient = P Consultant = C GAS = 25

The patient kept her eyes averted throughout most of the interview and was reluctant to answer questions. She made several gestures to leave the room and finally sat down curled in the "fetal position."

C: Can you tell me what frame of mind you're in just now?
P: I don't feel like talking. *(Pause)* Why are you talking to me?
C: I was hoping to be able to get acquainted with you and with the difficulties that led up to your coming here to the hospital.
P: I'd like some pills . . .
C: Pills?
P: . . . to go to sleep.
C: Is that to get away from something particular?
P: *(No response)*
C: Dr. Smythe had mentioned to me you had been bothered by disturbing voices shortly before coming here. Are they still . . . ?
P: *(Nods "no")* . . . I don't hear anymore. *(Pause)* I don't *feel* anymore.
C: Since you took a leave of absence from college?
P: *(Nods "no")*
C: Have you regrets about leaving college? . . . wished you were back there?
P: I don't wish I were anywhere. *(Pause)* I feel frozen *(sotto voce)*.
C: What was that again?
P: This is a refrigerator!
C: *(Pause)* Could you, I wonder, be talking about chilliness of a different sort? Have you in fact felt cold or frozen in some emotional way, for example?
P: *(No response: focuses her attention at some spot in the middle of the floor)*
C: Are you telling me you've felt somehow "dead" since you've been here? Or just before?
P: *(No response)*
C: Well, do you *ever* recall having felt distinctly alive?
P: Now and then.
C: When was the last "then"? When did things begin to take a turn for the worse with you?
P: I don't remember. *(She begins to shudder, as if with a chill)*
C: I notice you shuddering when I was asking you about . . .
P: *(Interrupting)* I'm *cold!* . . . That's all I care about *(whimperingly)*.
C: Well, but I've had the impression you might be saying something to the effect: "People have been cold toward me" . . . something of that sort.

P: No! *(Speaking for the first time in an ordinary conversational level)* Don't you understand!? I'm *cold!* Physically.
C: Well, it's awfully warm in the room . . . I couldn't help thinking you were hinting at some . . . spiritual sort of coldness.
P: *(Plaintively)* It's freezing . . .
C: Are you afraid of catching cold, literally?
P: Maybe. My father got pneumonia last year.
C: Were you very concerned whether he'd pull through?
P: I was sure he would. He wasn't that sick.
C: No?
P: No. He didn't take care of himself.
C: Why did you suppose he neglected himself?
P: He's a masochist.
C: A more thoroughgoing one than yourself, even?
P: You're very witty. *(Pause)* But I never said I was one. If I were, I'd be enjoying all this. I wouldn't . . . *(blocks)* . . . only here I am! *(Becomes tearful briefly)*
C: What was moving you to tears just then?
P: *(Wistfully, in a childlike voice) I* don't kno-o-ow. *(Pause)* Now can I leave?!
C: I think you're trying to avoid something.
P: *(Mumbling to herself in a barely audible way)* . . . avoid . . . a voice . . . where is my voice? . . .
C: I've noticed that since you became tearful, you've withdrawn into a shell; you keep your eyes more away from me than even before . . . I can scarcely hear you. . . . It makes me even more convinced that you're trying very hard to dodge some painful topic. I wonder what that could be . . .
P: *(More audibly)* That's enough now! I'm going to go now . . . *(begins to get up from her chair)*.
C: Just a moment there! Every time you don't like the way the conversation is headed, you start to take off. Why don't you "count to ten" and tell me what's going on!
P: *(Becomes tearful again)* I keep my eyes away from everybody's eyes *(spoken enigmatically, her face looking upwards and away from the consultant)*.
C: To shield you from what?
P: Their frosty glaze . . . *(spoken as if reciting a line of poetry)*.
C: Seriously, though, what is it that disturbs you about other peoples' looks?
P: *(Attempting once again to avoid the topic)* I dunno . . .
C: Well, they obviously don't please you.
P: They *frustrate* me!
C: In what way?

P: If they would smile at me . . . it makes me happy . . . *(pause, voice dropping to a whisper)*, but nobody ever smiles at me.
C: "Nobody"? Does that take in the whole family as well?
P: Um-hmm.
C: That amazes me. In fact I wonder if you're not telling me something about the atmosphere at home, rather than an actual fact—as if the five other people in your family never once smiled at you in twenty years . . .
P: *(Becoming more tearful and quite loud at this point)* I'm no good . . . why should they? . . . Nobody at school did either . . . Now I have to leave! Goodbye! *(And again begins to get up)*
C: Ah! We have gotten to a touchy subject again!
P: *(Sits down, but says nothing)*
C: Tell me something: Is what you're dishing out to me now—I'm referring to you clamming up and making as if to bolt from the room—are you showing me in effect your method of getting even with the family? They fail to smile and you give them the "silent treatment"?
P: Partly!
C: A technic you learned from your mother, one might wonder?
P: Oh, yeah! *(Facing the consultant for the first time as she acknowledged this; then lapsing back into silence)*
C: Again, I notice myself thinking: Were you telling me a factual truth . . . or just a kind of emotional truth, when you mentioned that no one smiled at you or . . .
P: Nobody likes me. Why should they smile?
C: But that strains my imagination! Does it seem to you possible that a young woman such as yourself *(alluding to her obvious attractiveness)* would end up with "no smiles" . . . from anyone!?
P: No one smiled.
C: *(Pause)* Well . . . let's assume for the moment that's how it really was. Just for the sake of argument, because it's still very hard to believe. . . . How have you accounted for this? You must have a dozen ideas in your mind how come no one seemed to like you . . .
P: No! *(Spoken rather testily)*
C: You're not giving yourself a chance, though. Think about it for a moment. I have a hunch some notion . . . some fantasy will occur to you about this rather unusual . . .
P: *(Interrupting)* No-o-o! *(Her voice now a mixture of defiance and seductiveness)* . . . I'll sit here for you . . . for hours! You can't make me talk!
C: *(Sympathetically)* No . . . that's very true.
P: *(Becoming tearful again and quite tense; she took a piece of paper from her purse and wrote something on it, shielding her work from the consultant's view. She then handed it to him, got up and left the room. On*

the slip of paper she had drawn a Cupid's heart and arrow with her initials underneath).

Anamnestic Data

The patient was the second of four children. She was born of a normal delivery and birth weight and showed normal milestones. At seven she was noted to be withdrawn by her grade school teachers, who remarked that she would often stare vacantly into space. At other times she could be quite disruptive in class, talking out of turn or throwing objects at the other pupils. This led to consultation with the school psychologist and some brief psychotherapy. Menarche was at thirteen, uneventful. During adolescence she became more withdrawn, secretive, and given to daydreaming, particularly after the hospitalization of her father (see Family History). Shortly before graduation from high school, she became depressed, tearful, anxious, and still more seclusive. She suffered a more serious breakdown in college six months later. This was characterized by panic, depression, insomnia, and hallucinations of her mother's voice speaking about her to her father in a depreciatory way. She had somatic delusions (of electricity running through her bones), periods of catatonia, and dreams of being strangled by her mother, so vivid that she awoke thinking she was dead by her mother's hand. She made a suicidal gesture with an overdose of sleeping pills before being hospitalized.

Psychological Test Data (during the early phase of hospitalization)

Full-scale IQ = 118 (verbal = 116, performance = 118). Fluidity of ideas, loss of boundary sense, and illogicality were noted on the Rorschach and TAT responses. Severe conflicts over dependency were suggested by the percept on card VI: " . . . two men with beards stuck back to back . . . I wish they could be free . . . I wish they weren't together. . . ."

Suicidal preoccupation and poor impulse control were suggested by certain sentence-completion responses, namely: Sometimes she wished . . . "she were dead."

The diagnostic impression was considered most compatible with a "chronic undifferentiated schizoaffective psychosis."

Comments

This patient is one of several (see case illustration 29) discussed in this section in whose background are first-degree relatives with both types of major psychoses, segregated in accordance with parental line. Here, there was a confluence of affective illness on the maternal side and schizophrenic illness on the paternal side. It is noteworthy that at the clinical level, the patient exhibited a fairly even mixture of the two tendencies. Depression, tearfulness, insomnia, suicide attempts, feelings of worthlessness existed side by side with auditory hallucinations (in which X talks to Y *about* the patient), concreteness, clang associations ("avoid . . . a voice"), boundary confusion, allusive, noncommunicative speech, and chronicity. Examples of many such signs and symptoms are to be found in the case material. She concretizes the feeling of being treated "coldly" as physical chilliness, even in the midst of a heat spell. Father caught cold last year; therefore, she might do so this year, as though he and she are the same and time is of no meaning (see Matte Blanco, 1976, on these forms of schizophrenic thinking). Her darting in and out of relatedness with the interviewer, along with the striking ambivalence (she rejects the consultant verbally, but then passes him a love note), are, in the context of her other interactions, also more in keeping with a schizophrenic disorder.

Although there can be little question about her psychostructural level, it should be noted that the consultant tried to confront the patient, for example, about her claim of being universally "disliked." This led to a worsening of her emotional state: she became even more anxious and tearful, and redoubled her denial. As with many largely uncommunicative patients, one finds oneself tempted, at times forced, to supply possible meanings out of one's own intuition. Occasionally one will "hit home," as when the consultant asked whether her silent treatment was a replica of her mother's behavior. Momentarily this led to greater relatedness in this fragile patient. Conceivably, and without her being able to acknowledge it, correct empathic hunches of this sort—or even the effort at such hunches—prompted in her a certain gratitude, of which the poignant Cupid note was perhaps an expression. It is of course of some diagnostic import—about the level of psychic structure—that one can struggle so long and expend such effort in trying to establish rapport with a patient, yet emerge with so little information.

Final Diagnostic Impressions

A. Categorical diagnoses
   1. Schizoaffective disorder, depressed type
   2. Psychotic structure
   3. Infantile personality with paranoid features

B. Dimensional assessments
   1. Region III of the Sz-MDP continuum
   2. GAS = 26
   3. Personality profile as shown in Table IV–1

FAMILY HISTORY

First-degree relatives =	5 (parents, plus 3 sibs)
affected members:	(1) father (chronic undifferentiated schizophrenic, hospitalized)
	(2) mother (manic-depressive illness, bipolar-I type; treated [successfully] with lithium)

Second-degree relatives =	7
affected member:	(1) maternal grandfather (violent rage attacks; depressive episodes [never hospitalized])
Third-degree relatives	(precise number unknown)
affected member:	(1) paternal cousin (hospitalized for a chronic schizophrenic reaction [unknown type])

Case Illustration 6

Patient = P Doctor = D GAS = 26

The patient begins by describing the disturbing feelings she experienced shortly before seeking hospitalization.

P: I was extremely depressed, um *(pause)*. Very frustrated because I couldn't really get rid of the painful feelings.

D: What painful feelings?

P: I can't remember. I mean, I know that it felt painful but I don't know what it was that made me feel painful.

D: You don't remember what you were angry at?

P: No. Well, I have a feeling I know but I don't; I didn't feel it then. The reason why I went into the other hospital was because one day I decided that I had the power to get rid of the pain and that was by taking a lot of sleeping pills and I did it. And the strange thing was that after I got out of the coma, um, I felt like I had gotten rid of all the painful feelings.

D: What do you mean by saying you had the "power" to get rid of the pain?

P: I thought I could do something *(pause)* to make people understand how bad it felt. *(Long pause)*

D: Are you talking about a feeling of very special power, or what?

P: *(Pause)* Well, I only felt powerful while I was taking them, ya know, like just popping the pills into my mouth and *(pause)* I felt kinda like God or something, ya know, I felt like . . . um, something very special was happening to me while I was taking them.

D: How would you characterize that?

P: Well, the only way I can describe it is to say I felt like a painting of a scene with a lot of, um, light coming out all around. I felt . . . I felt really alive and it was an incredible feeling because I hadn't felt very much of, uh, life in me the whole summer long.

D: And now that you were dying you felt a love of life?

P: Well, I wasn't dying, I was just putting pills in my mouth.

D: But the intent was that you would be dying?

P: Well, that the feelings would die, not me.
D: It didn't occur to you that you might die along with the feelings?
P: No.
D: Really?
P: Well the only time I had any sense of it was after the whole thing ended when I got out of the coma, they told me that . . . that I had almost died and . . .
D: That came as a great surprise to you.
P: Well, it was more of a . . . a shocking feeling, uh, when I found out about that, I . . . I had that same kind of light, that ya know, the-scene-with-the-light-coming-out feeling.

The interviewer tries to discover whether the patient is fully able to acknowledge the strength of her self-destructive wishes.

D: You were having no thoughts about death at the time . . .
P: *No.*
D: . . . whatsoever, never had in fact?
P: Had thoughts about *death?*
D: Yes, courting death as it were? Wishing it would come sooner than your allotted day.
P: No. Uh-uh. *(Very long pause)* I guess I felt like I didn't wanna get rid of myself completely: I just wanted to give myself another chance, like if I could try out being a different person, that's about all I thought I could do, ya know, but I didn't wanna just cut off all my chances.
D: Well, what sort of a "different person" did you hope you'd wind up?
P: *(Pause)* Well a person who would have an easier time. *(Long pause)* As a matter of fact, the day that that happened, it happened right after an incident where I met an old school friend of mine and she seemed like absolutely perfect. I'd never seen anybody as perfect as her. She was perfect in every way when I talked to her, and, uh, . . . there's something so entirely wrong with me, I just had to do something about it, ya know. I don't know if I really wanted to become like her but just. . . .
D: What was wrong with you?
P: *(Pause)* Well, I felt mean and angry and tied up in knots and, um *(pause)*, and pathetic.
D: *(Very long pause)* What was your understanding, then, about the sleeping pills that led you to entertain the hope that taking them would make you, literally, a "different person"?
P: *(Pause)* Well, I didn't . . . I really didn't . . . I didn't have too much understanding of what would happen if you took a whole lot of sleeping pills, I thought . . .
D: You somehow knew they were a *sleeping* pill?
P: I'd . . . I'd heard that people took sleeping pills and I guess, I guess I

knew that they could die from it. *(Pause)* But I just felt like I wanted to see what would happen, ya know, like I thought it might be, um, make me into a different person and really, in fact, it did . . .

D: Like *who* for example?

P: When I woke up from my coma, I was, um, restful, ya know, like . . . I was like an angel . . . felt like an angel. I felt (*pause*) happy and calm and at peace and things like that.

D: Well, you keep saying "make you a different person" as though you had some very distinct person in mind. Let's see what comes to mind about that?

P: Well, I guess my mother.

D: Let me hear.

P: I don't know what you wanna hear. *(Pause)* Um, well my mother is kinda a saint, in a way. Um, it's sorta hard to know how to talk to her sometimes because she's just so, she's so good, like . . . she never gets angry, very rarely gets angry. If she gets angry, she's completely justified. Um, she's . . . she's not a phoney, she's completely real. And she has these very good feelings all the time. And that's the way I understand it.

Moments later, the patient described some negative attributes of her mother, in a manner suggesting she was quite unaware how these impressions clashed with the saintly image she had spoken of shortly before. When the contradiction was pointed out to her, she became tearful. This constituted a turning point. Toward the end of the interview, she spoke poignantly of her apprehension about exposing her feelings of despair.

D: What are you afraid of—about being more "real" with us here?

P: *(Long pause)* Well . . . I'm afraid no one's gonna understand my feelings. Like, I get the feeling that my feelings, I mean, my feelings are very wrong, in a certain way, and they've gotta be understood very carefully.

D: Or else?

P: *(Sobbing)* Or else, ya know, I'm gonna really be in a bind because I've decided that I wanna *try* feeling, and I don't wanna go back to being that other person . . . and it's gonna be disaster, because I'm gonna be caught in the middle and I won't be able to do anything. I won't be able to be my old self, I won't dare to be my real self because people won't like me. I won't know *who* I'm gonna be.

Comments

The patient of this clinical vignette, a single woman of twenty-two, showed an appreciable deficit in ego integration. Allusive and concretistic speech, with evidence of sharply contradictory views on a number of important issues, were also noted. There were marked inconsistencies in her perceptions of others and of herself: She is "entirely wrong"; her friend is "perfect." There is more here than simply ambivalence (namely, toward her mother): the oppositely tinged feelings exist, to be sure, but she is not aware of them simultaneously. The negative side of her feelings toward others is, in fact, disavowed or denied outright: she supplies the clues to the interviewer but is surprised when the inescapable conclusion is interpreted back to her. The split in object representations suggests borderline structure (at best), but the severity of the split in self-representation is more suggestive of psychotic structure. There is further confirmation of the latter, in that she at first denied having any awareness of the implications of her otherwise self-evident *suicidal behavior*. This was a measure of faulty reality testing. The reality of death itself was denied, as though one could take a "fatal" overdose and simply enter a different world (as one might travel to a different continent) *called* "Death," where life goes on pretty much as usual—only with angels instead of neighbors.

In the midportion of the interview, the patient was confronted rather forcefully about the extent of her repudiating the truths of what she had been communicating. Her capacity to test reality, as it turned out, was not so impaired that she persisted in defending the unrealistic positions she had earlier been asserting. Unlike a patient with a borderline structure, she does not merely acknowledge the validity of the interviewer's confrontation (about discrepancies in the patient's comments) and henceforth become more organized and composed. Instead, one sees a measure of disorganization, not in her thinking (which happens to improve from this point forward) but in her affect—which becomes markedly unstable. She became able, after the turning point in the interview, to communicate something about the disorganization of her thinking, which she had been experiencing up till that moment. There was a marked improvement in her rapport with the interviewer, so that, even while she gave expression to the nature of her fragmentation, she was now actively in the process of knitting the pieces back together. Her capacity to work meaningfully with such material, even while being profoundly affected by the interchange, constituted a good prognostic sign, auguring well for improvement in her level of psychic organization. This impression was in time corroborated: at follow-up after one-and-a-half years of thrice-weekly psychotherapy plus medication, GAS level had risen to 55 and she showed a much more integrated conception of herself and of her interpersonal world. Characterological predominance by then had shifted away from the narcissistic, toward the depressive-masochistic.

Psychological Test Data

IQ was in the bright-normal range. There was a fair amount of variability in the subject scores (from 6 on picture arrangement to 14 on block design). There were no signs of organicity.

The nonstructured portions of the test battery suggested fluidity of ego boundary and distortions in body image (and, in addition, withdrawal from object relatedness). No examples of Rorschach percepts were offered in the written report.

Final Diagnostic Impressions

A. Categorical diagnoses
   1. Schizoaffective disorder
   2. Psychotic structure
   3. Narcissistic character with depressive-masochistic and hysterical features
B. Dimensional assessments
   1. Region II of the Sz-MDP continuum (Sz/MDP = 67/33)
   2. GAS (initial) = 26
   3. Personality profile as shown in Table IV–1

FAMILY HISTORY

First-degree relatives =	5 (parents, plus 3 sibs)
affected member:	(1) brother (hospitalized [age twenty-nine] for a schizophrenic disorder with predominantly paranoid features)
Second-degree relatives =	7
affected member	(1) maternal uncle (hospitalized for chronic undifferentiated schizophrenic disorder)
Other (including less seriously affected) members:	(1) mother (severe narcissistic character disorder with schizoid features)

Case Illustration 7

Patient = P Doctor = D GAS = 27

D: Hello, I'm Dr. Elsasser.[2]

P: *(Spoken rapidly with great pressure of speech)* What is it you want to know? The police bĕat me up black and blue. Black and bluish. Jack and Jewish? You don't look Jewish. Now what do you want to know?

D: Well, what led to . . .

P: I'd just bought some incense. The cops drove up. I said to the "super," "What do they want?" He said, "Don't worry! They're friends." I was praying for the super, for the son and the wife, who was pregnant . . .

D: You prayed for the . . . ?

[2]These names and all that follow are of course fictitious.

P: Yes, I'm Greek Orthodox. I'm a Jesus freak. I pray for myself because I'm afraid of *you!*
D: Of who?
P: You'd have me beaten up, like—you're surprised at me . . .
D: At . . . ?
P: . . . that I'm dirty and badly dressed. . . . Even tho' I pray, I get beaten up. I have a doctor . . . not the "Doctor" (*spoken with emphasis*) in the hospital—forget about *him!* Dr. Norman Efron, Butterfield 7 ——.
D: Let's . . .
P: *You want me to talk or not!?*
D: Yes, but . . . let's not talk about Dr. Efron; let's . . . has this happened to you many times before?
P: Since '58, in and out . . .
D: How many times?
P: I don't remember. I have had Dr. Emilio, Dr. Flint, Dr. Hamad, Dr. McGowan, Dr. Weintraub . . . I've been in Parker State, Island State, Oak Park State. . . . I almost lost my baby because they didn't believe I was pregnant. I had to miss his birthday because Dr. Weintraub wouldn't let me go home. . . . My mother's a strong Greek Orthodox . . . she'll drive me right outta here to the beach . . .
D: When were you first hospitalized?
P: At twenty.
D: How old are you now?
P: Thirty-six. . . . Here comes the real sadism!: They won't let me go to the bathroom. . . . Dr. Efron left two months ago but he called me once. . . . I'm interested in Dr. Efron right now . . .
D: Let's try to talk about what's going on right now . . .
P: No! You don't look pretty! I like to talk to pretty men. Dr. Efron is pretty . . . *Dr. McGowan* was pretty. . . . I was in love with him . . . I took an overdose when nothing happened.
D: What makes you love some and hate others?
P: What makes *you* love some and hate others!? Are you married?
D: Yes.
P: Does your wife love you?
D: Yeah . . .
P: Give me her phone number: I'll call her immediately!
D: That's getting off the subject!
P: *Dr. Efron* loves me!
D: How do you know?
P: He called me from miles and miles away. Now what else?
D: What were the hospitalizations mostly for?
P: Overdoses. Except this time. I felt suicidal. I feel *homicidal* at the moment because you won't light my cigarette! . . . What's your name?
D: Dr. Elsasser.

P: Elsasser? Hell-sasser? You related to Dachau people? . . . What else do you want to know, mister? I breast-fed my child who weighed ten pounds at birth. I worked for a blind psychiatrist, Dr. Per—— you can call him up—right now if you want—Commonwealth 3 ——— the last job I had was coding numbers . . . all homosexuals there.

Comments

This patient exhibits "pushed" speech, irritability, flight of ideas, grandiosity, and easy distractibility, therefore satisfying the criteria in common use for mania. The "clang-bang" associations and flight of ideas—which might be interpreted as loosening of associations—might lead to confusability with a schizophrenic disorder. But there is a haughty comicality about her speech, reminiscent of the patter of certain comedians, that seems much more consistent with a manic disorder: she picks up on various details of the interviewer's own speech and person, in order to make sport of him. This already betokens a degree of relatedness (however mocking in spirit) not ordinarily encountered in comparably ill schizophrenics. In the anamnesis, there is mention of several episodes of severe disturbance, some characterized by psychotic *depression,* others by *mania* (the latter accompanied by early morning awakening). Her condition might be said to exemplify a "bipolar" illness, though there are other aspects of her history which would make us tag her as "atypical."

This patient experienced psychotic episodes beginning around age twenty. Although many of these were characterized by suicide gestures and strong depressive (dysphoric mood, tearfulness) features, the earlier episodes were diagnosed "paranoid schizophrenia." This reflected not only the diagnoses that were the most popular when the patient was first seen at the hospital but also certain clinical features: her grandiose ideation, tangentiality, ideas of reference, and litigiousness. The paper of Abrams et al. (1974) on the paranoid element in certain manic cases is worth reading with the present example in mind.

It was of interest that during the many years clinicians were thinking of the patient as schizophrenic, a computer diagnosis based on a standardized mental-status questionnaire read "manic-depressive."

In retrospect, ever since the onset of her illness at least some symptoms of *both* schizophrenia and manic-depressive psychosis were present simultaneously. But the balance between the two tendencies may have shifted over the years from a more evenly divided "schizoaffective psychosis" to the current picture, a disorder of Region IV in the Sz-MDP continuum, where affective symptoms predominate. Sz/MDP ratio (modified Cohen scale) was 36/64: predominantly affective. For easier visualization of the shift in clinical diagnoses during the course of her illness, a diagnostic time cube (Figure IV–8) adapted to the time dimension accompanies this case.

Figure IV–8. Time-Cube Diagram for Case Illustration 7

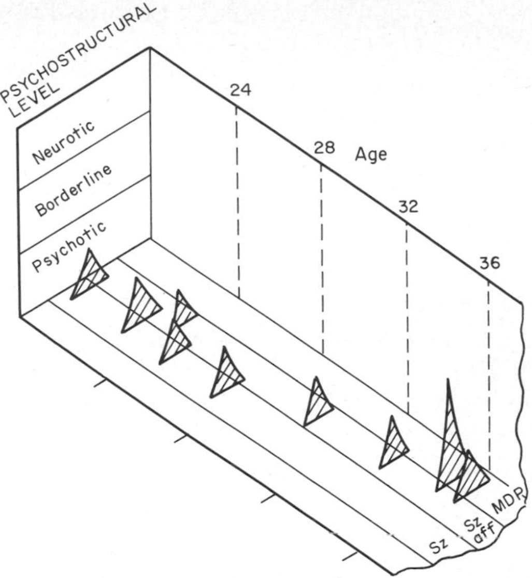

NOTE: Placement and height of the markers reflect clinical diagnoses made at various stages of the illness. It is unclear whether the apparent shift stemmed from factors intrinsic in the patient (''occasion variance'') or from changing standards of diagnosis on the part of the physicians in attendance.

Respecting the patient variables of significance in distinguishing psychotic from borderline structures, it will be apparent from the vignette that the quality of object relations was, if one were to judge from the interaction, exceedingly poor. The patient remained on her own wavelength and did not relate to the interviewer, except to use him as a fall guy for her own preoccupations and preconceptions. Overall severity of symptoms was quite high.

Psychological Test Data

Full-scale IQ = 120 (verbal = 121, performance = 120). Test results showed consistently well-preserved intellectual functioning, despite evidence of disorganization and faulty reality testing on the unstructured portions. There were many animal-eye percepts on the Rorschach, suggesting paranoid trends, and suicidal preoccupation was suggested by several of the TAT stories.

Five years later a repeat test battery showed the same IQ, along with abnormalities on the unstructured portions felt to be most compatible with "chronic undifferentiated schizophrenia." Clinically, at that time, at least one of Schneiders's first-rank symptoms was present, namely, a kind of thought insertion (" . . . someone is trying to push his personality into my mind, and to push my personality out . . .").

Final Diagnostic Impressions

A. Categorical diagnoses
   1. Schizoaffective disorder, manic type (affective symptoms predominate)
   2. Psychotic structure
   3. Paranoid personality

B. Dimensional assessments
   1. Region IV of the Sz-MDP continuum
   2. GAS = 27
   3. Personality profile as shown in Table IV–1

FAMILY HISTORY

First-degree relatives (none affected)	=	3 (parents, plus 1 sib)
Second-degree relatives	=	6
affected member:		(1) maternal aunt (hospitalized for what was considered to be an acute schizophrenic reaction [exact nature unknown])
		(nothing known concerning the father's parents)
Other (including less seriously affected) members:		(1) mother (irritable temperament with occasional bouts of depression)
		(2) brother (paranoid personality, irritable, never hospitalized)

Case Illustration 8

Patient = P Consultant = C GAS = 28

C: Tell me what feelings you're in touch with at the moment.
P: Only anxiety . . . I'm very anxious.
C: And is it clear to you what's provoking that anxiety?
P: Well . . . this interview, for one thing.
C: Anything else?
P: Well . . . there's the anxiety and the sadness I felt before coming to the hospital, that are still with me . . .
C: And what do those relate to?

P: *(Long pause)* . . . things having to do with feelings I have about my body. *(Long pause)* My body has a serious flaw. . . . Am I supposed to tell you about it?
C: You sound uncertain whether I would find it relevant.
P: You . . . I wasn't sure how I'd react to talking about all this . . . I pictured myself crying the whole time, which is what I feel like right now.
C: Why the tearfulness, do you think?
P: I don't know. I feel hopeless, mostly.
C: Well, but how would you put it into words, that feeling of hopelessness?
P: *(Long pause)* I suppose it has to do with exposing myself. Being vulnerable.
C: To what, though?
P: I have no idea.
C: Perhaps if you try to think of it right now, something will occur to you.
P: *(Long pause)* My mind is just blank when I try to think about it.
C: Really "blank"?
P: Yes.
C: Well, let's hear whatever you notice yourself experiencing just at the moment.
P: *(Long pause)* I'm feeling . . . threatened.
C: By . . . ?
P: By you . . . asking me to talk about my defect.
C: Uh-huh. *(Pause)* Of course, one effect of your telling me that is to make me feel that, as a gentleman, I should quietly withdraw my question about that subject. But, as a psychiatrist, my hunch is you're quite strong enough to tolerate speaking about it after all . . . even though you'd prefer not to. Where does this feeling of being bodily "defective" concentrate?
P: On my navel.
C: Let me hear.
P: I feel it's pulled to one side . . . misshapen . . . and that my appearance is damaged . . . beyond repair.
C: Well . . . let's assume for the moment your abdomen is distorted just as you describe it. What do you envision as the consequences?
P: *(Tearful)* . . . that I can never . . . that I can never be attractive any more.
C: "Any more." As though you once *did* feel attractive?
P: Yes . . . before this happened . . . up till last year when my navel moved toward the left side . . .
C: I see. But still, what are the consequences for you that really matter? Even if you see yourself as becoming less attractive because of it, I still don't quite know what is the "bottom line," as they say.
P: Well *(tearful)*, the primary thing is, I feel . . . less attractive . . . less

comfortable with myself . . . if I'm with men . . . or even just by myself.

C: In a way that would cast a pall over your whole future, do you mean?

P: No.

C: No?

P: I don't see that outwardly my life would be different.

C: Well . . . then I guess I don't understand where the feeling of desperation comes in. . . . You make it sound as though you'd have to settle for a man way beneath the level of fellow you could have attracted otherwise . . . or even for no man at all . . .

P: I don't see myself as all that damaged.

C: But from your tears, and what you say . . . it's like your life is "over."

P: You don't understand. It's not a matter of how a man might react to my abnormality. It's that I never can feel good about the state of my body . . . regardless of what he might think. *I* have to bear the burden of my imperfection.

C: You're not even sure a fellow would notice anything the matter?

P: Sometimes I think not. Sometimes I think a man would. . . . That's not the most painful part of it. . . . The most painful part of it *(tearful again)* . . . is that there's nothing that can be done about it . . .

C: How do you know that?

P: Well . . . suppose I tried to have a surgeon put it back where it should be, in the center . . . there would be a scar . . . maybe the scar would be uglier than what I have now . . . or easier to notice . . .

C: The cure would be worse than the disease, as it were.

P: Exactly.

C: Well . . . is it "exactly" like that? Or is it that you could be dwelling on these matters . . . having to do with your body . . . in a way that's exaggerated totally out of proportion? Have you ever had that impression? That your perception of your naval as being shifted anatomically, et cetera, is, however strongly you feel about it, just not valid?

P: I hope . . . yes . . . at times I think . . . it could all be a symptom of something else.

C: Do you at times regard yourself as *knowing* that your preoccupation has no reality except a symbolic one?

P: *(Pause)* Well . . . no . . . I'm too "in" it to be sure about that.

C: Have you allowed yourself to guess, ever, what your supposed defect might signify—in case it were largely a symbolic thing?

P: No. I have no idea. It's real to me . . . so I've never carried it any further than that . . .

Anamnestic Data

The patient was a single woman of twenty-three who had been working for a magazine after graduating *cum laude* from college.

Several months before admission to the hospital, she began to ruminate about suicide (though never injuring herself), feeling depressed and also hopeless about the prospects of ever meeting a man who would want to marry her. She based this fear on what she considered to be a "displacement of her naval toward the left side" and would examine and stare at her navel for hours at a time.

Less crippling forms of hypochondriasis and depression had troubled her for a number of years, going back to the time of graduation from high school. She complained at times of feeling "spaced out" or "cut off from the world," as well as of feeling "empty." This depersonalization, along with hypochondriasis and ideas of reference (which she exhibited at times) constitute the "triad" of symptoms Benedetti (1965) described under the heading, "borderline psychosis."

Throughout childhood, her parents noted her to be hypersensitive to criticism, shy, inhibited, ritualistic, and overattached to her mother. She always had one close friend at a time, but never more than the one. Separation from home, especially from her mother, always provoked severe anxiety and exacerbation of her symptoms.

The year before her admission to thc hospital, her grandmother, with whom she had been especially close as a child, died of pancreatic carcinoma. Her fixation on her "navel displacement" began shortly thereafter; in particular, her conviction that her naval had been pulled toward the left may have been related to her awareness that the grandmother's tumor was in the left side of the abdomen—though she had made no such conscious connection at the time of the interview.

In the family of this patient, there were no first- or second-degree relatives with psychiatric disorders.

Psychological Test Data

Full-scale IQ = 126 (verbal = 136, performance = 110). Subtest scores were all uniformly high with the exception of picture arrangement (= 11) and object assembly (= 5). Graphomotor coordination was adequate.

On the unstructured parts of the test battery, bizarre intrusions and primary-process ideation were noted. On card VII, which frequently elicits associations to the maternal figure, the patient saw a "pregnant Egyptian woman cut open below the navel and all empty inside." Suggestive of a severely damaged self-image as a woman was her response on card I, in an area typically seen as a woman: "an ugly miniature bulldog viewed from the front." The TAT cards evoked themes of rape, sadism, necrophilia. and political torture.

Reality testing appeared impaired even in some of the structured portions of the tests: the relatively low picture-arrangement score suggested an impaired capacity to perceive and judge the environment accurately. Even greater evidence of impaired reality testing emerged on the Rorschach, where she made many improbable responses, namely (to card II), " . . . iguanas dancing an old-fashioned waltz." There were very few popular percepts in the record.

Comments

This patient exhibited depressive symptoms in about equal measure with those associated more typically with schizophrenic syndromes. The differentiation between somatic delusions in schizophrenia versus those compatible with psychotic depression was not easily made; likewise, the distinction between somatic delusion and mere hypochondriasis—or even hysterical conversion—was difficult. The chronicity and bizarre quality of her symptoms were more in keeping with schizophrenia, as were many of the responses on the psychological test battery. Likewise there was a schizophrenic quality to the concreteness with which she assumed that the alleged and all-but-invisible body defect would have as devastating effects on the course of her life as though her body were totally "defective." Matte Blanco (1976) has drawn attention to the similarity of reasoning in the unconscious mind (one might even say, in the "nondominant" hemisphere) and in the mind of the schizophrenic. Both show a predilection for "symmetrical" equations, in which the converse of any relation is treated as if identical with the relation. The expression "Peter is the father of John," for example, cannot be reversed in everyday, Aristotelian logic. But in the unconscious, the two possibilities, "Peter is the father of John" and "John is the father of Peter," make equal "sense." In the patient under discussion, the propositions "my body includes a defect" and "my defect includes [or envelops] my body" were equally tenable.

This patient was unusually bright, which made the one area of idiosyncratic thinking stand out all the more glaringly against the background of her generally excellent grasp of the world. At the same time, her intelligence seemed to carry her almost to the point of recognizing the unreality of her claims: she almost (as we see in the interview), but not quite, sees through her symptoms—to their symbolic origins. Her behavior, incidentally, left little doubt that her feelings were of delusional force: she refused to have blood drawn for routine tests least she be irreparably "weakened," even though she was aware the amounts drawn were minuscule compared to a person's total blood volume. In a similar fashion, her hours-long absorption with her navel, like Freud's Wolf Man's with his nose, went well beyond neurotic worry. For these reasons her psychic organization, from the structural viewpoint, should be considered psychotic: just on the edge of being borderline (where there would be overvalued ideas instead of delusions), but still on the side of being psychotic.

In traditional nosology, the patient would be considered schizoaffective (depressed type).

There were many abnormal characterological features; at the time of the interview, the narcissistic traits overshadowed (but not to any striking degree) those of the obsessional, paranoid, infantile, and depressive subtypes.

Final Diagnostic Impressions

A. Categorical diagnoses
   1. Schizoaffective disorder, depressed type
   2. Psychotic structure (Kernberg); "borderline psychosis" (Benedetti)
   3. Narcissistic personality with infantile and paranoid features
B. Dimensional assessments
   1. Region III: schizoaffective area of the Sz-MDP continuum
   2. GAS = 28
   3. Personality profile as shown in Table IV–1

Case Illustration 9

Patient = P Interviewer = I GAS = 28

The patient is a twenty-year-old single woman. She was neatly dressed, intense and dramatic in her expression, and quite verbal. She related well to the interviewer and was comfortable and composed throughout.

I: Can you tell me what led up to your having been admitted to the hospital?
P: Well . . . I had an intense love relationship at the time with a boy, and we had just broken up. And, uh, I was really distraught. I'd gone to a party and gotten into hysterics.
I: What do you mean by "hysterics"?
P: We-ell *(dramatically),* I was at the top of the loft where this party was, and I started to scream, and I tried to cut myself; they held me down until a doctor came . . . and after that, I went to my family and said I was really very distressed . . .
I: Um-hmm.
P: . . . and I said I needed help, because I don't understand why I was doing all that . . .
I: That was the first such display of . . .
P: No, I had cut myself with a razor blade even before, while I was still going with that boy. So . . . um . . . ya know, I had been doing this "*stuff*" and I was really very confused and I didn't know what I was doing, and I wanted to get help very badly.
I: Now when was the very first time you recall having done something which—as you look back—would fall into this category of dramatic or self-injurious behavior?

P: Well, I think the first *dramatic* behavior started *way* back! When I was about . . . the first time I remember cutting myself was when I was fourteen . . .
I: In relation to this fellow?
P: Yes. I sort of thought of him as a father figure . . .
I: Hmm?
P: . . . and I sort of thought he was interested in the dramatics in me. And I felt I could keep him interested in me by cutting myself up, by telling wild stories . . .
I: Is that something that occurred to you spontaneously, or had you heard of people doing that? Who taught you the technics, so to speak?
P: Well, I didn't cut my wrists; I scratched on my hands . . .
I: Whatever . . .
P: . . . I'd been reading a lot of psychology . . . I read *I Never Promised You a Rose Garden* . . . so I think that's where I probably got the idea. I guess I thought it was romantic . . . ya know, the nineteenth century had all *these invalids,* Elizabeth Barrett and so . . . *so romantic* you know, like what's her-name that died all over the place for hours and hours . . . I tended to think of sick people as very *alluring,* and very interesting, very romantic.
I: Was that a notion that originated with you, or was that the family's philosophy, so to speak?
P: Well, about the time I had that first episode with the razor blade, my brother had just had a serious illness and had to go to the hospital. I think I felt somewhat jealous.

The patient went on to describe her family. She saw her father as volatile like herself, her mother as placid. She felt closer to her mother, although when she was in her most distraught state, her father "really came through." Later she described her intense and often inappropriate anger.

P: I've got such repressed anger in me; what happens is . . . I can't *feel* it; I get anxiety attacks. I get very nervous, smoke too many cigarettes. So what happens to me is I tend to *explode.* Into tears or hurting myself or whatever . . . because I don't know how to contend with all those mixed up feelings.
I: What was the more recent example of such an "explosion"?
P: I was alone at home a few months ago; I was frightened! I was trying to get in touch with my boyfriend and I couldn't. . . . He was nowhere to be found. All my friends seemed to be busy that night and I had no one to talk to. . . . I just got more and more nervous and more and more agitated. Finally, *bang!* I took out a cigarette and lit it and stuck it into my forearm,.I don't know why I did it because I didn't really care for him all that much. I guess I felt I had to do something very dramatic . . .

I: Might you have been even more disturbed over something else?
P: Well, you mean when I was burning myself and everything . . . I had been thinking of going away for a few months, which would have meant I had to leave my former therapist.
I: Ahh!
P: I think the thought of losing him was agitating me quite a bit: having to leave him.
I: But, you mention it almost as an aside, even though it might have been the key issue . . .
P: Well, I remember it as such; I remember one weekend I felt terribly keyed up and I called him up . . . like, for an extra session . . .
I: I notice whenever you've been upset, it seems to come at a time of separation from someone who means a lot to you.
P: . . . yes! Even when I was the one doing the "abandoning."

The patient mentioned several episodes of depersonalization during her early teens and during periods when she was using cannabis drugs at social gatherings. She also spoke of occasions when she experienced what sounded at first like hallucinations.

I: Did you ever have the feeling that you were being controlled, as it were, by something external to you altogether?
P: Oh, yes! When I, uh, first time I cut myself up when I was fourteen, with the cigarette in my hand, I remember someone *telling* me to go ahead. I heard a distinct voice saying, "Go burn yourself!" At times there'd be a lot of voices in my head that I couldn't identify or even make out what they're saying.
I: They seem to be *in* your head?
P: Yes, *in* my head. I *know* they're hallucinations because I know there isn't anybody speaking to me from afar.
I: Huh?
P: I mean, there's a difference hearing something in your head and hearing something from five feet away. Like, when you hear music in your head: it's different from hearing it at a concert.
I: You never had had the sensation that the voices *seemed* to come from afar?
P: No, never.
I: They don't come from outside, they come from inside but strike you as saying things different from how you might carry on a conversation with yourself in your head by way of daydreaming or whatever.
P: Yeah. That's why I can be rational when I'm having them. I know fully well they're hallucinations.
I: Or so you choose to call them!
P: Well, or maybe it's an illusion. I don't know what you would call it. But

I know fully well it's not a question of there being someone *out* there, and I'm not deluded about *that*.

The patient then gave examples of other nondelusional but abnormal experiences of reality, such as when she would "totally" identify herself with an actor in the movies, or get an uncanny feeling after hearing a certain unusual word three or four times on the same day—as though the "coincidence" might have had some special significance (she never felt these occurrences related specifically to her, however). Next she alluded to her unrealistically low image of herself.

P: I don't think I'm a very interesting person.
I: You don't.
P: No. I mean, maybe as a weird case for a psychiatrist, but I don't feel I have very much really to *offer* anybody.
I: What have you felt you might have to offer?
P: Well, I'm a fairly good artist. I'm pretty good at it when I put my mind to it, only that's not very often. I don't have much discipline. I don't think I'm pretty, and I don't think I'm vivacious or someone that anyone'd wanna be around.
I: No?
P: I think a lot of people could do just as well without me.
I: Have these feelings been reinforced by things people have said, or things your folks have said?
P: Oh, my parents think I'm beautiful. They certainly boost my ego. But I don't *feel* it.

Toward the end of the interview, the patient discussed her mood swings and her general pessimism.

I: Are there times you feel you can eventually recover, or do you mostly feel you'll be on the casualty list for keeps?
P: I *never* feel encouraged about life. I have my very high "highs." I can get extremely high.
I: How high is that?
P: Oh, ecstatic! I'm just out of bounds completely. Like I was yesterday: running around in highs and lows. Mostly I was full of energy, talking to all my friends, dashing off pictures. . . . It's like I'm doing that, though—in a frantic effort to hold onto something before I sink.
I: With thoughts of suicide hovering in the background?
P: Right! One of these days I can see myself doing something to myself I won't recover from so fast. That's pretty scary!
I: How have you been feeling here during the past week or so?
P: I'm premenstrual now, so I'm more tense than usual.

I: Your appetite's okay?
P: Yeah.
I: No aches or pains?
P: No *(smiling)*. Only my heart aches. I miss my friends, I miss everything. I'm just tryin' to relax. That's why I'm sitting here *(actually she was at this moment slouched very seductively in her chair)*.

Comments

Like many patients whose symptom picture is intermediate with respect to the paradigm cases of schizophrenia and manic-depressive illness, this patient was given a wide variety of diagnostic labels during the early weeks of hospitalization. Disappointment in a romantic relationship was the apparent precipitant of her illness, which was at first mostly of a depressive quality (suicidal ruminations, tearfulness). There was a history of mild marijuana use and one or two experiences with other drugs. Her response to cannabis was one of withdrawal, detachment, and a dreamlike preoccupation that led some observers to think of a schizophrenic or schizoaffective disorder.

Later in the course of her hospitalization, there was a shift in the nature of her symptoms. Giddiness, euphoria, hyperactivity, overfamiliarity, and flippancy replaced depression and depersonalization. A formal thought disorder was never present. There was a mild tendency toward allusiveness and punning, as in the reply, "only my heart aches," to the question about bodily aches and pains. A month before the interview, she had a brief period of manic psychosis with grandiose and paranoid features. On phenothiazines these symptoms subsided, but irritability and impatience remained. Later, on lithium, the remaining symptoms also disappeared.

There was a history of affective (including bipolar) illness in the family. It may be that the initial symptoms some regarded as schizophrenic in nature were an epiphenomenon related to drugs. In any case, they disappeared shortly after the admission.

The borderline features in this patient, in addition to the "nonspecific" signs, consisted in the impairment of ego integration, particularly along the narcissistic path of development. She showed a strong inclination, for example, to overidealize certain people and to see herself in devalued terms.

The patient here showed a good capacity to test reality. She knew, for example, that the voices she occasionally heard were illusory and were localized inside her head to begin with. Pseudohallucinations of this sort are compatible with borderline conditions (by any standard: structural, genetic, or clinical). What distinguishes her, psychostructurally, from the neurotic is her faulty ego integration: her sense of identity is not only shaky but quite at odds with how others would experience her. Self-esteem is seriously impaired; she sees herself as boring and unprepossessing, whereas most people would regard her as attractive and interesting. Related to these phenomena is her incapacity to handle compliments, a quality exhibited by many patients with the syndrome *hysteroid dysphoria* (D. Klein, 1972). Actually this designation fits the patient well: she demonstrates almost all the qualities described by Klein under this heading.

The main characterological features were hysterical, depressive/masochistic, infantile, explosive, and narcissistic (in decreasing order of importance).

Final Diagnostic Impressions

A. Categorical diagnoses
   1. Affective disorder, bipolar-I
   2. Borderline structure
   3*a*. Hysterical personality with narcissistic features
   b. Kraepelinian temperament: cyclothymic

B. Dimensional assessments
   1. Initially, Region IV, but the "schizophrenic" component apparently a manifestation of drug effect. Region V of the Sz-MDP continuum
   2. GAS = 28 (initially, at interview = 39)
   3. Personality profile as shown in Table IV–1

FAMILY HISTORY

First-degree relatives =	6 (parents, plus 4 sibs)
affected member:	(1) brother, age thirty-one (series of brief psychotic episodes, initially of uncertain diagnosis, later of manic-depressive [bipolar] character)
Second-degree relatives =	7
Other (including less seriously affected) members:	(1) mother (recurrent depression of moderate severity, never hospitalized) (2) sister, age twenty-two (mildly depressive, introverted) (3) maternal uncle (alcoholism)

Case Illustration 10

Patient = P   Therapist = T   GAS = 28

The following interchange took place after the patient, a single woman of twenty-one, had spent much of her session vilifying the various members of her family, especially her mother.

P: . . . how'd *you* like it, if you always got shot down?! What am *I* supposed to do?

T: Well . . .

P: *(Interrupting)* Can't I just "forget it," where she's concerned? Why can't I just forget it?

T: I don't see how you can . . .

P: *(Interrupting)* Everybody says she's no good for me; my friends say it; Dr. Grauber *(her previous therapist)* even said it . . .

T: You talk as though you had only one brand of feelings toward her. I really don't think that's so . . .

P: Why all this effort toward *her?* Where do *I* fit in? I don't owe her a damn thing!

T: Maybe not. But you certainly owe it to yourself to settle matters between you reasonably. You pretend she's nothing but an albatross around your neck, when the fact of the matter is, when she's away, you crawl the walls!

P: You make me feel like I'm two years old because I still need her!

T: You said it, not . . .

P: What she needs is a bomb under her bed! . . .

T: Oh come now; you act as if you can't make a lick of progress unless you literally get rid of her.

P: . . . what I'm trying to say is—something has to be *done* with her!!

T: And I'm trying to say—something has to be done with you to make you realize you have more down there than just hatred for her!

P: (*Becoming slightly tearful at this point*) Look, for Chrissake, I was trying to reach out to her . . . last night I really was: I couldn't get enough of her. . . . I wanted to be next to her every second. . . . And I was thinking . . . I had a very "tell-me-how-I-can-get-along" conversation. . . . I was polite—"Should I take Spanish lessons?" "Was I rude to Aunt Margaret?" . . . but she just gave me the back of her hand: "You're the Buttonhole Queen tonight, aren't you" . . . she said a lot of cruel shit like that, that really hurt my feelings. . . . And she wanted to drag me to Dr. Fox to do behavior therapy to get rid of my phobia . . . who the hell is Dr. Fox? I can't *stand* it when she makes up my mind for me: "*Well* now, Alexandra, the voice of reason must conquer the . . . " *(imitating her mother)* . . . as though I've been lying around the house accomplishing *nothing* . . . she has no right to throw it up to me that I haven't made an *obscene* amount of progress . . . "in my little cat way" *(interposing a phrase in baby talk suddenly)* . . . she tried to drag me to the restaurant over the weekend, saying "it's important to Daddy that. . . . " It was *not* important, 'cause he really *would* have preferred to stay home . . . so she called me a *witch* when I said, "No!"

T: And do you recall *why* you all had to be "dragged" to the restaurant?

P: Huh?

T: I'm referring to your having sprinkled Clorox over the chicken your mother was . . .

P: It was Lysol!

T: Oh, pardon me! . . . Lysol, over the chicken your mother was preparing. That was hardly calculated, do you think, to effect a rapprochement between you and her . . .

P: I *tried* to make a rapprochement . . . I just told you that . . . but when she called me "Buttonhole Queen" . . . I said "Okay, dammit, this is *war!*"

T: Wait a minute! Look . . . you're not going to win any "war" between you and her . . .

P: *(Interrupting)* Who are you? Ann Landers? The village priest? . . . Who's side are you on, anyway?

T: I'm on "your"-plural side: you and her, because I know you're not going to get better at all unless you make your peace with her. . . . You have to make an effort to . . .

P: (*Interrupting*) She doesn't *deserve* my effort!

T: You both have to make an effort. But you're the younger one, naturally, so you can't expect so much change from her, as we could expect from you . . .

P: Thanks a lot! Only I'm not gonna "change" for that bitch. . . . *She's* the sick one, goddammit . . . *she* should be here, not me . . . and don't be surprised if you find me floating in the river . . . because I can't *take* much more of this! What am I supposed to do? Feel sorry for *her*!?

Anamnestic Data

The young woman of this case illustration had functioned fairly well until leaving home to go to college. There, "homesickness" soon mounted to near panic proportions, and to this was added a more acute sense of loss in connection with a romantic disappointment. Concentrating on her studies became impossible at this point, and she returned home. There she developed a wide range of crippling "neurotic" symptoms: compulsions, rituals, agoraphobia, rage outbursts, and depressive episodes capped by suicidal ruminations and occasional minor self-injurious acts. In addition she withdrew from many (but not all) of her friends and spent many hours of the day in autistic reverie. At times she was so anxious she was scarcely able to engage in any structured activities around the house; at other times she was able to "lose herself" in reading. She was locked in a markedly ambivalent relationship with her mother, and alternated between petulance or outright abusiveneess and clinging dependency. At the time the case material was gathered, she had already been continuously ill for some fourteen months. Only after a brief period of residential treatment did the agoraphobic symptom subside, whereupon she made an excellent recovery. Antidepressant medication and phenothiazines had been given for extended periods during the course of her illness, but her responses to either type of agent were equivocal.

Comments

Evidence for borderline structure in this patient consisted of the "nonspecific" signs (gross inability to tolerate stressful situations without experiencing crippling anxiety; marked impulsivity as manifest by tantrums, rage outbursts, and even a few instances of assaultiveness; inability to attend either to schoolwork or avocational pursuits) in the presence of adequate reality-testing capacity. The latter was never impaired to the point of delusions but did show deficiencies in the interpersonal realm. She would continue, as in the vignette, to externalize, casting all blame on the family.

With respect to placement on the Sz-MDP continuum, the following clinical points were of relevance. On the affective side, she exhibited at various times self-depreciation, tearfulness, suicide ruminations and gestures, and depressive affect. On the schizophrenic side, again, at various times: ambivalence, bizarre behavior, chronicity, and inappropriate affect. According to my modification of Cohen's weighted rating scale (Chapter 8), her schizophrenia/affective disorder ratio = 67/33, placing her in Region II of the continuum diagram. Her peculiarities of speech, including preciosity, strangely incorrect usages of words, and so on, were also more compatible with schizophrenic predominance. The bizarre behavior mentioned above consisted of adopting strange postures (mostly of either a childlike or seductive quality) along with unusual forms of hostile or manipulative conduct at home.

She is one of the few patients from among the case illustrations whose profusion of erstwhile "neurotic" symptoms would remind one of the older designation, "pseudoneurotic schizophrenia." From the standpoint of *syndrome* diagnosis, this might be an apt label, although (1) there were never any productive signs and (2) her other symptoms were overshadowed by the agoraphobia.

Characterologically the predominant traits were narcissistic (grandiosity, condescension, exploitative object relationships, a combined exalted and denigrated self-image, and so on). As in many patients (especially those with strong schizophrenic propensities) who show *fragmentation* in the internal representation of the self, she could appear as quite different selves on different days. It was quite unpredictable whether one was going to see her in her haughty state (in which all "blame" was externalized) or in her childlike state or in her depressive, tearful state (in which she accepted blame for things she had not done).

Final Diagnostic Impressions

A. Categorical diagnoses
   1*a*. Schizoaffective disorder, depressed type
   b. Agoraphobia
   2. Borderline structure (schizotypal)
   3. Narcissistic personality (with phobic and infantile features)

B. Dimensional assessments
   1. Region II of the Sz-MDP continuum
   2. GAS = 28
   3. Personality profile as shown in Table IV–1

First-degree relatives =	3 (parents, plus 1 sib)
affected member:	(1) brother (hospitalized for an acute psychotic episode with predominantly schizophrenic symptoms)
Second-degree relatives =	7
Other (including less seriously affected) members:	(1) mother (narcissistic and rigidly obsessional personality; chronically given to rage outbursts but never hospitalized)

Case Illustration 11

Patient = P Doctor = D GAS = 30

P: I was alone about two hours while the wife was out shopping, and . . . I began to sing and dance and write stuff on the blackboard. I get a word in my mind and I say it over and over; I get to rhyming things. . . . I was getting this strange feeling again—of being watched from the living room. The more I got the feeling, the louder I sang.
D: Would that "drown out" the feeling?
P: Yeah! Sort of. Doesn't always work!
D: You were telling me the other day how you give yourself an "imaginary companion" in the form of a spy . . .
P: Oh, ya mean "Edward"?! *(The name he gives this figure)*
D: Is that something you do when you feel uncomfortably alone?
P: Yeah, though it happens without my ever trying. . . . I used to think the bell or the phone'd ring with someone there who'd wanna talk to me. Or if I'd be in the shower, I think I'd hear my wife calling me. When I was very young, I was left alone a lot: my sister was very ill as a baby; my folks'd be visiting Tina in the hospital and I'd be stuck outside in the car—seemed like for hours . . . when I was around six.

I used to hate it. And I still imagine people say my name when I'm alone. Also, there's the fear the house'd be broken into. I fear I'd *kill* them, whoever came in. It'd give me such pleasure . . . yet it's scary. I have these crummy dreams about killing, all the time. Like this one last night where I'm in the army, and I get the enemy in my sights . . . but the bullets bounce off 'em . . . I used to hit Emmy *(his wife)* a lot—till the Doc up in L—— *(where he'd been hospitalized six months earlier)* put me on eighteen hundred of Thorazine. . . . I was really pacing around the house last night . . . my thoughts were racing . . . though some of the time, I'd be so depressed, I'd just sit on the edge of my bed, and Emmy'd have to push me just to get me to brush my teeth.

One month later:

P: . . . I feel fragmented today.
D: How do you mean?
P: I dunno: it's like every time I take a step, I leave part of me behind . . . it's partly a feeling that you're like—all over the universe . . . or that someone's coming after me.

One month later:

P: I had a lousy weekend . . . felt closed off from the rest of the world . . . like when everything'd become "smooth" . . . could even read a book . . . but today, I feel *great! (He looked cheerful, was pacing back and forth in the room, instead of sitting despondently in his chair, as he had done in the past)*
D: Feeling maybe a little too "great," even?
P: "Too great?" What could be "too great" for my own good!? . . . I do feel a little "hyper." It's very unusual for me. My mind's going too fast.

One month later:

P: . . . I had this rotten dream: there were animals talking; there was this one animal, and someone cuts its head off. It still talked as it lay on the floor. I was some kind of animal myself, and I was married to a woman: a human being that was like, civilized. I think I'm gonna get depressed again! I feel *dead* again. Cold. Like my feet, legs . . . are dying. Or never existed before. Like time was beginning all over again . . .

One month later:

P: . . . Emmy picks on me whenever I feel depressed or "meek": I get tired of it! I don't usually get mad, ya know—but I did Monday! I . . .

(suddenly an inappropriate glee comes into his voice and expression; he takes on the demeanor of a monster in a horror film) tried to strangle her! . . . could've been frightening in retrospect. First time *(more sober and reflective now)* I tried to strangle her. I've hit her before.

D: That's pretty serious, don't you think?
P: No.
D: Why not?!
P: I have a right to get mad.
D: Mad is one thing; strangle is another!
P: It makes me nervous to think about it.
D: Makes you think of how your uncle killed your aunt?
P: Yeah, yeah . . .

One month later:

P: . . . felt *terrible* yesterday. . . . I was afraid to fall asleep. I cried all night. Tried to kill myself, with glass, or burn my arm with a cigarette lighter. Never felt so bad in *all* my life!

P: I get this thought; like a voice in my head that'll say, "Do you know where I'm going tomorrow?" If I get that, the *next* day I'll feel *bad.* But if I go the whole day without saying that, I'll feel OK the next day. I never told *anyone* that before! It sounds sorta ridiculous.
D: How come?
P: I dunno; a lot of things happen inside me that lay buried before, in silence—when I was with Dr. T——*(previous therapist).* I was reluctant to reveal certain things to him; sometimes I feel very detached—as though I watch myself from acrost a hallway. Other times I feel like my "self." Feel disconnected. Fragmented over time, if I get to thinking about the past days, weeks, years . . . feel cut off from my wife much of the time, though not from mother. My mother's my anchor.

One month later:

P: I still get the "unreal" feeling, especially before I go to sleep; had a nightmare last . . . got super-mad yesterday, like for ten to fifteen minutes I'd be in a rage. Afterwards I'd feel sorry, even. But I'd curse, feel loud and distant; Emmy begins to look huge and scary all of a sudden.

Anamnestic Data

This patient, a married man of twenty-five, had been in treatment for several years, and in a number of different settings, because of a refractory condition in which depression, a peculiar thought disorder, paranoid ideation, and aggressive and self-destructive outbursts seemed to alternate in dominating the clinical picture. This serious and constantly shifting disorder began without any demonstrable psychological precipitant and, once begun, persisted regardless of what was or was not occurring in the interpersonal field.

The case material presented here stems from the most recent change of therapist; beforehand, the patient had undergone several courses of ECT (with only temporary relief of his depression), taken psychotropic medications (chiefly phenothiazines or tricyclic antidepressants, and these were without discernible effect), and engaged in psychoanalytic psychotherapy on a five-times-a-week basis (without appreciable benefit). An endocrinological and neurological workup were unrevealing. These were obtained because of "unexplained" weight gain—that actually coincided with his taking chlorpromazine and which disappeared upon discontinuance of the drug.

Although a brilliant student, the patient had had to take a leave of absence from engineering school because there were few days when he was completely symptom free and able to concentrate. His demeanor was ordinarily shy, even meek, but at unpredictable times he would suddenly become assaultive or self-destructive, resorting at times to bizarre means of carrying out his impulses. This behavior would subside within a day or so as quickly and mysteriously as it came on.

At various times since his illness began, he experienced illusions, hallucinations, and persecutory delusions—all of a fleeting nature. More lasting was the imaginary companion who "accompanied" him when he was alone. At the height of any of these brief psychotic episodes, he also had severe insomnia and terrifying nightmares. He became addicted to the sleeping compound prescribed for these symptoms.

After he moved to a different city, he began seeing a different psychiatrist, who noted, after following him for several months, that the psychotic episodes recurred with clocklike regularity every twenty-eight days (and lasted thirty-six to forty-eight hours). For these reasons, all other medications were discontinued, and a trial of lithium was instituted. To this he responded dramatically, maintained rationality even during the critical phases of his cycle, and gradually returned to his former pursuits.

Comments

This patient illustrates certain difficulties in discerning the level of personality organization in someone recuperating rapidly from an episodically psychotic state. For several years his "true" level, as assessed by anyone interviewing him at the time, would appear to have been *psychotic*. In the initial stages of lithium therapy (the phase represented by the case material), sharply contradictory views of himself coexisted in his mind. Also, his anxiety tolerance and sublimatory capacity were still impaired (the impulsivity had disappeared). Hence he now appeared *borderline*. By a year later, at which time his GAS score had risen from 30 to 62, the primitive defenses were no longer manifest and he appeared, even in structural terms, as *neurotic*. Because of the tendency toward rapid shifts of state, the psychostructural framework is not ideally suited to the conceptualization of bipolar manic-depressive conditions.

Final Diagnostic Impressions (during the early stages of lithium therapy)

A. Categorical diagnoses
   1. Affective disorder, bipolar-I type, atypical[3]
   2. ? borderline (see "Comments")
   3. Paranoid personality with obsessive and depressive features[4]

B. Dimensional assessments
   1. Region IV of the Sz-MDP continuum
   2. GAS = 30
   3. Personality profile as shown in Table IV–1

FAMILY HISTORY

First-degree relatives = 4 (parents, plus 2 sibs)
affected members: (1) father (recurrent depressive episodes but nonpsychotic; not hospitalized)
(2) mother (treated with ECT for recurrent depressive psychotic episodes)

Second-degree relatives = 7
affected members: (1) maternal grandfather (violent rage outbursts leading to difficulties with the law; mood lability; irritable temperament)
(2) paternal aunt (hospitalized for many years for what was considered to be a schizophrenic episode; exact nature of illness is unclear)

Case Illustration 12

Patient = P Interviewer = I GAS = 30

The patient, a young woman of nineteen, sits rigidly in the chair, arms folded akimbo, dressed in a man's shift with pants and a man's sweater and

[3]"Atypical" because some symptoms more commonly associated with schizophrenia had been present at the outset: eccentric and disorganized thought (episodically), bizarre delusions, and also hallucinations. The Sz/MDP symptom ratio was 30/70; i.e., preponderantly but not exclusively affective.

[4]Further along in his recovery, the dominant character traits were no longer paranoid, but obsessive.

loafers, hair pulled back tightly; her voice is very soft, controlled, monotonous, at times barely audible; her manner is imperious, disdainful; she tends to look away from the face of interviewer—sometimes fixing her gaze on his shoe or on his legs or on his wristwatch.

After several minutes of verbal sparring with the interviewer, the patient began to speak of how uncomfortable she felt at any reference to sexuality or tender feelings.

P: The world would be a better place without sex.
I: In what way?
P: People talk as though it's everything. It isn't everything. There *are* other dimensions to a person's image of himself . . .
I: But that doesn't tell me what you had in mind when you said . . .
P: There'd be less danger without sex.
I: What are the dangers you're hoping to sidestep?
P: Right *now,* I'm not concerned about them . . . *(Pause)* I find sex something very uncomfortable. . . . I guess I just choose not to consider it at all.
I: Consider what?
P: Man's sexual nature.
I: *(Pause)* You *have* allowed yourself to contemplate *woman's* sexual nature?
P: Man *nor* woman.
I: Equally forbidding.
P: Yeah.
I: How is that?
P: Uncomfortable.
I: In what way?
P: I just find it very difficult to talk about. I can't specify any particular way, I can't put my finger on it.
I: Huh?
P: I can't put my finger on it. I can't specify any particular way it makes me uncomfortable.
I: Well, but what comes to mind?
P: Nothing. I think it's just an area I choose to block off.
I: I think you're trying to avoid something; perhaps, if you let yourself try, some thought, some impression will occur to you . . .
P: Well . . . I suppose it all seems cheap and vulgar.
I: All right, but what *is* the cheapness and the vulgarity of it all, anyway?
P: I don't really know. I find it frightening. I find it disgusting.
I: What is so frightening?
P: I don't really know.
I: I think you know *extremely* well!

P: I don't know what it is precisely that frightens me.

I: But you know in what way it frightens you, what things about it disturb you—even though you're not aware of how it all may have started, correct?

P: In vague ways, I know . . .

I: Well, let's hear what comes to mind. I'll be happy to accept a "vague" beginning in comparison to no beginning at all!

P: I think I have a lot of, umm, misconceptions about it . . .

I: Indeed! *(Alluding to her double entendre)*

P: I have a lot of the same feelings about childbirth: painful, it's bloody, it's disgusting. I realize also there's a pleasurable side *(spoken sotto voce and without conviction)* but . . . I guess I'm willing to forego that.

I: "Pleasurable" in what way?

P: *(Silence)*

I: What comes to mind on the "disgusting" side?

P: The blood. The nudity.

I: What about the blood? You put it ahead of nudity on the "disgusting" list.

P: *(Smiles nervously)* Yeah.

I: So what about blood?

P: I'm sure it ties in with menstruation, but . . . but I think it's more the blood, all by itself, than the menstruation.

I: As if what: What about blood gives it its special . . .

P: *(Pause)* I really don't know. And I can't remember.

I: Well, we don't have to rely on your memory alone. As you think about it right now, what comes to . . .

P: *(Pause)* One thing I remember—I don't know if it means anything or not—one day my mother cut her finger and she had to have stitches, and she almost fainted. . . . I don't actually recall if I *saw* it or just heard about it . . . that was a long time ago.

I: Were you concerned about the possibility she might have really hurt herself badly? Or that she might even die?

P: No, I don't . . . well, yes, I've had thoughts like that. The main feeling I got from that was, umm, *terror*. Being left alone. Like I'd have to pull myself together. . . . I had different fantasies of what'd happen if my parents were both dead. How I'd sort of march on . . . carry on from there . . . *(smiles nervously)*.

I: Sex is another bloody business, I guess: menstruation, defloration, childbirth. . . . A lot more "dangerous" than a cut finger!

P: Yeah *(long silence)*.

I: You'd prefer to banish sex, as it were, and just become a disembodied head . . . a brilliant mind not attached to a body of any sort.

P: I won't disagree with you because that's exactly how I feel.

She goes on to relate a few incidents from early adolescence when there were some pleasurable moments with her father: sitting on his knees, playing with his pipe collection, and so forth, enjoyment of which she subsequently felt the need to repudiate.

I: There was some fun between you and your dad back then; it wasn't all serious and unpleasant as it seems to be now.
P: Well, I'm not the same person who did those things in the past.
I: You make it sound as though there's no connection, no continuity between the "you" of six years ago and the "you" of today!
P: No, as I told you, I really felt there was a break somewhere. I guess that was when things became more serious.
I: What sort of "break"?
P: I don't know.
I: Could it be that this "break" was when your period came; that since then you've been "stuck" with being a woman?
P: (*Silence*)
I: At some point in your life, it dawned on you that you were inescapably a woman. Was that when things got "serious"? That's certainly when you began to lose weight. . . .
P: I wouldn't wanna be male . . . I don't wanna be female. I wanna be neuter.
I: Now, as a final question: if you simply had to *choose* one sex as being slightly more endurable to inhabit than the other—repugnant as they both seem—which might be, at the moment anyway, *preferable* to you?
P: Female *(spoken almost inaudibly)*.
I: Well, so there's hope. Okay. We'll stop at this point.

Comments

This patient was admitted to the hospital for treatment of a moderately severe anorexia nervosa syndrome.

There were no psychiatrically ill relatives in her immediate or extended family.

Psychological tests taken around the time of admission showed an IQ in the very superior range (136, with no difference between verbal and performance). There was no unevenness in the subtest scores. On the unstructured portions, she gave no evidence of impairment in reality testing. A number of Rorschach percepts centered on animal mouths with sharp teeth, but always with good awareness of form (i.e., there were no F− responses). The same fears she made manifest in the interview were expressed in the TAT stories. The only diagnostic impressions to emerge from the tests were characterological: "obsessive personality with passive-aggressive and narcissistic features."

In this patient there were no stigmata of a major functional psychosis of either schizophrenic or manic-depressive nature. Hence her condition, at least as far as one can tell, lies outside the Sz-MDP continuum.

With regard to psychic structure, only one of the nonspecific signs (reduced anxiety tolerance) was present, unless one wishes to include severe dieting as an impulse disorder. She did not exhibit any of the conventional forms of impulse disturbance or "acting-out" tendencies. Since reality testing was unimpaired, our chief concern would be with the distinction at the higher level—between borderline and neurotic organizations. In the vignette we can find considerable evidence of disturbance in identity sense (or "ego integration"), particularly in regard to matters of gender identity and sexual drive. The primary defense at work here is less primitive than denial: the patient shows conscious repudiation or disavowal (as Bergeret might refer to it) of feelings and fantasies which are nonetheless available to her at a conscious level. She makes a conscious attempt to split off the intellectual from the sensual aspect of her personality, so much so that the interviewer has to expend enormous effort to elicit from her any acknowledgment of the sensual. She once referred to this as an "area" she "chose to block off." A similar but less pronounced tendency to repudiate hostile feelings was also noted, although outwardly she was quite critical and condescending. Dependency feelings were somewhat less difficult to acknowledge, but without prodding she was unwilling to volunteer anything of emotional significance about herself. Disavowal and splitting, and the attendant defect in ego integration, all established the structural level as borderline. (Note that in this patient, even the unstructured psychological tests revealed no primitivity, unlike the situation with many borderline—especially schizotypal borderline—patients). Interview GAS at 30 reflected the still severe anorexia problem; as the latter abated through appropriate intervention, the global rating rose to approximately 60.

Final Diagnostic Impressions

A. Categorical diagnoses
   1*a*. No functional psychosis
   b. Anorexia nervosa
   2. Borderline structure
   3. Obsessive personality with passive-aggressive and narcissistic features

B. Dimensional assessments
   1. Sz-MDP continuum not relevant
   2. GAS initial = 30
   3. Personality profile as shown in Table IV–1

Case Illustration 13

Patient = P Consultant = C GAS = 35

C: You look rather anxious.
P: Well . . . *(pause)* I was expecting to be interviewed by Dr. T——.
C: What effect does it have on you that it's me instead of him?
P: Well, I suppose . . . well, somehow I have the impression that he wouldn't know as much about my progress here as you probably do.
C: Because he's from a different service in the hospital?
P: Yes, I'm not sure I can trust you to place internal signs above external signs.
C: I'm not sure I grasp what you mean.
P: Well, here I am, and it's a "progress conference." Felt weird about it.
C: How so?
P: Well, at this particular moment . . . ahh . . . I'd have to say my external self and my internal self are not in the same place. There's the question of how I view myself and how you view myself, ya see . . .
C: Perhaps you need to spell that out a bit more, I think.
P: Well, I'm not allowed out of this unit yet, so how can you think I've made "progress"? If I say I *have* made internal progress, how can I prove it to you?
C: From where you sit, people simply judge by appearances. Something like *that?*
P: Yuh.
C: Let's hear what that brings to mind: "appearances."
P: *(Pause)* Well . . . my family goes back to the Mayflower. Everybody my parents knew are in the Social Register. At the time I thought that was great. I felt a lot of pride and all that.
C: Uh-huh.
P: But I've also felt a lot of bitterness. A lot of bitterness in my soul, ya know . . .
C: Well, actually . . .
P: . . . because there was always something going on I was left out of. I spent half the evenings as a kid looking at bigwigs through the bannister.
C: They didn't let you come downstairs and meet the guests?
P: No. I had to stay upstairs with the nurse. But I'd sneak down just far enough to see. There was always a party *going*.
C: You say "party going."
P: So?
C: I thought you were about to say there was always a party going "on" . . .
P: *(Interrupting)* Well, yeah, "going on" . . .

C: . . . "party going" put me in mind of someone—some "party"—going . . . leaving . . . leaving you, perhaps. Does that bring anything to mind?

P: Well *(pause)* . . . you could say my father was away a good deal when I was young.

C: *I* could say?

P: Well, *I* could say! I mean, he was away four months at a time, sometimes.

C: You missed him?

P: When he was away, I missed him, yeah. . . . When he got back, he and my mother would be at each other's throats. And I couldn't do anything about it. I'd stand in a corner listening to them yell at each other, imagining I was Alexander.

C: Why Alexander?

P: 'Cause he conquered the world, man, and I couldn't conquer shit! I still spend a lot of time imagining I'm Alexander. If not Alexander, then some other superman type . . .

C: Like Hamlet? *(Alluding to a brief engulfment of the patient in the notion he might be Hamlet)*

P: No, man . . . more that I was Shakespeare writing *Hamlet* . . .

C: Uh-huh . . . The "who-you-are" and "who-you'd-like-to-be" have always been pretty far apart, I take it.

P: Yeah *(pause)* . . . Those supermen were the only source of strength I had, to help me put up with all the shit that was going on around me . . .

C: You really had *no* source of strength, in effect.

P: Huh?

C: You took "strength" from imaginary persons. Dead people. You invented people on one side of your brain and "borrowed strength" from them on the other side: the whole transaction was going on inside *you!*

P: I guess you could say that.

C: You seem reluctant to go along with the idea.

P: It means I had *nothing*. I got *nothing* from them.

C: Isn't that what you've been hinting at all along?

P: *(Sotto voce, reluctantly)* Yeah . . .

Anamnestic Data

The case material derives from an interview that took place about a month after hospitalization for a brief but acute psychotic episode. Florid symptoms were present for several days, including severe blunting of affect, grandiose delusions, auditory hallucinations (in which the phrase "rotten eggs" was repeated or else the phrase "Anna Karenina," which the patient took as a command to throw himself in front of a train). During this time he had experiences of depersonalization and derealization. Marked tangentiality and allusiveness temporarily made his speech difficult to understand. At the height of the initial episode, everything in the environment seemed to take on special meaning and relevance. Every act, even the most accidental, seemed imbued with symbolic overtones and cryptic messages. Thus, if he bent down and a pen fell out of his coat pocket, he construed this as signifying he no longer had any need for the object. If he crossed paths in the street with a Great Dane, he would suddenly feel identified with (the great Dane) Hamlet and would experience this as a message to "avenge" his father (though the latter was still living). At no time in the past had the patient used "hallucinogenic" or other illicit drugs.

Psychological Test Data

Full-scale IQ = 110 (verbal IQ = 115, performance IQ = 101). Intertest variability in subscores was moderately high (9 to 14). On the unstructured portions of the test battery, "autistic thinking" broke through; there was evidence of confusion about gender identity. There were a number of unusual Rorschach responses, namely, " . . . a sort of superannuated ugly cadaverous woman . . ." (card IX); " . . . a bashed-up body with lungs outside, no penis, so I supposed it must be that of a woman who's been in a car accident" (card II). His TAT stories were remarkable for their emphasis of two contrasting themes: general ineffectiveness side by side with grandiosity.

Comments

By the time of the interview, the patient had recompensated moderately well from his acute psychotic episode but was still quite unstable. His facade of superciliousness broke down under moderately intense confrontation. At one point, for example, he retreated into intellectualization, delivering a kind of "canned speech" to the interviewer rather than communicating his feelings. This was brought to his attention with the following remark: "I can't help noticing how you recite to me this, as it sounds to me, prearranged script—yet you look intensely forlorn, and about that you tell me nothing." To this mild intervention, he reacted with tearfulness and agitation, though ordinarily he took immense pains to sound detached and professorial.

It can be very difficult to say on which side of the continuum of psychoses an *acute* episode will settle (so many established manics start out with a seemingly schizophrenic break). This patient leans heavily in the direction of schizophrenia as his condition evolves. There is a profound disturbance of ego boundary (" . . . I'd have to say my external self and my internal self are not in the same place . . .") long after the grossly psychotic symptoms disappeared. Strange locutions crop up every so often in his speech, though admittedly not very frequently. Some of these are eccentric enough to alert the listener to the likelihood of a schizophrenic process. As Rochester, Martin, and Thurston (1977) mention in their paper on thought-process disorder in schizophrenia, many schizophrenics can communicate *adequately* on the whole, yet make occasional aberrant responses which are highly characteristic. They cite Joseph Jaffe's observation in this regard that sometimes "a few swallows *do* make a summer." The patient's remark, "[I've felt] a lot of bitterness in my *soul,* ya know," was, to cite one instance, most unusual from a speaker of his sociocultural background, and therefore came across as peculiarly "highfalutin" and at the same time elliptical: he took for granted that the interviewer would know exactly what he meant by this expression, as though the interviewer were already "in" on the patient's private world. Elsewhere, the patient retorted, as though announcing something of a philosophical profundity, " . . . truth is . . . is *real!*" Altogether in the interview there were about a dozen instances when the patient "did not take the point of view of the listener into account"—a failure Rochester et al. (1977, p. 111) consider typical of the schizophrenic "thought disorder."

Characterologically this patient had been described by those familiar with his premorbid personality as aloof, grandiose, imperious, and mannered. These same narcissistic qualities were again noted by the nursing staff of the hospital unit where his treatment was carried out. Usually he behaved condescendingly toward the female staff members, though he was rather easily intimidated by males in authority.

Final Diagnostic Impressions

A. Categorical diagnoses
   1. Schizophrenic reaction, acute undifferentiated with paranoid features
   2. Level of function initially psychotic; now recompensated
   3. Narcissistic personality with schizoid features

B. Dimensional assessments
   1. Region I of the Sz-MDP continuum
   2. Schizotypal borderline; GAS during acute episode = 22, at time of interview = 35
   3. Personality profile as shown in Table IV–1

FAMILY HISTORY

First-degree relatives = 2

affected member: (1) mother (chronic undifferentiated schizophrenia with three periods of decompensation; narcissistic personality)

Second-degree relatives = 5
Other (including less seriously affected) members: (1) father (schizoid personality)
(2) maternal grandfather (eccentric, irascible, never hospitalized)

Case Illustration 14

Patient = P Doctor = D GAS = 36

D: What are you experiencing at the moment?
P: *(His speech throughout is monotonous, calculated, ponderous, slow)* Uhh . . . a mild degree of trepidation . . . or rather *(pause)* there had been a degree of trepidation on the grounds that my family might have been present at this meeting. *(Pause)* Seeing that they're not here, I feel a measure of relief. Though it is unclear as yet whether I will have anything to say here.
D: Whether I will give you the chance?
P: Uhh . . . No. Whether I will be in a frame of mind to do any talking.
D: What was your apprehension about your folks possibly visiting?
P: Uhh . . . I have been . . . you could say, alienated from them. The only way they know I was still alive would be if I were in trouble and called them. I'm talking about our pattern of communication over the past six years . . . *(silence)* . . . *(The patient adopts a tense posture)*
D: You look ill at ease.
P: Uhh . . . I would say "cautious." Waiting for you to say something.
D: Well . . . you began a moment ago alluding to your family . . . some strain there. I found myself at the moment expecting you might enlarge on that theme, especially if it were relevant to your having come to the hospital.
P: It's hard for me to answer that question, because . . . uhh . . . my family has scarcely existed as a unit, going back even before six years . . . more like ten years. . . .
D: The family didn't seem to you much like a "family" in the ordinary sense of the word?
P: That would be one possible interpretation of my remark. . . . There was never any considerable degree of closeness. *(Pause)* My mother had a second family . . .
D: Oh? Ah, you mean she had been married once before . . .
P: Hardly! You appear to have missed my meaning entirely.
D: Quite possibly. But then I must ask you to explain what is no longer a clear allusion.
P: My mother was a schoolteacher . . .
D: Aha!

P: . . . and she had a "family" of some twenty or thirty other children on whom she concentrated most of her thoughts.

D: Ah . . . you were making a joke . . .

P: That is correct.

D: . . . which I did not catch at first. Well, I'd have to say I am also very uncertain about this trepidation you felt at the prospect of their coming. I mean, from what you've mentioned so far, I could understand *indifference* on your part—since no one was close to anyone else, but not fearfulness. Or even bitterness: I could understand your having felt bitter at what sounds like a lot of unavailability on her part when you were growing up . . .

P: I don't recall "bitterness," as you put it . . . I recall a certain contentment at being left to do as I pleased . . . *(Pause)* . . . though it's conceivable I may at times have wished for greater responsiveness . . .

D: "Conceivable"? One would think "inevitable," under the circumstances. Still, though, I don't get a feeling about your apprehensiveness at the idea of seeing them.

P: You're continuing to pressure me on an issue I prefer not to answer.

D: I sense that. Perhaps this means, however, that the issue is an important one and that you should try in spite of yourself to answer it.

P: *(Pause)* Confronting them would provoke a certain paranoia. . . . might provoke such a reaction on my part . . .

D: I'm not sure what you mean by that term.

P: They might laugh, or think of laughing, at seeing me . . .

D: Both equally?

P: My mother, somewhat more so, possibly.

D: But at what?

P: *(Pause)* Possibly the spectacle of seeing me in the hospital: "Lo, how the mighty are fallen" . . . that sort of thing.

D: As though they might be contemptuous of your suicide attempt, rather than sympathetic?

P: Correct.

D: Does it seem to you quite likely that they *would* smirk or laugh up their sleeves at the thought of your having landed here?

P: *(Pause)* Outwardly, possibly not . . .

D: Even inwardly? Can you easily picture them laughing themselves at your distress, even though they were to put on a show of concern?

P: *(Pause)* . . . Probably . . . from a purely statistical viewpoint . . . the odds are they would be sympathetic. This does not overcome my fear of ridicule on their part.

D: Well, now I'm beginning to wonder whether your real fear isn't so much of *their* ridicule but of your *own!* You may be quite contemptuous of whatever it is in yourself that led to your being hospitalized, isn't that possible? You seem to have felt you "failed" on the job, though neither your parents nor your boss felt that way from what I understand; you then tried to hurt yourself . . . I don't think the "demon"— that would laugh at your situation—is "out there." I think he's in you.

P: *(Pause)* That's possible. . . . Yes. That's possible . . .

D: That you're a harsher critic of yourself than your folks'd be.

P: Yes. I would have to agree with that.

D: You say that reluctantly . . . as though you'd prefer to hang on to the old notions.

P: *(Pause)* Well . . . one gets used to a certain view of the world . . .

Toward the end of the interview, the consultant drew attention to a rather striking quality of the patient's demeanor, namely, that he spoke and sat in the chair not as one would expect of a young man in his twenties, but more in keeping with an octogenarian in a nursing home.

D: Have you always been this "dead" emotionally?

P: *(Pause)* I don't think so. *(His expression grew more distant and irritable)*

D: Perhaps the question itself bothers you?

P: No. I can appreciate that the question is relevant. I have asked myself when was I alive emotionally. I have no answer for that. At the same time I hear a voice saying, "Maybe you were" . . .

D: A voice?

P: *(Smiles)* Not a hallucination, as you might call it. I am referring to an inner voice—my own voice, in the process of carrying out a conversation with myself. I was nervous when this interview began, so I controlled my feelings more than usual.

D: Uh-huh. But what about this image of being old, I was mentioning. Do you feel "old"?

P: *(No response)*

D: Is it clear to you how someone might react to you in that fashion?

P: Oh, yes, I can appreciate that.

D: How do you account for it?

P: Well . . . I have the feeling that there's nothing happening in my life at this time. Everything that did happen, happened a very very long time ago.

D: Whilst now, nothing is "happening" except some quiet decay?

P: Yeah *(becoming more engaged in the dialogue now)* . . . that'd be a good way of putting it. My life, I often think lately, is more or less "over" . . . and I . . . I tend to push away anything that would stir it *up* again.

D: Like our conversation, for instance.
P: Yes.
D: And if life *did* get "stirred up" again? What then?
P: I don't know.
D: All hell might break loose?
P: I've wondered about that possibility. Yes. Though I don't think it would occur.
D: No?
P: No: there have been times when I have gotten disturbed. Angry. But I never go around fighting or breaking things. I have a way of turning it inside.

Comments

The patient is a single man of twenty-nine, admitted to the hospital following a suicide gesture (overdose of some mild tranquilizers). He had been working as an engineer, but his work history was erratic: he would do well at one assignment for a few months, then begin to fail some task, whereafter he would quit and repeat this process at another company. Although he had a few heterosexual contacts, he rarely dated; he had few friends and usually kept very much to himself. He used neither alcohol nor illicit drugs. The problem of social isolation was noted by his parents when he was an adolescent.

When he was admitted, his clinical picture was rather confusing. He was very guarded, socially isolated, anhedonic, and markedly ambivalent about hospitalization. He externalized a great deal, and could at times be quite argumentative, even menacing. But at no time were productive signs of psychosis noted. The rest of the time he would sit by himself in a corner, communicating with no one. He was bitter and discouraged but not sad. Affect was usually restricted but never inappropriate. Speech flow was normal; his movements were somewhat slowed. Appetite and sleep pattern were undisturbed. Some described him as depressed, others as lacking in "energy" or goal directedness.

Psychological tests, when repeated in the hospital, showed good intellectual function (verbal IQ = 137, performance IQ = 108; full-scale IQ = 125). Performance was not remarkable except on the unstructured tests, where considerable anxiety and depression seemed to break through. Quite a number of unusual and disorganized responses were seen on the Rorschach. Thus on card V, "a ballerina imitating an insect, or a ballerina garbed in insect costume." On the so-called mother card: "two faces connected at their necks, or their necks are a couple of animal figures: two lumpish masses joined by a woman's vagina." To card X (alluding to a rather small element on the blot): "a creature with a rabbit's head, which has two kinds of snakelike appendages coming out of where the ears should be".[5]

The test interviewer felt the patient was harboring "explosive underlying rage" that might erupt in "paranoid panic or suicide." A TAT story was ended in this fashion:

> "He tried to be all things to all people; he tried to operate faster and faster, until finally he broke down. The story ends up with him sitting in a room in a basically catatonic state, not feeling anything too much or rather, feeling sort of numb, dead, burnt out."

A prestigious consultant very familiar with patients of this sort had considered the patient to have *pseudoneurotic schizophrenia,* when he was seen shortly before admission. The admitting psychiatrist gave a contrasting diagnosis: *"major recurrent depression,* functioning with *borderline personality organization."* Review by several attending psychiatrists a month after admission led to a shift in classification to *"borderline schizophrenia"* (Kety type) with *borderline personality organization.* This shift was based on their and the nursing staff's observations of the patient's evasiveness, guardedness, restricted affect, and chronicity of illness, along with the disorganized responses on the Rorschach (the results of testing having by then become available). It was admitted that the patient failed to meet research diagnostic criteria for schizophrenia, since his speech had no peculiarities and there were no productive signs. Still, a trial of phenothiazines was suggested, and he received up to 800 milligrams/day of Thorazine over a period of three months. No benefit was discernible.

His therapist moved to a different city. His new psychiatrist saw his symptoms in a different light: he saw the patient as exhibiting a *recurrent (unipolar) depressive illness with a paranoid personality,* again, functioning at a *borderline level.* The patient was given a trial of tricyclic antidepressants (Elavil, 300 milligrams/day). Over a period of several months he improved significantly and was able to find employment and leave the hospital. It was also noted that the patient was able to speak more candidly about his problems, and to utilize his psychotherapy more effectively. There was no longer a "stalemate" between him and his therapist.

[5]It is of interest that Rapaport, Gill, and Schafer discussed this very response some years ago (1945–1946, vol. II, pp. 332–333), as an example of "fabulized combinations":

> . . . on Card X in reference to the lower middle green areas, "a rabbit . . . worms coming out of his eyes." . . . However, worms do not come out of the eyes of a rabbit. . . . The fabulized character of these responses is apparent in the *impossibility* of the combination effected. . . . The autistic thinking in these fabulized combinations is usually quite striking.

The authors thought such responses constituted impressive evidence of underlying schizophrenic thought disorder.

The patient showed only the weakest signs of schizophrenia clinically; the most suggestive evidence came from the psychological testing. Characterologically, his more prominent features were paranoid, obsessive, schizoid, and narcissistic. This may have contributed to the schizophrenic coloration of his otherwise depressive picture. If one focused on the family history one would have been inclined toward a diagnosis within the spectrum of primary *depressive* illnesses. His very high intelligence may have softened the degree to which he might appear phenotypically schizophrenic.

In retrospect, and with the benefit of much time in which to observe this patient, the *Final Diagnostic Impressions* are:

A. Categorical diagnoses
   1. MDP: unipolar depressive
   2. Borderline personality organization
   3. Paranoid personality with obsessive features
B. Dimensional assessments
   1. Region IV on the Sz-MDP continuum
   2. Borderline personality organization with initial GAS = 36
   3. Personality profile as shown in Table IV–1

As a therapeutic footnote, one might add that visualizing him as a Region IV patient, with a positive family history for major depression, should have led the clinical staff to try antidepressants before the phenothiazines.

FAMILY HISTORY

First-degree relatives =	3 (parents, plus 1 sib)
affected member:	(1) mother (treated with ECT for severe depressive episodes)
Second-degree relatives =	7
affected member:	(1) maternal uncle (made a number of serious suicide attempts; frequent periods of deep depression)

Case Illustration 15

Patient = P Consultant = C GAS:
initial = 33
subsequent = 40

Anamnestic Data

The patient, a married man in his early thirties, made a serious suicide attempt two weeks before hospitalization. His illness occurred after a business reversal and a falling out with one of his partners. There were also a number of problems with his wife, the nature of which was as yet unclear, that appeared to contribute to his despondency. In the few weeks before the attempt, he had become restless and anorectic, had lost five pounds, and had complained of trouble falling asleep and of frequent frightening dreams.

As a child he had been rather isolated, lonely, and perfectionistic. He was enuretic till age ten and had a number of nervous tics throughout adolescence. He was extremely preoccupied with his physical appearance and would spend up to three-quarters of an hour brushing his hair till it was "just so."

At twenty-eight he impulsively married the first woman who paid him any real attention and was relieved at the opportunity because he was then developing a bald spot which he was sure would ultimately ruin his chances of attracting a woman.

The patient, like the other members of his immediate family, was given to histrionic exaggerations in language ("I'm in jail here," "my boss is a sadist," and so on), fluctuations of mood between sadness and euphoria, and episodes of irritable, even assaultive, behavior. Family life was characterized by raucousness: screaming, crying, coming to blows, hilarity, were all part of everyday life.

His relationships with others were superficially friendly but essentially shallow; he shared very little of his deeper feelings with anyone, including his wife.

He had occasional episodes of panic, and these would be followed by periods of relative calm in which he would deny that anything was the matter. Overt sadness had not been noted.

The patient had been phobic about heights and about bridges for as long as he could remember.

Upon admission he was intensely fearful and agitated; he was so preoccupied with certain fears that his ability to relate to others was compromised. Instead he would lead any conversation back to the subject of his anxiety.

P: I'm afraid you'll tell me there's nothing you can do about my condition. That I'm a hopeless case.

C: What would make you afraid that I'd come to that conclusion?

P: I don't know . . . I've just been going downhill . . . I've been this way three months . . . nothing's helped. The medication didn't help . . . nothing's helped. And I don't think the pills I'm on now are gonna help either.

The consultant attempted to explain to him something of the nature of his depressive condition. But since the patient was predominantly anxious and agitated, he (rather concretistically) refused to accept the notion that his symptoms were part of a depressive disorder.

P: I'm not depressed. I'm very nervous . . . but I'm not depressed.
C: I understand before you came here you made a serious suicide attempt.
P: Yuh . . .
C: You don't see that as possibly related to your having been depressed?
P: Am I gonna get better?

At the same time he was expressing apprehension about ever recovering, the patient was also importuning the consultant to let him be discharged from the hospital so he could return to work. At this time, all efforts to get him to see the contradictoriness of wanting to resume outside life as if nothing had happened—only days after a suicide attempt—failed.

The following extract reflects his condition two weeks after the first interview:

C: I understand you're feeling a good deal calmer now.
P: Yes.
C: Can you tell me something about the problems you were having; what led up to your coming here?
P: Well, a month or so before I came in here, I was having a lot of difficulties at work . . . with my partner. There was a sum of money I was counting on from the business that I needed for a down payment on a bigger apartment, that I thought our situation could . . . that it'd be all right to take it out of the firm. Only my partner said things weren't going that well, and that I couldn't. We had a scene over it . . . it wasn't calm and quiet like I'm telling you here . . .
C: Uh-huh.
P: The upshot of it was he decided definitely ''no''—which put me in a jam, because I already committed myself . . . and I got very restless. Very anxious. I would shake, at times; I couldn't sleep. I lost weight, which I never did before. I couldn't sleep; I couldn't *fall* asleep, and I'd wake up at 4:30, 5:30. . . . I didn't wanna go near my wife, which I couldn't understand, because we've always had such a perfect relationship . . .
C: Physically?
P: Every way. *(Pause)* Anyhow . . . I panicked . . . as the time came to actually take the new place, I couldn't face up to it and I panicked. That's when I took the overdose. If my partner had okayed the funds, I guess everything would've gone okay, and this wouldn't have happened . . .

The patient went on to describe his feeling of entrapment. He needed the money ''desperately'' because his wife had given him an ultimatum. Either they get a bigger place (suitable for starting a family), or she would leave him. He had not been at all in tune with her feelings for a long time; when she spelled them out, he was taken by surprise.

P: Well . . . she wanted . . . we've been married nine . . . almost ten years now. And it's been an ideal relationship up till now. In every way . . . I suppose she was thinking of . . . that it was about time to start having a family . . .

C: You say "I suppose." Do you know whether or not she was thinking definitely along those lines?

P: Well, she felt we'd waited pretty long . . . ten years . . . she wasn't getting any younger . . .

C: What was your attitude about it?

P: I didn't want the responsibility of it.

C: Could you have afforded it?

P: Well, if we had taken a less lavish place, I guess . . . we could.

C: Are you saying, in effect, that the money wasn't the only reason, perhaps not even the main reason why the idea of starting a family made you anxious? Could there be other reasons?

P: Well . . . *(Pause)* . . . I was afraid . . . I thought the marriage'd go downhill, once there was a kid . . . somehow. . . . The marriages I'd seen, it was that way. We were happy all the time before. Everything was perfect before . . .

C: You keep saying that, I notice.

P: It was. Far as I was concerned it was . . .

C: And what about her? As far as your wife was concerned, was it "perfect" all that time?

P: I thought she felt that way. Apparently I was wrong.

The consultant attempts to probe the area of self-contradictory thinking:

C: I'm reacting to the comment you made several times now: that your marriage is "ideal," "perfect," everything "hunky-dory," so to speak . . . isn't that what you've been telling me?

P: Yes.

C: And then in the next breath, you tell me your wife has thrown you an ultimatum: "Give me a baby or give me a divorce!" And it comes as if without a warning, as if you had no idea it mattered that much to her. Is that a correct way of putting it?

P: Yes.

C: Does that *add up,* to you? Could it have been so "perfect" as you're telling me?

Eventually the patient acknowledges that the consultant's portrayal of his family situation is most likely more accurate than his own previous picture of "reality."

C: It seems to me your wife's "ultimatum" was an ultimatum only because you were blind to what was staring you in the face for ten years. Isn't that what's been going on? That the marriage was "ideal" only because she kept quiet, waiting for you to get out of fool's paradise. And that in reality it's been on shaky grounds for a long time . . .

P: *(Becoming momentarily tearful)*

C: Could you have been fooling yourself?

P: Yeah . . . yeah . . . *(pause)* . . . I could have been. *(Pause)* I felt a lot more comfortable . . . a lot safer . . . when there was just the two of us. . . . My folks split up when I was four. I figured the same sort of thing'd happen all over again if we ever. . . . I guess I felt when a real kid came along, that'd be the day of reckoning for me.

Psychological Test Data

There was no evidence of organic impairment. Full-scale IQ = 120 (verbal IQ = 120, performance IQ = 118). There was considerable scattering on the subtests, where the scores ranged from 9 to 19. The MMPI was compatible with a depressive disorder. Performance on the unstructured portions was good with respect to reality testing. Thematically, suicidal preoccupation was noted, and also concern about bodily integrity (namely, card I: "a goat with a leg missing"; card VI: "a lobster with a big claw"). The tester was impressed also with the apparent impulsivity of the patient.

Comments

Psychostructurally this was a borderline patient by specific as well as nonspecific criteria. Interestingly, his psychological tests show good performances on the unstructured portions—better than what was noted on the structured tests. This is the opposite of what is expected in "borderline" patients according to Singer (Gunderson and Singer, 1975).

The combination of panic states, motor restlessness, vegetative signs, monomanic preoccupation with certain topics ("I'm okay," "You've gotta let me outta here," "Will I ever get better?"), in the wake of a suicide attempt, was compatible with the syndrome diagnosis of *"agitated depression."* Typical of patients in this state, there is no way to establish a dialogue.

By the time of the second interview, the patient was much more open and reachable. His baseline structure could be more readily ascertained. Eventually, the consultant was able to "get through"; the patient was able to integrate the previously split-off perceptions about his wife. The above extract demonstrates both the borderline structure (primitive defenses; pervasive contradictoriness in his perception of his wife's feelings, yet with capacity to test reality when confronted) and the positive response to appropriate confrontation. In retrospect, the panic state present on admission could be seen as part of a "brief psychotic episode" in a patient with borderline structure or (in Gunderson's terminology) with borderline personality disorder.

Final Diagnostic Impressions

A. Categorical diagnoses
   1*a*. Affective disorder; depressed type
   b. (Syndrome) agitated depression with panic states; phobic-anxious syndrome (see D. Klein, Chapter 9)
   2. Borderline structure
   3*a*. Narcissistic personality with passive-aggressive and phobic features
   b. (In Kraepelinian nosology) irritable temperament

B. Dimensional assessments
   1. Region V of the Sz-MDP continuum (pure affective disorder)
   2. GAS = 31 (initial) to 40 (at time of second extract)
   3. Personality profile as shown in Table IV–1

FAMILY HISTORY

First-degree relatives =	4 (parents, plus 2 sibs)
affected member:	(1) mother (four episodes of unipolar depression, one of which was treated with a short course of ECT)
Second-degree relatives =	6
affected members:	(1) paternal grandfather (died in a mental hospital; had delusions of persecution) (2) maternal grandfather (recurrent severe depressions though not hospitalized)

Case Illustration 16

Patient = P Doctor = D GAS:
on admission = 40
at time of interview = 33

D: Can you tell me what led to your coming to the hospital?

P: I have no self-discipline at all. I don't know what to expect from treatment here. I hope they can help me. If not . . . I'll just live out my life as best I can. I don't know where to begin telling you . . . I'd rather you ask *me* questions.

D: You've been here a few weeks already, I understand. What have you learned about yourself?

P: I haven't learned anything more since I've been here. I still pull at myself like I did before; I sneak food, disobey rules, talk about other people in front of them. The only thing I haven't done, is I haven't run away, like I used to. I have had the *urge* to, though I scarcely know what I'm running *from*. Certain things in my past I don't want to face, I suppose.

D: Like what?

P: I don't want to talk about them. I don't know if they really happened: someone trying to kill me with a pillow when I was in a crib; that's a memory I have. I've had a fear of being closed in. At three I tried to smother a baby in a carriage, and when the mother came out, I ran away.

D: What else?

P: I'd rather not say.

D: And if you did?

P: I'd feel disgusting, and want to walk out.

D: I don't understand . . .

P: I can't tell you any more.

D: I don't understand the nature of your fear. Are you keeping something from me that'd portray you in a bad light?

P: Not me. Someone else.

D: So why would you refrain . . .

P: Because it's someone I love . . . and he . . . *(trails off).*

D: You're keeping something from me you also keep from your therapist?

P: He didn't want to hear it.

D: Doesn't that sound strange?

P: Maybe he didn't think it was important.

D: How do you explain that?

P: I was angry; he said I shouldn't tell it—unless I could do so with *feeling*.

D: Still, it sounds strange that Dr. T—— wouldn't "let" you tell something so important.

P: Well, I think this is all planned out!

D: Yes!?

P: To get me to *feel* something . . . like, get *mad* at him . . . be *provoked*. Yet, I wouldn't show him the anger. I wouldn't do it. Like maybe he wanted me to break a vase in the office, the way I would've done in the past . . .

D: You thought he really wanted you to break those vases?

P: No. Though it seemed planned: like, I should express my anger in other ways than in words, or so I figured he meant *(spoken testily).*

D: You sound angry at me.

P: Yes . . . I am . . . I think you're doing this to see if I can be provoked or if I have self-control.

D: But perhaps this is your fantasy?

P: It's possible.

D: But what do you really believe?

P: I don't understand why you're doing this.

D: What do you imagine?

P: That you're putting me on the *spot*. Exposing me. I don't wanna tell ya. You might think it was for my good, but I'd wanna *leave*. I'd feel ashamed. But I *know* it all happened. I was eight at the time.

D: That was a long time ago.

P: Yes, but I was made aware of it in treatment, several years ago. I was running away from it. I was doing things other people wouldn't have done.

D: Yet, it seems a contradiction, not to tell about the things we'd really help you get better over, if you *could* let us know!

P: Well, I'm embarrassed; I'm scared to tell them.

D: Because people'd feel you were weird, crazy, strange . . . ?

P: Yes *(pause)*. Though I'm sure it's happened to others—obviously, I'm weird anyway! Because of what I do to myself . . .

D: You mean to your hair?

P: Yes. But I can't enjoy what other people get enjoyment from . . . because of what *happened*. *(Pause)* But I'd rather not talk about it.

D: You'd rather not talk about what's *important*. You're just going through this as a kind of empty exercise!

P: No! I *wanna* tell you. But I *can't*.

D: Perhaps what you can't talk about is that some of what you do is fun: maybe it's fun, pulling at your self. If you could just do it *secretly*, you'd be "OK."

P: For a while! I used to enjoy it. But I'm sick of that already. Now, I want everyone to see what I did to myself, and what everyone did to *me!*

D: Who did *what* to you?

P: My *friends*.

D: How?

P: They hurt me: embarrassed me in front of everyone. About my appearance.

D: What about your ap——?

P: My nose. It had a bump on it once, it's gone now *(becomes tearful)*.

D: You're upset now.

P: I never got over my adolescence.

D: It could be that you're upset over what's going on right here, isn't that possible? Upset at your having to be so indirect, and your being *aware* of that . . .

P: I dunno . . . *(sotto voce)*.

D: I don't see any sign of your being concerned about your situation.

P: You must *know* already . . .

D: How?

P: You can read my thoughts! You're smart, you're a doctor! You must have an *idea* of what it is already! *(Pause)* I feel "disgusted." Why? What could make a person "disgusted"? *(Pause)* If they were physically *abused* by someone!

D: You try to tell me indirectly; you feel I can really read your mind? I just do all this questioning to keep you "dangling"?
P: No, I don't feel you do that!
D: I try to get your secrets out of you, isn't that so?
P: I don't think you *want* to manipulate me.
D: So what does it mean that I press you to tell me about those things?
P: I don't think you're trying to manipulate me.
D: Actually, if you're suffering so much, one would think you'd want to play it straight!
P: I feel so stupid in front of you!
D: That's changing the subject.
P: I *liked* what it was that happened to me!, OK!? *That's* why I feel so disgusted!
D: So?
P: What'll happen to me if I don't tell you?
D: Nothing at all. Just that you'll have thrown away an opportunity, that's all.
P: I'd *tell* you if you weren't just a consultant. . . . I'll tell you—OK?—I *like* the feeling! No . . . I can't tell you.
D: I think you enjoy it more than you care to admit.
P: I've chosen this alternative because of what happened to me. If I expose myself, I couldn't face the other patients here, or anybody.
D: Actually, I understand you've already told a number of them beforehand.
P: Yes. *(Pause)* You can't figure it out yourself?
D: That's an illusion.
P: It's such a feeling of disgust!
D: I can't buy that. I think you hesitate, because you're afraid of losing a sense of *control* over me.
P: But I would be exposing someone else.
D: You've been the "victim," in other words, of what others have done to you?
P: I think of disfiguring the people who've hurt me . . . I think of killing them! I think of that a lot!
D: Still, couldn't one consider it absurd that something at age eight should continue to mess up your life?
P: I shouldn't *let* it affect my life. But I do.
D: What do you mean?
P: That I've learned to enjoy the things I do to myself, instead of the normal things.
D: You think people *want* to hurt you?
P: *(Pauses) Some* people.
D: As though it's a conspiracy?

P: No! not *now*. As a child. One girl used to organize the others to taunt me at school.
D: Are they continuing to fight against you?
P: No. They were adolescents then. They've found more constructive things to do with their lives. But I *haven't*. And I still do these adolescent things as a sort of a vengeance—even though they're not around to see what I do. So why do I bother?!
D: Do you see me in league with those people, to bother you?
P: No! You don't know any of them.

Comments

The patient, an unemployed woman of twenty-four, was considered a "difficult child" by her parents from the very beginning. In elementary school she alienated her peers by spreading hurtful rumors. She was restless, hyperactive, and nervous. She overate, sometimes pilfering the food for her overindulgence, although her family was well off. There were hints of unmentionable secrets in the family, apparently relating to sexual activities between the patient and some of her close relatives, shortly before puberty. It was not clear if her veiled hints referred to things that actually took place or merely to fantasies she had elaborated. There were physical fights between her and her parents, and tantrums throughout adolescence. Menarche was accompanied by feelings of ugliness and of being malformed. Trichotillomania developed as a symptom of her self-loathing. In high school there was a period of abusing illicit drugs, some of which triggered brief psychotic episodes of a paranoid quality. Her academic work was only fair. She had no close friends, despite superficial popularity. The latter was purchased through clownishness. On entering college she became depressed, though at times she was euphoric and giddy. She discontinued her courses to join a fringe religious sect for a brief time. Threats of violence continued at home. Relationships with men seemed never to last beyond a month or two; she picked very unsuitable partners. She supported herself with a succession of menial jobs. The termination of one particular romantic relationship prompted a suicide gesture; the latter precipitated hospitalization.

Mental status on admission was noteworthy insofar as her speech was coherent but pressured; there was a strong tendency to externalize, blame others for her chaotic life, and so on, but there was no formal thought disorder. Lability of affect (without inappropriateness) was noted: hypomania, alternating with crying spells. There was a tendency to identify strongly with certain members of her family, or with "forces of evil," which she would make known by phrases such as "I am Lucifer." Upon challenge, she would say that this was merely a figurative way of speaking.

Psychological tests revealed an IQ in the average range. The Rorschach showed only a few $F+$ responses and a loss of distance; personalized idiosyncratic associations were noted on many of the blots. For example, card X: " . . . scorpions fighting with a stick; a heap of dead scorpions below . . . "; card III (alluding to the white space not normally attended to): a "child in between her parents." The WAIS subtests showed much variability in performance.

A variety of consultants interviewed this patient shortly after her admission to the hospital; each came to a somewhat different diagnostic conclusion. The referring psychiatrist had spoken of "pseudoneurotic schizophrenia." One consultant labeled her condition "schizoaffective, with paranoid features"; he thought she exhibited a psychotic structure. Another diagnosed "manic-depressive illness: bipolar-II type, with narcissistic and paranoid features." This consultant thought her level of function was borderline because she reacted to confrontation with improvement in her reality testing. Still a third consultant, who diagnosed a "schizophrenic reaction, paranoid type, with narcissistic features," saw her as functioning at the psychotic level. He also drew attention to her weak ego boundaries (e.g., the confusing memories about smothering) and to her tendency toward "injustice collecting."

There seemed to be good evidence for a genetic factor operating in this patient: there were many relatives with depressive and manic-depressive illness, bilaterally; others had features (compulsive gambling) suggestive of manic-depressive illness.

With respect to her personality profile, narcissistic (grandiose side by side with self-depreciatory) and paranoid features were readily apparent. But these were overshadowed by the intensity of the patient's (often quite chaotic) histrionic qualities.

Her psychostructural type, at the time of the interview, could not be diagnosed with certainty, or at least not with unanimity. A "transitional" case, she appeared to be at the interface between *psychotic* and *borderline*. Her reality testing in interpersonal situations was often poor, but just as often could be improved by appropriate confrontation. An interviewer who touched on mostly neutral topics would come away with the impression that her structure was well within the *borderline* range. If someone challenged her on more sensitive issues, however, her structure appeared *psychotic*. Observer variance thus played a role in the diagnostic confusion she engendered.

Her clinical picture shows nearly equal schizophrenic and manic-depressive features. The latter seemed to be preponderant to the author. The case is reminiscent of Hoch and Polatin's "pseudoneurotic schizophrenia" (compulsions, obsessions, phobias, depressions, all being present over many years). One might also note that "hard" signs of schizophrenia are lacking: at the time of the interviews, none of Carpenter's twelve highly discriminating signs of schizophrenia were clearly discernible—only a pervasive paranoid cast to her ideation with moments of blurring of ego boundary.

Final Diagnostic Impressions

A. Categorical diagnoses
   1. Schizoaffective disorder, predominantly affective (mixed: depressive > manic).
   2. Transitional structure: psychotic ⟶ borderline
   3. Hysterical personality with paranoid and narcissistic features. *Syndromes:* trichotillomania; borderline personality disorder (Gunderson)

B. Dimensional assessments
   1. Region IV (Sz/MDP = 38/62)
   2. GAS range during first month of hospitalization: 33 to 40
   3. Personality profile as shown in Table IV–1

FAMILY HISTORY

First-degree relatives =	4 (parents, plus 2 sibs)
affected members:	(1) mother (severely alcoholic) (2) father (bipolar manic-depressive illness, treated with lithium; explosive personality)
Second-degree relatives =	7
affected members:	(1) paternal uncle (suicided) (2) maternal aunt (alcoholic)
Other (including less seriously affected) members:	(1) maternal cousin (explosive personality) (2) paternal cousin (severe character disorder, with compulsive gambling) (3) brother (severe personality disorder within the depressive spectrum; irritable temperament) (4) maternal aunt (panic attacks; fainting spells)

Case Illustration 17

Patient = P GAS = 42

A twenty-six-year-old divorced woman had the following to say to a consulting psychiatrist on the eve of her transfer from a medical to a psychiatric hospital. (She had been hospitalized for a medical condition that was self-induced, as a side effect of her ingestion of a large overdose of a drug the week before, in a suicide gesture.) She had agreed initially to the transfer but backed out at the last minute in a fit of pique against her parents, upon whom she was dependent financially and who she feared would attempt to regulate her life if she acquiesced.

P: I want to forget about them! Forget they exist, and forget about this hospital . . . that's all it is to them, this hospital: a chance to prove they're right. I'm not gonna sacrifice any more of my soul and my life. I'll forget they ever lived and go off on my own.

Father has to play his little games. I know what you [the consultant] are thinking: you're probably swayed by them [her parents], but as a human being, I have my rights! And I know in my heart what is right and what isn't right. I've paid a million times over to their games. . . . As soon as I realize they've never liked me and never will, I'll be okay. I don't know what *you've* been told, but I shouldn't be just put before judge and jury. . . . I've taken a lot of injustice and I won't be set up in a situation again. . . . I'll bust out of here and not let Father take his frustration out on me. I won't let him do it to me. My heart isn't in it. I'm not gonna play their game at the expense of my soul! I need to get outta this area and outta this kind of life. I've had enough!

So, you know, I'm not giving any more, till I know I'm gonna be given *to*. I've been through this trip before. I've tried hard to be honest within my own heart and that's what I have to follow. I have to lead *my* life *(becomes tearful):* it's in *my* body. I can't do it any more! It's not gonna work out. And you don't understand: I've got twenty-six years on my own life up on *you;* I'm not fooling myself, believe me!

I know what's coming up: Father travels a lot. Mother's alone: she wants me in her house to keep her company. No one's done more thinking about my life than me! My parents are as happy as two pigs in shit about my going to the hospital, and that's not normal to me! They're not gonna take it out on me any *more!* To be their "good little girl"! Well, fuck that! A leopard doesn't change its spots and they're not gonna change theirs.

Anamnestic Data

This patient was noted to have serious "behavior problems" while still in grade school. Chiefly these consisted of spreading malicious rumors at school and among neighbors about members of her family, and of feigning illness to get out of school. Tantrums and arguments with her family were frequent, and she was provocative enough that verbal abuse sometimes led to physical violence. This kind of behavior was not characteristic of the rest of the family, who regarded her as incomprehensibly different from themselves—"as though," in the words of one of her relatives, "there'd been a mix-up in the nursery."

She made few friends, and toward them behaved so exploitatively that she soon alienated them and had to seek new ones.

Marrying young to "escape the family," she quickly tired of the responsibilities, in addition to which, she found sex repugnant (the only problem she ever acknowledged openly). Divorced two years later, she embarked upon a series of jobs in different cities, never remaining in one place more than a year. She began to elaborate fanciful stories of being ill with all manner of obscure or fatal diseases. These became the pretext for urgent calls, mostly to her parents, for money and other assistance. Having worked briefly as a copy editor for a medical publishing house, she even acquired a degree of sophistication about blood dyscrasias. She pretended to have two rare blood disorders at different times; one led to the hospitalization from which the case material was derived.

The patient had a divisive effect on the hospital staff, tending to evoke sympathy from some (as though she were victimized by an uncaring family) and outrage from others (as they began to see through her manipulations). She could shift rapidly between meekness and abusiveness. The same consultant who was the target of her wrath in the case material was implored two days later, with equally impressive submissiveness, to help her start her life over on a good footing.

Side by side with these characterological problems were periods of genuine depression, in which dysphoria, insomnia, suicidal ruminations, tearfulness, and self-denigration were present.

Psychological Test Results

Full-scale IQ = 110 (verbal IQ = 111, performance IQ = 108). There was appreciable inter- and intrasubtest scatter and evidence of underlying depression against which she erected largely obsessional, intellectualized defenses. Responses to certain questions about social judgment suggested antisocial tendencies (Why should a person avoid bad company?: "You don't really have to"; Why do we have to pay taxes?: "I don't think people should have to, not if you can get out of it").

On the unstructured portions of the test battery, her responses were highly personalized, idiosyncratic, and pathological. "Primary-process" thought intruded, of a sort that showed preoccupation with decay and death. Thus on card III of the Rorschach: "an infant split down the middle with an axe"; and "two creatures ripping each other down the middle." On card VI: "a dog that's been run over or something, all split open where you can see the organs all rotting and mushed." The TAT stories often centered on the themes of suicide and open hostility toward both men and women.

Difficulty in integrating the disparate aspects of her personality was suggested by a number of contaminated responses to the blots (namely, fusion of incompatible concepts). On card I to the percepts "bat" and "woman" she added: "The woman has wings and is some sort of sorceress trying to harm me . . . or smother me."

Comments

In traditional nosology the patient's illness falls within the affective disorder realm and is depressive in character. Periods of rage outbursts, suicidal rumination, and restlessness were almost exclusively a premenstrual phenomenon. The psychological tests would have been compatible with a psychotic depressive reaction, but clinically she never exhibited psychotic signs—certainly no delusions or hallucinations. This point may be debatable to a degree, since some might regard the pseudologia and feigned illness as a kind of behavioral "psychosis."

Despite the adequacy of conventional reality testing and the absence of any thought disorder or linguistic peculiarities, there were glaring inconsistencies in her self-perception. This "splitting" was frequently acted out within the environment, as she went about creating two camps in her interpersonal world: those who saw her as cunning and untrustworthy "versus" those who (unaware of her other side) experienced her as the tragic victim of "hateful" parents and "lingering diseases." Grandiosity alternating with self-abasement formed another contradictory aspect of her personality.

The ominous aspect of her illness was not so much the affective disorder or even the "irritable temperament": medication (Diuril 500 milligrams/day, the week before her period) alleviated these aspects of her symptom picture fairly well (especially the premenstrual rage outbursts). Rather, it was the strong antisocial component in her character that constituted the limiting factor, prognostically. She had no motivation for psychotherapy and no interest in making amends with her beleagured family. Though less hostile and irritable than before, the pattern of factitious illness and frequent changes of locale has continued.

Final Diagnostic Impressions

A. Categorial diagnoses
   1*a*. Affective disorder: unipolar depression
   b. Factitious illness (the "Munchausen syndrome")
   2. Borderline structure
   3. Antisocial personality with narcissistic and hysterical features

B. Dimensional assessments
   1. Region V of the Sz-MDP continuum
   2. GAS = 42
   3. Personality profile as shown in Table IV–1

FAMILY HISTORY

First-degree relatives = 4 (parents, plus 2 sibs)
Second-degree relatives = 7

NOTE: No psychiatric disorders in the family with the exception of the patient's mother, who suffered mild depressive episodes beginning in the third decade of life, and also a number of "psychosomatic complaints" including irritable colon and migraine. Like the patient, the mother also experienced premenstrual aggravation of symptoms.

Case Illustration 18

Patient = P Doctor = D GAS = 43

The patient spent the early portion of the interview trying to give a coherent account of why she voluntarily admitted herself to the hospital's long-term intensive therapy unit. She manifested considerable concern about her condition, but even when challenged by the interviewer could not put very well into words what were the feelings she was struggling with. In addition, she could scarcely express her own wants and tended, knowingly or otherwise, to manipulate others in such a way that they acceded to her wishes without her having to verbalize them. As she put it:

P: It's hard for me to come right out and say, "Mama, I need help! so I'd create a situation where she'd have to come across . . . couldn't refuse me . . .

The difficulty she experienced in postponing gratification she expressed in this fashion:

P: I want a response immediately! And I know I can't get it. It's frustrating—that's *it!*

Regarding her lack of autonomy, she went on to say:

P: I used to try to get the therapist I was working with before I came here to give me a list of stuff to do that day.

Her mode of relatedness to others was still predominantly symbiotic in nature. She could not function to any extent except in the presence of some other person important to her. She was aware of this pattern and could articulate quite clearly her ambivalence about the "other":

P: . . . I stopped going to see that therapist. I really liked her, though. There was this same pattern of withdrawing from things: I'd isolate myself from *her,* even, after a certain period of time. I felt after a while that I just needed the structure of a hospital, where I can't "not go" just because I might not feel like seeing my doctor . . . I know since

I've been here that it's hard for me to get in touch with my feelings . . . *(she becomes tearful)*.

D: What's occurring to you now?

P: . . . it's, like . . . very frustrating if I can't convey the way I'm feeling: How can I get any *help* here? It's very *scary!* You can only go by what I *say*. It's what I *give*. If I can't make you understand, how can I help you to help myself?

D: Are you worried only about *me* understanding you?

P: *Anybody!* It's scary that . . . when I feel things, maybe there's so many feelings that'll come out all at once: all the feelings in me that seem all meshed together, that I don't separate out.

D: What affected you the *most* in your life?

P: My father's death. *(Pause)* I don't know how accurate that is, but I've just sensed that ever since then, I just stopped feeling. But it was just too painful to deal with, and I seemed to have blocked out all the feelings.

D: Tell me about him.

P: He was very special. Very gentle. I loved him very much. . . . He was a quiet man . . . I saw him, even though he was in his seventies when he died . . . I always saw him as very, very strong . . . almost, like he couldn't be destroyed. I feel that way about my mother . . . physically, my father really wasn't that well. But he overcame it. He went to work anyway.

Comments

Besides exhibiting no trace of formal thought disorder, this patient even demonstrated a measure of insight, albeit rather intellectual, into her condition. She was not propelled into hospital confinement out of the most urgent reasons, such as self-destructive behavior or psychotic disintegration of function. Instead she noticed that she was in the grip of a self-defeating pattern of relationships—that she was excessively dependent on certain key (usually mothering) figures and that she could not easily tolerate being alone. In fact she lost all motivation for work unless there was some familiar caring person almost literally by her side. These difficulties pointed, on the psychodynamic plane, to faulty resolutions of what Mahler has called the rapprochement subphase of the separation-individuation process in early life (1971). Furthermore, these difficulties, present since childhood, mounted in intensity following the death of her father.

This patient presented intriguing problems from the standpoint of structural diagnosis. Initial consensus was lacking after the admission conference interview. Two raters considered her "borderline." One drew attention to her demandingness, which he saw as more striking than her clinging, needy qualities; this seemed more in keeping with narcissistic than infantile character structure, although features of the latter were not lacking. (For example, she was noted by the nursing staff to eat lollipops frequently—unusual behavior in a woman of twenty-seven.) She was "aware of everything" but able do almost nothing. This quality was reminiscent of the term Stern used in 1938 for this sort of paralysis of coping: "psychic bleeding." The interviewer also felt that the patient did harbor considerable anger at those she worked for, but that this anger was largely dissociated from awareness (leaving her with the sort of bland facade Helene Deutsch drew attention to in connection with the "as if" patient; other "as if" features were not present here). This, in turn, constituted "splitting" (in object representations), enough to establish the presence of faulty ego integration (the syndrome of "identity diffusion" of Erikson), necessary for the diagnosis of borderline structure.

I was not struck by this aspect of her self-presentation at first, because of her relatively good insight, her good rapport with the interviewer, and her quite rational speech. (In comparison to most hospitalized patients, her ego integration was rather intact. It seemed more appropriate to place her as on the lowermost rung of what was still neurotic structure. Nevertheless, it is hard to imagine any young adult volunteering to be hospitalized for many months of intensive psychotherapy unless something serious is the matter: by "something serious" I mean psychopathology of no better than "borderline" level.)

In relation to the various criteria for a borderline condition, it becomes even clearer why the diagnosis was so difficult. In Grinker's classification, for example, she would be a type IV borderline (anaclitic depression). This is the "border with neurosis" and consists of patients who "search for a lost symbiotic relation with a mother figure which they do not achieve" (1968, p. 176). Hence, Grinker, too, would have seen her as on just the other side of the borderline-neurotic interface.

On psychological testing, her MMPI suggested psychoneurosis with depressive features. She handled the structured portion of the standard battery well but had some tendency to diffusion on the Rorschach (her responses were not at all bizarre in the manner of a schizophrenic's responses). On card I, for example, she saw a "bug in the middle of two ladies . . . swinging all around . . . " and then, turning the card upside down: "God blowing clouds away"; "a strangely formed fetus." The examiner saw these responses as suggesting "regressive retreat" and "nostalgia and longing for the past." Threatening imagery was seen on card V ("an ominous butterfly") and card VII ("bared teeth and piercing eyes"). The symbiotic quality of her relationships was suggested by a particular response on card IX: "a fetus in amniotic fluid." The test data in general were considered too well integrated for a schizophrenic impression but nevertheless too primitive for psychoneurosis.

On the Spitzer checklist she had six positive items. This is the minimum number for most persons with a "borderline" condition. Again, she represents something of a transitional case: the healthiest borderline or the sickest psychoneurotic, depending upon how the various criteria are assessed.

Final Diagnostic Impressions

A. Categorical diagnoses
   1. ———
   2*a*. Borderline structure
   b. Grinker type IV borderline (anaclitic depression)
   3. Narcissistic personality with depressive features

B. Dimensional assessments
   1. (?) Region V of the Sz-MDP continuum[6]
   2. GAS = 43
   3. Personality profile as shown in Table IV–1

Case Illustration 19

Patient = P Interviewer = I GAS = 44

The patient enters the interview room with an awkward, wobbly gait, sits down, and smiles at the interviewer and at the group of four others in attendance.

I: Can you tell me something about the problem for which you're seeking help in our hospital?

P: A lot of times I don't know there *is* a problem, and *that's* a problem! My father says I have a problem. He hasn't explained it real good so's I can understand what it is . . . *(stares blankly for a brief moment)* . . . it's that I can't *do* anything . . . *(blank stare for a few seconds)*. . . . Well . . . *(seems to "block" on something)* . . . since I'm in the church choir, and I work as a waitress in this night club . . . and I don't understand what he means when he says I'm "unreliable."

I: How is it you haven't been attending school of late?

P: I get upset at school and I cry; I suppose it's because nobody likes me there.

I: How do you mean?

P: Nobody'll have anything to do with me. I used to have a friend, Emily. When I say "Hi!" lately . . . she doesn't come over. Doesn't call me anymore. I dunno: maybe because I got *sick* so much. She might feel she had to take care of me too much.

I: Hmmm?

[6]The question mark relates to the uncertainty about what degree, if any, genetic liability for an affective disorder might be present.

P: Like, if I had a seizure.
I: What happens then?
P: Nuthin' much. There's different kinds! I used to think I was holding my breath, and I get all hunched over. That's *one* kind! . . . I'm all foggy at that time. Really I'm breathing out real slow. *(It has been noticed by now that her affective range is normal and that she has an engaging smile.)*
I: Have you had these spells right along?
P: Oh, I had a seizure this morning, and I played some music on the record player and that seemed to snap me out of it.
I: You sorta know how to stop some of these attacks yourself.
P: Yes. . . . *(She then suddenly hunches over in her chair, for about twenty seconds, as she says:)* I didn't hear you . . . I'm having a seizure! . . . *(and a few seconds later, regains her full consciousness with composure)*

This patient, a girl of fifteen, had been referred for hospitalization because of a strange malady consisting of frequent "spells" of altered consciousness, accompanied by occasional stereotyped acts that seemed quite out of keeping with her usual character. She would, for example, begin undressing in the street for no apparent reason. The spells occurred up to a hundred and fifty per day and were, for the most part, two- to ten-second "blackouts" where she would lose the thread of conversation and assume some unaccustomed posture. They were considered petit mal seizures by some neurologists, although some prehospital EEGs did not reveal a characteristic abnormality. These did reveal some diffuse abnormal patterns, but no special foci. Nasopharyngeal leads had not been obtained, so "psychomotor epilepsy" was not considered ruled out; neither could it be "confirmed." A trial of Dilantin had apparently stopped the stereotypic acts, but the brief blackouts continued unabated, necessitating her removal from school. The atypical picture led her neurology consultants to suspect a possible hysterical conversion reaction, especially since her blacking out often followed questions of a challenging or embarrassing nature. At other times they seemed to constitute appeals for attention and sympathy.

The attacks began shortly after her mother began to go to work to help support the family. This necessitated her being out of the house when the patient returned from school. The family itself was middle-class; there were six siblings besides herself. She was the eldest daughter, and the apple of her father's eye. The father was much older than the mother and was of a decidedly hot-tempered nature. There was much bickering at home, mostly over strained finances; in this chronic battle, the patient took her father's side, which in turn had led to a deterioration in her relationship with her mother (whom she already resented for being away from home so much). The patient's schoolwork had fallen off considerably since the mother's resumption of work; she was now failing three of five courses, whereas before she had gotten all B's.

There was no family history of functional psychoses, epilepsy, or alcoholism, although the father has an "explosive" personality. The father had behaved seductively toward the patient in recent months, according to the referring psychiatrist. At the same time the atmosphere at home was one of rigidity and prudishness, in keeping with its fundamentalist religious background; sex was a forbidden topic. The patient appeared caught between sexual excitation and stern prohibition against acknowledging it. The referring consultant considered the situation ripe for the development of a hysterical conversion reaction, and wondered if her "seizures" were not hysterical in nature.

Nonspecific signs of borderline structure were present: she grew anxious under the impact of minor stresses at home or at school; she was quite impulsive and was also unable to persevere at scholastic or recreational tasks. She showed considerable rigidity and contradictoriness in her views of her family members and of her own personality. Seductive behavior, for example, existed side by side with denial of any sexual fantasies or interest. She was able, however, to grasp the interviewer's point, when this discrepancy was related to her (this is not included in the brief extract). Her capacity to test reality was unimpaired, including in the interpersonal realm.

The case exemplifies the development of a borderline structure in the presence of an organic factor—and in the absence of any discernible genetic factor. The organic condition here is most likely temporal lobe epilepsy. She exhibited some signs of affective disturbance in addition—predominantly of a depressive nature. In this regard it should be noted that epileptics with this syndrome tend, if the lesion is in the "dominant" hemisphere (i.e., the hemisphere mediating linguistic tasks), to show schizophreniform sequelae. Those with nondominant hemisphere foci tend to show affective symptoms (Flor-Henry, 1969; Falconer and Serafetinides, 1963; Hughes and Schlagenhauff, 1961; Hambert and Willen, 1978).

Psychological test data were not available for this case, nor were there detailed data regarding the family history.

Final Diagnostic Impressions

A. Categorical diagnoses
   1. Temporal Lobe ("Psychomotor") Epilepsy
   2. Borderline Structure
   3. Hysterical Personality

B. Dimensional assessments
   1. Region "O" of the Sz-MDP Continuum (no known predisposition to either schizophrenia or primary affective disorders)
   2. GAS = 44
   3. Personality profile as shown in Table IV–1

Case Illustration 20

Patient = P Consultant = C GAS = 45

C: Let me hear in your own words what led to your coming to the hospital.

P: Well, I was having trouble at work; the work wasn't going as well as it should have. . . . This is back in August . . . and . . . there were a number of things happening at once. . . . I wasn't sure I could keep earning enough to pay for the expenses of myself and the person I've been living with . . .

C: The "person"?

P: My girlfriend.

C: Oh.

P: And . . . I was getting a lot of advice on both sides. . . . I was seeing a doctor on the outside and he said I just needed to pull myself together, look for new work after I'd become unemployed, and that if I did that, I'd be fine, on . . .

C: You mentioned "becoming unemployed" . . .

P: Well, I lost my previous position . . .

C: You say that as though you somehow misplaced it. Is that what you intended to convey, or was it that . . .

P: I was let go.

C: That is to say, your boss fired you?

P: I guess someone could say that.

C: You "guess"?

P: I *was* . . . I mean, he *did* fire me.

C: Uh-huh. *(Pause)* I notice, though, that I still have no very clear notion of what was going on inside you, what in your life was getting to be "too much" to handle—that then precipitated this admission.

P: Uh . . . my girlfriend . . . she felt I ought to come in, get a rest, get some things straightened out . . . although my doctor said if I just buckled down and got a job, I'd be all right. . . . I think if I realized what it would be like in the hospital . . . I mean, several people told me I'd have plenty of things to do here, that there would be hot and cold running psychiatrists that I could talk to every day . . . that's what I was looking for, if I was to go in, in the first place.

C: To hear you describe it, you would have been comfortable with the idea of hospitalization only if that meant being in a resort-hotel atmosphere.

P: Well, in the end, I couldn't make up my mind to come in or not to. I think if I knew, I certainly wouldn't have come in, in the first place . . .

C: But I think you're getting ahead of your story. I still don't have a grasp of what landed you at our door to begin with, where you had the decision to make: Shall I come in or shall I not?

P: *(Pause)* Well, in the end, I was getting confused about which way to go. . . . Some people were telling me to go one way, some were telling me to go another . . . and it was affecting my sleep. . . . I'd wake up several times a night . . . it was getting difficult to take care of myself properly. . . . I mean the person in front of you is not the person I was in December before I came in here . . .

C: Just how do you mean that?

P: Not literally, of course, but my appearance has always been tremendously important to me, and, what with the loss of sleep, there were circles under my eyes. . . . I felt I was less attractive to my girlfriend . . .

C: She commented on these changes?

P: No, she didn't say anything like that, but in the end, that's how I began to feel, and that was weighing on me a great deal. . . . I guess that's what led up to my going along with the suggestion to get a rest here and . . .

C: Yet, would it surprise you to hear that in my experience, it would be a very uncommon event precipitating a psychiatric hospitalization that someone should be fretting over his image in the mirror because of "circles" under his eyes?

P: Well, I told you I wasn't sure it was the right move . . .

C: I'm also mindful of the fact that, according to what the nurses mentioned, you had been given to burning your cheek with cigarettes before you came to the hospital . . .

P: Uh . . . well, I guess that was to relieve the tension I was under . . .

C: *What* tension? What indeed *is* the tension you have been in the grips of all this time? I'm at a loss . . .

P: Uh . . . you mean the tension now, or the tension in December? . . . *(Pause)* I don't really understand the nature of the tension over the fall months . . . *(looks away from the consultant)* . . . Uh . . . I guess I'm . . . what was the question, exactly? . . .

C: *(Does not respond)*

P: "What is the tension I've been in the grips of all this time?"

C: *(Nodding)*

P: Well . . . since I've been here, I've felt like an actor going through his paces, you know, like . . . I'm here for no reason, just going through the motions . . . a sort of pretend patient . . .

C: That doesn't answer my question, though. Nevertheless, I can't help jumping ahead for a moment and asking you how you square it with this being-here-under-false-pretense feeling that you burned yourself rather severely—and where it would show, too—several days after you got here? Does that strike you as the act of a man who's just cooling his heels here as a fake patient?

P: I didn't know how I could get out of here. The whole mechanism of getting myself discharged . . . I didn't know the ropes.

C: Are you saying in effect that you were "forced" to that extreme measure for want of knowing how to walk out of a voluntary hospital?

P: Uh . . . well, I guess I regressed once I got in here . . . I must have just let myself go . . .

C: You can appreciate how burning yourself would tend to convince a stranger that hospitalization was appropriate rather that unnecessary?

P: I guess that would be . . .

C: You *guess*?

P: That would be how it is . . .

C: The more so as you put great stock in your appearance, yet did something to scarify yourself. *(Pause)* Well, could it be, that you really *did* need to be here? That something *was* scaring you to death out there, that you began to think of suicide even before you came, and that you burnt yourself *not* out of desperation at being unable to find the "Exit" sign, but to show us how desperate you were, period! . . . that you wanted to make *sure* we got the message as to how sick you were, so we wouldn't be conned by your cool exterior . . . into letting you go too soon.

P: That's what my girlfriend said. I was very uncertain about things before I came in. But in the end . . . uh . . . because I had a hard time finding work, things fell apart. . . . it was like something was gnawing away at me . . .

C: "Gnawing away"?

P: Yeah.

C: What does that bring to mind, "gnawing away"?

P: Well, I dunno . . . something inside me . . .

C: Like what, for instance?

P: *(Pause)* You mean before I came in or right now?

C: *(Silence—again sidestepping his evasion)*

P: Uh . . . well . . . before I came in, I at times felt like there was something inside . . . I don't feel that so much now . . . that was dragging me down. . . . I don't know as I could characterize it any further than that . . . but it slowed me down . . . everything about my life seemed to just grind to a halt . . .

C: You know, up to this point you've been awfully vague. If I ask you what you felt, I only hear what your girlfriend felt. I really *don't* think you're here through some bureaucratic slipup, by the way; I think you're here for good reason . . . but to go back to this vagueness, I got to wondering whether the bewilderment and irritation I have been noticing in myself was perhaps a reflection of feelings *you* were up against before coming here—for whatever reason. . . . Have *you* in fact found yourself confused, bothered to distraction, by something occurring *in you,* that made hospitalization necessary and that you're trying to convey to me in this tortuously roundabout way?!

P: I guess I'd have to say there was.

C: You "guess," again, or . . .

P: There *was,* yes.

C: Ah! . . . *what* was going on inside you that made you feel you couldn't manage your life any longer outside the hospital? Where were you "hurting"?

P: *(Pause)* Well, like I think I said . . . things were okay up until August . . . and then I had problems on the job . . . problems with the boss. . . . They didn't seem too serious I didn't think, not at first, but along about October, he let me go. . . . I was hired to check out these precision instruments, and I kept reporting a lot of deficiences, minor ones, some of them, which I felt is what I was hired to do . . . but apparently my boss felt I was noticing too much for the good of the firm. So, I felt pretty hopeless . . . trying to find another job in my line of work. . . . I guess my girlfriend was concerned how all this would affect our situation if we were to go ahead with our plans to get married this spring . . .

C: Your plans to get married?

P: . . . well, we had been talking tentatively about this spring as a time to . . . all of which has been upset by my being here, which is another reason I felt I oughta get back to . . .

C: Well now, what about marriage? Was that what your anxiety and desperation were all about as the weeks were getting closer? . . .

P: Uh . . . well, I guess so. . . . I mean, after I lost the job . . . the whole question of how I was going to be able to support her and everything. . . . I mean, here I was, all through high school and even college, getting almost straight A's. . . . I wasn't popular in school . . . I was alone a good deal of the time, but I always was a success. . . . I didn't see how I could go on.

C: But was it only worries over work, I wonder, that made your thoughts turn in this suicidal direction? Did you have no doubts, no second thoughts about the marriage? Either about your girlfriend as a person, or about just what it meant to you to be somebody's husband?

P: *(Pause)* Well . . . uh . . . I guess I did. Yes, I did have second thoughts.

After this point in the interview, the patient became more candid about his feelings. He was eventually able to reveal his strong fear of marriage, because of its symbolic meaning, for him, of premature death: marriage seemed to him like an ending rather than a beginning.

Anamnestic Data

The patient was twenty-seven at the time of the interview. Suicidal ideation accompanied by self-mutilating acts of a repetitive but only moderately severe nature were the symptoms leading to his admission. In addition he manifested insomnia, mild anorexia, a modest weight loss (five pounds in three months), obsessive indecisiveness, loss of energy, and impairment in concentration.

He had been in the habit of using marijuana in small amounts, on weekends, for several years.

There were two previous depressive episodes, one several months after the death of his mother (whom he did not mourn to any appreciable extent at the time of her death), around the time of graduation from high school. He was treated with antidepressants and psychotherapy at the time, both of which were discontinued when he entered college. The other episode followed his failure to reach the ranks of the final contestants in a sports competition. Suicidal ruminations and self-destructive acts were not a part of either episode.

He was described by a previous therapist as alternatingly self-critical and grandiose, tremendously preoccupied with physical strength and appearance, passive and demanding, at times fearful and indecisive.

Psychological Test Data

Full-scale IQ = 120 (verbal IQ = 132, performance IQ = 101). There was no evidence of organic impairment. Performance on the subtests was poor only in those tasks relating to the understanding of peoples' motives.

On the unstructured portions there was evidence of marked obsessionalism (attention to tiny details, missing the sense of the overall form), as well as a tendency toward depression and suspiciousness (many animal eyes seen in the Rorschach). But there was no evidence of impaired reality testing. The diagnostic impression from the test responses was that of a severe character disorder with obsessive and paranoid features.

Comments

This patient illustrates some of the difficulties in establishing a psychostructural diagnosis in the presence of evasiveness. Ultimately he volunteered some material that seemed of high relevance to his current problems. But that emerged only after one managed, with a very intense confrontation (couched in the form of a "resistance interpretation"), to circumvent his denial. Reality sense and reality testing were intact with respect to the interview, nor had the patient ever experienced "productive signs" of psychosis. But at the height of his illness his behavior was overtly self-destructive. He had no awareness at first of the sharp discrepancy between his self-mutilating acts and his professed pride in his appearance. There was some question among those concerned with his treatment whether such behavior constituted evidence of psychotic structure or whether he was hiding delusional thoughts behind his facade of studied normality. His brief psychotic episodes and brief panic states do not by themselves indicate psychotic *structure,* given that his general relationship with reality, over all the intervening time, was free of gross abnormality. Because there were no stigmata of schizophrenic illness and because there was evidence of recurrent severe depressive episodes with moments of "psychotic" behavior, it seemed appropriate to place him diagnostically in Region V.

He showed features of several personality subtypes: narcissistic, passive-dependent, and obsessional, particularly. On the narcissistic side were his marked grandiosity and simultaneous self-perception as a "failure," his extreme preoccupation with his physical appearance, and his incapacity to involve himself except in a shallow fashion with other people, his fiancée included. Though isolation of affect, intellectualization, and other "obsessive" traits were prominent, they were overshadowed by the narcissistic features, as were his passive-dependent qualities (wanting to be waited on by the hospital staff, to get better without effort on his part, and so on). One may speculate prognostically what it portends that it was so hard to establish meaningful emotional contact with this man. For contrast, one can compare him with the patient in case illustration 28.

Final Diagnostic Impressions

A. Categorical diagnoses
   1. Primary affective disorder, depressed type
   2. Borderline structure ("unstable borderline" in terms of the DSM-III); borderline personality disorder (Gunderson)
   3. Narcissistic personality

B. Dimensional assessments
   1. Region V of the Sz-MDP continuum
   2. GAS = 30 on admission; 45 at time of interview
   3. Personality profile as shown in Table IV–1

FAMILY HISTORY

First-degree relatives =	3 (parents, plus 1 sib)
affected members:	(1) mother (tense, restless, depressed; no psychotic episodes, but treated with antidepressants several years before her terminal illness made its appearance)
	(2) father (moderately serious depressive episodes beginning at age thirty-five)
	(3) brother ([three years younger] three recurrent depressive episodes, one of which was treated with ECT)

Second-degree relatives = 6
Other (including less seriously affected) members: (1) paternal great-aunt (suicided)

Case Illustration 21

Patient = P Doctor = D GAS = 49

P: I was up until six this morning . . .
D: Got up so early? Or went to bed so late!?
P: Didn't get to bed. That's just it—I *just* can't seem to catch up with everything. Anyway . . . the window-washer guy promised to come this morning but . . . he never came and he never called. And Monday . . . Friday, the guy was supposed to come, and I said, "Gee, I hope he can come Monday" to the thing on the phone . . . it was pouring rain and I never know what window washers do . . . and it said, "We'll call you back: this is a recorded message" . . . I called five times, but no nothing! I said, well, can you come the *next* day? I called twice yesterday, and then I gave up; either they don't come *down* my way, or they do only industrial stuff. . . . And I had to lug all the window frames up from the subbasement—which is *one* per trip . . . ya know . . . 'cause they're rather heavy . . . plastic, corners are narrow and ya just can't manipulate them easily. . . . I guess it's for two people . . . and then my *neighbor* yesterday: gee, she drives me nuts! She said, "Well I don' *want* him!" *(imitates her high-pitched squeal)* . . . yeah! . . . "I don' *want* the guy!" "An hour or so before I hired the guy ya said ya *did* want 'im!" And I said, "Make your *own* plans after this: ya always wait for *me* to get hold of somebody, and ask, 'Oh, can *he* do this for me?!' " ya know . . . and, uh, I said, "You make your *own* plans after this"; so she said, "Oh, all right, I'll *take* him." She said, "But I can't push the bed"; so I said, "OK, I'll push it out for you"; she said, "Well the window's nailed up"—I said, "Well, I'll *un*nail it for you" *(laughs)* . . . she said, "Well, the flowerbox is there near the radiator"; I said, "OK, OK, between him and me, we'll get it" . . . ugh, what a complainer! Drivin' me crazy! . . . So then I *threw* on my clothes, and I ran across the street to get her some flowers for a centerpiece for her table, and there were these metal bands . . . I finally caught up with the sanitation men half way up the block. I didn't wanna leave it there—it's gonna get windy; you know—these big metal bands they put around big boxes and crates and stuff, the sort of wide metal bands? . . . well, about three of those things, eight feet long, just sitting in the middle of the street: that's just all they need, ya know—to have somebody get

wound up in that—or a dog, or a kid on a bike or something . . . so I picked those up and *ran* after the trash man.

P: I wanted to get something for my little nephew . . . some guy wrote a book, what was it called? *The Loch Ness Man?* . . . I don't know . . . six or eight years ago he wrote a book about popular mechanics; this new one is about science too, so I think it'll intrigue my nephew . . .

P: Anyway, I am so tired at the moment. And I have to put up all those storm windows and stuff, hang all my winter curtains, vacuum the room, wash the floor, and put all the furniture back and hang all the plants . . . I'm *so* just absolutely knocked out . . . and Martha called, said, "How are you?" I said, "Exhausted. Absolutely knocked out!". . . She said, "They're up to their ankles in rain after the last downpour up there". . . . She said, "How's everything?" I said, "Exhausting." She said, "Well it's the eclipse." I said, "Yeah, but it's past now . . . I got a very interesting astrology book yesterday . . . on my way to Johnson's Department Store where I went to get some shirts for my brother." . . . They put them aside for me. I said, "*Can* you hold them for me a couple a days?" What with the window washer and everything . . . so I saw this book, *The Bermuda Triangle*.

D: What's that?

P: Well, it's been *out* a year and a half, I think . . . and it tells about all the ships and airplanes that disappear without a *trace*. There've been over a thousand ships with airplanes, not to mention how many *people* . . . that have . . . anyway, it's a triangle between Bermuda and Long Island, and, I guess, Florida somewhere . . . that's very dangerous shipping, or something . . . and they *never* have found even *one* piece of *debris* and *any* of those ships! Or airplanes! Completely vanished without a *trace!* And . . . this guy who wrote the book has a thesis about it . . .

D: What idea does he have about those ships?

P: Well, I'm not sure, but I think he feels they've disappeared by some extraterrestrial *force*. Now, I *have* heard . . . somewhere in the *Enquirer* I read, two, or was it three or more years ago, I guess . . . that Coast Guard planes'd been in contact with them one minute and the next minute they just completely lose contact, without the pilot saying, "Help, I'm losing *power!*" or anything! Just, *from normal to nothing in a second!* . . . And I think now they think it might come from flying *saucers* or that . . . maybe there's even a *hole* somewhere . . . somewhere in the middle of the earth . . .

D: So you may go to Scranton again for the holiday?

P: I may . . . but, . . . just the idea of, ya know, fighting again . . . with . . . I won't have as much junk . . . the fighting, getting up early in the morning and not sleeping. . . . I just feel like staying here, making a chicken casserole and having a day of *peace! (chuckles)* . . . 'cause, you know what it is . . . I keep *pushing* myself, and I'm still *tired* . . . um . . . and Dr. C—— said maybe take another "pep pill" . . . but . . . and he's changing offices next week. I dunno, maybe the rent went up at the old place, or just what. Anyhow, there'll be the same phone number . . . *(pause)*. I'll try to get a hold of him Tuesday to see what's what. . . . I haven't noticed any difference on the extra pill, but, you know, things get more hectic . . .

D: You *have* been less depressed I notice, before your periods over the past six or seven months, so . . .

P: Well, it's the manganese that I read about in the diet book, you know: it's since I began taking *that,* that I've at least felt better around that time of the month. You oughta put some of your other hysterical females *(chuckles)* on it and see! I gave some to my niece, but she didn't take it.

D: She gets worse off before her periods, too?

P: Well, she gets a *temper* . . . she doesn't get weepy or emotional the way I did . . . she's very active.

Anamnestic Data

The patient, a single woman of thirty-nine, was nearing completion of college. There had been many delays along the way in this task. She complained chronically of a lack of energy; felt defeated, discouraged, depressed; and found it difficult to finish assignments on time. In addition many minor illnesses interfered with her scholastic pursuits. There was an equally sporadic quality to her work history. All the jobs she had held seemed uninteresting; those she was more attracted to seemed always beyond reach. Deficiencies in self-discipline and goal directedness contributed to this record of working below capacity.

The week before her menses she usually gained four to six pounds and became noticeably more irritable and depressed; suicidal ruminations frequently occurred at such times, though these were never acted upon. A number of medications were given without appreciable effect, including imipramine (up to 300 milligrams/day), Ritalin, and fluphenazine. A trial of lithium was also unsuccessful, but the use of Diuril (chlorothiazide) the week before the menses reduced the irritability and despondency that accompanied this phase of her cycle.

Comments

This patient's clinical picture does not satisfy research criteria for either an affective or a schizophrenic psychosis. By St. Louis criteria she would be considered an "undiagnosed patient" (see Welner et al., 1973). According to my modification of Cohen's rating scale, the ratio of schizophrenic to affective symptoms was 34/66, that is, slanting toward the affective. Specifically, she showed depressive affect, somatic complaints, insomnia, self-depreciation, tearfulness (on occasion), psychomotor retardation, and repeated episodes of depression with fairly good remissions. Premenstrual aggravation of symptoms was present for several years until brought under control with diuretics. On the "schizophrenic side" there was some disorganization of thought and chronicity (in the sense that this disorganization had persisted for years).

Her speech showed the kind of circumstantiality alluded to in Peck's article on "circumstantial schizophrenia" (1962). In the light of recent work, however, circumstantiality does not emerge as a strong indicator of schizophrenia. She was much given to eccentric pseudoscientific preoccupations. Though outwardly self-denigratory, she had a hidden grandiose "self" that became apparent in the course of psychotherapy. This was accompanied by a kind of perfectionism that interfered with her vocational progress. She would shy away from tasks unless she could excel in them. As a result she restricted her activities to such an extent that she denied herself the chance to acquire certain skills that would eventually have been within her grasp; her level of function was therefore below what her B+ average in college would have led one to suspect.

The relatives with distinct schizophrenic illnesses had a clinical picture different from the patient's: in them paranoid ideation overshadowed other symptoms, whereas in the patient there was never more than some consternation that "others were getting ahead"—and this only occurred premenstrually.

Most of the signs of borderline structure were present: the sharply contradictory views of self and others, the low stress tolerance, and so on. But of impulsivity there was none, except an overgenerosity toward friends and a tendency to spend more than was prudent on various gifts (actually, this would be a mildly "manic" sign).

Characterologically the patient presented some difficulties in assessment: the existence of a concealed and pathological grandiose self behind the self-depreciatory facade constituted a strong narcissistic character trait. Yet there was none of the vanity, selfishness, or empathic deficit seen in so many "conventional" narcissistic people. Instead, the patient was self-effacing, excessively generous, unusually solicitous of others, and little concerned with her appearance. The assignment of a 6 to the PPS band for "narcissistic" reflects the intensity of the pathological grandiose self, but does not do justice to her altruistic attributes.

Final Diagnostic Impressions

A. Categorical diagnoses
   1. ———
   2. Borderline structure
   3. Depressive-masochistic character with narcissistic features

B. Dimensional assessments
   1. Region IV of the Sz-MDP continuum (Sz/MDP ratio, Cohen's scale = 34/66)
   2. GAS = 49
   3. Personality profile as shown in Table IV–I

FAMILY HISTORY

First-degree relatives =	6 (parents, plus 4 sibs)
affected members:	(1) mother (eccentric, narcissistic, hospitalized at age thirty-five for several months for an emotional illness of unknown type, called "depressive" at the time)
	(2) brother (hospitalized for several months at twenty-eight for a psychotic illness characterized by litigiousness and referential ideation)
Second-degree relatives =	7
Other (including less seriously affected) members:	(1) maternal cousin (a female cousin of thirty-six with a serious depressive disorder, not hospitalized)

Case Illustration 22

Patient = P Consultant = C GAS = 50

C: Well, as I mentioned before, I'm really sorry that Dr. G—— *(initial consultant)* didn't have a chance to get in touch with me beforehand, because as it happens I'll only be able to see you for this consultation and then make sure your treatment can be continued by a colleague.

P: Well, will he keep up my Elavil, like Dr. T—— *(previous therapist)*?

C: Umm . . . I imagine your new doctor will want to evaluate your situation in his own way, and come to his own conclusions about what's best for you in the long run . . .

P: *(Petulantly)* But I'm concerned about today! The next week! The next hour! I know Elavil has a powerful reaction . . . I've been depressed for a long time. . . . I guess *(pause)* I wasn't well enough to leave the dermatologist.

C: The who?

P: The dermatologist . . . from Des Moines Medical. I had psoriasis, and . . . I got well so fast, I was still exhausted . . . I asked them to let me stay another four or five days . . . because I was just getting my strength back, but they said no, and I said, "Can't I go to the psychiatric unit?" To rest up. But they said no. . . . I still need physically to get better.

(Pause) I couldn't find a sort of . . . a good situation . . . I could . . . I'm jumping around too much . . . I'm living alone . . . other problems . . .

C: "Jumping around"?

P: Well, I also have sciatica, so it's not that easy to walk around that much. . . . My boyfriend and I rented a house in A—— . . . but I couldn't go that much, and I got frightened going out alone . . . I . . . I got *really* exhausted and . . . here I *am! (Pause)* . . . and I, uh, I've been leaning on my boyfriend way too much . . . and it ends up in confusion! I told him he's going much too fast for me.

C: Hmm?

P: His whole pace is just too fast; he has a lot of insight, but he isn't a therapist, so . . . *(pause)* but I've been leaning on him, and it's too much for him, too much pressure. . . . *(Pause)* I was extremely relieved about the Elavil . . . I was on lithium from Dr. G——, but I had a bad reaction to it. It did nothing for me anyway.

C: I'm not sure what you mean "relieved"?!

P: I was very relieved when Dr. T—— said I didn't need it. *(Pause)* Eight to ten days before my period, it becomes so *intense* . . .

C: *What* gets "intense"!?

P: *(Huffily, as though it should have been obvious)* . . . my depression! Usually the day I can't stand it any more, usually the *next* day my period comes. I went to an acupuncture specialist about it . . . but that didn't help . . .

C: Mmm.

P: Once I tried raising the Elavil myself but I got nervous and didn't follow through with it. *(Pause)* Since I talked to Dr. T——is that, umm . . . I feel I'm going to start feeling good again. And having been in other depressions . . . *(pause)* . . . By the way, I'll tell you for what it's worth, I once went to a quack, and it tore up my life. I don't mean just mentally. I mean physically . . .

C: Oh!?

P: I was down to ninety pounds. It's taken years to repair it . . .

C: "Repair it"?!

P: The thing I'll always have to guard against is not to let it make me upset. . . . I *do* think I'll feel better with the Elavil and not get consumed by the past again . . . by the things that've happened. Like, not crying over spilt milk: if you're crying, you're still spilling it!

C: Indeed!

P: I don't want to go through this again. I'm thirty-seven years old. I'm amazed I could discuss so much with Dr. T——. . . . Talking to different therapists is a form of jumping I can't handle . . . I'm getting confused . . . I want stability . . . just too many *things!* . . . The boyfriend

I've been seeing for over two years . . . *sexually* it isn't a good relation. I suggested we turn it into an open relationship a year ago. He's from a Stoish-Swedish background . . .

C: "Stoish-"?

P: Well, you know, the Swedes are so stoic, stuffy—he doesn't care about it that much . . .

C: About what?

P: Sex. *(Pause)* I go out with other men for sexual reasons. But I *stay* with J—— . . . and that's kind of confusing right there.

C: *(In an attempt to pull the conversation back toward its original purpose)* Look, as I said earlier, I would be happy to place a call to a colleague of mine who I'm sure will be able to see you . . . though, as I mentioned, he will have to be guided, so far as the medication is concerned, by his own impressions of you . . .

P: *(Interrupting)* Well . . . I don't know! I find it difficult to talk to *you* . . . and you're going to try to find someone I could work with. . . . How do I know I could relate to *them* any better?!

C: I'm sorry.

P: I mean, *you'll* call people *you* know, and they'll be like yourself, so I wouldn't be able to relate to them, could I? . . . any better!

C: Then all I can suggest is that you phone Dr. G—— again and ask him to give you the name of someone he knows who *does* have time.

P: Maybe if *you* call him . . . and the *combination* of you . . . would make a better *recommendation* . . . wouldn't . . .

C: In any case, since Dr. G—— is the man whom you saw first in consultation, you might better get back to *him* . . .

P: But you've been talking to me . . . can't you *tell* what sort of person . . . which of your colleagues I might be able to relate to *(plaintively)*? . . . If you're going to suggest someone, I guess I should *try* someone you suggest.

Comments

With this patient it was not possible to accumulate enough information to make the usual categorical and dimensional evaluations. The material is presented chiefly to demonstrate certain abnormalities of speech pattern suggestive of a schizophrenic disorder, whereas the patient presents herself as suffering from an (exclusively) affective disorder.

The most frequently noted abnormality consists in her assuming that the consultant, a total stranger to her, is so familiar with the minutiae of her past experience that he would automatically understand every oblique reference in her speech. The unexpected allusion to the dermatologist is one such reference. There are also a number of juxtaposed clauses presented as if logically connected but which are actually non sequiturs. The comment,

"His whole pace is just too fast; he has a lot of insight . . . " illustrates this illogicality. One also encounters frequent unaccountable changes of subject, some occurring in midsentence. These derailments give a spasmodic and bewildering aspect to her pattern of communication. The catchall word "it" is used very often, only the referents are omitted: " . . . *it* gets intense, . . ."; "it's taken years to repair *it*. . . ." On several occasions the patient grew visibly annoyed at having to explain what "it" related to.

Besides these abnormalities, there were also several instances of marked concreteness (" . . . if you're crying, you're still spilling it") and even one of neologism ("stoish" for stoic and Swedish).

Her assumption that she could not be comfortable with any colleague to whom the consultant might refer her—because she didn't feel comfortable with the consultant—is another example of concreteness, here arising from a faulty syllogism.

Finally, when the consultant urged her to go back to the referring physician for another recommendation, her ambivalence manifested itself: she suddenly wanted to cooperate with the consultant, whereas the moment before her attitude was quite negative.

In addition to all this evidence of a formal disorder of thought, there was a parallel abnormality in her behavior, though one that is hard to capture on the printed page. She does not respect the conventional gestures of closure, for example: the obvious end of the conversation ("I'm sorry [I can't be of help]; you'll have to phone Dr. G—— again and ask him to give you the name of someone . . .") is not the "end" for her at all. Unless the other person forces closure by a desperate maneuver (such as walking away, ordering her out, and so on), the patient would continue indefinitely to oscillate between one alternative and another. In the purer forms of affective illness, especially at nonpsychotic levels, it is most unusual for these kinds of cues to be ignored. If anything, depressive people are often exquisitely tuned in to the feelings of others, since they depend so heavily on winning their support.

In office practice, depressed patients may "cling" as the session draws to an end and remain seated, hoping for a few extra minutes, but more often will begin to leave before the time is up—at the first sign (a notebook being put away, a pen being put down) that the session is almost over. They are afraid to "offend" by overstaying their welcome. On the other hand, the patient who talks on, oblivious to the closing of the notebook, the replacement of the pen, the therapist's looking at the clock, his beginning to get up, and so on, is more apt to show at least an admixture of schizophrenic stigmata.

The patient in this vignette, then, may have an affective component to her illness; if the Elavil and lithium she mentions had been prescribed for valid reasons, there would appear to be compelling evidence for a schizophrenic component. This would mean that her illness would be better conceptualized as *schizoaffective,* at least symptomatically.

Although the patient's level of function at the time of the consultation was consistent with a GAS of 50, her psychostructural organization was not tested methodically, so it is unclear whether there was (still) a psychosis or whether she might exemplify a clinical state best conceptualized as a "borderline schizoaffective" disorder.

Case Illustration 23

Patient = P Interviewer = I GAS = 52

I: I'd be grateful if you could tell me in your own words what problems led to your being asked to see me today.

P: Problems? You'll have to rephrase your question. I have no problems. Redefine what you mean! I was referred to you after several tests, though I dispute the results. I was under emotional strain when I took the tests—which I found absurd.

I: Would I be correct in assuming, though, that your relatives felt you had some problems, at least in their eyes?

P: My feelings haven't conflicted with contemporary social values, if that's what you mean. Which is not to deny that another system can exist.

I: Still, I can't get away from the realization that you and your relatives, even if you have indeed been well . . . you and your relatives must not have been getting on as well as before, and in such a way that they got it into their heads to ask you to go through with this consultation.

P: If I've been frustrated in my goals, the reason is—which may be at variance with the attitude of my relatives—that I took a leave of absence from divinity school for various reasons, because of changes in my academic interests. I had to provide special proof of my interest in returning, because I took the leave three weeks too late. My relatives would not permit me to withdraw certain funds from my account, which eliminated all possibility of return to school. That is the main point of contention. I see no reason for their cutting off arbitrarily my academic and social potential in this manner.

I: Uh-huh . . . what do you suppose could have given them the impression you were under emotional strain?

P: What gave them the impression? I really can't answer that. Though I can see how being away from school could lead to emotional strain.

I: Something specific may have stimulated their interest in a consultation, I gather.

P: I look after my own needs. My relatives have radically different interests and outlooks. One of them said, "Don't tell anyone you're a theology student," when I had a job at a hardware store. They should give a logically sound reason why I'm being asked to see you. I doubt they can.

I: I understand their reluctance to release funds for your return to school may have been predicated on their concern you might have difficulties remaining in it, and functioning well . . .

P: I disagree!!

I: . . . inasmuch as you seemed to have a hard time last semester . . .

P: I disagree!!

I: . . . a hard time last semester with the course work, and you asked to leave after two weeks . . .

P: I disagree!! I indeed started the semester, with full intention of remaining, but I found the professors of poor quality. So I changed, or asked to change to a different school. But once there, I discovered their courses were also poor. So I asked to change again.

I: I understood you were having some difficulties getting along with people. Different people, at that school—something over and beyond the disadvantages you describe in the academic setup.

P: Perhaps you're referring to the fact that my roommate smoked marijuana, which I found objectionable, and listened to records till 1 A.M., which interfered with my attention to my studies.

I: That puts the emphasis on the "other fellow"; I was wondering if you experienced any difficulties in making friends and such, that seemed to stem from within yourself?

P: Certainly not!!

I: What friends do you have at the moment?

P: Just now I'm engrossed in studies; when I meet people who share my interests, I develop a friendship. At the moment, my interests have taken a different path, and I have grown apart from my former friends.

I: Yet your relatives gave me the impression you have scarcely left the house these past three months, as if you were not looking too vigorously to establish new acquaintances. Is that . . .

P: *(Interrupting)* That is perhaps a rationalization, which I find rather subjective; they may resent that my interests are not the same as their interests. In their milieu I am unable to find like-minded persons with whom I could form friendships.

I: You know, I have more and more the impression you're annoyed at something, maybe; annoyed at having to put up with this interview, even.

P: I disagree. I take no stand on such matters. I take an existential view of it: there are no absolutes in matters of this sort. If you wish to perceive my situation in a particular way, you are morally free to do so. I am of course under no obligation to see it the same way.

I: At least maybe you'll acknowledge you weren't brimming with enthusiasm about coming here today.

P: No, I wasn't.

I: But I have managed, I think, to put my finger on one problem I feel you have, although I hesitate to mention it, for fear of your response . . .

P: I don't see why you should . . .

I: . . . and it's this: Whenever anybody says anything to you, you immediately disagree!

P: *(Interrupting)* I don't go along . . .

I: You don't give yourself a chance to listen to what the other fellow has to say.

P: You're speaking in general terms! You have no right to apply as a general truth something that is based on experience with only one person, in this case yourself!!

I: Perhaps you have a point! But then, perhaps I'm not the only person with whom you've found yourself constantly disagreeing. I leave that for you to ponder later on, because I see our time is up.

Comments

The absence of delusions, hallucinations, incoherence, or eccentric speech means that research diagnostic criteria for schizophrenia are not satisfied. One is left with abnormalities of thought and relatedness which have a schizophrenic flavoring (paranoid ideation, in the absence of any affective symptoms, guardedness, evasiveness). The clinical picture would satisfy the less rigid criteria of "borderline" schizophrenia and happens also to be compatible with certain earlier descriptive terms such as "ambulatory schizophrenia" (Zilboorg) or "latent psychosis" (Bychowski). Compartmentalization of paranoid ideas and ability to function at intellectual endeavors were of a sort that permitted a relatively high global function score—one that is ordinarily not achieved by patients with psychotic structure, though typical of ambulatory borderline (-structure) patients.

Psychotic structure is established here on the basis of primitive defenses (pervasive denial, disavowal, projection), lack of identity integration (seeing others as only caricatures of their actual selves or as endowed with attributes actually projected onto them from the patient's own imagination; seeing himself in grandiose, unrealistic terms) and incapacity to test reality (particularly, an incapacity to "try out" the other person's opinion of himself even momentarily). Even the most cautious and tactful "confrontation" (here, in the sense of inviting him to consider alternative explanations for his reactions and behavior) had no effect in enhancing rapport or in diminishing the degree of argumentativeness.

Among the personality subtypes, paranoid and (to a lesser extent) obsessional features overshadow all others.

Never having shown productive signs, the patient would, to many clinicians, represent a condition just short of that diagnostic rara avis "pure paranoia." Winokur is of the opinion (mentioned in the June 1977 American Psychiatric Association *Clinical News*) that this illness is distinct from schizophrenia and that it can occur in persons of average intelligence, rather than being restricted to those of superior intelligence (as is customarily thought). The patient in this example comes from a family many of whose members suffered unequivocal schizophrenic episodes. My personal acquaintance is limited to three such cases, all in males of superior intelligence. Each, as in the present case, had one or more first-degree relatives with a clearly defined schizophrenic illness. Further study will be required to resolve the issue Winokur raises, but as far as I am concerned, the burden of proof is on him to demonstrate that this syndrome is *not,* in many instances, a "spectrum" manifestation of the schizophrenic genotype(s). Winokur also regards this as a predominantly male syndrome. I suspect this is true not only empirically but also theoretically. Recent research concerning hemispheric specialization seems to point toward a difference in predominance between the sexes: that by adult life many males end up left-hemisphere predominant, while females show superiority in functions mediated by the "nondominant" hemisphere. It is easy to grasp at least at the conceptual level how, if these tendencies become exaggerated for whatever reason, certain males will show an excessive preoccupation with logic, "reasoning," intellectualism, and so on, to the exclusion of attention to matters of feeling and empathy. This is the *obsessional,* par excellence. Rarely does one encounter in women the kind of emotional blindness demonstrated by the patient in the illustration, or in hyperobsessive males in general. With this same kind of exaggerated obsessive intellectualizing, given a schizophrenic twist through heightened genetic liability, and so on, a case of "pure paranoia" may result. With less liability, one may see, as in this patient, a nondelusional form: (pure) paranoid personality. Such patients are often unmotivated for psychotherapy, for which they would be handicapped in any case because of their incapacity to perceive and understand emotions. For similar reasons, their sense of humor is characteristically deficient.

In dimensional terms, placement in Region I of the Sz-MDP continuum reflects the absence of affective features, the borderline schizophrenic clinical picture, and the positive family history.

Final Diagnostic Impressions

A. Categorical diagnoses

1. ———
2*a*. Psychotic structure
b. "Borderline schizophrenia" (Kety's B-3 type)
3. Paranoid personality

B. Dimensional assessments
   1. Region I of the Sz-MDP continuum
   2. GAS = 52
   3. Personality profile as shown in Table IV–I

FAMILY HISTORY

First-degree relatives =	4 (parents, plus 2 sibs)
affected members:	(1) mother (eccentric, hospitalized on several occasions and treated with phenothiazines for what were considered schizophrenic episodes) (2) sister (hospitalized at age twenty-two for psychotic episode characterized by persecutory delusions; temperamentally shy and withdrawn)
Second-degree relatives =	7
Other (including less seriously affected) members:	(1) maternal grandfather (alcoholic)

Case Illustration 24

Patient = P Doctor = D GAS = 57

D: Tell me about how your emotional difficulties began.

P: *(Speaking with a casual air)* Oh, I guess I was a pretty straight arrow till I got to college. I went there thinking to take pre-law, and end up in my old man's firm, but I got into art in a big way, which was more my thing . . . and I got close with this art professor and his wife. . . . He got me into drugs—LSD, mescaline, peyote—and from then on I was in a different world.

D: What about this "different world"?

P: Well, I spent all my time painting instead of going to the courses I signed up for. I got very into abstract expressionism. . . . I turned out some canvases my teacher felt had a lot of potential. The "different world" part had to do with the art professor and his wife: I wound up living with them. After a while we all ended up in the same bed. I think each of us "had" the other two at some time or another, which really blew my mind . . .

D: What particular aspect of all that was "mind-blowing"?

P: Well, the homosexual part, mostly. . . . I was still a virgin when I went to Wisconsin, and here I was losing my cherry two ways at once. . . . at the time it was going on, it felt like a special thing . . . like "exalted," you know . . . it was a beautiful thing . . . except that after about six months of it, I got to being jealous of her if she paid attention to him and jealous of him if he paid attention to her . . . it was more than I could handle, and I freaked out . . .

D: By which you're referring to what sorts of experiences?

P: Well . . . and this could be from the LSD I was doing at that time . . . I felt I could look through other people's eyes . . . or that I looked like other people . . . I might be becoming my sister, was a major thought at the time. . . . I used to see this scene in my head . . . still do now and again . . . that seems like my whole life past and present . . . most of it's a blur, though, except for a de Kooning nude in a silver frame, far off in the distance. I can still see it with my eyes closed . . .

D: Are you describing "flashbacks" from the LSD?

P: Well, it's a hard-to-tell thing. . . . I haven't done any acid in three years now. The first year or so I'd get the scene every now and then without knowing it was coming on . . . I think those must've been flashbacks. But now I can summon up the scene just as a matter of recollection. . . .

D: This was a very chaotic period for you then . . . but what specifically led up to your getting psychiatric help? What in all that was going on was affecting you the most?

P: When I would be coming down from a "trip," or if I wouldn't be stoned, I would get completely torn up by the homosexual thing. I had to admit I liked it as much with my teacher as I did with his wife . . . and it was even an easier thing with him . . .

D: How do you mean?

P: I wasn't thinking, "Am I balling her as good as her old man?" See, what he and I had between us was "our thing," if you know what I mean. . . . But I couldn't stand the thought of being queer even though I was enjoying it. . . . It got to the place where I fled that whole scene, dropped out of their house, dropped out of college, and dropped out of life . . .

D: Meaning?

P: I avoided everybody . . . I went back home, but there were heavy scenes between my mother and me. . . . She threatened to send me to jail if I didn't go back to school or get a job. . . . I think she would've done it . . . my mother's a powerful dude . . .

D: So where did you wind up?

P: For the last year I've been in an apartment of my own . . .

D: Working?

P: Half working . . . that's it: I can't get my head together enough for a 9-to-5 life. . . . I did some volunteer art teaching in high school . . . right now, I've got a half-time job in a school, which is about as much as I feel up to right now.

D: You're off drugs now?

P: Yeah. I haven't touched anything in over a year. It wasn't like I was really hooked, see . . . I got in with a crowd that was heavily into drugs . . . I got caught up in it. I knew I had to get un-caught-up in it. After my folks threw me out, I said to myself, "Screw it, man, you gotta grow up!"

D: Were you still having these experiences where you felt you were becoming other people, looking through their eyes and such?

P: Only once over the last seven or eight months: there was this weird episode where I got it into my head that there was this invisible soul hovering over me. . . . I gave it the name "Daphne." . . . Daphne was the name of all the feelings going on in me that I couldn't name . . . but it seemed real. . . . This must've gone on for a week . . . and I'd carry on conversations with Daphne, wait up for her to come around. . . .

D: Are there times when you still get caught up in such feelings . . . or where you personify a part of yourself like that?

P: Oh, "Daphne" comes around every so often . . . she's the flicker in the light bulbs overhead. . . . we carry on many a weighty conversation about Karma, the meaning of life, the screwed-up feelings I get . . .

D: Well, are you talking of her as someone who is somehow invisibly *out there,* like a companion, who tells you things your own mind "couldn't" . . . like she really is a separate creat——?

P: *(Interrupting)* Oh, she's a companion, all right, but she's my imagination . . . just a piece of my imagination, see . . . that I just keep stationed out there to keep me company. With Daphne around, it's a lot less lonely.

The case material is derived from an interview conducted one year following the patient's discharge from the hospital.

Anamnestic Data

This patient came from a background that was favorable from a socioeconomic standpoint but chaotic with regard to the psychological environment. The patient's father, a successful lawyer, was given to rage outbursts in which he could be verbally or physically abusive to anyone in the family who happened to be present. The patient was frequently the butt of humiliating remarks. His mother, though a much more gentle person, was ineffectual either in preventing such outbursts or in softening their effect. The patient was shy throughout his school years and never had more than one or two friends. Academically he outperformed his brother and sister, until college, when his grades dropped off precipitously. The "problem child" in the family had been the older brother, not the patient.

There was no sexual intimacy until the college experiences related in the preceding material. Thereafter the patient's sexual fantasies were largely, but not exclusively, heterosexual, but his self-confidence was seriously undermined. He had little sexual interest until after he stopped taking marijuana and the various "hallucinogenic" drugs he had sampled. But when his sexual appetite returned, he kept himself aloof from women and as a result had almost no experience of intimate relationships, apart from the highly pathological ones in college with the art instructor and his wife.

Several of the patient's relatives had serious psychiatric disorders, largely within the realm of affective illness (see Family History, below). The father's irritable temperament and periodic rage outbursts probably represented a "spectrum" manifestation of an affective (bipolar) disorder.

According to the parents, the patient had normal milestones, following an uncomplicated birth, but showed signs of "nervousness" during childhood. These included enuresis till nine, frequent head banging till about three and a half, and difficulty with "separations" (going to school, going to camp, and so forth).

Comments

This patient had psychotic episodes, some lasting weeks at a time, under the influence of psychotomimetic drugs. The question arises, Were these episodes *induced* by the drugs? Or were they examples of preexisting vulnerability to psychosis merely precipitated (or aggravated) by the drugs?

There were some signs of vulnerability premorbidly (nervous "habits," difficulty with separation, pathological shyness), though it was an open question how much these were to be attributed to constitutional factors and how much to the adverse family environment. At all events, there were no stigmata of schizophrenia beforehand, and little direct evidence of affective disorder. Instead, there was only the "positive" family history, suggesting that the patient might be at greater than average risk for eventual affective disorder himself.

Thus, a conservative diagnostician might favor the notion of an induced psychosis; someone with a more speculative bent would incline toward the view that the psychosis was precipitated in a person with heightened vulnerability to a major psychiatric disorder. The conservative view is espoused in the excellent review of Davison (1976); the speculative view has been argued elsewhere by the author (Stone, 1973).

After cessation of drug intake, the patient wafted in and out of contact with reality, elaborated a kind of imaginary companion (as had the patient in case illustration 11, without drugs), that, at the time of the interview, had the force of an "overvalued idea."

Off drugs, the patient was not impulsive, whereas impulsivity was of chaotic proportions at the height of his illness. Stress tolerance was still low, in both the occupational and interpersonal realms. At the time of the interview the patient had regained his capacity for avocational pursuits. Earlier, his artwork was incoherent, even within the framework of abstract expressionism; he deluded himself about the brilliance of his canvases, which were really not regarded as "promising" by the art faculty of his college. His speech, which was so filled with "hippie" locutions and private allusions, was scarcely comprehensible during the drug phase of his illness. Now, one noted only occasional lapses into this private world; furthermore, his capacity to *test* reality now seemed adequate. But were these solipsistic intrusions the manifestations of an underlying psychotic structure or, like "flashbacks," a sign of prolonged toxicity from the psychotomimetic drugs? In the patient under discussion, psychotic intrusions had been brief and relatively uncommon events for almost a year and were not part of his premorbid picture. It may be fair to claim, then, that his organization is borderline—in the "state of nature"—but was temporarily pushed into seemingly psychotic structure by the hallucinogens. Psychological testing, done while he was still much more under the influence of the drugs, was not helpful in making this kind of trait-versus-state distinction.

Psychological Test Data

These were performed three weeks after admission, at a time when the patient was psychotic only intermittently. Full-scale IQ was "very superior": 138 (verbal IQ = 141, performance IQ = 126). His lowest subscore (though still well above average) was in the area of comprehension of conventional social situations. Apart from this suggestion of immaturity in social judgment, his reasoning, abstraction, and perceptual-motor abilities were unimpaired and above average.

On the unstructured portions, however, considerable intrusion of "primary process" was evident. On card II of the Rorschach, for example, his percepts were "a lobster mouth," "the face of a Hopi chieftain," and "two Italians dressed as Esquimaux." Unusual percepts relating to sex were noted as often as those relating to hostile and dependent themes; thus, on card I: "a couple doing sex in an odd position." To the "phallic" imagery in card VI: "a splattered penis pinned down as on a wax plate for classroom dissection." Even more striking were the patient's responses on the "color cards" (VIII, IX, and X), where he reversed figure and ground, included the white spaces—namely, "a Navajo chief with war paint and a yellow beard." Elsewhere on one of these cards he "saw" a sexual climax: "not anyone doing it, but just the *feeling* of it."

The diagnostic impression was "acute schizophrenic reaction with highly personalized perceptions suggesting faulty reality testing and depersonalization."

Final Diagnostic Impressions

A. Categorical diagnoses
   1. History of drug-"induced" psychosis—predominantly affective schizoaffective in type
   2. Borderline structure
   3. Passive-dependent personality with narcissistic features

B. Dimensional assessments
   1. Region IV
   2. GAS = 57 (at height of illness, would have been in the high twenties)
   3. Personality profile as shown in Table IV–I

FAMILY HISTORY

First-degree relatives =	4 (parents, plus 2 sibs)
affected members:	(1) father (paranoid, grandiose, hypomanic, sadistic; has had several brief psychotic rage outbursts) (2) brother (long history of severe emotional problems from adolescence onward; schizoid; depressed; a devotee of Eastern religion; graduated from college but unable to function up to potential; considered "schizoaffective" by his [outpatient] therapist; no history of drug abuse)
Second-degree relatives =	7
affected member:	(1) maternal aunt (suicided)

Case Illustration 25

Patient = P Therapist = P GAS = 60

P: Carabosse[7] called again last night! . . .

T: Uh-huh.

P: . . . to tell me the children needn't expect anything for Christmas from her, unless I promise to "rid the house of popery" . . .

T: To what?!

P: To promise to raise them High Church instead of Catholic . . . *(pause, as her face becomes livid with emotion)* . . . times like that, I just feel like *crushing* her . . . like mashing her the way they do in that . . . used car thing.[8] *(Pause)* I wished I knew which feeling was more something like a plague . . . or whatever it's called . . . like witchery, is there . . . and is hopeless . . . and I can't stand it. And then, too, I try to think like I think *you* tell me to think about her . . . I can hear you telling me, "What do you care what she says: your husband's on your side" . . . only I *do* care, goddammit, because . . . it's that "that's-how-people-*are*" sort of thing. . . . If that's how people are, I don't wanna be "people"!

T: But I'm not sure how she gets to you still, if Bill already told you it was

[7]The witch in "Sleeping Beauty"; her name for her mother-in-law.

[8]Referring to the giant press used to reduce abandoned cars to scrap iron.

fine with him to send them to the Lycée and to give them a Catholic upbr——

P: *(Interrupting)* I *know* she can't make them get brought up her own way, instead of the way I . . . it's the *image* of her, that . . . like if I go into the study to play Rameau or Debussy, then I'm not *"in life"* . . . but if Carabosse goes to her damned Anglican or whatever-it-is church and decries "popery" . . . you see what I mean? She's "living life" . . . it's like the whole battle of Agincourt's being fought all over again in my living room . . . and people like her are gonna get the credit . . . but if all you do is play music and let other people live their own life, you get . . . *walked on:* that's what it is! For Carabosse I'm just a stepping-stone to get wherever it is she's . . . wherever she thinks she's going. People like her . . . they're so *sure* of themselves . . . so "sure" we had to march into Vietnam . . . like the way the terrorists are "sure" they have to bomb this one or shoot that one . . . if "people" are so "sure," I wonder "what am I?" . . .

T: Like you must belong to some other "species."

P: Yeah! "Homo incertus," or something like that *(laughs)* . . . I don't know, it just seems to me I was born without a protective skin or something . . . people . . . you know . . . "regular" people rattle me . . . even if I know they can't really do anything to me. The worst of it is, I can't help knowing I am "people," just like they are . . . it galls me . . . I always imagine: What if a Martian were looking in through the window? He'd have to conclude that Bill and I and the kids belonged to the same crummy species as the rest of them.

Anamnestic Data

This patient, a married woman in her late thirties, was the eldest of three children from a family many members of which, especially in the paternal line, suffered either "core" or "spectrum" schizophrenic conditions. The family, of French Catholic descent, also contained a number of literati, inventors, and musicians, including several of considerable reputation.

The patient was the only one in her generation to make a stable marriage and was likewise the only one with what in everyday parlance would be considered an "agreeable" personality. Her siblings and cousins were for the most part difficult, in some instances grossly paranoid. Although a psychological test battery was never performed, the patient appeared to be, in addition, the one "gifted" member of her generation. She was an accomplished musician but distinguished herself equally, among her acquaintances, for her exquisite sensitivity to the feelings of other people. This was the source of some distress, paradoxically, because others frequently sought her out for advice, unaware that she had little confidence in her perceptions and was furthermore too shy to be at ease in their company and too polite to discourage their requests. Fairly comfortable within the confines of her own immediate family, she nevertheless sought psychiatric help in order to cope with the various intrusions from the outside. The case material derives from a time when she was struggling with feelings of unaccustomed anger, evoked by conflicts (about the rearing of her children) with her highly opinionated mother-in-law. At the height of her distress just before seeking help, she had been depressed, tearful, anxious, and unable to fall asleep; on occasion she would give vent briefly to a kind of helpless rage.

Comments

The most striking features of the patient's verbal productions are the frequent gaps in logical flow and the high degree of allusiveness in her speech: she depends a great deal on the history of her relationship with the therapist; namely, that he seize the meaning of her ideas even though these are often only half-communicated, at times merely hinted at through shared symbols. These phenomena are seldom noticeable except when the patient is unusually anxious. At such times she manages to be at once highly *articulate*—almost poetic—in describing her plight, and also *inarticulate,* in the sense that someone unfamiliar with her would have trouble following her discourse.

She has difficulty in assimilating the contrasts between various groups of people (those who are considerate but ill at ease versus those who are crass and intrusive but comfortable with themselves), experiencing mankind as composed of two distinct "species." Yet she is aware that such a thought is a peculiarity of hers and not really accurate: it is not quite an "overvalued idea," as in a borderline patient, because she does not cling to it with even moderate tenacity.

She has insight about her own vulnerability to stressful interpersonal situations, spontaneously choosing a metaphor reminiscent of Freud's comments about the thin stimulus-barrier *(Reizschutz)* in schizophrenia.

While her speech is like that of many "schizotypal" borderline patients, her overall function (as housewife and musician) is quite good, apart from certain social gatherings, nor does she exhibit the nonspecific criteria for borderline psychic structure, apart from diminished anxiety tolerance (i.e., heightened vulnerability).

It may be that the patient requires continual vigilance and the use of every ounce of her ample intelligence just to keep herself above the level of unreality and contradictory self-perceptions. The effortfulness with which she maintains herself at (or near) the neurotic level may itself be a measure of the degree to which she has had to contend with an extra measure of liability to schizophrenia—to which so many family members have succumbed outright.

Final Diagnostic Impressions

A. Categorical diagnoses
   1. ———
   2. Schizotypal; structure transitional[9]
   3. Schizoid personality
B. Dimensional assessments
   1. Region II of the Sz-MDP continuum
   2. GAS = 60 (typically, has ranged in the high forties to low fifties, episodically)
   3. Personality profile as shown in Table IV–I

FAMILY HISTORY

First-degree relatives =	4 (parents, plus 2 sibs)
affected members:	(1) father (eccentric, paranoid, narcissistic; "schizotypal borderline") (2) brother (narcissistic, chronic undifferentiated schizophrenic reaction)
Second-degree relatives =	10
affected members:	(1) niece, age twenty-three ("schizotypal borderline" [or Kety B-3 Sz]) (2) niece, age twenty (referential, bizarre ideation and behavior led to dismissal from college and psychiatric hospitalization) (both are daughters of the affected brother) (3) paternal grandmother (grandiose, severe narcissistic character disorder; not overtly schizophrenic)
Other (*including less seriously affected*) *members:*	(1) maternal cousin (alcoholic)

Case Illustration 26

Patient = P Therapist = T GAS = 62

The patient was a single woman in her early twenties referred for psychotherapy shortly after she completed nursing school and moved into an apartment with a roommate. She had become mildly depressed, anxious when alone, and withdrawn in relation to her peers during work. She was

[9]The patient functions at the interface between borderline and neurotic: shows five items positive on the Spitzer checklist (the minimum for "borderline" in this schema), one item positive on the Gunderson list (but psychological tests not done), and only two certain on Kernberg's criteria (with only an episodic tendency toward splitting and contradictory self-image).

extremely inhibited as well as very inexperienced in sexual matters. Having been raised in a strict Catholic family and educated by nuns, she felt considerable guilt about even discussing sexual subjects. Guilt about masturbation was particularly intense: therapy went on two years before she could bring herself to mention the subject, and then only fleetingly. If asked to make an effort to explore the subject a bit further, she would become mute, and her eyes would glaze over. Her guilt was all the more intense because she was convinced her father knew of her "transgressions" and rejected her for it. He had been markedly aloof and hostile toward her since her graduation.

A more accurate reading of events seemed to be that he was actually quite fond of her and was disappointed at her growing up and away from him. A proud and temperamental man, he could not express his deeper feelings, leaving her with the impression that he harbored only ill will. Many months later she was able to reveal that he had been quite seductive with her during her adolescence. It became clear that their relationship was much more complex, with warm as well as hostile feelings, than she was initially willing to admit. Meanwhile she was convinced all men were both predatory and rejecting; it was inordinately difficult for her to be trustful of men. Once when her therapist called in the evening to change the appointment time, she felt convinced at first that he was calling to "make a pass" at her, which temporarily made her more mistrustful than ever. The men she selected were for the most part predatory enough to justify her worst fears. At work she performed her duties very well, but often felt some of her co-workers were making innuendoes of a sexually compromising nature about her, and on a few occasions misconstrued what people within earshot were saying, as though they were casting aspersions on her. Sometimes she would become provocative and argumentative to the point where people really did make unpleasant remarks.

Though she was frequently evasive and guarded in sessions, there were no abnormalities in her speech. She had one "micropsychotic" episode, characterized by panic and overconcern with certain sexual themes, triggered by witnessing a very "frank" movie. Much of the time, nevertheless, she showed a toughness and humor that earned her the friendship of some of her co-workers, despite her shyness.

On a number of occasions she spoke of wanting to quit treatment on the spur of the moment. Usually this occurred when sexual themes were rising to the surface; she preferred to interrupt therapy rather than confront these issues. She was once able to speak more forthrightly about fantasies connected with masturbation:

P: When I do it, I have fantasies of being with Al or with Henry . . . of being loved by one of them . . . and not being alone.

T: So this dramatizes your feelings of loneliness? For a few minutes you're absorbed in ''being loved'' . . . of being ''with'' someone. Then—bang!—down to earth again!

P: *(Becoming tearful)* I'm like a hungry person who can forget he's hungry till he walks past a restaurant. Also, it'd be not so *bad,* except that you feel you're *stuck* having to be alone, always.

T: Yes, *I* don't feel it has to be that way, but *you* certainly do, at least up till *now*. It's like the misery you've felt for years is just a sample of what's in store for you for the rest of your life.

P: *(Tearfully)* Yeah . . . I know that's how I feel . . . but having to *talk* about it brings it all . . . it makes it seem *more* true instead of less true . . .

Final Diagnostic Impressions

A. Categorical diagnoses
   1. ———
   2. Borderline structure; schizotypal borderline personality (Spitzer)[10]
   3. Paranoid personality with obsessive, schizoid, and depressive-masochistic features

B. Dimensional assessments
   1. Region II of the Sz-MDP continuum (but low on severity scale)
   2. GAS = 62
   3. Personality profile as shown in Table IV–I

FAMILY HISTORY

First-degree relatives = 6 (parents, plus 4 sibs)
Second-degree relatives = 8
Other (including less seriously affected) members: (1) father (paranoid personality, seclusive, given to violent temper outbursts; [?] borderline [B-3 type] schizophrenic)
(2) paternal grandfather (eccentric, paranoid, seclusive)

[10]This patient does not exemplify Gunderson's borderline personality disorder (no impulsivity or self-damaging acts).

Case Illustration 27

Patient = P Doctor = D GAS = 65

P: I'm a person that likes a very structured existence; whenever anything deviates from that system, it bothers me. Like if I were to have an appointment, ya know, and an emergency came up . . .

D: Uh-huh . . .

P: . . . and I had myself oriented to the appointment, I'd get anxious. Like, this office party tonight, it takes me out of my routine for a Friday night. But still, it's a *change*. *(Pause)* I like to eat, go to bed, 'n' everything—at the same time. That may just be my "circuitry"! It could be there're others who actually like the unstructured life. Of course if I make a change on my *own,* it's OK.

D: But when there's a change imposed on . . .

P: Yeah! When there's a change imposed on me from the *outside,* I get anxious . . . even if *I* initiate something, though, the *newness* of it gets to me!

D: Even if that's a change you make yourself?

P: Yeah! There is something about *newness*. Like, when I first get a subscription to the Jets, it's something *new;* once I get there, I'm OK. Of course, I feel the most comfortable at home.

D: Your own or your . . . ?

P: Either my folks' or my own. *(Pause)* Another thing I noticed, when I went for my appraisal . . .

D: From work?

P: Yeah, every year's end they give you an appraisal, plus you appraise yourself. Your boss and you rate you from "1" to "4" on a lot of items. He rated me "4," which is "excellent," on fourteen of the twenty categories. I only gave myself a "4" nine times. Only once did I get a "2," and it was the same question I gave myself a "2" on.

D: Which thing was that?

P: "How does he take pressure?" I get anxious under pressure, and my boss picked it up, too.

D: What kind of "anxious" would you say it is, and is it part of the "dream feeling" you've so often complained of?

P: No, it's different: it's not like I get butterflies-in-the-stomach-"anxious." It's more like a band around the head. Then I think, aha! I'm getting nervous! So then, quick, I do something to try to control it, though I can't always manage to do it. Like, I might try to get absorbed in a book, or go home, or whatever. I think I may bring the anxiety states on *myself,* by letting them sort of get the upper hand, sometimes. Occasionally, I get insomnia, too.

D: Oh?

P: Yeah, I can't fall asleep at all. Though if I go to my folks, I go right to sleep! Other times I get nervous, often dreaming something scary even though I don't remember what it is . . .

D: Or, that might happen on a day when . . .

P: Well, yeah, like you've said in the past, it may be that I was anxious already the day before without realizing about *what,* and then I go have a dream that night that's scary. I feel my anxiety afterwards is from the dream, but, like you say, *both* could come from something bothering me the day before, even.

D: But you feel the "dream feeling" is something distinct? Something like feeling you're a part of someone's dream, or that everything is not quite real, or. . . .

P: Well, the dream feeling is first of all whenever I feel scared. My mother told me she had the same thing only she called it her "bad nerves." Anyhow, when I'm *in* it, I wonder: Is all that's around me *real?* It's pretty much caused by the fear.

D: But is it like also being as if still asleep and being caught up *in* a dream?

P: It's hard to describe. Of course, when I plug through it *(meaning, when he keeps busy to distract himself from the uncanny sensation)*, it disappears. I feel, like, choked up. And like I can't sit down. *I gotta keep moving*. Otherwise I go crazy! I gotta keep *busy!*

D: How do you mean, "otherwise I go cr . . . "?

P: My mind is constantly *going,* then.

D: Faster than usual?

P: Oh, much faster! My thoughts come very quickly. My mind is overworking a mile a minute. *(Pause)* I wonder if psychiatry's progressed enough to know if this stuff is hereditary? Because my mother says that's the way *she* had it. My father doesn't understand us, because this is all foreign to him. And of course *her* mother had it *before* her. I think there's a lineage there. I console myself that my mother and grandmother are still OK . . . despite their bad times.

D: But you have worried a good deal?

P: Well, sure: I always have this fear I'll break down like my mother and grandmother, even though theirs were brief . . . also, my grandmother broke down at her menopause, and my mother figured so would she. Actually hers came after . . . no . . . before I was born.

D: Well, it won't be the menopause that'll get ya.

P: *(Laughing)* I know *that!* But I do fear, what if my folks died, like in some tragedy, would I go off the deep end? Of course, I've always been able to function with it . . .

D: Right . . .

P: . . . I've been generally more anxious the past two years; probably there've been more bad days where I'd be blue or have the dream feeling . . . than there've been good days.

D: So it's subtle, something you keep hidden, even though it really bothers you?

P: Yeah, even the *"blue"* moments are subtle, because I don't get all *that* depressed. Or I go to a football game and forget the whole thing. I'm beginning to get a handle on it. Like, I try to *reason* with myself, take stock of the situation, and pull *out* of it. Which I can *do,* almost always, unless the fear is really strong. I figure this is my burden to bear, sort of. Like my father has his ulcer condition, so that's his burden to bear. Nobody else notices when I'm really nervous anyhow, except my mother. It takes one to know one! She and I have the same circuitry.

Comments

These extracts were taken from interviews with a twenty-nine-year-old male patient, seen originally at nineteen because of the "dream feeling" and episodic anxiety states. Treatment at that time consisted of medication with a mild antianxiety drug plus expressive psychotherapy twice weekly. Although the patient was well motivated for therapy, this method was not very successful because of a difficulty he had in free associating. At that time, many conflictual areas seemed inaccessible, walled off by disavowal or at times denial. Dreams were rare; those mentioned to the therapist, though suggestive of various conflicts, did not lead the patient to any greater awareness of the relevant issues (the latter related to problems in separating emotionally from his parents). The "dream feeling," as he tried to describe it originally, seemed like a mild phenomenon related to depersonalization or derealization, but it was so hard for him at that time to describe it in other words that it was unclear what this symptom most resembled. At that time his symptoms interfered mildly with his studies. He had many friends, including close ones; there was no interference in this sphere. After graduation from college, he settled for a time in a different community, where he did well in a large business concern, rising quickly to a "middle-management" level. His symptoms remained mild and under control, until his excellent record led him to be considered for still further promotion. At this point he experienced his anxiety and "dream feeling" more intensely and was quite conscious of apprehension at the prospect of having a great many men under his authority. He persuaded his superiors to let him remain at a level comparable to where he had worked for some time. This led to significant abatement of his symptoms but spurred him to reenter treatment.

By now he was able to define his symptoms more clearly, and added details which seemed to suggest a strong affiliation to the manic-depressive group of disorders. He spoke, for example, of *thought racing, hyperactivity* (though without irritability), *insomnia* (usually in falling asleep), along with mild-to-moderate *dysphoria,* and the episodes of *derealization* (their nature by now having become clear).

It is noteworthy that the patient's complex of symptoms satisfied the criteria neither for "anxiety neurosis" nor for "phobic neurosis," as defined by Feighner et al.(1972, p. 59). Dyspnea, palpitations, and the sense of impending doom were never present for the former diagnosis; true phobias were not present for the latter. Instead there was a pattern of avoiding certain key situations. Characterologically, he was predominantly obsessive, as is reflected in his personality profile (see Table IV–I, above).

The diagnosis of personality organization, from a structural standpoint, was just on the edge between *borderline* and *neurotic*, falling, however, on the higher-level side (neurotic). Ego integration was reasonably well preserved; there were some contradictions in the patient's images of others (he tended to see his parents in overidealized terms much of the time, despite evidence from dreams and other sources of having contrary views as well). But these were not so striking or severe, at least not during the second period of treatment, as to warrant a borderline diagnosis. There were only three definitely positive items on the Spitzer checklist (and two debatably positive).

What was of particular interest about this patient's description of his symptoms was his spontaneous allusion to a hereditary influence of some kind. To this he made direct reference as well as indirect reference through his recurring image of his own—and his relatives'—"circuitry." The normality of his speech and the intactness of his capacity to relate to the interviewer should also be apparent from the material.

Final Diagnostic Impressions

A. Categorical diagnoses
   1. None; does not satisfy RDC for a manic-depressive disorder
   2. Psychoneurosis; neurotic personality organization
   3. Obsessive personality with depressive and phobic-anxious features

B. Dimensional assessments
   1. Region V on Sz-MDP continuum (kinship to manic-depressive illness)
   2. GAS = 65
   3. Personality profile as shown in Table IV–I

FAMILY HISTORY

First-degree relatives =	2
affected member:	(1) mother (hospitalized for severe depressive episodes; on antidepressant medication ever since)
Second-degree relatives	(precise number unknown)
affected member:	(1) maternal grandmother (psychotic depressive episodes in involutional period responding to ECT)

Case Illustration 28

Patient = P Therapist = T GAS = 65

The following material derives from the treatment of a woman who had entered psychotherapy a year earlier. When first seen her Global Assessment Score was 50. In this session she had just reported a vivid, frightening dream in which a crocodile bit off her leg as she was crossing a river. The day residue included an announcement by her parents that they were about to visit the patient and her family. In her association to "crocodiles," she thought first of "crocks" (chronic complainers) and then of her mother's hypochondriasis.

P: Mother's getting to that age now where she seems to have a million physical complaints . . . it's very hard to tell which ones are genuine, which ones are exaggerated, which ones are made up out of whole cloth . . . and it has a very wearing effect on everyone in the family . . . especially my Dad, because he's with her all the time, whereas I'm living out here now. . . . I mean, I love her dearly, but she can really drag people down . . . crying over nothing. . . . Whenever I'd be home I always felt I had to stop whatever I was doing to shore her up in some way . . . I couldn't get on with my life . . . or if I tried to, I'd feel very guilty, as though "I'm letting Mama down" . . .

T: She got to you before you could get to the other side, in a manner of speaking?

P: *(Becomes tearful)* Yes.

T: So in effect, you see her as this interfering creature who "cuts you off" in midcourse—literally—but why might you be conjuring up such images *now?* Had she been on your mind in some way, of late, more than usual?

P: *(With a sudden start)* Oh! of course! She phoned me on the weekend and told us they'd both be coming to the city for a few days on their way to England, and could they stay with us!?

T: And will they?

P: Of course. They always do, whenever they come here . . . we put them up in the . . .

T: *(Interrupting)* Yes, yes, I realize . . . but since even the Louvre would be too small for you and her at this point, and since they're comfortably off, why doesn't it occur to you to suggest a hotel?

P: That would be impossible. Mother would feel I'd thrown her out in the cold. I can just see the expression on her face. I don't think Dad would object terribly . . . might even prefer it . . . but she'd be dissolved in tears . . . it would hang on my conscience forever. I'm better off letting them invade . . .

The patient had never been able to stand up to her mother; the visit was experienced as a murderous assault—but one which she nonetheless had to endure with a smile. Later in the session she was reminded of another stark and disturbing dream involving one of her sisters:

P: I'm remembering now another terrible dream I had on the weekend about Sybil *(the elder of her two sisters)*. *(Becoming tearful suddenly)* I don't know if I can talk about it . . . *(voice muffled, almost inaudible)* . . . it's very embarrassing . . .
T: My impression would be, if it's this close to the surface, it's going to be more comfortable your sharing it with me than if you keep it back . . .
P: It was a real queer sort of dream . . . *(pause)*. . . . We were on a boat. Sybil's there with me . . . and I don't know what she did or why I do what I do, but I *kill* her . . . I stab her to death, and stuff her in a footlocker. She had been looking at me very resentfully and I couldn't stand it . . . *(more tearful)* . . . I couldn't stand it any more, so I got rid of her . . . I don't know why she had been looking at me that way . . . *(pause)*. . . . The dream seems to be saying I hate Sybil enough to kill her. . . . I don't hate my sister . . . we're very different . . . she's got her *own* problems . . .
T: You mean with the drugs? *(This sister used mescaline and LSD extensively.)*
P: Not only that. She's promiscuous. She can't hold a job. She's more pathetic than . . . than hateful . . .
T: Well, might you not be highlighting the fact that you came, at least as you've always perceived it, from a ''kill-or-be-killed'' family?
P: I know I'm uncomfortable around her. I never am aware of . . . wanting to get rid of her. She drags me down when she's around.

Anamnestic Data

The patient was a married Catholic woman of twenty-six. She had sought psychiatric help because of mounting anxiety and depression at the prospect of having to start a family (as her husband was urging her to do).

As noted in the family history, at least four relatives (three, of the first-degree, on the maternal side) either suffered from recurrent depression or exhibited severe character disorders.

The patient herself had shown a pronounced tendency to tearfulness over the most minor criticisms ever since adolescence. In addition, she was inordinately sensitive to loss or separation, and although she managed never to have to live alone (marrying at a time when she had still been living with her parents), she grew restless and tearful if her husband had to absent himself briefly on business or if the therapist were about to go on vacation.

Her vulnerability to depression had been activated by her parents' frequent and prolonged absences during the first ten years of her life: they took extended trips, leaving the three girls in the care of servants. She experienced her childhood as bleak and felt particularly starved of motherly attention, though she was quite close to her father. He preferred her, apparently as the most attractive of his three daughters; there was much evidence that her sisters resented her greatly, as a result. At a conscious level, the patient remained oblivious of her sisters' envy and went so far as to imagine herself unprepossessing, therefore "unable" to excite their envy in this regard. Though she was short of being delusional on this point, her notion was firmly entrenched (an "overvalued idea") and contributed to the paradoxical situation of her being as intolerant of compliments as she was of criticism.

By the time she was sixteen or seventeen, her mother, who had often been either aloof or harsh with her before, had grown to depend on her inordinately, occasionally confiding in her about the near breakup of the marriage a few years earlier. The patient grew to regard the lot of a woman as consisting of two phases: one in which she bore children she then neglected, and a later one in which she clung to them tenaciously after they grew up. The prospect of being a mother seemed appalling, and as the time approached to start having children of her own, she grew tense and irritable, became lachrymose to the point of crying "over nothing" even when among friends and neighbors, lost weight (eight pounds in three months), and developed insomnia. During this period she had frequent terrifying dreams, usually of a primitive kind involving murder and dismemberment. For the most part she remained able to perform her usual household activities, although she had begun to avoid social gatherings. Her symptoms were aggravated premenstrually, but only to a modest degree. Shortly before psychotherapy began, she often felt despondent and spoke of "not minding if she didn't wake up the next morning," but did not contemplate suicide, in part because the notion was abhorrent to her religious convictions. Ordinarily self-effacing and gracious, she noticed herself becoming uncharacteristically "bitchy" and vituperative toward her husband.

Comments

From the case material, taken from a session in the eleventh month of intensive analytically oriented psychotherapy, it can be seen that the patient was coherent and well related. She was still subject to nightmares and easy tearfulness (though less so than at the beginning of treatment), but her depression and irritability were less intense and she was less withdrawn. Appetite had improved. Elavil, 100 milligrams a day, had been prescribed initially and she was currently taking 75 milligrams a day.

She was highly motivated for therapy and had an excellent capacity for self-reflection. Capable of some degree of candor, at this stage she still gave much evidence of lowered self-esteem. She was out of touch with a number of important feelings, especially with her extreme reluctance to assume the role of motherhood (she imagined herself quite "ready" to have children and at first had no awareness of the psychological issues that appeared to exacerbate her depressive tendencies). This defect of ego integration was not as serious as that noted in many of the preceding illustrations, yet was sufficient, at least in the beginning, to be consistent with borderline structure. The primitivity of her dreams and their frightening quality portrayed in visual terms the sharp contradictoriness of many aspects of the patient's personality. Nevertheless her capacity to benefit from intensive therapy was such as to raise her self-awareness and general adaptation to a level where a diagnosis of borderline structure no longer seemed justifiable. She eventually functioned at the neurotic level of personality organization.

From the standpoint of syndrome diagnosis, the patient showed the essential features of D. Klein's hysteroid dysphoria along with the required number of *associated* factors (histrionic, expansive and active, and over-idealized love objects).

Though life circumstances (early parental, especially maternal, deprivation) may have enhanced the likelihood that the patient would react with depressive symptoms under the impact of various life stresses, the marked family history of unipolar depression suggests strongly that the "choice of symptoms" was dictated in no small measure by genetic predisposition.

Final Diagnostic Impressions

A. Categorical diagnoses
   1*a*. Primary affective disorder, depressed type
   b. Syndrome diagnosis: hysteroid dysphoria
   2*a*. Borderline personality organization (initial diagnosis)
   b. Neurotic personality organization (final diagnosis 2½ years later)
   3. Depressive-masochistic character with infantile and passive-aggressive features

B. Dimensional assessments
   1. Region V: pure affective disorder, unipolar depressed type
   2*a*. GAS = 50, when first seen
   b. GAS = 66, at time case material was gathered
   2. Personality profile as shown in Table IV–I

FAMILY HISTORY

First-degree relatives = 4 (parents, plus 2 sibs)

affected member: (1) mother (recurrent depression, treated with antidepressants and [on one occasion] ECT)

Second-degree relatives = 6
Other (including less seriously affected) members:
(1) sister, age twenty-three (severe character disorder with impulsivity, drug abuse, rage outbursts)
(2) sister, age twenty-one (mild episodes of depression since eighteen)
(3) maternal cousin, age twenty-four (hospitalized for several months with a severe depressive episode)

Case Illustration 29

Patient = P Consultant = C GAS:
initial = 35
subsequent = 67

C: Can you tell me what led to your coming to the hospital several days ago?

P: Well, my doctor suggested I come in, to get some things straightened out. There were some things that needed to be put in order, and I agreed on that point, I really did, so I came in. . . . I came of my own volition, ya know . . . I signed myself in . . . *(then laughs nervously for a second)*. Though right now I'd like to sign myself out! . . . Does that answer your que—— I mean, I don't know . . . maybe *you* should ask me something! *(All this is spoken rapidly and with an air of some nonchalance.)*

C: Are you unsure whether you could give a good account of what happened, yourself? . . .

P: I don't know what you mean.

C: . . . plus I notice that you refer to "getting some things straightened out" in a rather casual fashion, considering that those "things" were enough to require being in a hospital.

P: Well *(still nonchalant and "stagy" in tone)*, there was this thing with the Cavaliers *(a jazz band that had recently come to town)* . . . I mean, the Cavaliers have always meant . . . like . . . "everything" to me, especially Johnny V——, the saxophonist . . . when I thought he got me kicked out of the backstage room where I was trying to meet him . . . but it turned out it wasn't *him,* see . . . I didn't know that till later. . . . He wasn't *aware* . . . so everything fell in. My *world* collapsed!

C: You say that as though it should be obvious to me that such a misadventure would naturally land one in a mental hosp . . .

P: Well, you don't understand! He and I had spent the . . . I had gotten very *close* . . .

C: On the surface, that would *still* not add up to sufficient reason, I don't think, to explain how . . .

P: *(Interrupting)* Well, I was . . . the Cavaliers . . . I mean, I've followed them *very closely* for, I don't know . . . ever since I was in the eighth grade, eight or nine years now . . . , *especially* Johnny V—— . . . I mean I've kept clippings of all his performances, I've written him letters, and I got two letters *back,* you know . . . *from* him, I mean . . . I've really built my *life* around them; I feel the stages I've gone through are like the stages they've gone through . . . over the years. . . . There's a kind of fundamental harmony, an ESP thing, between me and them, or me and Johnny V——, you see? I mean, when they wouldn't let me get through to him last week, I felt *suicidal.* I actually contemplated suicide, which I had never done before. Like he was my "hope," and that was *it!* No other way to go!

C: But if you tell me you could be pushed to suicide by an imaginary rebuff . . . let's even say, by a real rebuff . . . from someone you know more in your mind than in real life, you're still not telling me what made life so desolate at that moment as to make you inclined to destroy yourself! You're only telling me—indirectly—that inside *you* is some really big problem . . . or some really big deficit . . . that this man and the Cavaliers were making up for. They were an *antidote!* Only you haven't told me what the *sickness* is.

P: I don't know. I've never given it much thought *(laughs nervously again).*

C: Well, try to think about it now.

P: I just don't know. *(Pause)* Nothing comes to mind. I could go over the events of that evening with the Cavaliers. Should I do that? I need clues . . . I mean if you tell me what I should be getting into, maybe I can . . .

C: Look. You speak with great rapidity, I notice . . . with a certain facility, along with it . . . in a superficial and engaging way, yet the fact remains, you tell me nothing of substance. I get no sense of evident distress, yet I have to assume you didn't come here for trivial reasons.

P: No, I felt . . . empty. Should I tell you about that?

C: You're not sure I'd be interested beyond the openers, is that what you're trying to get across?

P: Well, there's a kind of . . . I'm aware of an . . . an . . . a feeling, like "emptiness" . . . being empty inside . . .

C: Let's hear what that brings to mind.

P: You mean "being empty"? Times I've *felt* that, you mean? Or . . .

C: Whatever you find occurring to you in that connection at the moment.

P: *(Pause)* These two friends of mine . . . I'm thinking about two girlfriends I have . . .

C: What about them? How do they tie up with this "emptiness"?

P: Uhh . . . Well, they finished college, too, only they have good jobs . . . they married guys they still get along with . . . one's working on her Ph.D.
C: They're not empty, I take it.
P: No. Next to them . . . I'm . . . I mean, they're getting on with their lives and I'm . . . here in a hospital.
C: Can you recall the very first time you noticed this feeling . . . this uncomfortable state you've called "emptiness"?
P: Well, I felt it last year after I broke up with my husband . . .
C: The *first* time, though . . .
P: When I was about . . . thirteen . . . in there, somewhere.
C: Is that when you became so attached to that jazz group?
P: Around then. Yes.
C: Does your use of marijuana et cetera go back to the same period?
P: Yes . . . one came a month or two before the other. I don't remember which was first.
C: The jazz group and the pot?
P: No, the empty feeling and both of those things. I think the empty feeling came first.
C: Uh-huh.
P: *(Long pause, during which she begins to look more sullen at the silence of the consultant, as though angry at his putting the burden of saying something on her; eventually she becomes somewhat tearful.)*
C: I notice you're reacting quite strongly to something.
P: *(Nods, but still says nothing)*
C: What's coming to mind?
P: *(Pause)* The "principal's office."
C: The "principal's office"?
P: It's like you're the principal, and you're judging me.
C: In itself a familiar feeling?
P: Depends who. Yeah. From my mother, it would be.
C: She frequently sits in judgment?
P: Yes.
C: What does she "judge" you about?
P: She didn't approve of my husband, is one thing. *Any* of the men I've gone with. You make me uncomfortable the same way.
C: As though I'm condemning you as far as men are concerned?
P: No. I haven't even told you about the men I've been with. Apart from Johnny V——. . . . You just disapprove of everything I *say*.
C: Only to encourage you to tell me what you haven't been able to say before!
P: Well it's a helluva way to go about it.
C: Perhaps. But if I hadn't used "tactics" like that, I have a hunch you'd still do what you do in every tense situation in your life.

P: What do you mean?

C: You'd run away from it. Not necessarily run out of the room. You'd run away into some "safe" topic . . . that had nothing to do with why you're here. I think I'm beginning to get to know why you *are* here this time. You're running out of places to run away to.

Anamnestic Data

The patient was a married woman in her middle twenties. She had one child by her first marriage. The first clinical extract derives from a time shortly after the breakup of that marriage. She had been living with her small daughter, attempting to support herself by secretarial work until it was interrupted by mounting depression and suicidal ruminations. Inability to tolerate being alone was very marked; one way in which she tried to combat a pervasive sense of loneliness was through the attachment, highly idealized and unrealistic, to the musician mentioned in the extract. When the unrealistic nature of this attachment was brought forcibly home to her, she became despondent and made a suicide attempt (overdose of sleeping pills). This led to several weeks of hospitalization where supportive psychotherapy and antidepressant medication (amitriptyline, 300 milligrams/day) were initiated. Though able to return to work, her social adjustment remained precarious. Analytically oriented psychotherapy, three sessions per week, was begun at this time; antidepressants were continued in a lower dose range.

A year later, she married again. Her husband was a successful but emotionally isolated lawyer, eight years older than herself. Shortly thereafter she began to grow irritable and depressed, ostensibly in relation to minor criticisms from her husband or to his relative emotional unavailability. But her reactions were out of proportion to the minor degree of disharmony between them. She was given to episodic outbursts of rage (in which she would destroy objects around the house) and to crying jags. In addition she made several suicidal gestures. The latter had a dramatic quality, which consisted of locking herself in the bathroom. There she would cut her wrist superficially or swallow a number of tranquilizers. On other occasions she would drink to excess. In between these episodes (which usually lasted from three to five days) she was vivacious, enthusiastic about her new life, and not ill at ease being alone at home during the day.

She herself was puzzled by the Jekyll and Hyde quality of her behavior, especially the unpredictable nature of her attitude toward her husband. During her "bad spells" she found him intolerable and thought of divorce; she would become convinced he found her ugly and was planning extramarital affairs. In her calm state, she felt comfortable with him and more confident of her attractiveness. It was noted that her moments of irritability and suicidal depression occurred the week before her menses, and subsided the same day her period came. Careful recording of her weight throughout her cycle revealed that she gained anywhere from four to six pounds before the onset of menses. Addition of Diuril 250 milligrams/day beginning ten days before her anticipated period led to reduction of premenstrual edema and was accompanied by marked diminution of her cyclical crises. She was now more able to utilize the psychotherapy to help resolve certain problems in her marital relationship.

The following material is excerpted from a session in which for the first time she realized the connection between her crises and her periods. She was twenty-six at this time; GAS level = 67.

P: I was at the concert last night with my husband, feeling tense as a cat at first. I didn't know how I'd get through the evening! I was crying at the drop of a hat all week. I had a crying jag yesterday afternoon over nothing . . . I mean, my daughter was making a racket in her room, but that doesn't usually get to me like it did yesterday . . . but then, all of a sudden, right during the concert, I felt this wave of relief, like an enormous sense of relief, and it was the beginning of my period. I had forgotten completely that it was almost due, even though I've been quite regular for some time now.

D: Were you aware of having put on any weight over the past week?

P: Oh, yes: I went from a size 8 to a size 10, I put on six pounds, felt bloated all over, . . . and I felt disconnected somehow.

D: I'm not sure what you mean, "disconnected."

P: Like . . .*erratic*. Jumpy, uncomfortable, outside myself, somehow, or like a different person, almost. My sleep was poor. I never have any cramps, you know, the way all the women I know who complain about their periods do. I figured if I have no cramps, I must not be having what you hear all the other women complain of. And the psychological problems I have before my period seem suddenly enormous; more than I can deal with. But if I could feel as calm as I do now, I could deal with anything, I think. The mood I'm in now, I don't feel rejected by Harry over trivial things, the way I do if I'm in my Mr. Hyde mood. I'm not superhappy and I'm not supersad. Just peaceful, relaxed. I used to feel this way only after I plugged myself full of tranquilizers.

Comments

At the time of this extract, the patient's Global Assessment Score was 67. This figure does not do justice to the seesaw nature of her course nor to the complexities of her clinical picture. During the interpsychotic phases, a careful diagnostic assessment would have revealed borderline structure, and a GAS in the sixties. Her course was consistent with the picture of bipolar manic-depressive illness, type II; besides severe depressions there were occasional periods of euphoria, pushed speech, and early morning awakening. Dreams were consistently primitive and filled with images of body fragmentation. Intensive psychotherapy, along with tricyclic antidepressants and diuretics premenstrually, led to a better and stable adaptation—still in the borderline range at first, but with global functioning near the neurotic level much of the time. Structurally, the patient was in transition from the *borderline* to the *neurotic* level.

After thirty months of intensive treatment, the patient no longer demonstrated a serious defect in ego integration. The initial splitting of image, regarding the analyst, into flagrantly idealized and grotesquely denigrated part images was no longer present. She became able to appreciate herself and others as blends of different coexisting qualities. Her life was now much less chaotic, whereas before her life was an unbroken string of crises. She grew able to tolerate being alone much better and has become involved in artistic pursuits, which hold her interest even when no one else is in the house.

Gradual integration of the once markedly contradictory nature of self- and object representations led to the elevation of structural level to the consistently neurotic. What continues to differentiate her from the straightforward psychoneurotic patient is her *vulnerability*. Her anxiety tolerance, especially without treatment, continues to be below the norm typical for neurotic personality organization.

The patient's stormy course during the initial phases of treatment is portrayed in the diagram of her clinical course (Figure IV–9), in which her

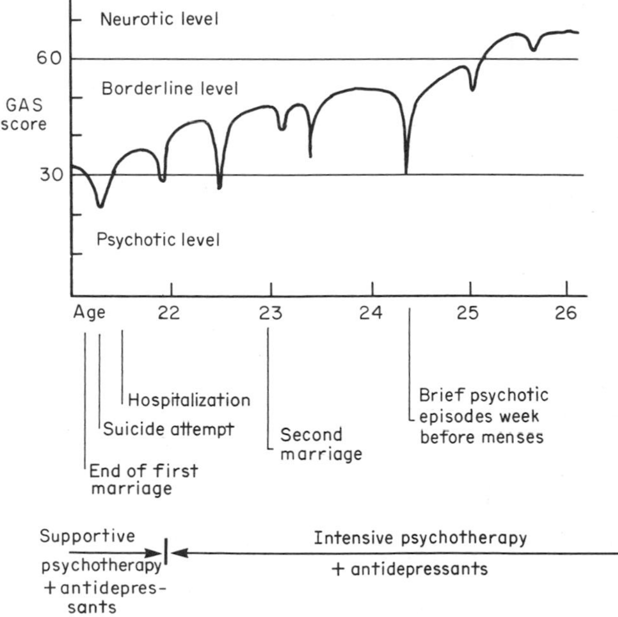

Figure IV-9. Clinical Course of Case Illustration 29

Global Assessment Scores are plotted at frequent intervals. The diagram takes advantage of the rough correspondence between structural level and the GAS: when the latter was below 60, the patient's level was (for the most part) borderline.

Final Diagnostic Impressions

A. Categorical diagnoses
   1. Primary affective disorder: bipolar-II type
   2*a*. Borderline structure (initially); neurotic structure (subsequently)
   2*b*. Syndrome diagnosis: borderline personality disorder (Gunderson), hysteroid dysphoria (D. Klein), "unstable" borderline personality (Spitzer)
   3. Hysterical personality with depressive-masochistic and narcissistic features

B. Dimensional assessments
   1. Region V of the Sz-MDP continuum
   2. GAS = 35 (initial), 67 (subsequent)
   3. Personality profile as shown in Table IV–I (the pathological aspects of the narcissistic traits diminished over the course of the psychotherapy)

FAMILY HISTORY

First-degree relatives =	4 (parents, plus 2 sibs)
affected members:	(1) father ("residual" schizophrenia with paranoid features)
	(2) mother (manic-depressive illness, bipolar-II)
	(3) brother (hospitalized for a schizoaffective episode)
	(4) brother (cyclothymic personality; one brief manic episode)
Second-degree relatives =	6
affected members:	(1) maternal grandmother (history of serious depressions, treated with ECT)
	(2) paternal grandmother (chronic paranoid schizophrenia)
Other (*including less seriously affected*) *members:*	(1) maternal cousin (unipolar depressive illness, several suicidal gestures)

Afterword

Borderline syndromes have come to assume a place of considerable importance in contemporary psychiatry. A number of factors contribute to this development. Patterns of psychopathology themselves evolve and change over the decades to the extent that the categories elaborated by our predecessors at the beginning of the century no longer adequately describe as great a percentage of patients in our generation as in the generation when these terms were first formulated. Some patients are now labeled "borderline" for being, in effect, the casualties of our anachronistic nomenclature. Paradoxically, another group of borderline patients is the creation of our efforts, in recent years, to improve upon the older categories by creating diagnostic criteria that meet research standards. These tend to be strict; many of the cases they exclude are subsequently designated borderline according to one or another schema. As discussed in Chapter 7, Strauss and his co-workers (1979) have drawn attention to these phenomena in their comparison of ideal or archetypal patients with actual patients.

Another important group of borderline patients reflects the time element in the unfolding of the classical schizophrenic and primary affective ("manic-depressive") illnesses: certain adolescent and young adult patients with ill-defined psychiatric disorders of moderate severity go on to exhibit clearly recognizable categories of illness (schizophrenia, bipolar manic-depression, and so forth) in their late twenties or thirties. In the meantime they are often called borderline. Besides these cases of "incipient" schizophrenia or manic-depression are others, with attenuated forms of those disorders, who never go on to develop the full-blown condition. Many of these patients have also been called borderline, and their alleged relationship to the parent condition often represents an educated guess on the part of the clinician. In some instances this educated guess is reinforced by the presence of a family history strongly positive for one of the unequivocal forms of a functional psychosis.

Finally, borderline syndromes are encountered where no kinship to schizophrenia or affective illness is discernible but where psychosocial factors have been unusually adverse. Samples of borderline patients, by whatever set of criteria they are diagnosed, tend for all these reasons to reflect etiological heterogeneity. Samples will also differ in the proportions with which the various subgroups are represented. This will be true even if the same criterion set is employed. Differences will be exaggerated still further if borderline samples are compared, when the samples were selected according to different criteria (say, those of Kernberg versus those of Grinker or Gunderson).

In this book, *borderline* syndromes have been discussed mainly from three vantage points: (1) conditions which are in between neurosis and psychosis (as defined in psychoanalytic terms), (2) those psychiatric disorders that are situated between the more categorical cases of schizophrenia and primary affective (manic-depressive) illness, and (3) attenuated or incipient forms of the classical psychoses not (or not as yet) meeting strict diagnostic standards for either schizophrenia or primary affective disorder. Included under the first heading are borderline conditions as understood by psychoanalytic theoreticians (Stern, Knight, Frosch, Grinker, Mahler, Bergeret, and Kernberg). The formulations of Gunderson are also of this variety, although he does not attempt to differentiate "borderline" from "psychosis" so much as from the specific psychosis of schizophrenia. Examples of the second variety include the schizoaffective disorders described by Kasanin and many cases of "pseudoneurotic schizophrenia" as depicted by Hoch and Polatin. The third variety, attenuated forms, presupposes the existence of a spectrum for each type of classical psychosis: one for schizophrenia, another for the primary affective disorders ("manic-depression"). The spectra consist of unequivocal or "core" cases, but then shade off into milder, less easily identified forms, to which the term "borderline" may be applied. Borderline schizophrenia has been described by Kety and his colleagues (see Chapter 7) and defined more rigorously by Spitzer and his co-workers (Chapter 9). Borderline variants of manic-depression have been described by the author and by Akiskal and his colleagues. Hysteroid dysphoria and a number of related syndromes outlined by Donald Klein (Chapter 9) may be said to constitute another group of conditions which are *borderline* with respect to the primary affective disorders.

In tracing the evolution of the term "borderline" since the beginning of the twentieth century, I have attempted to demonstrate that many of the earlier advocates of the term had the image of full-blown schizophrenia as their reference point (Chapter 1). More recently, specifically since the papers of Robert Knight appeared in the early 1950s, borderline has been used within the psychoanalytic community to denote a group of conditions that have greater affiliation with the affective disorders. This shift in connotation may derive from several sources. Progress in psychopharmacology since 1955 has shrunk the realm of conditions to which analytic psychotherapy is customarily applied. Among the more severe syndromes, it is mostly the depressive and schizoaffective disorders that now receive intensive psychotherapy (in addition to chemotherapy), especially their borderline counterparts, but these are usually within the domain of *affective* disorders. Also, the psychostructural definition of borderline personality organization rests (among other things) on the exclusion of chronically "poor reality testing," which in effect excludes overt schizophrenia and favors the remission-prone affective disorders.

Syndromes intermediate between the polar conditions of schizophrenia and manic-depression relate to the *constitutional* element in psychopathology: certain inborn factors, some specific, others nonspecific, appear to predispose to the development of these clinical syndromes (Chapters 3, 4, and 6). The same may be said for the attenuated or "borderline" forms of the classical psychoses (Chapters 7 and 9). When "borderline" is used to describe a type of personality organization intermediate between the neurotic and the psychotic, the focus is not so much on constitution as on the level of *adaptation*. My thesis has been that borderline syndromes must be evaluated according to both these frames of reference. Particularly from the standpoint of prognosis, a third frame of reference must be introduced, namely, that of *personality* type (Chapter 10). While not all "borderline" conditions (by whatever diagnostic criteria) exhibit constitutional elements reminiscent of either schizophrenia or manic-depression, they will exhibit features of one or another personality type. As mentioned in Chapter 10, certain personality types (such as paranoid, hypomanic, antisocial) are often associated with a poor prognosis, at least with respect to psychoanalytically oriented psychotherapy, while others (such as depressive, infantile, obsessive) are more often associated with a good outcome (in well-motivated borderline patients undergoing this form of psychotherapy).

Because conditions in the borderline realm are, by definition, difficult to diagnose within the framework of our standard nomenclature, a dimensional approach is taken alongside the customary approach emphasizing categories (Chapter 8). The dimensional approach requires a semiquantitative estimation of the similarity between any given (and equivocal) case and the paradigmatic (or unequivocal) case. Various methods of mapping the borderline conditions onto domains of standard or more familiar diagnostic entities are presented in the book (Chapter 2).

In Part II (Chapters 3 to 7), a survey of the data about the hereditary factor in the severer forms of mental illness, beginning with schizophrenia and moving through the schizoaffective region to the affective disorders, is presented. This ordering corresponds to my concept of a phenotypic continuum of clinical states stretching between schizophrenic syndromes devoid of affective derangements to manic-depressive disorders free of any schizophrenialike symptoms. In between are to be found all degrees of mixes of the two tendencies. The purer the schizophrenic nature of an illness in a proband, the greater the tendency for close relatives, if they are mentally ill, to exhibit a schizophrenic disorder either in full-blown (psychotic) or dilute (borderline) form. The more the illness in a proband is situated near the "pure" affective disorders, the more any ill relatives will tend to suffer, themselves, from an affective, or at the most "schizoaffective," disorder.

The term "borderline" is applied about twice as often to female as to male patients. This imbalance could be related in part to the uneven sex ratio noted among unipolar depressives. Unipolar depression (as opposed to bipolar mania) is more common in women, many of whom have illnesses of a lesser degree of severity than would be consistent with a "psychotic depressive reaction." They are often, in fact, borderline. If the other etiological routes to borderline organization are traveled equally by the two sexes, this factor alone could account for an excess of women within the borderline domain, perhaps to the level of 3:2. There may be a special relationship between schizoaffective illness, femaleness, and sex differences in the balance of right- versus left-hemisphere predominance, all conspiring to make women overrepresented within the schizoaffective realm and prognostically advantaged (over men) because of their apparently greater resistance to the affect-constricting potential of schizophrenic heredity. This relationship is still highly speculative but indicates one direction in which some of the more exciting psychiatric research is now headed.

In the sections devoted to the genetics of the major psychoses (Chapters 3 to 6), arguments were marshaled in support of the view that, within the realm of clinical schizophrenia, the majority of cases are idiopathic rather than phenocopies reflecting organic or other nonspecific origins. A similar argument can be made with respect to the primary affective disorders, though there appear to be more nonspecific conditions that mimic unipolar than mimic bipolar disorders. Among the severe forms of classical psychosis, a genetic factor probably constitutes a necessary but not sufficient condition for eventual breakdown.

The currently most tenable theoretical models of transmission are also discussed at some length in Part II. Our knowledge at this time does not permit definitive selection of one over another model, either for the schizophrenias or for the affective disorders. While both a polygenic or a single major gene model (with thresholds) may be made to fit family-study and twin-study data reasonably well, there is some reason to believe a polygenic model is more likely for schizophrenia (and possibly for MDP as well [Stabenau, 1977]). Furthermore, it may also be more reasonable to see in schizophrenia and the primary affective disorders not so much abnormalities totally askew to a normal development but rather gross exaggerations of otherwise normal neurophysiological endowments relating (in the case of schizophrenia) to attention, language function, and ego boundary, or (in the case of affective illness) to energy-, sleep-, and sexual-regulatory mechanisms.

What is important to realize with respect to the borderline syndromes is that the most favored genetic schemata are capable of embracing many

Figure 1. Genetic Loading and Clinical Syndromes: Possible Correlations

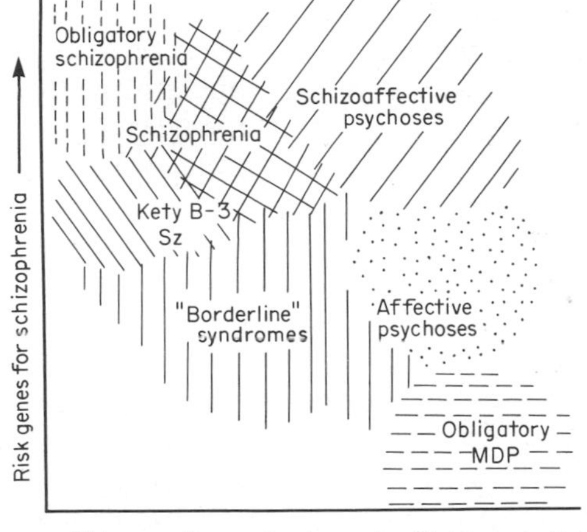

NOTE: Individuals can exhibit enhanced risk for either schizophrenia or for manic-depressive illness. Those with high loading for schizophrenia (Sz) will tend, if they fall ill, to exhibit a schizophrenic illness. Some will have such high loading that they will fall ill inevitably, regardless of favorable modifying influences (these are the "obligatory schizophrenes"). A similar situation holds for those with very high loading for MDP. In between, in the high (combined) loading region will be found schizoaffectives who have psychotic episodes. In the intermediate regions of risk are borderline conditions. These may exist as borderline Sz (Kety's B-3 group) if the increased risk is only for Sz. Many of the patients diagnosed as borderline according to the criteria of either Kernberg or Gunderson appear to have intermediate levels of risk for an affective disorder (or, in a few instances, for schizophrenia).

borderline conditions within the penumbra region around the unequivocal "core" conditions. Some individuals, including a number with mixed schizophrenia–affective-disorder pedigrees, appear to harbor significant liability to *both* a schizophrenic *and* an affective psychosis (Chapter 4). A hypothetical model that could account for these phenomena is shown in Figure 1. The relationship between genotype and phenotype in real life is, of course, not likely to be as close as that suggested by the model, just as real patients only occasionally conform to our hypothetical diagnostic constructs (Strauss et al., 1979).

The subject of minimal cerebral damage and its capacity either to expose an underlying schizophrenic vulnerability or to provoke a phenocopy of schizophrenia (see Thomas and Chess, 1975) is dealt with only briefly in this book, owing to the relative rarity with which this factor is encountered in office or even hospitalized borderline patients chosen for intensive analytically oriented psychotherapy.

Some space is devoted toward the end of Part II (in Chapters 5 and 6) to biological markers that may be of relevance in the major idiopathic psychoses. Many are outgrowths of the catecholamine hypotheses and other biochemical models of schizophrenia or MDP. As with the biochemical markers suggested in the 1950s and 1960s, many of the current candidates have shown initial promise only to become discredited later in a flurry of conflicting or negative results. Some results in the area of the affective disorders have withstood the test of time better than have the suggested endophenotypes of schizophrenia. Ideally one would hope to find a marker which yielded not only positive results in the "core" cases but also intermediate levels of abnormality in the dilute or borderline forms. As matters stand, it is difficult to find a biochemical lesion which holds up consistently from one laboratory to another.[1]

Matthysse (1977) has suggested that some of the positive findings reported for various proposed markers, about which the profession is at present skeptical, may be valid after all—in selected pedigrees. The major psychoses (and their borderline forms) may be quite heterogeneous etiologically. For the most part, it is not yet possible, confronted with very low or high readings in the laboratory, to know whether one is in the presence of the extreme ends of a normal distribution or a typical value for some truly separate and pathological condition. Certain enzymatic abnormalities found only in a small proportion of schizophrenics, for example, while not relevant to most of what is now being called schizophrenia, may be highly relevant to a small proportion of the cases. An example of the latter would

[1]Garver and his co-workers (1977) found, for example, that the dopamine agonist, apomorphine, elicited elevated growth hormone responses in schizophrenics of "good prognosis," whereas others (Rotrosen, Angrist, et al., 1976) found this elevation only in schizophrenics who failed to respond to neuroleptics (subnormal responses were noted in schizophrenics who did respond to neuroleptics).

be homocystinuria, some carriers of which exhibit a schizophrenialike psychosis and others an affective disorder with a high suicide risk (Spiro, Schimke, and Welch, 1965).

Part III concentrates on the criteria for diagnosis: of the major psychoses (including the schizoaffective) in Chapter 8, of borderline syndromes in Chapter 9, and of personality types (with attention to both characterological and temperamental elements) in Chapter 10. The approach to diagnosis advocated in this book devotes attention to traditional categories as well as to dimensions. Methods for evaluating patients according to their most appropriate locus on a sliding scale (or "spectrum") are proposed for each important axis. Borderline patients who are being considered for intensive psychotherapy are best served, according to the author, by a multiaxial approach involving constitution (here, as the degree of similarity to schizophrenia or manic-depression), level of adaptation, and personality type. It is recognized that other patient populations might be better served by a different multiaxial schema tailored to the nature of that population. A number of such models are outlined in Chapter 8.

Special attention was drawn in Chapter 8 to premenstrual disorders in women exhibiting borderline personality organization. Biological (including hormonal) factors contributing to symptom aggravation around the time of the period are often overlooked by therapist and patient alike. Yet in some women, fluctuation in state may be so marked during this phase of the cycle as to produce changes in psychostructural organization. Sudden shifts from neurotic to borderline or from borderline to psychotic may occur in certain cases, even though, as a general rule, one's level of personality organization is remarkably stable.

Chapter 9 is devoted to an examination of the more important current usages of the *borderline* concept. The systems of Bergeret, Gunderson, Kernberg, Klein, and Spitzer are discussed in detail. In the section dealing with Kernberg's work, a number of variables are described that are relevant to the assessment of psychic structure; among these, *integration of identity,* the nature of *predominant defenses,* and the *capacity to test reality* are of the most immediate importance in structural diagnosis. It is easier to make the distinction between borderline and psychotic structures, since this distinction depends on the evaluation of reality testing. This will generally be a less subtle task than assessing a patient's identity integration. To qualify as borderline in structure, integration must be faulty to the degree that important life functions (love, work, play) are seriously affected. Behavioral correlates such as impaired job performance, or diminished capacity for close relationships, will usually be present. The point at which the reasonably well-preserved identity integration of the neurotic shades into the impaired integration of the borderline is difficult to specify; because of this, clinicians will agree less often about which psychic structure is present in certain marginally adjusted ambulatory patients.

Defensive patterns in borderline structure involve chiefly splitting, projective identification, denial, and other primitive mechanisms—namely, omnipotence (grandiosity), projection, and devaluation (see Chapter 9). These are all seen in psychotic structures as well. In this respect the difference between borderline and psychotic structure lies not so much in the nature of the defenses as in their apparent function. Whether the patient is defending merely against the awareness of intrapsychic conflict (as in borderline structure) or against either fragmentation or merging of "self" with other(s) (as in psychotic structure) makes the difference in deciding which structure is present.

The capacity to test reality is preserved in the higher two structures and lost in the psychotic. This is a more subtle point than it appears to be on the surface, since the loss of capacity to test reality is a broader phenomenon than just the existence of well-defined delusions. The paradoxical situation can therefore arise in which productive signs are absent but capacity to test reality is still extremely poor. One may encounter patients who, though free of grossly delusory ideation, show a marked inability to put themselves in the situation of the interviewer, with complete blindness to glaring inconsistencies in their self-presentation and so forth. Some of these patients, nevertheless, satisfy the Gunderson criteria for "borderline personality disorder"—and are thus "borderline" in his system, but not in Kernberg's. Usually this phenomenon is encountered in patients at the schizotypal end of the clinical spectrum.

In neurotic structure, the capacity to evaluate the personalities of other people is well preserved; in borderline structure, it is faulty. From the standpoint of traditional nosology, psychotic structure is usually seen only in the schizophrenias, but there are exceptions: certain refractory cases of affective psychosis (melancholia, untreated or treatment-resistant bipolar patients) are accompanied by psychotic structure (on a continuous basis). Some severe cases of drug abuse are also in this category.

The notion of structure, specifically psychic structure, implies continuity over time. For that very reason, the utility of the structural concept remains high in those conditions characterized by relative stability of *state* and low in conditions that are markedly state dependent and variable. The prime example of the latter is of course bipolar manic-depressive illness, especially with rapid cycling.

The utility of the various metapsychologies and of the various approaches to diagnosis (the phenomenological, the genetic, the object-relations oriented, and so forth) depends in the last analysis upon the patient sample with which the clinician becomes most familiar. Psychoanalysts with an interest in the least well integrated ambulatory patients can scarcely do without a "borderline" concept. Experts in the treatment of bipolar mania have less need for this concept.

Clinicians who work frequently with affectively ill, particularly depressed, patients will find the classificatory system of Donald Klein especially useful. The syndromes Klein and his colleagues have elaborated (hysteroid dysphoria, endogenomorphic depression, and so forth; see Chapter 9) may be understood, in many instances, as borderline cases of primary affective disorder. Likewise, many of the patients exemplifying those syndromes satisfy Kernberg's and Gunderson's criteria as well.

Types of interviewing styles are also discussed in this book. The diagnosis of psychic structure depends heavily upon a particular type of clinical interview, called *structural* by Kernberg to emphasize its orientation toward the goal of psychostructural diagnosis. This interview involves meticulous attention to discrepancies between the patient's perceptions of self and others and the interviewer's view of the patient's world as the dialogue proceeds. The patient's responses to the compassionate but firm confrontation about any such discrepancies become a measure of his capacity—or lack of it—to test reality, especially in the interpersonal realm. The "structural" interview thus addresses itself primarily to cognitive processes and not to the grasp of obscure symbols or of psychodynamic issues. The special interviews and checklists devised by Gunderson, Klein, and Spitzer to objectify the diagnosis of *borderline* according to their schemata are also discussed in Chapter 9.

Subsequent portions of Chapter 9 deal with borderline adolescents, dreams in borderline and psychotic patients, and the impact of intellectual endowment on structure.

Figure 2*a* portrays the overlap of structural and nonstructural usages of "borderline." The large irregular shape in the upper diagram represents the realm of all patients exhibiting borderline structure. Oval 1, "borderline schizophrenia" (Kety's B-3 type) overlaps slightly: some patients in that category have borderline *structure;* many have psychotic *structure*. Oval 2 designates schizoaffective patients who, phenotypically, are predominantly schizophrenic. Again, a portion show borderline structure. The portions of 1 and 2 lying *within* the borderline-structure realm might be spoken of as the region of the *schizotypal borderline* patient. Oval 3 refers to patients with affective illnesses within the "spectrum" of MDP. This area includes oval 4, hysteroid dysphoria, most of which lies within the borderline-structure realm. Oval 5, which intersects with 4 and 3, contains patients with what Rado called *pharmacothymia*—an overwhelming need for alcohol or drugs. Oval 6 represents "as if" patients, some of whom exhibit borderline, some psychotic, structure. Oval 7 contains patients with the anorexia nervosa syndrome, many but not all of whom show borderline structure. Oval 8, shaded, shows the realm occupied by Gunderson's "borderline personality disorder." Patients with borderline structure who show no clear evidence of genetic factors, and who do not fall into any of the

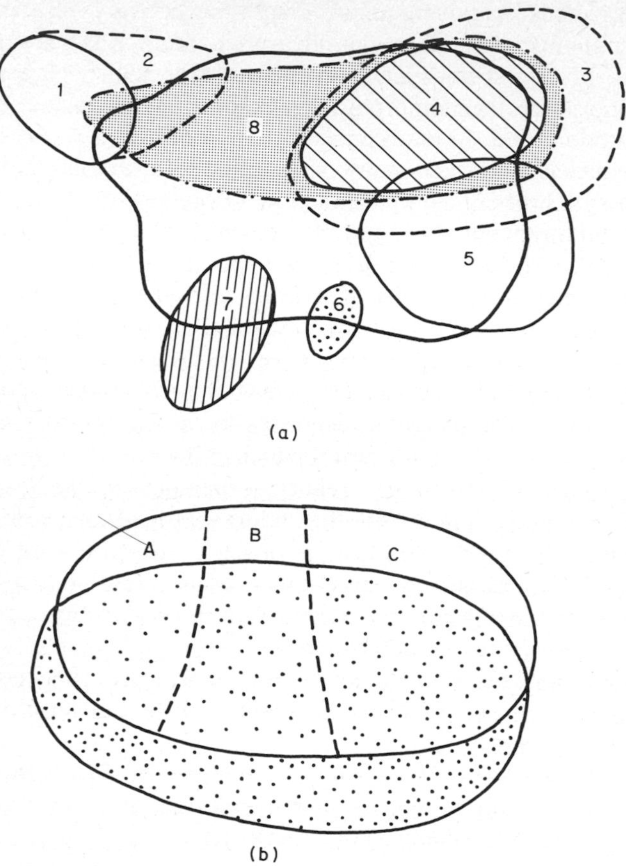

Figure 2. Relationships between Structural and Nonstructural Uses of the Term "Borderline

more popular syndrome types, occupy the "leftover" portions of the realm. Many sociopaths and addicted persons would be included in these portions.

The lower diagram (Figure 2*b*) highlights the two main usages in a different way. The dotted oval represents the realm of borderline *structure*. Intersecting this is the realm of borderline (in the clinical or genetic senses) schizophrenia (*A*), schizoaffective disorders of less severe types (*B*), and the borderline layer of affective illnesses (*C*). These two large realms do not overlap entirely because the clinical and genetic usages of borderline include some persons with psychotic structure; they do not meet research criteria for the classical psychoses but show severe impairment in the capacity to test reality.

In Chapter 10 we examined in some detail the dimension of personality type. Some of the more influential character typologies were reviewed, beginning with that of the Greeks in the classical period. Varieties of temperament were also discussed. As one compares the various typological models, both competing and complementary aspects become noticeable. The author advocates a typology combining certain elements from traditional psychiatry and others from psychoanalytic psychology for use in assessing borderline patients. Thirteen subtypes emerge and are used as the foundation for a Personality-Profile Scale in which space is provided for the placement of any given patient along separate axes designated for each subtype. It is assumed that many borderline patients will exhibit fairly strong features of several subtypes. One ordinarily predominates, and that subtype may serve as the personality-type label for quick reference (for example, a borderline patient with "narcissistic" personality). Fuller description of the patient requires, besides this categorical label, a dimensional evaluation in which the levels of all the subtypes are indicated in semiquantitative fashion. In this way the clinician may introduce greater precision into his diagnoses of character and temperament. Ordinarily one must content oneself with phrases like "phobic with hysterical and narcissistic features." On the Personality-Profile Scale, however, a number from zero to ten is assigned for each subtype. The numbers, if plotted on a grid, constitute a personality profile. The importance of such an exercise lies in the corresponding importance of this dimension in overall prognosis. This is especially true where a psychoanalytically oriented type of psychotherapy is being contemplated.

In the final section (Part IV) a series of diagrams and rating scales are described, each of which may be used in the appraisal of the major diagnostic dimensions. These include the Sz-MDP Continuum Diagram, Spitzer and Endicott's Global Assessment Scale, and the Personality-Profile Scale. Following this are a series of case illustrations arranged in order of severity (beginning with the most disturbed). Diagnostic impressions are given in both category-based and dimensional terms.

Highlights from the psychological test battery are also included in most of the cases. Variables of special importance to the understanding of borderline cases are illustrated and discussed in the different vignettes. These variables include reality testing, ego integration, the quality of object relations, vulnerability to stress (anxiety tolerance), impulse control, primitivity of defenses, and so forth.

The first item in the dimensional diagnosis appended to (most of) the case illustrations is the relative position on the phenotypic continuum (the Sz-MDP continuum) between "pure" schizophrenia (Region I) and a "pure" affective disorder (Region V). The method for selecting which region is most appropriate for any given patient relies on a modification of the schizoaffective weighted rating scale described by Cohen et al. (1972), as outlined in Chapter 8. There is an important practical aspect to this task: If the patient's condition can be construed as a dilute form of one or another major (psychotic) disorder, the medication most beneficial to the particular major disorder may also be of use (often in smaller amounts) in the borderline form of the illness. A two-dimensional approach, emphasizing only the adaptational level and personality type, by overlooking the constitutional component, may lead to inadequate treatment, namely, psychotherapy alone, when a combined program would have proved superior.

Another practical aspect of assessing genetic vulnerability relates to the risk of attempting depth therapy (especially on an office basis) in patients with subtle manifestations of either *bipolar* manic-depressive illness or of schizophrenia. Awareness of possible biological components in certain borderline syndromes will also reduce the tendency to ascribe to psychological causes phenomena more accurately attributable to predominantly organic changes, such as periodic mood shifts, periodic episodes of impulsivity, certain examples of premenstrual depression, and so forth.

Some patients who meet structural criteria for borderline organization do not exhibit discernible signs of hereditary predisposition. In them, other underlying factors appear responsible, such as severe parental neglect or abusiveness, death of a parent during early adolescence, and so forth. No systematic study of psychic structure in a random population has yet been performed, however, to determine the size of this group relative to the size of the borderline group in which predisposition does seem important.

The clinical portions of Part IV constitute the beginnings of a diagnostic dictionary in which each element is "defined" by actual dialogue with the patient as well as by the usual anamnestic and other data. Ideally the dictionary should serve as a nucleus to be fleshed out by the reader with additional cases of his own. The more complete such a lexicon becomes, the more precisely can the clinician objectify impressions about where any given patient "fits" diagnostically (in relation to those already included in the lexicon). Because the dictionary spans the continuum from severe to relatively mild psychiatric illness, it should also help in objectifying impressions about the level of a patient's progress. This is of special importance when one deals with patients in the borderline range, many of whom, under proper treatment, are capable of major shifts in occupational and social function.

From the standpoint of its theoretical framework, psychoanalysis has progressed from its origins as an id psychology to an ego psychology, and in recent years to a more interpersonally oriented object-relations psychology. The time seems now at hand to push on further to a psychoanalytic psychobiology—in which the newer genetic, biochemical, neuroendocrinological, and neurophysiological data are also integrated into a still broader theoretical framework. This kind of integration is particularly necessary in the realm of the borderline syndromes. It is hoped that this book will represent another step toward this goal.

References

Aarkrog, T. (1973). Conditions in adolescents who were borderline psychotics as children. *Acta Psychiat. Scand.*, **49**:377–385.

Abelin, T. (1972). Etiological implications of the distinction between process and reactive schizophrenia: The monogenic model involving intermediateness. In Kaplan, A. R. (Ed.), *Genetic Factors in "Schizophrenia."* Springfield, Ill.: Charles C Thomas, pp. 181–218.

Abrams, R., Taylor, M. A., and Gaztanaga, P. (1974). Manic-depressive illness and paranoid schizophrenia. *Arch. Gen. Psychiat.*, **31**:640–642.

———, and ——— (1976). Mania and schizo-affective disorder, manic type: A comparison. *Amer. J. Psychiat.*, **133**:1445–1447.

Akiskal, H. S., Bitar, A. H., Puzantian, V. R., Rosenthal, T. L., and Walker, P. W. (1978). The nosologic status of neurotic depression. A prospective three- to four-year follow-up examination in the light of the primary-secondary and unipolar-bipolar dichotomies. *Arch. Gen. Psychiat.*, **35**:756–766.

———, Djenderedjian, A. H., Rosenthal, R. H., and Khani, M. K. (1977). Cyclothymic disorder: Validating criteria for inclusion in the bipolar affective group. *Amer. J. Psychiat.*, **134**:1227–1233.

———, ———, Bolinger, J. M., Bitar, A. H., Khani, M. K., and Haykal, R. F. (1978). The joint use of clinical and biological criteria for psychiatric diagnosis, II: Their application in identifying subaffective forms of bipolar illness. In Akiskal, H. S., and Webb, W. L. (Eds.), *Psychiatric Diagnosis: Exploration of Biological Predictors*. New York: Spectrum Publications, pp. 133–145.

Alanen, Y. O. (1966). The family in the pathogenesis of schizophrenic and neurotic disorders. *Acta Psychiat. Scand.,* Supplementum **189**.

Alias, A. G. (1974). On the psychopathology of schizophrenia. *Biol. Psychiat.,* **9**:61–70.

Allen, M. G. (1976). Twin studies of affective illness. *Arch. Gen. Psychiat.,* **33**:1476–1478.

———, and Pollin, W. (1972). Schizophrenia in twins and the diffuse ego boundary hypothesis. In Cancro, R. (ed.), *Annual Review of the Schizophrenic Syndrome,* vol. 2. New York: Brunner/Mazel, pp. 285–293.

American Psychiatric Association Committee on Nomenclature and Statistics (1968). *Diagnostic and Statistical Manual of Mental Disorders* (DSM-11) (2nd ed.). Washington, D.C.: American Psychiatric Association.

Angst, J. (1966). *Zur Aetiologie und Nosologie endogener depressiven Psychosen.* Berlin: Springer-Verlag OHG.

———, and Perris, C. (1968). Zur Nosologie endogener Depressionen. *Arch. Psychiat. u. Z. Ges. Neurol.,* **210**:373–386.

Anthony, E. J. (1968). The developmental precursors of adult schizophrenia. In Rosenthal, D., and Kety, S. (Eds.), *Transmission of Schizophrenia.* Oxford: Pergamon Press, pp. 293–316.

——— (1972). A clinical and experimental study of high-risk children and their schizophrenic parents. In Kaplan, A. R. (Ed.), *Genetics of Schizophrenia.* Springfield, Ill.: Charles C Thomas, pp. 380–406.

Arieti, S. (1955). *Interpretation of Schizophrenia.* New York: R. Brunner.

——— (1970). The concept of schizophrenia. In Cancro, R. (Ed.), *The Schizophrenic Reactions.* New York: Brunner/Mazel.

Arlow, J., and Brenner, C. (1964). *Psychoanalytic Concepts and the Structural Theory.* New York: International Universities Press.

Asano, N. (1967). Clinico-genetic study of manic-depressive psychoses. In Mitsuda, H. (Ed.), *Clinical Genetics of Psychosis.* Kyoto.

Astrachan, B. M., Harrow, M., Adler, D., Bauer, L., Schwartz, A., Schwartz, C., and Tucker, G. (1972). A check-list for the diagnosis of schizophrenia. *Brit. J. Psychiat.,* **121**:529–539.

Astrup, C., Fossum, A., and Holmboe, R. (1962). *Prognosis in Functional Psychosis: Clinical, Social and Genetic Aspects.* Springfield, Ill.: Charles C Thomas.

———, and Noreik, K. (1966). *Functional Psychoses: Diagnostic and Prognostic Models.* Springfield, Ill.: Charles C Thomas.

Ayd, F. J. (1970). Prevention of recurrence (maintenance therapy). In DiMascio, A., and Shader, R. I. (Eds.), *Clinical Handbook of Psychopharmacology.* New York: Jason Aronson, pp. 297–310.

Bacon, F. (1640). *The Advancement and Proficience of Learning.* Oxford: Leon Lichfield.

Baillarger, M. (1850). Hereditary insanity. Reviewed in *Amer. J. Insanity,* **6**:367–369.

——— (1854). De la folie à double forme. *Ann. Med. Psychol.,* pp. 369 ff.

———, and Falret, J. (1855). On a new species of insanity. *Amer. J. Insanity,* **11**:230.

Bakan, P. (1975). Dreaming, REM sleep and the right hemisphere: A theoretical integration. Presented at the Second International Congress of Sleep Research, Edinburgh, June 30.

Baker, M., Dorzab, J., Winokur, G., and Cadoret, R. (1972). Depressive disease. *Arch. Gen. Psychiat.,* **27**:320–327.

Barcai, A. (1977). Lithium in adult anorexia nervosa. *Acta Psychiat. Scand.,* **55**:97–101.

Barchas, J. D., Ciaranello, R. D., Kessler, S., and Hamburg, D. A. (1975). Genetic aspects of catecholamine synthesis. In Fieve, R., Rosenthal, D., and Brill, H. (Eds.), *Genetic Research in Psychiatry.* Baltimore: Johns Hopkins Press, pp. 27–62.

Baron, M., Gershon, E. S., Rudy, V., Jonas, W. Z., and Buchsbaum, M. (1975). Lithium caronate response in depression. *Arch. Gen. Psychiat.,* **32**:1107–1111.

Beaumont, P. J. V., Richards, D. H., and Gelder, M. G. (1975). A study of minor psychiatric and physical symptoms during the menstrual cycle. *Brit. J. Psychiat.,* **126**:431–434.

Beck, A. T. (1967). *Depression: Causes and Treatment*. Philadelphia: University of Pennsylvania Press.

Beck, S. (1959). Schizophrenia without psychosis. *Arch. Neurol. Psychiat.*, **8**:85–96.

Beers, Clifford (1908). *A Mind that Found Itself*. Garden City, N.Y.: Doubleday.

Belfer, M. L., and d'Autremont, C. C. (1971). Catatonia-like symptomatology. *Arch. Gen. Psychiat.*, **24**:119–120.

Bellak, L. (1949). A multiple-factor psychosomatic theory of schizophrenia. *Psychiat. Q.*, **23**:738–755.

——— (1976). A possible subgroup of the schizophrenic syndrome and implications for treatment. *Amer. J. Psychother.*, **30**:194–205.

——— Hurvich, M., and Gediman, H. K. (1973). *Ego Functions in Schizophrenics, Neurotics and Normals*. New York: John Wiley.

———, and Loeb, L. (1969). *The Schizophrenic Syndrome*. New York: Grune and Stratton.

Belmaker, R. H., and Ebstein, R. P. (1977). The search for genetic polymorphisms of human biogenic-amine related enzymes. In Gershon, E. S., Belmaker, R. H., Kety, S. S., and Rosenbaum, M. (Eds.), *The Impact of Biology on Modern Psychiatry*. New York: Plenum Press, pp. 241–260.

———, Pollin, W., Wyatt, R. J., and Cohen, S. (1974). A follow-up of monozygotic twins discordant for schizophrenia. *Arch. Gen. Psychiat.*, **30**:219–225.

Bender, L. (1975). Schizophrenic spectrum disorders in the families of schizophrenic children. In Fieve, R. R., Rosenthal, D., and Brill, H. (Eds.), *Genetic Research in Psychiatry*. Baltimore: Johns Hopkins Press, pp. 125–134.

Benedetti, G. (1965). Psychopathologie und Psychotherapie der Grenzpsychose. Report of the Dikemark Seminar, Dikemark Sykhuset, Norway, Apr. 29–May 1, pp. 1–29.

Berg, I., Hullin, R., Allsopp, M., O'Brien, P., and MacDonald, R. (1974). Bipolar manic-depressive psychosis in early adolescence. A case report. *Brit. J. Psychiat.*, **125**:416–417.

Bergeret, J. (1974). *La Depression et les etats-limites*. Paris: Payot.

——— (1974a). *Abrégé de la psychologie pathologique*. Paris: Masson.

Bertelsen, A., Harvald, B., and Hauge, M. (1977). A Danish twin study of manic-depressive disorders. *Brit. J. Psychiat.*, **130**:330–351.

Biederman, J., Rimon, R., Ebstein, R., Belmaker, R. H., and Davidson, J. T. (1977). Cyclic A. M. P. in the cerebrospinal fluid of patients with schizophrenia. *Brit. J. Psychiat.*, **130**:64–67.

Blacker, K. H. (1966). Obsessive-compulsive phenomena and catatonic states: A continuum. A five-year case study of a chronic catatonic patient. *Psychiatry*, **29**:185–194.

Blashfield, R. (1973). An evaluation of the DSM-II classification of schizophrenia as a nomenclature. *J. Abnorm. Psychol.*, **82**:382–389.

Bleuler, E. (1950). *Dementia Praecox or the Group of Schizophrenias* (Tr. of the 1911 monograph by J. Zinkin). New York: International Universities Press.

Bleuler, M. (1974). The offspring of schizophrenics. *Schizophrenia Bull.*, no. 8:93–107.

Bloomgarden, J. (1978). A study of splitting and related phenomena on the Rorschach test. Unpublished thesis.

Bogen, J. E., and Bogen, A. (1969). The other side of the brain III: The corpus callosum and creativity. *Bull. Los Angeles Neurol. Soc.*, **34**:191–200.

Boklage, C. E. (1977). Schizophrenia, brain asymmetry development and twinning: Cellular relationship with etiological and possibly prognostic implications. *Biol. Psychiat.*, **12**:19–35.

Böök, J. A. (1953). A genetic and neuropsychiatric investigation of a north-Swedish population. *Acta Genetica*, **4**:1–100; 345–414.

Borland, B. L., and Heckman, H. K. (1976). Hyperactive boys and their brothers. *Arch. Gen. Psychiat.*, **33**:669–675.

Bradlow, P. A. (1971). Murder in the initial dream in psychoanalysis. *Bull. Phil. Assoc. Psychoanal.*, **21**:70–81.

Braff, D. L., and Beck, A. T. (1974). Thinking disorder in depression. *Arch. Gen. Psychiat.*, **31**:456–459.

Breakey, W. R., and Goodell, H. (1972). Thought disorder in mania and schizophrenia evaluated by Bannister's grid test for schizophrenic thought disorder. *Brit. J. Psychiat.*, **120**:391–395.

Breuer, J., and Freud, S. (1893–1895). Fraulein Anna O., *S.E.*, **2**:21–47. London: Hogarth Press.

Březinová, V., and Kendell, R. E. (1977). Smooth pursuit eye movements of schizophrenics and normal people under stress. *Brit. J. Psychiat.*, **130**:59–63.

Broen, W. E., Jr. (1968). *Schizophrenia: Research and Theory*. New York: Academic Press.

Brunswick, R. Mack (1928). A supplement to Freud's *History of an Infantile Neurosis*. *Int. J. Psycho-Anal.*, **9**:439–476.

Buchsbaum, M. (1975). Average evoked response augmenting/reducing in schizophrenia and affective disorders. In Freedman, D. X. (Ed.), *Biology of the Major Psychoses*. New York: Raven Press, pp. 129–142.

——— (1977). Techniques of clinical neurophysiology in the diagnosis and neuropharmacology of affective illness. Presented at the thirty-second annual meeting of the Society of Biological Psychiatry, Toronto, Apr. 30.

———, Goodwin, F. K., Murphy, D., and Borge, G. (1971). A.E.R. in affective disorders. *Amer. J. Psychiat.*, **128**:19–25.

Bunney, W. E., Jr., Goodwin, F. K., Murphy, D. L., House, K. M., and Gordon, E. K. (1972). The "switch process" in manic-depressive illness: I. A systematic study of sequential behavioral changes. *Arch. Gen. Psychiat.*, **27**:295–302.

Burnham, D. (1969). *Schizophrenia and the Need-Fear Dilemma*. New York: International Universities Press.

Bychowski, G. (1953). The problem of latent psychosis. *J. Amer. Psychoanal. Assoc.*, **4**:484–503.

Cade, J. (1974). Lecture on mania at N.Y. State Psychiatric Institute, Oct. 24.

Cadoret, R. J. (1973). Toward a definition of the schizoid state: Evidence from studies of twins and their families. *Brit. J. Psychiat.*, **112**:679–685.

———, Cunningham, L., Loftus, R., and Edwards, J. E. (1976). Studies of adoptees from psychiatrically disturbed biologic parents: II. Temperamental, hyperactive, antisocial and developmental variables. In Chess, S., and Thomas, A. (Eds.), *Annual Progress in Child Psychiatry and Child Development*. New York: Brunner/Mazel, pp. 258–268.

———, and Winokur, G. (1972). Genetic principles in the classification of affective illnesses. *Int. J. Mental Health,* **1**:159–175.

Cancro, R. (1975). Genetics, dualism and schizophrenia. *J. Amer. Acad. Psychoanal.*, **3**:353–360.

Cantwell, D. P., Sturzenberger, S., Burroughs, J., Salkin, B., and Green, J. K. (1977). Anorexia nervosa: An affective disorder? *Arch. Gen. Psychiat.*, **34**:1087–1093.

Carlson, G. A., and Goodwin, F. K. (1973). The stages of mania. *Arch. Gen. Psychiat.*, **28**:221–278.

———, and Strober, M. (1978). Manic-depressive illness in early adolescence. *J. Amer. Acad. Child Psychiat.*, **17**:138–153.

Carpenter, W. T., Jr., Bartko, J., Carpenter, C. L., and Strauss, J. S. (1976). Another view of schizophrenia subtypes. *Arch. Gen. Psychiat.*, **33**:508–516.

———, Gunderson, J. G., and Strauss, J. S. (1976). Considerations of the borderline syndrome from the vantage point of a longitudinal comparative study of borderline and schizophrenic patients. Unpublished manuscript.

———, Murphy, D. L., and Wyatt, R. J. (1975). Platelet monoamine oxidase activity in acute schizophrenia. *Amer. J. Psychiat.*, **132**:438–441.

———, Sacks, M. H., Strauss, J. S., Bartko, J. J., and Rayner, J. (1976). Evaluating signs and symptoms: Comparison of structured interview and clinical approaches. *Brit. J. Psychiat.,* **128**:397–403.

———, Strauss, J. S., and Bartko, J. J. (1973). Flexible system for the diagnosis of schizophrenia: Report from the W.H.O. International Pilot Study of Schizophrenia. *Science,* **182**:1275–1277.

———, ———, and Muleh, S. (1973). Are there pathognomonic symptoms in schizophrenia? *Arch. Gen. Psychiat.,* **28**:847–852.

Carrington, P. (1971). Dreams and schizophrenia. *Arch. Gen. Psychiat.,* **26**:343–350.

Carter, C. O. (1973). Multifactorial genetic disease. In McKusick, V. A. (Ed.), *Medical Genetics*. New York: H. P. Publishing Co., pp. 199–208.

Carter, L., and Rinsley, D. B. (1977). Vicissitudes of 'empathy' in a borderline adolescent. *Int. Rev. Psycho-Anal.,* **4**:317–326.

Cary, G. L. (1972). The borderline condition: A structural-dynamic viewpoint. *Psychoanal. Rev.,* **59**:33–54.

Cavalli-Sforza, L. L., and Bodmer, W. F. (1971). *Genetics of Human Populations*. San Francisco: W. H. Freeman.

Chapman, J. P. (1966). The early symptoms of schizophrenia. *Brit. J. Psychiat.,* **112**:225–251.

Chapman, L. J., and Chapman, J. P. (1973). *Disordered Thought in Schizophrenia*. Englewood Cliffs, N.J.: Prentice-Hall.

Chess, S., Thomas, A., and Birch, H. G. (1959). Characteristics of the individual child's behavioral responses to the environment. *Amer. J. Orthopsychiat.,* **29**:791–802.

———, ———, and ——— (1967). Behavioral problems revisited: Findings of an anterospective study. *J. Amer. Acad. Child Psychiat.*, **6**:321–331.

Chiarugi, V. (1789). *Regolamento dei Regi Spedali di Santa Maria Nuova e di Bonifazio*. Florence: G. Cambiagi.

Childs, B., and Der Kaloustian, V. M. (1968). Genetic heterogeneity. *N.E.J. Med.,* **279**:1205–1212; 1267–1274.

Chodoff, P. (1973). The depressive personality: A critical review. *Int. J. Psychiat.,* **2**:196–217.

——— (1974). The diagnosis of hysteria: An overview. *Amer. J. Psychiat.,* **131**:1073–1078.

———, and Lyons, H. (1958). Hysteria, the hysterical personality, and "hysterical" conversion. *Amer. J. Psychiat.,* **114**:734–740.

Clark, L. P. (1919). Some practical remarks upon the use of modified psychoanalysis in the treatment of borderland neuroses and psychoses. *Psychoanal. Rev.,* **6**:306–308.

Clayton, P., Rodin, L., and Winokur, G. (1968). Family history studies: III. Schizoaffective disorder, clinical and genetic factors including a one to two year follow-up. *Comprehen. Psychiat.,* **9**:31–49.

Cloninger, C. R., and Guze, S. B. (1973). Psychiatric illnesses in families of female criminals: A study of 288 first-degree relatives. *Brit. J. Psychiat.,* **122**:697–703.

———, Reich, T., and Guze, S. B. (1975). The multifactorial model of disease transmission: II. Sex differences in the familial transmission of sociopathy (antisocial personality). *Brit. J. Psychiat.,* **127**:11–22.

———, ———, and ——— (1975a). The multifactorial model of disease transmission: Familial relationship between sociopathy and hysteria (Briquet's syndrome). *Brit. J. Psychiat.,* **127**:23–32.

Cohen, D. J., and Young, J. G. (1977). Neurochemistry and child psychiatry. *J. Amer. Acad. Child Psychiat.,* **16**:353–411.

Cohen, S. M., Allen, M. G., Pollin, W., and Hrubec, Z. (1972). Relationship of schizo-affective psychosis to manic depressive psychosis and schizophrenia. *Arch. Gen. Psychiat.,* **26**:539–545.

Cohn, C. K., Dunner, D. L., and Axelrod, J. (1970). Reduced C. O. M. T. activity in red blood cells of women with primary affective disorder. *Science,* **170**:1323–1324.

Conolly, J. (1838). *An Inquiry concerning the Indications of Insanity*. London: John Taylor.

Cooper, J. E. (1975). Concepts of schizophrenia in the United States of America and in Great Britain. In Lader, M. H. (Ed.), *Brit. J. of Psychiatry Special Publication No. 10: Studies of Schizophrenia*. Ashford, Kent: Headley Bros., pp. 19–24.

———, Kendell, R. E., Gurland, B. J., Sharpe, L., Copeland, J. R. M., and Simon, R. (1972). *Psychiatric Diagnosis in New York and London*. Maudsley monographs, no. 20. London: Oxford University Press.

Coppen, A. (1965). The prevalence of menstrual disorders in psychiatric patients. *Brit. J. Psychiat.*, **111**:155–167.

Cornfield, R. B., and Malen, R. L. (1978). A multidimensional view of the obsessive character. *Comprehen. Psychiat.*, **19**:73–78.

Cromwell, R. L., Strauss, J. S., and Blashfield, R. K. (1975). Theoretical position. In Hobbs, N. (Ed.), *Issues in the Classification of Children—A Handbook on Categories, Labels and Their Consequences*. Los Angeles: Jossey-Bass.

Da Fonseca, A. F. (1963). Affective equivalents. *Brit. J. Psychiat.*, **109**:464–469.

Davis, J. M. (1976). Dopamine theory in schizophrenia. Abstracted in *Roche Report*, vol. 6, no. 17, Nov. 1.

Davison, K. (1976). Drug-induced psychoses and their relationship to schizophrenia. In Kemali, D., Bartholini, G., and Richter, D. (Eds.), *Schizophrenia Today*. Oxford: Pergamon Press, pp. 105–133.

De Alarcon, R. (1975). Detection and management of affective disturbances in schizophrenia. In Lader, M. H. (Ed.), *Brit. J. of Psychiatry Special Publication No. 10: Studies of Schizophrenia*. Ashford, Kent: Headley Bros., pp. 137–141.

DeLeon-Jones, F., Maas, J. W., Dekirmenjian, H., and Sanchez, J. (1975). Diagnostic subgroups of affective disorders and their urinary excretion of catecholamine metabolites. *Amer. J. Psychiat.*, **132**:1141–1148.

Deutsch, F., and Murphy, W. F. (1955). *The Clinical Interview*. New York: International Universities Press.

Deutsch, H. (1942). Some forms of emotional disturbance and their relationships to schizophrenia. *Psychoanal. Q.*, **11**:301–321.

Diamond, S. B., Rubinstein, A. A., Dunner, D. L. and Fieve, R. R. (1976). Menstrual problems in women with primary affective illness. *Comprehen. Psychiat.*, **17**:541–548.

Dickes, R. (1974). The concept of borderline states: An alternative proposal. *Int. J. Psychoanal. Psychother.*, **3**:1–27.

Didion, J. (1977). *A Book of Common Prayer*. New York: Simon and Schuster.

Dimond, S. (1972). *The Double Brain*. London: Churchill Livingstone.

Dince, P. (1977). Considerations in the psychotherapeutic treatment of "borderline" adolescents. Presented at the Panel on Psychotherapy of Adolescents, annual meeting of the American Academy of Child Psychiatry, Houston, Oct. 22.

Dunner, D. L. (1971). Unipolar versus bipolar affective disorders. Lecture at the New York State Psychiatric Institute, Aug. 4.

———, Goodwin, F. K., Gershon, E. S., Murphy, D. L., and Bunney, W. E., Jr. (1972). Excretion of 17-OHCS in unipolar and bipolar depressed patients. *Arch. Gen. Psychiat.*, **26**:360–363.

———, Fleiss, J. L., Addonizio, G., and Fieve, R. R. (1976). Assortative mating in primary affective disorder. *Biol. Psychiat.*, **11**:43–51.

———, ———, and Fieve, R. R. (1976). The course of development of mania in patients with recurrent depression. *Amer. J. Psychiat.*, **133**:905–908.

———, Gershon, E. S., and Goodwin, F. K. (1976). Heritable factors in the severity of affective illness. *Biol. Psychiat.*, **11**:31–42.

———, Levitt, M., Kumbaraci, T., and Fieve, R. R. (1977). Erythrocyte catechol-O-methyltransferase activity in primary affective disorder. *Biol. Psychiat.*, **12**:237–244.

Dyson, W. L., and Barcai, A. (1970). Treatment of children of lithium-responding parents. *Curr. Ther. Res.*, **12**:286–290.

Easser, R., and Lesser, S. (1965). Hysterical personality: A reevaluation. *Psychoanal. Q.*, **34**:390–402.

Easson, W. M. (1969). *The Severely Disturbed Adolescent*. New York: International Universities Press.

Eaton, E. M. (1977). Hemisphere processing of verbal and nonverbal visual information in process and reactive schizophrenia. Presented at the thirty-second annual meeting of the Society of Biologic Psychiatry, Toronto, Apr. 29.

Edwards, G. (1972). Diagnosis of schizophrenia: An Anglo-American experience. *Brit. J. Psychiat.*, **120**:385–390.

——— (1973). Diagnosis of schizophrenia: An Anglo-American comparison. *Int. J. Psychiat.*, **11**:442–452.

Eisenberg, L. (1968). The interaction of biological and experiential factors in schizophrenia. In Rosenthal, D., and Kety, S. (Eds.), *The Transmission of Schizophrenia*. Oxford: Pergamon Press, pp. 403–409.

Eitinger, L., Laane, C. L., and Langfelt, G. (1958). The prognostic value of the clinical picture and the therapeutic value of physical treatment in schizophrenia and the schizophreniform states. *Acta Psychiat. Scand.*, **33**:33–53.

Ekstein, R. (1955). Vicissitudes of the "internal image" in the recovery of a borderline schizophrenic adolescent. *Bull. Menninger Clin.*, **19**:86–92.

Elsässer, G. (1952). *Die Nachkommen geisteskranker Eltenpaare*. Stuttgart: Georg Thieme Verlag.

——— Lehmann, H., Pohlen, M., and Scheid, T. (1971). Die Nachkommen geisteskranker Eltenpaare. *Fortschr. Neur. Psych.*, **39**:495–522.

Endicott, J., Forman, J. B. W., and Spitzer, R. L. (1978). Research approaches to diagnostic classification in schizophrenia. *Birth Defects*, 14(5):41–57.

———, Spitzer, R. L., Fleiss, J. L., and Cohen, J. (1976). The global assessment scale. *Arch. Gen. Psychiat.*, **33**:766–771.

Erikson, E. H. (1951). Growth and crises of the healthy personality. In Senn, M., *Symposium on the Healthy Personality*. New York: Josiah Macy, Jr. Foundation, pp. 91–146.

Erlenmeyer-Kimling, L. (1968). Studies on the offspring of two schizophrenics. In Rosenthal, D., and Kety, S. (Eds.), *Transmission of Schizophrenia*. Oxford: Pergamon Press, pp. 65–83.

——— (1975). A prospective study of children at risk for schizophrenia. In Wirt, R., Winokur, G., and Roff, M. (Eds.), *Life History Research in Psychopathology*. Minneapolis: University of Minnesota Press, pp. 22–46.

———, and Nichol, S. (1969). Comparison of hospitalization measures in schizophrenic patients with and without a family history of schizophrenia. *Brit. J. Psychiat.*, **115**:321–334.

———, and Paradowski, W. (1971). Selection and schizophrenia. In Bajema, C. J. (Ed.), *Natural Selection in Human Populations*. New York: John Wiley.

———, Rainer, J. D., and Kallmann, F. J. (1966). Current reproductive trends in schizophrenia. In Hoch, P. H., and Zubin, J. (Eds.), *Psychopathology of Schizophrenia*. New York: Grune and Stratton.

Escalona, S. K. (1968). *The Roots of Individuality*. Chicago: Aldine.

Esquirol, E. (1838). *Maladies mentales* (2 vols.). Paris: Baillière.

Essen-Möller, E. (1941). Psychiatrische Untersuchungen an einer Serie von Zwillingen. *Acta Psychiat. Scand.*, Supplementum **23**:1–200.

——— (1970). Twenty-one psychiatric cases and their MZ co-twins: A thirty years' follow-up. *Acta Genet. Med. Gemellol.*, **19**:315–317.

——— (1977). Evidence for polygenic inheritance in schizophrenia. *Acta Psychiat. Scand.*, **55**:202–207.

Eysenck, H. J. (1947). *Dimensions of Personality*. London: Kegan Paul, Trench, Trubner.

——— (1952). *The Scientific Study of Personality*. London: Routledge and Kegan Paul.

——— (1960). *The Structure of Human Personality*. London: Methuen.

——— (1967). *The Biological Basis of Personality*. Springfield, Ill.: Charles C Thomas.

———, and Eysenck, S. B. G. (1969). *Personality Structure and Measurement*. San Diego: Robert R. Knapp.

Fairbairn, W. R. D. (1944). Endopsychic structure considered in terms of object relationships. In *An Object-Relations Theory of the Personality*. New York: Basic Books, 1952, pp. 82–136.

Falconer, D. S. (1965). The inheritance of liability to certain diseases, estimated from the incidence among relatives. *Ann. Hum. Genet.*, **29**:51–76.

Falconer, M. A., and Serafetinides, E. A. (1963). A follow-up study of surgery in temporal lobe epilepsy. *J. Neurol. Neurosurg. & Psychiat.*, **26**:154–165.

Fard, K., Hudgens, R. W., and Welner, A. (1978). Undiagnosed psychiatric illness in adolescents. *Arch. Gen. Psychiat.*, **35**:279–282.

Federn, P. (1947). Principles of psychotherapy in latent schizophrenia. *Amer. J. Psychother.*, **1**:129–139.

Feighner, J. P., Robins, E., Guze, S. B., Woodruff, R. A., Jr., Winokur, G., and Munoz, R. (1972). Diagnostic criteria for use in psychiatric research. *Arch. Gen. Psychiat.*, **26**:57–63.

Fieve, R. R. (1975). Lithium prophylaxis in affective disorders. *N.Y.S.J. Med.*, **75**:1219–1221.

———, Kumbaraci, T., and Dunner, D. L. (1976). Lithium prophylaxis of depression in bipolar I, bipolar II, and unipolar patients. *Amer. J. Psychiat.*, **133**:925–929.

———, Mendlewicz, J., Rainer, J. D., and Fleiss, J. L. (1975). A dominant X-linked factor in manic-depressive illness: Studies with color blindness. In Fieve, R. R., Rosenthal, D., and Brill, H. (Eds.), *Genetic Research in Psychiatry*. Baltimore: Johns Hopkins Press, pp. 241–255.

Fink, M. (1974). Psychiatric diagnosis: Phenotypic or pathophysiologic? *Biol. Psychiat.*, **9**:227–229.

Fischer, E. (1960). Hallucinogenic drugs: Their importance in the pathogenic investigation of schizophrenia. *Semin. Med.*, **117**:115–119.

Fischer, M. (1971). Psychoses in the offspring of schizophrenic monozygotic twins and the normal co-twins. *Brit. J. Psychiat.*, **118**:43–52.

——— (1973). Genetic and environmental factors in schizophrenia. *Acta Psychiat. Scand.*, Supplementum **238**:1–72.

———, Harvald, B., and Hauge, M. (1969). A Danish twin study of schizophrenia. *Brit. J. Psychiat.*, **115**:981–990.

Fish, B. (1975). Biologic antecedents of psychosis in children. In Freedman, D. X. (Ed.), *Biology of the Major Psychoses*. New York: Raven Press, pp. 49–80.

Fish, F. (1964). The cycloid psychoses. *Comprehen. Psychiat.*, **5**:155–169.

——— (1975). Clinical presentation and classification of schizophrenia. In Silverstone, T., and Barraclough, B. (Eds.), *Brit. J. of Psychiatry Special Publication No. 9: Contemporary Psychiatry*. Ashford, Kent: Headley Bros., pp. 3–10.

Fitzgerald, F. Scott (1920). *This Side of Paradise*. New York: Charles Scribner.

Flemenbaum, A. (1976). Pavor nocturnus: A complication of single daily tricyclic or neuroleptic dosage. *Amer. J. Psychiat.*, **133**:570–572.

Flor-Henry, P. (1969). Psychoses and temporal lobe epilepsy: A controlled investigation. *Epilepsia,* **10**:363–395.

Forssman, H., and Wolinder, J. (1970). Lithium effect as aid in psychiatric diagnosis. *Acta Psychiat. Scand.*, Supplementum **219**:59–66.

Fowler, R. C., Tsuang, M. T., Cadoret, R. J., and Monnelly, E. (1975). Non-psychotic disorders in the families of process schizophrenics. *Acta Psychiat. Scand.*, **51**:153–160.

Freides, D. (1976). A new diagnostic scheme for disorders of behavior, emotion, and learning based on organism-environment interaction. *Schizophrenia Bull.*, **2**:218–236.

Freud, S. (1900). The interpretation of dreams. *S. E.,* **5**:507; 541–542; 574–577. London: Hogarth Press.
——— (1918). From the history of an infantile neurosis. *S. E.,* **17**:7–122. London: Hogarth Press.
——— (1923). The ego and the id. *S. E.,* **19**:19–39. London: Hogarth Press.
Friedman, J., and Meares, R. (1978). Biologic aspects of personality. Abstracted in *Clin. Psychiat. News,* **6**:12 (June).
Frosch, J. (1960). Psychotic character. *J. Amer. Psychoanal. Assoc.,* **8**:544–551.
——— (1964). The psychotic character. *Psychiat. Q.,* **38**:81–96.
——— (1970). Psychoanalytic considerations of the psychotic character. *J. Amer. Psychoanal. Assoc.,* **18**:24–50.
———, and Wortis, S. B. (1954). A contribution to the nosology of the impulse disorders. *Amer. J. Psychiat.,* **111**:132–138.
Galin, D. (1974). Implications for psychiatry of left and right cerebral specialization: A neurophysiological context for unconscious process. *Arch. Gen. Psychiat.,* **31**:572–583.
Garmezy, N. (1974). Children at risk: The search for antecedents of schizophrenia. *Schizophrenia Bull.,* no. 8:14–90.
Garrone, G. (1962). Etude statistique et genetique de la schizophrenia à Geneve de 1901 à 1950. *J. de Genet. Humaine,* **11**:89–219.
Garver, D. L., Erickson, S., Casper, R., Pandey, G. N., and Davis, J. N. (1977). Schizophrenia of good prognosis: A distinct syndrome? Presented at the one hundred and thirtieth annual meeting of the American Psychiatric Association, Toronto, May 2.
———, Pandey, G., Dekermenjian, H., and DeLeon-Jones, F. (1975). Growth hormone and catecholamines in affective disease. *Amer. J. Psychiat.,* **132**:1149–1154.
Geleerd, E. (1958). Borderline states in childhood and adolescence. *Psychoanal. Study of the Child,* **13**:279–295.
Gero, G. (1953). An equivalent of depression: Anorexia. In Greenacre, P. (Ed.), *Affective Disorders.* New York: International Universities Press, pp. 117–139.
Gershon, E. S., Baron, M., and Leckman, F. (1975). Genetic models of the transmission of affective disorders. *J. Psychiat. Res.,* **12**:301–317.
———, and Bunney, W. E., Jr. (1976). The question of X-linkage in bipolar manic-depressive illness. *J. Psychiat. Res.,* **13**:99–117.
———, Dunner, D. L., and Goodwin, F. K. (1971). Toward a biology of affective disorders. *Arch. Gen. Psychiat.,* **25**:1–15.
———, ———, Sturt, L., and Goodwin, F. K. (1973). Assortative mating in the affective disorders. *Biol. Psychiat.,* **7**:63–74.
———, and Matthysse, S. (1977). X-linkage: Ascertainment through doubly ill probands. *J. Psychiat. Res.,* **13**:161–168.
Glassman, A. (1974). Personal communication.
Glover, E. (1932). Psychoanalytic approach to the classification of mental disorders. *J. Mental Sci.,* **78**:819–842.
Goetzl, U., Green, R., Whybrow, P., and Jackson, R. (1974). X-linkage revisited. *Arch. Gen. Psychiat.,* **31**:665–672.
Goldfarb, W. (1961). *Childhood Schizophrenia.* Cambridge, Mass.: Harvard University Press.
Goodwin, D. W., Schulsinger, F., Hermansen, L., Guze, S. B., and Winokur, G. (1973). Alcohol problems in adoptees raised apart from alcoholic biological parents. *Arch. Gen. Psychiat.,* **28**:238–243.
———, ———, ———, ———, and ——— (1975). Alcoholism and hyperactive child syndrome. *J. Nerv. Ment. Dis.,* **160**:349–353.
———, ———, Knop, J., Mednick, S., and Guze, S. B. (1977). Psychopathology in adopted and nonadopted daughters of alcoholics. *Arch. Gen. Psychiat.,* **34**:1005–1009.
Goodwin, F. K., Murphy, D. L., and Brodie, H. K. H. (1970). L-DOPA catecholamines and

behavior: A clinical and biochemical study in depressed patients. *Biol. Psychiat.*, **2**:341–366.

———, ———, and Dunner, D. L. (1971). Lithium response in unipolar versus bipolar depression. Read before the annual meeting of the American Psychiatric Association, Washington, D.C., May.

———, ———, ———, and Bunney, W. (1972). Lithium response in unipolar versus bipolar depression. *Amer. Psychiat.*, **129**:44–47.

Gottesman, I. I. (1968). Severity/concordance and diagnostic refinement in the Maudsley–Bethlehem schizophrenic twin study. In Rosenthal, D., and Kety, S. (Eds.), *Transmission of Schizophrenia*. Oxford: Pergamon Press, pp. 37–48.

———, and Shields, J. (1966). Contribution of twin studies to perspectives on schizophrenia. In Maher, B. A. (Ed.), *Progress in Experimental Personality Research*, vol. 3. New York: Academic Press, pp. 1–84.

———, and ——— (1972). *Schizophrenia and Genetics: A Twin Study Vantage Point*. New York: Academic Press.

———, and ——— (1976). A critical review of recent adoption, twin and family studies of schizophrenia: Behavioral and genetics perspectives. *Schizophrenia Bull.*, **2**:360–401.

———, and ——— (1977). Obstetric complications and twin studies of schizophrenia: Clarifications and affirmations. *Schizophrenia Bull.*, **3**:351–354.

Gottschalk, L. A., Gleser, G. C., Magliocco, E. B., and D'Zmura, T. L. (1961). Further studies on the speech patterns of schizophrenic patients. *J. Nerv. Ment. Dis.*, **132**:101–113.

Graff, H., and Mallin, R. (1967). The syndrome of the wrist cutter. *Amer. J. Psychiat.*, **124**:36–42.

Greenacre, P. (Ed.) (1953). *Affective Disorders*. New York: International Universities Press.

Grinker, R. R., Sr., and Holzman, P. S. (1973). Schizophrenic pathology in young adults. *Arch. Gen. Psychiat.*, **28**:168–175.

———, and Werble, B. (1977). *The Borderline Patient*. New York: Jason Aronson.

———, ———, and Drye, R. C. (1968). *The Borderline Syndrome*. New York: Basic Books.

Grunebaum, H. V., and Klerman, G. L. (1967). Wrist slashing. *Amer. J. Psychiat.*, **124**:527–534.

Gunderson, J. G. (1977). Borderline personality disorders. Lecture at New York Hospital, Westchester Division, Sept. 16.

——— (1977a). Characteristics of borderlines. In Hartocollis, P. (Ed.), *Borderline Personality Disorders*. New York: International Universities Press, pp. 173–192.

———, Autry, J. H., III, and Mosher, L. R. (1974). Special report: Schizophrenia, 1974. *Schizophrenia Bull.*, no. 9:15–54.

———, Carpenter, W. T., Jr., and Strauss, J. S. (1975). Borderline and schizophrenic patients: A comparative study. *Amer. J. Psychiat.*, **132**:1257–1264.

———, and Kolb, J. E. (1976). Diagnosing borderlines: A semistructured interview. Unpublished manuscript.

———, and ——— (1978). Discriminating features of borderline patients. *Amer. J. Psychiat.*, **135**:792–796.

———, and Singer, M. T. (1975). Defining borderline patients: An overview. *Amer. J. Psychiat.*, **132**:1–10.

Guze, S. B., Woodruff, R. A., and Clayton, P. J. (1971). Secondary affective disorders: A study of 95 cases. *Psychol. Med.*, **1**:426–428.

———, ———, and ——— (1975). The significance of psychotic affective disorders. *Arch. Gen. Psychiat.*, **32**:1147–1150.

Hakarem, G., and Lidsky, A. (1975). Characteristics of pupillary reactivity in psychiatric patients and normal controls. In Kietzman, M. L., Sutton, S., and Zubin, J. (Eds.), *Experimental Approaches to Psychopathology*. New York: Academic Press, pp. 61–72.

Halaris, A. E., and Freedman, D. X. (1975). Psychotropic drugs and dopamine uptake inhibition. In Freedman, D. X. (Ed.), *Biology of the Major Psychoses*. New York: Raven Press, pp. 247–258.

Hall, P., Hartridge, G., and Van Leeuwen, G. H. (1969). Effects of catechol-O-methyltransferase in schizophrenia. *Arch. Gen. Psychiat.*, **20**:573–575.

Hambert, G., and Willen, R. (1978). Emotional disturbance and temporal lobe injury. *Comprehen. Psychiat.*, **19**:441–447.

Hamburg, B. A. (1974). The psychobiology of sex differences: An evolutionary perspective. In Friedman, R. C., Richart, R. M., and VandeWiele, R. L. (Eds.), *Sex Differences in Behavior*. New York: John Wiley, pp. 373–392.

Hanfmann, E., and Kasanin, J. (1942). *Conceptual Thinking in Schizophrenia*. Nervous and Mental Disease Monograph no. 67. New York: Nervous and Mental Disease Publishing Co.

Harrow, M., and Quinlan, D. (1977). Is disordered thinking unique to schizophrenia? *Arch. Gen. Psychiat.*, **34**:15–21.

Hartmann, H. (1939). *Ego Psychology and the Problem of Adaptation*. New York: International Universities Press, 1958.

Hawk, A. B., Carpenter, W. T., Jr., and Strauss, J. S. (1975). Diagnostic criteria and five-year outcome in schizophrenia. *Arch. Gen. Psychiat.*, **32**:343–347.

Hayman, A. (1972). Some inferences with the analysis of an atypical child. *Psychoanal. Study of the Child*. **27**:476–504.

Hays, P. (1976). Etiological factors in manic-depressive psychoses. *Arch. Gen. Psychiat.*, **33**:1187–1188.

Hecker, E. (1871). Die Hebephrenie. *Archiv f. pathol. anat. u. Physiol.*, **52**:394–429.

Hedberg, D. L., Houck, J. H., and Glueck, B. C. (1971). Tranylcypromine-trifluperazine combination in the treatment of schizophrenia. *Amer. J. Psychiat.*, **127**:1141–1146.

Helmchen, H. (1975). Schizophrenia: Diagnostic concepts in the I.C.D.-8. In Lader, M. H. (Ed.), *Brit. J. of Psychiatry Special Publication No. 10: Studies of Schizophrenia*. Ashford, Kent: Headley Bros., pp. 10–18.

Helzer, J. E., Robins, L. N., Taibleson, M., Woodruff, R. A., Jr., Reich, T., and Wish, E. D. (1977). Reliability of psychiatric diagnosis: I. A methodological review. *Arch. Gen. Psychiat.*, **34**:129–133.

———, and Winokur, G. (1974). A family interview study of male manic depressives. *Arch. Gen. Psychiat.*, **31**:73–80.

Herz, M. I., Endicott, J., and Spitzer, R. L. (1976). Brief versus standard hospitalizations: The families. *Amer. J. Psychiat.*, **133**:795–801.

Heston, L. L. (1966). Psychiatric disorders in foster-home reared children of schizophrenic mothers. *Brit. J. Psychiat.*, **112**:819–825.

——— (1970). The genetics of schizophrenia and schizoid disease. *Science*, **167**:249–256.

Himmelhoch, J. M., Coble, P., Kupfer, D. J., and Ingenito, J. (1976). Agitated depression associated with severe hypomanic episodes: A rare syndrome. *Amer. J. Psychiat.*, **133**:765–771.

Himwich, H. E. (1971). Indoleamines and the depressions. In *Biochemistry, Schizophrenias and Affective Illnesses*. Baltimore: Williams and Wilkins, pp. 230–282.

Hirsch, S. R., and Leff, J. P. (1975). *Abnormalities in Parents of Schizophrenics*. London: Oxford University Press.

Hoch, P. H., and Cattell, J. P. (1959). The diagnosis of pseudoneurotic schizophrenia. *Psychiat. Q.*, **33**:17–43.

———, and Polatin, P. (1949). Pseudoneurotic forms of schizophrenia. *Psychiat. Q.*, **23**:248–276.

Hoffer, A., Osmond, H., and Sonythries, J. (1954). Schizophrenia: A new approach. *J. Ment. Sci.*, **100**:29–45.

Hollingshead, A. B., and Redlich, F. C. (1958). *Social Class and Mental Illness.* New York: John Wiley.

Holzman, P. S. (1975). Smooth-pursuit eye movements in schizophrenia: Recent findings. In Freedman, D. X. (Ed.), *Biology of the Major Psychoses.* New York: Raven Press, pp. 217–231.

———, Proctor, L. R., and Hughes, D. W. (1973). Eye-tracking patterns in schizophrenia. *Science,* **181**:179.

———, ———, Levy, D. L., Yasillo, N. J., Meltzer, H. Y., and Hurt, S. W. (1974). Eye-tracking dysfunctions in schizophrenic patients and their relatives. *Arch. Gen. Psychiat.,* **31**:143–151.

Hopkinson, G., and Ley, P. (1969). A genetic study of affective disorder. *Brit. J. Psychiat.,* **11**:917–922.

Horn, J. M., Green, M., Carney, R., and Erickson, M. T. (1975). Bias against genetic hypothesis in adoption studies. *Arch. Gen. Psychiat.,* **32**:1365–1367.

Hughes, J. R., and Schlagenhauff, R. E. (1961). Electroclinical correlation in temporal lobe epilepsy with emphasis on inter-areal analysis of the temporal lobe. *Electroencephalogr. Clin. Neurophys.,* **13**:333–339.

Inouye, E. (1961). Similarity and dissimilarity of schizophrenia in twins. *Proceedings Third Internat. Congr. Psychiat.,* **1**:524–530. Montreal: University of Toronto Press, 1963.

——— (1972). A search for a research framework of schizophrenia in twins and chromosomes. In Kaplan, A. R. (Ed.), *Genetic Factors in "Schizophrenia."* Springfield, Ill.: Charles C Thomas, pp. 495–503.

Ionescu-Tongyonk, J. (1978). Marginal depressive states and the borderline syndromes. *Thai Med. J.,* **2**:72–77.

Jablensky, A. (1976). Personality disorders and their relationship to illness and social deviance. *Psychiat. Annals,* **6**:375–386.

Jackson, D. D. (1960). A critique of the literature on the genetics of schizophrenia. In Jackson, D. D. (Ed.), *The Etiology of Schizophrenia.* New York: Basic Books, pp. 37–87.

Jacobson, E. (1953). Contribution to the metapsychology of cyclothymic depression. In Greenacre, P. (Ed.), *Affective Disorders.* New York: International Universities Press, pp. 49–83.

James, N. M. (1977). Early- and late-onset bipolar affective disorder. *Arch. Gen. Psychiat.,* **34**:715–717.

——— and Chapman, C. J. (1975). A genetic study of bipolar affective disorder. *Brit. J. Psychiat.,* **126**:449–456.

Janet, P. (1911). *L'Etat mental des hystériques.* Paris: Félix Alcan.

Johanson, E. (1964). Minor delusions. *Acta Psychiat. Scand.,* Supplementum **177**:1–100.

Johnson, G., Gershon, S., Burdock, E. I., Floyd, A., and Hekimian, L. (1971). Comparative effects of lithium and chlorpromazine in the treatment of acute manic states. *Brit. J. Psychiat.,* **119**:267–276.

Johnson, G. F. S., and Leeman, M. (1977). Analysis of familial factors in bipolar affective illness. *Arch. Gen. Psychiat.,* **34**:1074–1083.

Jones, J. E., Rodnick, F. H., Goldstein, M. J., McPherson, S. R., and West, K. L. (1977). Parental transactional style deviance as a possible indicator of risk for schizophrenia. *Arch. Gen. Psychiat.,* **34**:71–74.

Jones, M. B., and Offord, D. R. (1975). Independent transmission of IQ and schizophrenia. *Brit. J. Psychiat.,* **126**:185–190.

Jung, C. G. (1912). Wandlungen und Symbole der Libido. *Jahrbuch f. psychoanal. u. psychopath. Forsch.,* 3/4.

——— (1921). *Psychologische Typen.* Zurich: Rascher.

——— (1956). *Symbols of Transformation,* vol. 1 (Tr. R. F. C. Hull). New York: Harper.

Kales, A., Scharf, M., and Tan, T. L. (1970). Sleep laboratory and clinical studies of the effect of Tofranil, Valium and placebo on sleep stages and enuresis. *Psychophysiol.*, **7**:348–349.

Kallman, F. J. (1938). *The Genetics of Schizophrenia.* Locust Valley, N.Y.: J. J. Augustin.

——— (1946). The genetic theory of schizophrenia: An analysis of 691 schizophrenic twin index families. *Amer. J. Psychiat.*, **103**:309–322.

——— (1950). *Congrès International de Psychiatrie, Rapports,* **VI**:1–27. Paris: Hermann.

——— (1954). Genetic principles in manic-depressive psychosis. In Hoch, P. H., and Zubin, J. (Eds.), *Depression.* New York: Grune and Stratton, pp. 1–24.

Kanzer, M. (1957). Acting-out and its relation to the impulse disorders: Panel report. *J. Amer. Psychoanal. Assoc.*, **5**:136–145.

Kaplan, A. R. (1969). Chromosomes, mosaicism and schizophrenia. In Shankar, S. (Ed.), *Schizophrenia: Current Studies.* Hicksville, N.Y.: PJD Publications, pp. 322–335.

——— (1972). Genetics and schizophrenia. In Kaplan, A. R. (Ed.), *Genetic Factors in "Schizophrenia."* Springfield, Ill.: Charles C Thomas, pp. 555–578.

Karlsson, J. L. (1968). Genealogic studies of schizophrenia. In Rosenthal, D., and Kety, S. (Eds.), *Transmission of Schizophrenia.* Oxford: Pergamon Press, pp. 85–94.

——— (1972). A two-locus hypothesis for inheritance of schizophrenia. In Kaplan, A. R. (Ed.), *Genetic Factors in "Schizophrenia."* Springfield, Ill.: Charles C Thomas, pp. 246–255.

——— (1973). An Icelandic family study of schizophrenia. *Brit. J. Psychiat.*, **123**:549–554.

——— (1974). Inheritance of schizophrenia. *Acta Psychiat. Scand.*, Supplementum **247**:1–108.

Kasanin, J. (1933). Acute schizoaffective psychoses. *Amer. J. Psychiat.*, **97**:97–120.

Katan, M. (1953). Mania and the pleasure principle. In Greenacre, P. (Ed.), *Affective Disorders.* New York: International Universities Press, pp. 140–190.

Kay, D. W. K., Atkinson, M. W., Stephens, D. A., Roth, M., and Garside, R. F. (1975). Genetic hypotheses and environmental factors in the light of psychiatric morbidity in the families of schizophrenics. *Brit. J. Psychiat.*, **127**:109–118.

Keith, S. J., Gunderson, J. G., Reifman, A., Buchsbaum, S., and Mosher, L. R. (1976). Special report: Schizophrenia—1976. *Schizophrenia Bull.*, **2**:509–565.

Kendell, R. E. (1975). Schizophrenia: The remedy for diagnostic confusion. In Silverstone, T., and Barraclough, B. (Eds.), *Brit. J. of Psychiatry Special Publication No. 9: Contemporary Psychiatry.* Ashford, Kent: Headley Bros., pp. 11–17.

——— (1975a). *The Role of Diagnosis in Psychiatry.* Oxford: Blackwell Scientific Publications.

———, and Gourlay, J. (1970). The clinical distinctions between the affective psychoses and schizophrenia. *Brit. J. Psychiat.*, **117**:261–266.

Kernberg, O. F. (1967). Borderline Personality Organization. *J. Amer. Psychoanal. Assoc.*, **15**:641–685.

——— (1970). A psychoanalytic classification of character pathology. *J. Amer. Psychoanal. Assoc.*, **18**:800–822.

——— (1971). Prognostic considerations regarding borderline personality organization. *J. Amer. Psychoanal. Assoc.*, **19**:595–635.

——— (1974). Further contributions to the treatment of narcissistic personalities. *Int. J. Psycho-Anal.*, **55**:215–240.

——— (1975). *Borderline Conditions and Pathological Narcissism.* New York: Jason Aronson.

——— (1976). The diagnosis of borderline conditions in adolescence. Presented at the Eastern Seaboard Regional Meeting, American Society for Adolescent Psychiatry, Washington, D.C., Oct. 8.

——— (1976a). The structural diagnosis of borderline personality organization. Presented at the International Conference on Borderline Disorders, Topeka, Kans., Mar. 18.

——— (1977). The structural diagnosis of borderline personality organization. In Hartocollis,

P. (Ed.), *Borderline Personality Disorders*. New York: International Universities Press, pp. 87–121.

———, Burstein, E. D., Coyne, L., Appelbaum, A., Horwitz, L., and Voth, H. (1972). Psychotherapy and psychoanalysis: Final report of the Menninger Foundation's psychotherapy research project. *Bull. Menninger Clin.*, **36** (1/2): 1–274.

———, and Goldstein, E. (1975). A diagnostic study of borderline personality disorder. Unpublished grant proposal.

Kestenbaum, C. J. (1977). Psychotherapy of childhood schizophrenia. In Wolman, B., Egan, J., and Ross, A. (Eds.), *Handbook of Treatment of Mental Disorders in Childhood and Adolescence*. Englewood Cliffs, N.J.: Prentice-Hall.

——— (1979). Children at risk for manic-depressive illness. *Amer. J. Psychiat.* (in press).

———, and Bird, H. L. (1978). A reliability study of the Mental Health Assessment Form for school-age children. *J. Amer. Acad. Child Psychiat.*, **17**:338–347.

Kety, S. S. (1975). Progress toward an understanding of the biological substrates of schizophrenia. In Fieve, R. R., Rosenthal, D., and Brill, H. (Eds.), *Genetic Research in Psychiatry*. Baltimore: Johns Hopkins Press, pp. 15–26.

——— (1976). Genetic aspects of schizophrenia. *Psychiat. Annals*, **6**:11–32.

——— (1976a). Studies designed to disentangle genetic and environmental variables in schizophrenia: Some epistemological questions and answers. *Amer. J. Psychiat.*, **133**:1134–1137.

———, Rosenthal, D., Wender, P. H., and Schulsinger, F. (1968). Mental illness in the biological and adoptive families of adopted schizophrenics. In Rosenthal, D., and Kety, S. (Eds.), *Transmission of Schizophrenia*. Oxford: Pergamon Press, pp. 345–362.

———, ———, ———, and ——— (1971). Mental illness in the biological and adoptive families of adopted schizophrenics. *Amer. J. Psychiat.*, **128**:302–306.

Klein, D. F. (1967). Importance of psychiatric diagnosis in prediction of clinical drug effects. *Arch. Gen. Psychiat.*, **16**:118–126.

——— (1972). Drug therapy as a means of syndromal identification and nosological revision. In Cole, J. O., Freedman. A. M., and Friedhoff, A. J. (Eds.), *Psychopathology and Psychopharmacology*. Baltimore: Johns Hopkins Press, pp. 143–160.

——— (1975). Psychopharmacology and the borderline patient. In Mack, J. E. (Ed.), *Borderline States in Psychiatry*. New York: Grune and Stratton, pp. 75–92.

———, and Davis, J. (1969). *Drug Treatment and Psychodiagnosis*. Baltimore: William and Wilkins.

Klein, M. (1935). A contribution to the psychogenesis of manic-depressive states. In *Contributions to Psychoanalysis, 1921–1945*. London: Hogarth Press, 1948.

——— (1952). Notes on some schizoid mechanisms. In Riviere, J. (Ed.), *Developments in Psychoanalysis*. London: Hogarth Press, pp. 292–320.

——— (1960). *The Psychoanalysis of Children*. New York: Grove Press.

Knight, R. P. (1953). Borderline states. *Bull. Menninger Clin.*, **17**:1–12.

——— (1954). Management and psychotherapy of the borderline schizophrenic patient. In Knight, R. P., and Friedman, C. R. (Eds.), *Psychoanalytic Psychiatry and Psychology*. New York: International Universities Press, pp. 110–122.

Kohn, M. (1973). Social class and schizophrenia. *Schizophrenia Bull.*, no. 7: 60–79.

Kohut, H. (1971). *The Analysis of the Self.* New York: International Universities Press.

Kolata, G. B. (1977). Catastrophe theory: The emperor has no clothes. *Science*, **196**:287.

Kolb, L. C. (1973). *Modern Clinical Psychiatry* (8th ed.). Philadelphia: W. B. Saunders.

Kraepelin. E. (1896). *Psychiatrie: Ein Lehrbuch für Studierende und Aerzte*. Leipzig: Barth.

——— (1905). *Einfuehrung in die Psychiatrische Klinik* (2nd ed.). Leipzig: Barth.

——— (1921). *Manic-Depressive Insanity and Paranoia*. Edinburgh: E. and S. Livingstone.

——— (1925). *Dementia Praecox and Paraphrenia*. Edinburgh: E. and S. Livingstone.

Kretschmer, E. (1948). *Korperbau und Charakter*. Berlin: Springer-Verlag OHG.

Kringlen, E. (1968). An epidemiological-clinical twin study on schizophrenia. In Rosenthal, D., and Kety, S. (Eds.), *Transmission of Schizophrenia*. Oxford: Pergamon Press, pp. 49–63.

——— (1968a). *Heredity and Environment in the Functional Psychoses*. Oslo: Universitetsforlaget.

——— (1975). A multifactorial view of schizophrenia. In Lader, M. H. (Ed.), *Brit. J. of Psychiatry Special Publication No. 10: Studies of Schizophrenia*. Ashford, Kent: Headley Bros., pp. 42–47.

Kripke, D. F., Mullaney, D. J., Atkinson, M., and Wolf, S. (1978). Circadian rhythm disorders in manic-depressives. *Biol. Psychiat.*, **13**:335–351.

Kupfer, D. J. (1967). REM Latency: A psychobiologic marker for primary depressive disease. *Biol. Psychiat.*, **11**:159–174.

———, and Bowers, M. D. (1972). REM sleep and central monoamine oxidase inhibition. *Psychopharmacologia*, **27**:183–190.

———, and Foster, F. G. (1972). Interval between onset of sleep and R.E.M. sleep as an indicator of depression. *Lancet*, **2**:684.

Langfeldt, G. (1937). The prognosis in schizophrenia and the factors influencing the course of the disease. *Acta Psychiat. Scand.*, Supplementum **13**.

——— (1969). Diagnosis and prognosis of schizophrenia. *Proc. Royal Soc. Med.*, **53**:1047–1052.

Leonhard, K. (1934). Atypische endogene Psychosen im Lichte der Familienforschung. *Z. Ges. Neurol. Psychiat.*, **149**:520–562.

——— (1963). Die Temperamente in den Familien der monopolaren euphorischen Psychosen. *Psychiat. Neurol. u. Med. Psychol.*, **15**:203–206.

———, Korff, I., and Schulz, H. (1962). Die Temperamente in den Familien der monopolaren und bipolaren phasischen Psychosen. *Psychiat. Neurol.*, **143**:416–434.

Lesse, S. (1970). *Anxiety: Its Components, Development and Treatment*. New York: Grune and Stratton.

——— (1974). *Masked Depression*. New York: Jason Aronson.

Levitt, M., and Mendlewicz, J. (1975). A genetic study of plasma dopamine-β-hydroxylase in affective disorder. In Mendlewicz, J. (Ed.), *Genetics and Psychopharmacology*. Basel: S. Karger, pp. 89–98.

Lewis, A. (1968). Perception of self in borderline states. *Amer. J. Psychiat.*, **124**:1491–1498.

Lewis, D. O., and Shanok, S. S. (1978). Delinquency and the schizophrenic spectrum of disorders. *J. Amer. Acad. Child Psychiat.*, **17**:263–276.

Lewis, N. D. C., and Piotrowski, Z. A. (1954). Clinical diagnosis of manic-depressive psychosis. In Hoch, P. H., and Zubin, J. (Eds.), *Depression*. New York: Grune and Stratton, pp. 25–38.

Lichtenberg, J. D. (1978). Is there a line of development of narcissism? *Int. Rev. Psycho-Anal.*, **5**:435–447.

Lidz, T., Fleck, S., and Cornelison, A. (1965). *Schizophrenia and the Family*. New York: International Universities Press.

Liebowitz, M. R. (1979). Is borderline a distinct entity? *Schizophrenia Bull.*, **5**:23–38.

Lilliston, L. (1973). Schizophrenic symptomatology as a function of probability of cerebral damage. *J. Abnorm. Psychol.*, **82**:377–381.

Lipkin, K. M., Dyrud, J., and Meyer, G. G. (1970). The many faces of mania. *Arch. Gen. Psychiat.*, **22**:262–267.

Lombroso, C. (1876). *L'uomo delinquente in rapporto alla antropologio, alla giurisprudenza ed alle discipline carcerarie*. Rome: Fratelli Bocca.

——— (1880). Claustrophobia e claustrofilia. *Archivio d. Psi., Antrop.*, **1**:37 ff.; 176 ff.

Loranger, A. W. (1975). X-linkage and manic-depressive illness. *Brit. J. Psychiat.,* **127**:482–488.

Lorr, M., and Klett, C. J. (1969). Psychotic syndromes across cultures. *J. Abnorm. Psychol.,* **74**:531–543.

Luborsky, L. (1962). Clinicians' judgments of mental health. *Arch. Gen. Psychiat.,* **7**:407–417.

Luxenburger, H. (1928). Vorläufiger Bericht ueber psychiatrische Serienuntersuchungen an Zwillingen. *Z. Ges. Neurol. Psychiat.,* **116**:297–326.

Lynch, H. T., Cohen, L., Kaplan, A. R., and Lynch, J. (1972). Report on a pair of male monozygotic twins concordant for schizophrenia. *Acta Genet. Med. Gemellol.,* **21**:99–106.

Maas, J. W., Fawcett, J., and Dekirmenjian, H. (1968). 3-Methoxy-4-hydroxy phenylglycol (MHPG) excretion in depressive states. *Arch. Gen. Psychiat.,* **19**:129–134.

Mack, J. E. (Ed.) (1975). *Borderline States in Psychiatry.* New York: Grune and Stratton.

MacKinnon, R. A., and Michels, R. (1971). *The Psychiatric Interview in Clinical Practice.* Philadelphia: W. B. Saunders.

MacMahon, B. (1968). Gene-environment interaction in human disease. In Rosenthal, D., and Kety, S. (Eds.), *Transmission of Schizophrenia.* Oxford: Pergamon Press, pp. 393–402.

Mahler, M. S. (1968). *On Human Symbiosis and the Vicissitudes of Individuation.* New York: International Universities Press.

——— (1971). A study of the separation-individuation process, and its possible application to borderline phenomena in the psychoanalytic situation. *Psychoanal. Study of the Child,* **26**:403–424.

——— (1972). On the first three subphases of the separation-individuation process. *Int. J. Psycho-Anal.,* **53**:333–338.

Malek-Ahmadi, P., and Fried, F. E. (1976). Biochemical correlates of schizophrenia. *Comprehen. Psychiat.,* **17**:499–509.

Maricq, H. R. (1975). A two-gene model for schizophrenia with the possibility to detect carriers of the modifier gene. *Acta Psychiat. Scand.,* **52**:264–282.

———, and Jones, M. B. (1976). Visibility of the nailfold plexus and heredity. *Biol. Psychiat.,* **11**:205–215.

Masterson, J. F. (1971). Treatment of the adolescent with borderline syndrome: A problem in separation-individuation. *Bull. Menninger Clin.,* **35**:5–18.

———, and Rinsley, D. B. (1975). The borderline syndrome: The role of the mother in the genesis and psychic structure of the borderline personality. *Int. J. Psycho-Anal.,* **56**:163–177.

Matte Blanco, I. (1976). Basic logico-mathematical structures in schizophrenia. In Kemali, D., Bartholini, G., and Richter, D. (Eds.), *Schizophrenia Today.* Oxford: Pergamon Press, pp. 211–233.

Matthysse, S. W. (1976). Theoretical commentary on Gottesman and Shields' review. *Schizophrenia Bull.,* **2**:445–446.

——— (1977). Etiological diversity of the psychoses. Lecture at the New York State Psychiatric Institute, Sept. 23.

———, and Baldessarini, R. J. (1972). S-adenosylmethionine and catechol-O-methyltransferase in schizophrenia. *Amer. J. Psychiat.,* **128**:1310–1312.

———, and Kidd, K. (1976). Estimating the genetic contribution to schizophrenia. *Amer. J. Psychiat.,* **133**:185–191.

May, P. R. A. (1968). *Treatment of Schizophrenia.* New York: Science House.

McCabe, M. S. (1975). Reactive psychoses: A clinical and genetic investigation. *Acta Psychiat. Scand.,* Supplementum **259**:1–133.

———, Fowler, R. W., Cadoret, R. J., and Winokur, G. (1971). Familial differences in schizophrenia with good and poor prognosis. *Psychosom. Med.,* **33**:326–332.

———, ———, ———, and ——— (1972). Symptom differences in schizophrenia with good prognosis. *Amer. J. Psychiat.,* **128**:1239–1243.

———, and Strömgren, E. (1975). Reactive psychoses. *Arch. Gen. Psychiat.*, **32**:447–454.

McClure, J. N., Jr., Reich, T., and Wetzel, R. (1971). Premenstrual symptoms as an indicator of bipolar affective disorder. *Brit. J. Psychiat.*, **119**:527–528.

McCully, R. S. (1962). Certain theoretical considerations in relation to borderline schizophrenia and the Rorschach. *J. Projective Tech.*, **26**:404–418.

McGaffin, C. G. (1911). A manic-depressive family—A study in heredity. *Amer. J. Insanity,* **68**:263–269.

McGlashan, T. H., and Carpenter, W. T., Jr. (1976). An investigation of the postpsychotic depressive syndrome. *Amer. J. Psychiat.*, **133**:14–19.

McKnew, D. H., Cytryn, L., and White, I. (1974). Clinical and biochemical correlates of hypomania in a child. *J. Amer. Acad. Child Psychiat.*, **13**:576–585.

McKusick, V. A. (1973). The nosology of genetic disease. In McKusick, V. A., and Claiborne, R. (Eds.), *Medical Genetics*. New York: H. P. Publishing Co., pp. 211–219.

Meares, R., and Horvath, T. (1973). A physiological difference between hallucinosis and schizophrenia. *Brit. J. Psychiat.*, **122**:687–688.

Mednick, S., and Schulsinger, F. (1968). Some premorbid characteristics related to breakdown in children with schizophrenic mothers. In Rosenthal, D., and Kety, S. S. (Eds.), *The Transmission of Schizophrenia*. Oxford: Pergamon Press, pp. 267–291.

Meehl, P. E. (1972). A critical afterword. In Gottesman, I. I., and Shields, J. (Eds.), *Schizophrenia and Genetics*. New York: Academic Press, pp. 367–415.

Meissner, W. W. (1978). Notes on some conceptual aspects of borderline personality organization. *Int. Rev. Psycho-Anal.*, **5**:297–312.

Melamud, N. (1967). Psychiatric disorder with intracranial tumors of the limbic system. *Arch. Neurol.,* **17**:113–124.

Meltzer, H. Y., and Stahl, S. M. (1976). The dopamine hypothesis of schizophrenia: A review. *Schizophrenia Bull.,* **2**:19–76.

Mendlewicz, J. (1974). A genetic contribution toward an understanding of affective equivalents. In Lesse, S. (Ed.), *Masked Depression.* New York: Jason Aronson, pp. 41–52.

———, Fieve, R. R., and Stallone, F. (1973). Relationship between the effectiveness of lithium therapy and family history. *Amer. J. Psychiat.,* **130**:1011–1013.

———, Fleiss, J. L., and Fieve, R. R. (1972). Evidence for X-linkage in the transmission of manic-depressive illness. *J.A.M.A.*, **222**:1624–1627.

———, ———, and ——— (1975). Linkage studies in affective disorders: The Xg blood group and manic-depressive illness. In Fieve, R. R., Rosenthal, D., and Brill, H. (Eds.), *Genetic Research in Psychiatry*. Baltimore: Johns Hopkins Press, pp. 219–232.

———, and Stallone, F. (1975). Genetic factors and lithium response in manic-depressive illness. In Mendlewicz, J. (Ed.), *Genetics and Psychopharmacology (Mod. Probl. Pharmacopsych.,* vol. 10). Basel: Karger, pp. 23–29.

Mirsky, I. A. (1958). Physiologic, psychological and social determinants in the etiology of duodenal ulcer. *Amer. J. Digestive Dis.*, **3**:285–314.

Mitsuda, H. (1962). The concept of atypical psychoses from the aspect of clinical genetics. *Folia Psychiat.* (Japan), **16**:214–221.

——— (1965). The concept of "atypical psychosis" from the aspect of clinical genetics. *Acta Psychiat. Scand.*, **41**:372–379.

——— (1967). *Clinical Genetics in Psychiatry*. Osaka, Japan.

——— (1972). Heterogeneity of schizophrenia. In Kaplan, A. R. (Ed.), *Genetic Factors in "Schizophrenia."* Springfield, Ill.: Charles C Thomas, pp. 276–293.

Modell, A. (1963). Primitive object relationships and the predisposition to schizophrenia. *Int. J. Psycho-Anal.*, **44**:282–292.

Moore, T. V. (1921). The parataxes: A study and analysis of certain borderline mental states. *Psychoanal. Rev.*, **8**:252–283.

Moreau de Tours, J. J. (1852). Observations on hereditary influences. Reported in *Amer. J. Insanity,* **9**:79. (Review of the *Gazette des Hopitaux* for Dec. 21, 1851.)

Morel, M. (1860). *Traité des maladies mentales* (2nd ed.). Paris: Masson.

Morgan, D. W., Porzio, R. J., and Hedlund, J. L. (1968). Schizophrenic symptom change with rehospitalization. *Arch. Gen. Psychiat.,* **19**:227–231.

Morrison, J. R., Clancy, J., and Crowe, R. (1972). The Iowa 500: I. Diagnostic validity in mania, depression and schizophrenia. *Arch. Gen. Psychiat.,* **27**:457–461.

———, and Minkoff, K. (1975). Explosive personality as a sequel to the hyperactive-child syndrome. *Comprehen. Psychiat.,* **16**:343–348.

———, Winokur, G., Crowe, R., and Clancy, J. (1973). The Iowa 500: The first follow-up. *Arch. Gen. Psychiat.,* **29**:678–682.

Mosher, L. R., and Gunderson, J. G. (1973). Special report: Schizophrenia. *Schizophrenia Bull.,* no. 7:12–52.

Moyer, K. E. (1974). Sex differences in aggression. In Friedman, R. C., Richard, R. M., and VandeWiele, R. L. (Eds.), *Sex Differences in Behavior.* New York: John Wiley, pp. 335–372.

Murphy, D. L., and Beigel, A. (1974). Depression, elation and lithium carbonate responses in manic patient subgroups. *Arch. Gen. Psychiat.,* **31**:643–648.

———, Brodie, H. K. H., and Goodwin, F. K. (1971). Regular induction of hypomania by L-DOPA in "bipolar" manic-depressive patients. *Nature,* **229**:135.

———, Donnelly, C. H., Miller, L., and Wyatt, R. J. (1976). Platelet monoamine oxidase in chronic schizophrenia. *Arch. Gen. Psychiat.,* **33**:1377–1381.

———, and Weiss, R. (1972). Reduced monoamine oxidase activity in blood platelets from bipolar depressed patients. *Amer. J. Psychiat.,* **128**:1351–1357.

———, and Wyatt, R. J. (1972). Reduced monoamine oxidase activity in blood platelets from schizophrenic patients. *Nature,* **238**:225–226.

———, and ——— (1975). Neurotransmitter-related enzymes in the major psychiatric disorders: I. Catechol-O-methyltransferase, monoamine oxidase in the affective disorders, and factors affecting some behaviorally correlated enzyme activities. In Freedman, D. X. (Ed.), *Biology of the Major Psychoses.* New York: Raven Press, pp. 277–288.

Nadzharov, R. A. (1972). Course forms. In Snezhnevsky, A. V. (Ed.), *Schizophrenia.* Moscow: Meditsina, pp. 16–76.

Noble, D. (1951). A study of dreams in schizophrenia and allied states. *Amer. J. Psychiat.,* **107**:612–616.

Nunberg, H. (1932). *Principles of Psychoanalysis.* New York: International Universities Press, 1955.

Oberndorf, C. P. (1930). The psychoanalysis of borderline cases. *N.Y.S.J. Med.,* **30**:648–651.

Ødegaard, O. (1963). The psychiatric disease entities in the light of genetic investigation. *Acta Psychiat. Scand.,* Supplementum **169**:94–104.

——— (1972). The multifactorial theory of inheritance in predisposition to schizophrenia. In Kaplan, A. R. (Ed.), *Genetic Factors in "Schizophrenia."* Springfield, Ill.: Charles C Thomas, pp. 256–275.

Offord, D. R., and Cross, L. A. (1969). Behavioral antecedents of adult schizophrenia. *Arch. Gen. Psychiat.,* **21**:267–283.

Ollerenshaw, D. P. (1973). The classification of the functional psychoses. *Brit. J. Psychiat.,* **122**:517–530.

Omenn, G. S. (1975). Alcoholism: A pharmacogenetic disorder. In Mendlewicz, J. (Ed.), *Genetics and Psychopharmacology (Mod. Probl. Pharmacopsych.,* vol. 10). Basel: Karger, pp. 12–22.

Ornitz, E. M., Brown, M. B., Mason, A., and Putnam, N. H. (1974). Effect of visual input on vestibular nystagmus in autistic children. *Arch. Gen. Psychiat.,* **31**:369–375.

Osmond, H., and Smythies, J. (1952). Schizophrenia: A new approach. *J. Ment. Sci.,* **98**:309–315.

Overall, J. E., Hollister, L. E., and Pichot, P. (1967). Major psychiatric disorders: A four-dimensional model. *Arch. Gen. Psychiat.*, **16**:146–151.

Owen, F., Bourne, R., Crow, T. J., Johnstone, E. C., Bailey, A. R., and Hershon, H. I. (1976). Platelet and monoamine oxidase in schizophrenia. *Arch. Gen. Psychiat.*, **33**:1370–1373.

Palmer, J. D. (1975). Biologic clocks of the tidal zone. *Scient. Amer.*, **232**:70–80.

Pandey, G. N., Garver, D. L., Tamminga, C., Ericksen, S., Ali, S. I., and Davis, J. M. (1977). Postsynaptic supersensitivity in schizophrenia. *Amer. J. Psychiat.*, **134**:518–522.

Pardue, L. H. (1975). Familial unipolar depressive illness: A pedigree study. *Amer. J. Psychiat.*, **132**:970–972.

Pauleikhoff, B. (1974). Psychopathological classification of the atypical psychoses. In Mitsuda, H., and Fukuda, T., (Eds.), *Biological Mechanisms of Schizophrenia and Schizophrenia-like Psychoses*. Tokyo: Igaku Shogun, pp. 272–277.

Payne, R. W., and Hewlett, J. H. G. (1960). Thought disorder in psychotic patients. In Eysenck, H. J. (Ed.), *Experiments in Personality*, vol. 2. New York: Frederick A. Praeger, p. 223.

Peck, R. E. (1962). Circumstantial schizophrenia. *Psychiat. Q.*, **30**:655–664.

Perris, C. (1966). A study of bipolar (manic-depressive) and unipolar recurrent depressive psychoses. *Acta Psychiat. Scand.*, Supplementum **194**:1–189.

Perry, J. C., and Klerman, G. L. (1978). The borderline patient. *Arch. Gen. Psychiat.*, **35**:141–150.

Peterfreund, E. (1971). Information, systems, and psychoanalysis. *Psychol. Issues*, monograph 25/26. New York: International Universities Press.

Pétrement, S. (1976). *Simone Weil: A Life*. New York: Pantheon Books.

Pfeiffer, E. (1974). Borderline states. *Dis. Nerv. Syst.*, **35**:212–219.

Pinel, P. (1806). *A Treatise on Insanity* (Tr. D. Davis). New York: Hafner (1962), facsimile edition.

Pines, M. (1976). Genetic profiles will put our health in our own hands. *Smithsonian*, **7**:86–90.

Planansky, K. (1972). Phenotypic boundaries and genetic specificity in schizophrenia. In Kaplan, A. R. (Ed.), *Genetic Factors in "Schizophrenia."* Springfield, Ill.: Charles C Thomas, pp. 141–172.

Pollack, M. (1960). Comparison of childhood, adolescent and adult schizophrenics. *Arch. Gen. Psychiat.*, **2**:652–660.

Pollin, W. (1971). A possible genetic factor related to psychosis. *Amer. J. Psychiat.*, **128**:311–317.

———, Allen, M. G., Hoffer, A., Stabenau, J. R., and Hrubec, Z. (1969). Psychopathology in 15,909 pairs of veteran twins: Evidence for a genetic factor in the pathogenesis of schizophrenia and its relative absence in psychoneurosis. *Amer. J. Psychiat.*, **126**:597–610.

———, Stabenau, J. R., and Tupin, J. (1965). Family studies with identical twins discordant for schizophrenia. *Psychiatry*, **28**:60–78.

Pope, H. G., Jr. (1976). From schizophrenia to affective illness: A question of diagnosis. *McLean Hosp. J.*, **1**:108–117.

———, and Lipinski, J. F. (1978). Diagnosis in schizophrenia and manic-depressive illness. *Arch. Gen. Psychiat.*, **35**:811–828.

Post, R. M., Fink, E., Carpenter, W. T., Jr., and Goodwin, F. K. (1975). Cerebrospinal fluid amine metabolites in acute schizophrenia. *Arch. Gen. Psychiat.*, **32**:1063–1069.

Price, J. S. (1972). Genetic and phylogenetic aspects of mood variation. *Int. J. Mental Health*, **1**:124–144.

——— (1975). Genetics of affective illness. In Silverstone, T., and Barraclough, B. (Eds.), *Brit. J. of Psychiatry, Special Publication No. 9: Contemporary Psychiatry*. Ashford, Kent: Headley Bros., pp. 67–75.

Prichard, J. C. (1835). *A Treatise on Insanity*. London: Sherwood, Gilbert and Piper.

Procci, W. R. (1976). Schizo-affective psychosis: Fact or fiction? *Arch. Gen. Psychiat.,* **33**:1167–1178.

Pull, C., Pichot, P., Overall, J. E., and Pull, M. C. (1976). Validations conceptuelle d'une classification psychiatrique syndromique. *Ann. Méd. Psychol.,* **2**:353–370.

Quitkin, F., Rifkin, A., and Klein, D. F. (1976). Neurologic soft signs in schizophrenia and character disorders. *Arch. Gen. Psychiat.,* **33**:845–853.

———, ———, and ——— (1978). Imipramine response in deluded depressive patients. *Amer. J. Psychiat.,* **135**:806–811.

Rado, S. (1956). *Psychoanalysis of Behavior: Collected Papers.* New York: Grune and Stratton.

——— (1962). Theory and therapy: The theory of schizotypal organization and its application to the treatment of decompensated schizotypal behavior. In *Psychoanalysis of Behavior, Collected Papers,* vol. 2. New York: Grune and Stratton, pp. 127–140.

Rainer, J. D. (1972). The contributions of genetics to problems of nosology and interrelationship in psychiatry. *Int. J. Mental Health,* **1**:28–41.

Rangell, L. (1955). The borderline case: Panel report. *J. Amer. Psychoanal. Assoc.,* **3**:285–298.

Rapaport, D. (1957). Cognitive structures. In *Contemporary Approaches to Cognition.* Cambridge, Mass.: Harvard University Press, pp. 157–200.

———, Gill, M. M., and Schafer, R. (1945–1946). *Diagnostic Psychological Testing* (2 vols.). Chicago: Year Book Publishers.

———, and ——— (1959). The points of view and assumptions of metapsychology. *Int. J. Psycho-Anal.,* **40**:153–162.

Raskin, E. E. (1975). Bleuler and schizophrenia. *Brit. J. Psychiat.,* **127**:231–234.

Raymond, F., and Janet, P. (1903). *Les Obsessions et la psychasthenie.* Paris: Félix Alcan.

Reed, S. C., Hartley, C., Anderson, V. E., Phillips, V. P., and Johnson, N. A. (1973). *The Psychoses: Family Studies.* Philadelphia: W. B. Saunders.

Reich, T., Cloninger, R., and Guze, S. B. (1975). The multifactorial model of disease transmission: I. Description of the model and its use in psychiatry. *Brit. J. Psychiat.,* **127**:1–10.

Reich, Walter (1975). The spectrum concept of schizophrenia. *Arch. Gen. Psychiat.,* **32**:489–498.

Reich, Wilhelm (1925). *Der Triebhafte Charakter.* Leipzig: Internationaler Psychoanalytischer Verlag.

——— (1949). *Character Analysis* (3rd ed.). New York: Farrar, Straus and Giroux.

Reilly, F., Harrow, M., Tucker, G., Quinlan, D., and Siegel, A. (1975). Looseness of associations in acute schizophrenia. *Brit. J. Psychiat.,* **127**:240–246.

Reis, D. J. (1974). Consideration of some problems encountered in relating specific neurotransmitters to specific behaviors or disease. *J. Psychiat. Res.,* **11**:145–148.

Reiser, D. E., and Willett, A. B. (1976). A favorable response to lithium carbonate in a "schizo-affective" father and son. *Amer. J. Psychiat.,* **133**:824–827.

Rickarby, G. A. (1977). Four cases of mania associated with bereavement. *J. Nerv. Ment. Dis.,* **165**:255–262.

Rieder, R. O. (1974). The origin of our confusion about schizophrenia. *Psychiatry,* **37**:197–208.

———, Rosenthal, D., Wender, P., and Blumenthal, H. (1975). The offspring of schizophrenics: Fetal and neonatal deaths. *Arch. Gen. Psychiat.,* **32**:200–211.

Rifkin, A., Levitan, S. J., Galewski, J., and Klein, D. F. (1972). Emotionally unstable character disorder: A follow-up study, I. Description of patients and outcome. *Biol. Psychiat.,* **4**:65–79.

———, Quitkin, F., Carillo, C., Blumberg, A. G., and Klein, D. F. (1972). Lithium carbonate in emotionally unstable character disorders. *Arch. Gen. Psychiat.,* **27**:519–523.

Rimon, R., Roos, B. E., Räkkölaiken, V., and Alanen, Y. (1971). The content of 5-hydroxyindoleacetic acid and homovanillic acid in the C.S.F. of patients with acute schizophrenia. *J. Psychosom. Res.,* **15**:375–378.

Rinsley, D. B. (1972). A contribution to the nosology and dynamics of adolescent schizophrenia. *Psychiat. Q.,* **46**:159–186.

——— (1978). Borderline psychopathology: A review of aetiology, dynamics and treatment. *Int. Rev. Psycho-Anal.,* **5**:45–54.

——— (1978a). Borderline and narcissistic disorders: Clinical and developmental aspects. Unpublished manuscript.

Robins, E. (1976). Categories versus dimensions in psychiatric classification. *Psychiat. Annals,* **6**(8):39–55.

Rochester, S. R., Martin, J. R., and Thurston, S. (1977). Thought-process disorder in schizophrenia: The listener's task. *Brain & Language,* **4**:95–114.

Roemer, R. A., Shagass, C., Staumanis, J. J., and Amadeo, M. (1977). Pattern evoked potential measurements suggesting lateralized hemispheric dysfunction in chronic schizophrenics. Presented at the thirty-second annual meeting of the Society of Biologic Psychiatry, Toronto, Apr. 29.

Rorschach, H. (1951). *Psychodiagnostics* (5th ed.). New York: Grune and Stratton.

Rosanoff, A. J., Handy, L. M., Plesset, I. R., and Brush, S. (1934). The etiology of so-called schizophrenic psychoses with special reference to their occurrence in twins. *Amer. J. Psychiat.,* **91**:247–286.

———, ———, and ——— (1935). The etiology of manic depressive syndromes with special reference to their occurrence in twins. *Amer. J. Psychiat.,* **91**:725–762.

———, and Orr, F. I. (1911). A study of heredity in insanity in the light of the Mendelian theory. *Amer. J. Insanity,* **68**:221–261.

Rosen, J. N. (1947). The treatment of schizophrenic psychosis by direct analytic therapy. *Psychiat. Q.,* **21**:3–37.

Rosenthal, D. (Ed.) (1963). *The Genain Quadruplets.* New York: Basic Books.

——— (1970). *Genetic Theory and Abnormal Behavior.* New York: McGraw-Hill.

——— (1971). A program of research on heredity in schizophrenia. *Behav. Sci.,* **16**:191–201.

——— (1972). Three adoption studies of heredity in the schizophrenic disorders. *Int. J. Mental Health,* **1**:63–75.

——— (1975). The concept of subschizophrenic disorders. In Fieve, R. R., Rosenthal, D., and Brill, H. (Eds.), *Genetic Research in Psychiatry.* Baltimore: Johns Hopkins Press, pp. 199–208.

——— (1975a). The spectrum concept in schizophrenic and manic-depressive disorders. In Freedman, D. X. (Ed.), *Biology of the Major Psychoses.* New York: Raven Press, pp. 19–25.

———, and Van Dyke, J. (1970). The use of monozygotic twins discordant as to schizophrenia in the search for an inherited characterological defect. *Acta Psychiat. Scand.,* Supplementum **219**:183–189.

———, Wender, P. H., Kety, S. S., Schulsinger, F., Welner, J., and Østergaard, L. (1968). Schizophrenics' offspring reared in adoptive homes. In Rosenthal, D., and Kety, S. S. (Eds.), *The Transmission of Schizophrenia.* Oxford: Pergamon Press, pp. 371–391.

———, ———, ———, Welner, J., and Schulsinger, F. (1971). The adopted-away offspring of schizophrenics. *Amer. J. Psychiat.,* **128**:307–311.

Rotrosen, J., Angrist, B. M., Gershon, S., Sachar, E. J., and Halpern, F. S. (1976). Dopamine receptor alteration in schizophrenia: Neuroendocrine evidence. *Psychopharmacology,* **51**:1–7.

Rubin, L. S., and Barry, T. J. (1976). Amplitude of pupillary contraction as a function of intensity of illumination in schizophrenia. *Biol. Psychiat.,* **11**:267–282.

Rüdin, E. (1916). *Zur Vererbung und Neuenstehung der Dementia Praecox.* Berlin: Springer-Verlag OHG.

——— (1923). Ueber Vererbung geistiger Stoerungen. *Z. Ges. Neurol. Psychiat.,* **81**:459–496.

Rush, B. (1812). *Medical Inquiries and Observations upon the Diseases of the Mind.* Philadelphia: Kimber and Richardson.

Sachar, E. J. (1975). Evidence for neuroendocrine abnormalities in the major mental illnesses. In Freedman, D. X. (Ed.), *Biology of the Major Psychoses.* New York: Raven Press, pp. 347–358.

———, Finkelstein, J., and Hellman, L. (1971). Growth hormone and responses in depressive illness: Response to insulin tolerance test. *Arch. Gen. Psychiat.,* **24**:263–269.

Sacks, M. H., Carpenter, W. T., Jr., and Strauss, J. S. (1974). Recovery from delusions. *Arch. Gen. Psychiat.,* **30**:117–120.

Salzinger, K., Portnoy, S., and Feldman, R. S. (1964). Verbal behavior of schizophrenic and normal subjects. *Ann. N. Y. Acad. Sci.,* **105**:845–860.

———, ———, and ——— (1966). Verbal behavior in schizophrenics and some comments toward a theory of schizophrenia. In Hoch, P., and Zubin, J. (Eds.), *Psychopathology of Schizophrenia.* New York: Grune and Stratton, pp. 98–128.

Salzman, L. F., Goldstein, R. H., Atkins, R., and Babigian, H. (1966). Conceptual thinking in psychiatric patients. *Arch. Gen. Psychiat.,* **14**:55–59.

Sandy, W. C. (1910). Studies in heredity, with examples. *Amer. J. Insanity,* **66**:587–598.

Sartorius, N., Shapiro, R., and Kimura, M. (1975). Towards an international definition of schizophrenia. In Lader, M. H. (Ed.), *Brit. J. of Psychiatry Special Publication No. 10: Studies of Schizophrenia.* Ashford, Kent: Headley Bros., pp. 25–28.

Scharfetter, C. (1975). The historical development of the concept of schizophrenia. In Lader, M. H. (Ed.), *Brit. J. of Psychiatry Special Publication No. 10: Studies of Schizophrenia.* Ashford, Kent: Headley Bros., pp. 5–9.

Schildkraut, J. J. (1965). The catecholamine hypothesis of affective disorders: A review of supporting evidence. *Amer. J. Psychiat.,* **122**:509–522.

——— (1971). Catecholamine metabolism and affective illnesses. In Himwich, H. E. (Ed.), *Biochemistry, Schizophrenias and Affective Illnesses.* Baltimore: Williams and Wilkins, pp. 198–229.

——— (1978). Biochemical tests in diagnosing depression. Abstracted in *Clin. Psychiat. News,* **6**:1 (June).

Schmideberg, M. (1947). The treatment of psychopaths and borderline patients. *Amer. J. Psychother.,* **1**:45–55.

Schneider, K. (1959). *Clinical Psychopathology* (Tr. M. W. Hamilton). New York: Grune and Stratton.

Schuckit, M. A., Daly, V., Herrman, G., and Hineman, S. (1975). Premenstrual symptoms and depression in a university population. *Dis. Nerv. Syst.,* **36**:516–517.

Schulsinger, F., and Mednick, S. A. (1975). Nature-nurture aspects of schizophrenia: Early detection and prevention. In Lader, M. H. (Ed.), *Brit. J. of Psychiatry Special Publication No. 10: Studies of Schizophrenia.* Ashford, Kent: Headley Bros., pp. 36–41.

Schulz, B. (1932). Zur Erbpathologie der Schizophrenie. *Z. Ges. Neurol. Psychiat.,* **143**:175–293.

Schuyler, D., Klein, D. F., Secunda, S. R., Wallingford, J., Di Giacomo, N., and Weissman, M. (1977). A clinician's guide to the treatment of depression. Panel, One hundred and thirtieth annual meeting of the American Psychiatric Association, Toronto, May 9.

Scott, D. F., and Schwartz, M. S. (1975). EEG features of depressive and schizophrenic states. *Brit. J. Psychiat.,* **126**:408–413.

Searles, H. F. (1969). A case of borderline thought disorder. *Int. J. Psycho-Anal.,* **50**:655–664.

Sechèhaye, M. (1956). *A New Psychotherapy in Schizophrenia.* New York: Grune and Stratton.

Serban, G., and Gidynski, C. B. (1975). Differentiating criteria for acute-chronic distinction in schizophrenia. *Arch. Gen. Psychiat.*, **32**:705–712.

Shagass, C. (1976). An electrophysiological view of schizophrenia. *Biol. Psychiat.*, **11**:3–30.

———, Amadeo, M., and Overton, D. A. (1974). Eye-tracking performance in psychiatric patients. *Biol. Psychiat.*, **9**:245–260.

———, Roemer, R. A., Straumanis, J. J., and Amadeo, M. (1977). Evoked potential correlates of psychosis. Presented at the thirty-second annual meeting of the Society of Biological Psychiatry, Toronto, Apr. 30.

Shakhmatova-Pavlova, I. V., Akopova, I. L., Golovan, L. I., Kozlova, I. A., Lobova, L. K., Moskalenko, V. D., Rokhlina, M. L., Rudenko, G. M., Siryachenko, T. M., and Shenderova, V. L. (1975). Non-manifest disorders in closest relatives of schizophrenic patients. In Arieti, S., and Chrzanowski, G. (Eds.), *New Dimensions in Psychiatry*. New York: Wiley, pp. 373–396.

Shein, H. M. (1975). Tissue and cell-culture models in the study of neurotransmitter and synaptic function. In Ingle, D. J., and Shein, H. M. (Eds.), *Model Systems in Biologic Psychiatry*. Cambridge, Mass.: M.I.T. Press, pp. 80–96.

Shields, J. (1968). Summary of the genetic evidence (in schizophrenia). In Rosenthal, D., and Kety, S. (Eds.), *Transmission of Schizophrenia*. Oxford: Pergamon Press, pp. 95–126.

——— (1972). Concepts of heredity for schizophrenia. In Cancro, R. (Ed.), *Annual Review of the Schizophrenic Syndrome,* vol. 2. New York: Brunner/Mazel, pp. 319–336.

———, Heston, L. L., and Gottesman, I. I. (1975). Schizophrenia and the schizoid: The problem for genetic analysis. In Fieve, R. R., Rosenthal, D., and Brill, H. (Eds.), *Genetic Research in Psychiatry*. Baltimore: Johns Hopkins Press, pp. 167–198.

———, and Gottesman, I. I. (1972). Cross-national diagnosis of schizophrenia in twins. *Arch. Gen. Psychiat.*, **27**:725–730.

———, and Slater, E. (1975). Genetic aspects of schizophrenia. In Silverstone, T., and Barraclough, B. (Eds.), *Brit. J. of Psychiatry Special Publication No. 9: Contemporary Psychiatry*. Ashford, Kent: Headley Bros., pp. 32–40.

Siever, L. J., and Gunderson, J. G. (1979). Genetic determinants of borderline conditions. *Schizophrenia Bull.*, **5**:59–86.

Singer, M. T. (1977). The borderline diagnosis and psychological tests: Review and research. In Hartocollis, P. (Ed.), *Borderline Personality Disorders*. New York: International Universities Press, pp. 193–212.

Skodol, A., Buckley, P., and Salamon, I. (1976). The ubiquitous symptoms of schizophrenia. *Comprehen. Psychiat.*, **17**:511–516.

Slater, E. (1938). Zur Periodik des manisch-depressiven Irreseins. *Z. Ges. Neurol. Psychiat.*, **162**:794–801.

——— (1938a). Zur Erbpathologie des manisch-depressiven Irreseins: Die Eltern und die Kinder von Manisch-Depressiven. *Z. Ges. Neurol. Psychiat.*, **163**:1–47.

——— (1953). Psychotic and neurotic illnesses in twins. *Medical Research Council Special Report No. 278*. London: Her Majesty's Stationery Office.

——— (1958). The monogenic theory of schizophrenia. *Acta Genet. et Statistica Med.*, **8**:50–56.

Sletten, I. W., and Gershon, S. (1966). The premenstrual syndrome: A discussion of its neurophysiology and treatment with lithium ion. *Comprehen. Psychiat.*, **7**:197–206.

Snyder, S. H. (1976). Dopamine and schizophrenia. The Pauline Goodman Seminar, New York Medical College, New York, Nov. 5.

———, Banerjee, S. P., Yamamusa, H. I., and Greenberg, D. (1974). Drugs, neurotransmitters and schizophrenia. *Science,* **184**:1243–1253.

Sovner, R. D., and McHugh, P. R. (1976). Bipolar course in schizoaffective illness. *Biol. Psychiat.*, **11**:195–204.

Sperber, M. A., and Jarvik, L. F. (1976). *Psychiatry and Genetics*. New York: Basic Books.

Spiker, D. G., Coble, P., Cofsky, J., Foster, F. G., and Kupfer, D. J. (1978). EEG sleep and severity of depression. *Biol. Psychiat.,* **13**:485–488.

Spiro, H. R., Schimke, R. N., and Welch, J. P. (1965). Schizophrenia in a patient with a defect in methionine metabolism. *J. Nerv. Ment. Dis.,* **141**:285–290.

Spitzer, R. L., and Endicott, J. (1968). DIAGNO: A computer program for psychiatric diagnosis utilizing a differential diagnostic procedure. *Arch. Gen. Psychiat.,* **18**:746–756.

———, and ——— (1975). A schedule for affective disorders and schizophrenia (2nd ed.). *Biometrics Research.* New York State Psychiatric Institute.

———, and ——— (1979). Justification for separating schizotypal and borderline personality disorders. *Schizophrenia Bull.,* **5**:95–100.

———, ———, and Gibbon, M. (1979). Crossing the border into borderline personality and borderline schizophrenia. *Arch. Gen. Psychiat.,* **36**:17–24.

———, ———, and Robins, E. (1975). Clinical criteria for psychiatric diagnosis and DSM-III. *Amer. J. Psychiat.,* **132**:1187–1192.

———, ———, and ——— (1975a). Research diagnostic criteria (R.D.C.). *Psychopharm. Bull.,* **11**:22–24.

———, ———, and ——— (1978). Research diagnostic criteria: Rationale and reliability. *Arch. Gen. Psychiat.,* **35**:773–782.

———, and Fleiss, J. L. (1974). A re-analysis of the reliability of psychiatric diagnosis. *Brit. J. Psychiat.,* **125**:341–347.

———, Gibbon, M., and Endicott, J. (1971). The family evaluation form (F. E. F.). *Biometrics Research,* New York State Psychiatric Institute, December.

———, ———, and ——— (1978). Global Assessment Scale (GAS). Unpublished manuscript.

Srole, L., Langer, T. S., Michael, S. T., Opler, M. K., and Rennie, T. A. C. (1962). *Mental Health in the Metropolis: The Midtown Manhattan Study,* vol. 1. New York: McGraw-Hill.

Stabenau, J. R. (1977). Genetic and other factors in schizophrenic, manic-depressive and schizo-affective psychoses. *J. Nerv. Ment. Dis.,* **164**:149–167.

———, and Pollin, W. (1969). The pathogenesis of schizophrenia: II. Contributions from the N.I.M.H. study of sixteen pairs of monozygotic twins discordant for schizophrenia. In Sankar, S. (Ed.), *Schizophrenia: Current Concepts.* Hicksville, N.Y.: PJD Publications, pp. 336–351.

Stein, L., and Wise, C. D. (1971). Possible etiology of schizophrenia: Progressive damage to the noradrenergic reward system by 6-hydroxydopamine. *Science,* **171**:1032–1036.

Stenstedt, A. (1952). A study in manic-depressive psychosis: Clinical, social and genetic investigations. *Acta Psychiat. Scand.,* Supplementum **79**:1–111.

Stephens, D. A., Atkinson, M. W., Kay, D. W. K., Roth, M., and Garside, R. F. (1975). Psychiatric morbidity in parents and sibs of schizophrenics and non-schizophrenics. *Brit. J. Psychiat.,* **127**:97–108.

Stern, A. (1938). Psychoanalytic investigation and therapy in the borderline group of neuroses. *Psychoanal. Q.,* **7**:467–489.

Stevenson, A. C., Davison, B. C. C., and Oakes, M. W. (1970). *Genetic Counseling.* Philadelphia: Lippincott.

Stone, M. H. (1970). Cultural factors in the treatment of an obsessive handwasher. *Psychiat. Q.,* **44**:627–636.

——— (1971). Mania: A guide for the perplexed. *Psychiatry and Soc. Sci. Rev.,* **5**:14–18.

——— (1973). Drug-related schizophrenic reactions. *Int. J. Psychiat.,* **11**:391–441.

——— (1973a). The history of child psychiatry before 1900. *Int. J. Child Psychother.,* **2**:264–307.

——— (1974). Mesmer and his followers: The beginnings of sympathetic treatment of childhood emotional disorders. *Hist. of Childhood Q.,* **1**:659–679.

——— (1975). The role of loss in borderline and psychotic conditions. *J. Thanatol.,* **3**:207–222.

——— (1976). Madness and the moon revisited: Possible influence of the full moon in a case of atypical mania. *Psychiat. Annals,* **6**:47–60.

——— (1977). Dreams, free-association and the right-brain. *J. Amer. Acad. Psychoanal.,* **5**:255–284.

——— (1977a). The borderline syndrome: Evolution of the term, genetic aspects and prognosis. *Amer. J. Psychother.,* **31**:345–365.

——— (1978). Toward early detection of manic-depressive illness in psychoanalytic patients. *Amer. J. Psychother.,* **32**:427–439.

——— (1978a). Turning points in psychotherapy: Some clinical and theoretical considerations. Presented at the annual spring meeting of the American Academy of Psychoanalysis, Atlanta, May 7; for publication in *J. Amer. Acad. Psychoanal.*

——— (1978b). A psychoanalytic approach to abnormalities of temperament. Presented at the Association for Advancement of Psychotherapy, Atlanta, May 7; for publication in *Amer. J. Psychother.*

——— (1978c). Etiological factors in schizophrenia: A reevaluation in the light of contemporary research. *Psychiat. Q.,* **50**(2):83–119. Abstracted in *Behavior Today,* **8**(39):3–5, 1977.

——— (1979). Dreams of fragmentation: A manifestation of vulnerability to psychosis. *Psychopharmacol. Bull.,* **15**:12–14.

——— (1979a). Genetic aspects of borderline syndromes (discussion of Siever and Gunderson's article). *Schizophrenia Bull.,* **5**:105–110.

———, and Oestberg, B. (1979). Survey of borderline patients in Norway, using the Spitzer checklist. Dikemark Seminar, Apr. 25. Unpublished data.

———, and ——— (1979a). Survey of Norwegian psychiatrists on borderline conditions. Unpublished data.

Strauss, J. S. (1975). A comprehensive approach to psychiatric diagnosis. *Amer. J. Psychiat.,* **132**:1193–1197.

———, and Carpenter, W. T., Jr. (1972). The prediction of outcome in schizophrenia: I. Characteristics of outcome. *Arch. Gen. Psychiat.,* **27**:739–746.

———, and ——— (1974). Prediction of outcome in schizophrenia: II. Relationships between predictor and outcome variables. *Arch. Gen. Psychiat.,* **31**:37–42.

———, and ——— (1975). The key clinical dimensions of the functional psychoses. In Freedman, D. X. (Ed.), *Biology of the Major Psychoses.* New York: Raven Press, pp. 9–17.

———, ———, and Bartko, J. J. (1974). The diagnosis and understanding of schizophrenia: III. Speculations on the processes that underlie schizophrenic symptoms and signs. *Schizophrenia Bull.,* no. 11:61–69.

———, Gabriel, K. R., Kokes, R. F., Ritzler, B. A., VanOrd, A., and Tarana, E. (1979). Do psychiatric patients fit their diagnoses? *J. Nerv. Ment. Dis.,* **167**:105–113.

———, and Gift, T. E. (1977). Choosing an approach for diagnosing schizophrenia. *Arch. Gen. Psychiat.,* **34**:1248–1253.

Sullivan, H. S. (1931). Treatment of schizophrenia. *Amer. J. Psychiat.,* **11**:519–540.

Tausk, V. (1919). Uber den Beeinflussingsapparat in der Schizophrenie. *Int. Z. Psychoanal.,* **5**:1–33.

Taylor, M. A. (1972). Schneiderian first-rank symptoms and clinical prognostic features in schizophrenia. *Arch. Gen. Psychiat.,* **26**:57–64.

———, and Abrams, R. (1973). A genetic study of early and late onset affective disorders. *Arch. Gen. Psychiat.,* **28**:656–658.

———, and ——— (1975). A critique of the St. Louis Psychiatric Research Criteria for schizophrenia. *Amer. J. Psychiat.,* **132**:1276–1280.

———, and ——— (1975a). Acute mania: Clinical and genetic study of responders and nonresponders to treatments. *Arch. Gen. Psychiat.,* **32**:863–865.

Theophrastus (1947). *Charaktere* (Tr. W. Plankl). Vienna: Verlag der Ringbuchhandlung–A. Sexl.

Thomas, A., and Chess, S. (1975). A longitudinal study of three brain-damaged children. *Arch. Gen. Psychiat.*, **32**:457–462.

Tienari, P. (1963). Psychiatric illness in identical twins. *Acta. Psychiat. Scand.*, Supplementum **171**:1–195.

——— (1975). Schizophrenia and Finnish male twins. In Lader, M. H. (Ed.), *Brit. J. of Psychiatry Special Publication No. 10: Studies of Schizophrenia.* Ashford, Kent: Headley Bros., pp. 29–35.

Tonks, C. (1968). Premenstrual tension. *Brit. J. Hosp. Med.*, **7**:383–387.

Tourney, G., and Gottlieb, J. S. (Eds.) (1971). *Lafayette Clinic Studies on Schizophrenia.* Detroit: Wayne State University Press.

Tsuang, M. T. (1967). A study of pairs of sibs both hospitalized for mental disorder. *Brit. J. Psychiat.*, **113**:283–300.

———, Dempsey, G. M., Dvoredsky, A., and Struss, A. (1976). A family history study of schizoaffective disorder. *Biol. Psychiat.*, **12**:331–338.

———, ———, and Rauscher, F. (1976). A study of "atypical schizophrenia." *Arch. Gen. Psychiat.*, **33**:1157–1160.

———, and Winokur, G. (1973). Criteria for subtyping schizophrenia. *Arch. Gen. Psychiat.*, **31**:43–47.

———, and ——— (1975). The Iowa 500: Field work in a 35-year follow-up of depression, mania, and schizophrenia. *Canad. Psychiat. Assoc. J.*, **20**:359–365.

Turner, W. J. (1979). Genetic markers for schizotaxia. *Biol. Psychiat.*, **14**:177–206.

Vaillant, G. E. (1963). The natural history of remitting schizophrenias. *Amer. J. Psychiat.*, **120**:367–375.

——— (1963a). Manic depressive heredity and remission in schizophrenia. *Brit. J. Psychiat.*, **109**:746–749.

Van Praag, H. M. (1976). About the impossible concept of schizophrenia. In *Comprehen. Psychiat.*, **17**:481–497.

Venables, P. H. (1964). Input dysfunction in schizophrenics, *Prog. Exp. Pers. Res.*, **1**:1–47.

Vercelletto, P. (1972). The hereditary factor in generalized epilepsy. *Int. J. Mental Health,* **1**:207–220.

Vigotsky, H. (1934). The Concept-Formation Test. *Arch. Neurol. Psychiat.*, **31**:1063–1077.

Von Domarus, E. (1927). Zur Theorie des schizophrenien Denkens. *Z. Ges. Neurol. Psychiat.*, **108**:703–714.

Von Greiff, H., McHugh, P. R., and Stokes, P. E. (1975). The family history in sixteen males with bipolar manic-depressive illness. In Fieve, R. R., Rosenthal, D., and Brill, H. (Eds.), *Genetic Research in Psychiatry*. Baltimore: Johns Hopkins Press, pp. 233–240.

Wahl, O. F. (1976). Monozygotic twins discordant for schizophrenia. *Psychol. Bull.*, **83**:91–106.

Watson, C. G. (1973). Abstract thinking deficit and autism in process and reactive schizophrenics. *J. Abnorm. Psychol.*, **82**:399–403.

Weil, A. P. (1970). The basic core. *Psychoanal. Study of the Child,* **25**:442–460.

Weinberg, I., and Lobstein, J. (1936). Beitrag zur Vererbung des manisch-depressiven Irreseins. *Psychiat. Neurol. Bull.* (Amsterdam), **1a**:339–372.

Weingarten, L., and Korn, S. (1967). Psychological test findings on pseudoneurotic schizophrenics. *Arch. Gen. Psychiat.*, **17**:448–454.

Weissman, M. M., and Klerman, G. L. (1977). Sex differences and the epidemiology of depression. *Arch. Gen. Psychiat.*, **34**:98–111.

Welner, A., Croughan, J. L., and Robins, E. (1974). The subgroup of schizoaffective and related psychoses: Critique, record, follow-up, and family studies: I. A persistent enigma. *Arch. Gen. Psychiat.*, **31**:628–631.

———, ———, Fishman, R., and Robins, E. (1977). The group of schizoaffective and related psychoses: A follow-up study. *Comprehen. Psychiat.*, **18**:413–422.

———, Liss, J. L., and Robins, E. (1973). Undiagnosed psychiatric patients: III. The undiagnosible patient. *Brit. J. Psychiat.,* **123**:91–98.

———, Reich, T., Robins, E., Fishman, R., and Van Doren, T. (1976). Obsessive-compulsive neurosis: Record, follow-up, and family studies: I. Inpatient record study. *Comprehen. Psychiat.,* **17**:527–539.

———, Welner, Z., and Fishman, R. (1979). The group of schizoaffective and related psychoses: IV. A family study. *Comprehen. Psychiat.,* **20**:21–26.

———, ———, and Leonard, M. A. (1977). Bipolar manic-depressive disorder: A reassessment of course and outcome. *Comprehen. Psychiat.,* **18**:327–332.

Welner, J., and Strömgren, E. (1958). Clinical and genetic studies on benign schizophreniform psychoses based on a follow-up. *Acta Psychiat. Scand.,* **33**:377–399.

Wender, P. H. (1977). The contribution of the adoption studies to an understanding of the phenomenology and etiology of borderline schizophrenia. In Hartocollis, P. (Ed.), *Borderline Personality Disorders.* New York: International Universities Press, pp. 255–269.

———, Rosenthal, D., and Kety, S. S. (1968). A psychiatric assessment of the adoptive parents of schizophrenics. In Rosenthal, D., and Kety, S. S. (Eds.), *The Transmission of Schizophrenia.* Oxford: Pergamon Press, pp. 235–250.

West, A. (1973). Concurrent schizophrenia-like psychosis in monozygotic twins suffering from a CNS disorder. *Brit. J. Psychiat.,* **122**:675–677.

Wetzel, R. D., Reich, T., and McClure, J. N., Jr. (1971). Phase of the menstrual cycle and self-referrals to a suicide prevention service. *Brit. J. Psychiat.,* **119**:523–524.

Wiesert, K. N., and Hendrie, H. C. (1977). Secondary mania? A case report. *Amer. J. Psychiat.,* **134**:929–930.

Wing, J. K. (1976). The uses of classification in psychiatry. *Psychiat. Annals,* **6**(8):10–21.

———, and Nixon, J. (1975). Discriminating symptoms in schizophrenia. *Arch. Gen. Psychiat.,* **32**:853–859.

Winokur, G. (1974). The use of genetic studies in clarifying clinical issues in schizophrenia. In Mitsuda, H., and Fukuda, T. (Eds.), *Biological Mechanisms of Schizophrenia and Schizophrenia-like Psychoses.* Tokyo: Igaku-Shoin, pp. 241–247.

——— (1975). Relationship of genetic factors to course and drug response in schizophrenia, mania and depression. In Mendlewicz, J. (Ed.), *Genetics and Psychopharmacology (Mod. Probl. Pharmacopsych.,* vol. 10). Basel: Karger, pp. 1–11.

——— (1976). Chronic schizophrenia: How many separate illnesses are there? *Frontiers of Psychiatry,* **6**:3.

———, Cadoret, R., Baker, M., and Dorzab, J. (1975). Depression spectrum disease versus pure depressive disease: Some further data. *Brit. J. Psychiat.,* **127**:75–77.

———, Clayton, P. J., and Reich, T. (1969). *Manic Depressive Illness.* St. Louis: C. V. Mosby.

———, Morrison, J., Clancy, J., and Crowe, R. (1972). The Iowa 500: II. A blind family history comparison of mania, depression and schizophrenia. *Arch. Gen. Psychiat.,* **27**:462–464.

———, and Reich, T. (1970). Two genetic factors in manic-depressive disease. *Comprehen. Psychiat.,* **11**:93–99.

———, and Tanna, V. L. (1969). Possible role of X-linked dominant factor in manic depressive disease. *Dis. Nerv. Syst.,* **30**:89–94.

Wise, C. D., Baden, M. H., and Stein, L. (1974). Postmortem measurements of enzymes in human brain: Evidence of a central noradrenergic deficit in schizophrenia. *J. Psychiat. Res.,* **11**:185–198.

———, and Stein, L. (1973). Dopamine-beta-hydroxylase deficits in the brain of schizophrenic patients. *Science,* **181**:344–347.

Wittenborn, J. R., and Maurer, H. S. (1977). Persisting personalities among depressed women. *Arch. Gen. Psychiat.,* **34**:968–971.

———, and Smith, B. K. (1964). A comparison of psychotic dimensions in male and female hospital patients. *J. Nerv. Ment. Dis.,* **38**:375–382.

Wittgenstein, L. (1933–1935). *The Blue and Brown Books* (edited with a preface by R. Rhees). Oxford: Blackwell, 1958.

Wolf, S., and Berle, B. B. (Eds.) (1976). *The Biology of the Schizophrenic Process.* New York: Plenum.

Woodruff, R. A., Jr., Goodwin, D. W., and Guze, S. B. (1974). *Psychiatric Diagnosis.* New York: Oxford.

Wyatt, R. J., Belmaker, R., and Murphy, D. (1975). Low platelet monoamine oxidase and vulnerability to schizophrenia. In Mendlewicz, J. (Ed.), *Genetics and Psychopharmacology (Mod. Probl. Pharmacopsych.,* vol. 10). Basel: Karger, pp. 38–56.

———, and Murphy, D. L. (1975). Neurotransmitter-related enzymes in the major psychiatric disorders: II. MAO and DBH in schizophrenia. In Freedman, D. X. (Ed.), *Biology of the Major Psychoses.* New York: Raven Press, pp. 289–296.

———, ———, Belmaker R., Cohen, S., Donnelly, C. H., and Pollin, W. (1973). Reduced monoamine oxidase activity in platelets: A possible genetic marker for vulnerability to schizophrenia. *Science,* **173**:916–918.

Zeeman, E. C. (1976). Catastrophe theory. *Sci. Amer.,* **234**:65–83.

Zehnder, M. (1940). Uber Krankheitsbild und Krankheitsverlauf bei schizophrenen Geschwistern. *Mschr. Psychiat. Neurol.,* **103**:230–277.

Zeller, E. (1844). Die Einheitspsychose. *Allg. Z. Psychiat.,* **1**:1–79.

Zerbin-Rüdin, E. (1967). Endogene Psychosen. In Becker, P. E. (Ed.), *Humangenetik, ein kurzes Handbuch,* vol. V/2. Stuttgart: Georg Thieme Verlag, pp. 446–577.

——— (1968). Zur Genetik der depressiven Erkrankungen. Presented at a symposium on genetics, Berlin, Feb. 16.

——— (1971). Genetische Aspekte der endogenen Psychosen. *Fortschr. Neur. Psych.,* **39**:459–494.

——— (1972). Genetic research and the theory of schizophrenia. *Int. J. Mental Health,* **1**:42–62.

——— (1974). Genetic aspects of schizophrenia (a survey). In Mitsuda, H., and Fukuda, T. (Eds.), *Biological Mechanisms of Schizophrenia and Schizophrenia-like Psychoses.* Tokyo: Igaku-Shoin, pp. 250–256.

Zetzel, E. (1971). A developmental approach to the borderline patient. *Amer. J. Psychiat.,* **127**:867–871.

Ziegler, V. E. (1977). Personal communication.

Zigler, E., and Levine, J. (1973). Premorbid adjustment and paranoid-nonparanoid status in schizophrenia. *J. Abnorm. Psychol.,* **82**:189–199.

Zilboorg, G. (1941). Ambulatory schizophrenia. *Psychiatry,* **4**:149–155.

——— (1941a). *A History of Medical Psychology.* New York: Norton.

Zubin, J. (1976). Vulnerability: A new concept in the diagnosis of schizophrenia. Lecture at the New York State Psychiatric Institute, Apr. 9.

———, Salzinger, K., Fleiss, J. L., Gurland, B., Spitzer, R. L., Endicott, J., and Sutton, S. (1975). Biometric approach to psychopathology. In Rosenzweig, M. R., and Porter, L. W. (Eds.), *Annual Review of Psychology,* vol. 26. Palo Alto: Annual Reviews, pp. 621–671.

———, and Spring, B. (1977). Vulnerability: A new view of schizophrenia. *J. Abnorm. Psychol.,* **86**:103–126.

———, and Sutton, S. (1970). Assessment of physiological, sensory, perceptual, psychomotor, and conceptual functioning in schizophrenic patients. *Acta Psychiat. Scand.,* Supplementum **219**:247–263.

Name Index

Subject Index